RUSSIA IN BRITAIN, 1880–1940

Russia in Britain, 1880–1940

From Melodrama to Modernism

Edited by
REBECCA BEASLEY AND PHILIP ROSS BULLOCK

OXFORD
UNIVERSITY PRESS

Great Clarendon Street, Oxford, OX2 6DP,
United Kingdom

Oxford University Press is a department of the University of Oxford.
It furthers the University's objective of excellence in research, scholarship,
and education by publishing worldwide. Oxford is a registered trade mark of
Oxford University Press in the UK and in certain other countries

First Edition published in 2013

Impression: 1

Published in the United States of America by Oxford University Press
198 Madison Avenue, New York, NY 10016, United States of America

British Library Cataloguing in Publication Data

Data available

Library of Congress Cataloging Control Number: 2013941139

ISBN 978–0–19–966086–5

Printed and bound in Great Britain by
CPI Group (UK) Ltd, Croydon, CR0 4YY

Acknowledgements

It is a pleasure to have the opportunity to thank the many friends and colleagues who have contributed to this book. It has its origin in a conference we organized at the Institute of English Studies of the University of London in June 2009: 'Russia in Britain, 1880–1940: Reception, Translation and the Modernist Cultural Agenda'. In this volume, and in our 2011 special issue of *Translation and Literature* (*Translating Russia, 1890–1935*), we are able to present a more permanent, if necessarily partial, record of the remarkable research and inspiring discussions in which we were privileged to take part that summer. We are grateful to all the contributors to the conference, and particularly to our keynote speakers, Ol′ga Kaznina, Laura Marcus, and Laurence Senelick, for their support of the project and their advice on both the conference and this book. It is with great pleasure that we publish here Laura Marcus's and Laurence Senelick's essays based on their papers, and are able to acknowledge the influence of Ol′ga Kaznina's *Russkie v Anglii: Russkaya emigratsiya v kontekste russko-angliiskikh literaturnykh svyazei v pervoi polovine VV veka* (Nasledie, 1997) in both the conference and the volume's title. We are delighted that Ken Hirschkop, one of the contributors to our roundtable on 'The new international modernism' agreed to write an afterword to this volume. We gratefully acknowledge the generous financial support of the British Academy, the British Association of Slavonic and East European Studies, Birkbeck College, University of London, the John Fell OUP Fund, University of Oxford, and the Modern Humanities Research Association. At Oxford University Press, we thank Jacqueline Baker and Rachel Platt, and the Press's readers for their insightful comments about the manuscript at various stages of its evolution. Our greatest debts are to Markman Ellis and Stefano Evangelista, who are neither British nor Russian, but have left their own transnational, cosmopolitan imprints on this book, and on the lives of its editors.

Rebecca Beasley
Philip Ross Bullock
Oxford, 2012

Contents

List of Illustrations

List of Contributors

Charlotte Alston is Senior Lecturer in History at the University of Northumbria. She is the author of *Russia's Greatest Enemy: Harold Williams and the Russian Revolutions* (I.B. Tauris, 2007), and *Piip, Meierovics and Voldemaras: The Baltic States* in the series 'Makers of the Modern World: The Peace Conferences of 1919–23 and their Aftermath' (Haus, 2010). She has also published articles about the British press and the Russian civil war, Russian émigré organizations in the west, and Russia's border states at the Paris Peace Conference. She is currently working on a study of the international Tolstoyan movement in the late nineteenth and early twentieth centuries.

Rebecca Beasley is Tutorial Fellow in English at The Queen's College, Oxford, and University Lecturer in English at the University of Oxford. She is the author of *Ezra Pound and the Visual Culture of Modernism* (Cambridge University Press, 2007) and *Theorists of Modernist Poetry* (Routledge, 2007), and is currently working on a book-length study of the impact of Russian culture on British literary modernism. With Philip Ross Bullock, she is the editor of *Translating Russia, 1890–1935*, a special issue of *Translation and Literature* (2011). She has also published essays on modernism and translation, the British 'intelligentsia', and the history of comparative literature.

Philip Ross Bullock is Fellow and Tutor in Russian at Wadham College, Oxford, and University Lecturer in Russian at the University of Oxford. The author of *The Feminine in the Prose of Andrey Platonov* (Legenda, 2005), and *Rosa Newmarch and Russian Music in Late Nineteenth and Early Twentieth-Century England* (Royal Musical Association Monographs/ Ashgate, 2009), he has most recently edited and translated *The Correspondence of Jean Sibelius and Rosa Newmarch, 1906–1939* (Boydell, 2011). With Rebecca Beasley, he is the editor of *Translating Russia, 1890–1935*, a special issue of *Translation and Literature* (2011).

Ramsay Burt is Professor of Dance History at De Montfort University. His publications include *The Male Dancer* (Routledge, 1995, rev. 2007), *Alien Bodies* (Routledge, 1997), *Performative Traces: Judson Dance Theater* (Routledge, 2006), and, with Valerie Briginshaw, *Writing Dancing Together* (Palgrave, 2009). In 1999 he was Visiting Professor at the Department of Performance Studies, New York University. With Susan Foster, he is founder editor of *Discourses in Dance*.

Robert Henderson worked for a number of years as a curator of the Russian collections at the British Library before, in 2008, completing his doctorate at Queen Mary, University of London. He has published articles on the Russian revolutionary emigration in Britain and is currently Honorary Research Associate in the School of History at Queen Mary where he is working on a book-length study of the revolutionary publisher and historian Vladimir Burtsev.

Ken Hirschkop is Associate Professor of English at the University of Waterloo, and has previously taught at the Universities of Southampton and Manchester. He is co-author of *Benjamin's Arcades: An unGuided Tour* (Manchester University Press, 2005) and the author of *Mikhail Bakhtin: An Aesthetic for Democracy* (Oxford University Press, 1999), as well as many articles on cultural politics. He is now working on *Linguistic Turns, 1890–1950: Writing on Language as Social Theory*, and a history of Toronto's dream-images.

Caroline Maclean is Departmental Lecturer in English at the University of Oxford. She is the author of *The Vogue for Russia: Mysticism and Modernism in Britain, 1900–1930*, which will be published by Edinburgh University Press in 2014. Her article on Eisenstein and the fourth dimension appeared in *Literature and History* in 2012, and a chapter on Mary Butts and Petr Uspensky is forthcoming in *Modernism's Fourth Dimensions*, edited by Bruce Clarke and Linda Dalrymple Henderson for Penn State Press.

Laura Marcus is Goldsmith's Professor of English Literature at the University of Oxford and a Fellow of New College. She is the author of *Auto/biographical Discourses: Theory, Criticism, Practice* (Macmillan, 1994), *Virginia Woolf* (British Council/Northcote House 1997/2004), *The Tenth Muse: Writing about Cinema in the Modernist Period* (Oxford University Press, 2007; awarded the 2008 James Russell Lowell Prize of the Modern Language Association) and, as co-editor with Peter Nicholls, *The Cambridge History of Twentieth-Century English Literature* (2004). Her current research projects include a book on British literature 1910–1920, and a study of the concept of rhythm in the late nineteenth- and early twentieth-centuries, in a range of disciplinary contexts.

Michael Newton is Lecturer in English at the University of Leiden. He is the author of *Age of Assassins: A History of Conspiracy and Political Violence, 1865–1981* (Faber, 2012), *Savage Girls and Wild Boys: A History of Feral Children* (Faber, 2002) and a book on *Kind Hearts and Coronets* in the BFI's Film Classics series (2003). He has edited Edmund Gosse, *Father and Son* for Oxford University Press's World's Classics series, and Joseph Conrad, *The Secret Agent* and *The Penguin Book of Ghost Stories* for Penguin Classics.

Ian Patterson is a Fellow and Director of Studies in English at Queens' College, University of Cambridge. He is the author of *Guernica and Total War* (Profile, 2007) and translator of Marcel Proust, *Finding Time Again* (2003), the final volume of the Penguin edition *In Search of Lost Time*. His latest volume of poetry is *The Glass Bell* (Barque, 2009). He has recently published essays on New York little magazines of the 1950s, modernism and time, the sublime in the 1930s, the literature of pacifism and conscientious objection, John Rodker's unpublished satire on Wyndham Lewis, and the poetry of Veronica Forrest-Thomson.

Laurence Senelick is Fletcher Professor of Drama and Oratory at Tufts University. His publications include *A Historical Dictionary of Russian Theatre* (Scarecrow, 2007), *The Changing Room: Sex, Drag, and Theatre* (Routledge, 2000) (received Honourable Mention for the Freedley Award of the Theatre Library Association), *The Chekhov Theatre* (Cambridge University Press, 1997) (awarded the Barnett Hewitt Award of the American Society for Theatre Research), *Gender in Performance* (University Press of New England, 1992), and *Gordon Craig's Moscow Hamlet: A Reconstruction* (Greenwood, 1982). Among the books he has translated and edited are *The American Stage: Writing on Theater from Washington Irving to Tony Kushner* (Library of America, 2010), *The Complete Plays of Chekhov* (Norton, 2005), *Cabaret Performance: Sketches, Songs, Monologues, Memoirs, 1890–1940*, 2 vols (Johns Hopkins University Press, 1993), *Wandering Stars: Russian Émigré Theatre, 1905–1940* (University of Iowa Press, 1992), and *Russian Dramatic Theory from Pushkin to the Symbolists* (University of Texas Press, 1981).

James Smith is Lecturer in English Studies at Durham University. He is the author of *Terry Eagleton: A Critical Introduction* (Polity, 2008) and has published articles examining the impact of government surveillance, censorship, and propaganda on twentieth-century British culture. His most recent book is *British Writers and MI5 Surveillance, 1930–1960* (Cambridge University Press, 2013).

Matthew Taunton is a Leverhulme Early Career Fellow in the School of Literature, Drama and Creative Writing at the University of East Anglia. He is the author of *Fictions of the City: Class, Culture and Mass Housing in London and Paris* (Palgrave, 2009), and numerous articles and book chapters on twentieth-century British literature and culture. His present research project explores the cultural resonances of the Russian Revolution (in its various stages) in Britain.

Stuart Young is Associate Professor and Head of the Theatre Studies programme at the University of Otago. He has published extensively on Russian drama and its reception abroad, translation studies and translation for the theatre, modern British drama and theatre, and New Zealand drama and theatre in journals including *Modern Drama*, *New Theatre Quarterly*, *Theatre Journal* and the *New Zealand Slavonic Journal*. He is also a translator and director, and has recently been engaged in practice-led research on documentary/verbatim theatre.

Note on Transliteration

Wherever possible, the original Russian titles of works are given after their first English citation. In some cases, it has been impossible to trace the putative original, not least because some English versions are in fact free adaptations of or responses to the relevant source text. In the main body of the text and in bibliographical references, Cyrillic has been transliterated according to British Standard 2979 (1958), omitting diacritics and using –y to express -й -ий and -ый at the end of personal names, for example, Tolstoy, Dostoevsky, Bely. (In cited material, the transliteration of the original has of course been preserved.) In many cases, this decision produces versions of Russian names that will be immediately evident to the reader, but in other cases, it has a distinctly estranging effect. Diaghilev, for instance, becomes Dyagilev, Benois—Benua, Nijinsky—Nizhinsky, and Yavorska—Yavorskaya. By using this system consistently throughout the volume, even where individuals themselves preferred transliterations that were intimately shaped by Western European languages, we eschew the practice of domestication of a foreign culture in favour of a foreignizing approach. This approach, in keeping with the broader aspirations of this volume, is designed to encourage readers to look at familiar figures with new eyes and in a new context, and to reconsider the ideologies, mechanisms, and institutions that first brought Russia to Britain.

Introduction
Against Influence: On Writing about Russian Culture in Britain

Rebecca Beasley and Philip Ross Bullock

THE CHALLENGE OF RUSSIAN CULTURE

Russia in Britain explores the transformative effect of Russian and Soviet culture on British intellectual life from the 1880s, the decade that saw the first sustained interest in Russian literature, to 1940, the eve of the Soviet Union's entry into the Second World War. It builds on a rich field of previous research that has been effective in highlighting the role of particular individuals in disseminating Russian culture, and aims to take the discussion into new territory by shifting attention to the contribution of institutions, disciplines, and groups—libraries, periodicals, government agencies, concert halls, universities, publishing houses, theatres, and film societies. It substitutes a methodological model of influence with one more attentive to issues of circulation, translation, and mediation. While the majority of chapters here are written by scholars of literature, the volume draws attention to the limitations of working within an exclusively literary framework, and emphasizes the relevance of research undertaken within the disciplinary frameworks of history, art history, film studies, performance, dance, and music.

It has long been recognized that critical assessment of the impact of Russian culture presents particular difficulties, despite the wealth of evidence of its intensity. As Gilbert Phelps remarked in one of the earliest attempts to account for Russia's literary impact in Britain, *The Russian Novel in English Fiction* (1956), 'when one looks back over the volume of comment, a curious fact emerges: that however enthusiastic it may be, it rarely goes beyond the vaguest of generalizations'.[1] His solution was to trace a genealogical narrative of the British novel that provided a longer literary

[1] Gilbert Phelps, *The Russian Novel in English Fiction* (London: Hutchinson's University Library, 1956), 12.

history than had been allowed by what he saw as the excessive critical attention paid to the 'Dostoevsky cult'. But even if he expanded on Helen Muchnic's meticulously researched study *Dostoyevsky's English Reputation* (1939), his own focus on the influence of Turgenev replicated her methodology.[2] Subsequent critics and editors have built on these early studies, to which should be added Royal Gettmann's *Turgenev in England and America* (1941) and Dorothy Brewster's historical overview *East-West Passage: A Study in Literary Relationships* (1954).[3] Almost twenty years ago the 'Anglo-Russian Affinities' series edited by Anthony Cross, as well as including a volume by Cross himself that sets out the pre-history of the current volume, produced books on Turgenev, Dostoevsky, and Tolstoy (edited by Patrick Waddington, W. J. Leatherbarrow, and W. Gareth Jones, respectively), which gathered important accounts of the reception of these authors in Britain and added a distinctive body of new research that widened the study of literary influence to include some of the institutional factors examined in the present volume.[4] Waddington and Glyn Turton have contributed further studies of Turgenev's impact on English fiction, Patrick Miles and Laurence Senelick have examined the performance of Chekhov in Britain, and Liisa Byckling has traced the impact of the work of the actor Mikhail Chekhov on Western theatre and cinema through his studio at Dartington.[5] The impact on individual British modernist writers has been thoroughly documented in many essays, and more recently in books by Neil Cornwell (on James Joyce), Roberta Rubenstein (on Virginia Woolf), Joanna Woods (on Katherine Mansfield), and Peter Kaye (on Dostoevsky's influence on Lawrence, Woolf, Arnold Bennett, and Joseph Conrad).[6]

Implicitly or explicitly, much English-language scholarship on the British reception of Russian literature is indebted to and in dialogue with Russian scholarship that looks on this question from a different disciplinary and cultural perspective. Russian literary culture has long seen itself in a global, as well as a national, context, whether in the form of Gor′ky's attempt to translate the canonical works of world

[2] Helen Muchnic, *Dostoyevsky's English Reputation, 1881–1936*, Smith College Studies in Modern Languages, 20, no. 3/4 (Northampton, MA: Smith College, 1939), 63.

[3] Royal A. Gettmann, *Turgenev in England and America* (Urbana, IL: University of Illinois Press, 1941), Dorothy Brewster, *East-West Passage: A Study in Literary Relationships* (London: Allen & Unwin, 1954).

[4] Anthony Cross, *Anglo-Russica: Aspects of Cultural Relations between Great Britain and Russia in the Eighteenth and Early Nineteenth Centuries* (Oxford: Berg, 1993), Patrick Waddington, ed., *Ivan Turgenev and Britain* (Oxford: Berg, 1995), W. J. Leatherbarrow, ed., *Dostoevskii and Britain* (Oxford: Berg, 1995), W. Gareth Jones, ed., *Tolstoi and Britain* (Oxford: Berg, 1995).

[5] Patrick Waddington, *Turgenev in England* (London: Macmillan, 1980), Glyn Turton, *Turgenev and the Context of English Literature, 1850–1900* (London: Routledge, 1992), Patrick Miles, *Chekhov on the British Stage* (Cambridge: Cambridge University Press, 1993) and *Chekhov on the British Stage, 1909–1987: An Essay in Cultural Exchange* (Cambridge: Sam & Sam, 1987), Laurence Senelick, *The Chekhov Theatre: A Century of Plays in Performance* (Cambridge: Cambridge University Press, 1997), Liisa Byukling, *Mikhail Chekhov v zapadnom teatre i kino* (St Petersburg: Akademicheskii proekt, 2000).

[6] Neil Cornwell, *James Joyce and the Russians* (Basingstoke: Palgrave, 1992), Roberta Rubenstein, *Virginia Woolf and the Russian Point of View* (Houndmills: Palgrave, 2009), Joanna Woods, *Katerina: The Russian World of Katherine Mansfield* (Auckland: Penguin, 2001), Peter Kaye, *Dostoevsky and English Modernism, 1900-1930* (Cambridge: Cambridge University Press, 1999).

literature for Soviet readers in his *Vsemirnaya literatura* project, the publication of journals devoted to foreign literature, the activity of poets obliged to undertake translation when their own work was banned, or outward-facing work produced by scholars despite little or no opportunity to travel abroad until the collapse of the Soviet Union.[7]

Russian literature, and indeed history, criticism, and news, was of course encountered in a variety of translations, including translations into French and German, as well as English. But this volume also foregrounds instances of non-linguistic mediation: visual representation, corporeal gesture, sonic imagination, and new ways of living. Although literary and historical studies dominate the study of Russo-British cultural relations, a growing body of work in other disciplines is beginning to offer both new bodies of primary material, and alternative approaches to the field. In particular, recent research on the impact of Russian music in Britain has opened up important new areas of enquiry, as has work on the dissemination of Russian visual culture and the applied arts.[8] Indeed, this latter field is particularly relevant for our aims in the present volume: given the ways in which paintings, drawings, sculptures, and even folk art are embedded in and disseminated through a transnational context of training, exhibitions, and publication, their study necessarily involves a comparative framework, attentive to institutional circumstances. Although it is less concerned with the Western reception of Russian art than with 'the process and products of artistic encounters and exchanges', Rosalind P. Blakesley and Susan E. Reid's co-edited volume *Russian Art and the West* (2007) exemplifies a methodological perspective that is of relevance here. Similarly, a notable feature of Carol Adlam and Juliet Simpson's *Critical Exchange: Art Criticism of the Eighteenth and Nineteenth Centuries in Russia and Western Europe* (2009) is the prominence that many contributions afford to Russia's integral place within European artistic discourse, a point also borne out by

[7] Susanna Witt, 'Between the Lines: Totalitarianism and Translation in the USSR', in Brian James Baer, ed., *Contexts, Subtexts and Pretexts: Literary Translation in Eastern Europe and Russia* (Amsterdam: Benjamins, 2011), 155, Nailya Safiullina, 'Window to the West: From the Collection of Readers' Letters to the Journal *Internatsional'naya literatura*', *Slavonica*, 15, no. 2 (2009), 128–61, Nailya Safiullina and Rachel Platonov, 'Literary Translation and Soviet Cultural Politics in the 1930s: The Role of the Journal *Internacional'naia literatura*', *Russian Literature*, 72, no. 2 (2012), 239–69, Leon Burnett and Emily Lygo, eds, *The Art of Accommodation: Literary Translation in Russian Culture* (Oxford: Peter Lang, 2013), and Maurice Friedberg, *Literary Translation in Russia: A Cultural History* (University Park, PA: Pennsylvania State University Press, 1997); K. N. Lomunov, 'Lev Tolstoi on English Writers', in Jones, ed., *Tolstoi and Britain*, 43–60, Iurii D. Levin, 'Dostoevskii and Shakespeare', Leonid Grossman, 'Dostoevskii and the Chartist Novel', and A. N. Nikoliukin, 'Dostoevskii in Constance Garnett's Translation', in Leatherbarrow, ed., *Dostoevskii and Britain*, 39–81, 123–138, 207–27.

[8] Philip Ross Bullock, *Rosa Newmarch and Russian Music in Late Nineteenth and Early Twentieth-Century England* (Farnham: Ashgate, 2009), Anthony Cross, ed., *'A People Passing Rude': British Responses to Russian Culture* (Cambridge: Open Book Publishers, 2012), Laura Marcus, *The Tenth Muse: Writing about Cinema in the Modernist Period* (Oxford: Oxford University Press, 2007), Gareth James Thomas, 'The Impact of Russian Music in England, 1893–1929', PhD thesis, University of Birmingham, 2005.

Blakesley's *The Arts and Crafts Movement* (2006), which incorporates Russia into a pan-European context from which it has often been excluded.[9]

These more recent studies and collections have made available a wealth of detail about the British encounter with Russian culture, and indicated how our understanding of cultural exchange has been, especially in literary studies, somewhat straitened by its attempts to trace direct lines of influence.[10] As early as 1965, Donald Davie, in the astute introduction to his anthology *Russian Literature and Modern English Fiction* (1965), described the impact of Russian fiction as not primarily 'a *formal* influence', but rather 'a challenge presented to Anglo-American literary culture'.[11] It is worth noting that the formalist critical approach had always been profoundly out of sympathy with late nineteenth- and early twentieth-century explanations of the distinctiveness of the Russian impact. From the first wave of translations made during and immediately after the Crimean War, it was a commonplace to read Russian literature as a peculiarly unmediated account of contemporary history—particularly in Britain, as Rachel May amongst others has discussed. So, notoriously, Mikhail Lermontov's *A Hero of Our Time* (*Geroi nashego vremeni*) was retitled *Sketches of Russian Life in the Caucuses* (1853) and presented as a factual account by a 'Russe, Many Years Resident Among the Mountain Tribes', Nikolay Gogol''s *Dead Souls* (*Mertvye dushi*) appeared as *Home Life in Russia* (1854), accompanied by a preface claiming it had been written in English by a Russian nobleman 'to give an insight into the internal circumstances and relations of Russian society', and Ivan Turgenev's *Sportsman's Sketches* (*Zapiski okhotnika*), translated via a French version as *Russian Life in the Interior, or The Experiences of a Sportsman* (1855), was first serialized under the heading 'Photographs from Russian Life'.[12] E. M. de Vogüé's pioneering study *Le roman russe* (1885, 1886), first translated into English as *The Russian Novelists* in 1887, and first published in Britain in 1913, was immensely influential in presenting the Russian novel as a moral and truthful alternative to French naturalism. It argued that the Russian novel 'fascinated not by its local colour or its foreign savour, but by the "breath of life," the sincerity and compassion which animates all these books' ('Ce qui l'a séduite, ce n'est point la couleur locale et le ragoût d'étrangeté; c'est l'esprit de vie qui anime des livres, l'accent de sincérité

[9] Rosalind P. Blakesley and Susan E. Reid, 'A Long Engagement: Russian Art and the "West"', in Rosalind P. Blakesley and Susan E. Reid, eds, *Russian Art and the West: A Century of Dialogue in Painting, Architecture, and the Decorative Arts* (Dekalb, IL: Northern Illinois University Press, 2007), 3–20 (p. 8), Carol Adlam and Juliet Simpson, eds, *Critical Exchange: Art Criticism of the Eighteenth and Nineteenth Centuries in Russia and Western Europe* (Oxford: Peter Lang, 2009), Rosalind P. Blakesley, *The Arts and Crafts Movement* (London: Phaidon, 2006), 159–75.

[10] See Muchnic, *Dostoyevsky's English Reputation*, 171–2, Brewster, *East-West Passage*, 195–7, and Part II in general. Kaye's study is interesting in relation to this point, because its aim to delineate what happens when 'when novelist meets novelist', and to offer 'an explanation of Dostoevsky's power that accommodates form as well as content' is theorized not through Anglo-American formalist criticism, but the rediscovery of Russian formalism, in the guise of Bakhtin, that began in the mid-1980s (27–8).

[11] Donald Davie, introduction in *Russian Literature and Modern English Fiction: A Collection of Critical Essays* (Chicago, IL: University of Chicago Press, 1965), 9.

[12] Rachel May, *The Translator in the Text: On Reading Russian Literature in English* (Evanston, IL: Northwestern University Press, 1994), 14–15, 18–19.

et de sympathie').[13] This interpretation of Russian literature reappears throughout this volume in various guises—in the pamphlets and journals of the British Tolstoyans described by Charlotte Alston, to the Modern Language Association's report on the teaching of Russian discussed by Rebecca Beasley, and the blurring of art and life is fundamental to the British government's anxiety about Soviet cinema examined by Laura Marcus and James Smith.

This deliberately uncritical, even anti-critical, approach to Russian culture—literature in particular—is a component in the generalization typical of British enthusiasm about Russian culture that Phelps noted in 1956, and it is not easily analysed by a form of specialized criticism that focuses above all on formal influence. It is, however, much more susceptible to the pressure of questions that studies of the transnational and the global have taught us to ask. Indeed, it is precisely the vagueness of the generalizations noted by Phelps that draws attention to the ideological content of Britain's interpretation of Russian culture, and the mobility of 'Russia' as a signifier in British discourse.

The British zeal for Russian culture was, after all, a product of the tensions surrounding the political and diplomatic relations between the two countries during the nineteenth and twentieth centuries. As is routinely observed, sustained British interest in Russian culture came about as a result of the perceived need to learn more about an enemy recently defeated in the Crimean War, but which nonetheless still posed a considerable threat to British territorial possessions in Asia and the Far East. This colonial dimension generates many of the distinctive features of the British reception of Russian culture that set it apart from responses on the continent.[14] Relations were regularized to a certain extent by the signing of the Anglo-Russian Convention in 1907, and during the Great War, Russia, Britain, and France found themselves allied in the Triple Entente against the Axis powers—a relationship partially facilitated by pro-Russian propaganda disseminated by Russophiles in the cultural sphere, as Michael Hughes has argued.[15] Following Britain's participation in the failed intervention on the side of the White forces in the Russian Civil War,

[13] E. M. de Vogüé, *The Russian Novel*, trans. H. A. Sawyer (London: Chapman and Hall, 1913), 23, E. M. de Vogüé, *Le Roman russe* (Paris: Plon, 1886), lii. The first translation into English is abridged: E. M. de Vogüé, *The Russian Novelists*, trans. Jane Loring Edmands (Boston, MA: Lothrop, 1887).

[14] John Howes Gleason, *The Genesis of Russophobia in Great Britain: A Study of the Interaction of Policy and Opinion* (Cambridge, MA: Harvard University Press, 1950) remains a useful account. For a study of the latter half of the century that concentrates on the literary representation of this phenomenon, see Jimmie E. Cain, Jr., *Bram Stoker and Russophobia: Evidence of the British Fear of Russia in 'Dracula' and 'The Lady of the Shroud'* (Jefferson, NC: McFarland, 2006). For a comparative study of the German context, see Troy R. E. Paddock, *Creating the Russian Peril: Education, the Public Sphere, and National Identity in Imperial Germany, 1890–1940* (Columbia, SC: Camden House, 2010).

[15] Michael Hughes, 'Searching for the Soul of Russia: British Perceptions of Russia during the First World War', *Twentieth Century British History*, 20, no. 2 (2009), 198–226. For broader political histories of this general period, see Michael Hughes, *Diplomacy before the Russian Revolution: Britain, Russia and the Old Diplomacy, 1894–1917* (Basingstoke: Macmillan, 2000), Keith Neilson, *Britain and the Last Tsar: British Policy and Russia, 1894–1917* (Oxford: Clarendon Press, 1995), Fiona Tomaszewski, *A Great Russia: Russia and the Triple Entente* (Westport, CT: Praeger, 2002), and Keith Wilson, *The Policy of the Entente: Essays on the Determinants of British Foreign Policy 1904–1914* (Cambridge: Cambridge University Press, 1985).

the political relationship between the two countries reverted to a degree of tension, notwithstanding Britain's diplomatic recognition of the Soviet Union in 1924.

Yet rather than repeat the conclusions of the extensive body of secondary literature on Russo-British historical relations to paint an account of tension and détente, accommodation and resistance—or indeed use them to sketch a broad historical context as 'background' before turning to the discussion of specific works—we note here instead that studies of diplomatic, political, military, and even ecclesiastical relationships are particularly important because they point the way to the kind of detailed and nuanced history of institutions that this volume explores in relation to culture and the arts.[16] As fields shaped by contingent negotiations between individuals with contrasting and often competing ideologies and agendas, they offer an important methodological framework for the institutional analysis of cultural production. Moreover, as the chapters in this volume by Alston and Robert Henderson suggest, even the presence of large numbers of Russian political and religious émigrés in Britain need not necessarily be seen in the black-and-white terms of opposition to Russian autocracy and religious persecution inherited from such influential accounts as those of, say, Sergey Stepnyak-Kravchinsky or Petr Kropotkin. Rather, by setting aside such tempting binary oppositions and focusing on practical and institutional factors that shaped access to and disseminated knowledge and information, such accounts further contribute to our understanding of the complex mechanics of cultural mediation and exchange.

THE GLOBAL TURN

As Ken Hirschkop's afterword explores, this volume sits in complex relation to the theories of globalization and cosmopolitanism that have been expanding studies of early twentieth-century culture for the last two decades. Despite the substantial existing scholarship on the cultural relationship between Britain and Russia, the subject has been largely absent from studies generated by the 'global turn', which have focused principally on the exchange between Britain, France, and the United States on the one hand, and India, China, Africa, the Caribbean, and the Arab world on the other. In literary, art historical, and cultural studies, the contribution of postcolonial theory to defining global modernity has highlighted the urgency of rereading colonial and imperial encounters, and Russo-British relations have seemed a somewhat old-fashioned topic, affiliated to an earlier methodology. Yet introducing Russia to this framework opens up a distinctive seam of enquiry. As Andrew Wachtel has argued, Russia's entry into cultural modernity occurred within an unusual matrix of imperial power and cultural inferiority that led its cultural

[16] Michael Hughes, 'The English Slavophile: W. J. Birkbeck and Russia', *Slavonic and East European Review*, 82, no. 3 (2004), 680–706, Jeffrey Bibbee, 'The Church of England and Russian Orthodoxy: Politics and the Ecumenical Dialogue, 1888–1917', PhD thesis, University of London, 2008.

elite to emphasize 'their nation's peculiar sponge-like ability to absorb the best that other people had to offer as the basis for a universal, inclusive national culture'. We may expect, therefore, that other nations' reception of Russian culture will involve a complex encounter with familiar ideas made strange, made to seem distinctively Russian, in fact, while at the same time coded as universal.[17]

In the introduction to their influential collection *Geomodernisms*, Laura Doyle and Laura Winkiel note that the global turn 'requires a rethinking of periodization, genealogies, affiliations and forms'.[18] The trajectory such rethinking will follow in this volume appears in very condensed form in our subtitle, 'from melodrama to modernism'. The juxtaposition of these terms encodes a cluster of contrasts: a formal or generic contrast (drama/ experimental poetry and prose), a temporal contrast (nineteenth century/ twentieth century), and a contrast in audience and market (mass culture/ high culture). But the prepositions of the subtitle should not imply any easy route between the main terms, nor any settled idea of what those terms connote. Our subtitle should be seen, instead, as raising a series of questions.

What are the national and cultural imperatives that shape and define a form or a genre? A list of the genres, or sub-genres, imported from Russia to Britain between 1880 and 1940 would conventionally include the anti-classical ballets of the Ballets Russes, the Chekhovian drama, the psychological (or 'Dostoevskyan') novel, and the montage film as developed by Sergey Eizenshtein. But those importations were substantially transformed for their new audience. For example, Laurence Senelick demonstrates in his chapter on the presentation of Russia and Russians on the British stage that Chekhov's plays were initially interpreted through the stereotypes of nineteenth-century British melodramas on Russian themes, which were closely keyed to political events. Stuart Young's chapter indicates how the eventual success of Chekhov's plays was not only due to Fedor Komissarzhevsky's notorious romanticizing of Chekhov, but also a contemporary context which saw a far wider and more diverse range of Russian plays performed than has hitherto been understood. The British conception of Chekhovian drama is not the same as the Russian—though, of course, even before Chekhov's work was transformed by its British dissemination, reception, and translation, what appeared to be a distinctively Russian import was already a hybrid product, responding to the short stories of Guy de Maupassant, and the plays of Shakespeare and Ibsen.[19] Similarly, Dostoevsky's novels, the works most closely associated with the dissemination of the peculiarly 'Russian soul' in early twentieth-century Britain, are in fact deeply engaged with the British and French

[17] Andrew Wachtel, 'Translation, Imperialism, and National Self-Definition in Russia', in Dilip Parameshwar Gaonkar, ed., *Alternative Modernities* (Durham, NC: Duke University Press, 2001), 61.

[18] Laura Doyle and Laura Winkiel, 'Introduction: The Global Horizons of Modernism', in *Geomodernisms: Race, Modernism, Modernity* (Bloomington and Indianapolis, IN: Indiana University Press, 2005), 3.

[19] See Andrew Baruch Wachtel, *Plays of Expectations: Intertextual Relations in Russian Twentieth-Century Drama* (Seattle, WA: University of Washington Press, 2006), 29–49.

realist traditions.[20] The 'Russian soul' itself is by no means the pristine Slavic concept it appeared: informed in its nineteenth-century Russian context by German Romanticism, its meaning shifted substantially as it moved into a predominantly literary context in twentieth-century Britain.[21]

This process of transformation not only governs the works within certain genres and categories, but the boundaries of the genres and categories themselves. Peter Brooks has drawn attention to the importance of retaining distinctions between national traditions of melodrama, though Louise McReynolds and Joan Neuberger's collection of essays on melodrama in Russia finds that 'what made Russia melodrama unique was Russia, not melodrama'.[22] Modernism is a more problematic term in the history of cultural exchange between Russia and Britain: nineteenth-century Russian realism presented a model to modernist British fiction, but British modernists had less knowledge of, and interest in, Russian literary modernism. Indeed, 'modernizm' itself is a term that sits somewhat uncomfortably within the vocabulary of Russian literary history, not least because it was often used as a term of abuse in the Soviet era. Movements as diverse as symbolism, acmeism, and futurism can all be seen as local versions of pan-European cultural phenomena, yet they rarely map directly onto their apparent cognates in other languages and cultures.[23] Caroline Maclean's chapter shows that British modernists knew something of contemporary experiments in Russian visual art, but that their selection of artists in reviews, reproductions, and exhibitions was governed by the promotion of a 'spiritual aesthetics' of modernism, which excluded the more avant-garde work that 'Russian modernism' would normally be understood to include.

As this mismatch between modernisms (and the uneasy distinction between modernism and the avant-garde in that last sentence) suggests, the transferral of cultural material and cultural categories across national borders also entails temporal disparities. If British modernism is conventionally associated with the period

[20] See Nathalie Babel Brown, *Hugo and Dostoevsky* (Ann Arbor, MI: Ardis, 1978), Donald Fanger, *Dostoevsky and Romantic Realism* (Cambridge, MA: Harvard University Press, 1965), I. M. Katarsky, *Dikkens v Rossii* (Moscow: Nauka, 1966). For further discussion of the British impact on nineteenth-century Russian literature, see Catherine Brown, *The Art of Comparison: How Novels and Critics Compare* (London: Legenda, 2011), W. Gareth Jones, 'George Eliot's "Adam Bede" and Tolstoy's Conception of "Anna Karenina"', *Modern Language Review*, 61, no. 3 (1966), 473–81, and Rachel Polonsky, *English Literature and the Russian Aesthetic Renaissance* (Cambridge: Cambridge University Press, 1998).

[21] Robert C. Williams, 'The Russian Soul: A Study in European Thought and Non-European Nationalism', *Journal of the History of Ideas*, 31, no. 4 (1970), 573–88, Catherine Brown, 'The Russian Soul Englished', *Journal of Modern Literature* 36, no. 1 (Fall 2012), 132–49.

[22] Peter Brooks, *The Melodramatic Imagination: Balzac, Henry James, Melodrama, and the Mode of Excess* (New Haven, CT: Yale University Press, 1976), xii, Louise McReynolds and Joan Neuberger, eds, *Imitations of Life: Two Centuries of Melodrama in Russia* (Durham, NC: Duke University Press, 2002), 11.

[23] Nevertheless, modernism, as term and idea, has found considerable purchase in Anglo-American Russian studies. See, for instance, George Gibian and H. W. Tjalsma, *Russian Modernism: Culture and the Avant-Garde, 1900–1930* (Ithaca, NY: Cornell University Press, 1976), Stephen C. Hutchings, *Russian Modernism: The Transfiguration of the Everyday* (Cambridge: Cambridge University Press, 1997), Irina Paperno and Joan Delaney Grossman, eds, *Creating Life: The Aesthetic Utopia of Russian Modernism* (Stanford, CA: Stanford University Press, 1994), Hilary L. Fink, *Bergson and Russian Modernism, 1900–1930* (Evanston, IL: Northwestern University Press, 1999), Peter I. Barta, with Ulrich Goebel, eds, *The European Foundations of Russian Modernism* (Lampeter: Mellen, 1991).

between 1910 and 1930, its Russian equivalent is generally dated slightly earlier.[24] In the literary field, the development of a self-consciously modern (if not definitively modernist) aesthetic is often attributed to Dmitry Merezhkovsky's two lectures entitled 'O prichanakh upadka i o novykh techeniyakh v sovremennoi russkoi literatury' ('On the Reasons for the Decline and on the New Trends in Contemporary Russian Literature'), delivered in 1892.[25] Significantly, this period is often referred to as Russia's 'Silver Age' (distinguishing it from the 'Golden Age' in the first half of the nineteenth century)—a temporal rather than an aesthetic definition of the movement.[26] The terminal point of Russian modernism is harder to pinpoint, both because the Bolshevik revolution of 1917 has often served as a political justification for an aesthetic preference, and because the early Soviet avant-garde seems to effect a radical break with its immediate precursors. Nonetheless, recent revisionist studies have begun to posit profound continuities between Russian symbolism, the Soviet avant-garde, and Stalinist socialist realism that further problematize normative accounts of Russian literary evolution.[27]

Temporal disparity of a different sort occurs within the reception of individual works. Dyagilev's ballets, Kandinsky's paintings, Stravinsky's music, and the montage film all arrive in Britain seeming more recognizably 'modern' than any of their British equivalents. But in all four cases an important element of that modernity was, paradoxically, their perceived or intended primitivism. The discourse of modernist primitivism had been established in Britain at least by 1910, when Desmond MacCarthy's catalogue essay for Roger Fry's exhibition, *Manet and the Post-Impressionists*, explained the painting of Cézanne, Van Gogh, and Matisse as a return to the expressiveness of 'primitive art', and, as Maclean indicates, this discourse directed the choice of Russian artists included in the *Second Post-Impressionist Exhibition* (1912).[28] But in the case of the Russian arts, unlike the French, the

[24] For debates about the dating of modernism, see Fredric Jameson, *A Singular Modernity* (London: Verso, 2002), Susan Stanford Friedman, 'Periodizing Modernism: Postcolonial Modernities and the Space/Time Borders of Modernist Studies', *Modernism/Modernity*, 13, no. 3 (2006), 425–43; Raymond Williams, 'When Was Modernism?', *New Left Review*, 175 (1989), 48–52, Mark Wollaeger, introduction in Mark Wollaeger and Matt Eatough, eds, *The Oxford Handbook of Global Modernisms* (Oxford: Oxford University Press, 2011), 10–14.

[25] Avril Pyman, *A History of Russian Symbolism* (Cambridge: Cambridge University Press, 1994), 7–10.

[26] The historical validity of this widely used term has been disputed by Omry Ronen in *The Fallacy of the Silver Age in Twentieth-Century Russian Literature* (Amsterdam: Harwood Academic Press, 1997).

[27] Still the most important study in this respect is Boris Groys, *The Total Art of Stalinism: Avant-Garde, Aesthetic Dictatorship, and Beyond*, trans. Charles Rougle (Princeton, NJ: Princeton University Press, 1992). See also Bernice Glatzer Rosenthal, ed., *Nietzsche and Soviet Culture: Ally and Adversary* (Cambridge: Cambridge University Press, 1994), and Bernice Glazer Rosenthal, *New Myth, New World: From Nietzsche to Stalinism* (University Park, PA: Pennsylvania State University Press, 2002). Catriona Kelly's anthology of modernist literary works takes the period up to the eve of the Second World War: see *Utopias: Russian Modernist Texts, 1905–1940* (London: Penguin, 1999).

[28] [Desmond MacCarthy], 'The Post-Impressionists', in *Manet and the Post-Impressionists* (London: Ballantyne & Company, 1910), 7, 10, 11. See Rebecca Beasley, 'Vortorussophilia', in Mark Antliff and Scott Klein, eds, *Vorticism: New Perspectives* (Oxford: Oxford University Press, forthcoming 2013), and Marianna Torgovnick, *Gone Primitive: Savage Intellects, Modern Lives* (Chicago, IL: University of Chicago Press, 1990), 85–104.

primitive was understood as indigenous: it was seen not as an engagement with the colonial (principally African) 'other', but an invocation of a native heritage, variously understood as either the Byzantine, oriental, or even pre-Christian, heritage of the Eastern Slavs. The principal reason for the distinction lies in the fact that Russia's empire was, unlike the British and French overseas possessions, a contiguous one, and hence played a prominent role in the formation of domestic national identity.[29] Nizhinsky's 1913 ballet *Le Sacre du printemps*, the subject of Ramsay Burt's chapter, is structured around an imaginary Slavonic tribe's rituals, interpreted by Russian critics in nationalist terms, but in Britain as more emphatically, and transnationally, modern.

Thus so-called primitive and folk cultures become the preserve of high art, through a process variously viewed as inspired experiment, colonialist raid, absorption of mass culture, and capitalist opportunism. Certainly, in many of the chapters here, there is a strong awareness of how 'Russia' and Russian cultural products are sold in the British marketplace, whether in melodramas for the masses, as Senelick discusses, or in theatre, music, art, and film for the cultural elite, as Young, Bullock, Maclean, and Marcus explore, or in Soviet-sanctioned translations for the political left wing, as Ian Patterson describes. But of course one of the distinctive characteristics of the dissemination of Russian culture is that instances of cultural capitalism are simultaneous with, and sometimes indistinguishable from, instances that are directly anti-capitalist. So in Alston's chapter we see Tolstoy's Christian anarchist writings circulating in a milieu that might well be characterized as a marketplace, organized by the entrepreneurial genius of Tolstoyans such as John Kenworthy and Vladimir Chertkov, yet this marketplace is structured against the cultivation of capital; Tolstoy renounced his copyright on these works, and the Tolstoyan community eschewed definition on lines of class or wealth. Henderson's examination of the Free Russian Library set up in London by Aleksey Teplov also highlights a particular community, one predominately made up of impoverished Russian expatriates. But its boundaries were porous enough to enable the participation of individuals beyond that community, such as Constance Garnett, the period's most prolific translator of Russian literature into English, and Charles Hagberg Wright, the Librarian of the London Library.

Although our focus away from individuals means that Garnett is a far less visible figure in this volume than one might expect, she is representative of connections between the Russian émigré community and the socialist literary elite, as is Virginia Woolf. Marcus's chapter on British film culture discusses how Soviet film reached diverse audiences, shown by both 'bourgeois' and workers' film societies, which found common cause in opposing censorship. Patterson's chapter on the Soviet literary agency, the Press and Publisher Literary Service (PresLit), presents a compelling picture of how Soviet culture was disseminated through a mixture of Soviet propaganda, socialist idealism, and financial need. The market for Russian culture in Britain, then, was both highbrow and lowbrow, elite and mass, wealthy and poor.

[29] See Vera Tolz, *Russia's Own Orient: The Politics of Identity and Oriental Studies in the Late Imperial and Early Soviet Periods* (Oxford: Oxford University Press, 2011), Harsha Ram, *The Imperial Sublime: A Russian Poetics of Empire* (Madison, WI: University of Wisconsin Press, 2003), and Alexander Etkind, *Internal Colonization: Russia's Imperial Experience* (Cambridge: Polity, 2011).

This mixing of audiences within small communities is a typical feature of the way Russian culture circulated in Britain: the role of revolutionary émigrés like Teplov, and the involvement of British socialist movements, made the reception of Russian culture structurally distinct from the reception of French, German, Spanish, and, even, Italian culture in the era before 1917. Britain's relationship with Russian culture continued to be distinct from that of the European continent after 1917, too. Many of the political exiles and other émigrés of the pre-revolutionary period left the country, and few of those who chose—or were forced—to leave Soviet Russia elected to settle in Britain in the interwar years, preferring the major centres of Russian émigré life, such as Paris, Berlin, Prague, and Sofia, to London.[30] In comparison to France, Germany, Czechoslovakia, or even Bulgaria, the Russian diaspora in Britain was relatively small in number and the range and influence of its activities remained limited. It is for this reason that the present volume differs from many of the recent studies that have been produced on Russian culture's relationship to and place in the West. To be sure, an important role was played by a number of émigré Russians in Britain in the interwar period, as works by G. S. Smith and Ol′ga Kaznina have demonstrated, yet it was certainly not as vital and decisive as that played by their contemporaries in continental Europe. Accordingly, in this volume, the role of the host culture

[30] On the French, especially Parisian scene, see Aleksey Gibson, *Russian Poetry and Criticism in Paris from 1920 to 1940* (The Hague: Leuxenhoff, 1990), F. W. J. Hemmings, *The Russian Novel in France, 1884–1914* (Oxford: Oxford University Press, 1950), Leonid Livak, *How it was Done in Paris: Russian Émigré Literature and French Modernism* (Madison, WI: University of Wisconsin Press, 2003) and *Russian Émigrés in the Intellectual and Literary Life of Inter-War France: A Bibliographical Essay* (Montreal: McGill-Queen's University Press, 2010), Annick Morard, *De l'émigré au déraciné: la 'jeune génération' des écrivains russes entre identité et esthétique (Paris, 1920–1940)* (Lausanne: L'Age d'Homme, 2010), Zh.-F. Zhakkar (Jean-Philippe Jaccard), A. Morar (Annick Morard) and Zh. Tassis (Gervaise Tassis), eds, *Russkie pisateli v Parizhe: vzglyad na frantsuzskuyu literaturu, 1920–1940* (Moscow: Russkii Put′, 2007), and Aleksey Zverev, *Zhizn′ russkogo literaturnogo Parizha, 1920–1940* (Moscow: Molodaya gvardiya, 2003). On Germany, see Karl Schlögel, ed., *Russische Emigration in Deutschland, 1918–1941: Leben im europäischen Bürgerkrieg* (Berlin: Akademie Verlag, 1995), and Amory Burchard, *Klubs der russischen Dichter in Berlin, 1920–1941: Institutionen des literarischen Lebens in Exil* (Munich: Sagner, 2001) Prague was a particularly important intellectual centre, not least because of its role in bringing Russian formalism, and subsequently structuralism, to the West: see Catherine Andreyev and Ivan Savický, *Russia Abroad: Prague and the Russian Diaspora, 1918–1938* (New Haven, CT: Yale University Press, 2004), Alastair Renfrew and Galin Tihanov, eds, *Critical Theory in Russia and the West* (London: Routledge, 2010), and Galin Tihanov, 'The Birth of Modern Literary Theory in East-Central Europe', in *History of the Literary Cultures of East-Central Europe*, i, ed. M. Cornis-Pope and J. Neubauer (Amsterdam: John Benjamins, 2004), 416–24, and 'Why Did Modern Literary Theory Originate in Central and Eastern Europe? (And Why Is It Now Dead?)', *Common Knowledge*, 10, no. 1 (2004), 61–81. For a survey of émigré literary culture more generally, see Maria Rubins, ed., *Twentieth-Century Russian Émigré Writers*, Dictionary of Literary Biography 37 (Detroit, MI: Thomson Gale, 2005). Although most research in this area concerns literature, there is substantial body of work on the political and philosophical movement known as Eurasianism, which had a particular impact in musical circles: see Richard Taruskin, *Stravinsky and the Russian Traditions: A Biography of the Works through 'Mavra'*, 2 vols (Oxford: Oxford University Press, 1996), I. G. Vishnevetsky, *'Evraziiskoe uklonenie' v muzyke 1920–1930–kh godov: istoriya voprosa, stat′i i materialy A. Lur′e, P. Suvchinskogo, I. Stravinskogo, V. Dukel′skogo, S. Prokof′eva, I. Markevicha* (Moscow: Novoe literaturnoe obozrenie, 2005), and Ekaterini Levidou, 'The Encounter of Neoclassicism with Eurasianism in Interwar Paris: Stravinsky, Suvchinsky and Lourié', DPhil thesis, University of Oxford, 2008.

receives greater attention than has been the case in recent studies of the Russian diaspora.[31]

However, Katerina Clark's recent argument that, as late as the 1930s, the Soviet Union continued to be associated with a form of political action that transcended the merely national is borne out by Marcus's and Patterson's chapters in this volume. In *Moscow, The Fourth Rome: Stalinism, Cosmopolitanism, and the Evolution of Soviet Culture, 1931–41*, Clark seeks to 'supplement the standard account, which analyses the decade in terms of a turn to Great Russian nationalism—already well argued and documented—by pointing to a simultaneous, if more precariously flourishing, internationalism'.[32] Although the essays in this volume focus on the British, rather than the Soviet, context, Clark's emphasis comes as a timely reminder of the importance of philosophy, politics, and the history of ideas as transnational, even international, spaces that can shape both the receiving and exporting culture in complementary ways. PresLit's activity provides an example of how the Soviet Union intensified its commitment to promoting an image of itself in the 1930s through the dissemination of its most recent literature in English translation. As a visual form with strongly revolutionary associations, film was even better placed to benefit both from Western interest in Russian culture, and Soviet cosmopolitanism in the Stalin era. Perhaps paradoxically, patterns of reception may even have shaped the production of Russian culture itself. Take, for instance, Ivor Montagu's publication of a number of essays by Vsevolod Pudovkin in London in 1929 and 1933, both with the short title *On Film Technique*.[33] Neither directly corresponds to any single Russian publication in the Soviet Union; indeed, these editions were for a long time the only available sources for these works, which circulated as English-language versions of an otherwise unavailable Russian text in a kind of transnational space made possible by translation and cultural exchange.[34]

However, while the products, ideas, practices and people discussed in this book cross national boundaries, and in that sense are transnational, most of the chapters in this volume are at least as interested in exploring their nationality. No one working on Russian culture can fail to register that cultural borders do not correspond to national borders, but this volume is explicitly concerned with Britain and Russia not only as cultural spaces but as nation states with a historical reality. The impact of the political relationship between Britain and Russia is everywhere evident in the following chapters: it generates curiosity about the enemy during the Crimean War and the ally during the Great War (Senelick); it shapes the role of university Russian

[31] G. S. Smith, *D. S. Mirsky: A Russian-English Life, 1890–1939* (Oxford and New York: Oxford University Press, 2000), and O. A. Kaznina, *Russkie v Anglii: Russkaya emigratsiya v kontekste russko-angliiskikh literaturnykh svyazei v pervoi polovine XX veka* (Moscow: Nasledie, 1997).

[32] Katerina Clark, *Moscow, the Fourth Rome: Stalinism, Cosmopolitanism, and the Evolution of Soviet Culture, 1931–1941* (Cambridge, MA: Harvard University Press, 2011), 7.

[33] Vsevolod Pudovkin, *On Film Technique: Three Essays and an Address*, trans. and ed. Ivor Montagu (London: Gollancz, 1929) and *Film Technique: Five Essays and Two Addresses*, trans. and ed. Ivor Montagu (London: Newnes, 1933).

[34] On the textual history of the essays, see Richard Taylor, 'Introduction: Pudovkin Revisited', in Vsevolod Pudovkin, *Selected Essays*, ed. Richard Taylor (London: Seagull Books, 2006), xiii–xiv.

departments and their curricula (Beasley); it determines which Russian texts are translated (Patterson), and it controls the distribution of Soviet films (Marcus, Smith). The history of the reception of Russian culture provides particularly clear examples of how profoundly mediated cultural material is when it moves across borders, how partial our access to the source culture must be, even while it circulates within a rhetoric that suggests precisely the opposite, that Russian culture is characterized by its immediacy, its authenticity, its connection to universal ideas of 'life' and 'the soul'.

One of the effects of this rhetoric is the transformation of Russia, the nation in history, into 'Russia', a British intellectual commodity that bears little relation to its ostensible source. Several chapters in this volume demonstrate how Russia is deployed as a sign to connote other, domestic, concerns. Michael Newton discusses how Oscar Wilde's first play, *Vera; or The Nihilists* (1880), covertly discusses domestic politics by presenting a plot about Russian nihilism as a substitute for the more immediate threat of Irish Fenianism. Ramsay Burt argues that Vatslav Nizhinsky's *Le Sacre du printemps* (*The Rite of Spring*, 1913) becomes, in reviews of its London performance, a debate about the performance of gender closely tied to the suffrage campaign. And Matthew Taunton examines how, in the 1934 debate in the *New Statesman* about H. G. Wells's interview with Stalin, Soviet Russia operates as an imaginary space in which the political fantasies of British intellectuals are staged. As Hirschkop remarks, 'it's tempting to say that Russia was *already* in Britain, its appearance in imported plays, films, and ballet obliquely reminding its audience that Britain was a more confused space than they were willing to admit'.

INSTITUTIONS OF TRANSLATION

Twenty years ago, Susan Bassnett concluded her canonical *Comparative Literature: A Critical Introduction* with the contentious argument that 'comparative literature as a discipline has had its day'. 'Writing does not happen in a vacuum', she wrote, 'it happens in a context and the process of translating texts from one cultural system into another is not a neutral, innocent, transparent activity... We should look upon translation studies as the principal discipline from now on, with comparative literature as a valued but subsidiary subject area'.[35] This argument, also made by several other critics, including Gayatri Spivak and David Damrosch, has met with sustained rebuttal, and an assertion of comparative literature's continued relevance and its difference from the straw man presented in Bassnett's argument.[36] But the argument's prioritizing of translation is nevertheless instructive for

[35] Susan Bassnett, *Comparative Literature: A Critical Introduction* (Oxford: Blackwell, 1993), 160–1.

[36] Gayatri Spivak, *Death of a Discipline* (New York: Columbia University Press, 2003), David Damrosch, *What is World Literature?* (Princeton, NJ: Princeton University Press, 2003).

modernist studies, which has had surprisingly little to say about translation, despite its well-known centrality to the creative work of the period.[37]

Our 2011 special issue of the journal *Translation and Literature*, *Translating Russia, 1890–1935*, presented five essays on translators and mediators who are largely absent from this volume, including Maurice Baring, Korney Chukovsky, Edward Garnett, Constance Garnett, Jane Harrison, S. S. Kotelyansky, D. S. Mirsky, and Virginia Woolf.[38] In the introduction to that collection, we drew attention to the under-developed connections between the fields of cultural or descriptive translation studies and literary modernist studies. In particular, we were interested in relating literary studies' increased interest in institutions of cultural transmission to translation studies' account of literature as a system or network that includes various forms of translation or rewriting.[39] For example, although translators are not a focus of Lawrence Rainey's *Institutions of Modernism* (1998) the terms in which he sets out his argument are clearly relevant for studies of translation and reception. Definitions of modernism derived from formalist and ideological analysis, he argues, pay insufficient attention to

> the intervenient institutions that connect works to readerships, or readerships to particular social structures. To focus on those institutions, instead, is to view modernism as more than a series of texts or the ideas that found expression in them. It becomes a social reality, a configuration of agents and practices that converge in the production, marketing, and publicization of an idiom, a shareable language in the family of twentieth-century tongues.[40]

Rainey's argument echoes those of translation theorists writing over a decade before, who had also rejected a critical practice that evaluates formal features of the text in favour of one that describes its production in social terms. Theo Hermans described the contributors to his influential collection *The Manipulation of Literature* (1985) as sharing

> a view of literature as a complex and dynamic system; a conviction that there should be a continual interplay between theoretical models and practical case studies; an

[37] Exceptions are Emily Dalgarno, *Virginia Woolf and the Migrations of Language* (Cambridge: Cambridge University Press, 2012), Daniel Katz, *American Modernism's Expatriate Scene: The Labour of Translation* (Edinburgh: Edinburgh University Press, 2007), Steven G. Yao, *Translation and the Languages of Modernism: Gender, Politics, Language* (Basingstoke: Palgrave, 2002). See Rebecca Beasley, 'Modernism's Translations', in Mark Wollaeger and Matt Eatough, eds, *The Oxford Handbook of Global Modernisms* (New York: Oxford University Press, 2012), 551–70, and 'On Not Knowing Russian: The Translations of Virginia Woolf and S. S. Kotelianskii', *Modern Language Review*, 108, no. 1 (2013), 1–29.

[38] Helen Smith, 'Edward Garnett: Interpreting the Russians', Marilyn Schwinn Smith, '"Bergsonian Poetics" and the Beast: Jane Harrison's Translations from the Russian', Claire Davison-Pégon 'Samuel Solomonovich Koteliansky and British Modernism', Philip Ross Bullock, 'Untranslated and Untranslatable? Pushkin's Poetry in English, 1892–1931', Anna Vaninskaya, 'Korney Chukovsky in Britain', in Rebecca Beasley and Philip Ross Bullock, eds, *Translating Russia, 1890–1935*, special issue of *Translation and Literature*, 20, no. 3 (2011)), 301–13, 314–33, 334–47, 348–72, 373–92.

[39] Rebecca Beasley and Philip Ross Bullock, 'Introduction: The Illusion of Transparency', in Beasley and Bullock, eds, *Translating Russia, 1890–1935*, 283–300.

[40] Lawrence Rainey, *Institutions of Modernism: Literary Elites and Public Culture* (New Haven, CT: Yale University Press, 1998), 5.

> approach to literary translation which is descriptive, target oriented, functional and systemic; and an interest in the norms and constraints that govern the production and reception of translations, in the relation between translation and other types of text processing, and in the place and role of translations both within a given literature and in the interaction between literatures.[41]

Although neither Hermans' nor Rainey's statements are recent, since their publication remarkably few studies of early twentieth-century translation culture have appeared; the aim of *Translating Russia* was to collect a body of essays that focused not on the merit of individual translations, but on the dynamic network in which they were produced.

Russia in Britain develops this project. Although it has little to say about individual translations of Russian texts, it is centrally concerned with networks of translation, not only directly, as in Beasley's and Patterson's chapters, but also in more general terms. Hermans' representation of translation as one among many forms of 'manipulation', and André Lefevere's similarly expansive concept of translation as only one element of the 'rewriting' a text undergoes when it moves between audiences, provide enabling models for studies of international and transnational encounters dissatisfied with the binary structures of comparison, reception, and influence.[42]

Russia in Britain is organized roughly chronologically. The traditional account of Russian culture's British reception tends to begin with the arrival of groups of Russian émigrés in the 1880s and the translations of Russian realist classics they published and promoted. The first chapter in the volume demonstrates that this left-leaning and highly literary dissemination of Russian culture developed in the context of more popular forms with a quite different political agenda: Victorian popular theatre and melodrama. Reminding us that the history of Russia on the British stage begins well before the twentieth century's productions of Chekhov, Laurence Senelick's wide-ranging chapter, '"For God, for Czar, for Fatherland": Russians on the British Stage from Napoleon to the Great War', shows the significance of non-Russian-authored plays, which absorbed and reflected the changing political opinion about Russo-British relations. Instituting a more variegated and complete theatrical history of Russia in Britain, this chapter's approach aptly summarizes the aims of the volume as a whole, breaking down divisions between high and low culture, and considering the reception of Russian culture not as a passive experience, but as an active engagement, in which British and Russian cultural materials transform each other. Chapters two and five provide further revisions of Russia's importance to British theatre history. Drawing out one element of Senelick's account, the appearance of the Russian nihilist as a stock character on the late Victorian stage, Michael Newton's chapter, '"Nihilists of Castlebar!": Exporting Russian Nihilism in the 1880s and the case of Oscar Wilde's *Vera; or the Nihilists*', examines how this figure comes to summarize British fears about political violence, and in Wilde's

[41] Theo Hermans, 'Introduction: Translation Studies and a New Paradigm', in *The Manipulation of Literature: Studies in Literary Translation*, ed. Theo Hermans (London: Croom Helm, 1985), 10–11.

[42] André Lefevere, *Translation, Rewriting and the Manipulation of Literary Fame* (London: Routledge, 1992).

play becomes a locus for displaced anxieties generated by the more direct threat of Irish Fenianism. Exploring the reasons for the play's withdrawal before its first performance, Newton raises the issue of censorship, an issue addressed throughout the volume, most directly in the final two chapters of the volume, on cinema. Jumping forward to chapter five, in '"Formless", "Pretentious", "Hideous and Revolting": Non-Chekhov Russian and Soviet Drama on the British Stage', Stuart Young provides a twentieth-century counterpart to Senelick's chapter, detailing the variety of Russian and Soviet drama on the British stage, preceding and accompanying the better-known cult of Chekhov.

Chapters three and four present new research on groups central to the dissemination of Russian literature and thought in the late nineteenth and early twentieth centuries. In 'Britain and the International Tolstoyan Movement, 1890–1910', Charlotte Alston explores the British Tolstoyan movement's integration of Tolstoy's philosophy with local British concerns, and the way its connections with international movements shaped its ideology. In '"For the Cause of Education": A History of the Free Russian Library in Whitechapel, 1898–1917', Robert Henderson uncovers the history of the library founded by Aleksey Teplov in 1898 to educate and support East European immigrants in the East End of London. These chapters shed new light on the circumstances in which the translation and reading of Russian literature occurred by insisting on the importance of popular movements and working-class activism, and at the same time, provide further information about the contacts of more well-known translators and writers. Tolstoy's major translators, Aylmer and Louise Maude were members of the Tolstoyan communities in Croydon and subsequently Purleigh; Constance Garnett, Edward Garnett, and Ford Madox Ford lived close by. Ford's mother was a member of the Free Russian Library's committee and Constance Garnett was a borrower of the Library's books.

Moving into the early twentieth century, Young's chapter describes the rarely discussed range of Russian drama performed in Britain in the early twentieth-century, showing that British audiences were able to see more contemporary drama, including naturalist, symbolist, and, later, socialist realist works, than standard narratives relate. Chapters six, seven, and eight present new perspectives on the reception of Russian music, dance, and the visual arts during the first two decades of the twentieth century. Philip Ross Bullock's chapter, 'Tsar's Hall: Russian Music in London, 1895–1926', shows how the vogue for performances of Russian music at the turn of the century became the site of a debate about whether academic institutions or popular taste should determine the canon. It also sheds light on the evolving status of modernism in music, with Russia at first representing the latest development in European music, yet later being partially eclipsed by the rise of a transnational and cosmopolitan form of neoclassicism that sat uneasily with the late romanticism characteristic of the first wave of Russia music that had found popularity in Britain. In '*Le Sacre du printemps* in London: The Politics of Embodied Freedom in Early Modernist Dance and Suffragette Protest' Ramsay Burt looks at the sensational first British performance of *Le Sacre du printemps* by the Ballets Russes in the new context of the contemporaneous militant suffrage campaign, examining the political construction of the female body. In 'Russian Aesthetics in Britain: Kandinsky,

Sadleir, and *Rhythm*' Caroline Maclean is concerned with the role Russian culture played in modernist critical debates. She explores responses to Russian visual art and aesthetics in the British periodical press, focusing in particular on the promotion of Vasily Kandinsky's art and writings in *Rhythm*, the modernist journal edited by John Middleton Murry and Michael Sadleir. Like Skryabin, Kandinsky was associated with the theosophical movement, and the work of both artists became a focal point for debates about the relationship between spirituality and modernism in art and in criticism.

In the next three chapters the discussion turns to literary canons and the role intellectuals played in determining British responses to the Soviet Union. Chapters nine and ten expand knowledge about the translation and dissemination of Russian and Soviet literature in Britain by moving beyond the study of well-known amateur translators, to bring to light the work of teachers, academics, and professional translators. In 'Reading Russian: Russian Studies and the Literary Canon', Rebecca Beasley investigates the development of Russian studies in schools and universities during the early twentieth century, in order to analyse the shaping of curricula and the creation of an academic literary canon of Russian and Soviet literature. In 'The Translation of Soviet Literature: John Rodker and PresLit', Ian Patterson reveals the central importance of the official Soviet literary agency, and the role played by its London agent, the modernist poet, novelist, and publisher, John Rodker, who was employed to find translators and publishers for Soviet-approved books, essays, short stories, screenplays, and music during the 1930s. In chapter eleven, 'Russia and the British Intellectuals: The Significance of *The Stalin-Wells Talk*', Matthew Taunton analyses the 1934 debate on Soviet Russia in the *New Statesman and Nation* between three of Britain's leading intellectuals—H. G. Wells, George Bernard Shaw, and John Maynard Keynes—occasioned by H. G. Wells's interview with Stalin published that year. His chapter records the polarized opinions about the Soviet Union among the British left in this period, and analyses the continued importance of the Soviet Union in the British political imagination.

In the 1920s and 1930s, Soviet film became of major interest to British writers and artists, its formal techniques suggesting wholly new directions for the arts, and its development as a mass medium offering new possibilities for entertaining and instructing a new, far larger, audience. Soviet Russia seemed to present not only a new political system for the modern world, but also a new art to represent it, one that synthesized and superseded the old forms, genres, and media. Chapters twelve and thirteen examine the reception of Soviet cinema in Britain. Laura Marcus's 'The Tempo of Revolution: British Film Culture and Soviet Cinema in the 1920s' surveys the diverse routes through which Soviet film and film theory were disseminated in Britain, and argues that government censorship shaped the character of early British film culture, its film societies, its journals, and its criticism. James Smith looks at one particular instance of such censorship in 'Soviet Films and British Intelligence in the 1930s: The Case of Kino Films and MI5'. Drawing on recently declassified intelligence files, he discusses MI5's monitoring of the film section of the Workers' Theatre Movement, founded in order to make Soviet films available in Britain. The volume concludes with an afterword by Ken Hirschkop,

'A Time and a Place for Everything: On Russia, Britain, and Being Modern', which explores the distinctiveness of the British encounter with Russian culture in the context of recent debates about global modernity and cosmopolitanism.

Hirschkop concludes with a measured and somewhat equivocal account of the fate of many of the Russian-inflected projects studied here:

> Perhaps the difficulty of the task can be gauged by the temporary and provisional nature of so many of the projects recounted in this collection. The Tolstoyan collectives faded away, Rodker lost his job, Wells' dreams came to naught, Russian drama remained—outside Chekhov, Turgenev, and Bulgakov's *Dni Turbinykh* (*Days of the Turbins*)—an alien body, and Kinofilms went bust. . . . For Russian culture may not have been the kind of material its host culture could adapt or amalgamate. Perhaps it was, in fact though not in intention, the critique of Britain's modernity, to be accepted or rejected. From the evidence of this volume, the critique did not fall on deaf ears, but those who listened most attentively were not in a position to make it stick.

Such a cautionary note is welcome in the longer historical perspective, and it is an important corrective to the more extravagant yet unsubstantiated claims that are sometimes made for the impact of Russian culture in Britain during the early twentieth century. At the same time, the readiness with which British intellectuals responded to Russian cultural models is compelling. Rebecca West claimed that 'Russia is to the young intellectuals of to-day what Italy was to the Victorians.'[43] Virginia Woolf remarked that 'the most elementary remarks upon modern English fiction can hardly avoid some mention of the Russian influence, and if the Russians are mentioned one runs the risk of feeling that to write of any fiction save theirs is a waste of time'.[44] The film critic Bryher (Winifred Ellerman) wrote of Eizenshtein's *October* (*Oktyabr'*), 'Of all the films I know, I feel it to be the greatest.'[45] And in 1917 D. H. Lawrence wrote to his friend, the translator S. S. Kotelyansky, 'I feel that our chiefest hope for the future is Russia. When I think of the new young country there, I love it inordinately. It is the place of hope.'[46] Hirschkop's point, like Davie's remarks about the 'challenge' presented by Russian fiction, reminds us that the impact of Russian culture in Britain is not easily discovered, and that the record of enthusiastic response can act as a smokescreen that conceals more obscure domestic transformations. But thinking laterally, thinking institutionally, thinking across the disciplines, it is that obscurity the current collection aims to illuminate.

[43] Rebecca West, 'The Barbarians', *New Republic* (9 January 1915), 20.

[44] Virginia Woolf, 'Modern Fiction', in *The Common Reader* (London: Hogarth Press, 1925), 193.

[45] Bryher, *Film Problems of Soviet Russia* (Territet: POOL, 1929), 37–8.

[46] D. H. Lawrence, letter to S. S. Kotelyansky, 1 May 1917, in *The Letters of D. H. Lawrence*, iii, *1916–21*, ed. James T. Boulton and Andrew Robertson (Cambridge: Cambridge University Press, 1984), 121.

1

'For God, for Czar, for Fatherland'

Russians on the British Stage from Napoleon to the Great War

Laurence Senelick

In August 1867, the fairground theatre in Nizhnii Novgorod housed the troupe of F. K. Smol′kov, a manager more concerned with box-office success than production values. Rough-hewn as Smol′kov's productions may have been, they were much to the taste of a certain Oxford don on a tour of Russia. In his diary, the Englishman, struck by the theatre's plain whitewashed interior, noted in his journal that

> It was very large, & not more than a tenth full, so that it was remarkably cool & comfortable. The performance, being entirely in Russian, was a little beyond us, but by working away diligently at the play bill, with a pocket dictionary, at all intervals, we got a tolerable idea of what it was all about. The first & best piece was 'Aladdin and the Wonderful Lamp', a burlesque that contained some really first-rate acting, and very fair singing and dancing. I have never seen actors who attended more thoroughly to the drama & the other actors, & looked less at the audience.[1]

He singled out the *jeune premier* Aleksandr Lensky, just beginning his professional career, as the best actor, and would later prefer the offerings of this provincial theatre to those he would see at the Malyi (Small) Theatre in Moscow.[2]

Since the Rev. Charles Lutwidge Dodgson was a seasoned playgoer, this was high praise indeed. The fortuitous encounter of the future author of *Alice's Adventures in Wonderland* and the future luminary of the Imperial theatres is all the rarer for being one of the few accounts we have of Englishmen going to the theatre in tsarist Russia. Russian actors were not permitted to travel abroad to perform and, in any case, there would have been scant audiences for shows performed in Russian. To experience a native drama of Russian life, one would perforce have to visit the Empire itself.

Unfamiliarity with the Russian stage was simply one minor aspect of the general ignorance about Russia in Great Britain. Rare are the references to it in British plays

[1] Charles Lutwidge Dodgson, *The Russian Journal and Other Selections from the Works of Lewis Carroll*, ed. John Francis McDermott (New York: Dutton, 1935), 97. The other pieces on the bill were *Cochin China* and *The Hussar's Daughter*.

[2] N. Zograf, *Aleksandr Pavlovich Lensky* (Moscow: Iskusstvo, 1955), 18–21. Lensky had joined the company the previous autumn.

before the nineteenth century. Shakespeare's masque of the Muscovites in *Love's Labours Lost* (1598) may be the earliest. News of Boris Godunov's stormy reign and the Time of Troubles (*smutnoe vremia*) filters through to a few Jacobean plays, such as John Fletcher's tragi-comedy *The Loyal Subject* (1618, pub. 1647). The scene is set in 'Moscovia', there is talk of the Volga and Tartars, and a few of the characters bear names like Theodore, Burris, Putskie, and Boroskie, but the facts are sketchy and local colour almost entirely absent. There is more authenticity in Fletcher's source, Lope de Vega's *El gran duque de Moscovia.* As shown in the frontispiece to the 1711 publication of *The Loyal Subject,* the characters are envisaged more as antique Romans than as Slavs.[3] In other words, the dramatic portrayal of events taking place in what English visitors called the 'rude and barbarous Kingdom' were no better informed than is Dryden's picture of a Mughal court in his tragedy *Aurengzebe.*[4] These far-away places provide primarily a picturesque novelty as well as a setting in which bloody deeds and dynastic struggles, given an exotic veneer, can comment on politics while avoiding offense to the government at home.

This state of affairs changes when Britain becomes an ally of Russia during the Napoleonic Wars. What Patrick Waddington calls 'Russomania' overwhelmed the streets and salons in the years 1812 and 1813. As bulletins arrived of Napoleon's ignominious retreat from Moscow, the theatres were quick to capitalize on public curiosity. The first of at least nine such plays, Henry Brereton Code's *The Russian Sacrifice; or, The Burning of Moscow*, offered a simulated conflagration and a subsequent snowstorm. Charles-Louis Didelot choreographed ballets on Russian subjects.[5] However, the most powerful effect was made by the hippodrama, the equestrian spectacles put on at such non-patent playhouses as Astley's Amphitheatre.

A characteristic of dramas about war is that those composed while the conflict is raging tend to be ephemeral in their topicality; it requires a certain amount of distance before the events can be treated with the degree of objectivity needed to get beyond mere exploitation of popular sentiment or patriotism. J. H. Amherst's *Bonaparte's Invasion of Russia, or The Conflagration of Moscow* which opened at Astley's on 4 April 1825 as the Easter offering demonstrates this. Napoleon, recently deceased and no longer a bogeyman, is now depicted as 'a sympathetic figure who dashes through the flames of a burning building to rescue a woman and her child'.[6]

[3] John Fletcher, *The Loyal Subject: A Tragi-Comedy*, in *The Works of Mr Francis Beaumont, and Mr John Fletcher*, 7 vols (London: Jacob Tonson, 1711), ii, 923–1016. Its sources are examined exhaustively in Ervin C. Brody, *The Demetrius Legend and its Literary Treatment in the Age of the Baroque* (Madison, NJ: Fairleigh Dickinson University Press, 1972). For Russian references in other pre-nineteenth-century plays, see Anthony G. Cross, *The Russian Theme in English Literature from the Sixteenth Century to 1980: An Introductory Survey and a Bibliography* (Oxford: Meeuws, 1985), 18–23; Cross's list of works for the stage is far from complete, because he relies solely on printed works.

[4] A useful compendium of early English accounts of Russia, in modern spelling, is Lloyd E. Berry and Robert O. Crummey, eds, *Rude & Barbarous Kingdom: Russia in the Accounts of Sixteenth-Century English Voyagers* (Madison, WI: University of Wisconsin Press, 1968).

[5] Patrick Waddington, *From 'The Russian Fugitive' to 'The Ballad of Bulgarie': Episodes in English Literary Attitudes to Russia from Wordsworth to Swinburne* (Oxford: Berg, 1994), 20; based on M. P. Alekseev, *Russko-angliiskie literaturnye svyazi (XVIII vek-pervaya polovina XIX veka)* Literaturnoe nasledstvo 91 (Moscow: Nauka, 1982), 168, 186, note 171.

[6] Michael R. Booth, *English Melodrama* (London: Jenkins, 1965), 95.

In contrast, the Cossacks, Britain's former allies, are played as bellowing bullies on horseback, savagely lashing and murdering their French prisoners. A stage direction describes the final rout of the French:

> *The ragged and desolate remains of the French endeavour to rally; but, frozen and perishing, they can scarcely stand to their colours—a sudden yell of the Cossacks is heard, and they are furiously attacked—a powder wagon is blown up. The Cossacks enter—perform their wild evolutions, and trample life out of the feeble French soldiery. NEY makes a last and grand attack, but is defeated—wild pursuit—grand tableau—white and blue fire.*[7]

The audience would leave the theatre with the residual impression of the French as noble victims and the Russians as mustachioed ogres familiar from the earlier caricatures of James Gillray. The ahistorical imbalance was not lost on the press. The patriotic newspaper *John Bull* published an indignant letter allegedly from a paterfamilias upset by the portrayal of the Russians as bestial, even though they were expelling the French from their own land.[8]

Not much had changed thirty years later at the time of the Crimean War. Between 1854 and 1855, ten London theatres, mainly on the Surrey side or in the East End, had twenty-five plays licensed for production which dealt with the conflict, even though audiences showed little enthusiasm until the British victory at Alma. The allied forces were portrayed as freedom fighters combating tyranny. This interpretation was borrowed from the French stage: in Paul Meurice's *Schamyl* (1854), the French army is greeted by the Caucasian rebels with the words: 'Welcome, soldiers of thought, I have been waiting for you.... The Orient extends its hand to the Occident for this war of the peoples.'[9]

Thirty years of cheap illustrated newspapers had made the general public somewhat better informed about events in Europe, but distrust of Russia, portrayed as despotic, militaristic, and semi-Tartar by such popular journals as *Punch*, dated from the 1840s. The stereotypes of Russians already in place were hard to dislodge. In plays about the Crimean conflict, Russian names were a source of punning (Gruffenough) or insult: Prince Menshikov becomes Mendaciakoff and is depicted on stage as a blustering bantam with enormous yellow epaulettes and a shrewish wife. The Russian soldier, subsisting on a diet of train oil and candles, was shown driven into battle by the knout.[10] *The Battle of Alma,* Astley's updated sequel to *The Invasion of Russia*, drew on *Henry V* for scenes in the Russian camp displaying the febrile vanity and 'moral inferiority' of Russian leadership. Their ladies rebuke

[7] Quoted in Booth, *English Melodrama*, 96. Also see A. H. Saxon, *Enter Foot and Horse: A History of Hippodrama in England and France* (New Haven, CT: Yale University Press, 1968), 142, and his *The Life and Art of Andrew Ducrow & the Romantic Age of the English Circus* (Hamden, CT: Archon Books, 1978), 129.

[8] Saxon, *The Life and Art of Andrew Ducrow*, 134.

[9] Quoted in Jean-Marie Thames, *Le Mélodrame* (Paris: Presses universitaires de France, 1984), 86–7 (my translation).

[10] The filthiness of the Russian peasant was a cliché that later informed the comic opera *Faddimir; or, The Triumph of Orthodoxy* by Arthur Reed and Oscar Neville, produced at the Vaudeville Theatre in 1889. A proclamation that a cake of soap must be bought by every member of the populace incites a rebellion.

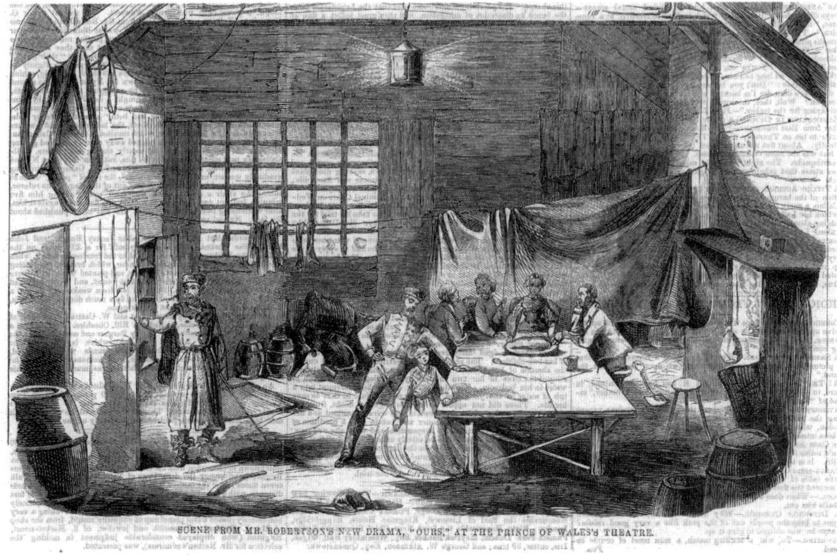

Fig. 1. The cabin in the Crimea scene of *Ours* (1866), *Illustrated Sporting and Dramatic News*. Laurence Senelick Collection.

officers for their cowardly skulking on the heights to watch the battles from a safe distance.

At the same time, a new respect for the Cossack as a warrior can be observed in London theatres with working-class audiences. In *The Fall of Sebastopol* the Russian private soldier is congratulated for serving in a force where promotion by merit, rather than rank, is available (a shaft aimed at the inept high command of the British armies), and in *The Siege of Silestria* he is shown burying his dead comrades to the March from Handel's *Saul.* Gallant officers with names like Romanoff acknowledge 'England's rule to offer a home to all who seek it in the hour of peril' (*The Storming of Hango*) or rescue British officers who turn out to be their brothers-in-law (*The Battle of Inkermann*).[11]

This recognition of the enemy's humanity grows with the passage of time. The best play about the Crimean War appeared a decade after it ended: Tom Robertson's *Ours* of 1866. Robertson is best known as the founder of the 'teacup and saucer' school of playwriting, author of domestic comedies full of conversational banter and everyday objects. In *Ours,* the warfare is kept offstage: Act Two ends with the female leads watching through windows as the unseen troops leave for the Crimea to the rousing tune of 'The Girl I Left Behind Me'. Act Three takes place in a cabin 'liberated' from

[11] This paragraph is greatly indebted to J. S. Bratton, 'Theatre of war: The Crimea on the London stage, 1854–5', in David Bradby, Louis James, and Bernard Sharratt, eds, *Performance and Politics in Popular Drama: Aspects of Popular Entertainment in Theatre, Film and Television, 1800–1976* (Cambridge: Cambridge University Press, 1980), 119–37.

the Cossacks, where 'you can drink as much liquor as you like and it doesn't have any effect on you! It's the climate!' (Fig. 1).[12] The first-night audience was astonished that every time the door opened, a flurry of snow (simulated by sand) would blow in.[13] The other astonishing effect was the making of a roly-poly pudding on stage, a touch of home confected from the primitive appurtenances of the snowbound hut.

Robertson's temperate view of Russians is personified in the only Russian character, Prince Petrovski. He is characterized as complacently patriotic—'No war with Russia ever lasts long... When the snow falls to envelop our enemies, we burn our Moscows'—and proposes to the heroine just before the war is declared:

PRINCE.	Should you honour me by favourable consideration of my demand, in return for the honour of your hand, I offer you rank and power. On our own lands we hold levees—indeed you will be queen of the province—of 400,000 serfs—of your devoted slave—my queen!
BLANCHE (*sits on sofa, L.*).	Queen! If I should prove a tyrant?
PRINCE (*standing*).	I am a true Russian, and love despotism!
BLANCHE (*smiling*).	And could you submit to slavery?
PRINCE.	At your hands—willingly (*sits on her R.H.*). I assure you slavery is not a bad thing.
BLANCHE.	But freedom is better.[14]

The pertinence of this exchange rests on the fact that serfdom had been abolished in Russia only a few years before. In the finale, the Prince, now a prisoner, gives up his claim to Blanche and lets her marry a man of limited income with the remark, 'In youth no man is poor.' John Hare's performance was accounted a small masterpiece, specially commended by the Prince of Wales who praised the accuracy of the uniform, decorations, and deportment.[15] Petrovski seems to be the prototype of the unflappable, autocratic but superlatively polite foreign adversary from Erich von Stroheim to Fu Manchu and Dr No.

However, the most congenial genre for displaying Russia on the Victorian stage was not society comedy but melodrama. Russia provided a wildly romantic background for extreme behaviour. A great empire, reputed for its cruelty, vast wealth, and enslaved populace, a climate distinguished for its inhospitality, a people supposed to be subject to overwrought emotions and only half-civilized, had much to offer in the way of determinant conditions for spectacular situations. Many of the standard topoi of Russified sensation drama were foreshadowed in Sophie Cottin's popular romance *Elisabeth* (1806). The novel has the virginal Elisabeth travelling from Siberia, where her Polish parents have been unjustly banished by an evil

[12] T. W. Robertson, *Ours*, in *The New York Drama*, 4, no. 43 (Washington, DC: Wheat & Cornett, 1878), 16. Also see *Plays by Tom Robertson*, ed. William Tydeman and Martin Banham (Cambridge: Cambridge University Press, 1982).

[13] T. Edgar Pemberton, *The Life and Writings of T. W. Robertson* (London: Bentley, 1893), 194. This effect quickly became common (W. C. Fields parodied it in the film *The Fatal Glass of Beer*, getting hit in the face with pellets of paper every time he sought to leave his Alaskan hut with the remark, 'Tain't a fit night out for man nor beast!').

[14] Quoted in M. Willson Disher, *Melodrama: Plots That Thrilled* (London: Rockliff, 1934), 39.

[15] Clement Scott, *The Drama of Yesterday & To-day*, 2 vols (London: Macmillan, 1899), i, 511.

official, to obtain a pardon from the all-merciful tsar. Along the way she meets with many misadventures, including marauding Tartars and a raging river. Elisabeth's purity wins over everyone she meets, protects her from danger and overcomes all obstacles. What were to become clichés about Russia in fiction were transferred to the stage in 1819 when Guilbert de Pixérécourt, the inventor of melodrama, adapted the romance as *La fille de l'exilé*. However, he had been anticipated in 1808 by Frederick Reynolds, whose *The Exile, or The Deserts of Siberia*, a three-act 'melodramatic opera' was played at Covent Garden.

Cottin's plot is faithfully followed by Pixérécourt.[16] Reynolds, however, changed the heroine's name to Alexina and, to protect her chastity, endowed her with an Indian protector who turns out to be her sweetheart in disguise. Whatever the alterations, certain features remain constant: unjust exile to the mines of Siberia, venal officials, political intrigue, struggle with the elements, and the deus-ex-machinal intercession of the tsar. *The Exile* remained something of an anomaly for over fifty years; but in the 1870s and 1880s these tropes were to flourish in a glut of melodramas about Russia.[17]

The British stage in the nineteenth century was largely dependent on French drama for inspiration: adaptations and translations of Parisian hits, diluted to satisfy the censorship of the Lord Chamberlain's office and often sentimentalized to suit British taste, dominated the repertoire. One of the first French melodramas of Russian life to be so transmuted, *Les Danicheff* (1876), was set in the 1850s, before serfdom was abolished, and so presented a picture of bygone abuses rather than current events. It is a sub-Dostoevskyan tale of a saint-like manumitted peasant who enables the marriage of his ex-serf wife and his noble ex-master by entering a monastery. Because one of the authors, the journalist Petr Korvin-Krukovsky, was Russian-born, the play is studded with local colour, such as an on-stage Orthodox wedding and a newly-rich peasant who builds churches with his filthy lucre. The *raisonneur* is a French diplomat who makes a long speech delineating the contrasts and contradictions in the Russian character.[18] In an abridged form, this would become a staple of such plays.

Translated, *The Danicheffs* was produced at the St James Theatre in June 1876, but did not make a stir with its prosiness and lack of action. The profusion of

[16] See Julie A. Buckler, 'Melodramatizing Russia: Nineteenth-century Views from the West', in Louise McReynolds and Joan Neuberger, eds, *Imitations of Life: Two Centuries of Melodrama in Russia* (Durham, NC: Duke University Press, 2002), 55–78.

[17] It was revived in 1874 as *The Exiles of Siberia*. The comic opera *Narensky; or, The Road to Yaroslaf* (1814) was also based on a French original. It had a libretto by Charles Armitage Brown, a friend of Keats who had spent time in St Petersburg as a clerk, but it nevertheless presented a peasant hut shaded by both a pine-tree and a palm. See Waddington, *From 'The Russian Fugitive' to 'The Ballad of Bulgarie'*, 20.

[18] Pierre Newsky, *Les Danicheff: Comédie en quatre actes* (Paris: Calmann Lévy, 1879). Alexandre Dumas *fils* chose to conceal his collaboration with Korvin-Krukovsky under a pseudonym; the latter was to write the first history of the Russian theatre in French. See 'Various dramatic topics', *Musical World* (6 January 1877), 27 and *New York Times* (25 July 1899), 5. An earlier melodrama of servitude, *The Serf* by Robert Talbot, had been produced at Covent Garden in 1828, adapted from a German play, *Isidor und Olga*, by Ernst Raupach: see Maurice Willson Disher, *Blood and Thunder: Mid-Victorian Melodrama and its Origins* (London: Muller, 1949), 108–9.

pseudo-Russian plays does not begin for another two years. In January 1878 news arrived of the attempted assassination of General Trepov by Vera Zasulich. The *Times* reported that her nihilist lover was imprisoned and a female friend flogged. Love among the nihilists and the corporal punishment of young women suddenly became popular themes.

London was a haven for escaped liberals and radicals who influenced public opinion about Russian tyranny and oppression. Although the presence of Aleksandr Gertsen (Herzen) seems to have gone unnoticed by the English literati, Sergey Mikhailovich Kravchinsky, alias Stepnyak, the assassin of the chief of the secret police General Mezentsev, was befriended by William Morris, Walter Sickert, Bernard Shaw, Oscar Wilde, and the Garnett family; his opinions coloured their views of his homeland. Britain was twice on the verge of war with Russia in 1878, in April after the Treaty of San Stefano at the close of the Russo-Turkish War, and again in July over Russia's intervention in Afghanistan.

The melodramas of this period fall into two distinct categories: the spectacular and the drawing-room. Both were cultivated by Victorien Sardou in Paris and both were rapidly adapted to British tastes. The spectacular, which capitalized on the ethnographic magnitude and exoticism of the Russian Empire, was launched with *Les Exilés*, written in collaboration with Eugène Nus and Grigory Lubomirsky, and staged at the Porte St-Martin in 1877. It featured a pet goat, reindeer and dog teams, barking wolves, a conflagration in the governor's house, a battle on a riverbank, and a city square illuminated at night. A phenomenal success in New York and Boston, it seems never to have been produced in London.[19]

The honour of setting the pattern for such plays in Britain falls to *Michel Strogoff*, Jules Verne's dramatization of his own popular novel. It had been written specifically to celebrate the visit of the Alexander II to Paris in 1875; five years later it was seized upon by a manager looking for a show grandiose enough to fill the Théâtre du Châtelet. The title character is an Imperial courier who must deliver a message to the farthest reaches of the Empire to prevent a Tartar uprising; he departs to the rousing cry, 'For God! For Czar! For Fatherland!' In this paean to an imperative sense of duty, Strogoff, in the course of his errand, is horsewhipped, saves his mother from a flogging, and is seemingly blinded by a white-hot sword; the astounding effects exploited hundreds of extras, horses, a moving panorama, and the bombardment of a telegraph office that disintegrated into 370 separate pieces (Fig. 2).[20] Despite the absurdity of the premise (most Russians knew Tartars as waiters in taverns), the play exemplifies Peter Brooks' formula for classic melodrama: a quest, an escape, a fall, and a theme of expulsion and redemption.[21]

[19] 'Karma', 'Exiles', *The Theatre* (New York) (1890), 59; John Bouvé Clapp and Edwin Francis Edgett, *Plays of the Present* (New York: Dunlap Society, 1902), 104–6.

[20] See Jules Verne and Adolphe d'Ennery, *Michel Strogoff*, ed. Louis Bilodeau (Exeter: University of Exeter Press, 1995). 'A new spectacular play: the success of "Michel Strogoff" in Paris', *New York Times* (9 December 1880), 1. Léon Marais, who played Michel Strogoff, had formerly played Osip the saintly serf in *Les Danicheff*.

[21] Peter Brooks, *The Melodramatic Imagination: Balzac, Henry James, Melodrama and the Mode of Excess* (New Haven, CT: Yale University Press, 1995), 30.

Fig. 2. Poster for the American production of *Michael Strogoff* (1882), showing the hero whipped by the villain Ivan Ogareff. Laurence Senelick Collection.

In March 1881, when *Michael Strogoff* opened at the London Adelphi, a house specializing in melodrama, the final tableaux celebrating the Franco-Russian alliance were omitted. The British public had a more jaundiced view of the Russian autocracy, but could not help but admire

> A gaily dressed ballet, a procession of Bokharan warriors, and a number of horses, [which] diversified the scenes. The picture of the battlefield after the walls of the telegraph office had fallen was skilfully composed and exceedingly realistic. The panorama along the banks of the Angura [*sic*] was extremely well painted, and the destruction of part of the city of Irkutsk was one of those scenes which always arouse the enthusiasm of impressionable persons. Here deference was made to modern discoveries, and the villain of the piece, being aware that petroleum exists in large quantities in the neighbourhood, turns a stream of it on to the river, down which the fierce flames travel unquenched.[22]

The spectacular element was so predominant that the critic for *The Theatre* complained it overwhelmed the actors.[23] Even though many twists of the plot relied on modern phenomena such as the telegraph, roving reporters, and the aforesaid naphtha conflagration, its political sentiments of feudal loyalty and tribal rebellion were such that it could as easily have been set in the Middle Ages or darkest Africa.

[22] Austin Brereton, 'Dramatic Notes, 1881', in *Dramatic Notes: A Chronicle of the London Stage, 1879–1882* (London: Bogue, 1883), 17.

[23] 'Michael Strogoff', *The Theatre* (1 April 1881), 240–3.

Profitable they might be, but such productions entailed high costs and were less common than Sardou's other innovation, the play of espionage and intrigue. Inspired by a spy scare that occurred as the new fortifications of Paris were completed, he penned *Dora*, a vehicle for Sarah Bernhardt. In this, secret papers entrusted to the heroine have been read and replaced; the telltale clue is the lingering perfume left by the *femme fatale. Dora* demonstrated that a drawing-room play could provide as much suspense as a panoramic spectacular, and, as the critic Clement Scott put it, 'the day of the document' had arrived.[24] Scott himself, with the actor-manager Squire Bancroft and B. C. Stephenson, adapted *Dora* as *Diplomacy*, leaving out much of the discussion of international politics.[25] With its Russian spy couple, the Count and Countess Zicka, it became a frequently revived staple of the repertory.

The assassination of Alexander II in 1881 kept Russian revolutionary movements in the forefront of the popular imagination. As a political and artistic conservative, Clement Scott opined 'Nihilism is a subject that it would perhaps be best to leave alone.'[26] No one heeded his advice. For the next generation, nihilism bore the same relation to melodrama that Roman Catholicism had to the Gothic novel or terrorism has to the action film: it was deep-dyed villainy in an up-to-date guise. With only the vaguest idea of its ideological principles, confusing it with anarchism, playwrights concocted midnight gatherings of conspirators plotting the assassination of tsarist officials and the bombing of public works. They might espouse noble purposes and thus attract misguided idealists, but their means were always underhand. Yet the secret police who tracked them down were depicted as dogged and merciless agents of a despotic regime. Between these millstones, the heroes (or more often heroines) were ground to powder.

This template was set by Sardou's hugely influential *Fédora*, carpentered as yet another vehicle for *la divine* Sarah—Sardou once said the easiest way to compose a play was to write, 'The curtain rises on Sarah Bernhardt.' The title character is a wealthy Russian widow whose noble but impoverished fiancé is murdered. Grech, chief of the secret police, begins an investigation. The clues lead to Loris Ipanoff, suspected of nihilism, so Fédora intends to seduce him into a confession and hand him over to the authorities. He does confess the murder to her, though not his reasons, and a tryst, which is also a trap, is appointed. At the rendezvous Loris explains that he murdered Fédora's betrothed because the latter had seduced Loris's wife; Fédora, now disabused, must save Ipanoff by keeping him in her bed overnight. The authorities execute Ipanoff's family instead; responsible for this crime, Fédora pleads her case to him as if it were that of an unknown woman. Loris attempts to strangle her, but, to prevent this crime, she takes poison.

What one reviewer called this 'tissue of improbabilities of the most impossible character' was a triumph for Bernhardt at the Paris Vaudeville in 1882.[27] It was

[24] Scott, *The Drama of Yesterday & To-day*, ii, 59.

[25] 'French authors and English adapters', *The Theatre* (1 December 1878), 329–32.

[26] Scott, *The Drama of Yesterday & To-day*, ii, 59

[27] W. F. Waller, 'Fédora', *The Theatre* (1 February 1883), 85–93.

pirated, parodied, and eventually made into an opera and a hat. The English adaptation, for which Squire Bancroft had purchased the rights, had been forestalled by a pirated version at Whitehaven a month before it opened at the Haymarket in June 1883. The reviews were mixed, but the audience adored it. As usual, bowdlerization had to be applied: affairs became engagements, there was no offstage torturing, Ipanoff did not throttle Fédora, and, to justify the heroine's indiscretion, the one-night stand became a notarized marriage. Not even a kiss was exchanged. It sounds more like Gilbert and Sullivan than Sardou. Moreover, the Slavonic coloration that had tinctured the Parisian performance had evaporated: Ipanoff was clean-shaven and Grech the police chief had a 'moustache and whiskers like a solicitor', his frock coat and notebook 'more suggestive of an assessor of ecclesiastical dilapidations than of a sub-Nemesis of Nihilism'.[28] Russianness and the hirsute were seen as inextricable.

Whether Oscar Wilde conceived his play *Vera; or The Nihilists* before or after he heard of *Fédora* is unclear. Although he makes use of such popular paraphernalia as dissident conspirators, railway trains, and emancipated serfs, he sets the action in 1800 in the court of the fictional Paul II. The title role was obviously tailored to provide a diva with an opportunity to display a kaleidoscope of emotions; its plotters come across as comic-opera banditti and the convolutions of the plot strain even the conventions of melodrama. Wilde himself admitted to Marie Prescott, the actress he hoped to lure to star in it, 'modern Nihilistic Russia, with all the terror of its tyranny and the marvel of its martyrdoms, is merely the fiery and fervent background in front of which the persons of my dream live and love'.[29] As Michael Newton discusses in the next chapter of this volume, it never received a London production, owing to difficulties with the censor, and failed in New York in 1883.[30]

Fédora and, to some degree, the trial of the *narodnik* (populist) Vera Figner in 1884, ushered in a spate of nihilistic melodramas. Fifteen years later, Max Beerbohm recalled it as a period 'when the scent of Nihilist gunpowder was being wafted through Europe, and when knouts, knives, and the White Terror were the awful topic of our conversation... I well remember how deeply I was stirred by such plays as *Lost for Russia*, *The Secret Track*, and *The Red Lamp*, with their loyalists ending in -off and their conspirators ending in -ski.'[31] *The Red Lamp*, by William Outram Tristram, which opened at the Comedy Theatre in April 1887, was memorable as the first venture in actor-management of Beerbohm's half-brother, Herbert

[28] 'Our Omnibus-Box', *The Theatre* (1 March 1883), 190–1; W. F. Waller, 'Fédora', *The Theatre* (1 June 1883), 362–9.

[29] Letter to Marie Prescott [? Mar.–Apr. 1883], *The Letters of Oscar Wilde*, ed. Rupert Hart-Davis (New York: Harcourt, Brace & World, 1962), 142–3.

[30] Richard Ellmann, *Oscar Wilde* (London: Hamish Hamilton, 1987), 146, 228–9. In 1890, a stir was created when *Vera: A Russian Story in Four Acts* opened in London. Its author Ellis Smith was erroneously thought to be a pseudonym of Wilde. The sensational incest plot—the heroine, a former mistress of the tsar, makes love to a confidence man who is masquerading as her son to gain her estate, while an intriguing minister of police tries to get everyone exiled to Siberia—was condemned as crude and sketchy. See Cecil Howard, 'Vera', *The Theatre* (1 August 1890), 35–6.

[31] Max Beerbohm, 'Two Plays', *Saturday Review* (18 June 1898), in *More Theatres, 1898–1903* (New York: Taplinger, 1969), 36–9.

Beerbohm Tree, but not his first venture into Slavonic dastardliness. Tree had played a Russian villain the year before in Maurice Barrymore's *Nadjezda*, a work which had nauseated both the critics and the public with its 'modern Zolaism'. A deep-dyed sensation drama, it told of a wife who, to save the life of her anarchist husband, agrees to sleep with the infamous governor Prince Zoubaroff. His post-coital act is to send her her husband's corpse on its bier. This is the prologue. The child of this brief encounter grows up to be the female avenger, who entangles Zoubaroff in her toils and stabs him to the heart. The reviewers complained that 'The sufferings of the victims are regarded with indifference—at most with curiosity'. On opening night, the cheap seats greeted the arrival of the corpse with a storm of protest and hoots, resisted by a counter-demonstration from stalls, dress circle, and boxes. Only Tree as Zoubaroff emerged from this debacle with credit.[32]

No doubt instructed by this failure, Tree avoided such graphic horrors in *The Red Lamp*. Its plot clearly hailed from the realm that Shaw called 'Sardoodledom'. A monarchist princess discovers that her beloved brother is chief of the Nihilists, and so finds she must station a red lamp to warn him against raids by the secret police. The *scène à faire* involved the princess and her son-in-law-to-be, an American journalist, having to infiltrate the Nihilists' lair to forestall a raid and prevent a cache of dynamite from being discovered. Meanwhile, the prince turns out to be a double agent.[33] The hit of the play was not so much the tortuous intrigue but Tree's performance as Demetrius the head of the secret police. Instead of a moustache-twirling bulldog, the audience saw a stout, bald, bespectacled old man, in the words of one memoirist, 'fat, feline, ponderous but sinister' (Fig 3).[34] His catchphrase 'I wonder' swept all London.[35] Proof is hard to come by, but it seems at least possible that Tree, a reader of taste, might have based his detective on Porfiry Petrovich in Fedor Dostoevsky's *Crime and Punishment* (*Prestuplenie i nakazanie*). The type of the soft-spoken, overweight, 'but sinister' investigator would become familiar in the character of the detective Nero Wolfe and the acting of Sydney Greenstreet.

[32] Percy Fitzgerald, 'Nadjezda', *The Theatre* (1 February 1886), 104–5; William Archer, *About the Theatre: Essays and Studies* (London: Unwin, 1886), 151–3; W. Macqueen-Pope, *Haymarket: Theatre of Perfection* (London: Allen, 1948), 327. The play led to a good deal of litigation: Barrymore unsuccessfully sued Sardou, claiming that his plot had been stolen for *La Tosca*; while Helena Modjeska claimed half-authorship and hence rights to performance. She also stated that *Nadjezda* was based on Ibsen's *A Doll House*. See Helena Modjeska, *Memoirs and Impressions* (New York: Macmillan, 1910), 464.

[33] This plot device seems to have been copied two years later in the comic opera *Faddimir*, in which a proscribed prince joins the anarchists under a false identity and is ordered to kill his royal self. One critic saw a similarity between *The Red Lamp* and *Lady Windermere's Fan*, since both their plots hinge on the placement of inanimate objects: review of *Lady Windermere's Fan*, *Black and White*, 3 (27 February 1892), 264.

[34] Macqueen-Pope, *Haymarket*, 328. Also see Marie de Mensiaux [Clement Scott?], 'The Red Lamp', *The Theatre* (1 June 1887), 335–9; she was pleased that nihilism was not glorified.

[35] Tree's wife recalled, 'The phrases of the play lent fun to our daily life. We did not ask for the bell to be rung—we cried, "One touch to the communicator, and oh! how hideous a ruin!" Questions as to time were answered, "It is the dawn, mad woman—it is the dawn!" We must sometimes have astonished our own and other people's servants. "Ay, the dawn of blood!" is no sort of answer to the meek question, "Will you call in the morning, ma'am?".' See Maud Tree, 'Herbert and I', in Max Beerbohm, ed., *Herbert Beerbohm Tree: Some Memories of Him and His Art* (New York: Dutton, n.d.), 28.

Fig. 3. Herbert Beerbohm Tree as the police spy Paul Demetrius in *The Red Lamp* (1887). Photograph by Burford. Laurence Senelick Collection.

The fashionable success of *The Red Lamp* combined with news coming out of Russia about the persecution of the Jews gave fresh impetus to melodramas on Russian themes. Since North America was a more sought-after haven for Jewish immigrants than Britain, the earliest play touching on the theme came from there. Bartley Campbell's *Siberia* had first opened in San Francisco in 1881, possibly in an attempt to spike the guns of a touring production of *Michael Strogoff*, for it covers much the same ground with forecasts of *Nadjezda*. There is the inevitable libertine governor who forces his attentions on a Jewish maiden, oddly named Marie, and, in pursuance of his dastardly ends, stirs up a pogrom. Marie's father is beaten to death, she is abducted and loses her reason, and her sister Sara stabs the governor, who, as he falls, grievously wounded but not dead, accuses her of being a nihilist. She is condemned to Siberia, where the commandant's cruelty leads the prisoners to revolt successfully. As the heroic characters are about to embark for the United States, the wicked governor has them re-arrested, but the Governor-General, who has observed all in disguise, à la *Measure for Measure*, allows them to depart for the New World. Only six years after its premiere did this play appear in London, but with nothing like the success it had

had in the United States.[36] It was observed that the most impressive scene in *Siberia* was the departure of the convicts for their long journey to the mines. This was not lost on Beerbohm Tree in 1902 when he produced Michael Morton's adaptation of Henri Bataille's adaptation of Tolstoy's *Resurrection* (*Voskresenie*), with himself as a 'cold repentant Neklyudoff' and Lena Ashwell as the outcast Katya. Tolstoy's preachments were conspicuous by their absence.[37]

The Jewish theme, so central to *Siberia,* rarely appeared in English plays about Russia. The exception was Joseph Hatton's *By Order of the Tsar*, originally a novel banned in Russia and Finland. In the standard overwrought fashion, the 1904 dramatization presents the oppression of the Jews as the result of personal motivation: a lustful governor, spurned by Anna Klostock, the beauteous 'Queen of the Ghetto', orders her flogged and her co-religionists persecuted. From this point on, the plot turns Ruritanian rather than Russian. The abused maiden, a variant of the romantic Beautiful Jewess, is metamorphosed into the mysterious and powerful Countess Stravensky and, aided by Ferrari, the Venetian agent of an unnamed secret society, a Jewish Pimpernel with a wardrobe of disguises, she has her revenge. At the end the tsar's decree pardons all. At one point, a character remarks, 'It is only in London where it may be said the Jew is equal to the Christian'.[38]

By Order of the Tsar is a very belated specimen. As Max Beerbohm pointed out in an 1898 review of Sergey Stepnyak's *The Convert*, melodramas of nihilism were out of date.[39] Spectacular melodrama itself still throve in West End theatres like Drury Lane and domestic melodrama in the cheaper houses, but a factor in the decline of the Russian setting was the availability of the works of Russian authors in translation. With Aylmer and Louise Maude's proselytizing for Tolstoyanism and the bookstalls flooded by the copious renderings of Isabel Hapgood and Constance Garnett, a more authentic Russian voice could be heard by the educated and well-informed portion of the British public. Between 1903 and 1914, the Independent Stage Society offered performances of plays by Gor'ky, Tolstoy, Gogol', Turgenev, and Chekhov, as well as Jacques Copeau's adaptation of Dostoevsky's *The Brothers Karamazov* (*Brat'ya Karamazovy*).[40]

Seven plays in eleven years may not seem much, and even then the press rebuked the Stage Society for some of these choices. The fastidious Max Beerbohm was as put off by Gor'ky *The Lower Depths* (*Na dne*) as the London critics had been by Ibsen's *Ghosts* a generation earlier, though his condemnation of these mere 'gobbets, not a slice of life' was dismissive, not outraged. 'Gorki on stage is merely a bore, and a disgusting

36 Cecil Howard, 'Siberia', *The Theatre* (2 January 1888), 45–6.

37 'Tolstoy staged', *The Independent* (1903), 344–6.

38 Joseph Hatton, *By Order of the Czar: A Drama in Five Acts* (London: Hutchinson, 1904), 23.

39 Beerbohm, 'Two plays', 37.

40 Specifically, Gor'ky, *Lower Depths* (*Na dne*), November 1903; Tolstoy, *Power of Darkness* (*Vlast' t'my*), December 1904; Gogol', *The Inspector General* (*Revizor*), June 1906; Turgenev, *The Bread of Others* (*Nakhlebnik*), January 1909; Chekhov, *The Cherry Orchard* (*Vishnevyi sad*), May 1911; Copeau-Croué, *Brothers Karamazov* (*Brat'ya Karamazovy*), February 1912; Chekhov, *Uncle Vanya* (*Dyadya Vanya*), May 1914.

bore . . . Gorki's work is to dramaturgy as snap-shot photographs are to the art of painting.'[41] Beerbohm was more forgiving to *The Power of Darkness* (*Vlast' t'my*) because of its ethical bent, but still could not stomach the plot nor the Maudes' translation, couched in the idiom of the Old Kent Road and the Bowery.[42] *The Cherry Orchard* (*Vishnevyi sad*) completely baffled Stage Society audiences; accustomed to melodrama and the problem play, they took Lopakhin to be a brutish villain, the Gaev family to be charming victims, and Epikhodov to be the raisonneur. The critics assumed that the play was so rooted in specific social types and conditions as to be indecipherable to the average Englishman. In particular, the characters' melancholy and sense of futility seemed inimical to English common sense.[43]

Bernard Shaw recognized that 'the imbecilities and outrages of the old anti-Ibsen campaign' were being revived against Gor'ky and Chekhov. His own interpretation of the Russian dramatists was, typically, to see them all as proto-Shaws, in whose plays 'the men appear as more tragically sacrificed by evil social conditions and their romantic and idealistic disguises than the women'.[44] *The Power of Darkness* aside, Tolstoy he regarded as a comedian; and he called *Fruits of Enlightenment* (*Plody prosveshcheniya*) a presage of Granville-Barker, the first of the Heartbreak Houses.[45] As for Chekhov, Shaw granted that *The Cherry Orchard* was 'a novel and delicate picture' and his own *Arms and the Man* a 'bag of the oldest stage tricks', but would not concede that Chekhov was the better playwright or *The Cherry Orchard* the better play.[46]

In the light of such misunderstanding and tendentiousness, the Russian character was better interpreted to the British playgoer by three Englishmen who had spent time in Russia and sought to convey its special attributes to their fellow countrymen. They were Maurice Baring, George Calderon, and, to a lesser extent, Laurence Irving, with his bowdlerized adaptation of *Crime and Punishment* as *The Unwritten Law.* Calderon had spent the years 1895 to 1897 in Russia learning the language, immersing himself in the literature, and absorbing an expertise in Russian thought, supporting himself by writing articles and giving lessons in English. Calderon's translation of *The Seagull* (*Chaika*), performed in Glasgow in November 1909, was the first British production of a Chekhov play, and it was his *Cherry Orchard* that the Stage Society offered two years later. Calderon sought the advice of no less an expert on current trends in Russian drama than Vsevolod Meierkhol'd (Meyerhold), and his ensuing essay in the

[41] Max Beerbohm, 'The Lower Depths', *Saturday Review* (5 December 1903), in *Around Theatres* (London: Rupert Hart-Davis, 1953), 302–4.

[42] Max Beerbohm, 'The Stage Society', *Saturday Review* (3 December 1904), in *Last Theatres, 1904–1910* (New York: Taplinger, 1970), 113–5

[43] Laurence Senelick, *The Chekhov Theatre: A Century of the Plays in Performance* (Cambridge: Cambridge University Press, 1997).

[44] Bernard Shaw, *The Quintessence of Ibsenism,* in Bernard F. Dukore, ed., *The Drama Observed, iv: 1911–1950* (University Park, PA: Pennsylvania State University Press, 1993), 1261.

[45] G. B. Shaw, 'Tolstoy: Tragedian or Comedian?', *London Mercury* (May 1921), in *The Drama Observed,* iv, 1378–9.

[46] G. B. Shaw, 'I am a Classic, but Am I a Shakespear Thief?', *Arts Gazette* (31 January 1920), in *The Drama Observed,* iv, 1344–5.

July 1912 *Quarterly Review* was the best informed article on the subject in any Western language.[47]

Oddly enough, for someone whose analyses of Chekhov were subtle, insightful, and poetic, Calderon's one play on a Russian theme perpetuates the melodrama tradition, almost *Grand-Guignolesque* in its treatment. *The Little Stone House*, produced by the Stage Society in the same season as *The Cherry Orchard*, presents a peasant mother who has been saving up for twenty years to purchase a monument for the grave of her son, who died heroically in battle. When the son suddenly shows up, she learns that all that time he had been a fugitive Siberian convict, turns him over to the police and spends the money on the specious monument.[48] Calderon's contribution to the British understanding of Russia is therefore more valuable in his translations, articles, and lectures than in his own creations.

The same holds true, though to a lesser extent, in the case of Maurice Baring. A seasoned diplomat as well as a veteran theatre buff, Baring's intention was, in the words of one reviewer, specifically to combat 'a Russia of fiction and imagination. This is the Russia of the "Danicheffs" and of "Michael Strogoff", the Russia of the Third Section and the knout and the half-shaved convict train dragging bloody chains across the snowy steppe. Yet this fake Russia is the real Russia for most of the world'.[49] In Baring's society comedy of 1911, *The Grey Stocking*, set in an English country-house, the only Russian character is young Count Peter Velichkovsky, a former prisoner of war in Japan, who dresses exactly like an Englishman, looks like an Italian, speaks English with barely an accent because he had an English nurse, but speaks Russian with an English accent, smokes, and plays the piano. Like Chekhov's Elena in *Uncle Vanya*, he feels like a second violin in life. His function in the plot is to act as catalyst: he falls in love with his hostess, the younger wife of a man who was her tutor (shades of *Vanya* again). He seduces her but she decides not to elope with him and settles into her everyday life.

In his gallantry and reticence, Velichkovsky is a direct descendant of Prince Petrovski in *Ours*. In a speech that is clearly Baring instructing his audience, the Count explains, 'In Russia the *intelligenzia* people, like writers and professors, are quite apart. They never strive or pretend anything except what they are. They live very simply in uncomfortable surroundings; but here I find this beautiful place, the Tudor house, the lovely garden, the books, make it all so much worse—or more tiresome.'[50] Tiresome is evidently Baring's introduction of the then current Russian literary concept of *skuchnost'* (the word 'boring' did not become fashionable until after the Great War). Later, the Count describes the prevalent inertia, so familiar in Chekhov:

> For years in Russia anybody with brains has been obliged to look on and do nothing but talk, knowing that the talking will lead nowhere; and the people are so used to knowing this that they still go on talking now, and doing nothing but talk, when their

[47] Percy Lubbock, *George Calderon: A Sketch from Memory* (London : Grant Richards, 1921), and 'George Calderon', *Dictionary of National Biography, 1912–1921* (Oxford: Oxford University Press, 1927), 105.

[48] George Calderon, *The Little Stone House* (London: Sidgwick and Jackson, 1913).

[49] William Churchill, review of Maurice Baring, *The Russian People* (1911), *Bulletin of the American Geographical Society*, 44, no. 3 (1912), 218.

[50] Maurice Baring, *The Grey Stocking and Other Plays* (London: Constable, 1911), 41.

> talk might lead somewhere. Consequently, he puts his faith in the radical revolutionaries, the bomb throwers.

Velichkovsky's presence and his sentiments seem a quaint device in a drawing-room comedy. Baring decided to depict the intelligentsia and the bomb throwers *in propria persona* in his later play *The Double Game.* This takes place in Moscow in the home of a schoolmaster in January 1907; the characters are meant to be a cross-section of the educated classes, who discuss politics endlessly: a university student, an army doctor, an ex-civil engineer, a doctor, a man of letters, a schoolboy, and their wives and girlfriends, even an English journalist, once liberal but now conservative. The heroine is the daughter of an aristocratic family, ostensibly studying medicine but actually a terrorist, a Social Revolutionary in love with an anarchist. At the final curtain she is about to be arrested, but shoots herself offstage.[51]

Despite the closely-observed middle-class milieu and the idea-rich discussions, even Baring could not avoid melodramatic conventions. The incendiary heroine, the love among the anarchists, the police as a constant threat are familiar almost as far back as Cottin's *Elisabeth*. Only the unhappy ending is more common to Russian drama than to English melodrama. Edmund Gosse made this point at the time, saying that the aristocratic girl in a nest of revolutionaries threw one's mind back to *The Red Lamp* and its ilk, and only the last act showed the play to be more subtle than that.[52] This demonstrates how difficult it was, even for the best-intentioned playwrights, to overcome the ingrained stereotypes of the previous century.

[51] Baring, *The Double Game* in *The Grey Stocking and Other Plays*, 263–366.

[52] Edmund Gosse, 'Mr. Baring's Plays: They Show a Decided Improvement on His Previous Work (From the *Morning Post*)', *New York Times Review of Books* (21 April 1912), 247.

2

'Nihilists of Castlebar!'

Exporting Russian Nihilism in the 1880s and the case of Oscar Wilde's *Vera; or the Nihilists*

Michael Newton

In St. Petersburg on 24 January 1878, petitioners were queuing for an audience with Fedor Fedorovich Trepov, Governor-General of the city. Among the crowd a young woman waited her turn. When she finally stood before the Governor-General, she drew out a gun from under her cloak, and fired a shot directly at him. The bullet tore into his pelvis, wounding but not killing him. She then stood back and calmly awaited arrest. She was Vera Ivanovna Zasulich, a young nihilist. At her trial, the motivation for the attempted assassination became clear. Some time before, after a petty act of insubordination, Trepov had ordered that a young man, unfairly incarcerated in the city's prison, should be flogged. The beating was severe and illegal, a strikingly vicious act of summary injustice. Unable to bear the cruelty of the deed, Zasulich vowed to perform a deed of her own. She fired at Trepov, not caring if he were killed or not, in order to show that such brutal acts would not go unpunished in Russia. Her trial should have been a straightforward matter. The government banked on a conviction, risking a jury trial for the young offender. After all, there was little doubt that she had shot Trepov. Instead, disgusted by Trepov, enthused by the speeches of the defence counsel, stirred by Zasulich, and roused by the zeal and integrity of her deed, within minutes the jury voted that the young would-be assassin was innocent of her crime.[1]

Along with the scandalous matter of her being a woman, what made Vera Zasulich famous was not her abortive assassination attempt, but her acquittal.[2] When the Russian jury found her innocent, it announced a moral paradox: it was entirely just and right for someone as ardent as Vera Zasulich to attempt to murder

[1] The fullest account of Vera Zasulich's crime can be found in Ana Siljak, *Angel of Vengeance: The 'Girl Assassin,' the Governor of St. Petersburg, and Russia's Revolutionary World* (New York: St Martin's, 2008).

[2] In the United States, at least one critic found it scandalous, or absurd, that Wilde's play should have a woman at its centre: 'A peculiarity of the piece is that it contains but one female character, Vera, the heroine…To make a woman the leader of a national insurrection is foolish' (quoted in Oscar Wilde, *Oscar Wilde's 'Vera; or, The Nihilist'*, ed. Frances Miriam Reed (Lampeter: Edwin Mellen, 1989), xxxiii.

someone as corrupt as General Trepov. The acquittal made Zasulich a ten days' wonder, her case celebrated across Europe. She stood as a modern Charlotte Corday, a passionate avenger and a champion for justice. Versions of her story proliferated: a theatre company in Italy staged her life; she inspired Tolstoy, and also Dostoevsky (who was present at her trial).[3] The vogue for Zasulich as the archetypal 'nihilist' assassin was an element in a wider European fascination in these years with things Russian: as Laurence Senelick's essay in this collection shows, in the last decades of the nineteenth century plays about Russia's nihilists were chic.

A single definition of nihilism proves elusive. In his novel, *Fathers and Children* (*Ottsy i deti*, 1862) (published in French in 1863 and English in 1867), Ivan Turgenev had popularized both the word, 'nihilist', and the character-type, in his portrait of the young rebel, Evgeny Bazarov.[4] For Turgenev, the epithet carried a trace of his ambivalence: it was a means of designating a younger generation whom he simultaneously admired and deemed disturbing and alien. Dmitry Pisarev, one of the editors of the radical journal the *Russian Word* (*Russkoe slovo*), proudly reclaimed the word used by Turgenev with all its equivocally pejorative overtones; definition by others had become an act of self-definition. By declaring that he too was a nihilist, Pisarev embraced—and thereby attempted to invert—the term's negative connotations: what was needed was a generation who would criticize and attack the status quo rather than accept and preserve it. As Arkady Kirsanov, Bazarov's friend and disciple in *Fathers and Sons*, explains to his father and uncle:

> 'He is a nihilist.'
> 'What!' asked his father. As to Paul Petrovich, he raised his knife, on the end of which was a small bit of butter, and remained motionless.
> 'He is a nihilist,' repeated Arcadi.
> 'A nihilist,' said Nicholas Petrovich. 'This word must come from the Latin *Nihil*, nothing, as far as I can judge; and consequently it signifies a man who . . . who recognizes nothing?'
> 'Or rather who respects nothing,' said Paul Petrovich; and he began again to butter his bread.
> 'A man who looks at everything from a critical point of view,' said Arcadi.
> 'Does not that come to the same thing?' asked his uncle.
> 'No, not at all; a nihilist is a man who bows before no authority, who accepts no principle without examination, no matter what credit the principle has.'

Soon the word caught on, even though it was misleading. As the above exchange suggests, it seemed to imply the refusal to believe in anything, when in fact the 'nihilists' themselves were fervent believers in their own brands of positivism and materialism (see, for instance, Barazov's quip that 'a good chemist is twenty times more useful than the best poet').[5] Only later, did the term come to be associated primarily with political sedition.[6]

[3] Jay Bergman, *Vera Zasulich: A Biography* (Stanford, CA: Stanford University Press, 1983), 55; Richard Garnett, *Constance Garnett: A Heroic Life* (London: Sinclair Stevenson, 1991), 85.

[4] Ivan Tourguenef, *Pères et enfants*, [trans. Hippolyte Delaveau?], ed. Prosper Mérimée (Paris: Charpentier, 1863); Ivan Turgenef, *Fathers and Sons*, trans. Eugene Schuyler (New York: Leypoldt & Holt, 1867).

[5] Turgenef, *Fathers and Sons*, trans. Schuyler, 25–6.

[6] On the origins of nihilism, see in particular Peter C. Pozefsky, *The Nihilist Imagination: Dmitrii Pisarev and the Cultural Origins of Russian Radicalism, 1860–1868*, Middlebury Studies in Russian

In Britain, the name began to be used in the 1850s as a term in philosophy, and only in 1866 took on its later meaning of a supporter of a revolutionary movement in Russia with the attempted assassination of tsar Alexander II by Dmitry Karakozov. From then, interest in Russian nihilism peaked and fell away in connection with a series of acts of political violence: the arrest of the archetypal terrorist, Sergey Gennadievich Nechaev; the case of Vera Zasulich; the repeated assaults on the tsar by the People's Will (*Narodnaya volya*). In this way, nihilism came to stand in journalistic discourse for assassination and acts of political violence. In tandem with this, however, there were a number of more sober considerations of nihilism, focusing on its resemblance to western liberalism, or sometimes socialism; it was a commonplace of such essays that Russian autocracy produced a more fervent and vicious form of radicalism, directing to foul ends a hunger for reform that in western Europe would look rational and unexceptional.[7]

British commentary on nihilism, therefore, was poised between representing it as, on the one hand, the most extreme form of political violence, and, on the other, a desperate version of modern rational liberalism. Yet most of all, it was the fact that nihilism was tied so intimately to violence, and to an ongoing campaign of assassination in the years 1878 to 1882, that secured its place in British discourse. As such, nihilism was seen to represent a peculiarly Russian excess. Yet this essay will argue that in the 'United Kingdom', the figure of the Russian nihilist could simultaneously be adopted for concerns that were closer to home.

When the Russian émigré writer 'Stepnyak' (Sergey Mikhailovich Kravchinsky) declared that 'Zassulic has nothing about her of the heroine of a pseudo-Radical tragedy', it is probable that he was thinking of a play by Oscar Wilde, one that had attempted to make Vera Zasulich precisely that.[8] *Vera; or the Nihilists*, was Wilde's first play, scheduled for its debut at the Adelphi Theatre on 17 December 1881. It is likely that it was in part nihilism's currency that stimulated Wilde, always keen to be *à la mode*, to make his first play a Russian one. Moreover, the play's origin was very likely Vera Zasulich's fame. Shortly before its first performance, it was suggested that the lead figure was modelled on Zasulich: 'It appears that Mr. Oscar Wilde has written a drama about Russian life and Russian secret societies with a tremendous heroine in it, of whom the original is no other than the celebrated Mddle. Sassulitch.'[9] However, this remark was made not in 1881, but 1883: in November 1881, the performance at the Adelphi was cancelled just as rehearsals were about to

Language and Literature, 27 (New York: Peter Lang, 2003). Older, although still useful, accounts include Ronald Hingley, *Nihilists: Russian Radicals and Revolutionaries in the Reign of Alexander II, 1855–81* (London: Weidenfeld and Nicolson, 1967) and Franco Venturi, *Roots of Revolution: A History of the Populist and Socialist Movements in Nineteenth Century Russia*, trans. Francis Haskell (London: Weidenfeld and Nicolson, 1960).

[7] For example, see Henry Alexander Butler-Johnstone, 'A Trip up the Volga to the Fair of Nijni-Novgorod', *Daily News* (19 September 1874), 3.

[8] Stepniak, *Underground Russia: Revolutionary Profiles and Sketches from Life* (London: Smith, Elder, 1883), 117.

[9] 'Theatres', *The Graphic* (28 July 1883), 94.

begin. Biographers and critics have long speculated that this was because the plot of the play, dealing with the assassination of a tsar, was deemed liable to upset the Russian authorities, and thereby damage Anglo-Russian relations. This essay argues that, in fact, the cancellation was due to two reasons that had their origin within Britain. First, that Wilde had written the play in order to mark a shift in his public image, and stake a claim for himself as a radical political writer. And, second, that though Russian settings were fashionably exotic, they also presented opportunities for social critique of domestic matters. In this play, Russia, I will argue, was a substitute for Ireland, and that it was largely the perceived Irish context that delayed the play's British premiere. To suggest that Wilde positions his work as a contribution to British-Irish politics is not to deny that Wilde's *Vera* depends upon its Russian setting, nor that the themes and mood of the drama do not derive from conventional notions of 'the Russian character' and situation. It is this dual vision that characterized much of the British and Irish discourse about Russia, asserting foreignness even as they let its strangeness seep into domestic concerns. Russia remains Russia, nihilists stay nihilists, even as they evoke thoughts of Ireland and 'Fenianism'.

Although it stands as a key intervention in the network of allusions and tropes situating Russian nihilism, the play itself is among the least engaging of all Wilde's literary productions. Wilde wished his play to represent 'realistic not operatic conspiracy'; it is not clear that he succeeded.[10] It unsuccessfully attempts to combine paradoxical wit and radical passion, professing republican sentiment, while in actual fact being far more equivocal. The list of the 'Persons of the Play', for example, follows custom by offering a strictly hierarchical ordering, with 'The Palace' above 'The People' and Vera (in the latter category) below both her father and her brother. It imagines 'assassination as a method of political reform', but nonetheless ultimately endorses self-sacrifice over murder.[11] Possibly the most vital element in Wilde's appropriation of Zasulich's tale was the misreported and untrue supposition that the man that she had sought to avenge had been her lover.[12] The first act takes place in 1795, when Vera Sabouroff witnesses the exile of her brother, Dmitri, to the mines of Siberia. Dmitri makes her swear vengeance and political commitment to the nihilists. Five years pass, and in 1800, Vera, now the leader of the nihilists, falls in love with a co-conspirator, apparently a medical student named Alexis. The young man, however, turns out to be the heir to the throne, a would-be enlightened ruler ready to bring in reforms. The nihilists kill the tsar and Alexis succeeds to the throne. It is decided that the new tsar must also be killed, and the responsibility for the murder falls to Vera. She is poised to stab the young man, but cannot do it, her love or her womanliness triumphing over her rectitude, and instead she plunges the knife into her own heart.

[10] Oscar Wilde, letter to Richard D'Oyly Carte, March 1882, in *The Complete Letters of Oscar Wilde*, ed. Merlin Holland and Rupert Hart-Davis (London: Fourth Estate, 2000), 151.

[11] Wilde, *Oscar Wilde's 'Vera; or, The Nihilist'*, 18.

[12] Richard Ellmann, *Oscar Wilde* (London: Hamish Hamilton, 1987), 122.

As this summary perhaps indicates, the play is a broody melodrama stuffed with stagey declamation. Wilde aims at tragedy, and achieves portentousness. The energy of the play mostly derives from the cynical witticisms—themselves revolutionary in their caustic power—of the aristocratic Prince Paul. This Satanic cynic is at once the enemy of the nihilists, and yet, when necessity demands, ready to become a nihilist himself. But he is still for a reader the hero of the play—a prototype for the paradox-making wit that would eventually emerge with greater force in Wilde's later work (though also there generally balanced by more stolid and good-hearted dramatic foils). That Prince Paul should be taken as a forerunner of the central later Wildean persona is a critical commonplace. What is noteworthy is that in this play, as in other later works of Wilde, wit allies itself with villainy and opportunism, here of a political kind; narrative (as opposed to aesthetic) sympathy belongs to the heartfelt, the compassionate, and the radical.

In July 1883 Wilde wrote to Marie Prescott, the actor then set to play its leading role,

> It deals with no theories of government, but with men and women simply; and modern Nihilistic Russia, with all the terror of its tyranny and the marvel of its martyrdoms, is merely the fiery and fervent background in front of which the persons of my dream live and love. With this feeling was the play written, and with this aim should the play be acted.[13]

Although this relegates the Russian setting to a mere necessary background in front of which wild feelings are acted out, clearly the play requires Russia to exist, and needs the fact of autocracy, the image of Russian passion, and its intimations of a political and spiritual intensity. Yet while emerging from a culturally constructed model of another nation, at the same time *Vera* is a work whose meanings disrupt the contextual limits of one nation state. It is a play set in Russia, about Ireland, written first for the British public, and eventually played in the United States where its target audience included the Irish diaspora. It is a work that migrates between international and local contexts, responses, and meanings.

Though *Vera* is keyed to Russian themes, and was certainly provoked by the popular image of the sensationalism of Russian politics, Wilde's covert interest was in Ireland. Writing about Russia was an oblique means of exploring internal politics; Russia's famed penchant for extremity was something easily translatable into the extremity of British and Irish relations. Following the failure of the play, Wilde would adopt a different approach in handling his radical sentiments, an approach best displayed in his other literary representation of Russian nihilists, his short story, 'Lord Arthur Savile's Crime'.

In 1880, Wilde was largely considered a figure of fun, sneered at by the press. Simply to drop Wilde's name was thought sufficient to provoke laughter; he was a comic standby in the uninspired pages of the 'funnies', the mere mention of his supposed catchword 'utterly' a lazy means to a laugh.[14] Wilde seemed a living

[13] Oscar Wilde, letter to Marie Prescott, [? July 1883], in *Complete Letters*, 214.

[14] See 'Pilferings from *Funny Folks*', *Bristol Mercury and Daily Post* (4 June 1881), 6, 'A Royal Two Years', *Funny Folks* (24 September 1881), 300, and 'Floats and Flies', *Fun* (30 November 1881), 228.

caricature, the embodiment of exaggerated aesthetic attitudes.[15] In the summer of 1881, the publication of Wilde's first book of poems merely added fuel for the derision: *Punch*, for instance, deemed it 'a volume of echoes'.[16] In fact, among the echoes were resonant expressions of his mother's politics. Under the significantly Italianate pen name of 'Speranza', Wilde's mother, Jane Francesca Algee, had been a beacon of Irish nationalism; his mother's passionate example served as a model both for the young writer and for the central female role in his new play. Wilde's early verses contained fumbling attempts to express his political radicalism, some of those poems bearing the stamp of a confused republicanism. In August 1880, having sent Violet Hunt a copy of his poem 'Ave Imperatrix', Wilde wrote a letter to her mother, Mrs. Alfred Hunt. The poem ends with a plainly republican last stanza, and Wilde remarked, 'I hope she will see some beauty in it, and that your wonderful husband's wonderful radicalism will be appeased by my first attempts at political prophecy'. He used the latter term again around a year later, in late 1881, in order to describe *The American Irish* (1879), his 'mother's pamphlet on the reflux wave of *practical* republicanism which the return of the Irish emigrants has brought on Ireland. It was written three years ago nearly, and is extremely interesting as a political prophecy.'[17]

As Algernon Charles Swinburne had done before him, in his first volume Wilde was searching for a way to meld aestheticism and radical politics; he may even have imagined himself at this stage of his career as a political artist.[18] After the publication of his poems, Wilde sought to deepen his radical reputation with *Vera*; in November 1881, in a letter to George Curzon that accompanied a handbill advertising the first performance, Wilde wrote, 'I send you a bill of my first attack on Tyranny.'[19] In comments to his future wife, Constance Lloyd, he remarked that 'he wrote it to show that an abstract idea such as liberty could have quite as much power and be made quite as fine as the passion of love'.[20] In choosing a political subject, Russian themes were enticing; the focus on individual deeds, and the extravagant gestures of the nihilists rendered them ideal subjects for dramatic treatment. Moreover, nihilism was in the news, and, sanctioned by the example of Turgenev, an up-to-date choice for a literary debut.[21]

15 'The Drama in America', *The Era* (8 September 1883), 3.

16 'Swinburne and Water', *Punch* (23 July 1881), 26.

17 *Selected Letters of Oscar Wilde*, ed. Rupert Hart-Davis (Oxford: Oxford University Press, 1979), 26, 28–9.

18 Wilde sent Swinburne a presentation copy of his *Poems*: see *More Letters of Oscar Wilde*, ed. Rupert Hart-Davis (New York: Vanguard Press, 1985), 35–6.

19 Wilde, *Complete Letters*, 117. Wilde hoped that Curzon would hang the poster on the High Street in Oxford, a self-publicizing gesture intended to respond to the insolence of the Oxford Union that had, earlier that autumn, voted to refuse a presentation copy of his poems.

20 Letter from Constance Lloyd to Otho Holland Lloyd, 23 November 1883, in Wilde, *Complete Letters*, 222.

21 In the May 1886 edition of *Macmillan's Magazine*, Wilde translated a short story by Turgenev (from the French), and in 1886–7 he praised Turgenev on two occasions in the *Pall Mall Gazette*—once in a review of Dostoevsky's *Crime and Punishment* (*Prestuplenie i nakazanie*). The articles suggest some considerable interest in Turgenev on Wilde's part: see Patrick Waddington, *Turgenev and George Sand: An Improbable Entente* (Basingstoke: Macmillan, 1981), 81, and Oscar Wilde, *Selected Journalism*, ed. Anna Clayworth (Oxford: Oxford University Press, 2004), 200.

Wilde wrote this apprentice work late in 1880; that autumn, almost immediately on completion, it was printed with the title, *Vera; or, the Nihilists*, Wilde himself paying for the privilege of publication. He promptly posted out the play to influential friends and theatre people, sending, for example, an inscribed copy to Ellen Terry.[22] The aim was to stimulate interest; the work was to be a calling card, a pledge for greater things to come. On 21 November 1881, the forthcoming production of Oscar Wilde's 'drama of Russian life and manners' was publicized in the press. It was declared that Mrs Bernard Beere would play the heroine, while the younger Dion Boucicault (the son of the Irish playwright) would also play a significant role. Both actors were connected to Boucicault senior.[23] The play was to be presented at a daytime performance on Saturday, 17 December at the Adelphi Theatre.[24] Given Wilde's current reputation as a poet, the play was variously, and wrongly, predicted to be 'poetical' and even a 'blank-verse drama'.[25] By the end of the month, with its premiere still some weeks away, the play was already being ridiculed: 'I suppose everyone will be Russian to see it; will it be quite too utterly Botticellian, I wonder?'[26]

However, with less than three weeks to go before the premiere, the play was cancelled. On 30 November 1881, a notice, probably written by Oscar's brother, Willie Wilde, appeared in *The World*: 'Considering the present state of political feeling in England, Mr. Oscar Wilde has decided on postponing, for a time, the production of his drama Vera.'[27] On Saturday 3 December 1881, *Bell's Life in London and Sporting Chronicle* believed that it could supply more information concerning the delay, reporting the story as follows:

> Mr. Oscar Wilde's drama, 'Vera,' will not be performed as announced, at the Adelphi after Christmas. Mr Wilde has admitted his play to a committee of literary persons, who have advised him to keep it from the stage. The work, composed about four years ago, abounds in revolutionary sentiments, which it is thought might stand in the way of its success with loyal British audiences.[28]

[22] Wilde, *Selected Letters*, 27; Letter to Ellen Terry, ca. September 1880, in Wilde, *Complete Letters*, 96.

[23] Young Mrs Bernard Beere was already a leading figure in Dion Boucicault's company; despite the cancellation of *Vera*, she went on to great success, including a hit in Victorien Sardou's *Fédora* (1882), another play on a Russian theme, as Laurence Senelick discusses in this volume, which opened in London in June 1883. See 'The Theatres', *Daily News* (23 July 1883), 2. She remained a friend of Wilde's and appeared in the first production of *A Woman of No Importance*.

[24] 'The Theatres', *Daily News* (21 November 1881), 2; 'Theatres', *The Graphic* (26 November 1881), 534. *The Stage* declared that the play, described as a 'melodrama of Russian life', would be given a first performance two mornings after Christmas: see 'The Stage', *Bell's Life in London and Sporting Chronicle* (26 November 1881), 11. However, this was probably an error on the part of the paper, as that day's edition of *The Era* repeated the earlier announcement of a first performance on the afternoon of 17 December: see 'Theatrical Gossip', *The Era* (26 November 1881), 5; see also 'The Philistine Lover to his Æsthetic Fair', *Funny Folks* (10 December 1881), 386.

[25] 'Theatres', *The Graphic* (26 November 1881), 534; 'The Philistine Lover to his Æsthetic Fair', 386.

[26] 'Floats and Flies', *Fun* (30 November 1881), 228.

[27] Quoted in Wilde, *Oscar Wilde's 'Vera; or, The Nihilist'*, xxvii. On Willie Wilde's connection to *The World*, see H. Montgomery Hyde, *Oscar Wilde: A Biography* (New York: Farrar, Straus and Giroux, 1975), 49–50.

[28] 'The Stage', 11.

It is difficult to gauge how much credence should be given to this report or from whom it may have come: *Bell's* had already proved stubbornly incorrect about the projected date of *Vera*'s premiere. The statement that the play had been written about 'four years ago' is intriguingly false. That would place its writing at the end of 1877, long before the murder of the tsar, and even before Vera Zasulich's attempt on Trepov. Was this a smokescreen started by Wilde himself to obscure his own intentions in writing the play?

On Monday, yet more gossip concerning the play's withdrawal appeared:

> The same authority which announced last week that Oscar Wilde's play 'Vera' would be produced on the 17th of the month to-day states that the intention has been abandoned, for the reasons that it contains speeches of a very violent and revolutionary character, and that they were considered to be too risky for the 'loyal English gallery and pit.'. The preparations for its production had proceeded so far that the characters had been cast, the Adelphi Theatre had been taken, and all was ready. As a matter of fact I understand that this marvellous detail of information had come with greater surprise on no one more than on the author, especially as regards the theatrical arrangements, the essential preliminary to which, in the eyes of those who have plays to dispose of, not even being seriously approached. The 'fable,' as the mild Oscar designates it, has all arisen out of a visit paid by him to Twickenham, where he met Mrs. Langtry at Mr. Labouchere's charming Thames retreat, which promises to vie with Strawberry Hill in its bright memories.[29]

This rather incoherent statement of the matter raises a number of issues. It emphasizes the Englishness of the audience and therefore their presumed hostility to the play's political message. Even the location of the anecdote is relevant, being the home of Henry Du Pré Labouchère, the radical MP for Northampton, who would introduce the clause in the Criminal Law Amendment Act that would cause Wilde's imprisonment. It suggests the possibility that Wilde felt insecure about the quality of the play. It is unclear whether or not Wilde was surprised by the cancellation: it is plausible that he was stage-managing a shift in his public perception, and therefore was responsible for the postponement. However, it could as convincingly be suggested that he had to be persuaded to it: here was gossip that Wilde had been 'induced' by others to withdraw his play.[30]

George Rowell has persuasively argued that the play was not put on simply because Wilde was too hard up to finance what may have been no more than a daytime, one-off trial production.[31] If so, the allusions to the political volatility of the drama might be no more than an excuse, or even a means of assuring publicity for any later performance. Nevertheless, Wilde's written comments and the web of rumour around the production all suggest that politics became enmeshed in the reasons given or imagined for its cancellation.

Was it, after all, Wilde's Russian theme that had prompted the postponing of the play? One of those supposedly talking Wilde into delaying the premiere, as

[29] 'Private Correspondence', *Birmingham Daily Post* (5 December 1881), 5.

[30] 'Frederick the Great', *Moonshine* (17 December 1881), 300.

[31] George Rowell, 'The Truth About *Vera*', *Nineteenth Century Theatre*, 21, no. 2 (1993), 96.

both H. Montgomery Hyde's and Richard Ellmann's biographies suggest, may have been the Prince of Wales.[32] If this was indeed the case, the Prince's intervention may have been due to sensitivities regarding the fact that the Danish-born Princess of Wales's sister was married to the new tsar, whose father had been murdered in March: the fact that the play was expressly set in the years 1795 to 1800 presumably altered nothing.[33] Like Irish nationalism and anarchism, royalty offered a vision of an international, cosmopolitan network. But this supposed reason is improbable: the tsar's assassination had taken place nearly nine months before, and of course would have been even fresher in the minds of theatre-investors, actors, and the author when the idea for the performance was first mooted. (It is not clear whether or not the Lord Chamberlain approved the play.) Moreover, in February 1880, and again in November of the same year, as Wilde was mobilizing interest in his play, there had been earlier abortive assassination attempts on the tsar: long before the tsar's actual murder, these attempts had made the subject a controversial one. Similarly, Johann Most's conviction for incitement to violence had occurred on 26 May 1881, months before the projected premiere. (The anarchist editor Most had been arrested following the publication in *Freiheit* of an inflammatory article on the tsar's assassination, which ended with a call for further political murders, going so far as to name likely targets.) It remains unclear why, if the worry was that Wilde's play would cause offence, it took so long to realize the risk involved. Some have considered that the assassination of the tsar had in fact piqued interest in things Russian still further, and had contributed to the possibility of a dramatic success.[34] A few weeks later, however, Wilde left Britain for the United States. He expressly hoped to have *Vera* staged there.

It is probable that the reason for Wilde's anxiety about the play had less to do with Russia than, as the phrasing of the announcements in both *The World* and the *Birmingham Daily Post* suggests, the current escalating Land War in Ireland. Here was a play by a noticeably Irish author, equivocally praising sedition, assassination, and republican rule. Wilde's decision to cancel the performance of *Vera* militates against the current critical image of him as an arch-subversive. Rather, his action allows a glimpse of his more tentative desire simultaneously to shock, placate, and amuse his audience. At this stage in his career at least, he had not yet mastered the finesse that would later enable him to achieve this aim. It is possible that Wilde suppressed *Vera* in Britain due to his awareness of the interpretation his own nationality might elicit. Moreover, it is likely that a tacit link between Russia and Ireland would have been implicitly understood and resented by the 'loyal English gallery'.

What evidence is there that in *Vera* Russia is a mask for Ireland? After all, it could be thought that it was merely the play's republicanism that might offend. There is one telling trace of Wilde's Irish concerns in the history of the text of *Vera*. In the first draft of the play, held in the Clark Library at the University of California, Los Angeles, Wilde has the Seventh Conspirator declaim, 'Our mission is to give

[32] Ellmann, *Oscar Wilde*, 146.

[33] Rowell, 'The Truth About Vera', 95.

[34] Hesketh Pearson, *The Life of Oscar Wilde*, rev. edn (London: Methuen, 1954), 54.

freedom to three millions of people now enslaved to one man.'[35] In the first edition of the play, this number, roughly equivalent to the population of Ireland at the time, has been upgraded to a more Russian-sounding, 'one hundred millions'. It is possible that the casting of the young Irishman, Dion Boucicault, for a major role in the aborted London presentation, would have invited audiences to interpret the play in an Irish context. His father's known sympathies with Irish Nationalism (in 1881, he claimed that the English newspapers were too hostile to permit his playing there), and the notion that Boucicault senior was in some way connected to the proposed production could also cause speculation about the play's perceived Irish context.[36] Furthermore, by early 1882, there are explicit indications that Wilde's Irishness had become an target for his parodists and attackers: an impersonator asserts, ' "Oh, yes! I speak most languages; in the sweet, honey-tinted brogue my own land lends me." '[37]

Almost from the first, in England Vera Zasulich's acquittal was understood in Irish terms. When *The Times* offered an editorial on Zasulich's release, it remarked, 'We could have understood the trial if it had happened in Dublin, but how is it to be explained when its scene is the City of PETER THE GREAT?'[38] In England, it argued, a compassionate jury would have balked at charging her with attempted murder, but would have upheld the law with a charge of wounding; the verdict would have come with a plea for mercy. In this, presumably, the pragmatic English would not resemble the irresponsible Irish.

In 1886 W. Earl Hodgson paid a visit to the London home of Stepnyak-Kravchinsky, the illustrious nihilist exile, literary lion, and himself an assassin. Hodgson describes his meeting with trepidation, as though he were to be introduced to a monstrous fanatic; instead he discovers a plump and benign man of good sense and order. He reports Stepnyak as remarking:

> '*Nihilist* is a nickname given to us by the thick-headed Saxon. It reminds me of a cartoon in one of your funny journals—a picture of two of us met in a ruined building. "Is all blown up already?" says one. "No," says the other. "The globe remains firm." "Well, let us blow up the globe, then!" answers the first. We don't want to blow up the globe.'

Stepnyak describes his activities as evidence of the Liberal spirit. Hodgson concludes:

> In short, the Nihilists are aglow with the same spirit that would send the British Tories into rebellion were our fatherland suddenly to come under the absolute rule of the soulless and self-seeking caucus that lives to do the behests of Mr Chamberlain. Let me, then, conclude with the hope that no one in these Isles will cast a slur on Victoria's reign by denouncing Nihilism under the impression that the British Monarchy and the Russian Autocracy are akin.[39]

[35] Wilde, *Oscar Wilde's 'Vera; or, The Nihilist'*, xiv.

[36] Richard Fawkes, *Dion Boucicault: A Biography* (London: Quartet Books, 1979), 196–7, 219. Later, in 1882, Boucicault senior certainly offered financial help to Wilde to help him escape from his connection to Carte (220).

[37] 'Oscar Interviewed', *Punch* (14 January 1882), 14.

[38] *The Times* (23 April 1878), 7.

[39] W. Earl Hodgson, *A Night With A Nihilist* (Cupar: Fifeshire Journal, 1886), 8, 19.

Here the nihilist example serves as a way of separating Britain from Russia. However, it was precisely by stressing the existence of British autocracy or imperial domination of Ireland, that a connection between the two nations could be demonstrated. If the Irish Fenians were sometimes understood as nihilists, this involved, for Home Rulers, Republicans, and anti-imperialists, the fact that British domination in Ireland was as anti-democratic as the knout, the secret police, or exile to Siberia. For supporters of British rule, describing the Irish as nihilists was to focus on the other side of the matter, alluding to their reliance on conspiracy and political violence.

In September 1880, during the violence of the Land War—just as Wilde was writing *Vera*—two presumed Russian assassination plots were discovered in Britain, one to blow up the tsar's yacht, *Livadia*, the other to bomb the Grand Duke Konstantin's train.[40] Nihilist plots had apparently come to Britain, and from this nearer view, the close resemblance of their tactics to those of the revolutionary Irish was unmistakable. Also that month a prominent Irish landlord, Lord Mountmorres, was assassinated on the road to his house at Ebor Hall on the northern shore of Lough Corib. The murder emerged from the context of the land agitation in rural Ireland that had brought the country close to violent rebellion. There is no way of telling if Wilde was influenced by Mountmorres's murder, though, given its prominence in the newspapers, he could hardly have been unaware of it. Yet the incident is an evocative one when considering the composition of *Vera*. Mountmorres was Anglo-Irish, as Wilde was, but an enemy to nationalist aspirations and republicanism; his murder was seen as a degraded and degrading act, but there were also indications that he may have been a tyrannical landlord: the tensions contained in these facts are at least analogous to the ambiguities present in Wilde's play.

The conjunction of Irish violence at home and nihilist violence in Russia meant that 'Fenians' and nihilists could be seen as parallel cases. The continued use of the name 'Fenian' was an anachronism; Fenianism in its original form as a nationalist movement was a relic of the previous decades. Yet in the popular imagination it lingered on—the emblem of Irish conspiracy and nationalist hopes. Many outside the movement felt Charles Parnell's and Michael Davitt's Irish Land League to be no more than a continuation of Fenianism under another name.

Although in the newspapers, journals and magazines of the day, the nihilist could on occasion seem interchangeable with the socialist or anarchist, it was very rare for the word to be used of rebels or revolutionaries of nations other than Russia.[41] It was only in an Irish context that commentators and journalists habitually resorted to a comparison with Russia. From the late 1870s, 'Fenians' and nihilists began

[40] 'Chronicle of Events in 1880', in *The Annual Register: A Review of Public Events at Home and Abroad for the Year, 1880*, NS (London: Longman's, 1881), 97–8; 'The Supposed Attempt to Wreck a Railway Train', *The Times* (16 September 1880), 8.

[41] In one rare exception, the *Belfast News-Letter* (27 July 1877), 2, talks of French Jesuits combating atheist, socialist, and nihilist ideas. This is the earliest authentic political use of the term I have found that refers to non-Russians. However, in the mid-1860s, nihilists were sometimes improbably linked to the political movement of 'Know Nothingism' in the United States: see, for instance, 'Nihilism in Russia', *Pall Mall Gazette* (10 December 1866), 1. As Russian nihilism was better understood, this practice rightly dropped away; the nihilists had very little in common with the Know Nothings.

to be grouped together by journalists. An article from an August 1879 edition of *The Examiner* listed a common American problem of 'German socialists, Russian Nihilists, and Irish Fenians'.[42] The assertion that America's Irish nationalists were nihilists soon became a commonplace; one periodical lightly talked of 'Yankee Irish Nihilists'.[43] In Britain, an editorial from December 1880 in a local paper found common ground for Russians and Irish Land-Leaguers in their attitude to property: 'the *genius* of the Irish nation appears to approach that of the Russian peasant rather than that of the French *bourgeoisie*'.[44] In September 1881, it was reported, with questionable accuracy, that throughout Castlebar in Ireland a placard had been distributed calling on the 'Nihilists of Castlebar!', declaring 'Nihilism is not confined to Russia' and signed by 'CAPTAIN (on behalf of the Irish Nihilists)'. The same placard promised 'Perdition to Victoria', a clear incitement to assassination, and, given the context of the other placards, a reference to the recent murder of the tsar.[45] In the autumn of 1881 newspapers carried the story that the 'Irish Nihilists' had vowed to embark on a programme of assassination and bombings.[46] In January 1881, in a *Punch* article entitled 'Our New Bogeys', the 'domestic demon' the 'Fenian' is imagined as the brother of the Russian nihilist; later in the summer of that year, a much-reprinted joke in *Punch* played on the idea of 'Irish Nihilists'.[47] In fact, during the years when *Punch* initiated its satirical attacks on Wilde, the magazine was consistently describing the land-leaguers as 'Irish Nihilists'. As early as December 1879, it was commenting: 'The leaders of the Irish Land Agitation may be congratulated on having developed Nihilism amongst a section of their compatriots. Nihilism in Ireland is essentially just the same as Russian Nihilism, and, indeed, Nihilism as practised by Nihilists all the world over, on the principle of assassinating, so as to annihilate, everyone they object to.'[48]

As had been the case with the caricature version of Wilde, this image of the 'Irish Nihilist' spread throughout British-based comic journals and magazines. In October 1880, a cartoon in *Funny Folks* imagined 'The Arch-Plotter—Nihilist, Socialist, and Fenian!', though this dangerous character is only a tousled pamphleteer.[49] Likewise, on many occasions *The Times* explicitly compared the 'Fenians' with nihilists, or linked the two groups, or reported the words of others who did so. In 1881, at a Christmas pantomime version of *Dick Whittington*, King Rat made the connection clear:

> Your duties, Sharpteeth, I am sure you're clear in,
> You go and help the Land League in Old Erin.

[42] 'The Mormon Embargo', *The Examiner* (16 August 1879), 1050.

[43] 'Dynamite Done Up', *Funny Folks* (17 September 1881), 291.

[44] 'Russian Nihilists and Irish Land Leagues', *Hull Packet and East Riding Times* (10 December 1880), 4.

[45] Reported in 'Ireland', *Bristol Mercury and Daily Post* (16 September 1881), 2, and in 'The State of Ireland', *Liverpool Mercury* (16 September 1881), 6, and then again in 'Ireland', *Trewman's Exeter Flying Post or Plymouth and Cornish Advertiser* (21 September 1881), 8.

[46] 'The State of Ireland', *Hampshire Telegraph and Sussex Chronicle* (26 October 1881), 3.

[47] 'Our New Bogeys', *Punch* (22 January 1881), 34; *Punch* (6 August 1881), 54: 'The Dynamite came over from America in barrels labelled "Cement." The skirmishing Irish Nihilists have a playful idea of cementing the friendship between the two countries'.

[48] 'Blood Relations and Brothers', *Punch* (13 December 1879), 275.

[49] 'Plots and Rumours of Plots', *Funny Folks* (9 October 1880), 325.

> You'll be a Nihilist, all you've to do,
> Is just to kill an Emperor or two.[50]

At the trial of Parnell in January 1881, the defence counsel had to deny specifically that there was anything resembling nihilism in the Land League.[51]

Though explicit connection between the nihilists and the Land-Leaguers or 'Fenians' had been circulating since 1879, it was in 1882, in the immediate aftermath of the Phoenix Park murders (the assassination in Dublin of Lord Frederick Cavendish, Chief Secretary for Ireland, and Thomas Henry Burke, the Permanent Undersecretary) that the connection became most emphatic. *The Belfast News-Letter* (hardly a neutral observer) reported a Unitarian minister who described the killings as the 'answer of Irish Nihilism to Mr. Gladstone's statement'.[52] The subject seems to have remained a pulpit favourite. In a sermon of July 1882, an East Anglian vicar connected 'the American rowdy, the French Communist, the Russian Nihilist, the Irish Fenian and the English rough' in a union of perfidy.[53] An editorial in the *Birmingham Daily Post and Journal* pilloried 'Irish Nihilists'; the London newspaper, the *Daily News*, spoke of the murder as 'a last convulsive effort of Irish Nihilism'.[54]

In that summer of 1882, outside Britain and Ireland, the link between nihilism and 'Fenianism' was also noted. There were reports in Britain that the Austrian press were speculating 'that it is the Nihilist-Fenian combination in America which has organized the Moonlighters' bands and provides dynamite and infernal machines.'[55] It was widely reported that a French newspaper had written, 'Irish Fenianism has decidedly many features in common with Russian Nihilism.'[56] In both the Hungarian and Spanish press, a similar link was suggested.[57] In June 1882, the British newspapers reported the revolutionary views of the *American Industrialist Liberator*, an American paper, as containing a medley of Irish Nationalism, Socialism, and Nihilism.[58]

So it was that the 'Fenians'—and certainly the Irish Republican Brotherhood—could easily be identified with Russian nihilists. Both employed practices and techniques derived from the secret societies of the earlier nineteenth century. The glamour of the conspirator hung about them both. Both groups shared a resemblance to the tactics of the Italian Carbonari and other Nationalist groups—in particular a commitment to the Mazzinian revolutionary adventure (the Fenians in America improbably attempted two invasions of Canada in 1866 and 1870), and

[50] Quoted in 'The Standard Theatre', *The Times* (27 December 1881), 4.
[51] 'Ireland: The State Prosecutions', *The Times* (14 January 1881), 10.
[52] 'The Reception of the News in Ireland', *Belfast News-Letter*, 2nd edn (8 May 1882), 6.
[53] 'Bawdsey', *Ipswich Journal* (22 July 1882), 9.
[54] 'News of the Day', *Birmingham Daily Post and Journal* (8 May 1882), 5; 'Public Feeling in America and on the Continent', *Daily News* (9 May 1882), 6.
[55] 'Austria', *The Times* (9 May 1882), 5.
[56] See, for instance, 'Reception of the News on the Continent', *Daily News* (8 May 1882), 5.
[57] 'Spanish Opinion on the Explosion', *Freeman's Journal and Daily Commercial Advertiser* (Dublin) (20 March 1883), 7; 'Austria', 5.
[58] 'The American-Irish Press', *The Times* (21 June 1882), 5.

furthermore a Blanquist readiness for violence.[59] Both were 'secret societies' with a public profile. The 'Fenians' were simultaneously hidden and a nationalist beacon, precisely akin to the nihilists themselves.

Nihilists resembled 'Fenians' above all in the fact that both were committed to a project whose limits were circumscribed by the idea of the nation: both sought the reform or liberation of their own country. Yet, as we have seen, nihilism seemed apt to leap over national borders. The international basis of Irish identity in the later nineteenth century—the product of over seventy years of emigration—also lent to the Fenians something of the anarchist and communist cosmopolitanism; the fact of the Irish diaspora internationalized the movement. There were Irish nationalists at work in most of the English-speaking colonies, particularly the United States, as well as in Paris and the British mainland itself. However, although international in scope and organization, in practice the 'Fenians' were very different from their anarchist counterparts. Although widely dispersed, they all looked towards a nationalist idea of home: their own beleaguered and suffering island. The exile of Russian political refugees had a similar effect on the nihilist movement; a national struggle planted adherents across the globe.

Denied his premiere in London, Wilde himself was about to exploit the international interest in nihilism and the Irish struggle. Late in 1881, rumours circulated that Wilde would soon visit America. It was suggested, not seriously, that Wilde's visit was an elaborate means of preparing America for the advent in the New World of Lily Langtry.[60] Langtry's name was certainly entangled with Wilde's. A fake interview with Oscar Wilde in *Punch* had the young aesthete declare, '"Who are my neophytes? Well, I fancy the LONSDALES and the LANGTRYS would never have been known if I hadn't placed them on a pedestal of daffodils, and taught the world to worship."'[61] Two days after the mention of Wilde meeting with Langtry at Labouchère's, the story had thickened into a rumour that she was to play Vera in the play's debut in New York.[62] Even without the imagined casting of Lily Langtry, the idea that *Vera* would receive its first performance in New York quickly gathered weight. By mid-December 1881, it was suggested that the play would indeed appear in New York, rather than Britain, where 'it will not receive so se-Vera reception as was expected of it here'.[63] A cartoon image of Wilde setting sail for the United States has him leaving 'with his tragedy' (*Vera*), depicted as a scroll being dropped by the writer as he stumbles on the boarding-plank: 'the tragedy will thus be played out of England, and the movement with which his name is associated will be played out too'.[64]

During his first stay in America, Wilde was involved in plans with the theatre impresario Richard D'Oyly Carte for a new edition of *Vera*, intended to generate

[59] See R. F. Foster, *Modern Ireland, 1600-1972* (London: Penguin, 1988), 391–3.

[60] 'The Lily and the Lecturer', *Funny Folks* (3 December 1881), 382.

[61] 'Oscar Interviewed'.

[62] 'London Gossip', *Hampshire Telegraph and Sussex Chronicle* (7 December 1881), 3.

[63] 'Floats and Flies', *Fun* (14 December 1881), 248.

[64] 'Exodus of the Æsthetes', *Funny Folks* (7 January 1882), 4.

interest in a theatrical production.[65] These overtures, however, came to little. By March 1883, it seemed unlikely that Wilde's play would ever be produced.[66] Yet a few months later, it was confirmed that *Vera* would finally have her debut. As had long been thought the case, *Vera* would first face an audience in the United States: the play was to be performed at the Union Square Theatre in New York. The play was retitled *Vera; or, The Nihilist*.[67] It was now plainly reported that the play had initially been withdrawn 'by the author on the ground of its strongly marked political character and of the special inopportuneness of its allusions to recent events in Russia'; around the same time, the idea that the play had been withdrawn from performance at the Adelphi for political reasons was reiterated in *The Graphic*: 'Originally this piece was to have been brought out at the Adelphi Theatre in London; but the inflammatory nature of its politics appears to have alarmed even the author himself, who accordingly, for reasons of State, withdrew it at the last moment'.[68] Though no more trustworthy than earlier statements, these reports place the responsibility for postponing the play firmly in Wilde's hands.

Now Wilde seemed more prepared than before to acknowledge to the republican and revolutionary sentiments voiced in the play. It was reported that on his second trip to the United States 'he took occasion to explain that this was his first attempt at a dramatic expression of the principles to which he had dedicated his youth.'[69] This strongly suggests a radical context for the play's politics, and, depending on how far back we take his 'youth', an Irish context too, though it is also possible that the reference is to his aestheticism. Some doubted that Americans would grasp the basic premise of the play, since 'its theme [was] one that is not understood, and evoking no sympathy in this country, where Nihilism is an almost meaningless term, except that it is generally regarded as a synonym of Communism and Socialism'.[70] Carte had similarly complained that Americans would know nothing about Russian politics; at his insistence, Wilde wrote a prologue for the play designed to inform them.[71]

On 20 August 1883, *Vera* finally had its premiere; Marie Prescott played Vera. If Wilde had hoped for a readier reception from an American audience than from 'the loyal English gallery', he was to be disappointed. American audiences had picked up the British sense that Wilde was inherently ridiculous; on the play's first night, the jeering began early.[72] The reviews were scathing, and, surprisingly, even included indications of finding fault with the republicanism of the play: 'It is a foolish, highly peppered story of love, intrigue, and politics, with Russian accessories of fur and dark lanterns, and overlaid with bantam gabble about freedom and the people. It was little better than fizzle.'[73] Worst of all, one of the more well-known members

[65] Wilde, *Selected Letters*, 36.
[66] 'Dramatic Notes', *Funny Folks* (10 March 1883), 78.
[67] 'Theatres', *The Graphic* (28 July 1883), 94.
[68] 'The Theatres', *Daily News* (23 July 1883), 2; 'Theatres', *The Graphic* (28 July 1883), 94.
[69] 'American Affairs', *Birmingham Daily Post* (29 September 1883), 5.
[70] 'The Drama in America', *The Era* (8 September 1883), 3.
[71] Ellmann, *Oscar Wilde*, 163.
[72] 'Theatres', *The Graphic* (25 August 1883), 187.
[73] Review from *The Tribune*, quoted in 'Mr. Oscar Wilde's Play', *North-Eastern Daily Gazette* (22 August 1883), 3.

of the audience, Charles T. Mills, a figure in New York theatre, died on Broadway shortly after leaving *Vera*'s premiere. The death was a gift to journalistic sarcasm, as it was inevitably inferred that the quality of the play had killed him.[74] The play was a financial disaster. $500 had been spent on the costumes, and over $15000 invested in its production. This investment gained no return, and the play's early closure made Marie Prescott's commitment to perform the play 100 times pointless.[75]

Back in Britain, the press enjoyed the New York debacle.[76] There were political elements to the *Schadenfreude*: 'Will the Æsthetic give some more *Impressions du Théâtre?* If so, he will probably have something to tell of "my Soul's dread weariness," and not very much to say in favour of "my freedom and my life Republican".'[77] These last phrases quote the last lines from Wilde's sonnet, 'Queen Henrietta Maria', and suggest that the press had perceived that one reason Wilde had shown *Vera* first in the United States was that it was a republican country. *The Sporting Times* characterized the play as 'a tale of treason, Nihilism, dynamite, murder, hate, conspiracy, love, furs, kümmel, and other pleasing Muscovite novelties.'[78]

Nonetheless, among these bad reviews, some prominent people, notably the American actress Mary Anderson, began to praise the young Irishman; there was also some encouragement from the wider press, and there followed something of a rally in Wilde's favour.[79] It was not enough, however, to save poor *Vera*. Wilde's attempt to write a topical play had broadly failed. At this stage of his career, his attempt to juggle his need to establish himself as a professional writer with his desire to replicate the radical vocation of his mother had misfired. This direct engagement with contemporary politics had left him with little success—the play had taken three years to be staged, and then had met with a decidedly cool reception when it first appeared. If, as I am arguing, in the early 1880s Wilde had attempted directly to combine, in the mode of Swinburne, 'pagan' aestheticism and Republican radicalism, then the attempt had proved both an artistic and a commercial failure. It seems that, learning from the debacle, Wilde mastered instead another means of combining his political interests with his art, in a manner that would please, and confuse, a paying public. He would better fuse his radical concerns with wit, irony, and playfulness. It is possible therefore that it was the failure of *Vera* that led him in the direction of indirection—he would never again, as he had in *Vera*, so obviously write about contemporary politics.

The first signs of this new approach were the short stories that eventually made up the 1891 volume, *Lord Arthur Savile's Crime and other Stories.* The title story in this volume, originally published in May 1887 in *Court and Society Review*, displays most readily Wilde's advance, in so far as it too, like *Vera*, has Russian nihilists (and German bomb-makers) standing in for Irish revolutionaries. The story depicts a

74 'Public Amusements', *Reynolds's Newspaper* (9 September 1883), 5.

75 'Music and the Drama', *Illustrated Police News* (22 September 1883), 2.

76 'Oscar's "Vera" ', *Moonshine* (1 September 1883), 112.

77 ' "The Play's Not the Thing" ', *Punch* (1 September 1883), 100.

78 'Playhouses Without Plays', *Sporting Times* (15 September 1883), 3.

79 'Music and the Drama', *Illustrated Police News* (22 September 1883), 2; 'American Affairs', *Birmingham Daily Post* (29 September 1883), 5.

society in contented moral collapse, where, in a precursor of radical chic, aristocrats signal their distance from the bourgeois by forming an alliance with other anti-bourgeois elements—Jews, criminals, 'Inverts' and 'Uranians', artists—and fortune-tellers. In this world, murderers become celebrities. Wilde's role in society was of course itself embroiled in just such a relationship—a position to which he responded as both snob and rebel. Wilde's story makes a joke about goodness and murder, it explores a moral confusion: to be good enough to marry his fiancée, Lord Arthur Savile must first kill someone. Savile doesn't know that his thoughts about his position are funny; the humour arises from the seriousness with which he takes things; it is his earnestness in pursuit of murder that makes him ludicrous. In this way, the story turns on the paradox of the assassin, the paradox of Vera Zasulich herself; for Lord Arthur Savile, as for Vera, murder becomes a duty. Like Vera, Savile must look upon the crime as an unpleasant task that is not to be shirked: 'His heart told him that it was not a sin, but a sacrifice; his reason reminded him that there was no other course open.'[80]

Lord Arthur Savile is therefore entangled in the moral paradox experienced by both the Russian nihilists and the Irish Republican Brotherhood. As with these late nineteenth-century terrorist groups, a worthy and idealistic aim is to be reached by violent and cruel means. Though Savile goes for instructions in murder to Count Rouvaloff, an aristocratic spy for the Russian nihilists, for the British reading public at the end of the 1880s, the recent bombing campaigns of the 1880s had made dynamite equally synonymous with Irishness. Here, as he had in *Vera*, but this time entirely successfully, Wilde was seeing Ireland in Russia, and using her image as a means of implicitly fusing his moral, political, and aesthetic concerns.

For Wilde, then, as for those journalists who glimpsed Ireland there, Russia was a malleable icon. It could serve as a screen for many contexts, changing its meaning as it interacted with different locales. Above all, from the point of view of this essay, it gifted the writers and the political activists of the 1880s a new character type: the hard, self-abnegating, violent, high-minded nihilist. To the British press, nihilism came to serve as a label for all that was understood as hostile and inimical to the status quo. In particular, it provided the exemplum of the rigorous assassin. To name the 'Fenians' as nihilists was to link them to an international spirit of revolt; nihilism became a moveable noun apt to be only a little modified by its transposition to another culture. The appeal of the term was greater than the need for accuracy; the British press both imagined the United States as a source of Irish 'nihilism' and a place where everyone was ignorant of nihilism and Russian politics. For the Irish Republican Brotherhood and other Irish nationalists ready to adopt violent tactics, the link with Russian nihilism cannot merely have been a slur. It associated the nationalist movement with a terrorist group that were signally successful in pursuing their aim: in the years 1878–1882, it seemed that a small committed group could transform history. Above all, nihilism provided the Irish republicans and nationalists with a model of how to be a committed revolutionary; the great examples were Vera Zasulich, and her one-time lover, the extraordinary Nechaev.

[80] Oscar Wilde, *Complete Short Fiction*, ed. Ian Small (London: Penguin, 2003), 181.

Wilde glimpsed the artistic and political possibilities of Russian nihilism, the chance of fashioning a work of art that would itself strike a blow against tyranny and intervene in the possibilities of mainstream theatre, making a drama that would bring together romantic love and revolutionary fervour. Clearly the idea of a nihilist is historically contingent, a personality best understood in relation to the cultural context that fostered its creation, though that context could operate with equal fertility in Ireland as in Russia. Yet Wilde's play imagines a timeless, unchanging Russia outside history; his nihilists plot anachronistically in a late eighteenth-century world, some sixty years before their movement came into existence. In Wilde's Russia, no matter what the period, there are always nihilists to plot and tsars to assassinate. Conflating 1795 and 1878, merging Vera Zasulich with some other Vera, her precursor, the history of Russia shimmers and ceases to matter. Things there are fabulously changeless. The play is not only outside history, it also embraces a peculiar placelessness, set in a St Petersburg that it names as Moscow.[81] The two cities become interchangeable, neither a specific place, both merely elements in a necessary fiction named 'Russia'. Wilde productively embraced the idea that nihilism itself was a fiction, the creation of Ivan Turgenev and Fedor Dostoevsky.[82] That signalled too the supremacy of art and imagination over hard fact, the well-spring for a play that happily conflates past and present, Moscow and Petersburg, Ireland and Russia.

[81] Wilde, *Oscar Wilde's 'Vera; or the Nihilist'*, xv–xvi.

[82] Dostoevsky's *Demons* (*Besy*, 1872) had been translated into French, by Victor Derély as *Les Possédés*, in 1886, one year before Wilde wrote 'Lord Arthur Savile's Crime'.

3

Britain and the International Tolstoyan Movement, 1890–1910

Charlotte Alston

In 1898 Percy Redfern was a low-level activist in the socialist movement. 'Steward at slum concerts, Socialist writer, Labour church worker, debater at the university settlement... like others of the time,' he later wrote, 'I was all of these.'[1] His introduction to Tolstoy's works—unusually via *What is Art?* (*Chto takoe iskusstvo*) and *The Christian Teaching* (*Khristianskoe uchenie*)—transformed his outlook on life.[2] 'Throughout a period of about five years', he commented, 'Tolstoy was my university and my church.'[3] Like other aspiring Tolstoyans, Redfern sought to acquaint himself with the movement and the possibilities for action in his area. In his autobiography he described the situation in Britain at the time as follows:

> the missionaries were in the field and active. Railway bookstalls were distributing the great writer's own pamphlets in the well-produced, threepenny editions of the Free Age Press founded by Tolstoy's exiled friend, Vladimir Tchertkoff, and his competent English partner and publisher A. C. Fifield. And through that pioneer, spare-time compilation by the civil servant, Joseph Edwards, *The Labour Annual*, I heard of a Tolstoyan colony amongst the different, small, socialist settlements in Essex. To detach oneself from all this stir and work was impossible.[4]

Redfern's description conveys something of the breadth of enthusiasm for Tolstoy's moral philosophy at this time, and of its place in a broader stream of reform movements. Tolstoy's philosophy, outlined in the body of work he produced from the late 1870s onwards, was essentially a form of Christian anarchism, based on the doctrine of non-resistance to evil. Tolstoy rejected the state (because it could only exist on the basis of physical force) and all institutions derived from it—the police, law courts, the army, and the Russian Orthodox Church. He condemned private property and money, and advocated living by one's own physical labour. He also came to believe in vegetarianism, complete chastity, and abstinence from tobacco

[1] Percy Redfern, *Journey to Understanding* (London: Allen and Unwin, 1946), 47–8.
[2] Leo Tolstoy, *What is Art?* (London: Brotherhood Publishing Company, 1898) and *The Christian Teaching* (London: Brotherhood Publishing Company, 1898).
[3] Percy Redfern, *Tolstoy: A Study* (London: A. C. Fifield, 1907), 5.
[4] Redfern, *Journey to Understanding*, 90.

and alcohol. In Russia a vigorous Tolstoyan movement emerged during the 1880s, with colonies in the provinces of Smolensk, Tver', Samara, Kursk, Perm', and Kyiv, and with the publishing house *Posrednik* (*The Intermediary*) and later the Moscow vegetarian society as centres of activity.[5] In the rest of Europe and in the United States, Tolstoyism gained dramatically in influence a decade later, in the 1890s. The remarkable increase in overseas engagement with Tolstoy's Christian anarchism is apparent in the volume and content of letters received by Tolstoy from correspondents across Europe and the United States from this decade onwards.[6] British correspondents were amply represented. In the 1890s and 1900s Britain became a major centre for Tolstoyan activity, facilitating publication of texts censored elsewhere, and hosting a community of Russian Tolstoyans in exile. Home-grown British Tolstoyans fostered close links with Tolstoy and with his Russian followers. However, they also operated as part of a vigorous international movement with centres across Europe and the USA, which developed correspondence networks and exchanged personnel and ideas. While there are numerous regional studies of Tolstoy's influence, there have been few attempts to place these local movements in their international context.[7] This chapter focuses on the structures, strategies, and concerns that the British Tolstoyans shared with other international Tolstoyan groups. It also examines their multiple local contexts, and explores the extent, and limits, of their cooperation with sympathetic British reformist groups.

As William Edgerton has pointed out, the delay in publishing foreign translations of Tolstoy's earlier work meant that English-, French-, and German-speaking audiences were introduced to Tolstoy's novels and his philosophical writings almost

[5] On the Tolstoyan movement in Russia, see Paul D. Steeves, 'Tolstoyans in Russia and the USSR', in Joseph L. Wieczynski, ed., *The Modern Encyclopaedia of Russian and Soviet History*, xxxix (Gulf Breeze, FL: Academic International, 1985), 114–21; William Edgerton, *Memoirs of Peasant Tolstoyans in Soviet Russia* (Bloomington, IN: Indiana University Press, 1993), xi–xv; Mark Popovsky, *Russkie muzhiki rasskazyvayut: posledovateli L. N. Tolstogo v Sovetskom Soyuze, 1918–1977: dokumental'nyi rasskaz o krest'yanakh-tolstovtsakh v SSSR po materialam vyvezennogo na Zapad krest'yanskogo arkhiva* (London: Overseas Publications Interchange, 1983).

[6] Almost every letter Tolstoy wrote, and summaries of some that he received, are published in the jubilee edition of his collected works: L. Tolstoy, *Polnoe sobranie sochinenii* (Moscow: Khudozhestvennaya literatura, 1935–64), lxiii–lxxxix (hereafter *PSS*). Letters written to Tolstoy by his international sympathizers are preserved in the Manuscripts Department of the Gosudarstvennyi muzei L. N. Tolstogo (State Tolstoy Museum) in Moscow (hereafter GMT).

[7] Two brief accounts of the international scope of the movement are William B. Edgerton, 'The Artist Turned Prophet: Leo Tolstoj after 1880', in W. E. Harkins, ed., *American Contributions to the Sixth International Congress of Slavists*, ii: *Literary Contributions* (The Hague: Mouton, 1968), 61–85, and Steven Marks, *How Russia Shaped the Modern World: From Art to Anti-Semitism, Ballet to Bolshevism* (Princeton, NJ: Princeton University Press, 2003), 102–39. Local studies include M. J. de K. Holman, 'The Purleigh Colony: Tolstoyan Togetherness in the late 1890s', and W. H. G. Armytage, 'J. C. Kenworthy and the Tolstoyan Communities in England', both in W. Gareth Jones, ed., *Tolstoi and Britain* (Oxford: Berg, 1995), 135–51 and 153–83; Rudolf Jans, *Tolstoj in Nederland* (Bussum: P. Brand, 1952); A. Nokkala, *Tolstoilaisuus Suomessa* (Helsinki: Kustannusosakeyhtiö Tammi, 1958); N. Velikanova and R. Whittaker, eds, *Tolstoy i SShA* (Moscow: IMLI RAN, 2004); Antonella Salomoni, *Il pensiero religioso e politico di Tolstoj in Italia, 1886–1910* (Florence: L. S. Olschki, 1996); Peter Brock, 'Tolstoyism and the Hungarian Peasant', *Slavonic and East European Review*, 58, no. 3 (July 1980), 345–69; and William B. Edgerton, 'The Social Influence of Lev Tolstoj in Bulgaria', in Jane Gary Harris, ed., *American Contributions to the Tenth International Congress of Slavists: Literature* (Columbus, OH: Slavica, 1988), 123–38.

simultaneously, effectively 'telescoping' thirty years of the author's literary development.[8] Early translations and publications of Tolstoy's moral tracts were a by-product of the broader late-nineteenth-century western European enthusiasm for Russian literature. Translators, publishers, and literary critics impatient for the arrival of Tolstoy's next great novel could not ignore the work he was producing at that time. Despite their dependence on reading his works in translation (and often in an intermediary language, usually French), enthusiastic recipients of Tolstoy's works on non-resistance, vegetarianism, and bread-labour embraced his ideas not simply as an expression of Russian spirituality or utopianism, but as directly relevant to their own experience. They deliberately and effectively crossed national borders, and fell on fertile ground amongst individuals disillusioned with modern industrial society and the politics of the time. By the turn of the century these individuals and their enterprises dominated the publication of Tolstoy's philosophical works, prioritizing the accurate representation of Tolstoy's message over fluency in the target language—whether by staying as close as possible to the author's own words, or relying on their own understanding and representation of the message. Both the perceived proximity of their relationship to Tolstoy, or Tolstoy's approval, were markers of a definitive translation.[9]

Percy Redfern was just one among many readers who found their lives changed by their introduction to Tolstoy. A reading of *What Then Must We Do?* (*Chto zhe nam delat'?*) subjected Jane Addams, the founder of Chicago's Hull House settlement, to a period of intense doubt about the value of her work. As an activist at the centre of the American peace and social reform movements, the book's focus on poverty and inequality in society spoke to her particularly—she believed its impact was a result of the 'sum of influences and of social trends under which it [was] read'.[10] *The Kingdom of God is Within You* (*Tsarstvo Bozhie vnutri vas*), Tolstoy's principal work on non-resistance and its application to war, spurred individuals in Austria-Hungary (Albert Škarvan) and in the Netherlands (Johannes Van der Veer) to refuse military service. But it seems that virtually any of Tolstoy's philosophical tracts had the power to produce a kind of 'conversion experience'—there are accounts of this phenomenon based on *On Life* (*O zhizni*), on *The Christian*

[8] Edgerton, 'The Artist Turned Prophet', 63.

[9] Vladimir Chertkov insisted on the most literal translation possible, and relied on a hierarchy of competent and sympathetic individuals to translate or approve a translation. Chertkov to Alexander Sirnis, 'How to Translate Tolstoy', 26 October 1909, MS 1381/641, Tuckton House Papers, Brotherton Collection, University of Leeds. At the other extreme Bolton Hall published simplified paraphrased versions of Tolstoy's works, as he believed Tolstoy's religious books were 'quite unreadable'. Bolton Hall, *What Tolstoy Taught* (London: Chatto and Windus, 1913), 5–8. Free Age Press pamphlets proudly displayed a statement by Tolstoy praising the company's publications from 1901 onwards: see Michael J. de K. Holman, 'Translating Tolstoy for the Free Age Press: Vladimir Chertkov and his English Manager Arthur Fifield', *Slavonic and East European Review*, 66, no. 2 (April 1988), 193.

[10] Jane Addams, 'A Book that Changed My Life', *Christian Century* (13 October 1927), 1196–8. Addams also describes the impact of Tolstoy's works upon her thought in *Twenty Years at Hull House* (New York: Macmillan, 1911), 259–60.

Teaching, or even in Redfern's case *What is Art?*[11] As Addams points out, there were many readers who 'without defying well-established custom . . . lived through miserable days and sleepless nights tormented by the simple question of "what to do?" Most of these, whether they finally worked through the problem to their own satisfaction or whether they gave it up and lived on as best they could without having solved it, found their lives in greater or lesser degree modified'.[12] For a number of conscience-stricken readers, however, nothing but a break with their existing way of life would suffice. These individuals formed the core of the Tolstoyan movement, whether in Croydon or Derby, Connecticut or Georgia, the Hague or Budapest; running publishing houses or newspapers, cooperative projects, or colonies.

Most of the individuals who appear in this chapter would have insisted that the teaching they followed and sought to promote was not Tolstoy's, but Christ's.[13] They were most often educated people who had read widely and drew on the ideas of a range of writers and reformers of their day. Nevertheless, several things united them: the profound impact of their first reading of Tolstoy's works; their acceptance of Tolstoy's core beliefs; their dedication to publicizing Tolstoy's works abroad; and their sense that they were part of a growing, international movement for which Tolstoy was a figurehead. Although he also refuted the existence of a specifically 'Tolstoyan' movement, Tolstoy played a pivotal role in the development of these international connections, and was delighted at the emergence of groups who were 'in complete agreement with our view and with one another, although they all look at things from their own particular aspect'.[14] He regularly recommended that his correspondents make contact with the centres in their locality that he valued most, and he sought to put these larger hubs of sympathetic thought in touch with one another. In time the connections between these groups were maintained independently of their initiator—through correspondence, the exchange of newspapers, and literature, and occasional visits. W. T. Stead described the movement Tolstoy had founded as 'something that is midway between a Church, a school, and a socio-political organisation'.[15]

THE TOLSTOYAN MOVEMENT IN BRITAIN

In Britain, the Croydon Brotherhood Church and its associated colony at Purleigh in Essex were the best known Tolstoyan groups.[16] This major centre for British

[11] Leo Tolstoy, *On Life*, trans. Mabel and Agnes Cook, ed. A. C. Fifield (Christchurch: Free Age Press, 1902); Russian Journal, April 1896, box 4, MS 218, Ernest Howard Crosby Papers, Michigan State University Library; John I. Kolehmainen, 'When Finland's Tolstoy met his Russian Master', *American Slavic and East European Review* 16, no. 4 (December 1957), 535; Redfern, *Journey to Understanding*, 47–50.

[12] Addams, 'A Book that Changed my Life', 1196.

[13] See for example *The Tolstoyan*, 1, no. 4 (February 1903), 121, and Lodewijk van Mierop, 'Geen Tolstoyaan maar Christen', *Vrede*, 2, no. 15 (15 May 1899), 108–10.

[14] Tolstoy to D. A. Khilkov, 12 March 1895, in *Tolstoy's Letters,* ii: *1880–1910*, ed. R. F. Christian (London: Athlone Press, 1978), 515–16, and in Tolstoy, *PSS*, lxviii, 45–7.

[15] W. T. Stead, *The Truth about Russia* (London: Cassell, 1888), 393.

[16] See Holman, 'The Purleigh Colony', 152–83.

Tolstoyism emerged from a venture established by the former businessman John Kenworthy, and the Congregationalist preacher John Bruce Wallace. Wallace was the editor of *Brotherhood,* a cooperative journal that began publication in Limavady in 1887, and continued for almost fifty years, from a variety of locations.[17] He was the first to set up a 'Brotherhood Church', in Southgate Road in North London, in 1891. Around the same time, Kenworthy's introduction to the works of Henry George, John Ruskin, and finally Tolstoy prompted him to give up his commercial career in America and return to London, where he worked on a series of cooperative ventures in Canning Town.[18] In 1893 they jointly established the 'Brotherhood Trust', a cooperative enterprise aimed at setting an example of industry and production run by workers for workers.[19] Kenworthy established his own 'Brotherhood Church' in Croydon in the spring of 1894, and his own newspaper, the *New Order* (initially the *Croydon Brotherhood Intelligence*) a year later.

In the following years a gradual divergence took place in the Brotherhood movement, as Kenworthy's Croydon group embraced the Tolstoyan position of non-resistance, while Wallace's programme remained focused on demonstrating to the current industrial system what could be done in a new socialist society. Kenworthy's first contact with Tolstoy was in 1894, when he sent him a copy of his 1893 book *The Anatomy of Misery*. Tolstoy had in fact already had a copy translated into Russian: he told Kenworthy that he felt him to be a 'kindred spirit'.[20] Kenworthy later described the day that he received this letter as 'one of the happiest in his life'.[21] A key turning point was a visit Kenworthy made to Tolstoy in January 1896. His intention, he said, was 'to see Leo Tolstoy and friends of his; to arrange with them ways and means of carrying forward in England the work to which they in Russia give themselves'.[22] If Tolstoy could only feel the earnestness and spirit of those involved in the Croydon Brotherhood, Kenworthy was sure he would know that his work was not in vain.[23] Kenworthy's return, and his report of his visit to Tolstoy, generated enormous enthusiasm in Croydon.[24]

In 1896 the Croydon Brotherhood's activities centred around two Sunday meetings, attended, in Kenworthy's estimation, by 'four or five score' people.[25] In addition there were discussion groups (for example on the Sermon on the Mount), physical education classes, a small school, and a rambling club. Branch meetings

[17] A. G. Higgins, *A History of the Brotherhood Church* (Stapleton: Brotherhood Church, 1982) 2; Patrick Smylie, '"Socialism of a mild type": The Political Thought and Action of Reverend J. Bruce Wallace and Radical Politics in Belfast, 1884-91', MA Thesis, Queen's University Belfast, 2008.

[18] John Kenworthy, *My Psychic Experiences* (London: Office of 'Light', 1901), 5–7; John Kenworthy, *Tolstoy: His Life and Works* (London: Walter Scott, 1902), 12–13.

[19] J. Bruce Wallace, *Towards Fraternal Organisation: An Explanation of the Brotherhood Trust* (London: Brotherhood Trust, [1894]), 3.

[20] Tolstoy to Kenworthy, 5 March 1894, *PSS*, lxvii, 61–2.

[21] Ernest Howard Crosby to Tolstoy, 15 June 1894, TS 211/25, GMT.

[22] John Kenworthy, *A Pilgrimage to Tolstoy* (London: Brotherhood Publishing Co., 1896), 1–2.

[23] Kenworthy, *Pilgrimage to Tolstoy*, 18.

[24] Nellie Shaw, *Whiteway: A Colony on the Cotswolds* (London: C. W. Daniel, 1935), 29–30.

[25] Kenworthy, *Pilgrimage to Tolstoy*, 18.

were held at Thornton Heath, Addiscombe, Norwood, Penge and Sydenham.[26] A Brotherhood store in Croydon sold 'honestly produced goods' including tea, stationery, sugar, dried fruit, and soup, and provided a meeting place where it was possible to 'meet friends who can talk to you about our principles and work'.[27] Brotherhood dressmaking, tailoring, and boot-making businesses catered to the sartorial needs of sympathizers.

These kinds of cooperative industries and enterprises were a central part of the Brotherhood vision, and they remained so. While in Russia, Kenworthy told the Tolstoyans he met that only exceptionally able or fortunate people were able to make a living on the land in England. So 'we are compelled to organise ourselves to carry on shopkeeping and such industries as become convenient to us, hoping thus to build up a round of industries in which we can, some day, work for one another, freeing ourselves, and all who choose to come with us, from the present wrong conditions of work and commerce'.[28] Nevertheless in the months that followed his visit the Croydon group's focus gradually shifted from their earlier industrial projects towards the establishment of a basis for agricultural work. The Purleigh Colony, established in the spring of 1897, sought to put into practice the principle of 'bread-labour', as advocated by Tolstoy. The *New Order* described itself as a special channel between British readers and Tolstoy, printing letters from him and reprints of his work. The split in the Brotherhood movement was complete by the autumn of 1897, when the Croydon group (acting on Tolstoy's advice) dropped the name 'Brotherhood Church' in order to 'dispense with names as we do with creeds'.[29] When Bruce Wallace accused Tolstoy's British followers of trying to apply in Britain ideas that were appropriate only to the Russian political system, and of handing over power to reactionary forces by abstaining from political involvement, Kenworthy responded with a vigorous defence of the non-resistant, Tolstoyan position—for him involvement in any political process was an impossibility.[30]

Kenworthy's Brotherhood Church was the leading centre for British Tolstoyism, but it was not the only one. The Croydon and Purleigh groups had links with groups established on similar lines, and they also fostered splinter and successor groups. One of the most important was the Whiteway colony near Stroud, which was funded by Samuel Veale Bracher and attracted an international membership over its long lifetime.[31] In Leeds, George Gibson and D. B. Foster collaborated in the establishment of a workshop at Victoria Road, Holbeck, which was 'owned and run by the workers ... [and] where no capitalist employer could interfere'.[32] Besides

[26] *New Order* (July 1895), 2.

[27] *New Order* (November 1895), 8.

[28] Kenworthy, *Pilgrimage to Tolstoy*, 24.

[29] John Kenworthy, 'A Change of Name', *New Order*, 3, no. 10 (October 1897), 73–4. Kenworthy to Tolstoy, 25 June 1896, TS 223/78, GMT; Tolstoy to Kenworthy, 27 June 1896, *PSS*, lxix, 107–8.

[30] John Bruce Wallace, 'Tolstoyism and its English Parody', *Brotherhood* (October 1897), 63; John Kenworthy, 'The Basic Christian Principle', *New Order*, 3, no. 11 (November 1897), 1.

[31] On the Whiteway colony, see Shaw, *Whiteway*, and Joy Thacker, *Whiteway Colony: The Social History of a Tolstoyan Community* (Stroud: J. Thacker, 1993)

[32] D. B. Foster, *Socialism and the Christ. My Two Great Discoveries in a Long and Painful Search for the Truth* (Leeds: D. B. Foster, 1921), 40–1.

electrical work, carpentry, and bicycle repairs, they offered workspace and accommodation for sympathizers, and a meeting space for a new Brotherhood Church. The group organized larger Sunday lectures at St. James's Hall in Leeds, and during the summer of 1898 took these to the city's parks, with Foster and Kenworthy, visiting from London, alternately addressing the assembled crowd.[33] In Blackburn, the Christian Communist Friends led by William Murray circulated Tolstoy's literature 'because his conception of life is nearest to ours', and displayed his works in the window of their workshop at 35 Victoria Street.[34] Ernest Ames and Tom Ferris of the Leeds group met with the Blackburn Friends in the autumn of 1898, and were confident that their cooperation would have good results.[35]

A group of Tolstoyans including Jack Goring and Charles Daniel met regularly at the Central Vegetarian Restaurant, and they initiated a colony at Wickford—Goring stated that although 'no confession of faith was demanded or expected from intending members... the group was essentially, so far as their mutual relationship was concerned, a group of non-resisters, in the Tolstoyan sense of that term'.[36] William Hare, who had been a contributor to the *New Order,* established his own Tolstoyan newspaper, *The Candlestick,* in Derby in 1900, and Brotherhood meetings took place at the city's Temperance Hall. In the same year Percy Redfern's Manchester Tolstoy Society was established; it held regular meetings either in buildings owned by philanthropic or trade organizations in Manchester, or outdoors in the summer—at its largest Redfern estimated that there were 150 attendees.[37] The London Tolstoyan Society, which operated in 1898–9 in the premises of the West London School of Music on Edgware Road, accommodated an audience of between twenty to fifty (and only very occasionally a hundred) in their dusty lecture hall.[38] Charles Daniel and Florence Worland, who were key players in that society, directed a series of periodicals in the 1900s which addressed the broad range of Tolstoyan concerns—*The Tolstoyan,* which aimed 'to break the record of its kind, and live beyond the sunset into another day',[39] but in fact survived only for a year; *The Crank* (until 1907), and *The Open Road* (until 1911). Daniel was tried for publishing radical pacifist literature during the First World War, and in his defence presented the courtroom with a pamphlet edition of Tolstoy's *Thou Shalt Not Kill* (*Ne ubii*), to demonstrate the kind of literature the government sought to ban.[40] Tolstoy made an appearance in peace literature in the late 1930s too, and in the 1950s and

33 D. B. Foster, 'Notes from Leeds', *New Order*, 4, no. 5 (June 1898), 55.

34 'The Blackburn Brotherhood', *New Order*, NS 2, no. 19 (August 1899), 115.

35 'Leeds Notes', *New Order*, 4, no. 10 (November 1898), 116.

36 Jack Goring, 'Wickford Notes', *New Order*, 4, no. 7 (August 1898), 76.

37 Percy Redfern to Tolstoy, 4 August 1901, TS 235/54, GMT.

38 F. E. W., 'Meetings and Partings II', *Focus* (February 1926), 97–107. The Tolstoyan Society's meetings are also described by Dorothy Richardson in *Pilgrimage*, 4 vols (New York: Knopf, 1967), iii, 373–4.

39 *The Tolstoyan*, 2, no. 1 (May 1903), 1.

40 Imogen Gassert, 'Charles Daniel: Maverick Pacifist Publisher in the First World War', *Publishing History*, 48 (2000), 5–40.

1960s his message was promoted by devotees like Harold Bing, the son of one of the original members of the Croydon group.[41] So while the 1890s and early 1900s were the high point of the organized movement in Britain, Tolstoy's influence and the physical and ideological remnants of the movement lasted much longer. Many individuals toyed with Tolstoyism or acknowledged its influence on their lives—the prolific radical writer John Morrison Davidson, for example, the pacifist Stephen Hobhouse, and the Irish anarchist Captain Jack White.[42]

In the years when their correspondence was at its height (1894–7), John Kenworthy was one of those with whom Tolstoy was most likely to recommend contact. In the local context, for example, he wrote to the Baptist pastor Kenneth Bond, 'Do you know John Kenworthy and his church and his paper? His address is Croydon. I think you will find spiritual help in putting yourself in communications with him and his people'.[43] And to Alexander McDonald, 'Are you acquainted with the activity of John Kenworthy? He is one of the most near to me in his views and has written excellent articles about questions, which will probably interest you.'[44]

BRITISH TOLSTOYISM AND THE INTERNATIONAL MOVEMENT

In the international arena, there were a number of other key groups and individuals that ranked alongside the Brotherhood Church in Tolstoy's esteem, and with which the British Tolstoyans were soon in touch. Ernest Howard Crosby, the leading advocate of Tolstoy's thought in the United States, visited Kenworthy as early as 1894, on his way back to Connecticut from Tolstoy's estate at Yasnaya Polyana. He found Kenworthy to be unheard of in literary circles in London, but enjoyed a conversation with him about the work of the Brotherhood churches.[45] Crosby had been a judge in the international court at Alexandria, and resigned his post after reading Tolstoy's *On Life* in French translation. He went on to conduct what Kenworthy described as 'a wide campaign upon our principles'; writing prolifically and lecturing on Tolstoyism at churches and reform societies across America. Around half of the lecturing engagements Crosby undertook in the years 1904 to 1906 were specifically devoted to Tolstoy and his thought; the others dealt either with other non-resistant heroes (William Lloyd Garrison, for example) or with political and social questions from a Tolstoyan standpoint.[46] He was a fervent anti-imperialist and

[41] See introduction to L. Tolstoy, *The Inevitable Change* (Saxmundham and Thorpeness: Peace Pamphlets by Ruth Fry, 1937), and postcards, notes and pamphlets in MS 486, Harold F. Bing Collection, University of Nottingham.

[42] John Morrison Davidson to Tolstoy, 12 July 1894 and 25 June 1895, TS 231/19, GMT; Stephen Hobhouse, *Forty Years and an Epilogue* (London: James Clarke, 1951), 57–68; Jack White, *Misfit* (London: Jonathan Cape, 1930) 145–58.

[43] Tolstoy to Kenneth Bond, 2 March 1897, *PSS*, lxx, 42–3.

[44] Tolstoy to Alexander McDonald, 26 July 1895, *PSS*, lxviii, 123–7.

[45] Crosby to Tolstoy, 15 June 1894, TS 211/25, GMT.

[46] Crosby diaries, 1904, 1905, 1906, box 2, MS 218, Ernest Howard Crosby Papers, Michigan State University Library.

anti-militarist, and satirized the absurdities of warfare in his anti-militarist novel *Captain Jinks: Hero* (1902). He was involved with the Christian Commonwealth, a colony founded on Tolstoyan lines in Georgia, and he also engaged in a kind of civic Tolstoyism, working with democratic and labour organizations for social reform. Crosby's writings regularly appeared in the *New Order*, *The Candlestick*, and, later, in *The Crank;* likewise he published contributions from international Tolstoyans in his own journal *The Whim.* Crosby visited the Tolstoyans in London and the Purleigh colony in the autumn of 1900, and remained in touch with key figures in the British movement even while it began to decline.[47]

On Tolstoy's advice Crosby also began a correspondence with Jenö Henrik Schmitt, another leading figure in the international movement. Schmitt was a Hungarian philosopher who had a well-developed Christian anarchist philosophy even before his introduction to Tolstoy. He had a significant following in Budapest, large enough to support twice-weekly meetings, and published two newspapers during the course of the 1890s—*Die Religion des Geistes* and later *Ohne Staat.*[48] Despite his relatively large local following Schmitt was not initially widely known abroad. His newspapers were more introspective than other vehicles of Tolstoyism, and they were constantly in financial difficulty. Dushan Makovitsky reported to Tolstoy on Schmitt that 'if you had not told me about him neither I nor my friend [Albert Škarvan] would ever have heard of him'.[49] It was Tolstoy who put Schmitt in touch with Makovitsky, with Crosby, with Ralph Albertson and George Gibson at the Christian Commonwealth in Georgia, with J. K. Van der Veer in Holland, and with Morrison Davidson in England.[50] Crosby was 'delighted with [Schmitt's] writings', and suggested to Kenworthy that he might translate some of them into English.[51] By the spring of 1897 Schmitt was in direct contact with Arnold Eiloart, the main benefactor of the Purleigh colony, sharing details of his activities in Budapest. Kenworthy reported in the *New Order* that the British Tolstoyans desired 'a close intercourse with him and his friends'.[52]

Van der Veer and Škarvan, mentioned here, came into the Tolstoyan orbit when their reading of Tolstoy's *The Kingdom of God is Within You* prompted them to refuse military service—Van der Veer in the National Guard in Holland, and Škarvan in the Austro-Hungarian army. Škarvan, a young Slovak doctor, had associated with a group of Tolstoyans (including Makovitsky) as a student in Prague and Innsbruck. In February 1895 he wrote to his commanding officer stating that he could no longer perform military service, wear military uniform, or carry out

[47] Crosby to Tolstoy, 5 September 1900, TS 211/25, GMT.

[48] On Schmitt and the Religion des Geistes group, see András Bozóki and Miklós Sükösd, *Anarchism in Hungary: Theory, History, Legacies* (Boulder, CO: Social Science Monographs, 2006), 79–86; and Peter Brock, 'Tolstoyism and the Hungarian Peasant', 345–69.

[49] Brock, 'Tolstoyism and the Hungarian Peasant', 348.

[50] Tolstoy to Schmitt, 29 September 1895, *PSS*, lxviii, 189–90; Tolstoy to Schmitt 24 November 1896, *PSS*, lxix, 212–13; Tolstoy to Schmitt, 25 February 1898, *PSS*, lxxi, 295–6.

[51] Crosby to Tolstoy, 15 July 1896, TS 211/25, GMT.

[52] Jeno Henrik Schmitt to Arnold Eiloart, *New Order* (May 1897), 38.

hospital duties.[53] Van der Veer, a 'Free socialist' and certainly not a Christian, wrote to the Commander of the National Guard declaring that 'he abhorred killing of any kind, either of his fellow-men or of animals, but above all he detested murder committed at the word of command, such murder as he should be required to commit if he obeyed the orders of government'.[54] An interesting third case was that of František Sedlák, a Czech conscientious objector whose actions were motivated by concern for freedom of thought and action rather than the horror of war. In military prison Sedlák was questioned about whether he had read any of Tolstoy's works. He had not, but the doctors' conviction that he must have been 'seduced' by Tolstoy's writings suggests the notoriety of cases of this kind, if not their frequency.[55]

Škarvan was sent first to a psychiatric ward in the military hospital in Vienna, and then to military prison. On his release in 1896 he left the Austro-Hungarian Empire and spent the subsequent years visiting Tolstoy and Tolstoyan groups across Europe before settling in Switzerland, where he forwarded news from Tolstoyan groups internationally, keeping up to date with the British and Dutch Tolstoyans and in regular correspondence with Schmitt.[56] Van der Veer served only a month in the military prison at Middelburg, and by the summer of 1897 was in The Hague, at the centre of a circle of propagandists for peace, vegetarianism, temperance and anti-vivisection.[57] This group included the Protestant pastor Louis Bahler, Professor Jacob van Rees of Amsterdam University, and Felix Ortt, who had given up a position in the government's water department as a result of his Tolstoyan beliefs.[58] Their journal *Vrede* issued its first number in October 1897, and in 1901 they began publication of the *Arbeiders Weekblad,* a paper aimed more specifically at the working classes. The group founded their own colony at Blaricum, near The Hague.[59] Van der Veer continued to correspond with Tolstoy, and from the end of 1898 was in England, associating himself with the Purleigh colonists and with Vladimir Chertkov and his family. He wrote regular (and rather scathing) letters for *Vrede* on the progress of the

[53] Peter Brock, 'Tolstoyism, Cultural Nationalism, and Conscientious Objection: A Slovak Case Study', in *Freedom from War: Non-Sectarian Pacifism, 1814-1914* (Toronto, ON: University of Toronto Press, 1991), 236. On Škarvan, see also Peter Brock, 'The Škarvan Case: The Trial and Imprisonment of a Slovak Tolstoyan', in *Against the Draft* (Toronto, ON: University of Toronto Press, 2006), 172–87, and Peter Brock, trans. and ed., *Life in an Austro-Hungarian Military Prison: The Slovak Tolstoyan Albert Škarvan's Story* (Syracuse, NY: Syracuse University Press, 2002).

[54] Albert Škarvan, 'The Peace Movement in Holland', *New Order*, 3, no. 13 (January 1898), 97.

[55] Francis Sedlak, 'My Military Experiences', *New Order* (May 1900), 81–3.

[56] Škarvan's correspondence with Tolstoy, between 1895 and 1906, is full of the news and activities of the various European Tolstoyans with whom he corresponded: see TS 240/18, GMT. He also wrote regularly for all the major Tolstoyan newspapers.

[57] Škarvan, 'The Peace Movement in Holland', 97; Rudolf Jans, *Tolstoj in Nederland,* 76; Dirk Jan Verdonk, *Het Dierloze Gerecht: Vegetarische Geschiedenis van Nederland* (Amsterdam: Boom, 2009), 75–113.

[58] Harold Williams, 'Notes from Holland and Germany', *New Order*, NS 7, no. 40 (June–July 1901), 73–4.

[59] On the Blaricum colony, see Jans, *Tolstoi in Nederland,* 99–108, and Henriette Hendrix, *Een Week in de Kolonie te Blaricum* (Amsterdam: Cohen Zonen, 1901).

British movement.[60] Sedlák visited Tolstoy upon his release, and on his advice travelled to England where he joined the Whiteway colony, in Gloucestershire.

The British Tolstoyans, then, were part of a vigorous international network. For many, the contradiction between their convictions and their surroundings, and the desire to demonstrate what might be achieved by brotherhood and bread-labour meant that establishing or joining a colony seemed a logical step. This was particularly true in Britain and America, where there was already a strong tradition of back-to-the-land utopian communities, many contemporaneous with the Tolstoyan movement. Although they were criticized for seeking to separate themselves from society, in fact these enterprises had grander aspirations—to act as an example and spread their light into the community at large. Explaining the Christian Commonwealth's plans to an audience in Chicago in 1898, one of the founder members, George Gibson, said, 'We have not put ourselves away from the world and its needs, but have taken it upon our hearts, and are pouring ourselves out to meet human needs'.[61] Land colonies were not a universal feature, however. In Finland, however, where the influence of Tolstoy's thought was very strong, communitarian experiments were conspicuous by their absence, and Germany was described by one aspiring Tolstoyan as 'a country of scholars' where new thought 'finds its way into books, pamphlets, and articles, rarely into colonies'.[62]

As an international movement, Tolstoyism operated in many other ways than through colonies. Individuals wrote and lectured on the subject. Reading groups, lecture societies, and centres for discussion attracted and consolidated support in particular localities, and their publications and correspondence networks connected them to other similar centres. Pilgrimages to Tolstoy (part of a wider phenomenon not confined to Tolstoy's devotees) and visits to other Tolstoyan groups or colonies cemented the international movement, as did campaigns and common causes. Translators and publishing houses disseminated Tolstoy's works as well as those of sympathetic figures and lower-level writers within the movement. Most major centres of Tolstoyism ran their own publishing house and besides books and pamphlet literature published their own newspaper, disseminating news about their own activities and those of other sympathetic groups. Prominent Tolstoyans contributed to each other's papers, and from 1898 the *New Order, Vrede, Ohne Staat* and the Christian Commonwealth's newspaper the *Social Gospel* carried advertisements for one another. Stories of Tolstoyan awakening or conversion and accounts of the refusal of military service made good copy for Tolstoyan newspapers and publishing houses. Tolstoy's article on the Van der Veer case, 'The Beginning of the End', circulated widely in the Tolstoyan press.[63] František Sedlák's 'Military Experiences'

[60] J. K. Van der Veer, 'Brieven uit Engeland', *Vrede*, 2, no. 5 (15 December 1898), 38–40, 2, no. 7 (15 January 1899) 52–3, 2, no. 9 (15 February 1899), 67–69, 2, no. 10 (1 March 1899), 76–8, 2, no. 13 (15 April 1899), 100–2, 2, no. 14 (1 May 1899), 102–4, 2, no. 18 (1 July 1899), 133–5, 2, no. 21 (15 August 1899), 156–8, 3, no. 1 (15 October 1899), 7–8.

[61] 'Our Chicago Trip', *The Social Gospel* (December 1898), 22.

[62] Williams, 'Notes from Holland and Germany', 74.

[63] Leo Tolstoy, 'The Beginning of the End', in *On Civil Disobedience and Non-Violence* (New York: Bergman, 1967), 9–28

were serialized by the *New Order* over a number of months in 1900. Škarvan's *Moi otkaz ot voennoi sluzhby* was published by Vladimir Chertkov's Svobodnoe slovo press in 1898.[64] The letters of Russian non-resister Petr Ol'khovik, which recounted his refusal to enter into military service, were serialized by the *New Order*, published in a Russian edition by Chertkov's press, a French edition in Geneva, and a Dutch edition, issued by the Vrede publishing house.[65]

While Van der Veer spent the years 1898 to 1900 at Purleigh and Sedlák took up residence at Whiteway, the Leeds Brotherhood group also received requests to join from as far afield as Holland.[66] The status of the British movement was given a significant boost by the arrival in England in 1897 of Vladimir Chertkov and his family. The colony of Russian Tolstoyans, first at Purleigh and later at Tuckton near Christchurch, hosted at various times Pavel Biryukov, Dmitry Khilkov and Albert Škarvan. It also had a long life—Ludvig Perno, the manager at Tuckton House during the last years of the First World War remained in Bournemouth until his death in 1970.[67] Britain was also the centre of operations for the Tolstoyan movement's largest and most successful campaign—the relocation of seven thousand members of the non-resistant Dukhobor sect from Russia to Canada during 1898 and 1899. Tolstoyan groups and newspapers across the international network publicized the Dukhobor cause, suggested locations, and raised subscriptions for the emigration from their readers.[68] Van der Veer's relocation to Britain was partly motivated by a desire to assist in this enterprise. He told an audience at the Purleigh colony in 1898 that

> we have been talking about the brotherhood of man for centuries, but today there exist groups who have broken down the frontiers of nationalities and a bond of union is felt... We believe this bond will become stronger. Such a meeting as this is evidence of that bond and will help us in our work in Holland. If it gives us courage to know we are working with God, it gives us even more courage to know we are working in unity with others who are trying to live honestly in accordance with Christ's teaching. I can now go back to Holland with a happy heart and tell the brothers there how you live and work together here.[69]

[64] Albert Škarvan, *Moi otkaz ot voennoi sluzhby: zapiski voennogo vracha* (Purleigh: V. Tchertkoff, 1898).

[65] 'Letters of P. V. Olkhovik', *New Order* (June 1899), 84–5, (July 1899), 102–3, (August 1899), 109–11; *Pis'ma P. V. Ol'khovika, krest'yanina Khar'kovskoi gubernii, otkazavshegosya ot voinskoi povinnosti v 1895 godu* (London: V. Tchertkoff, 1897); *Lettres de Pierre Olchowik, paysan du gouvernement de Kharkoff, qui a refusé de faire son service militaire en 1895* (Geneva: M. Fischer, 1898); *Een Volgeling van Jezus: Peter Olchowik. Een jonge Russische boer* (The Hague: Vrede, 1899).

[66] Foster, *Socialism and the Christ*, 41.

[67] Harold F. Bing, 'Tolstoyans in England', *One and All* (May 1972), 6.

[68] See for example *Ohne Staat*, 1, no. 11 (12 March 1897), 4, 1, no. 12 (19 March 1897), 3–4, 1, no. 14 (May 1897), 4.

[69] 'The Peace Movement in Holland', *New Order*, 4, no. 4 (May 1898), 37–8.

BRITISH TOLSTOYISM AND LOCAL CONTEXTS

Tolstoyans conceived of their own contemporary context very broadly. Almost without exception their newspapers featured a section on 'news of the movement', which documented the progress of sympathetic enterprises both locally and internationally. Each of the international centres operated within the context of local concerns and reform movements. Schmitt's Budapest group probably had the most influence on any popular political movement, through their relationship with the Hungarian Independent Labour Party, which incorporated some of Schmitt's anti-state ideas into its 'statement of principles'.[70] The Dutch Tolstoyans were particularly close to both vegetarian and anti-vivisectionist groups, having overlapping membership with both. The same was true of vegetarianism and the thriving Tolstoyan movement in Bulgaria.[71] The Christian Commonwealth entertained a range of political and religious views, including, uncharacteristically, a member who aimed at reunion between the Commonwealth and the Episcopal Church, in which he was a minister.[72] Before George Gibson joined the Christian Commonwealth he was the editor of Nebraska's Populist newspaper, and he believed that Populist and Christian principles were (or ought to be) essentially the same.[73]

The British Tolstoyans also operated in multiple contexts and shared literature, venues, and personnel with a variety of sympathetic movements. Nellie Shaw commented that 'every kind of crank' came to the church at Tamworth Road: 'Atheists, Spiritualists, Individualists, Communists, Anarchists, ordinary politicians, Vegetarians, anti-vivisectionists, and anti-vaccinationists . . . every kind of "anti" had a welcome and a hearing, and had to stand a lively criticism in this discussion which followed.'[74] They advertised Clousden Hill, the anarchist colony outside Newcastle, and hosted Petr Kropotkin at Croydon and Purleigh on several occasions. In correspondence with Tolstoy, Kenworthy insisted that the non-religious anarchist groups in England were losing their violent character, beginning to advocate voluntary cooperation, and moving closer to the Tolstoyan position. 'They have, as it were, found us out'; he wrote, 'and now often ask me to write and speak for them, which I do as far as I can.'[75] In editorials Kenworthy and his associates insisted that 'If we wish to-day to discover men with clear purpose and earnestness for . . . salvation . . . we shall find them, not in the "house of God" . . . but rather among the contemned Socialists and Anarchists of the street corner.'[76] The broader social reform movement was a strong recruiting ground, and Tolstoyans moved

[70] Brock, 'Tolstoyism and the Hungarian Peasant', 350–53; Bozóki and Sükösd, *Anarchism in Hungary*, 86.

[71] Edgerton, 'The Social Influence of Lev Tolstoj in Bulgaria', 123–38.

[72] Ralph Albertson, 'The Christian Commonwealth in Georgia', *Georgia Historical Quarterly*, 29 (September 1945), 133.

[73] Samuel Walker, 'George Howard Gibson, Christian Socialist Among the Populists', *Nebraska History*, 55, no. 4 (Winter 1974), 553–65.

[74] Shaw, *Whiteway*, 21.

[75] Kenworthy to Tolstoy, 25 June 1896 (22 October 1896), TS 223/80, GMT.

[76] 'A Plain Issue for Christians', *Croydon Brotherhood Intelligence*, 1, no. 3 (March 1895), 1.

in and out of these contexts—returning for example to cooperative enterprises (Redfern became editor of *The Wheatsheaf* and a historian of the cooperative movement), or becoming interested in other popular philosophies of the time, such as spiritualism (as Kenworthy, Tom Ferris, and even Bruce Wallace did). British socialists, however, did not always take such a positive view of the Tolstoyan philosophy. Nellie Shaw remembered that Kenworthy's increasing insistence on Tolstoyan 'Communist Anarchism' alienated many local socialists from the group.[77] Many, like Bruce Wallace, regarded joining a Tolstoyan colony and separating oneself from society as an abnegation of political duty.[78] In 1901 John Spargo wrote in the *Social Democrat* of a visit to Whiteway that their colony had 'wrecked the socialist movement there and brought it to ridicule. How long', he asked, 'will socialist societies continue to engage colony agents and Tolstoyan lecturers whose labours bear such fruit?'[79]

The breadth of their interests did not make Tolstoyans unusual in nineteenth-century reform circles, in which it was common to find activists with broad reformist consciences embracing numerous sympathetic causes—vegetarianism, temperance, anti-imperialism, and the peace movement, for example. This phenomenon was captured in the late nineteenth-century in the term 'anti-everythingarianism'.[80] But while Tolstoyans shared literature and speakers with all these causes, in these interactions the fundamental Tolstoyan worldview, based on the doctrine of non-resistance, held them slightly apart.

Tolstoyan relations with the vegetarian movement provide a good example. In their vegetarianism Tolstoyans borrowed for the most part from arguments already well developed by the vegetarian movement. They embraced a wide range of positions on dietary matters, from vegetarianism to fruitarianism to a raw-food diet. While for some vegetarianism was a central part of their belief system—Felix Ortt, for example, was president of the Dutch vegetarian society—others appeared not to engage with it at all. The members of the Christian Commonwealth enjoyed both chicken and turkey for their thanksgiving dinner. But their belief in non-resistance influenced their vegetarianism in several ways. For one thing they could not separate it from their other interests, including peace. Vladimir Chertkov told an audience at the Vegetarian Society that it was impossible to regard the killing of animals for food as an evil, but not to condemn the killing of men through war or capital punishment.[81] 'The most urgent task which lies before each of us', he argued, 'consists not so much in the dissemination of vegetarianism amongst mankind as in the deepening of that humane aspiration which lies at the basis of Vegetarianism and its expansion over all the field covered by our consciousness and our conduct.'[82]

[77] Shaw, *Whiteway*, 23.

[78] 'The Case of Hammond', *New Order*, 3, no. 3 (March 1897), 19–20.

[79] John Spargo, 'My Visit to the "Tolstoyan Colony" Whiteway', *Social Democrat* (15 September 1901), 275.

[80] James Gregory, *Victorians and Vegetarians: The Vegetarian Movement in Nineteenth-Century Britain* (London: I. B. Tauris, 2007), 115–16.

[81] Vladimir Chertkov, 'Words to Vegetarians', *New Order*, 4, no. 11 (December 1898), 118.

[82] Chertkov, 'Words to Vegetarians', 118.

Secondly, they could not join vegetarians or animal rights activists in lobbying for penalties or changes to the law. 'Fear of punishment', John Kenworthy assured an audience at the Humanitarian League, 'is the lowest appeal that can be made to man's nature, and one which is of outward force only...would it not be better to labour directly for more just and humane social conditions, rather than to resort to the "eye for an eye and a tooth for a tooth" of the law?'[83]

Similar frictions were apparent in the Tolstoyan relationship with the international peace movement, which although it encompassed many different forms of pacifism, concentrated its efforts in the late nineteenth century on lobbying for arbitration and disarmament. When refusal to bear arms was discussed by peace congresses, it was usually rejected.[84] For Tolstoyans, as for Tolstoy, the peace societies' emphasis on 'reading addresses, writing books, choosing presidents, vice-presidents, and secretaries, and meeting and talking first in one city and then in another' made them irrelevant; the question was 'solely one of the personal relation of each man to the moral and religious question now facing us all—the question of the rightness or wrongness of taking part in military service'.[85] Tolstoyan newspapers advertised peace literature (Bertha Von Suttner's *Lay Down Your Arms*, for example) and conceded the role that both congresses and literature had to play in popularizing the cause of peace, but in the end they believed there was only one way to render war impossible, and that was for those who were called to fight to refuse to do so.[86] Chertkov was disappointed that the international peace organizations proved so unsympathetic to the Doukhobor cause. He sent copies of *Christian Martyrdom in Russia*, the handbook for the emigration, to representatives of the peace movement who informed him that they did not advocate the refusal of military service as a means of action. Chertkov concluded that

> there must be something radically wrong in the movement of the Peace Societies. If representatives of these Societies do not understand the spiritual motive, consisting in the consciousness of the moral unlawfulness of oneself taking part in that which one believes to be wrong, if they do not understand this motive, which is the only one that can ever make war impossible, they are certainly not fitted to participate in the case they are advocating.[87]

As in the case of diet, Tolstoyan attitudes to sex, marriage, and divorce encompassed a broad spectrum of beliefs and practices. The orthodox position was that chastity was the ideal, but as in all things it was recognized that an ideal was something to aim towards, not necessarily achieve—a monogamous marriage was regarded as the next best alternative. Given their opposition to government and to the established church, an increasingly common practice in the British movement

[83] John Kenworthy, 'Man and the Animals', *New Order*, NS 5, no. 15 (April 1899), 56.

[84] Sandi Cooper, *Patriotic Pacifism: Waging War on War in Europe, 1815–1914* (Oxford: Oxford University Press, 1991), 60–1, 128.

[85] Leo Tolstoy, *The Kingdom of God and Peace Essays* (London: Oxford University Press, 1935), 177.

[86] Leo Tolstoy to Bertha Von Suttner, 9 October 1891, *PSS*, lxvi 66, 58.

[87] Vladimir Chertkov, 'The League of Peace in relation to the Nazarenes and the Spirit Wrestlers', *New Order*, 4, no. 1 (February 1898), 1.

was the 'Free Union', in which a marriage was celebrated by a declaration at a group meeting. Ernest Ames of the Leeds group described the rationale as follows:

> We could not agree to take part in the legal-religious marriage of society, because of the implied lowering of standard. Marriage to us is a religious concern, and not a legal contract. It consists in a spiritual bond of union between two people, and whomsoever God hath joined together let no man put asunder. We accepted Christ's standard of marriage; that of a permanent union and did not admit the rightness of divorce. This, of course, put us at variance with Church and State, which made marriage a legal contract, and allows the possibility of dissolution.[88]

Ames admitted that this position caused consternation not only amongst outsiders but amongst some of their own people. Tom Ferris and Lillian Hunt, who entered a Free Union at Leeds in December 1898 were disowned by their Quaker families. The Quakers and Tolstoyans had a generally cooperative relationship but this was an issue on which they could not agree. Several members of the Croydon Brotherhood Church objected to the statement by May Pinnell and William MacDonald that the principles taught there had determined them in their action.[89] The dissolution of their Free Union while at Whiteway caused even greater controversy, leading to a visit and a sermon on the subject from Kenworthy, and the withdrawal of all cooperation from the main benefactor of the colony.[90]

The 'no-money' movement was another controversial fever that swept the British movement in the late 1890s. Early no-moneyites undertook 'penniless pilgrimages', travelling from London to Oxford, for example, without funds. This sparked a vigorous debate about what this achieved—was it really a demonstration of the Christian life, or just taking advantage of the good nature of the people they met on their way?[91] The Leeds group had run their engineering workshop on communal principles, with all needs being met from a shared supply of money. But their external relations were still governed by money, not goodwill. The decision to adopt a no-money position was 'not so much a solution, as a complete clearing away of all the troubles... It would provide a means for extending the communism, which we had shared within our group, to all we came into contact with, by extending to all alike the same relation—that of freely giving according to *need*. All our transactions would be on a basis of brotherhood, and not of business.'[92] The *New Order* introduced a 'rational exchange project', aimed at the abnegation not only of money but of all exchange; goods advertised in each issue were available to anyone who needed them. In a polemic on the 'no-money movement' Florence Holah made a direct comparison between this withdrawal from the competitive system and the refusal of military

[88] Ernest Ames, 'The Brotherhood Church', *The Tolstoyan*, 1, no. 6 (April 1903), 217–25.

[89] W. P. Swainson, Letter to the editor, *New Order*, 2, no. 12 (December 1896), 6.

[90] Thacker, *Whiteway Colony*, 17–18.

[91] 'Should I use Money? Correspondence between X who uses it, and E who does not', *New Order*, NS 5, no. 16 (May 1899), 70; Louise Maude, 'The Root of All Evil', *New Order*, NS 5, no. 17 (June 1899), 79; Florence Holah, 'The Root of All Evil', *New Order*, NS 5, no. 18 (July 1899), 101.

[92] Ames, 'The Brotherhood Church', 121.

service. 'In continental countries', she wrote, 'men are being called upon to face this fundamental principle of Christianity (and, indeed, of humanity) in connection with the military service, and many are suffering persecution to the death, rather than violate their conscience. We, in England, have to face the same question in a less direct, but no less real form. Are we prepared to meet it in the same heroic spirit?'[93] In a letter supporting the movement in 1901, Tolstoy agreed that no-moneyism was 'almost the same as refusal of military service', and 'undoubtedly right'.[94]

Putting their principles into practice was perhaps the hardest task that British Tolstoyans faced. Their efforts to do so, and their desire to publicize and further the Tolstoyan worldview, brought them into a dialogue with individuals and enterprises internationally that were operating along the same lines. Tolstoy was the central figure in an international network which was increasingly able to operate under its own steam, and in which the centres influenced each other, sharing literature, ideas, and problems, and exchanging membership. Crosby described Tolstoyism as 'my ism'.[95] Tolstoyans like Chertkov, Biryukov, and Škarvan dedicated themselves to translating, publishing and promoting Tolstoy's works abroad; others, like Crosby and Kenworthy, to furthering Tolstoy's vision.

At the same time the British Tolstoyans operated within multiple local contexts. Their belief in non-resistance carried them into all sorts of spheres of interest—vegetarianism, animal welfare, temperance, and peace, for example—and they shared common beliefs and aspirations with all of these movements. However, their belief in non-resistance also held them slightly apart. In 1901 Percy Redfern justified the establishment of the Manchester Tolstoy society as follows. Having of his own free will and learning come to a view of life broadly the same as Tolstoy's, he wished to act according to his thoughts and feelings, and to help others avoid the delusions he had escaped. The practical value of these thoughts and feelings was increased, he felt, through association:

> Now I can temporarily associate with different groups—vegetarians, socialists, land reformers, 'rationalists', theosophists, Wesleyans and so forth. If I had some definite bias towards any particular material reform that might content me. But I want to face life as a whole. That we cannot do in mixed societies in which we must not introduce controversial subjects foreign to the particular aims of that society. So in addition to working occasionally with particular bodies one seeks society with others who also wish to face life as a whole. Hence a Tolstoy socy.[96]

To be a Tolstoyan meant to apply the principles of brotherhood and non-resistance in all aspects of life, and to follow one's own conscience, at the expense of church and state. As Redfern makes clear, and as the examples above have demonstrated, the fundamental Tolstoyan worldview placed limits on their ability to cooperate

[93] Florence Holah, 'Money—An Instrument of Compulsion', *New Order*, 4, no. 12 (January 1899), 5.
[94] 'The No Money Movement', *New Order*, NS 7, no. 35 (May 1901), 51.
[95] Crosby to Tolstoy, 28 May 1899, TS 211/25, GMT.
[96] Redfern to Tolstoy, 4 August 1901, TS 235/54, GMT.

with the other movements they overlapped with. In some cases it caused rifts within the movement as those who sought to follow their convictions to their logical conclusion alienated more moderate Tolstoyans. It gave their movement in Britain and elsewhere its own distinct character and purpose, even while its members operated within wider local and global reformist networks.

4

'For the Cause of Education'

A History of the Free Russian Library in Whitechapel, 1898–1917

Robert Henderson

In the early spring of 1915 a number of stylish posters appeared on the streets of London advertising a forthcoming West-End production of a little-performed play, *The Convert: A Drama in Four Acts* by the late Sergey Stepnyak.[1] The performance was to be followed by a grand ball and dancing until three in the morning with all proceeds intended for the benefit of a small institution which carried out its business just off the busy Commercial Road in the East End and which went by the name of The Free Russian Library and Reading Room *(Besplatnaya russkaya biblioteka i chital'nya)*.[2] Thanks to the generous sponsorship of the Nestlé Company an elegant programme for the performance was produced, drawn up in both English and Russian to cater for the widest possible audience.[3] As well as listing the names of the director—Fanny Stepnyak, the playwright's widow—and the dramatis personae—all drawn from London's Russian émigré community—the programme also provided detailed information on the Free Library itself, showing that its interests stretched to far more than simple book-lending to the Russian expatriate community. Apart from engaging in purely library matters the staff at the institution had already arranged a number of cultural excursions to museums, zoos, and botanical gardens; had worked out a series of lectures and talks, and were planning to organize entertainments of an educational nature for children. They had also opened a library for sailors and claimed to have helped found other workers' libraries in Britain. In addition, the Free Library acted as an employment agency, advertising the services of experienced foreign language teachers and generalists, competent

[*] This paper is based on research carried out in the State Archive of the Russian Federation, Moscow and the National Archives, Paris. My thanks are due to the staff at these two institutions for their invaluable assistance.

[1] Sergei Stepniak, *The New Convert: A Drama in Four Acts*, trans. Thomas B. Eyges (Boston: Stratford, 1917).

[2] Gosudarstvennyi arkhiv rossiiskoi federatsii (hereafter GARF) f. 1721, op. 1, ed. khr. 87, l. 269. The performance of Stepnyak's play was scheduled to take place on Saturday 17 April at 107 Charlotte Street, Fitzroy Square, WC. The contact address for the Library was given as 14, Union Street Mansions, Union Street (now Adler Street), Commercial Road.

[3] GARF, f. 1721, op. 1, ed. khr. 87, l. 270.

translators from and into all European languages, good copyists, guides, and so on. What the programme omitted to mention, however, was that one member of the cast, a certain A. Teplov (who was to play the role of the self-serving Count Mentirov, Russian Minister of the Interior) had, some seventeen years earlier, been responsible almost single-handedly for the foundation of the Free Library and from that day had humbly served in the capacity of its Chief Librarian.[4]

It is almost certain that the staging of this performance, the only attempt at dramatic composition by the Russian émigré writer and political activist Sergey Mikhailovich Kravchinsky ('Stepnyak') was Teplov's brainchild and, as such, was merely the latest in a long line of his efforts to raise funds for his Library, and in so doing, draw the attention of the British public to the plight of his countrymen under the tsar. *The Convert* fitted the bill perfectly in its depiction of the oppressive political climate in a Russia ruled by corrupt officials and secret policemen, and in its unqualified support for radical solutions to the problems portrayed. During the first performance of the play in London it was noted that its 'incendiary sentiments were loudly applauded' and there is little doubt that Fanny Stepnyak's production would have fared just as well although no review has yet been discovered.[5] The Chief Librarian's personal participation in the event is an example of his enthusiasm for the cause of revolution that he showed throughout his London emigration. Given the extensive range of his activities during the period and the numerous contacts he developed it is surprising that almost no mention has been made of this tireless individual or his Free Russian Library, in Russia or the West, from the date of its foundation to the present. Now however, following the recent discovery of Teplov's papers in the State Archive of the Russian Federation in Moscow, it is possible to describe the Library's operations in detail and to reveal the important role it played in Anglo-Russian social and political interaction in the British capital in the early years of the twentieth century.[6]

Aleksey L'vovich Teplov was born on 5 April 1852 in the small village of Agramakovo near Penza, some 600 kilometres to the south-east of Moscow. As a student in St Petersburg in the 1870s he was introduced to the radical ideas of the political opposition and soon joined the 'going to the people' movement, finding work on the railways in Saratov province where he engaged in the distribution of illegal populist literature among his co-workers.[7] Unfortunately, like the majority of his fellow propagandists, Teplov soon found himself under arrest. Sentenced to five years exile to Eastern Siberia he served his term in full and on its completion returned home to Penza where he obtained employment as a scribe in the local conservatory.[8] In 1889 he fled Russia for France where, together with a group of fellow

[4] Robert Henderson, 'Aleksei Teplov and the Free Russian Library in Whitechapel', *Solanus*, NS, 22 (2011), 5–26. See also my 'Russkaya besplatnaya biblioteka v Ist-Ende', in O. Morgunova, ed., *Russkoe prisutstvie v Britanii* (Moscow: Sovremennaya ekonomika i pravo, 2010), 59–68.

[5] 'The Theatres: Avenue', *The Times* (15 June 1898), 13.

[6] GARF, f. 1721, op. 1. Teplov's extensive archive comprises 212 files, each containing up to 400 individual documents.

[7] GARF, f. 1721, op. 1, ed. khr. 1.53. ll. 1–6.

[8] V. L. Burtsev, *Za sto let 1800–1896: Sbornik po istorii politicheskikh i obshchestvennykh dvizhenii v Rossii* (London: Russian Free Press Fund, 1897), 96.

émigrés in Paris, he became involved in a dangerous programme of conspiratorial action directed against the tsar. His plans suffered an almost immediate setback when, in February 1890 in a forest on the outskirts of Paris, he received a serious wound to the thigh caused by the premature explosion of one of the experimental bombs he had been testing. His misfortunes did not end there, for, a few months into his convalescence, in the early hours of the morning of 29 May, he was woken by the French police and taken into custody, together with sixteen of his compatriots, on charges of illegal possession of explosives.

This, the 'Paris Bomb Plot', received wide coverage in the international press and, as the story unfolded with reports of the discovery of a veritable terrorist bomb factory in the centre of Paris, it became clear that the group had fallen victim to an act of provocation by a Russian police agent, who had betrayed his compatriots to the authorities and fled before any arrests were made. At the trial the judge sentenced Teplov and another five of the accused to three years' imprisonment.[9]

TO LONDON

On his release from Angers prison in the spring of 1893 Teplov was met by his close friend, the bibliographer and 'historian of the Russian Revolution', Vladimir Burtsev, who immediately took him to London. There he found a welcoming public who, thanks in large part to the efforts of the émigrés Sergey Stepnyak, Nikolay Chaikovsky, and other members of the Society of Friends of Russian Freedom (SFRF), were already sympathetic to the plight of the Russian people, and aware of the oppressions of Alexander III's regime. What the young revolutionary also found, amongst the Russian and Polish immigrants in the East End of London, was poverty and illiteracy on a staggering scale. Teplov, a firm believer in the need to raise the political consciousness of the masses, as evidenced by his earlier propaganda work in Russia, now turned his attention to this new-found constituency.

What initially attracted Teplov to the idea of setting up a free library is unknown, but he was certainly encouraged in the endeavour by Chaikovsky and, in equal measure, by Burtsev, a truly bookish individual and passionate champion of the cause of mass education and libraries for all. The origins of the Library are obscure but Teplov's archive does contain references to an earlier incarnation which went by the name of the Russo-Jewish Free Reading Room of the 'Progress' Group (*Russko-evreiskaya bezplatnaya chital'nya—gruppy 'Progress'*) of which, unfortunately, little is known.[10] It would appear that after his arrival in London (and possibly with Chaikovsky's assistance), Teplov took over the running of this institution and for the next few years concentrated on expanding its collections.[11] Finally, on 13

[9] The others imprisoned were Boris Reinshtein, Aleksandr Lavrenius, Mikhail Nakachidze, Ivan Kashintsev, and Evgeny Stepanov. In absentia, the police agent, whom the judge had identified as ringleader, was given the maximum sentence permissible of five years. See 'Trial Of Nihilists In Paris', *The Times* (5 July 1890), 7.

[10] GARF, f. 1721, op. 1, ed. khr. 26, ll. 1–16.

[11] GARF, f. 1721, op. 1, ed. khr. 26, ll. 17–25.

Fig. 4. Free Russian Library stamp. The National Archives, HO 144/272/A59222B/21.

July 1898, five years after his arrival in Britain, the revolutionary was able at last to announce the opening of his Free Russian Library and Reading Room at 15 Whitechapel Road, Stepney (Fig. 4).

The inaugural notice promised that the Library would contain the best works of Russian literature published in Russia and abroad, and that books could be read on the premises or taken home on loan. Teplov's proposed opening hours were ambitious, from 10 a.m. till 10 p.m., and to ensure the reading public were properly served during this time a 'Corporation of Orderlies' (*Korporatsiya bibiliotechnykh dezhurnykh*) was established.[12] This collective, numbering up to ten individuals, was responsible for the day-to-day running of the Library, holding regular meetings at which special sub-committees reported on topics such as cataloguing, bookbinding, and also the organization of balls and entertainments which were to prove essential in providing enough funds for the maintenance of the Library and the payment of wages.[13]

No description remains of this first home of the Library but the premises were clearly inadequate, in particular with regard to the provision of a hall big enough to accommodate the audiences which took advantage of the second service provided, namely a series of lectures by figures such as Chaikovsky, Petr Kropotkin, and David Soskice. So popular was this series of Friday and Sunday talks, and so cramped were the Library premises, that public halls had to be hired for the purpose.[14] To deal with the growing demand for these events it became necessary to set up a Lectures' Committee, whose influence on the affairs of the Library would grow considerably over the years.

[12] GARF, f. 1721, op. 1, ed. khr. 4, l. 1, 2. 13 July 1898.

[13] GARF, f. 1721, op. 1, ed. khr. 46, l. 46. Orderlies' wages were set at fifteen shillings to £1 per week.

[14] GARF, f. 1721, op. 1, ed. khr. 84, ll. 27, 28.

The foundation of the Free Library had been achieved solely through the financial support of Teplov's fellow revolutionaries including Burtsev and, most notably, Chaikovsky. The Library also received monies from Vladimir Chertkov, Tolstoy's literary agent and disciple, newly arrived in Britain to found the *Svobodnoe slovo* (Free Word) publishing house.[15] However, finding continued funding from a community which was itself impoverished was problematic. Teplov turned therefore to his homeland with an appeal in which he explained that his intention was to give his impoverished fellow workers in the East End 'the opportunity to maintain a spiritual relationship with their mother country and to retain contact with its literature and life'. He stressed that this was a free library that existed on donations from private individuals alone but also promised that, as a social institution, it would never be allowed to become the property of a private individual or group.[16] The appeal was published in two Russian journals and apparently met with some limited success for, by the turn of the century, the Library had managed to relocate a few hundred yards along the road to a small house at 16 Church Lane.

CHURCH LANE

Teplov would later describe these humble premises in a letter to an unknown English woman, who had expressed a wish to pay a visit:

> I must prepare you not to expect too much. The Library consists of two small rooms on the third floor admitting no more than 30–35 readers. The entrance is up a dark narrow staircase so that it might be said that the premises are unsuitable and even not permissible [*sic*]. We should require a better place but we live in accordance with the Russian proverb: *Po odezhdu protiagivai nozhki*. Which translated in English would be 'Cut your coat according to your cloth.'[17]

The Librarian, however, had no intention of doing such a thing.

It is clear that Teplov's aim on his arrival in London had been simply to educate and proselytize amongst the émigré population. Initially, at least, he showed no interest in continuing Stepnyak's propaganda work amongst the British, in attracting British support, or in strengthening Anglo-Russian relations. This changed, however, with the dawning of the new century and Teplov's realization that more reliable sources of funding were urgently required if his project was to succeed. He therefore turned to his associates in the SFRF and asked them for help to get his appeal published in the British press. Unfortunately, the Society felt that the ordinary press would reject it for 'not being picturesque enough', and instead forwarded his request to J. Frederick Green at the Russian Free Press Fund for inclusion in their journal, *Free Russia*.[18] Green, in turn, put Teplov in touch with two contacts in the publishing industry and as a result sparked a sudden flurry of activity.

15 GARF, f. 1721, op. 1, ed. khr. 27ll. 5–6, January 1899. Chaikovsky made an initial donation of £10 with regular monthly supplements thereafter of £5.

16 GARF, f. 1721, op. 1, ed. khr. 4, l. 56.

17 GARF, f. 1721, op. 1, ed. khr. 84, l. 104, 105, 27 February 1903.

18 GARF, f. 1721, op. 1, ed. khr. 84, l. 60, 2 July 1901, Letter from E. Pease, Fabian Society.

The contacts in question were Ernest Foster of the Editorial Department of Cassells, and the playwright, journalist, and social activist George R. Sims who had long been concerned with the appalling living conditions of London's poor and who, at that instant, was engaged in a project with Cassell to publish a series of vignettes of London life. Therefore, in early August 1901 Sims paid a personal visit to Church Lane to see if he might discover some original materials for his project. Teplov was quick to take advantage of this opportunity. Shortly after Sims' visit the librarian sent him some further details of the Free Library's activities, including a listing of the lectures already delivered on topics as diverse as: 'The government and the working classes'; 'The Boers and the English'; 'The labour movement in Europe'—all by David Soskice—and 'Imperialism, the savages of civilization & the working class' by Isaak Shklovsky. He noted also that Mrs Sophie Kropotkin was due to lecture soon on 'ants and bees' and 'life and its phenomena'. Teplov then described his Library's requirements: a lecture hall, a reading room, a reference room, and a school room, and finally begged a favour of the journalist:

> I take the liberty of asking you to do the utmost in your power to make the Library more widely known among English societies who take interest in educational matters and to bring it to the notice of men of means, as well-to-do people can do much towards obtaining more and better books and a separate building for the use of the Library... Should the contents of your book, about to be published, allow something to be mentioned about the Library, I hope you will give a good description of this useful institution.[19]

Three months later, in November 1901, the first volume of Sims' project was published under the title *Living London: Its Work and its Play, its Humour and its Pathos, its Sights and its Scenes*. It contained an article entitled 'Russia in East London' written by Count E. Armfelt, who devoted a few pages to the Free Library describing its premises thus:

> This Library is unique in its way... A long table, two wooden benches, and two rough writing tables, a few chairs and several dozen shelves, about two thousand books, Russian newspapers and periodicals about five days old, with a few prints on the walls. This comprises all the furniture, and all there is to admire.

Then, under a photograph of the Reading Room (Fig. 5), Armfelt included a description of its clientele:

> At the Russian Library you meet men belonging to every class of society and men of every type: naval cadets of the imperial service, students and literary men, tradesmen, men without occupation who do not know a word of English, all congregate there and the smoke which issues from cigars and pipes and cigarettes welds all these atoms of Russian society into an indistinct mass.[20]

Shortly after publication Teplov contacted Cassell for permission to reprint part of the article since it had 'produced a good impression at the time and we would like to make a leaflet out of it to make the Library known to a wider circle of interested

[19] GARF, f. 1721. op. 1, ed. khr. 86, ll. 153, 154. Undated letter to George R. Sims.

[20] Count E. Armfelt, 'Russia in East London', in *Living London: Its Work and its Play, its Humour and its Pathos, its Sights and its Scenes,* i (London: Cassell, 1901), i, 24–8.

Fig. 5. The Free Russian Library, reproduced in Count E. Armfelt, 'Russia in East London', in *Living London: Its Work and its Play, its Humour and its Pathos, its Sights and its Scenes* (London: Cassell, 1901), i, 27.

public in the East End and elsewhere'.[21] As the March 1902 issue of *Free Russia* showed, permission was granted for, as well as reporting on Chaikovsky's 'interesting account of the Russian Free Library in Whitechapel, founded and managed by Mr Teplov, which it was now proposed to place on a permanent footing', the journal also carried a one-page supplement entitled, 'An Appeal for the Cause of Education in the East End of London'.[22] This document called for help from outside sympathizers to allow the Organizing Committee (which included such notable British liberals as Gertrude Toynbee, Catherine Hueffer, Herbert Burrows, and J. Frederick Green) to procure larger premises and extend the services already on offer to the foreign community in the East End, namely 'free lessons in the English language, composition, literature, history, and constitution, as well as free legal advice to the poor, a free labour bureau, free concerts, and a social club'. The verso of the appeal carried that same photograph of the cramped interior of the Library that had appeared a few months earlier in the pages of *Living London*.

Proof of the success of the appeal can be gauged by the immediate interest it sparked amongst the British public, some of whom contacted the Library directly

[21] GARF, f. 1721. op. 1, ed. khr. 84, l. 70, 71, 13 August 1901. Also l. 81 (undated).

[22] 'Meetings and Lectures', *Free Russia*, 13, no. 3 (1 March 1902), 36. Teplov's original draft of the appeal had been entitled 'To Friends of Russian Working Jews of East End of London', but, perhaps wisely, the organizing committee had toned this down to appeal to a wider public. (See GARF, f. 1721, op. 1, ed. khr. 86, l. 100.)

with offers of monetary assistance. In its issue of June 1902 *Free Russia* published a listing of the donations they too had received 'in response to the appeal on behalf of the Russian Free Library (containing English books as well) and popular lectures organized for the East End Hebrews.' These donations alone amounted to £12.[23]

SOME INFLUENTIAL FRIENDS

One keen early supporter was Aylmer Maude, the translator and biographer of Tolstoy, who contacted the Organizing Committee with a donation of £5 and expressed his hope that his Resurrection Fund Committee would be able to make a further grant. It is interesting to note that Maude also asked if he might borrow some Russian journals from the well-stocked Library.[24] He, of course, was not alone in this request: an indication of the Library's remarkable success and popularity is an archival note stating that at any given moment the number of readers borrowing books could be anything up to 400.[25]

Another famous client of the Free Library and one with whom Teplov was evidently on very friendly terms was Constance Garnett who was one of the first British visitors to Church Lane. The archive contains a fascinating letter from the translator dated September 1902 in which she writes:

> Dear Mr. Teploff, I have to thank you for letting me have the use of the volume of Tolstoy, which I post you back with this. I am ashamed to have kept it over a year. It has been of great use and I enclose a small subscription for your Library. Yours truly Constance Garnett.[26]

Garnett does not specify the volume in question but it may well have included *Smert' Ivana Il' icha* (*The Death of Ivan Ilyich*), since a collection containing Garnett's translation of that short story was published that year. Alternatively, it may have been the edition of *Voina i mir* (*War and Peace*) used by Garnett for her translation of Tolstoy's masterpiece which first appeared in print in 1904.[27] In passing, it might be noted that Teplov's archive contains a draft copy of rules for the use of the Library which stipulated that borrowed books should be returned within two weeks otherwise a fine would be incurred of one penny for every day overdue. Whether Garnett's 'small subscription' would have been enough to cover that substantial fine is not recorded.[28]

On 3 February 1903 Garnett wrote to Teplov again to say she had recommended him as a competent teacher to a woman studying Russian and then, later still, in May 1907, sent another letter, passing on her warmest good wishes and asking to

[23] 'For the Cause of Education in East London', *Free Russia*, 13, no. 6 (1 June 1902), 68.

[24] GARF, f. 1721, op. 1, ed. khr. 86, l. 126, 28 June 1904.

[25] GARF, f. 1721, op. 1, ed. khr. 153, l. 3.

[26] GARF, f. 1721, op. 1, ed. khr. 84, l. 91, 29 September 1902.

[27] Leo Tolstoy, *The Death of Ivan Ilyitch and Other Stories*, trans. Constance Garnett (London: Heinemann, 1902), and *War and Peace*, trans. Constance Garnett, 3 vols (London: Heinemann, 1904).

[28] GARF, f. 1721, op. 1, ed. khr. 4, ll. 99–100.

borrow an issue of Vladimir Burtsev's journal *Byloe* (*The Past*) which contained an article by Sof'ya Savinkova.[29] Garnett's translation of that article, 'Vospominaniya materi', appeared shortly thereafter in the *Albany Review* as 'A Russian Mother'.[30]

Teplov also entered into correspondence with other notable Russophiles such as Charles Hagberg Wright of the London Library and the two developed a mutually beneficial relationship that would last right through almost till 1917. Their correspondence is rich and varied, with Hagberg Wright not only turning to Teplov with requests for information on Russian social issues such as marriage customs, working conditions, wages, and the like, but also asking to borrow specific books by Russian authors such as Dmitry Grigorovich and Dmitry Stakheev.[31] This, from the curator of one of the best collections of Russian literature outside Russia, is itself testimony to the richness of the Free Library's holdings and to Teplov's achievement. Indeed, the popularity of the Free Library amongst such experts as the Maudes, Garnett, and Hagberg Wright was in large part due to its extensive holdings of Russian books and journals, which some considered not only better than the London Library but, in some areas, surpassing even those of the British Museum.[32]

But not only did the Free Library provide invaluable assistance to such established Russianists as those mentioned above, it also attracted a host of new British readers. Teplov's archive contains three folders of letters in English amounting to almost 800 sheets.[33] Much of this correspondence is from individual British men and women wishing simply to borrow Russian books or to perfect their language.[34] The Free Russian Library had appeared at a most propitious time and Teplov was more than happy to assist in the spread of this feverish interest in his country's culture.

Almost from the moment it opened its doors the Library received a steady flow of requests from those keen to learn this exotic and newly popular language, such as the enthusiastic Mr Joseph Jones of Covent Garden who wished to be sent Russian newspapers, and Miss Emily Whenn of Whitechapel, who had tried to memorize the alphabet but discovered what she had was incomplete, and the somewhat petulant but colourful Captain J. Sartorius of Surbiton who wished to have classes in conversational Russian but only at a rate of one shilling an hour plus travelling expenses.[35] Chaikovsky encouraged Teplov to take up the challenge of Russian language instruction and wrote to discuss the merits of the available teaching aids,

[29] GARF, f. 1721, op. 1, ed. khr. 84, l. 119, 8 February 1903. GARF, f. 1721, op. 1, ed. khr. 86, l. 269 May 24 1907, S. A. Savinkova, 'Na volosok ot kazni (Vospominaniya materi)', *Byloe*, 1 (January 1907), 247–71.

[30] S. A. Savinkov, 'A Russian Mother: A Personal Narrative (1897–1905)', trans. Constance Garnett, *Albany Review*, 1, no. 1 (April–May 1907), 86–101, 214–40: see Richard Garnett, *Constance Garnett: A Heroic Life* (London: Sinclair-Stevenson, 1991), 384, note 7.

[31] See GARF, f. 1721, op. 1, ed. khr. 84. l. 169, and ed. khr. 85, ll. 100, 104–5, 139–41, 145–7, 192.

[32] On a number of occasions the Museum was in fact pleased to accept donations of rare Russian material from Teplov. See, for example, GARF, f. 1721, op. 1, ed. khr. 84, ll. 33–4.

[33] GARF, f. 1721. op. 1, ed. khr. 84, 85, 86.

[34] GARF, f. 1721, op. 1, ed. khr. 84, l. 14,15, 10 September 1898.

[35] GARF, f. 1721. op. 1, ed. khr. 84, ll. 14,15, 10 September 1898, ll. 82–5, 1 September 1902. From other correspondence it would appear that the standard rate for such lessons varied from 2*s*. 6*d*. to 5*s*. per hour.

expressing a preference for the five shilling *Russian Reader* published by Nutt rather than Henry Riola's more expensive grammar.[36] And the interest of the British public in Russia did not stop at its language. A Mr F. A. Fawkes, researching Siberia, wrote requesting information on how the internal exile system had been affected by the construction of the Trans-Siberian railway.[37] At the other extreme, a Cardiff Boarding Master by the name of Poll sent in a rather badly spelled postcard asking for 'Russian newspapers in Estonian langwish or Russian (proper) and any accounts of Kamps at the Goldfields'.[38]

From all of the above it is clear that Teplov and his Free Russian Library had not only succeeded in arousing the interest of the poor Jewish émigrés in London's East End, but had also attracted the sympathies of, and in turn been of some considerable help to, a wide section of the British public. These groups, however, were by no means the only ones to take an interest in the Library's business.

A HOTBED OF REVOLUTION

The archives of the Sûreté Générale (General Security) in Paris contain a series of reports compiled by one of their London agents in early 1902, in which the 'Whitechapel Group' was described as one of the main Russian political émigré associations in England, and the Free Library as the 'rallying centre of the Russian revolutionary movement in London'.[39] Moreover, Teplov, the manager of the Library was deemed to be 'one of the most influential members of the revolutionary party here'.[40]

According to this police report, the 'Whitechapel Group' had a fairly mundane and limited programme which centred on two things: furthering the education of its members and finding work for new arrivals.[41] The police agent also submitted copious newspaper extracts and a variety of notices and handbills advertising a range of entertainments offered by and on behalf of the Library. But he went on to provide much more alarming news when he described how the Library was offering courses in practical chemistry and giving instruction in complex substances,

[36] GARF, f. 1721. op. 1, ed. khr. 31, l. 25, 4 May 1899. The works in question are Henry Riola, *How to Learn Russian: A Manual for Students of Russian, Based Upon the Ollendorffian System of Teaching Languages, and Adapted for Self-Instruction* (London: Kegan Paul, Trench Trübner, 1878), and G. Werkhaupt, *Russian Reader with Exercises of Conversation* (London: Nutt, 1902).

[37] GARF, f. 1721. op. 1, ed. khr. 84, ll. 272, 273, 31 August 1911.

[38] GARF, f. 1721. op. 1, ed. khr. 84, l. 38, 17 January 1900.

[39] Archives nationales, Paris (hereafter AN), F/7/12521/2: Angleterre (1887-1908), reports for 21 January, 28 February, and 15 March 1902.

[40] AN, F/7/12521/2: Angleterre (1887–1908) 17 May 1902, p. 1; AN, F/7/12521/1: Suisse (1882–1909), 17 February 1904.

[41] The archive contains numerous documents pointing to the institution's secondary role as a Labour Bureau staffed on a rota basis by certain members of the Lectures' Committee and their wives. See, for example, GARF, f. 1721, op. 1, ed. khr. 26, ll. 335, 346. The Library was approached not only by London tailors seeking the expertise of the Polish Jewish community (GARF, f. 1721. op. 1, ed. khr. 86, l. 92), but also, perhaps surprisingly, by Vickers who offered employment in their armaments factory at Crayford to qualified fitters and turners and also to unskilled labourers (GARF, f. 1721. op. 1, ed. khr. 27, l.335.)

including formulas for nitro-glycerine. Furthermore, he reported on the group's plans to organize Sunday trips to the countryside and, in passing, offered his own opinion that such excursions might give 'to those revolutionaries following a higher calling, the opportunity to perfect their skills in the manipulation of chemical compounds by carrying out open-air experiments'.[42]

According to this agent, then, Teplov, the notorious Paris bomber, was in fact still practising his art under the guise of mild-mannered librarian. However, there is no evidence in any of the archives examined so far that substantiates such an allegation. But it was not only the Sûreté who took an interest in the activities of the Free Library. One aspect of the history of 'Russia in Britain' which to date has received scant attention concerns the operations of the Russian secret police's Foreign Agency in the capital. A separate London office of the *agentura* had been established in the early 1890s and its members and activities were well known to Scotland Yard.[43] The principal tsarist agent in the capital at this time was a French citizen by the name of Edgar Jean Farce whose meticulous reports to his superiors covered the activities of all the revolutionaries in London and in much more detail than his counterpart in the Sûreté.[44] The agent's detailed submissions on Teplov in particular were helped by the fact that, as he boasted, one of his informants was 'a regular reader at the Russian Library'.[45] This would have come as no surprise to the émigrés who were well aware of spies in their midst. On one occasion in early 1905 Teplov himself was interviewed by the *London Daily News* for a long item describing the arrival in London of 'a special staff of Russian Police spies'. Teplov was dismissive, saying only, '"We are used to spies by this time. A few extra cannot make a difference to us." And he laughed merrily as he recalled some of his own experiences with the detectives.'[46]

Indeed, at this point Teplov was much more concerned with the immediate problems he faced within the Library itself. In the summer of 1904 he had been obliged to quit Church Lane at short notice and had decided to enter into a part-share agreement with the owners of a terraced house at number 16 Princelet Street, just off Brick Lane.[47] Unfortunately, the owners were the East London Jewish Branch of the Social Democratic Federation who intended to turn their part of the building into a *Dom naroda* or 'People's Home' (also often referred to as the '*Maison du Bund*') and, indeed, the opening of this club was duly celebrated on 30 July 1904 with an International Socialist Banquet chaired by the founder of the SDF, Henry Mayers Hyndman.[48] This move of the Library to its new address and its new association with the SDF was roundly criticized. Chaikovsky in

[42] AN, F/7/12521/2: Angleterre (1887–1908), 12 July 1902.

[43] In fact, it is clear they cooperated in a number of areas. Farce himself in a later report outlined his relationship with Special Branch, explaining that, thanks to his ability to read and understand Yiddish, he was able to pass on information from the local newspapers to Scotland Yard officers who in turn passed on information that would otherwise have been impossible for him to obtain.

[44] The National Archives (hereafter TNA) KV 6/47, 8 December 1904 (274/B).

[45] Archives of the Hoover Institution (hereafter HIA), Okhrana Archive, 54/VI/k/23 c. 20 September 1905.

[46] 'Spies in London: Watching Russian Refugees', *London Daily News* (27 January 1905), 6.

[47] AN, F/7/12521/2: Angleterre (1887–1908), report of 4 June 1904.

[48] GARF, f. 1721, op. 1, ed. khr. 87, l. 10. In fact Teplov's relations with the SDF stretched as far back as April 1900 when he received a letter from the Federation's London Organizer, George Hewitt, proposing the foundation of an international branch and asking for Teplov's help. See GARF, f. 1721. op. 1, ed. khr. 84, l. 41, 14 April 1900.

particular opposed the move on the grounds that it contradicted the non-party nature of the institution.[49] Sadly, it would appear that, following this disagreement, relations between the two cooled considerably.

These events were duly recorded by agent Farce in his dispatches. He and his Sûreté compatriots continued to follow Teplov's movements and also filed reports on his reactions and those of his comrades in the East End to the tumultuous events unfolding in Russia, which, in 1905, appeared to be building to a climax. By November these reports contained news of an increase in the British police presence in the East End with constables and detectives almost permanently stationed at the doors of the revolutionary and anarchist clubs and at the *Maison du Bund*.[50] Then, on 13 November 1905, Farce filed his final report on Princelet Street recording simply that 'For some days now red and black flags have been flying from the windows of the Russian Library.'[51]

In Russia the scent of victory was in the air. With the publication of the tsar's October Manifesto and his subsequent declaration of an amnesty for certain political refugees, many in the Russian East End decided to make an immediate return to their homeland, abandoning both the *Maison du Bund* and the Free Library. By the end of the year the house in Princelet Street had been vacated.[52] Whether Teplov also left for Russia at this time is unclear although in one contemporaneous newspaper report his name does appear alongside those of Kropotkin and Chaikovsky as members of the refugee colony who were 'actively completing arrangements to return to their native land'.[53] In Teplov's papers, however, there is no evidence to support this. Indeed, his archive contains hardly a mention of his or his library's activities for the rest of the decade. The next documents of relevance to the Free Library date from January 1911, a period of some significance not only for Teplov but for the Russian East End as a whole.

On 16 December 1910 a gang of Latvian 'revolutionary expropriators' murdered three policemen in Houndsditch, East London. The situation was further inflamed in the first days of the New Year when, after a long and violent gun battle, the infamous siege at 100 Sidney Street, Stepney ended with the death of two of the gang members and an innocent neighbour. The supposed leader of the gang, the so-called 'Peter the Painter', escaped capture and sparked an outcry for revenge in the national press. The *Daily Express,* in particular, was quick to articulate the British public's feelings of anger and disgust. In leading articles it denounced 'foreign aliens', criticized the weakness of the Liberal government for letting the 1905 Aliens Act drift, and called for its immediate enforcement. Then, three days after

[49] GARF, f. 1721, op. 1, ed. khr. 31, ll. 72, 73, 5 July 1903, and ed. khr. 46. l. 66 (undated).

[50] AN, F/7/12521/2: Angleterre (1887–1908), 16 November 1905. In this context it is interesting to note that Teplov's archive contains the visiting cards of two CID officers: Inspectors McNamara and McCarthy, and also that of Ernest Nicholls of the City Police. See GARF, f. 1721. op. 1, ed. khr. 27, ll. 142, 145, 151.

[51] HIA, Okhrana Archive, 54/VI/k/23 c, 13 November 1905.

[52] GARF, f. 1721, op. 1, ed. khr. 4, l. 20, 4 January, 1906.

[53] 'Russian Refugees in England', *The Observer* (5 November 1905), 7. Teplov is described as 'organizer of the free libraries for Jews in Whitechapel'.

the siege, on Friday 6 January 1911, the *Express* carried a front-page story in which it made the startling claim that the elusive gang leader was none other than Teplov himself. This astonishing story continued for several more paragraphs detailing Teplov's involvement in the Paris Bomb Plot, his imprisonment and expulsion from France, and his subsequent supposed leadership of a seventeen-strong group of Russian terrorists currently headquartered in Stepney.[54] The following day the *Express* revealed their source to be Dr Eugene Henniger, head of Berlin's political police.[55] Furthermore, they carried another story corroborating the libel. Their source this time was M. Xavier Guichard, chief of the 'Anarchist Brigade' of the Paris police force.[56] Teplov reacted quickly, appointing a firm of solicitors and issuing a high court writ.[57] Perhaps not surprisingly, two months later *The Express* openly admitted their error, agreed to pay damages of £100 and printed an apology for their libel, which they buried at the foot of the paper's second page.[58] However, in deciding to contribute a mere £5 from his award to the defence fund for the émigrés accused in the Houndsditch affair, Teplov caused much annoyance amongst the community and their supporters. J. Frederick Green, for example, was disgusted at this act of meanness, stating that Teplov had no moral right to keep the money. Thus it was that Teplov lost another influential friend.[59]

These unfortunate events marked the beginnings of a decline in Teplov's health and in the fortunes of the Free Library itself. During his periods of convalescence Teplov received numerous reports from staff complaining that others had failed to turn up for duty and that, as a consequence, the Library had been unable to open to the public.[60] The situation did not improve with the outbreak of war and, eventually, in February 1915, the Library was again obliged to close temporarily. Teplov tried to raise funds by arranging public entertainments such as the performance of Stepnyak's play referred to earlier, but, increasingly, expressions of discontent were voiced by members of the Lectures' Committee, most noticeably David Soskice, who believed a 'restructuring' was long overdue. Soskice had offered his services as lecturer shortly after his arrival in emigration in London in 1898, and had become increasingly involved in the Library's other affairs. His correspondence with Teplov was marked by a seriousness and lack of humour for which he was noted. This was apparent particularly in those letters in which he expressed his concerns over the poor organization of the Library's administration.[61] He made no secret of his desire to wrest control of the Library's finances from Teplov. Soskice believed it was all the more important that the Library's affairs should be set in order before it reopened its doors at its next new address—27 Sandy's Row, Whitechapel. It may be that he

[54] 'Peter the Painter', *Daily Express* (6 January 1911), 1.

[55] 'Berlin Experts' Cure for Anarchy', *Daily Express* (7 January 1911), 1.

[56] '"Peter the Painter" in Paris', *Daily Express* (7 January 1911), 1.

[57] GARF, f. 1721, op. 1, ed. khr. 84, ll. 294–6. Teploff v *Daily Express,* High Court King's Bench. Writ issued 10 January 1911.

[58] 'Peter the Painter', *Daily Express* (31 March 1911), 2. In fact, the newspaper did little more than express their regret that 'the information given to our correspondents was inaccurate'.

[59] GARF, f. 1721, op. 1, ed. khr. 84, ll. 267–8, 7 April 1911.

[60] GARF, f. 1721. op. 1, ed. khr. 46.

[61] GARF, f. 1721, op. 1, ed. khr. 52, l. 15–17, 23 December 1914 to 6 January 1915.

suspected some financial impropriety on Teplov's part, and although this was not made explicit it led inevitably to a cooling of relations to the point where the two could only communicate via an intermediary.[62]

By the time of the Library's relocation in October 1916 Soskice had succeeded in winning the support not only of the Corporation of Orderlies but also of Hagberg Wright, Green, and others on the Lectures' Committee, which had now transformed itself into an 'Organizing Committee'. One of the first acts of the new management was to change the institution's name to 'The Russian Institute and Library', and to cut its opening hours by fifty per cent.[63] While Teplov retained his title of Librarian and Secretary, he lost control of the Institute's financial administration to a newly appointed treasurer. Worse was to follow in two months when, after another meeting of Soskice's Committee, Teplov and his wife were informed they had until February to leave the apartment they had been occupying in Sandy's Row 'in order to free the rooms which are urgently required for the work of the Institute'.[64] The devastated couple were offered some financial assistance to help them find new lodgings but whether this aid was accepted is not recorded.

DEMISE OF THE FREE RUSSIAN LIBRARY

In early 1917, as Russia teetered on the brink of revolution, unpleasant letters continued to be exchanged between the Librarian and the Organizing Committee until 15 March when Teplov received the following note from L. Sagal, a library assistant who, due to his composure, had been appointed to act as intermediary between the two warring factions. On this occasion, however, he was barely able to contain his excitement: 'Midnight: I have only just heard that revolution has broken out in Russia and that Nicholas has been overthrown. Hurrah! Three cheers! I am so happy that I don't even want to talk about our petty squabbles.'[65] With the exhilarating news of the February revolution many émigrés had already started to return to Russia, and, in due course, but with rather more mixed emotions, Teplov and his wife and daughter followed suit, arriving back on Russian soil on 29 August 1917.[66] The family spent a few months in St Petersburg and then, in 1918, returned home to Penza. There is some evidence that Teplov took an interest in the affairs of the new post-October government, writing a handful of letters to the Head of State, Mikhail Kalinin and, indeed, to Lenin himself, in which he complained about the state of affairs in Turkestan, and commented on the situation in Fergana following

[62] From the archive it would appear that Teplov made no distinction between public and private accounting, with numerous of his wife's bills from Debenhams and other West End stores interfiled with the Library's other business receipts. See, for example, GARF, f. 1721, op. 1, ed. khr. 26, l. 339, etc.

[63] GARF, f. 1721, op. 1, ed. khr. 24, l. 29.

[64] GARF, f. 1721, op. 1, ed. khr. 85, l. 196. Letter from Green, 27 Feb 1917.

[65] GARF, f. 1721. op. 1, ed. khr. 78, l. 7, 15 March 1917.

[66] GARF, f. 1721, op. 1, ed. khr. 153, ll. 7–8.

the famine.[67] But nothing more is known of the last two years of Aleksey L′vovich's eventful life. He passed away on 17 October 1920 at the age of 68. Neither the cause of his death nor the place of his burial are recorded.

The fate of Teplov's beloved Library is equally uncertain. The librarian B. P. Kanevsky referred to a study of British public libraries in the early 1920s carried out by the Soviet scholar, I. Zvavich, who had uncovered a collection of over 500 Russian books in Whitechapel Public Library.[68] To Kanevsky it was 'evident' that these books had originally formed part of the Free Russian Library but, in fact, this was not the case for, as the same study stated, the Whitechapel Library's main source of Russian material for some years had been gifts of duplicates from Hagberg Wright at the London Library.[69] Be that as it may, after 1917 and the return of large numbers of East End émigrés to Russia demand for such books had decreased significantly. Zvavich, on leaving the East End, pointed out that the new inhabitants of the area no longer had any need for Russian books and it would appear he was right.[70] On 7 February 1921 *The Times* carried the following small notice:

> Many people who can read Russian will be glad to know that the Russian Library, which has existed for 20 years, has moved to a more accessible neighbourhood. It is now installed with its 8,000 books at 116 New Oxford Street, and Dr Hagberg-Wright, Librarian at the London Library has become its president. As it needs funds to cover the expense of moving, to bind old books and to purchase new ones, it has arranged a *Bal masqué* at the Portman Rooms on February 18th for which tickets may be had at the Library any evening except Wednesday, between 5 and 7.[71]

Teplov, then, had seen his Library's collections grow substantially since its inception and had also witnessed an exponential growth in its readership, but from this notice it is unclear whether the institution still managed to uphold its principle of free access. Moreover, one wonders whether the masked ball in question would have brought in sufficient funds to maintain the Library in business and to meet the rental payments on its expensive, new West End location. Many of its original readers, like its Chief Librarian, had long since returned to their motherland or passed on, and the 'Russomania' which had swept Britain some twenty years earlier, which Teplov had done so much to encourage, had now been replaced by a fascination for Soviet Russia and its new literature. Whether this latest incarnation of the Russian

[67] GARF, f. 1721, op. 1, ed. khr. 137, ll. 1–25. Under the command of Ya. K. Peters between 1920 and 1922, the Turkestan Bureau of the Revolutionary Communist Party violently suppressed all signs of anti-bolshevism in the region. At this time, Fergana and much of the rest of Uzbekistan suffered a famine as a result of collectivization.

[68] B. P. Kanevsky, 'Russkaya kniga v Britanskom muzee v XIX veke', in *Gosudarstvennaya biblioteka SSSR im. V. I. Lenina: Trudy* (Moscow: Kniga, 1969), xi, 124–5; I. Zvavich. 'Russkaya kniga v Anglii (Pis′mo iz Londona)', *Pechat' i revolyutsiya*, 6 (1923), 98–114.

[69] Zvavich, 'Russkaya kniga v Anglii (Pis′mo iz Londona)', 101. In June 1913 alone Hagberg Wright donated 390 Russian items to the Library: see Stepney Libraries and Museums Committee, Registers of Donations, 1891–1922 (STE/731), 195, and 'Books for Russian Emigrants', *The Times* (4 November 1912), 4.

[70] Zvavich, 'Russkaia kniga v Anglii (Pis′mo iz Londona)', 103, 104.

[71] 'Ball for the Russian Library', *The Times* (7 February 1921), 8.

Library succeeded in attracting a new clientele is uncertain since, following this brief notice in *The Times*, it appears to have sunk without trace.

Throughout the twenty years of its existence the Free Russian Library met with remarkable success in its efforts to raise the educational levels and political awareness of the East European inhabitants of the Whitechapel slums. This was the primary aim of the institution and, as documents in Teplov's archive demonstrate, there is no doubt that it was achieved in part thanks to the enthusiastic support which its appeal for the cause of education found in the drawing rooms and literary salons of London's West End. In turn, this small circle of Bloomsbury intellectuals, as active borrowers and readers, also benefitted greatly from the activities of the Library. But perhaps of greater interest is the ample evidence contained in the archive of the services provided by the Free Library to a much wider sector of the British public. For, alongside its laudable work in the Russian East End, the Library also managed to satisfy the curiosity of many ordinary men and women in the streets of London and elsewhere and bring to them a much clearer understanding of the realities of Russian life and culture—a considerable achievement for such a small institution and one which deserves some belated recognition.

5

'Formless', 'Pretentious', 'Hideous and Revolting'

Non-Chekhov Russian and Soviet Drama on the British Stage

Stuart Young

> This race... thinks so differently from our own. Russia is a queer, big place, where queer, big things happen (James Agate).[1]

Writing in 1951 about the previous two decades of British theatre, Audrey Williamson remarks, 'in England Russian plays fall into roughly three categories: Tchehovian revivals (in which we may include *A Month in the Country* by the earlier but not dissimilar writer Turgenev); adaptations of the great Russian novelists... Tolstoy and Dostoievsky; and contemporary plays, which rarely reach us'.[2] Indeed, by the 1940s the history of Russian drama on the British stage had become pre-eminently the adoption of Chekhov, for whom audiences and particularly actors, initially resistant, quickly developed a special and enduring affinity. Meanwhile, the appeal of adaptations of Tolstoy and, even more, Dostoevsky stemmed from the popularity of the great nineteenth-century Russian novels, and it anticipates Dostoevsky's emergence as the second most performed Russian writer in the British theatre. At the time Williamson was writing, that theatre had become rather insular: during and immediately after the Second World War the repertoire was relatively unadventurous—symptomatic of the malaise that Kenneth Tynan and others bemoaned in the 1940s and 1950s.[3] However, Williamson significantly misrepresents and diminishes the Russian presence on the British stage. From the mid-1920s until well into the 1930s there was considerable interest in Russian drama, both contemporary plays and the nineteenth-century canon. Moreover, even in the early years of the century an impressive series of Russian plays and adaptations of Russian novels was staged in London. This attention was symptomatic of both a wider curiosity, from the 1890s, about modern European drama and, of

[1] James Agate, review of *The Seven Who Were Hanged*, Yiddish Art Theatre, New Scala, 1924, *Sunday Times* (18 May 1924), 6.

[2] Audrey Williamson, *Theatre of Two Decades* (London: Rockliff, 1951), 193.

[3] See, for example, Kenneth Tynan, *Tynan on Theatre* (Harmondsworth: Penguin, 1964), 31.

course, the contemporary vogue for Russian art and literature, which swept Europe like an 'epidemic of influenza',[4] and to which this volume attests.

Lawrence Venuti and other theorists note the tension, in the traffic of cultural exchange and translation, between the impulse to 'domesticate' and respect for the alterity of the foreign.[5] The ethnocentric British theatre has often been strongly inclined to domesticate: in the terms of Patrice Pavis's 'hourglass' model of cultural transmission, it tends to blend—or grind—foreign plays like a mill.[6] However, as Denise Merkle argues, in Britain in the late nineteenth and early twentieth centuries there was a conspicuous degree of openness to alternative ways of seeing and representing the world as a means of stimulating renewal in art and culture.[7] Consequently, the introduction of Russian drama to the British stage encouraged audiences to 'travel abroad'.[8] Nevertheless, the tolerance of difference has its limits: not surprisingly, when set alongside expressions of Ibsenian and Shavian drama, English positivism, and enduring notions of Victorian propriety, some of those Russian plays proved baffling and alien. In due course theatre-makers and audiences developed a distinct preference for plays and playwrights that conformed, or proved conformable, to familiar models and perspectives on the world.

As befits the playwright who for well over half a century has occupied a place second only to Shakespeare in the British classical repertoire, the English embrace of Chekhov is well documented. However, the wider context of that adoption—the larger story of Russian drama on the British stage—has been but patchily told: Aleksey Bartoshevich has written on Anglo-Russian theatrical contacts in the 1910s; Cynthia Marsh has catalogued excerpts of reviews of Gor′ky productions; Kate Sealey Rahman has examined productions of Ostrovsky up to 1928; and I have looked at the history of Turgenev's *A Month in the Country* (*Mesyats v derevne*) in the British theatre.[9] This chapter documents the range of productions of Russian plays in London from 1900 until the Second World War—productions which occurred variously in progressive theatrical societies, the 'little' theatres that developed after World War One, and the West End. It examines the early fascination with, and horror at, the 'in-yer-face' naturalism of Gork′y and Tolstoy; the belated, rather tentative acknowledgement of Ostrovsky; the bemusement at the

[4] Somerset Maugham, *Ashenden or the British Agent* (London: Heinemann, 1928), 273.

[5] Lawrence Venuti, *The Translator's Invisibility: A History of Translation* (London: Routledge, 1995), 19–20.

[6] Patrice Pavis, *Theatre at the Crossroads of Culture*, trans. Loren Kruger (London: Routledge, 1992), 4–5.

[7] Denise Merkle, 'Secret Literary Societies in Late Victorian England', in Maria Tymoczko, ed., *Translation, Resistance, Activism* (Amherst and Boston, MA: University of Massachusetts Press, 2010), 108.

[8] Gunilla Anderman, *Europe on Stage: Translation and Theatre* (London: Oberon, 2005), 8.

[9] See Alexei Bartoshevich, 'The "Inevitability" of Chekhov: Anglo-Russian Theatrical Contacts in the 1910s', in Patrick Miles, ed., *Chekhov on the British Stage* (Cambridge: Cambridge University Press, 1993), 20–8; Cynthia Marsh, *File on Gorky* (London: Methuen, 1993); Kate Sealey Rahman, 'Ostrovskii on the British Stage: 1894–1928', *Toronto Slavic Quarterly*, 9 (Summer 2004), <http://www.utoronto.ca/tsq/09/rahman09.shtml>; and Stuart Young, 'A Month in the Country in the British Theatre', *New Zealand Slavonic Journal* (1994), 207–27.

symbolists; and the emerging, distinct preference for realist, psychological drama in the mould of Chekhov and Turgenev. It also looks at the contribution of the notable Russian émigrés Lidiya Yavorskaya and especially Fedor Komissarzhevsky to the production, reception, and perception of Russian drama.

For the British, Russian drama denotes intellectual gravitas. Reflecting in the late 1930s, Agate maintained that 'Russia's plays' are irrefutably superior to England's because they 'are written by her best minds'; 'your Russian dramatist writes for adults, whereas your English playwright sets out merely to amuse adolescents!'[10] Like Russian art and literature generally, Russian drama was regarded from the outset as intrinsically philosophical. According to Ashley Dukes, writing in 1911, whereas 'most of our dramatists are content to accept the fact of life without demur', Russian playwrights propound 'a peculiar questioning of life and a criticism of fundamentals. They set their note of interrogation... against life as an existing fact. They question its meaning and seek first its place in their philosophy.'[11] This preoccupation with the metaphysical meant that Russian drama acquired the reputation of being emphatically highbrow: confessing to being deeply unimpressed by Nikolay Evreinov's *A Merry Death* (*Veselaya smert'*) (Pioneer Players, 1916), the *Star* reviewer acknowledged that it was 'both philistine and unpatriotic to fail to be enraptured with everything Russian'.[12] That association with the highbrow and the esoteric was signified by the early championing of Russian drama by the Incorporated Stage Society of London.

1900–1913: GRITTY REALISM AND NATURALISM

Although the Stage Society, the leading London theatrical society and 'incubator' of the New Theatre movement, did not mount the first English production of Chekhov until 1911, in the meantime it staged four other Russian plays.[13] Founded in 1899, the Society continued the pioneering work of the Independent Theatre (1891–7) in producing contemporary Continental dramatists, including Maeterlinck, Hauptmann, and especially Ibsen, alongside new plays by British and Irish playwrights, such as Granville Barker, Yeats, and Shaw. French and German plays are conspicuous in that early repertoire, but it is perhaps a measure of the modishness of things Russian that, for its first decade at least, the Society staged more playwrights from Russia than from any other country. It launched its fifth season, in 1903, with *The Lower Depths* (*Na dne*), less than a year after the play's première in Moscow. Therefore, Gor'ky was performed in Britain six years before George Calderon's production of *The Seagull* (*Chaika*) in Glasgow, in 1909, and

[10] James Agate, *The Amazing Theatre* (London: G. G. Harrap, 1939), 193, 192.

[11] Ashley Dukes, *Modern Dramatists* (London: Frank Palmer, 1911), 180.

[12] Review of *A Merry Death*, Pioneer Players, 1916, *The Star* (3 April 1916), Victoria and Albert Museum Department of Theatre and Performance Collections (hereafter V&A).

[13] Cary M. Mazer, 'New Theatres for a New Drama', in Kerry Powell, ed., *The Cambridge Companion to Victorian and Edwardian Theatre* (Cambridge: Cambridge University Press, 2004), 215.

eight years before the first Chekhov production in London. The Stage Society then opened its sixth season with Tolstoy's *The Power of Darkness* (*Vlast' t'my*), with which, incidentally, *The Lower Depths* had played in repertoire at the Moscow Art Theatre. It closed the following season, in 1906, with an abridged version of Gogol''s *The Inspector-General* (*Revizor*, also known as *The Government Inspector*), preceded by John Pollock's one-act 'The Invention of Dr. Metzler', and in 1909 it staged Turgenev's two-act *The Bread of Others* (*Nakhlebnik*, more commonly known as *The Hanger-On* or *Alien Bread*) in a double bill with Giuseppe Giacosa's *The Rights of the Soul* (*I diritti dell'anima).*

Meanwhile, in 1906, a German production of *The Lower Depths* (*Nachtasyl*) appeared at the Great Queen Street Theatre and the Mermaid Society presented Gor'ky's *The Bezsemenovs* (*Meshchane*, also known as *Philistines*). Then, in 1911, the year that the Stage Society eventually produced *The Cherry Orchard* (*Vishnevyi sad*), Gor'ky's now 'famous' *Lower Depths* was revived in London, receiving its first 'public'—that is non-theatrical society—production.[14] In this period adaptations of two great Russian novels were also staged: Henri Bataille's version of Tolstoy's novel *Resurrection* (*Voskresenie*), adapted by Michael Morton and starring Herbert Beerbohm Tree as Prince Dmitry Nekhlyudov, in 1903 (three years later Bataille's own 'bald... plainer' French production also played in London); and, in 1910, *The Unwritten Law*, an adaptation of Dostoevsky's *Crime and Punishment* (*Prestuplenie i nakazanie*) by Laurence Irving, who had translated *The Lower Depths* for the Stage Society.[15] Irving played Raskol'nikov, and his wife, Mabel Hackney, played Sonya.

As one might expect, given Tree's and Irving's involvement, *Resurrection* and *The Unwritten Law* were substantial productions. On the other hand, the series of theatrical society productions, which included two other Tolstoy plays in 1912—*The Cause of It All* (*O nei vse kachestva*) by the Adelphi Stage Society and *The Living Corpse* (*Zhivoi trup*), under the title *The Man Who was Dead*, by the Literary Theatre Society—and *The Brothers Karamazov* (*Brat'ya Karamazovy*) by the Stage Society in 1913, were much more modest. They were mounted with limited resources and inadequate rehearsals, those rehearsals often compromised by the performers' other, commercial engagements, and the casting conditional upon the permission of the producers of those prior engagements. Stage Society productions received only two or three performances, while the Adelphi and Literary Societies' Tolstoys were each presented just once. Performances were usually on Sunday or Monday evenings or at matinees, when the main production at the venue was not playing. Audiences comprised a small, self-conscious, intellectual coterie, characterized, according to Max Beerbohm, by their 'literary tea-party attitude' and their 'gushing superficial curiosity'.[16]

Although they were accused of the 'unutterable pessimism' and 'relentless... almost unrelieved gloom' seemingly common to all Russian writers, Gor'ky,

[14] 'The Lower Depths', *The Times* (22 November 1911), 11.

[15] Review of *Resurrection*, Royalty, 1906, *Illustrated London News* (24 February 1906), 258.

[16] Max Beerbohm, review of *The Lower Depths*, Stage Society, 1903, *Saturday Review* (5 December 1903), 699.

Tolstoy, and Turgenev offered, unlike Chekhov, the element of social and political comment which the English sought in Russian art and literature, and which was expected of serious theatre, as exemplified by the New Drama presented at the Court by Granville Barker and Vedrenne.[17] Moreover, they epitomized the realism and naturalism that the English valued so highly, distinctly preferring Russian expressions over the French.[18] The *Daily Mail* reviewer found *The Bread of Others* 'intensely interesting' as 'a study of the times some twenty-two years before the liberation of the serfs', 'because Turgèniv's people are so real; because that was Russia that we saw on the stage'.[19] However, this Russian realism and naturalism also proved extremely challenging.

Whereas Ibsen and New English Drama explore social problems in middle-class milieus, Tolstoy and Gor′ky portray 'the degradation of the lower classes in Russia', Tolstoy focusing on the peasantry and Gor′ky on the impoverished urban proletariat.[20] Their plays pull no punches: they are 'full of hideous and revolting details'. Describing the 'mimic representation of Russian village life' in *The Power of Darkness* as 'a hideous medley of swinish drunkenness and satyr-like lust and fiendish crime', the *Times* reviewer invoked Aristotle's 'objection to the tragic use of *miaron*, the disgusting': 'For disgusting this tragedy of Tolstoy's is, to our taste, at any rate, and we feel after seeing it as though we ought to go into quarantine'. After outlining the narrative, he continues, 'into the details we forbear to enter. We merely hint that they leave no element of the nauseous neglected. There are coarse oaths and torrents of vile abuse;...everybody smells of drink; we are invited to listen to the crack-cracking of the murdered infant's bones.' So, we are prompted 'to avert our eyes and hold our noses'.[21] If Tolstoy is disgusting, 'Gorky need only be referred to as an advance in grime'—'a Zola of the doss-house'.[22] In its 1903 and 1911 productions *The Lower Depths* was deemed 'nothing but bald and unseemly horror', 'an interesting experiment in the hideous', and 'the last word in the macabre. It turns the theatre into a chamber of horrors. It haunts you like a nightmare.'[23] (It is interesting that, a century later, the trio of Vasily Sigarev's plays staged at the

[17] Review of R. E. C. Long's translation of Chekhov's short stories, *Outlook* (14 November 1903), 433, in Victor Emeljanow, ed., *Chekhov: The Critical Heritage* (London: Routledge and Kegan Paul, 1981), 69.

[18] Dorothy Brewster, *East-West Passage: A Study in Literary Relationships* (London: George Allen and Unwin, 1954), 151.

[19] Review of *The Bread of Others*, Stage Society, 1909, *Daily Mail* (23 February 1909), production file of *The Bread of Others* and *The Rights of the Soul* (by Giuseppe Giacosa) at Kingsway Theatre, 1909, V&A.

[20] Max Beerbohm, review of *The Power of Darkness*, Stage Society, 1904, *Saturday Review* (31 December 1904), 823.

[21] Review of *The Power of Darkness*, Stage Society, 1904, *The Times* (21 December 1904), 13.

[22] George Saintsbury, *The Later Nineteenth Century* (Edinburgh: Blackwood, 1907), quoted in Brewster, *East-West Passage*, 141; John Palmer, 'Gorki's Masterpiece', review of *The Lower Depths*, Kingsway, 1911, *Saturday Review* (9 December 1911), 731.

[23] Beerbohm, review of *The Lower Depths*, 1903, 700; 'A Mixed bag: Sporting Stories from Here and There', *The Tatler*, no. 546 (13 December 1911), 106; Review of *The Lower Depths*, Kingsway, 1911, *The Times* (4 December 1911), 6.

Royal Court from 2002 to 2004 was described in strikingly similar terms: 'nightmarish', a 'catalogue of horrors', and 'a play from hell'.)[24]

Notwithstanding his distaste for Gor'ky's and Tolstoy's plays and his disdain for their seemingly pretentious audiences, the *Times* reviewer acknowledges that *The Lower Depths* 'demands a serious effort' not only 'from every individual player', but 'from every individual playgoer—the effort to overcome the instinctive preference for the merely agreeable and to recognise that human misery and pain also have their claims to be interpreted in terms of art'.[25] He also appreciates that 'it is the business of stage societies, with their picked audiences and their closed doors, to produce, now and then, just such plays' as *The Power of Darkness*. Although his own response to Tolstoy's tragedy would be, like Voltaire's Candide, to take 'the first train back to his garden—with the silent resolve never to leave it again', he concedes that 'underneath the squalid horror' there is a profound moral lesson.[26] For Beerbohm too, the 'hideousness' of Tolstoy's play is redeemed by the 'fine moral idea' expressed in the writing.[27] However, whereas Tolstoy satisfies the English desire for a discernible moral perspective, Gor'ky is more problematic because, as John Palmer notes, he is 'the poet who looks on life as it is, and not on his vision of what it should be'; his plays are not vehicles for 'a homily or a system'.[28]

The challenge presented by Tolstoy and Gor'ky was not only the 'ugliness', the grim violence, and the 'listless despair' that was at odds with the confidence and optimism of Britain before the First World War; their and Turgenev's plays were disconcertingly 'formless', contravening the 'laws of the drama' with their lack of action or strong narrative.[29] In his survey of modern Russian literature, published in 1925, D. S. Mirsky remarks that Russian drama 'is even more undramatic than the Russian novel is un-narrative'.[30] Meanwhile, Dukes avers, 'There is little technical accomplishment in Russian drama', attributing the 'incompleteness and incoherence' that characterizes most plays to the Russian writer's overriding preoccupation with interrogating the meaning and fundamentals of life.[31] 'Gorkism' was especially vexing.[32] However, when *The Lower Depths* was revived in 1906 and more particularly in 1911, critics appreciated that the novelty of Gor'ky's dramatic purpose resides outside 'the compass of a conventionally constructed four-act play'.[33] The *Illustrated*

[24] John Gross, review of *Black Milk* (*Chernoe moloko*), Royal Court Upstairs, 2003, *Sunday Telegraph* (9 February 2003), in *Theatre Record*, 23, no. 3 (2003), 127; Kate Bassett, review of *Plasticine* (*Plastisin*), Royal Court Upstairs, 2002, *Independent on Sunday* (23 March 2002), in *Theatre Record*, 22, no. 6 (2002), 343; John Peter, review of *Plasticine*, Royal Court Upstairs, 2002, *Sunday Times* (31 March 2002), in *Theatre Record*, 22, no. 6 (2002), 346. The third play was *Ladybird* (*Bozh' i korovki*).

[25] Review of *The Lower Depths*, 1911, *The Times*, 6.

[26] Review of *The Power of Darkness*, 1904, *The Times*, 13.

[27] Beerbohm, review of *The Power of Darkness*, 1904, 823.

[28] Palmer, 'Gorki's Masterpiece', 731.

[29] E. F. S. ('Monocle'), review of *The Lower Depths*, Kingsway, 1911, *The Sketch* (13 December 1911), 298; Review of *The Lower Depths*, 1911, *The Times*, 6; Beerbohm, review of *The Lower Depths*, 1903, 700; Review of *The Bezsemenovs*, Mermaid Society, 1906, *The Times* (24 April 1906), 12.

[30] D. S. Mirsky, *Modern Russian Literature* (London: Oxford University Press, 1925), 66.

[31] Dukes, *Modern Dramatists*, 181.

[32] Beerbohm, review of *The Lower Depths*, 1903, 700.

[33] Palmer, 'Gorki's Masterpiece', 731.

London News's reviewer of the Kingsway production noted that the play is 'scarcely possessed of anything approximating to story or plot or development of action' and so is 'hardly a play in the technical sense of the term'. Nevertheless, he insisted that it 'is more impressive than many an elaborate and carefully planned drama that may have been worked out according to formula' and that it 'ought not to be missed by anyone who is interested in the drama of ideas'.[34] Consequently, in comparison to the Bataille-Tolstoy *Resurrection*, which 'endeavours to take the shape of an ordinary play, and fails', *The Lower Depths* 'apparently seeks to avoid every stage convention and succeeds'.[35]

SOMETHING A LITTLE MORE SALUBRIOUS: LIDIYA YAVORSKAYA AND ADAPTATIONS OF RUSSIAN NOVELS

In the same period as these early productions of Russian plays, there was considerable British interest in the theatre in Russia itself, stimulated by the reports of, among others, Calderon, Irving, and Maurice Baring, who had spent time in Russia. Tree and others made attempts to arrange a visit to London by the Moscow Art Theatre, which had established a high reputation internationally. Those plans never came to fruition, but, in the meantime, another exponent of Russian theatre came to England, Lidiya Yavorskaya (also known as Lydia Yavorska), one of several Russian émigrés and exiles who helped to bring Russian plays and productions to the stages of Europe and North America, more especially after the Russian Revolution. Otherwise known as Princess Baryatinskaya, Yavorskaya had enjoyed a successful career as an actress in St Petersburg, although Chekhov prevented her from performing in any of his plays because of her 'showy, melodramatic acting style'.[36] After the 1905 Revolution she left Russia and toured abroad, initially appearing principally in Paris. With her St Petersburg company she visited London in 1909, performing in Russian. During its season of *La Dame aux Camélias* at His Majesty's (Tree's theatre), the company presented three matinees that each included the fifth act of *Vassilissa Melentieva* (*Vasilisa Melent'eva*), Ostrovsky's early historical drama about a young widow who poisons the Tsarina and marries Ivan the Terrible. The performances were accompanied by a talk on the play and the author by Yavorskaya's husband, Prince Baryatinsky.[37]

[34] Review of *The Lower Depths*, Kingsway, 1911, *Illustrated London News* (9 December 1911), 976.

[35] Review of *Nachtasyl* (*The Lower Depths*), Great Queen Street Theatre, 1906, *The Times* (17 February 1906), 6.

[36] Simon Karlinsky, in Anton Chekhov, *Letters of Anton Chekhov*, ed. Simon Karlinsky, trans. M. H. Heim in collaboration with Simon Karlinsky (London: Bodley Head, 1973), 267.

[37] On the first two occasions the Ostrovsky was preceded by Prince Baryatinsky's talk and the final three acts of Dumas fils's play; on the third, the bill included Baryatinsky's 'conference', Strindberg's *The Stronger Woman*, and a programme of music (Programmes for *Vassilissa Melentieva*, His Majesty's, 1909, production file of *La Dame aux Camelias* at His Majesty's, 1909, V&A).

Yavorskaya then settled in London, where she produced and acted in several English productions of Russian plays. She produced and played the role of Nastya in the 1911 *Lower Depths*. Later that year she produced Chekhov's *The Bear* (*Medved'*), and in 1912, at the age of 43, she played Nina in the Adelphi Stage Society's *Seagull*, and appeared in *The Man Who was Dead*. Bartoshevich claims that Yavorskaya 'was not remotely the person to represent Russian dramatic art in London', that, ironically, 'the English public's acquaintance with the Russian stage began not with Chekhov in a Moscow Arts production, but with the actress who was the prototype of the *cabotine* Arkadina in *The Seagull*'.[38] In fact, opinion was divided about her acting: what some deplored as histrionic extravagance, others admired as virtuosity. Given her reputation as something of a prima donna, it is perhaps fitting that her most prominent English performance in a Russian play was the title role in *Anna Karenina* in 1913, a part she had played previously in both Russian and French. On this occasion Tolstoy's novel was adapted for the stage by the playwright John Pollock, with whom Yavorskaya had previously collaborated and whom she married in 1920, the year before she died.[39]

Along with Tree's *Resurrection*, Irving's *The Unwritten Law*, and the Stage Society's production of Jacques Copeau and Jean Croué's version of *The Brothers Karamazov*, Pollock's *Anna Karenina* institutes what Williamson identifies as the second strand of Russian drama on the English stage: adaptations of the great Russian novels. (The one previous adaptation was Robert Buchanan's version of *Crime and Punishment*, *The Sixth Commandment*, which was staged at the Shaftesbury in 1890.) Whereas *The Brothers Karamazov* was a typically modest theatrical society venture—and 'not one of the lucky discoveries of the Stage Society' thanks to the play's being 'too gloomy, violent, lengthy and disconnected'—the others were all major productions.[40] *Resurrection* ran at His Majesty's for three months (93 performances); *The Unwritten Law* opened in Manchester and transferred first to the Garrick and then to the Kingsway, running in London for over three months; and *Anna Karenina* played at the Ambassadors and La Scala for over six months, with 221 performances.[41] The public profile for *Anna Karenina* was demonstrated by a photo spread in *The Tatler* that showed Yavorskaya '"resting" and revelling' and 'taking the English summer in her arms' while studying the part of Tolstoy's heroine in 'a secluded spot on the south coast'.[42]

[38] Bartoshevich, 'The "Inevitability" of Chekhov', 25.

[39] In the triple bill featuring 'The Bear', Yavorskaya played the title role in Pollock's 'Rosamond' and was Presenter in 'Mrs Pleasance', written under a nom de plume for Pollock, Frederick Defell. Pollock (Frederick John Pollock of Hatton, 4th Baronet) was also co-director (with Frank Collins) of the Kingsway *Lower Depths* and co-translator (with Zinaida Vengerova) of *The Man Who was Dead*. Yavorskaya divorced Prince Baryatinsky in 1916.

[40] 'Things New: At the Theatres', review of *The Brothers Karamazov*, Stage Society, 1913, *The Sketch* (26 February 1913), 236.

[41] The production was revived and presented in Edinburgh in November 1914.

[42] '"Resting" and Revelling in the Simple Life: Princess Bariatinsky Prepares for a Strenuous Autumn', *The Tatler*, no. 633 (13 August 1913), 204.

The three large-scale novel adaptations were more admired for their high production values than for capturing the various essential elements of the source texts. However, a 'well-known Russian journalist' thought that the attention devoted to 'the local colour' in *Resurrection* was 'to the detriment of the "portée" of the whole play.' Moreover, some of that 'colour' was inauthentic: the conventions with kissing; leather rather than felt boots; and the gaiety of the singing and dancing during Easter night, which 'would be quite impossible... as the people are too exhausted by fasting and prayer'.[43] There were no such reservations about *Anna Karenina*, though. The souvenir programme marking the production's 101st performance cites endorsements from Russian correspondents: 'most scrupulous' in its 'fidelity to local colour', it 'surpasses all previous attempts to represent Russian life in Western Europe'; 'there has, to my knowledge, never been in London a play in which the social, emotional and pictorial sides of upper-class Russian society were shown with such fidelity. Not only in numerous small touches, but broad lines, too'.[44] Moreover, Yavorskaya was congratulated on the 'real greatness' and 'real genius' of her performance: 'she plays the more hysterical scenes with a great deal of intensity'.[45] Perhaps inevitably, verdicts on the adaptations themselves were more qualified, given the difficulty of condensing the action and thematic scope of such sprawling novels into a single evening's drama. Attempts to convey narrative sweep were generally at the expense of dramatic focus, detailed characterization, and, in the case of *Crime and Punishment*, the spiritual dimension. In Pollock's *Anna Karenina* Levin's story was eclipsed by Anna's.

1914–1940: AN OVERVIEW

During and immediately after World War One, Russian plays continued to appear in small-scale productions: Edith Craig introduced audiences to the Symbolist drama of Nikolay Evreinov and Leonid Andreev, and there were stagings of Tolstoy's comedy *The First Distiller* (*Pervyi vinokur*), directed by Nigel Playfair, at the Queen's in 1917, and of *Michael*, an adaptation by Miles Malleson of Tolstoy's short story 'What Men Live By' ('Chem lyudi zhivy'), at St Martin's and at the Old Vic in 1920.[46] There was also a major production of *Reparation*, an adaptation of *The Living Corpse* by Aylmer and Louise Maude, at the St James's in 1919; J. A. Fraser's designs were based on the Moscow Art Theatre's production, and the cast included Henry Ainley, Marion Terry, Ion Swinley, Athene Seyler, and Claude Rains. The next year *The Government Inspector* was revived at the Duke of York's,

[43] 'A Russian Critic of "Resurrection" ', unattributed press clipping about *Resurrection*, His Majesty's, 1903, production file of *Resurrection* at His Majesty's, 1903, V&A.

[44] G. de Wesselitsky, London correspondent of *Novoe Vremya*, and A. Werner, correspondent of *Russkoe Slovo*, in Souvenir Programme, *Anna Karenina*, Ambassadors, 1913, production file of *Anna Karenina* at Ambassadors Theatre, 1913, V&A.

[45] Excerpt from a review in *The Financier*, in Souvenir Programme, *Anna Karenina*, 1913; Review of *Anna Karenina*, Ambassadors, 1913, *Illustrated London News* (6 December 1913), 976.

[46] The production had been staged at the Birmingham Rep the previous year.

with Rains playing Khlestakov and Maurice Moscovitch the Mayor. Then, from the mid 1920s, Russian drama became a much more conspicuous presence on the London stage, due in particular to the fortuitous coincidence of the work of the 'little' theatres that sprang up around the country and to the significant contribution of the director of that *Government Inspector* of 1920, another Russian émigré, Fedor Komissarzhevsky, a former director of Moscow's Imperial Theatres who arrived in Britain in 1919.

During 1925 and 1926 a notable series of Chekhov productions in London sealed the playwright's enthusiastic adoption by the British. Following the success of James Bernard Fagan's *Cherry Orchard*—first presented by the Oxford Players in January 1925 and then revived at the Lyric, Hammersmith, and the Royalty—the producer Philip Ridgeway decided to mount a season of Chekhov's plays in London. This led to the famous sequence of Komissarzhevsky productions in a 'cramped', converted cinema at Barnes, arguably the most important British theatrical event of the decade.[47] However, Chekhov's were not the only Russian plays to appear at this time. The Barnes season also included Andreev's *Katerina* (*Ekaterina Ivanovna*), *The Government Inspector*—both directed by Komissarzhevsky—and *The Idiot* (*Idiot*), in 1926. In the same year the Birmingham Rep produced Andreev's *He Who Gets Slapped* (*Tot, kto poluchaet poshchechiny*), and Turgenev's *Month in the Country* received its British première in a production so successful that it was revived.

This series of Russian plays was part of a wider theatrical renaissance. Reviewing the theatrical 'situation in 1926', James Agate remarked that, thanks to inane musical comedy and plays about dope fiends and jazz-maniacs, 'roughly speaking, three-quarters of the London stage is closed to persons possessed of the slightest particle of intellect or the least feeling for drama.' Yet, thanks to a number of 'little', 'intellectual' theatres, there had never been a time 'when the general interest in, and preoccupation with, the drama was bigger both in London and throughout the country'.[48] As well as the various Sunday-play producing theatrical societies this burgeoning 'other theatre', to use Norman Marshall's term, comprised a series of non-commercial companies that were established in the 1920s and 1930s. Among those companies, the Everyman Theatre Guild in Hampstead, the Little Theatre, the Arts Theatre Club, the Mercury, the Left Theatre, and the Group Theatre, together with the Stage Society and theatres beyond London (such as the Birmingham Rep, the Oxford Players, and the Cambridge Festival Theatre), staged a variety of Russian plays, alongside works by Ibsen, Strindberg, Pirandello, Hauptmann, Cocteau, and O'Neill. It is interesting that, just as in subsequent years it became fashionable to use Chekhov—the metonym for ensemble—to launch new companies or projects, Russian plays were sometimes chosen to inaugurate inter-war theatrical ventures or particular seasons. For example, Dmitry Merezhkovsky's *Paul I* (*Pavel I*) at the Royal Court was the first—and only—project of Sloane Productions Limited, and Mikhail Bulgakov's *The White Guard* (*Belaya gvardiya*, also known as *The Days of the*

[47] Norman Marshall, *The Other Theatre* (London: John Lehman, 1947), 11.

[48] James Agate, *A Short View of the English Stage, 1900–1926* (London: Herbert Jenkins, 1926), 113–14.

Turbins (*Dni Turbinykh*)) was chosen to launch both the Ray Roddcliffe Players, in 1934, and Bronson Albery and Michel Saint-Denis's season at the Phoenix in 1938. (Their single performance of *The White Guard* was the Ray Roddcliffe Players' only production, while Albery and Saint-Denis's season extended to a second play, *Twelfth Night*.)

Notwithstanding their impressive output, these little theatres were driven by a relatively small group of theatre-makers. Particular names recur among the personnel involved in the Russian plays, including, for instance, Malcolm Morley and Milton Rosmer, actors, directors, and managers, associated especially with the Everyman; Barbara Nixon, translator, actor, and director; the Russian-born actor, director, and producer Michael Sherbrooke; the producer and director Anmer Hall (an alias of Alderson Burrell Horne); and such actors as Rains, Charles Laughton, and the coterie who worked with Komissarzhevsky, among them Elliott Seabrooke, Lydia Sherwood, W. E. E. Jenkins, and Vivian Beynon.

Amidst this activity, the Prague Group of the Moscow Art Theatre, established after the original company split in two in 1922, made two visits to London. Its productions impressed deeply, above all for the 'astonishing naturalism of the acting' that 'almost beggars description'.[49] In 1928 the Group presented eight plays during a four-week season at the Garrick, and in 1931 it staged nine bills at the Kingsway. The programmes included familiar works from the Russian repertoire—*The Government Inspector*, *The Lower Depths*, *The Power of Darkness*, *The Live Corpse*, *Brothers Karamazov*, *Crime and Punishment*, and Chekhov—as well as Ostrovsky's *Poverty is No Crime* (*Bednost' ne porok*), Gogol''s *Marriage* (*Zhenit'ba*), Bulgakov's *The White Guard*, and the Soviet satirical writer Valentin Kataev's *Quadrature of the Circle* (*Kvadratura kruga*). Other foreign productions of Russian plays and stage adaptations that visited London in the 1920s and 1930s included Andreev's *The Seven Who Were Hanged* (*Rasskaz o semi poveshennykh*) by the Yiddish Art Theatre of America (1924), Gaston Baty's (French) adaptation of *Crime and Punishment* (1934), and the Ohel Players' *Lower Depths* in Hebrew (1934).

So, from the mid 1910s to the mid 1930s, audiences were introduced to a rather different, much wider Russian repertoire from that of the early years of the century. Accordingly, even as Chekhov was being adopted by the 'priests of the sacred art', British audiences encountered, in stark opposition to the elegiac listlessness of his world, the 'vigour', 'vitality', and 'primitive local colour' of Ostrovsky, and a strong tradition of comedy, not only in Gogol' and Ostrovsky, but also in Kataev.[50] Moreover, in contrast to the naturalism exemplified by Chekhov, Gor'ky, and Tolstoy, they were introduced to symbolism and early socialist realism.

[49] Review of *The Marriage*, Prague Group, Garrick, 1928, *Times* (21 April 1928), 10.

[50] Treplev, in A. P. Chekhov, *The Seagull*, in *Polnoe sobranie sochinenii i pisem*, xiii (Moscow: Nauka, 1986), 8; Review of *Poverty is No Crime*, Prague Group, 1928, *The Times* (14 April 1928), 14; Review of *Bargains in Brides*, Charta Theatre, 1933, *The Times* (10 April 1933), 10; H. H., review of *The Storm*, Everyman, 1929, *The Observer* (8 December 1929), 15.

RUSSIAN SYMBOLISM

What was understood as Russian symbolism was represented on the English stage by the theatricalist plays of Evreinov and the neo-romantic drama of Andreev. These writers' work was first presented by the Pioneer Players, which was founded by Edith Craig in 1911 'with the object of producing Plays which may be outside the province of the commercial Theatre, as at present constituted, yet are none the less sincere manifestations of the dramatic spirit'.[51] In 1915–16 Edith Craig directed Evreinov's 'monodrama' *The Theatre of the Soul* (*V kulisakh dushi*), his harlequinade *A Merry Death*, and Andreev's satire *The Dear Departing* (*Lyubi soseda svoega*, literally *Love Thy Neighbour*) in a series of mixed bills. She directed *The Theatre of the Soul* again in 1931, for the People's Theatre, and in 1929 Evreinov's *The Theatre of Life* (*Teatr kak takovoi*, literally *The Theatre as Such*), adapted from a French translation, was staged by the Arts Theatre Club. Meanwhile, Andreev, who exemplified the Slavic focus on the spiritual and philosophical, emerged as the most performed Russian writer on the London stage after Chekhov during the 1920s. Apart from *The Dear Departing*, the Yiddish Art Theatre's *The Seven Who Were Hanged*, and Komissarzhevsky's *Katerina*, there were productions of: *The Painted Laugh* (an adaptation of the fragmentary novel *The Red Laugh* (*Krasnyi smekh*), a response to the Russo-Japanese War of 1904–5), which featured the American actress Khyva St Albans and received seven performances at the Garrick in 1921; *He Who Gets Slapped* and the anti-bourgeois satire *The Sabine Women* (*Prekrasnye sabinyanki*), staged at the Everyman (1927, 1928), which also planned a production of *The Seven Who Were Hanged*; and *Betrayal* (*Mysl'*, literally *Thought*), Andreev's dramatization of his story about the internal workings of the psyche, performed at the Little Theatre in 1931.[52]

Despite the relative popularity of Andreev, the reception of his and Evreinov's plays, like the modesty of their London productions, points to the limited compass of English interest in Russian modernist drama beyond the broadly naturalistic or realistic. Although there was grudging recognition of Evreinov's dramatic skills, his plays were generally dismissed as pretentious, portentous, and humourless; 'The Theatre of the Soul' 'did no more than dress up banality in unaccustomed robes'.[53] The 'curious' form and style of Andreev's plays proved similarly perplexing and irritating, and their emotional violence and darkness was off-putting.[54] Andreev's best known play was the highly theatrical and enigmatic *He Who Gets Slapped* (1915), which was made into a well regarded and popular film, directed by Victor Sjöström

[51] Programme note, 'A Merry Death' and *Ellen Young*, Pioneer Players, 1916, production file of *A Merry Death* at Savoy in 1916, V&A.

[52] *The [Fair] Sabine Women* was a curtain raiser for *The Dumb Man of Manchester*. The programme for this production refers to the plan to stage *The Seven Who Were Hanged*.

[53] M. D., 'It's Not Artistic', review of 'The Theatre of the Soul', People's Theatre, 1931, unidentified newspaper (3 June 1931), production file of 'Final *Rag of The Season*' ('The Theatre of the Soul', 'The Queen, God Bless Her!', 'Coals of Fire', and 'The Lost Silk Hat') at Fortune Theatre, 1931, V&A.

[54] Review of *The Sabine Women*, Everyman, 1928, *The Times* (4 April 1928), 12.

and starring Lon Chaney and Norma Shearer, and released in 1925. The play was staged at the Birmingham Rep in 1926, the year before it was produced at the Everyman, where it was directed by Milton Rosmer. Rosmer also played the role of He—a wealthy man who, deserted by his wife and cheated by his friend, seeks self-abasement as a clown in a circus. With its disconcerting mixture of realism and symbolism—involving abrupt changes in mood and tone, and a slyly ironic attitude towards symbolism—*He Who Gets Slapped* was deemed 'pretentious, and even twaddling', a 'morbid little play' that 'seemed to have the trappings and the suits of meaning but not meaning itself.'[55] The darkness of Andreev's vision was also evident in *The Seven Who Were Hanged*, which examines the vengeance wreaked on the tsarist government's opponents in the wake of the 1905 Revolution, and in *Katerina*.

FEDOR KOMISSARZHEVSKY

It is perhaps significant that, from Andreev's oeuvre, Komissarzhevsky and Ridgeway chose *Katerina* (1912) as the first alternative to Chekhov in their Russian season at Barnes. Although still philosophical and, to a degree, symbolist, it is less abstract and more naturalistic than Andreev's circus plays; it belongs, like *Thought*, to the strain of his drama that is intensely psychological and contains a distinct element of social criticism. Nevertheless, for one critic at least, the change from Chekhov to Andreev was 'unnerving'.[56] Indeed the reception of *Katerina* recalls the response to those early productions of Gor′ky and Tolstoy. Although the play was admired, its story of marital disintegration proved very foreign to an English sensibility. It represented a 'sickening study in degeneration', thanks to, according to Agate, its 'sex-obsession,... maundering delight in debauch,... maudlin itch for fine living and thinking... and morbid delight in revolvers and six-storey windows as means of compassing death'.[57] Notwithstanding their consternation at the play, critics praised the production for the qualities they had come to appreciate in Komissarzhevsky's Chekhovs: the careful orchestration and virtuosity of the direction and the quality of the acting.

Despite acquiring the reputation of a 'radical modernist' in England, especially for his Shakespeare productions at Stratford in the 1930s, on the whole Komissarzhevsky was conservative both in his choice of Russian plays and in his approach to their mise-en-scène on the English stage.[58] His shrewdness in reading

[55] See Andrew Barratt, 'Leonid Andreyev's *He Who Gets Slapped*: Who Gets Slapped?', in Robert Russell and Barratt, eds, *Russian Theatre in the Age of Modernism* (Houndmills: Macmillan, 1990), 101; St. J. E., review of *He Who Gets Slapped*, Everyman, 1927, *Observer* (13 November 1927), 15; Review of *He Who Gets Slapped*, Everyman, 1927, *Sunday Times* (13 November 1927), 6.

[56] H. H., review of *Katerina*, Barnes, 1926, *The Observer* (4 April 1926), biographic file of Cecil Madden, V&A.

[57] H. H., review of *Katerina*; James Agate, *The Contemporary Theatre, 1926* (London: Chapman and Hall, 1927), 61.

[58] Alexei Bartoshevich, 'Theodore Komisarjevsky, Chekhov, and Shakespeare', in Laurence Senelick, ed., *Wandering Stars: Russian Emigré Theatre, 1905–1940* (Iowa City, IA: University of Iowa Press, 1992), 103.

English audiences and his deftness in synthesizing different theatrical ideas was exemplified, of course, by his shameless romanticizing of Chekhov, whose drama this most un-Chekhovian of directors filtered 'through a mist of loveliness' in order 'to suit the public taste'.[59] His repertoire of Russian plays in England was very different from the one he pursued in St Petersburg and Moscow, at his sister Vera's Komissarzhevskaya Theatre, Nezlobin's Theatre, and his own studio. The only native realist work Komissarzhevsky staged in Russia was Ostrovsky's *Not a Farthing and Suddenly a Sixpence* (*Ne bylo ni grosha, da vdrug altyn*, or A *Change in Fortune*), which he staged in an iconoclastically non-naturalistic manner.[60] Otherwise, as well as Dostoevsky, he had directed a series of symbolist pieces by Remizov, Sologub, Andreev, and Kuzmin. *Katerina* was his only foray into that territory in England. When, in 1927 he staged Merezhkovsky, it was not one of the mystical, symbolist works more typical of the writer, but the old-fashioned, historical melodrama *Paul I*.

Although, in London, he forbore the avant-garde drama of the early twentieth century, with his second production of Gogol''s play Komissarzhevsky did offer English audiences a distinct taste of the expressionistic 'Synthetic Theatre' he fashioned in pre-Revolutionary Russia. Whereas his first production was fairly conventional and realistic, emphasizing broad comedy, at Barnes—in the same year as Meierkhol'd's seminal production—he turned *The Government Inspector* into 'a cubist ballet'.[61] The set was reminiscent of the fairground or toy-shop, with gaudy colours and a brass band: occupying most of the tiny stage was a brightly painted merry-go-round, which was used as a revolve to change scenes. This 'dynamic' approach to décor both complemented and helped to facilitate a distinctly expressionistic style of acting, very different from the naturalistic mode of Komissarzhevsky's Chekhovs and *Katerina*: the actors moved in a puppet-like manner, gesticulating extravagantly, and they declaimed their lines.[62] For Agate, who remembered the 1920 production as 'very funny', this 'frenzied', highly stylized staging was the 'dampest of squibs', which 'killed the play stone dead'; for 'Omicron', on the other hand, the production was a '*tour de force*', whose only jarring note was the translation, which was 'not stylized enough to suit the treatment.'[63]

From the outset Komissarzhevsky's British productions were hugely admired for their mise-en-scène, groupings, and stage pictures; the attention to detail in the design of sets, costumes, and lighting; the thorough preparation in rehearsal; and the calibre of the acting and the cohesive ensemble playing. *The Government Inspector* was rewarded with a transfer to the West End. Meanwhile the acting and pictorial qualities of *Paul I*, which featured Laughton as Count Pahlen, the military governor of St Petersburg, and the Shakespearean actor George Hayes (not to be

[59] Theodore Komisarjevsky, *Myself and the Theatre* (London: William Heinemann, 1929), 67.

[60] See Komisarjevsky, *Myself and the Theatre*, 92–3.

[61] 'Omicron', review of *The Government Inspector*, Barnes, 1926, *Nation and Athenaeum*, 22 May 1926, 176.

[62] Komisarjevsky, *Myself and the Theatre*, 148.

[63] Agate, *The Contemporary Theatre, 1926*, 50, 53; 'Omicron', review of *The Government Inspector*, 1926.

confused with the American film actor) as the tsar, served to flatter and enhance Merezhkovsky's rather pedestrian narrative of Paul I's assassination, such that some reviewers found the play 'remarkable'.[64] 'Omicron' insisted that it was 'the first play to see at the present moment'.[65]

Although *Paul I* and *The Brass Paperweight*—Komissarzhevsky's adaptation of *The Brothers Karamazov*, produced at the Apollo in 1928—enjoyed greater resources than the Barnes season, on the whole Komissarzhevsky was obliged to work in less than propitious circumstances. Like those of the theatrical societies and most 'little' theatre productions, the conditions were, in his description, 'cramping'. Comparing his experiences in England with those in Russia, Komissarzhevsky complained of the difficulties in working in the 'highbrow' English theatre, in particular problems with casting, insufficient rehearsals, and meagre resources for production.[66] Seldom was a rehearsal held on stage, or with the set ready before the sole dress rehearsal. For *Katerina* there were no sets for the dress, and on opening night, still with nothing finished, Komissarzhevsky had to improvise the set during the intervals, as well as prompt.[67]

ADAPTATIONS OF DOSTOEVSKY AND THE NINETEENTH-CENTURY CANON

The only common element to Komissarzhevsky's Russian repertoire in his homeland and in London was Dostoevsky. He had adapted and directed *The Idiot* at Nezlobin's Theatre in Moscow. For his production of *The Brass Paperweight* he also dramatized *The Brothers Karamazov* himself. This was one of five stage adaptations of Dostoevsky (apart from foreign productions) during the 1920s and 1930s, which points to the consolidation of the Russian novelist's position in the British theatre. *The Brothers Karamazov* was also staged at the Gate in 1925, in a version by George Merritt, and there were two productions of *Crime and Punishment*: a dramatization by Lena Ashwell and Roger Pocock, directed by Leslie Banks at the Century in 1927, and John Fernald's 1935 staging of the version by Gaston Baty (translated by D. L. Orna), whose more accomplished French production had transferred to London the previous year. The Barnes production of *The Idiot* was adapted and directed by Michael Hogan (the adaptation was under the alias Leahcim Nagoh, his name in reverse).

As with the adaptations of Tolstoy and Dostoevsky earlier in the century, reviewers noted the seemingly 'hopeless', 'impossible' task of condensing and shaping Dostoevsky's rambling, fragmented novels into satisfying drama as well as the

[64] E. A. Baugham, review of *Paul I*, Court, 1927, *Daily News* (6 October 1927), production file of *Paul I* at Royal Court, 1927, V&A; St. J. E., review of *Paul I*, Court, 1927, *The Observer* (9 October 1927), 15.

[65] 'Omicron', review of *Paul I*, Court, 1927, *Nation and Athenaeum* (15 October 1927), 84.

[66] Komisarjevsky, *Myself and the Theatre*, 160, 155.

[67] Komisarjevsky, *Myself and the Theatre*, 156–8.

tendency for melodrama to take precedence over psychological depth in characterization.[68] *The Brass Paperweight* was generally the most esteemed. Although Komissarzhevsky gave *The Brothers Karamazov* a happy ending by acquitting Dmitry, 'Omicron' appreciated that the play 'is not intended to be a representation of the novel' and credited Komissarzhevsky with extracting the original's 'violent nucleus'. He was also impressed that the characters 'remain the complicated creatures of Dostoevsky's imagination'.[69] Meanwhile, J. T. Grein considered the play 'perhaps the most effective' of all stage versions of *The Brothers Karamazov*—including Russian, French, and German (coincidentally, the Prague Group included its adaptation in its London season earlier that year).[70]

While Komiszarzhevsky was helping to cement the place of Dostoevsky, *The Government Inspector*, and Chekhov on the British stage, another key work of the nineteenth-century canon established itself in the repertoire. It is appropriate that, in the immediate wake of Ridgeway's sequence of Chekhov's plays in 1925–6, the 'Chekhovian' *Month in the Country* received its British première. As Agate observed, having come to appreciate Chekhov, the English could now understand Turgenev's play: 'the drawing-up of the curtain discloses one of those melancholy, sun-lit verandahs with which Mr. Komisarjevsky has made us familiar'.[71] The production, directed by Anmer Hall and produced by Michael Sherbrooke, who also played Shpigel′sky, ran for sixteeen performances at the Royalty in July 1926 and then, in October, transferred to the Fortune for another month. In 1930 Tyrone Guthrie directed the play at the Cambridge Festival Theatre, but the measure of its stature was Hall's choice to revive *A Month in the Country* to open the Group Theatre's season of 'unusual modern and classical plays' at the Westminster Theatre in 1936.[72] Three actors from the 1926 production, including Gillian Scaife, who played Natal′ya Petrovna, reprised their roles for the revival, while Dennis Arundell played Rakitin and Hall played Bol′shintsov, under another stage name: Waldo Wright. The production, which was directed by Michael MacOwan, emphasized the play's Chekhovian qualities: the languorous lack of action, the pathos and sweet melancholy commingled with comedy, and the fine characterization and focus on the ensemble. Proving 'even more exquisite' than it seemed ten years before, this *Month in the Country* ran for a month and then returned, for another month, to close the Group Theatre's season in May 1937.[73]

The next year at the Westminster, Hall produced Gogol′'s *Marriage*, also playing (as Waldo Wright) the central role of Podkolesin. The play had also been in both London seasons of the Prague Group and it had been staged at the Cambridge

[68] Review of *Crime and Punishment*, Century Theatre, 1927, *The Times* (8 February 1927), 12; Review of *The Idiot*, Barnes, 1926, *The Times* (24 August 1926), 8.

[69] 'Omicron', review of *The Brass Paperweight*, Apollo, 1928, *Nation and Athenaeum* (27 October 1928), 141.

[70] J. T. Grein, review of *The Brass Paperweight*, Apollo, 1928, *The Sketch*, (31 October 1928), 246.

[71] Agate, *The Contemporary Theatre, 1926*, 69.

[72] 'The Theatres', *The Times* (22 July 1936), 10.

[73] Agate, review of *A Month in the Country*, Westminster, 1936, *Sunday Times* (4 October 1936), 6.

Festival Theatre in 1929, directed by Guthrie, and at Oxford.[74] Although very funny, *Marriage* was deemed a much lesser play than *The Government Inspector*. Meanwhile, the other great nineteenth-century Russian playwright, Ostrovsky, a writer who has remained relatively overlooked in Britain, finally received his first professional, English-language productions. There had in fact been an abridged reading of *The Storm* (*Groza*) at the Opera Comique in 1894, organized by J. T. Grein. The play was read poorly by the thickly accented émigré Sergey Stepnyak, who also delivered a lecture on Russian drama.[75] In the late 1910s and early 1920s, several of Ostrovsky's plays were performed in London in amateur productions in both English and Russian, and the Prague Group presented *Poverty is No Crime* in its 1928 season.[76] The next year Malcolm Morley directed *The Storm* at the Everyman, and in 1933, at the Charta Theatre, he directed *Bargains in Brides* (*Bogatye nevesty*), paired with Hubert Griffith's *The People's Court*, a play about justice in the Soviet Union.

In his 1927 *History of Russian Literature from the Earliest Times to the Death of Dostoevsky*, Mirsky states that Ostrovsky's plays 'have not universal significance'; 'the saturation of the atmosphere with the very essence of Russian *byt* [everyday life] and Russian poetical feeling' makes a play like *The Storm* 'hardly understandable to a foreigner'.[77] This view of Ostrovsky as peculiarly alien and inaccessible in his Russianness has become a recurring theme of his reception in Britain. However, in the theatre in the late 1920s and 1930s that perception was not so apparent. The *Times* reviewer of the Prague Group's *Poverty is No Crime* and the Everyman's *Storm* conceded that Ostrovsky depicts a class of provincial merchants and denizens who are somewhat unfamiliar, and he and Agate acknowledged that Ostrovsky may lack the poignancy and poetry of Turgenev or the 'technical subtlety' of 'the brilliant, but not very representative,' Chekhov.[78] However, they found Ostrovsky's characterization and story-telling refreshingly direct and vital, and they appreciated his modernity in pioneering naturalism on the stage. Moreover, the plays (including *The Storm*) proved comic and entertaining. All these attributes were evident in Morley's productions.

It is curious that, while works by Chekhov, Dostoevsky, Gogol′, and Turgenev were consolidating their place in the British repertoire, and while attempts were made to claim a place for Ostrovsky, the two playwrights who had been so

[74] See 'The Theatres: Gogol's *Marriage*', *The Times* (6 June 1938), 8.

[75] J. T. Grein, review of *The Storm*, Everyman, 1929, *The Sketch*, (18 December 1929), 604.

[76] In 1919 the Russian Dramatical Society staged *Poverty is No Crime* and *Christmas Comes But Once a Year* (*Ne vse kotu maslenitsa*, literally *It's Not All Shrovetide for the Cat*) in Russian; and the Pax Robertson Salon, an amateur group led by Miss Pax Robertson, presented *It's a Family Affair* (*Semeinaya kartina*, or *It's All in the Family*) in 1922 and *Poverty is No Crime* in 1923. See Sealey Rahman, 'Ostrovskii on the British Stage: 1894–1928'.

[77] D. S. Mirsky, *A History of Russian Literature from the Earliest Times to the Death of Dostoevsky (1881)* (London: George Routledge & Son, 1927), 306, 310–11.

[78] Review of *The Storm*, Everyman, 1929, *The Times* (4 December 1929), 12; Review of *Poverty is No Crime*, Prague Group, *The Times*, 14. See also James Agate, 'An Early Masterpiece', review of *The Storm*, Everyman, 1929, *Sunday Times* (8 December 1929), 6.

prominent in the first two decades of the twentieth century were largely eclipsed. Gor′ky almost disappeared: the sole local production was Barbara Nixon's adaptation of his novel *The Mother* (*Mat′*) for the Left Theatre in 1935. Meanwhile, in 1928 the Arts Theatre Club, in collaboration with the Tolstoy Society and the theatre impresario (and founder of the Independent Theatre) J. T. Grein, marked the centenary of Tolstoy's birth with a revival of *The Power of Darkness* and a production of *The Fruits of Enlightenment* (*Plody prosveshcheniya*). Although the Club's *Power of Darkness* suffered by comparison with the Prague Group's production six months earlier, the pairing proved instructive: the tragic tone and severe portrayal of peasant barbarism in the former, familiar play were usefully offset by its companion piece's lighter, humorous tone and much more affectionate representation of the peasants.

SOVIET DRAMA

As well as a growing selection of plays from the nineteenth-century Russian canon, a range of contemporary, Soviet plays was also staged in London in the 1920s and 1930s. However, although often intriguing as a window on life in the Soviet Union and on Bolshevik ideology, like the 'Decadent' drama of Evreinov and Andreev they largely failed to make a significant or lasting impression. Given the English theatre's predilection for social and psychological realism, it is not surprising that producers overlooked the epic or romantic-heroic strain of Soviet drama exemplified by Vsevolod Vishnevsky and Nikolay Pogodin in favour of the plays of Aleksandr Afinogenov and Vladimir Kirshon, whose writing links back to the nineteenth-century realist tradition, and who laid the foundations for the socialist realism that duly became the prescribed form of artistic expression. Three years after its Russian première, Kirshon and Aleksandr Uspensky's schematic *Red Rust* (*Rzhavshchina*) was staged at the Little in 1929; its story of a false communist and an heroic idealist (played by Ion Swinley and John Gielgud) proved to be melodramatic, 'Bolshevist' 'propaganda'.[79] *Fear* (*Strakh*), Afinogenov's most popular play, which premièred at the Moscow Art Theatre in 1931, was presented by the Stage Society in 1932. The play was controversial in the Soviet Union for its story of a scientist, Ivan Borodin, who is not in tune with the new regime and whose research reveals that the principal stimulus determining the behaviour of Soviet citizens is fear. Although a more complex dialectical work than *Red Rust*, *Fear* nevertheless follows orthodox Marxist logic in identifying Borodin as anti-proletarian and counter-revolutionary. Consequently, 'there is no life in the characters' and no drama in the scenario.[80] Three years previously the Stage Society also produced an example of Bolshevik historical revisionism: *Rasputin*, an adaptation by the playwright Clifford Bax of

[79] Richard Jennings, review of *Red Rust*, Little Theatre, 1929, *The Spectator* (16 March 1929), 417; Review of *Red Rust*, Little Theatre, 1929, *The Times* (1 March 1929), 14.

[80] Review of *Fear*, Stage Society, 1932, *The Times* (28 November 1932), 12. See also review by John Pollock, *Saturday Review* (3 December 1932), 588.

Aleksey Tolstoy's and the historian Pavel Shchegolev's play *The Empress's Conspiracy* (*Zagovor Imperatritsy*), which Erwin Piscator had adapted in Berlin in 1927. Again the play failed to impress, offering neither 'imaginative insight into character' nor 'pageantry'.[81] More dramatically satisfying and entertaining than these plays was Kataev's *Squaring the Circle*, the most popular comedy in the Soviet repertoire, whose story of two mismatched young couples obliged to share a single room because of a severe housing shortage satirizes both communist idealism and shallow bourgeois values.[82] Having been presented by the Prague Group in 1931, the play was staged at the Mercury Theatre in 1934.

The most highly regarded of these new Russian plays, and an exemplar of modern Russian realism, was Bulgakov's *The White Guard*, based on his novel about members of the Turbin family—intellectuals and officers of the tsarist army—during the civil war of 1918–19. It was given a single performance by the Ray Roddcliffe Players at the Ambassadors Theatre in 1934 and then a much more substantial, and acclaimed production, directed by Michel Saint-Denis, at the Phoenix in 1938. Coming in the wake of Saint-Denis's similarly esteemed *Three Sisters* (*Try sestry*) earlier that year at the Queen's, and including several of the same cast (Michael Redgrave, Peggy Ashcroft, Glen Byam Shaw, and George Devine), the second production especially highlighted the play's Chekhovian qualities: its essential inaction and lack of plot, and its finely detailed relationships and emphasis on the ensemble. For Peter Fleming there was no play in London that was 'better written, better acted, or better produced'.[83]

While many of the more modest productions of Russian plays were also highly praised despite their limited resources, some did not do justice to their scripts. For example, the Everyman's stage seemed 'too small for realizing the theatrical possibilities' of *He Who Gets Slapped*, and the theatre's production of *The Storm*, notwithstanding the case it made for Ostrovsky's play, was 'tentative and untidy'.[84] On the whole, however, despite any shortcomings in performance, producers were commended for their enterprise and 'the sincerity and liveliness of their attempt[s]' in staging Russian drama.[85] Some of those plays—such as Gogol''s *Marriage*—were deemed 'flimsy',[86] but they were more likely to be judged pretentious and highfaluting, for Russian art continued to be thought of as intellectual and esoteric. The *Spectator*'s reviewer approached *Paul I*, for instance, in trepidation, anticipating that Merezhkovsky's melodrama would prove 'both highbrow and obscure': 'The title frightened me—it sounded so eminently instructive. The names of the author and producer terrified me still more—they were so uncompromisingly Russian'.[87]

[81] Review of *Rasputin*, Stage Society, 1929, *Times* (23 April 1929), 14.

[82] Harold B. Segel, *Twentieth-Century Russian Drama: From Gorky to the Present* (New York: Columbia University Press, 1979), 182.

[83] Ivor Brown, review of *The White Guard*, Phoenix, 1938, *The Spectator* (14 October 1938), 603.

[84] 'Omicron', review of *He Who Gets Slapped*, Everyman, 1927, *Nation and Athenaeum* (19 November 1927), 277; H. H., review of *The Storm*, 1929, 15.

[85] Review of *He Who Gets Slapped*, Everyman, 1927, *The Times* (9 November 1927), 12.

[86] Review of *The Marriage*, Westminster, 1938, *Illustrated London News* (25 June 1938), 1180.

[87] F. Y-B., review of *Paul I*, *The Spectator* (15 October 1927), 603.

Although the foreignness of these Russian plays and their worldview sometimes provoked dismay and even resistance, there was also recognition of the need to respect that foreignness. In 1921 Agate observed that Chekhov's characters 'are, oh, so exasperatingly Russian!' Consequently, 'We watch these people curiously, but without comprehension and almost without pity.'[88] However, less than four years later he scorned such insularity: ' "These Russians have a very un-English way of looking at things," I heard a lady say at the conclusion of [*The Cherry Orchard*]. That's our trouble. "If people are not English, they ought to be," puts our view in a nutshell.'[89] Moreover, he registered the need to respect the difference of these Russians and their world from the English. Confronted by Andreev's 'studies of a way of life so utterly foreign and antipathetic to our own', Agate advised, 'We must not be too English if we would get the best out of the[m].'[90] He and others even advocated marking that otherness in performance. Both Agate and Fleming noted the failure of the actors in Saint Denis's *White Guard*, in which the acting was otherwise 'above praise', to 'behave like Slavs'.[91] This was impressed upon them and Ivor Brown by the exceptional performance of George Devine, who, as Viktor Mishlaevsky, 'is the Russian woolly bear itself'.[92]

Although Agate and others might crave greater authenticity in the portrayal of Russian character and colour (however dubious such authenticity might actually be), the growing appreciation of Russian drama in Britain in the first decades of the twentieth century was due in no small part to the identification of dramatic forms and of a sensibility that corresponded to English tastes. Consequently, the English developed a clear preference for the 'Europeanized sophistication of Chekhov', Turgenev, Bulgakov, and plays in their mould.[93] In time even Gor′ky would be re-imagined to fit that mould, as plays such as *Summerfolk* (*Dachniki*) and *Philistines*, which focus on the gentry, displaced *The Lower Depths* in the repertoire. However, in the earlier part of the twentieth century, the English also discovered something of the richness and freshness of Russian modernist alternatives to naturalism as well as a very different sensibility and worldview, which Marsh describes as 'localised, sometimes barbaric, sometimes cruel'.[94] As a reviewer of the Prague Group's 1928 presentation of *Poverty is No Crime* registered, that other view of Russian culture is actually much more representative of Russian drama than is Chekhov.[95] The Royal Court's recent flirtation with the works of Sigarev suggests that a fascination with that other tradition resurfaces from time to time, prompting the more genteel once more to avert their eyes and hold their noses.

[88] James Agate, *At Half-Past Eight: Essays of the Theatre, 1921–1922* (London: Jonathan Cape, 1923), 183.

[89] James Agate, *The Contemporary Theatre, 1925* (London: Chapman and Hall, 1926), 77.

[90] Agate, *The Contemporary Theatre, 1926*, 60.

[91] Peter Fleming, review of *The White Guard*, Phoenix 1938, *The Spectator* (14 October 1938), 603. See also Agate, *The Amazing Theatre*, 194.

[92] Brown, review of *The White Guard*, 1938.

[93] Cynthia Marsh, *Maxim Gorky: Russian Dramatist* (Bern: Peter Lang, 2006), 358.

[94] Marsh, *Maxim Gorky*, 358.

[95] Review of *Poverty is No Crime*, Prague Group, 1928, *The Times*, 14.

APPENDIX

Productions of Russian Plays and Adaptations of Russian Novels on the London Stage, 1900–1940

This is as complete a record of productions at professional theatres as I have been able to compile, drawing principally from the relevant series of volumes of J. P. Wearing, *The London Stage: A Calendar of Plays and Players*, 1900–1909, 1910–19, 1920–29, and 1930–39 (Metuchen, NJ: Scarecrow Press, 1981–90); the Victoria and Albert Museum Department of Theatre and Performance Collections; and Patrick Miles, *Chekhov on the British Stage 1909–1987: An Essay in Cultural Exchange* (England: Sam & Sam, 1987). A number of significant productions from other British cities have also been included.

Playwright	Play	Director	Company/ Theatre	First performance
Tolstoy, adpt. Henri Bataille (trans. and adpt. Michael Morton)	*Resurrection* (*Voskresenie*)	Percy Nash	His Majesty's	17 Feb. 1903
Gor'ky	*The Lower Depths* (*Na dne*)	Max Behrend	Stage Society, Royal Court; Great Queen St.	29 Nov. 1903
Tolstoy	*The Power of Darkness* (*Vlast' t'my*)	Max Behrend	Stage Society, Royalty	18 Dec. 1904
Tolstoy, adpt. Henri Bataille	*Resurrection* (in French)	Gaston Mayer	New Royalty	12 Feb. 1906
Gor'ky	*Nachtasyl* (*The Lower Depths*, in German)		Great Queen St.	16 Feb. 1906
Gor'ky	*The Bezsemenovs* (*Meshchane*, also known as *Philistines*)	Philip Carr	Mermaid Society, Terry's Theatre	23 Apr. 1906
Gogol'	*The Inspector-General* (*Revizor*)	Charles Rock	Stage Society, Scala	17 June 1906
Turgenev	*The Bread of Others* (*Nakhlebnik*)	William Haviland	Stage Society, Kingsway	21 Feb. 1909
Chekhov	*The Seagull* (*Chaika*)	George Calderon	Repertory Theatre, Glasgow	2 Nov. 1909

(*Continued*)

(*Continued*)

Playwright	Play	Director	Company/ Theatre	First performance
Ostrovsky	*Vassilissa Melentieva* (*Vasilisa Melent'eva*; Act V; in Russian)		His Majesty's	30 Nov. 1909
Dostoevsky, adpt. Laurence Irving ('H. M. Clark')	*The Unwritten Law* (*Crime and Punishment* (*Prestuplenie i nakazanie*))	Laurence Irving	Gaiety, Manchester; Garrick; Kingsway	15 Aug.; 14 Nov.; 26 Dec. 1910
Chekhov	*The Bear* (*Medved'*)	Lidiya Yavorskaya	Kingsway	13 May 1911
Chekhov	*The Cherry Orchard* (*Vishnevyi sad*)	Kenelm Foss	Stage Society, Aldwych	28 May 1911
Gor'ky	*The Lower Depths* (*Na dne*)	John Pollock and Frank Collins	Kingsway	2 Dec. 1911
Chekhov	*The Seagull* (*Chaika)*	Maurice Elvey	Adelphi Stage Society, Little	31 Mar. 1912
Tolstoy	*The Cause of It All* (*O nei vse kachestva*)		Adelphi Stage Society, Little	28 Apr. 1912
Tolstoy	*The Man Who was Dead* (*The Living Corpse* (*Zhivoi trup*))	A. Andreev	Literary Theatre Society, Court	6 Dec. 1912
Dostoevsky, adpt. Jacques Copeau and Jean Croué	*The Brothers Karamazov* (*Brat'ya Karamazovy*)	Frederick Whelen	Stage Society, Aldwych	16 Feb. 1913
Tolstoy, adpt. John Pollock	*Anna Karenina*		Ambassadors; La Scala	1 Dec. 1913; 13 Apr. 1914
Chekhov	*Uncle Vanya* (*Dyadya Vanya*)	Guy Rathbone	Stage Society, Aldwych	10 May 1914
Evreinov	*The Theatre of the Soul* (*V kulisakh dushi*)	Edith Craig	Pioneer Players, Little; Shaftesbury; Savoy	7 Mar. 1915; 3 Dec. 1915; 7 Apr. 1916
Andreev	*The Dear Departing* (*Lyubi soseda svoega*)	Edith Craig	Pioneer Players, Court	6 Feb. 1916
Evreinov	*A Merry Death* (*Veselaya smert'*)	Edith Craig	Pioneer Players, Savoy	2 Apr. 1916
Tolstoy	*The First Distiller* (*Pervyi vinokur*)	Nigel Playfair	Birmingham Rep; Queen's	26 Oct. 1916; 26 June 1917
Chekhov	*The Wedding* (*Svad'ba*)	Nigel Playfair	Russian Exhibition, Grafton Galleries	May 1917
Chekhov	The Proposal (*Predlozhenie*)	A.E. Drinkwater	St James's	3 Dec. 1918

(*Continued*)

(*Continued*)

Playwright	Play	Director	Company/ Theatre	First performance
Chekhov	*The Seagull* (*Chaika*)	Vera Donnet	Art Theatre, Haymarket	2 June 1919
Tolstoy	*Reparation* (*The Living Corpse* (*Zhivoi trup*))	Stanley Bell	Grand Theatre, Leeds; St James's	18 Aug.; 26 Sept. 1919
Chekhov	*The Bear* (*Medved'*), *On the High Road* (*Na bol'shoi doroge*), *The Wedding* (*Svad'ba*)	A. E. Filmer; Edith Craig; Craig	Pioneer Players, St Martin's	25 Jan. 1920
Chekhov	*Three Sisters* (*Tri sestry*)	Vera Donnet	Art Theatre, Court	7 Mar. 1920
Gogol'	*The Government Inspector* (*Revizor*)	Fedor Komissarzhevsky	Duke of York's	13 Apr. 1920
Tolstoy, adpt. Miles Malleson	*Michael* (*Chem lyudi zhivy*)		St Martin's-in-the-Fields Players, St Martin's	28 Apr. 1920
Chekhov; Tolstoy, adpt. Miles Malleson	*The Proposal* (*Predlozhenie*); *Michael* (*Chem lyudi zhivy*)	Stockwell Hawkins	1920 Players, Old Vic	18 May 1920
Chekhov	*The Cherry Orchard* (*Vishnevyi sad*)	Vera Donnet	Art Theatre, St Martin's	11 July 1920
Chekhov	*The Anniversary* (*Yubilei*)	C. Graham-Cameron	Repertory Players, Kingsway	8 May 1921
Andreev	*The Painted Laugh* (*Krasnyi smekh*)	Oswald Marshall and Khyva St. Albans	Garrick	16 Nov. 1921
Chekhov	*Uncle Vanya* (*Dyada Vanya*)	Fedor Komissarzhevsky	Stage Society, Royal Court	27 Nov. 1921
Andreev	*The Seven Who Were Hanged* (*Rasskaz o semi poveshennykh*, in Yiddish)	Maurice Swartz and Leonid Sniegoff	Yiddish Art Theatre of America, Scala; Prince of Wales	28 Apr. 1924
Chekhov	*The Cherry Orchard* (*Vishnevyi sad*)	J. B. Fagan	Oxford Playhouse; Lyric Hammersmith; Royalty	Jan.; 25 May; 22 June 1925
Dostoevsky, adpt. George Meritt	*Crime and Punishment* (*Prestuplenie i nakazanie*)		Gate	1925
Chekhov	*The Seagull* (*Chaika*)	A. E. Filmer	Little	19 Oct. 1925
Chekhov	*Ivanov* (*Ivanov*)	Fedor Komissarzhevsky	Stage Society, Duke of York's; Barnes	6 Dec.; 23 Dec. 1925

(*Continued*)

(*Continued*)

Playwright	Play	Director	Company/ Theatre	First performance
Chekhov	*Uncle Vanya* (*Dyadya Vanya*)	Fedor Komissarzhevsky	Barnes; Duke of York's	16 Jan.; 15 Feb. 1926
Chekhov	*Three Sisters* (*Tri sestry*)	Fedor Komissarzhevsky	Barnes	16 Feb. 1926
Andreev	*He Who Gets Slapped* (*Tot, kto poluchaet poshchechiny*)	H. K. Ayliff	Birmingham Rep	21 Feb. 1926
Andreev	*Katerina* (*Ekaterina Ivanovna*)	Fedor Komissarzhevsky	Barnes	30 Mar. 1926
Gogol′	*Government Inspector* (*Revizor*)	Fedor Komissarzhevsky	Barnes; Gaiety	28 Apr.; 22 May 1926
Chekhov	*The Bear* (*Medved′*)	Nancy Price	Everyman	24 May 1926
Turgenev	*A Month in the Country* (*Mesyats v derevne*)	Anmer Hall	Royalty; Fortune	5 July; 6 Oct. 1926
Dostoevsky, adpt. Michael Hogan	*The Idiot* (*Idiot*)	Michael Hogan	Barnes; Little	23 Aug.; 7 Sept. 1926
Chekhov	*The Cherry Orchard* (*Vishnevyi sad*)	Fedor Komissarzhevsky	Barnes	28 Sept. 1926
Dostoevsky, adpt. Lena Ashwell and Roger Pocock	*Crime and Punishment* (*Prestuplenie i nakazanie*)	Leslie Banks	Century	7 Feb. 1927
Merezhkovsky	*Paul I* (*Pavel I*)	Fedor Komissarzhevsky	Court	4 Oct. 1927
Andreev	*He Who Gets Slapped* (*Tot, kto poluchaet poshchechiny*)	Milton Rosmer	Everyman	8 Nov. 1927
Chekhov	*The Proposal* (*Predlozhenie*)	Boris Ranevsky	International Theatre Society, Arts	26 Feb. 1928
Andreev	*The Sabine Women* (*Prekrasnye sabinyanki*)	Milton Rosmer and Malcolm Morley	Everyman	3 Apr. 1928

Moscow Art Theatre Prague Group visit to London, Garrick, April 1928:

Gogol′, *The Marriage* (*Zhenit′ba*); Ostrovsky, *Poverty is No Crime* (*Bednost′ ne porok*); Gor′ky, *The Lower Depths* (*Na dne*); Tolstoy, *The Power of Darkness* (*Vlast′ t′my*), *The Live Corpse* (*Zhivoi trup*); Dostoevsky, *Brothers Karamazov* (*Brat′ya Karamazovy*); Chekhov, *Uncle Vanya* (*Dyadya Vanya*), *The Cherry Orchard* (*Vishnevyi sad*).

Dostoevsky, adpt. Komissarzhevsky	*The Brass Paperweight (Brothers Karamazov (Brat'ya Karamazovy))*	Fedor Komissarzhevsky	Apollo	15 Oct. 1928
Tolstoy	*The Power of Darkness (Vlast' t'my)*	Michael Orme	Arts Theatre Club	30 Oct. 1928
Tolstoy	*The Fruits of Enlightenment (Plody prosveshcheniya)*	W. Keith Moss	Arts Theatre Club	2 Nov. 1928
Chekhov	*The Seagull (Chaika)*	A. E. Filmer	Arts Theatre Club; Fortune	16 Jan.; 25 Sept. 1929
Vladimir Kirshon and Aleksandr Uspensky	*Red Rust (Rzhavshchina)*	Frank Vernon	Little	28 Feb. 1929
Evreinov	*The Theatre of Life (Teatr kak takovoi)*	Frank Birch	Arts Theatre Club	5 Apr. 1929
Aleksey Tolstoy and Pavel Shchegolev	*Rasputin (The Empress's Conspiracy (Zagovor imperatritsy))*	Robert Atkins	Strand	21 Apr. 1929
Chekhov	*Three Sisters (Tri sestry)*	Fedor Komissarzhevsky	Fortune	23 Oct. 1929
Ostrovsky	*The Storm (Groza)*	Malcolm Morley	Everyman	3 Dec. 1929
Andreev	*Betrayal (Thought (Mysl'))*	David Horne	Little	7 Jan. 1931
Evreinov	*The Theatre of the Soul (V kulisakh dushi)*	Edith Craig	People's Theatre, Fortune	31 May 1931

Moscow Art Theatre Prague Group visit to London, Kingsway, November–December 1931: Gogol', *The Government Inspector* (*Revizor*), *The Marriage* (*Zhenit'ba*); Bulgakov, *The White Guard* (*Belaya gvardiya*, also known as *The Days of the Turbins* (*Dni Turbinykh*)); Kataev, *Quadrature of the Circle* (*Kvadratura kruga*); Dostoevsky, *Crime and Punishment* (*Prestuplenie i nakazanie*); Gor'ky, *The Lower Depths* (*Na dne*); Chekhov, *The Proposal* (*Predlozhenie*), *The Jubilee* (*Yubilei*), *Forgotten* (*Zabyl!!*), *The Physician* (*Khirurgiya*), *The Cherry Orchard (Vishnevyi sad).*

Afinogenov	*Fear (Strakh)*	Claud Gurney	Stage Society, Westminster	27 Nov. 1932
Ostrovsky	*Bargains in Brides (Bogatye nevesty)*	Malcolm Morley	Charta	9 Apr. 1933
Chekhov	*The Cherry Orchard (Vishnevyi sad)*	Tyrone Guthrie	Old Vic	9 Oct. 1933
Kataev	*Squaring the Circle (Kvadratura kruga)*		Mercury	27 Feb. 1934

(*Continued*)

Chekhov	*A Swan Song* (*Lebedinaya pesnya*)	Leonard Gibson Cowan	St Martin's	4 Mar. 1934
Bulgakov	*The White Guard* (*Belaya gvardiya*, also known as *The Days of the Turbins* (*Dni Turbinykh*)	Claud Gurney	Ray Roddcliffe Players, Ambassadors	11 Mar. 1934
Chekhov	*The Proposal* (*Predlozhenie*)	Oliver Reynolds	Arts; International One-Act Play Theatre, Kingsway	13 May 1934; 27 Jan. 1935
Dostoevsky, adpt. Gaston Baty	*Crime and Punishment* (*Prestuplenie i nakazanie*, in French)	Gaston Baty	New	14 May 1934
Gor′ky	*The Lower Depths* (*Na dne*, in Hebrew)	M. Halevy	Ohel Players, Scala	10 July 1934
Dostoevsky, adpt. Gaston Baty	*Crime and Punishment* (*Prestuplenie i nakazanie*)	John Fernald	Embassy	26 Feb. 1935
Chekhov	*Three Sisters* (*Tri sestry*)	Henry Cass	Old Vic	12 Nov. 1935
Gor′ky, adpt. Barbara Nixon	*The Mother* (*Mat′*)	Barbara Nixon	Left Theatre, Phoenix; various town halls	17 Nov. 1935
Chekhov	*The Seagull* (*Chaika*)	Fedor Komissarzhevsky	New	20 May 1936
Turgenev	*A Month in the Country* (*Mesyats v derevne*)	Michael MacOwan	Group Theatre, Westminster	30 Sept. 1936; 25 May 1937
Chekhov	*Uncle Vanya* (*Dyadya Vanya*)	Michael MacOwan	Westminster	5 Feb. 1937
Chekhov	*Three Sisters* (*Tri sestry*)	Michel Saint-Denis	Queen's	28 Jan. 1938
Gogol′	*The Marriage* (*Zhenit′ba*)	Rollo Gamble	Westminster	15 June 1938
Bulgakov	*The White Guard* (*Belaya gvardiya*, also known as *The Days of the Turbins* (*Dni Turbinykh*))	Michel Saint-Denis	Phoenix	6 Oct. 1938

6

Tsar's Hall

Russian Music in London, 1895–1926

Philip Ross Bullock

On 1 April 1897, the following piece of doggerel was published in the *Musical Times*:

Though critics say what I compose
Is generally good,
My name is one that no one knows,
Although you'd think they would.

Not one that ends in 'reff' or 'koff'
The present writer owns;
I wish my name was Goodenoff,
Unhappily it's Jones.

Glazounoff, Balakireff, some
Think very gifted men;
Liadoff, Rachmaninoff, come
Among the upper ten;

But at my name folks simply scoff,
It lacks Slavonic tones;
If only it were Goodenoff
Unhappily it's Jones!

Tschaïkowsky, now, they well may praise,
I could not rival him,
His music is no passing craze,
No fashionable whim.

But I might almost be a toff
In such exalted zones,
If only I were Goodenoff
Instead of simply Jones.

Borodine and Korsakoff make,
In ev'ry sense, a noise
In England now; I can't mistake
What all the world enjoys.

Great bangs, like cannon going off,
And melancholy moans,

That I should do as Goodenoff,
    But cannot do as Jones.

So for the future I'll be dumb,
    Composing nothing more,
Because, you see, I do not come
    From any foreign shore.

Nor will I play, unless at 'golf,'
    Or on the nigger's bones;
My name is never Goodenoff,
    I can't succeed as Jones.[1]

'Russian Rivalry' may read like an April Fools' skit, yet it also points to key themes in the reception of Russian music in Britain from the late nineteenth century onwards. Not only does it propose a list of the kind of composers then likely to be heard in British concert halls, but it also characterizes Russian music in terms of its emotional intensity ('Great bangs, like cannon going off, / And melancholy moans'), its appeal to popular audiences (Chaikovsky's music 'is no passing craze, / No fashionable whim'), and its tendency to cast local composers into the shade ('My name is never Goodenoff, / I can't succeed as Jones').

Although the poem does not mention it by name, the principal venue for performances of Russian music in London (and, indeed, Britain as a whole) was Queen's Hall, Langham Place. Opened in 1893, it hosted the Promenade Concerts from 1895 under the management of Robert Newman and musical direction of Henry Wood. One of Wood's greatest features was, in Robert Elkin's description, 'the extraordinary catholicity of his musical sympathies', something most evident in his espousal of Russian music. Indeed, so frequent were performances of Russian works at Queen's Hall that it prompted 'one critic of the eighteen-nineties to remark that the Hall ought to be renamed "Tsar's Hall"'.[2] Wood's dedication to Russian music has sometimes been attributed to his marriage to a Russian singer, and certainly Olga Wood appears with considerable frequency in the programmes of the Promenade Concerts at Queen's Hall. Yet to attribute the prominence of Russian music there solely to Wood's personal predilections would be to underestimate financial and institutional factors shaping the selection of repertoire. As Leanne Langley argues, 'Newman was a commercial animal, shrewdly promoting events and managing people like shares on the market.'[3] The volume of Russian works heard at Queen's Hall would have been unthinkable had audiences not wanted to hear it, and it was this sense of popular demand that constitutes one of the Proms' principal contributions to musical life in turn-of-the-century Britain.[4]

[1] 'Russian Rivalry', *Musical Times*, 38, no. 650 (1 April 1897), 234.

[2] Robert Elkin, *Queen's Hall, 1893–1941* (London: Rider & Co., 1944), 29.

[3] Leanne Langley, 'Building an Orchestra, Creating an Audience: Robert Newman and the Queen's Hall Promenade Concerts, 1895–1926', in Jenny Doctor and David Wright, eds, *The Proms: A New History* (London: Thames & Hudson, 2007), 39.

[4] Beyond the scope of the present chapter is the study of the presence of Russian music outside London, particularly at the provincial festivals and music societies that were such a feature of Victorian and Edwardian British musical life. On this growing field of scholarly enquiry, see in particular Pippa

At the opposite end of the institutional spectrum were the old universities of Oxford and Cambridge, as well as the more recently founded Royal College of Music in London (1883). Here, emphasis was placed on the established Austro-German repertoire, which was held up as a model for performers, composers, and students alike.[5] In particular, establishment figures such as Hubert Parry (director of the Royal College from 1895 and professor at Oxford from 1900) and Charles Stanford (professor of composition at the Royal College from 1882 and professor at Cambridge from 1885) advocated what they saw as the structural integrity and formal abstraction of the symphonies of Schumann and Brahms as the highest point of musical development. This view led them to regard newer and more unconventional repertoires as artistically substandard. Parry, for instance, suggested that 'it seems to be the rule with the artistic work of Slavs that the power of creating intrinsic interest is considerable, but that the faculties which are needed for concentration and systematic mastery of balance of design are proportionately weak'.

Furthermore, Parry's arguments rested on a racial historiography that drew on Darwinist theories to argue for the inherent inferiority of Russian music:

> The qualities of races but little advanced from primitive temperamental conditions are even more conspicuous in the Russian music which has almost submerged the world, especially England, in the closing years of the century. The music has naturally appealed to the awakening intelligence of the musical masses by vehement emotional spontaneity, orgiastic frenzy, dazzling effects of colour, barbaric rhythm, and unrestrained abandonment to physical excitement which is natural to the less developed races.[6]

Yet Parry's anxiety was not based solely on the national character of Russian music itself. Rather, his concern was that such music might appeal to an audience that he saw as immature, impressionable, and easily influenced, and that public susceptibility to the seductive charms of Russian music might alter the development of Western European music itself:

> it must be admitted that the conspicuous entrance of such art upon the scene affects the attitude of the very big audience of the big public. They get accustomed to the devices of the composers who are in closer contact with beings that are hardly raised above savagery, and finding they flatter their mental indolence and satisfy their desire for excitement, naturally think their own western composers should supply them with music made after the manner of the semi-oriental races.[7]

The emotional vitality of Russian music, allied with its evident allure for a new and untutored audience represented to its critics a negative influence that British music

Drummond, *The Provincial Music Festival in England, 1784–1914* (Farnham: Ashgate, 2012), Antje Pieper, *Music and the Making of Middle-Class Culture: A Comparative History of Nineteenth-Century Leipzig and Birmingham* (Basingstoke: Palgrave, 2008), and Paul Rodmell, ed., *Music and Institutions in Nineteenth-Century Britain* (Farnham: Ashgate, 2012).

[5] On the cultural and ideological allegiances of British musical academia, see Meirion Hughes and Robert Stradling, *The English Musical Renaissance, 1840–1940: Constructing a National Music*, 2nd edn (Manchester: Manchester University Press, 2001), 52–82, 115–63.

[6] C. Hubert H. Parry, *Summary of the History and Development of Mediæval and Modern European Music*, revised edn (London: Novello, 1905), 89, 119.

[7] C. Hubert H. Parry, *Style in Musical Art* (London: Macmillan, 1911), 406.

would find hard to resist. For all the apparent slightness of 'Russian Rivalry', the poem with which this chapter opened, its publication in Britain's leading music journal indicates that its diagnosis was more representative of prevailing establishment opinion than its humorous tone might at first suggest.

The 'rivalry' between Russian and Western music was, then, not simply a cultural rivalry between two different traditions viewed through the prism of race and geography and influenced by questions of imperial politics. Rather, the reception of Russian music in turn-of-the-century Britain rested on an internal opposition between the institutions of academic authority on the one hand, and a culture of performance and appreciation on the other. As Raymond Williams argues: 'The metropolis housed the great traditional academies and museums and their orthodoxies; their very proximity and powers of control were both a standard and a challenge'.[8] At a time when few scholarly studies of Russian music were available (and those that did exist were usually translated from the French), Russian repertoire owed its success principally to figures who worked outside of and even against scholarship and criticism, and who derived their authority by appealing directly to popular taste.[9] Unlike Parry's condescending attitude to concert audiences, Newman had greater confidence in the aesthetic potential of the individuals who attended Queen's Hall, as Wood later recalled:

> I was greatly impressed with Newman...I had never met a manager who knew anything about music. Newman did. He possessed both business acumen and artistic ideals. *He wanted the public to come to love great music.*
>
> 'I am going to run nightly concerts and train the public by easy stages,' he said. 'Popular at first, gradually raising the standard until I have *created* a public for classical and modern music.'[10]

The prominence of Russian music at Queen's Hall was not so much the result of Wood's and Newman's own individual preferences (although that clearly played a part); rather, it was based on their sense that this repertoire could form the basis for encouraging and establishing an intelligent and committed audience for serious music.

The Russian works programmed at Queen's Hall exemplify Newman's vision of 'a public for classical and modern music'. The opening 1895 season, for instance, contained relatively little Russian music, as did the 1896 season (notwithstanding the British premieres of Rimsky-Korsakov's *Capriccio espagnol* and Glazunov's *Scènes de ballet* on 24 September).[11] 1897, however, represented a major breakthrough, with a far greater number of performances of Russian works throughout

[8] Raymond Williams, 'Metropolitan Perception and the Emergence of Modernism', in Tony Pinkney, ed, *The Politics of Modernism* (London: Verso, 1989), 45.

[9] See, for instance, Alfred Habets, *Borodin and Liszt*, trans. Rosa Newmarch (London: Digby, Long, 1895) [Fr. orig. *Alexandre Borodine d'après la biographie et la correspondance publiées par M. Wladimir Stassoff* (Paris: Fischbacher, 1883)], and Arthur Pougin, *A Short History of Russian Music*, trans. Lawrence Haward (London: Chatto & Windus, 1915) [Fr. orig., *Essai historique sur la musique en Russie* (Paris: Fischbacher, 1904)].

[10] Henry J. Wood, *My Life of Music* (London: Gollancz, 1938), 91–2.

[11] Here, and subsequently, details of concert programmes at Queen's Hall are derived from the BBC's on-line 'Proms Archive', <http://www.bbc.co.uk/proms/archive>, with additional material based on the collection of concert programmes held at the British Library, Analytical Programmes and Words of the Queen's Hall Promenade Concerts, h.5470.

the season. Most striking was the inclusion of a 'Tschaikowsky Night' (two were held that year, on 1 and 29 September respectively)—evidence of the composer's appeal at the box office. 'Tschaikowsky Nights' rapidly established themselves at the heart of subsequent seasons and ran until 1905; the only other composers to receive more attention in this way were Beethoven and Wagner.[12] In many senses, the Proms were merely reacting to a long-standing vogue for Chaikovsky's music; a large number of his major works had already been premiered in Britain and the composer himself had visited London and Cambridge in 1893.[13] Yet in the wake of these performances came important British premieres of works by other composers, as the following selective list demonstrates:

1897: Arensky, Suite *Silhouettes* (17 September)
Kiui, *Suite Miniature* (1 September)
1899: Balakirev, *Overture on Russian Themes* (26 September)
Kiui, Scherzo No. 1 (29 September)
Glazunov, Fantasia *From Darkness to Light* (8 September)
Ippolitov-Ivanov, *Caucasian Sketches* (7 September)
Lyadov, *A Musical Snuffbox* (26 August)
1900: Rakhmaninov, Piano Concerto No. 1 (4 October)
Rimsky-Korsakov, Symphony No. 2 (19 September)
1901: Balakirev, Symphony No. 1 (26 September)
Glazunov, *Ouverture solonnelle* (29 October)
Lyapunov, *Ouverture solennelle* (21 September)
1906: Arensky, *Variations on a Theme of Tchaikovsky* (16 October)
Glier, Symphony No. 1 (28 August)
Lyadov, *8 chants populaires russes* (25 August), *Baba Yaga* (30 August)

The changing profile of Russian music in the first decade of the Proms at Queen's Hall amply demonstrates Newman's strategy of starting with popular works before moving onto more unfamiliar repertoire. Taking advantage of the widespread vogue for things Russian at the time, Wood and Newman established an alternative canon of musical value to the one promoted in universities and colleges.

The decisive role played by the audience in shaping the choice of repertoire can also be seen in the work of Rosa Newmarch, who, in 1908, took over as the author of the programme notes at Queen's Hall. By this time, Newmarch had published a series of books, articles and lectures that had established her as the leading authority on Russian music in Britain.[14] Yet what is most important about Newmarch's

[12] As Langley notes: 'By 1914, Tchaikovsky would even approach Beethoven in total number of Proms performances—an extraordinary rise—although neither of them came anywhere near Wagner, whose real and fashionable hold on London orchestral audiences continued through the Great War and beyond' ('Building an Orchestra, Creating an Audience', 67).

[13] Gerald Norris, *Stanford, The Cambridge Jubilee and Tchaikovsky* (Newton Abbot, London, and North Pomfret: David & Charles, 1980).

[14] Philip Ross Bullock, *Rosa Newmarch and Russian Music in Late Nineteenth and Early Twentieth-Century England* (Farnham: Ashgate, 2009).

programme notes is not the prominence that they accord to Russian music; her work in this regard was decidedly eclectic, reflecting the wide range of music heard at the Proms. Rather, Newmarch's notes reflect a profound challenge to the source of authority in matters of music appreciation in early twentieth-century Britain. Discussing the history of the programme note in Britain, Christina Bashford singles out 'its undisputed educational function as an aid to music appreciation, in an age when self-improvement was, for many, virtually a way of life'.[15] Similarly, Catherine Dale suggests that 'programme notes were intended for the musical amateur and may be regarded more realistically as symptoms of the Victorian philanthropic concern to educate and to make music accessible to the masses'.[16] Newmarch herself alluded to the ability of the programme note to act as 'a force in musical education'.[17] Yet such top-down accounts of the function of programme notes give a misleading impression of Newmarch's own contribution to the genre. Just as Newman and Wood based their work on an astute appeal to popular taste, so too are Newmarch's notes centred on the cultivation of the audience's own aesthetic appreciation, rather than on the display of her own authority as a critic.

This distinction is clear from a letter that Wood wrote to Newmarch in June 1907, in which he raised the possibility of her taking over the task of providing the programme notes at Queen's Hall. Describing the approach of the two previous annotators, Alfred Kalisch and Percy Pitt, as 'purely technical', he suggested a different model of writing that Newmarch might adopt: 'What we require is simple, short notices, without musical examples, giving the mood and dramatic purport of the piece, and not mentioning first and second subjects, modulations and episodes, as the public have no time in the concert-room to read such things.'[18] Newmarch was clearly inclined to this particular style (she was, after all, the author of two volumes of poetry), and a subsequent interview published in the *Musical Times* gives a good impression of how her notes were perceived:

> She does not trouble us with meticulous details, our attention is not drawn to the resolution of the very last diversion of the supertonic minor 13th on the Polish 6th, but her appeal is always aesthetic and seeks to lay bare the underlying poetic bases of the music. She does not attempt to paint the lily, but she is enthusiastic over the charm of its tints.[19]

Newmarch's notes are not intended to be absolute interpretations for the audience to follow, but rather function as stimuli for a new form of independent and imaginative listening.[20]

[15] Christina Bashford, 'Not just "G": Towards a History of the Programme Note', in Michael Musgrave, ed., *George Grove, Music and Victorian Culture* (Basingstoke: Palgrave, 2003), 127.

[16] Catherine Dale, *Music Analysis in Britain in the Nineteenth and Early Twentieth Centuries* (Aldershot: Ashgate, 2003), 36.

[17] M., 'Mrs. Rosa Newmarch', *Musical Times*, 52, no. 818 (1 April 1911), 225.

[18] Quoted in Langley, 'Building an Orchestra, Creating an Audience', 58.

[19] M., 'Mrs. Rosa Newmarch', 227.

[20] This argument is traced greater detail in Philip Ross Bullock, '"Lessons in Sensibility": Rosa Newmarch, Music Appreciation and the Aesthetic Cultivation of the Self', in Stefano Evangelista and Catherine Maxwell, eds, *The Arts in Victorian Literature*, special issue of *Yearbook of English Studies*, 40, nos. 1–2 (2010), 295–318.

Within this context, Russian music played a particularly important role. Much Russian music of the nineteenth century actively resisted the principles of 'pure' or 'absolute' music that were often associated with the Austro-German symphonic tradition, favouring instead extra-musical details, programmatic elements, and an intense appeal to the emotions.[21] This distinction between 'absolute' and 'descriptive' elements in music was sometimes interpreted in terms of a contrast between classicism and romanticism. Writing in 1898, for instance, E. A. Baughan (editor of the *Musical Standard*) established just such an opposition: 'classical music, however many descriptive touches it may have, is abstract and is the expression of feeling or is descriptive of it; modern non-classical music attempts to describe things, events, actions'. In particular, Russian music was perceived as just one of the most striking and successful instances of this 'modern non-classical music':

> The modern men, Dvorák [*sic*], Bruneau, Richard Strauss, Saint-Saëns, Tchaïkovsky, Rimsky-Korsakov and the Russian school generally have carried descriptive music to its limits, and have been laughed at for their pains, but who shall say that their efforts will not bear good fruit in due season? The blossoms are a little frost-bitten, perhaps, but he would be rash who would affirm that they will never fructify. Descriptive music is the modern movement, and no movement, religious, political or moral, can take place without leaving some result behind it.[22]

Baughan is here proposing a quasi-evolutionary narrative of music history from classicism to romanticism (and even beyond). To be sure, Russia was far from being the only musical culture to embody this shift, as the inclusion of Dvořák, Bruneau, Richard Strauss, and Saint-Saëns in Baughan's list suggests; yet Russian music nonetheless represented a modern form of composition that demanded new modes of listening. Loyalty to one school or another was, therefore, not merely a question of national allegiance (Parry on the German side, Newmarch on the Russian). Rather, it revealed a struggle for authority between rival institutions, with academic scholarship advocating the cause of classicism and absolute music on the one hand, and concert promoters preferring the descriptive ambitions of romanticism on the other.[23]

[21] Marina Frolova-Walker, 'Against Germanic Reasoning: the Russian Search for an Alternative Means of Symphonic Development', in Harry White and Michael Murphy, eds, *Musical Constructions of Nationalism: Essays on the History and Ideology of European Musical Culture, 1800–1945* (Cork: Cork University Press, 2001), 104–22.

[22] E. A. B[aughan]., 'What is "Classical"', *Musical Standard*, 9, no. 221 (26 March 1898), 195. On Baughan's attitude to Russian music, see Stephen Muir, '"About as Wild and Barbaric as Well Could be Imagined...": The Critical Reception of Rimsky-Korsakov in Nineteenth-Century England', *Music and Letters*, 93, no. 4 (2012), 513–42.

[23] Although it is beyond the scope of this chapter, the British reception of Wagner's music is fundamental to an understanding of the debate about classicism and romanticism. Parry, for instance, explicitly linked the popularity of Russian music to a decline in interest in Wagner, whilst admitting that Wagner's music itself rendered the distinction between classical and romantic uncertain: 'The exact date when the Russian musical invasion commenced may be given as the performance of his [Chaikovsky's] 'Pathetic' Symphony (in B minor, No.6) by the Philharmonic Society under the conductorship of Sir Alexander Mackenzie on February 28, 1894. From that moment Wagner's supremacy

The competing claims of classicism and romanticism were conditioned by the development of European music over the course of the nineteenth century, as well as by historiographical attempts to theorize that same development (especially by Eduard Hanslick and Guido Adler, his immediate successor as professor of music at the University of Vienna). In many ways, the repertoire at Queen's Hall continued to reflect this nineteenth-century legacy well into the twentieth century; in the decade before the Great War, programmes continued to favour Chaikovsky and the nationalists, with notably few premieres of new orchestral compositions by younger composers. Yet at precisely this time, Paris was beginning to establish a context for the performance of newer, more modernist works in the form of Sergey Dyagilev's Ballets Russes, as well as for productions of operas that had yet to be seen outside Russia. In 1908, for instance, Newmarch reported on the Paris premiere of Musorgsky's *Boris Godunov* (with Fedor Shalyapin (in the title role), and wondered: 'When may we hope to see anything so new, so instructive, and so profoundly interesting in London?'[24] It was not until 1911 that the Ballets Russes made their British debut, and in advance of the company's summer 1913 season, Newmarch was still able to remark that in France the operas of Musorgsky 'seem to have found permanent anchorage; whether they will sail into the haven of our affections and remain there, is a question that the next few weeks will decide one way or the other'.[25] An anonymous review of this season in the *Musical Times* suggests that the British were more conservative in their attitude to the works presented by the Ballets Russes than the French. The three operas that were presented (Musorgsky's *Boris Godunov* and *Khovanshchina*, and Rimsky-Korsakov's *Pskovityanka*) were welcomed, whereas reaction to the ballets was dismissive. Stravinsky's *Rite of Spring* met with particular hostility: 'The music baffles verbal description. To say that much of it is hideous as sound is a mild description. There is certainly an impelling rhythm traceable. Practically it has no relation to music at all as most of us understand the word'.[26] Nonetheless, Stravinsky's name began to figure more prominently in British musical life, with concert premieres of the suite from *The Firebird* and the *Scherzo fantastique* being given at Queen's Hall on 4 September 1913 and 26 August 1914 respectively.

Yet rather than rehearse a widespread account of British resistance to the European avant-garde (a narrative questioned by Ramsay Burt's discussion of the London premiere of *The Rite of Spring* in this volume), it is worth emphasizing the institutional factors that influenced aesthetic considerations. Dyagilev's two 1911

in the concert-room ceased to be uncontested. Public taste gravitated from the subtle emotionalism of the great Teutonic musical dramatist to the more obvious and highly accentuated passion of the more primitive and plain-speaking Russian. But, as has been before pointed out, Wagner had prepared the way, and had unintentionally led public taste away from the purity of abstract Art and created a craving which could only be satisfied with draughts of stimulants of ever-increasing strength' (Parry, *Summary of the History and Development of Mediæval and Modern European Music*, 119–20).

[24] Rosa Newmarch, 'Russian Opera in Paris: Moussorgsky's "Boris Godunov"', *Monthly Musical Record*, 38, no. 451 (July 1908), 149.

[25] Rosa Newmarch, 'Moussorgsky's Operas', *Musical Times*, 54, no. 845 (1 July 1913), 439.

[26] 'Russian Opera and Ballet at Drury Lane', *Musical Times*, 54, no. 846 (1 August 1913), 535.

seasons took place at Covent Garden; coinciding with the coronation of George V, they were primarily society affairs at which, to quote Lynn Garafola, 'the British ruling class displayed its brilliant plumage'.[27] Yet when Dyagilev returned to London in the summer of 1913, it was in collaboration with the young British conductor and impresario, Thomas Beecham. The heir to a large pharmaceutical fortune that allowed him to indulge both his own career and his sense of artistic idealism, Beecham shifted the focus of the Ballets Russes from Covent Garden to the more commercial and democratic venue of the Drury Lane Theatre. Beecham's memoir, *A Mingled Chime*, gives a good impression of the rivalries and agendas that lay behind his decision to shift his allegiance from Covent Garden:

> I began to feel that the alliance with an organization whose whole scheme of values as well as policy was so dissimilar to my own had outlived whatever utility it had at first contained, and I was convinced that what was vital to the operatic situation in London was some new visitation of striking originality. It was impossible to overlook the undiminished popularity of the Ballet, and it was at least imaginable that another one hundred per cent Russian institution might be the solution of the problem. I accordingly resigned my position at Covent Garden, requested Diaghileff to negotiate the visit of a company from the Imperial Opera of St. Petersburg to include singers, chorus, new scenery and costumes, indeed everything except the orchestra, and took a lease of Drury Lane Theater.[28]

Beecham's interest in the Ballets Russes rested on a belief that the artistic values of the company could be successfully grafted onto a British context that was itself desperately in need of reform. The repertoire of the 1913 season may have consisted of a diverse range of Russian and European ballets and operas, yet its sense of idealism was entirely Russian, and reveals the extent to which the Russian arts were less an exotic product to be consumed as a social model to be emulated.[29]

The key to realizing such ambitions was, of course, a steady source of income, whether from Beecham himself or from commercial success at the box office. Beecham's collaboration with Dyagilev thus brought together two figures with a keen sense for what was commercially viable, as well as artistically innovative. At once idealistic and pragmatic, Beecham's sponsorship of the Ballets Russes sought to effect a profound institutional transformation in British musical life, as Garafola suggests:

> Beecham's undertakings in these immediate prewar years proposed to do more than simply upgrade the style and quality of offerings at Covent Garden. They sought to transform the character of the public, to weld music-lovers, socialites, theatregoers, and artistic enthusiasts of modest means into an audience more closely attuned to Britain's

[27] Lynn Garafola, *Diaghilev's Ballets Russes* (New York: Oxford University Press, 1989), 300. See too Sjeng Scheijen, *Diaghilev: A Life*, trans. Jane Hedley-Prôle and S. J. Leinbach (London: Profile Books, 2009), 231–3.

[28] Thomas Beecham, *A Mingled Chime* (New York: Putnam's, 1943), 193.

[29] For a comparative study of both Beecham and Wood that looks at French, rather than Russian, influences on British orchestral practice, see Leanne Langley, 'Joining Up the Dots: Cross-Channel Models in the Shaping of London Orchestral Culture, 1895–1914', in Bennett Zon, ed., *Music and Performance Culture in Nineteenth-Century Britain: Essays in Honour of Nicholas Temperley* (Farnham: Ashgate, 2012), 37–58.

> middle-class social order. Neither the provincial troupes, which played at most a brief and occasional London season, nor Covent Garden, which catered almost exclusively to the haut monde, managed to make the necessary social and artistic adjustments. Beecham was able to do so, only in part because of his family's pharmaceutical empire. Thanks to Diaghilev and the revelation of Russia's lyric theater, Beecham found an artist and a repertory whose appeal transcended divisions of class and differences of taste.[30]

Rather like the Promenade concerts at Queen's Hall a generation earlier, the pre-war seasons of the Ballets Russes owed much of their success to the involvement of a perspicacious musical entrepreneur with a sense for what might appeal to a diverse and culturally voracious public rather than to the critical and academic establishment. In the class-conscious context of late nineteenth and early twentieth-century Britain, figures such as Newman, Wood, Newmarch, and Beecham were sometimes dismissed as vulgar popularizers. Yet, taking advantage of the widespread vogue for all things Russian, they were able to fashion for themselves a form of artistic authority that did not depend on canons of critical respectability, drawing instead on a growing middle-class audience for a sense of their own identity. The British reception of Russian music in the two decades before the Great War depended, then, on the work of a group of committed Russophiles, many of whom worked outside the main centres of learning and criticism. It would clearly be an overstatement to call them outsiders; they were often well connected to society patrons who afforded them access to wealth and influence. Yet despite the vogue for Russian culture that had come into being in the second half of the nineteenth century, their position was—at least in institutional terms—relatively marginal.

With the outbreak of the Great War, however, their work was to play a rather different role in British society. Where once Russia had been the object of suspicion and hostility (at least in terms of politics and diplomacy), it was now an ally, with culture becoming one of the primary vehicles for bringing about this necessary rapprochement.[31] There had always been a profound rivalry between the German and Russian repertoires at Queen's Hall, to which the war added a political dimension. The lessees of the hall, Chappell & Company, seemed minded to respond to a call by the popular press to boycott German music, as Elkin observes:

> Chappell brought pressure on Robert Newman to substitute a Franco-Russian programme for the Wagner programme which had come to be regarded as traditional on Monday nights at the Proms. Newman, however, issued a statement in which he announced his determination to adhere to the original scheme as nearly as possible, and declared, very properly, that 'the greatest examples of Music and Art are world possessions and unassailable even by the prejudices and passions of the hour.'[32]

[30] Garafola, *Diaghilev's Ballets Russes*, 313.

[31] This process is examined in detail in Michael Hughes, 'Searching for the Soul of Russia: British Perceptions of Russia during the First World War', *Twentieth Century British History*, 20, no. 2 (2009), 198–226.

[32] Elkin, *Queen's Hall*, 31–2.

Nonetheless, military conflict did lead to some modifications in the repertoire performed. From the very inception of the Promenade concerts in 1895, it had been traditional to open and close the season with the national anthem. The 1914 season, which opened just ten days after Britain declared war on Germany, featured a daily performance of 'God Save the King', as well as regular performances of the French, Belgian, and Russian anthems (thirty-two, nineteen, and fourteen times each). This nationalistic upswing continued in more measured form the following year; opening and closing with the British national anthem, it added Italian, Japanese, and Serbian to the allied anthems performed, as well as Canadian and Australian patriotic songs. The 1916 season, by contrast, showed a marked interest in Russia above all as Britain's chief military ally. Alongside just three performances of the British national anthem, Wood conducted Glazunov's *Paraphrase sur les hymnes des nations alliés*, as well as his own arrangements of Glazunov's setting of 'The Song of the Volga Boatmen' (both works featured in the 1917 and 1918 seasons too).[33] In fact, 1917 turned out to be the highpoint of British interest in Russian music at the Proms (possibly as a result of the February Revolution that year). For the first time in more than a decade, the series included a dedicated 'Russian Night'; strikingly, Russia was the only country to be honoured in this way. Notices in the programmes from this season show that Mondays and Fridays were reserved for Wagner and Beethoven respectively, Thursday and Saturdays were so-called 'popular nights', and Wednesdays were given over to performances of symphonies.

In large measure, the Russian repertoire performed during the war years was based on the nineteenth-century canon that had been established at the Proms over the previous two decades or so. Nonetheless, a number of new works, some by younger and less familiar composers, were heard at this time:

1915: Bagrinovsky, *From Russian Fairytales* (19 August)
Musorgsky, *Pictures from an Exhibition*, orchestrated by Wood (28 August)
Rakhmaninov, *Isle of the Dead* (25 August)
1916: Musorgsky, *Pictures from an Exhibition*, orchestrated by Tushmalov (7 September)
Prokof'ev: *Scherzo for four bassoons* (2 September)
Rebikov, Suite from *The Christmas Tree* (28 September)
Rimsky-Korsakov, *Suite* from *Pan Voevoda* (10 October)
1917: Gnesin, *From Shelley* (19 September)
Lyadov, *Kikimora* (18 September)

The inclusion of these works was clearly conditioned by the war effort; in comparison to many of the Russian works first heard at the Proms before 1914, some of them seem slight and, with the exception of Musorgsky and Rakhmaninov, have

[33] A further instance of how Russian composers became the most prominent musical advocates of the military alliance can be seen in Aleksandr Kastal'sky's *Requiem for the Fallen Heroes of the Allied Armies*. Premiered in Moscow in 1916 and performed in Birmingham in November 1917, it is a polyglot text drawing on the musical traditions of the various religious cultures represented by the alliance. See Rosa Newmarch, 'A Requiem for the Allied Heroes', *Musical Times*, 58, no. 897 (1 November 1917), 496–7.

failed to establish themselves in the performing repertoire. Nonetheless, they are striking evidence not just of contingent political circumstances, but also of the effective advocacy of figures such as Newman, Newmarch, and Wood, as well as the cosmopolitan tastes of London's popular metropolitan audiences for the latest in classical music, all of which constitute important factors in the rise to prominence of Russian music at Queen's Hall around the turn of the century.

Initially, the immediate post-war situation suggested a degree of continuity with the past. Led by Chaikovsky, the nineteenth-century repertoire continued to dominate the Promenade concerts at Queen's Hall, complemented by a small number of new works (such as Prokof'ev's Piano Concerto No.1 and Katuar's Piano Concerto on 24 and 25 August 1920 respectively). Yet in the wake of the October Revolution of 1917, the Russian musical landscape had been radically transformed. Metner, Prokof'ev, Rakhmaninov, and Stravinsky were just the most famous composers to go into emigration, and with the relocation of some of the most significant Russian composers to Paris came a shift away from the nationalism of the second half of the nineteenth century to an apparently more international form of modernism.[34] Within Soviet Russia, politics was beginning to transform the arts, and a variety of avant-garde movements vied for ideological and aesthetic supremacy.[35] Both factors led to a fragmentation of what was known and understood about the latest developments in Russian music. Despite sporadic reports about musical life in the specialized musical press (as in, for instance, *The Chesterian* or *The Sackbut*), it was not until the publication of Leonid Sabaneev's *Modern Russian Composers* in 1927 that any attempt was made to provide a reasonably coherent (if highly partial) summary of the contemporary state of affairs.[36]

Within Britain itself, developments in criticism were beginning to alter the ways in which Russian music was perceived. Looking back on the early years of the Proms in 1928, Newmarch suggests that it was 'only gulps of what was then very modern orchestral music (Tchaikovsky and the other Russians, Richard Strauss, Elgar and Sibelius)' that could satisfy an 'awakening hunger for a vital, secular art'.[37] Newmarch's qualified reference to 'then very modern' is telling; by the late 1920s, Russian music had evidently lost much of its novelty value. In particular, the romanticism that had been so crucial to its success with audiences and broad-minded critics around the turn of the century now looked decidedly old-fashioned. Writing in 1931, Cecil Gray offered the following highly tendentious account of

[34] This evolution is traced in detail in Richard Taruskin, *Stravinsky and the Russian Traditions: A Biography of the Works through 'Mavra'*, 2 vols (Oxford: Oxford University Press, 1996). The role of music in the interwar emigration is only now beginning to be studied in proper detail: see, for instance, Ekaterini Levidou, 'The Encounter of Neoclassicism with Eurasianism in Interwar Paris: Stravinsky, Suvchinsky and Lourié', DPhil thesis, University of Oxford, 2008.

[35] Amy Nelson, *Music for the Revolution: Musicians and Power in Early Soviet Russia* (University Park, PA: Pennsylvania University Press, 2004).

[36] Leonid Sabaneyeff, *Modern Russian Composers* (London: Lawrence, [1927]).

[37] [Rosa Newmarch], 'The Promenade Concerts', in *BBC Handbook, 1928* (London: British Broadcasting Corporation, 1928), 101. The nature of modernism in British music is currently the subject of renewed interest: see in particular Matthew Riley, ed., *British Music and Modernism, 1895–1960* (Farnham: Ashgate, 2010).

recent music history: 'music, for better or for worse—and quite possibly for neither—has for the last hundred years been in essence romantic, with all that this much misused but nevertheless indispensable adjective implies: namely, amongst other things, the predominance of sensation over intellect, of colouristic over linear interest, of expressiveness over formal balance and proportion'.[38] Writing a few years later, Constant Lambert echoed Gray's account, this time writing explicitly about what he perceived as the shortcomings of Russian music. Acknowledging its 'wealth of vitality, colour, and primitive nostalgia which breaks through the stuffy conservatoire tradition of the central European composers as refreshingly as the painting of Gauguin and Van Gogh breaks through the traditions of the French Salon', he nonetheless suggested that 'in its lack of any genuinely architectural element it carried with it the seeds of its own ultimate collapse'.[39] What Gray bemoaned in contemporary music as 'the predominance of sensation over intellect, of colouristic over linear interest, of expressiveness over formal balance and proportion', Lambert saw as inherently Russian musical characteristics: 'There is an extraordinary lack of formal as opposed to merely colouristic progress in Russian progress, and during the seventy years that separate *Russlan* from *Le Sacre du Printemps* there is less real advance, save of a purely decorative and two-dimensional order, than there is in the thirty years that separate Beethoven's first symphony from his ninth.'[40] The emphasis placed by both Gray and Lambert on formal rather than decorative elements in music recalls Parry's earlier condemnation of the dubious appeal of Russian music. Much as writers such as Newmarch had tried to argue both for Russian music's inherent importance and its relevance to the modern British context, aesthetic prejudices ran deep. The modernist turn in music criticism had, ironically enough, late-Victorian antecedents.

The most obvious victim of this shift in aesthetic ideology was Skryabin. On the eve of the Great War, a number of his vast orchestral works had seemed to promise a new phase in the British appreciation of Russian music. *Prometheus* received its British premiere at Queen's Hall on 1 February 1913 (at one of the winter season of Symphony Concerts, where more challenging repertoire was performed than at the Promenade Concerts in the summer); so important was this work deemed to be that it was, in fact, given twice on the same evening. Newmarch wrote to the composer, excitedly giving her impression of the concert:

> It is impossible to speak of 'success' in the usual sense of the word. But I can tell you that the impression was quite shaking, strange, and the work aroused unusual interest... The hall was packed, but not with the usual audience of free tickets for musicians. THIS WAS THE UNDERSTANDING PUBLIC, composed of people who really love music and who buy the cheapest seats several weeks in advance....
>
> After the first performance there was fortunately no apathy. Several whistles (virtually unknown here) along with sincere and spontaneous applause... I must tell you,

[38] Cecil Gray, *Sibelius* (London: Oxford University Press, 1931), 187–8.

[39] Constant Lambert, *Music Ho! A Study of Music in Decline* (London: Faber & Faber, 1934), 169.

[40] Lambert, *Music Ho!*, 169–70.

> that knowing the London musical public, I was more surprised at the great number who stayed for the second playing...After the indifferent and/or antipathetic group left, Sir Henry began again. Second time, everything went *much better* than the first....The applause was really warm and rapturous. Wood had to come out three times (after novelties, this is quite unusual).[41]

Newmarch's enthusiasm was not misplaced. Later that year, on 18 October 1913, Wood conducted the first British performance of the Symphony No. 3 (the so-called *Divine Poem*), and on 14 March 1914, Skryabin himself appeared at Queen's Hall to perform the solo piano part in *Prometheus*, as well as the Piano Concerto in F sharp minor. Writing in the *Saturday Review* two months later, John Runciman discussed Skryabin (as well as Stravinsky and Schoenberg) in an article entitled 'The Most Modern Musicians', seeing him as one of the figures most likely to transcend the still dominant cult of Wagner and prepare the ground for a new music of the future.[42] However, by 1922, a letter in the *Musical Times* objected to a planned performance of *The Poem of Ecstasy* at the Gloucester Three Choirs' Festival on the grounds that Skryabin's music was 'thoroughly morbid, erotic, and sensational in the worst sense of these terms'. Although clearly influenced by religious considerations, the author's argument was not atypical of 1920s reactions to Skryabin's music and can be seen as instance of the kind of purity and classicism that were characteristic of a certain strain of modernist criticism (see, for instance, the assertion that 'At present the tendency of taste in Church music is, happily, towards a return to those ideals of dignity and sanity which are embodied in the glorious heritage of English music that has come down to us from the 16th century').[43] Even Stravinsky's move towards a seemingly more objective musical language in the 1920s failed to accord with British interest in a classically inflected modernism. Gray, for instance, dismissed him as 'little more than an artistic weathercock who turns in whatever direction the wind is blowing', and argued that 'the self-conscious neo-classicism of the later Stravinsky... is hopelessly sterile because it is artificial and *voulu*'.[44] Ultimately, the main beneficiary of the classical turn in modernist music criticism was to be Sibelius, who became the object of an entire cult in the 1920s and 1930s, sidelining not just Russian but a whole range of other repertoires.[45]

[41] Quoted in Faubion Bowers, *Scriabin: A Biography*, 2nd edn, 2 vols (New York: Dover, 1996), ii, 242.

[42] John F. Runciman, 'The Most Modern Musicians', *Saturday Review of Politics, Literature, Science and Art*, 117, no. 3055 (16 May 1914), 629–31.

[43] Cambrensis, 'Scriabin's Music and the Three Choirs Festival', *Musical Times*, 63, no. 948 (1 February 1922), 124. For this, and the preceding reference, I am grateful to Charlotte Purkis, whose unpublished paper, '"Thought in a Glow": Scriabin's Challenge to Music Criticism' (read at the conference *Russia in Britain, 1880–1940: Reception, Translation and the Modernist Cultural Agenda*, London, June 2009), has informed my argument here.

[44] Cecil Gray, *A Survey of Contemporary Music* (London: Oxford University Press, 1924), 148; Gray, *Sibelius*, 198.

[45] Peter Franklin, 'Sibelius in Britain', in Daniel M. Grimley, ed., *The Cambridge Companion to Sibelius*, (Cambridge: Cambridge University Press, 2004), 182–95; Byron Adams, '"Thor's Hammer": Sibelius and British Music Critics', in Daniel M. Grimley, ed., *Jean Sibelius and His World* (Princeton, NJ: Princeton University Press, 2011), 125–57; and Philip Ross Bullock, ed. and trans, *The Correspondence of Jean Sibelius and Rosa Newmarch, 1906–1939* (Woodbridge: Boydell, 2011), 1–48.

As in the turn-of-the-century shift from classicism to romanticism, the postwar swing from romanticism to modernism entailed more than simply a debate about which particular national schools should be preferred. It also involved a reevaluation of attitudes to writing about music. Gray, for instance, proposed a new type of criticism that was distinctly formalist in its emphasis on authorial intention as the sole criterion of artistic value:

> A work of art should not be judged primarily from the point of view of its contemplator; it should be approached from the artist's standpoint. The best critic is he who is able to efface his personal idiosyncrasies and to identity himself with the creator in the act of creation. His task is not to observe the effect the work has upon himself but rather to efface himself altogether. Certain works may have for each of us a peculiarly personal significance, through association of ideas perhaps psychological, perhaps literary or historical, but that does not constitute æsthetic significance, being something quite fortuitous, extrinsic to the work itself... Criticism is first of all a re-creation of the work of art.[46]

Gray's belief that 'ideas perhaps psychological, perhaps literary or historical' were 'something quite fortuitous, extrinsic to the work itself' did not just shape the practice of criticism, but had profound consequences for how audiences might be encouraged to listen to music too. Russian music had established itself in British concert life precisely because its extra-musical, programmatic elements made it amenable to appreciation by popular audiences who lacked the specialist technical knowledge to understand it in abstract terms (terms that much nineteenth-century Russian music had, in any case, rejected). Newmarch, Newman, and Wood had seized on this potential in order to establish for themselves a form of influence and authority that bypassed the categories of academic writing and evaluation; now, new canons of criticism were downplaying both the inherent significance of Russian music, as well as its role in promoting an audience-based form of imaginative appreciation. Russian music naturally continued to feature in concert programmes throughout the 1920s and well into the 1930s, but the unclear picture of its most recent developments, the lack of consistent advocates, and an uncertain sense of its place in contemporary aesthetics meant that its status was distinctly ambiguous.

A final factor that influenced the reception of Russian music in Britain after the war was an institutional one. Queen's Hall had, both before and during the war, served as a leading venue for the promotion of works by Russian composers. Yet in the 1920s, its decisive influence over British musical life began to wane. Granted, Wood remained at the conductor's podium, but Newmarch handed over the provision of programme notes to Eric Blom (and, in any case, had abandoned writing about Russia, shifting the focus of her attention to the newly independent state of Czechoslovakia instead). Then, in the years before Newman's death in November 1926, the viability of the concerts themselves began to be questioned, largely on financial grounds (in 1925, it was even suggested that the hall could be turned into

[46] Cecil Gray, 'The Task of Criticism', *The Sackbut*, 1 (1920), 13.

'a picture house').[47] A number of reasons might be adduced for the problems of the early 1920s, but perhaps the principal threat came from the foundation of the British Broadcasting Company (later, Corporation) in 1922. Not only did this establish a powerful rival in terms of concert promotion (the BBC eventually took over the running of the Proms in 1927) and the way that audiences could access music by means of live broadcasts, it also led to a transformation in the kind of repertoire that was promoted. As Jennifer Doctor has demonstrated, the BBC was particular committed to the latest in contemporary European music, especially the so-called Second Viennese School (Berg, Schoenberg, and Webern), but also composers such as Hindemith, Bartók, and the French group known as 'Les Six' (Auric, Durey, Honegger, Milhaud, Poulenc, and Tailleferre).[48] Partly responding to the agenda of the newly founded International Society for Contemporary Music (ISCM), and partly promoting its own commitment to educate as well as to entertain, the BBC promoted a diverse range of challenging works both through its broadcasts and its associated publications (such as *The Listener* and the *Radio Times*).

Admittedly, Russian composers did feature in BBC concerts, most notably Prokof'ev and Stravinsky, but the prominence of Russian music was markedly less than it had been before. Moreover, because both Prokof'ev and Stravinsky were resident in Western Europe and their musical language had undergone a process of apparent internationalization, it is not immediately clear that their works would have been perceived as Russian in any specifically national sense at all. Ultimately, it would not be until the middle of the 1930s that Russian music would once again begin to feature as prominently in British concert programmes as it had in the late nineteenth and early twentieth centuries. With performances of Shostakovich's Concerto for Piano, Trumpet, and Strings and Symphony No. 1 at the Proms in 1935, and a concert performance of his opera, *Lady Macbeth of the Mtsensk District* at Queen's Hall in 1936, the Soviet Union made good its claim to consider itself the home of Russian music from now on, something corroborated by Prokof'ev's eventual return to his homeland.[49] Subsequently, Cold War politics would re-establish a quasi-national context that would, for all its ideological baggage, serve to promote the cause of Russian music in the West.[50] But to stay with the 1920s and early 1930s, it is a telling paradox that the cosmopolitanism that had been so propitious to the cause of Russian music in Britain around the turn of the century now threatened to efface national difference within the framework of a broad and receptive transnational modernism that Russia itself had done so much to bring into being.

[47] Langley, 'Building an Orchestra, Creating an Audience', 64.

[48] Jennifer Doctor, *The BBC and Ultra-Modern Music, 1922–1936: Shaping a Nation's Tastes* (Cambridge: Cambridge University Press, 1999).

[49] Simon Morrison, *The People's Artist: Prokofiev's Soviet Years* (New York: Oxford University Press, 2009). See Ian Patterson's chapter in this volume on the practical difficulties of bringing Russian music, and this opera in particular, to Britain.

[50] Pauline Fairclough, 'The Old Shostakovich: Reception in the British Press', *Music and Letters*, 88, no. 2 (2007), 266–98.

7

Le Sacre du printemps in London

The Politics of Embodied Freedom in Early Modernist Dance and Suffragette Protest

Ramsay Burt

Le Sacre du printemps is now generally recognized as a key work in the development of early modernist choreography. This is a consequence of the gradual rehabilitation of the reputation of Vatslav Nizhinsky (Vaslav Nijinsky) by dance scholars since the 1970s, and in particular the revelatory impact of Millicent Hodson's 1987 reconstruction of *Sacre* for the Joffrey Ballet. But from the outset, the ballet and its music were associated with radical innovation and modernity. The riot on 28 May 1913 at the first performance in Paris is, of course, infamous; the ballet consequently received a great deal of press attention, far more than was usual at that time even for Sergey Dyagilev's Ballets Russes. Yet the fact that London audiences in July 1913 seem generally to have been quietly appreciative of *Sacre* is not so well known. In 1913 the ballet's French title had not yet acquired its present English translation as *The Rite of Spring*, and was referred to as *The Crowning of Spring*, *The Spring Ritual*, and *The Spring Rite*, or even simply by its French title in the British press. An examination of reviews reveals the extent to which British responses to Nizhinsky's *Sacre* are aligned with contemporary concerns about the impact of modernity. As I shall show in this chapter, the modernist dancing body in *Sacre* became a site for contested notions of grace and the natural, underlying which were ideas about gender performance, nationalism, and modernism.

London audiences for *Sacre* were sufficiently appreciative for Nizhinsky to thank them publicly. In an interview published in the *Daily Mail* after the last of three performances of the work, he cordially thanked the British public for its serious interest in and attention to his ballet. Pointedly, however, he did not thank the British press:

> I am accused [by the Press] of a 'crime against grace' among other things. It seems because I have danced in ballets like 'The Pavilion of Armide' and 'The Spectre of the Rose'... that I am tied down to 'grace' for ever. Really I have a horror of the very word; 'grace' and 'charm' make me feel seasick.[1]

[1] Vaslav Nijinsky, 'M. Nijinsky's critics: "The word 'grace' makes me feel seasick"', *Daily Mail* (14 July 1913), 7.

The vocabulary of dance movements that Nizhinsky had devised for *Sacre* challenged these normative ideas about grace. But while some of the British newspaper critics dismissed the ballet, none were as derogatory as their French colleagues, with some reviews mentioning the audience's surprisingly positive response.[2] It seems that Nizhinsky may not have realized how many thoughtful and serious reviews his ballet had received in Britain.

Nonetheless, *Sacre* was received in a very different way from the earlier ballets that Dyagilev's company had presented there. At the time, there were no specialist ballet critics in Britain; reviews were generally written by a newspaper's music critic who would also cover opera performances. Ballets were either evaluated by reference to their composer (thus, *The Firebird* (*L'Oiseau de feu*) was a Stravinsky ballet and *Schéhérazade* a Rimsky-Korsakov one), or a ballet review would focus on star performers (for example, Nizhinsky, Tamara Karsavina, or Anna Pavlova). *Sacre* was the third ballet that Nizhinsky choreographed, but the first in which he did not himself perform. The first two—*Prélude à l'après midi d'un faune* (1912) and *Jeux* (1913)—were both discussed as Debussy ballets, but *Sacre* was the first ballet to be widely discussed in Britain as a new ballet by Nizhinsky, thus acknowledging for the first time the status of choreographer as author.[3]

Sacre consisted of a series of scenes in which a tribe enacts—unsuccessfully—several rituals in order to bring about the end of winter, finally resorting to the sacrifice of a young virgin who dances herself to death. This narrative, however, was not acted out or mimed, and could not therefore be easily followed by spectators. Where reviews of previous ballets by Dyagilev's company focused on their plots, critics reviewing *Sacre* found themselves having to write about the dance movement itself, as well as its relation to Igor′ Stravinsky's uncompromisingly modernist music. In Russia, ballet under imperial patronage was accepted as a serious art form, although this had not been the case for some time in Western Europe. Russian critics discussed the formal qualities of dancing and were therefore disappointed by the European reception of the ballets that Dyagilev's company had presented. As Hanna Järvinen has noted, some Russian commentators were highly critical of

[2] The anonymous critic of the *Daily Telegraph*, having thoroughly condemned *Sacre* noted, 'The audience, it is true, loudly applauded; no matter for the few who did otherwise' ('Russian Ballet: "Le Sacre de Printemps"'; *Daily Telegraph* (12 July 1913). Richard Capell in the *Daily Mail* observed that *Sacre* 'had success at Drury Lane last night: those who hissed this "Festival of Spring" (Le Sacre du Printemps) were a tiny minority. On the principle that anything new is good or the M. Nijinsky can do no wrong' (Richard Capell, 'Cannibal music: Amazing production of Russian Ballet', *Daily Mail* (12 July 1913), 5).

[3] Leonard Inkster, writing about Nizhinsky's choreography in the *New Statesman*, became confused about who was responsible for the ballet's choreography: 'The inseparability of certain gestures and certain musical gestures in *Le Sacre du Printemps* startled me until I discovered that the choreography was not by Nizhinsky, but by the composer of the music, Stravinsky' ('The Russian ballet, II', *New Statesman* (19 July 1913), 470). He corrected himself in the next issue: 'It has been pointed out to me that I was mistaken in saying last week that the choreography of *Le Sacre du Printemps* was by Stravinsky as well as the music. Readers of my article will have gathered that I was certainly seeing all the Nijinsky touches and was then presented with the statement on the programme "Ballet by Stravinsky"' ('The Russian ballet: A postscript', *New Statesman* (26 July 1913), 501). What is interesting here is, first, that authorship of the choreography mattered, but second, that it was evidently not listed in the programme.

Dyagilev for disseminating abroad a stereotype of Russia as exotic, pagan, barbaric, and child-like.[4] Paradoxically, however, many of these same Russian commentators welcomed Nizhinsky's *Sacre* as a work that was at the cutting edge of modernism but, at the same time, rooted in Russian traditions. Sergey Volkonsky, for instance, noted that *Sacre* had been described as '"cubist icon-painting" in which the archaic angularity of the movement unravels itself in front of us to the pipes of a Slavonic Pan'.[5] He hoped that Europeans, by appreciating the modernism of Russian ballets such as *Sacre*, would recognize Russian culture as modern and progressive. The appreciative reception of *Sacre* in Britain suggests just such a willingness, largely absent in France, to accept progressive Russian artists as members of an international modernist movement in the arts, although very few of the British reviews mention either Russian or Slavonic culture as important elements of the ballet. For Londoners in the eighteenth and nineteenth centuries, ballet was French. For much of the twentieth century, it became Russian.

Early British reviews of Nizhinsky's *Sacre*, favourable or not, betray a range of responses to modernity and to modernism in the arts. They are, of course, almost entirely written by men. Women's responses to modernism and modernity, as Janet Wolff and others have pointed out, had little impact at the time and received less attention than men's responses.[6] Where there is evidence of women's responses to *Sacre,* they appear to have been enthusiastic. In order to examine these, it is useful to place the ballet's theme of sacrifice in relation to ideas about sacrifice circulating at that time within the British women's suffrage movement and, in particular, among members of the militant Women's Social and Political Union. The London premiere of *Sacre* took place a few weeks after one of the grimmest events in the suffragettes' campaign. On 4 June Emily Wilding Davison had stepped in front of the King's horse, 'Anmer', during the Derby, dying of her injuries a few days later. On 14 June, a long suffragette procession followed her coffin as it was taken through the West End to King's Cross Station on its way to her funeral in Morpeth, Northumberland. Dyagilev's company arrived in London to present a season of ballets and operas that opened at the Theatre Royal, Drury Lane on 24 June. This would include, on 11 July, the first of three London performances of *Sacre,* which ended with a sacrificial solo danced by a young ballerina, Mariya Pil'ts (Piltz). Though Davison's intention remains unclear, her fellow suffragettes saw her death as a sacred gift or sacrifice. Apart from an isolated letter to the *Daily Mail,* there is no direct connection between *Sacre* and the suffragettes; yet reading their histories side by side allows similarities and parallels between the reception of the ballet and responses to suffragette actions to appear. Issues concerning the modern body were central to both militant protests and avant-garde dance at a time when the body was becoming the focus of social and political concern.

[4] Hanna Järvinen, 'The Russian Barnum: Russian Opinions on Diaghilev's Ballets Russes, 1909–1914', *Dance Research*, 26, no. 1 (2008), 18–41.

[5] Quoted in Järvinen, 'The Russian Barnum', 33.

[6] Janet Wolff, *Feminine Sentences: Essays on Women and Culture* (London: Polity Press, 1990).

MODERNISM, RUSSIANNESS, AND THE BRITISH RECEPTION OF *SACRE*

To understand British responses to *Sacre*, it is instructive to place it in the broader context of the Ballets Russes and their European reception. Dyagilev is now remembered as a key promoter of modernist and avant-garde art in the first three decades of the twentieth century. His 1917 production of *Parade,* with set and cubist costumes by Pablo Picasso, libretto by Jean Cocteau, and music by Erik Satie seems to exemplify this. But although none of *Parade*'s choreography by Leonid Myasin (Massine) has survived, dance scholars suspect that it was relatively conventional in comparison with the music and design, and that generally the choreography for the ballets Dyagilev produced was far less radical than their visual and musical elements. Lynn Garafola has looked in detail at the British reception of the Ballets Russes in the 1920s, while Susan Jones has written about the interest the company aroused among British writers and intellectuals at that time.[7] During the post-war period Dyagilev commissioned set and costume designs from the modernist painters Roger Fry was championing, including Picasso, Braque, Gris, and Matisse. Whereas the 'look' of the 1920s ballets that were so popular with Fry and members of the Bloomsbury group might have been modernist, their choreography was, in comparison, relatively conservative; they are all, in effect, narrative ballets. By contrast, very few members of the Bloomsbury group saw *Sacre* and none wrote about it.[8] Yet *Sacre* was far more radical, in choreographic terms, than any other ballet Dyagilev produced, especially in the way that it deconstructed the movement language of classical ballet.[9] Marie Rambert, who assisted Nizhinsky while he was making *Sacre*, notes that he needed to work with dancers who had 'a perfect ballet technique and then broke it down consciously for his own purposes'.[10] After he sacked Nizhinsky, Dyagilev never again allowed his choreographers to explore avant-garde approaches to dance movement. Evidence suggests he himself was never entirely happy with Nizhinsky's experiments.[11]

[7] See Lynn Garafola, *Diaghilev's Ballets Russes* (New York: Oxford University Press, 1989), 300–29; Susan Jones, 'Virginia Woolf and the Dance,' *Dance Chronicle*, 28, no. 2 (2005), 169–200, and 'Diaghilev and British Writing', *Dance Research*, 27, no. 1 (2009), 65–93.

[8] According to Michael Holroyd, Lytton Strachey found *Sacre* boring, and Roger Fry first wrote about the Ballets Russes in 1914, a year after the British performance of *Sacre*. See Michael Holroyd, *Lytton Strachey: A Critical Biography*, 2 vols (New York: Holt, Rinehart and Winston, 1968), ii, 94–5, and Roger Fry, 'Stage Setting', *New Statesman* (27 June 1914), 2. On Forster's documented reactions to the two performances of *Sacre* that he saw, see Michelle Fillion, *Difficult Rhythm: Music and the Word in E. M. Forster* (Urbana, Chicago, and Springfield, IL: University of Illinois Press, 2010), 9 (as well as 'Appendix A: Forster's Known *Ballets Russes* Attendance', 145).

[9] Arguably, Bronislava Nizhinskaya's *Svadebka* (*Les Noces*, 1923) is more innovative choreographically, but it is nevertheless stylistically neo-classical, rather than avant-garde, in its approach to movement.

[10] Marie Rambert, *Quicksilver* (Basingstoke: Macmillan, 1972), 61.

[11] When Nizhinsky married Romola Pulski in Buenos Aires in September 1913, Dyagilev sacked him from the Ballets Russes. His younger sister, Bronislava Nizhinskaya (Nijinska), who was also a dancer in Dyagilev's company, writes about the worsening relations between the two men in the preceding months, suggesting that Dyagilev rejected the choreography of both *Sacre* and *Jeux* as artistic failures (although some dance scholars have questioned the reliability of Nizhinskaya's memoirs). See Bronislava Nijinska, *Early Memoirs* (London: Faber and Faber, 1982), 472–6.

Whereas after the war ballet sets and costumes were designed by European modernist painters, the pre-war seasons featured the work of Russian painters associated with *World of Art* (*Mir iskusstva*), the influential luxuriously produced art journal that Dyagilev co-founded in 1899 with Leon Bakst and Aleksandr Benua (Benois): *Sacre* was designed by one of the artists close to *World of Art*: the painter, archaeologist, and later religious mystic, Nikolay Rerikh (Roerich). In comparison to the 1920s, less scholarly attention has been paid to the British reception of the pre-war Ballets Russes. The first season of the Imperial Russian Ballet, as Dyagilev's company was initially called in Britain, was in 1911 at the Opera House, Covent Garden, during the celebration of King George V's coronation. For this Dyagilev presented relatively conservative ballets, including the late nineteenth-century classic, *Swan Lake* (*Lebedinoe ozero*), with music by Chaikovsky. In 1912, *Schéhérazade*, choreographed by Mikhail Fokin (Fokine), was the most talked about of the company's ballets, establishing its reputation for spectacularly lavish, decadent, orientalist exoticism. That year Nizhinsky also performed his signature role in *Spectre de la rose,* also choreographed by Fokin to music by Carl Maria von Weber. His bravura solo ended with a famous leap out of a window, establishing his reputation as an exceptional and spectacularly agile male dancer. It was as a result of popular acclaim for this relatively accessible ballet that Nizhinsky felt he was limited to associations with 'grace'. For the 1913 season, during which *Sacre* was presented, Dyagilev went into partnership with Thomas Beecham and moved to the Theatre Royal, Drury Lane. During this season, Modest Musorgsky's opera *Boris Godunov* received its London premier with Fedor Shalyapin (Chaliapin) in the title role, and it is fair to say that in London at the time Dyagilev's company was as well known for its operas as it was for its ballets. The list of subscribers for this season suggests a shift from the aristocratic and conservative political elite audiences of previous seasons to a more liberal and artistically progressive one.[12]

When *Sacre* was first performed in Paris on 29 May 1913, some British devotees travelled to see it, which gave London audiences advance warning of its controversial nature. On 25 June, *Jeux*, the other new ballet Nizhinsky created that year, was performed With a commissioned score by Claude Debussy, *Jeux* was a largely story-less ballet about a triangular relationship between a man (Nizhinsky) and two women (Karsavina and Lyudmila Shollar), which the programme suggested was set ten years in the future. The scene was a tennis court in a public park at dusk, lit by electric light, and with an aeroplane passing overhead. This modern subject puzzled audiences in both Britain and France. Hanna Järvinen has suggested that for the British, compared with *Jeux*, *Sacre*'s more obviously Russian subject would have fitted better with audience expectations of the company's work.[13] *Sacre* was therefore presented in London at a time when the identity of Dyagilev's company was in transition: some of the reviews of *Sacre* betray antagonism or hostility

[12] Garafola, *Diaghilev's Ballets Russes*, 307.

[13] Hanna Järvinen, 'The Myth and Genius in Movement: Historical Deconstruction of the Nijinsky Legend', PhD thesis, University of Turku, 2003.

towards Nizhinsky's alleged crime against grace, while others welcome its embrace of the new.

Sacre's presentation of an imaginary prehistoric Slavonic tribe's rituals, a narrative devised by Stravinsky and Rerikh, included Slavonic imagery that Russians would have interpreted in nationalist terms. British critics however focused mostly on its modernism: the ballet did not act out the limited narrative but generated a strong, ritualistic intensity. Stravinsky's radical music was composed in cells using complex irregular rhythms and what was, at the time, unorthodox orchestration. Nizhinsky's choreography, it is now thought, responded to the expressive possibilities suggested in the score by creating heavy, jagged, asymmetrical movement material.

Some of the critics in the London papers, like their Parisian counterparts, disliked *Sacre*. Adolphe Julien had written in the *Journal des débats* that the ballet mocked the public, and dismissed both Stravinsky's 'bizarre' music and Nizhinsky's 'monotonous', 'insignificant', and 'pretentious' choreography.[14] Richard Capell in the *Daily Mail* called it 'Cannibal Island Dancing', while the *Daily Telegraph* complained that 'all this primordial, logical business revealed no beauty, save momentarily when... Miss Piltz danced amazingly'.[15] *The Standard* called the choreography 'anti-curvilinear', complaining that 'The subject—primitive man—is ugly, and his movements are ugly as the ugliest duckling'—probably alluding to the more conventionally beautiful *Swan Lake* or to Pavlova's famous solo, *The Dying Swan*.[16]

Lacking a vocabulary with which to create a critical discourse about choreography, London critics drew parallels between *Sacre* and developments in either the visual arts or contemporary music. Capell wittily suggested that the ballet's appeal 'is allied to recent manifestations in the other arts, and may perhaps be called cubist dancing' according to a recent definition—'twenty-four dances danced by twenty-four dancers to twenty-four different tunes played simultaneously'.[17] But more positive connections were made too. The anonymous *Times* critic appreciated 'the employment of rhythmic counterpoint in the choral movements', giving as an example the end of the first scene 'where figures in scarlet run wildly round the stage in a great circle while the shaking masses within are ceaselessly splitting up into tiny groups revolving on eccentric axes'.[18] 'The old ballet and the new: M. Nijinski's revolution', the first of two articles about Nizhinsky in *The Times*, placed the radical turn taken by his choreography in a broad art-historical context. It proposed that ballet as an art form had, since the time of Louis XIV, exemplified notions of grace and beauty that conformed to the same ideas about beautiful curves William Hogarth had discussed in his 'Analysis of Beauty' (1753), and which one might also find in

[14] 'Le plus fâcheux, dans *le Sacre du Printemps*, n'est pas qu'il ait composé en scenario et réglé une chorégraphie d'une pauvreté désespérante, c'est que cette monotonie et cette insignifiance si prétentieuse, aient entrainé M. Stravinsky à vouloir lutter de bizarrerie avec son collaborateur' (Adolphe Julien, 'Musique', *Journal des débats* (8 June 1913), 1–2).

[15] Capell, 'Cannibal music', 5, 'Russian Ballet: "Le Sacre de Printemps"'; *Daily Telegraph* (12 July 1913).

[16] Quoted in Nesta Macdonald, *Diaghilev Observed by Critics in England and the United States, 1911–1929* (New York: Dance Horizons, 1975), 97.

[17] Cappell, 'Cannibal music', 5.

[18] 'The fusion of music and dancing: "Le sacre du printemps"', *The Times*, (26 July 1913), 8.

classical Greek sculpture. There was something in Nizhinsky's choreography, however, that brought to mind the 'massive strain of weight and force which the square abrupt figures of Assyrian and archaic Hellenic sculpture convey to us'. Nizhinsky's revolution, it suggested, had led the choreographer to ' "Post-Impressionism" and the sacrifice of beauty to expressiveness, while the effort to infuse into dancing a genuinely barbaric quality of emotion has led him to follow the "Cubists" in their return to the sculptural ideals of ages which were too rude to appreciate the languorous charm of curves'.[19] The second article in *The Times*, which appeared three weeks later, argued that *Sacre* represented a new kind of fusion of music and dancing: 'The combination of the two elements of music and dancing actually produce a new compound result, expressible in terms of rhythm—much as the combination of oxygen and hydrogen produces a totally different compound, water'.[20]

For Geoffrey Whitworth, whose *The Art of Nijinsky* was published in late 1913 by Chatto and Windus, Nizhinsky's choreography was evidently a revelation. But he noted that 'this new phase of ballet-dancing, for all its power to shock or amuse a certain section of the public, here and in Paris, is no isolated venture', connecting it to post-impressionist painting and the new music of Debussy and Stravinsky. Nizhinsky's choreographic innovations, Whitworth went on, 'have shown us dancing stripped of its conventional attributes, a thing of accent rather than of rhythm, and almost destitute of grace, though still dancing essentially', so that 'almost every quality of beauty or dramatic interest which we had grown to expect in a ballet was absent from this one'. This, he argued, was 'not a destruction of what had been valued in the past... but a gradual evolution towards a new expressiveness and a new technique.'[21]

Like Whitworth, Leonard Inkster, writing in the *New Statesman*, believed that *Sacre* offered new potential for cultural renewal. Through a comparison of Nizhinsky's choreography with Fokin's choreography of the ballets Dyagilev had presented in earlier seasons, Inkster argued that Nizhinsky's approach produced a new synthesis in the arts:

> In *Le Sacre du printemps* you may see the barbaric Russian gestures and dances not, as in *Schéhérazade* and *Prince Igor*, used for their own natural oddness and barbarity, or as features in a barbarous story, but used to build up a synthesis in movement of a barbaric idea, the sacrifice of a young girl to spring. The literalness of the plot is gone; we do not rely on an unforeseen dénouement to excite us; we look for the unfolding of an idea... Here there was much more nearly a synthesis of the arts, neither in service to the other, but both expressing one idea.[22]

Moreover, for Inkster, ballet was particularly well suited to modernity, 'as a complex of music, pantomime scene and dance... it contains a refinement of all the most

[19] 'The old ballet and the new: M. Nijinski's revolution', *The Times* (5 July 1913), 11.

[20] 'The fusion of music and dancing, *The Times*, 8.

[21] Geoffrey Whitworth, *The Art of Nijinsky* (New York: Blom, 1972 [1913]), 82, 85, 98, 99. Whitworth worked for Chatto, and was also involved with the modernist poetry magazine, *The Open Window.* In retrospect, he is best known as a tireless campaigner in the 1920s and 30s for the establishment of the National Theatre; he seems to have written nothing else about dance.

[22] Leonard Inkster, 'The Russian ballet, II', *New Statesman* (19 July 1913), 470.

insistent elements of modern city existence', he wrote. 'We move today like figures in a kaleidoscope that is noisy, and our movements are incoherent—we have no form.'[23]

Although these writers all embraced the new choreography as positive and necessary, there was also a widespread discussion in Britain about 'natural dancing', in which modernity was perceived as a negative and unhealthy influence. Writing in 1912 about recent developments in theatre dance, J. E. Crawford Flitch sums up what was at stake in contemporary anxieties about the natural and the modern: 'the modern world has lost the old graceful motions natural to man in a less artificial state'. He proposes that 'the characteristic of natural movement is undulation', and relates the movement of water, wind, and trees to that of pre-industrial work activities like scything, rowing, and horse riding. However, Crawford Flitch notes that 'in the modern civilized world the body is usually exercised either too little or too continuously in a single occupation... Human motion nowadays tends to be not flowing but angular, abrupt, disjointed, full of gestures not flowing imperceptibly one into another but broken off midway.'[24] I noted earlier that *The Standard* called *Sacre*'s choreography 'anti-curvilinear': Crawford Flitch was writing before *Sacre* was created, but this passage seems to anticipate the movement qualities of Nizhinsky's choreography. Crawford Flitch's discussion is a useful reference point because of the direct correlation he perhaps unintentionally infers between the experience of modern, metropolitan lifestyles, and a particular modernist movement aesthetic. Because he felt that the practice of healthy dancing could remedy the ills of modern life, he would be unlikely to have agreed that, as Inkster suggested, modern choreography could express the experience of modernity.

An unsigned 'Letter of An Englishman', printed in the *Daily Mail* on 19 July, five days after Nizhinsky's interview in the same paper cited at the start of this chapter, takes a similar position to that of Crawford Flitch. This anonymous letter is typical of righteous tirades to conservative newspapers by outraged citizens. I quote at length its opening:

> M. Nijinski, the most highly accomplished dancer of our time, declared on the morrow of his new ballet that 'grace and charm made him sea-sick'. The confession is ingenuous and characteristic. The spirit of the age has gone to M. Nijinski's head, as it has gone to the head of many other artists. The same lawlessness, the same contempt of order which afflicts the politics of to-day afflicts also the humanities. The virtue most highly prized is the virtue of novelty. A fierce hatred of beauty drives the advanced champions of all the arts into a wild revolt against tradition. True image-breakers, they would destroy if they could all the trophies of the past. Discarding the wise lessons of centuries, they would re-create the world anew. And the implements of their creation are the hammer and the bomb. M. Marinetti, the Italian Futurist, and the militant suffragette differ only in the object of their attack.[25]

[23] Leonard Inkster, 'The Russian ballet, I', *New Statesman* (5 July 1913), 406.
[24] J. E. Crawford Flitch, *Modern Dancing and Dancers* (London: Grant Richards, 1912), 103, 104.
[25] 'Letter of an Englishman', *Daily Mail* (19 July 1913).

Seven more paragraphs follow during which the writer gradually shifts his target from ballet to post-impressionist, cubist and futurist painting. For him, modern art from abroad falls short of the principle of grace and beauty proposed by that quintessentially English painter Hogarth, who had also been compared with Nizhinsky in *The Times*.

In his condemnation of the suffragette leadership, Marinetti, and Dyagilev, the anonymous writer of the 'Letter of An Englishman' draws parallels between these disparate figures on the basis of their shrewd manipulation of publicity and the use of shock tactics to gain public attention. In this context, the mention of suffragism is distinctly suggestive, since Emily Wilding Davison's fatal intervention had taken place only a few weeks before. Like the Chosen One (l'élue) in the ballet, Davison appeared to have sacrificed herself. Mariya Pil′ts, who danced this role, was singled out for praise in a number of the newspapers, yet underlying anxieties about her solo also sometimes surfaced in the press.

From a British point of view, the modernist dancing body had become a site for contested notions of grace and the natural. What is striking is the complex socio-political matrix through which British writers recognized and responded to the new ways of moving in *Sacre*. The anonymous letter-writer in the *Daily Mail* was anxious about the spectacle of the lawless bodies of suffragettes and modernist ballet dancers, whose unnaturalness threatened to contaminate society. For him modernist art was generically foreign. What to him seemed uncontrollable, however, Whitworth welcomed warmly. Inkster valued the shift *Sacre* marked from the exoticism of ballets like *Schéhérazade* towards a new synthesis that transcended an older, primitive, Russian essence. At the heart of this appreciation was a willingness, largely absent in France, to accept Nizhinsky as a serious modern choreographer.

WOMEN'S RESPONSES TO *LE SACRE DU PRINTEMPS*

Nizhinsky was not considered as a serious modern choreographer for most of the twentieth century. Many of the more conservative members of Dyagilev's circle used the fact that, after 1918, Nizhinsky spent his life under medical supervision for mental health problems, to dismiss his avant-garde choreography as the work of an idiot. The way Nizhinsky was presented in Sergey Grigor′ev's memoirs exemplifies this.[26] For much of his life, Stravinsky also dismissed Nizhinsky as an imbecile, and his choreography for *Le Sacre du printemps* as a failure. In 1913, however, his letters and interviews show that he was extremely enthusiastic about Nizhinsky's response

[26] Sergey Grigor′ev was the rehearsal director for the Ballets Russes and a close friend of Fokin. In 1913 Dyagilev sacked Fokin in order to present a programme of ballets choreographed by Nizhinsky, which explains much of Grigor′ev's hostility towards him: see S. L. Grigoriev, *The Diaghilev Ballet, 1909–1929* (Harmondsworth: Penguin, 1960). Romola Nijinsky, in her deliberately sensational biography of her husband, shows no understanding or sympathy for his avant-garde aesthetics and, as Joan Acocella has shown, had her own reasons for giving a distorted account of his mental health: see Romola Nijinsky, *Nijinsky* (London: Sphere Books, 1970), and Joan Acocella, introduction in Joan Acocella, ed., and Kyril Fitzlyon, trans. *The Diary of Vaslav Nijinsky: Unexpurgated Edition* (New York: Farrar, Strauss and Giroux, 1999), vii–xlvi. The fairest account of the situation is Peter Oswald, *Vaslav Nijinsky: A Leap into Madness* (New York: Citadel Press, *1991*).

to his music, and at the end of his life he admitted that Nizhinsky's ballet had been better than any subsequent production.[27]

That there has been continuing interest in Nizhinsky's choreography, despite Stravinsky's contradictory statements, is largely due to the women who were involved in its production. Nizhinsky initially worked closely with his sister Bronislava Nizhinskaya, who subsequently became an important choreographer in her own right. With her he created *Sacre*'s final solo, which he then used as a stylistic template for the rest of the choreography. Dyagilev also hired Marie Rambert to assist Nizhinsky. A teacher of Jaques-Dalcroze's system of rhythmic gymnastics, Rambert's role was to help the dancers learn the complex irregular rhythms of Stravinsky's music, and she also danced in the ballet. Born in Poland, Rambert spoke several languages including Russian and, as the only dancer with an overview of the ballet as a whole, she seems to have acted as a sounding board for Nizhinsky's ideas. Both she and Nizhinskaya record in their memoirs Nizhinsky's furious reaction when he learnt of his sister's pregnancy and realized she would not be able to dance the role of the Chosen One in his ballet. This role was taken over by the promising, young, but largely unknown ballerina, Mariya Pil′ts. Pil′ts spoke at length about this experience during interviews in the 1960s with the Russian ballet historian Vera Krasovskaya. All these influential women's testimonies attested to the importance of *Sacre* at a time when Nizhinsky's choreography was being dismissed as a failure.

A further important source of information about women's responses to the ballet is a group of drawings by Valentine Gross, a French artist who subsequently joined the Surrealist group. Gross believed that the ballet was so important that she attended all nine of its performances, sketching it. She published an illustration in the glossy performing arts magazine *Montjoie*, which combines drawings of moments from the final solo with extracts from the music. In that illustration, the figure has been formalized in a way that gives it an almost art nouveau-like appearance, whereas her pencil sketches of individual dancers and pastels of group scenes have a more jagged, energetic quality that is closer to the fragmented modernist vitality of the choreography. Significantly, it is the idea of the Chosen One's final sacrifice that seems to have fascinated Gross.

The dance historian Tim Scholl notes similarities between the plot of *Sacre* and two other ballets that stage death scenes: the 1841 Romantic ballet *Giselle* and Anna Pavlova's famous 1905 solo, *The Dying Swan*. He argues that whereas these works sentimentalized death in a romantic way, the fragmented choreography of *Sacre* disrupted the ballet tradition and 'dealt an anarchic death blow to the nineteenth-century academic ballet'.[28] Scholl explores correlations between the ballet's anarchic theme and similar concerns in early twentieth-century Russian literature. But the ballet should also be analysed in relation to the ways in which it provided a vehicle

[27] See Stephanie Jordan, *Stravinsky Dances* (London: Dance Books, 2007).

[28] Tim Scholl, *From Petipa to Balanchine: Classical Revival and the Modernization of Ballet* (London: Routledge, 1994), 77.

for mediating specifically female experiences of modernity. A ballet devised by men about the sacrifice of a young virgin does not seem to present the kinds of ideas about femininity that would inspire the important and influential women who have been responsible for preserving its memory, yet Nizhinskaya remembered that 'the exciting rhythms of Stravinsky's music and the precision of rendering these rhythms were challenging. I was inspired by the innovations in the music and in the choreography'.[29]

Many of the British critics reviewing *Sacre* admired the intensity with which Pil′ts performed its difficult, modernist dance movements, and yet there is a hint in the way they did so that suggests they thought her performance may have been excessive. Their anxiety seems to have been inspired both by the feminine freedom that Pil′ts's solo signified, and by the modernism of its choreography. There is a parallel here with the suffragette campaign. Writing in 1912 in the suffragette newspaper *Votes for Women*, Teresa Billington-Grieg summed up the attitude of a large part of the general public towards the militant suffragettes: 'they admire the agitator, they resent the wrong against which she agitates; but they condemn the methods of agitation'.[30] Admiration for both Pil′ts and the suffragettes' strength was tempered by feelings that they were too extreme. Anxiety about Pil′ts's solo surfaced in an item in the *Daily Telegraph* which stated that she had been forbidden by the medical profession from dancing the solo again 'owing to the detrimental effect it had upon her, the physical strain being overwhelming'.[31] The cause of Pil′ts's supposed strain seems to be the fragmented nature of the choreography, its unnatural, modern quality. Nizhinskaya and Rambert in their memoirs, and Pil′ts in her interviews with Vera Krasovskaya, all attest to their continuing fascination with the very qualities in Nizhinsky's modernist choreography that many contemporary critics found unacceptable. While these critics feared change, the dancers eagerly embraced it. *Sacre* offered these women opportunities to explore, through dancing, a continual process of creative re-invention at a time when the world around them was rapidly changing.

Vera Krasovskaya records Pil′ts's memory of the tumultuous first performance concluding, in a poignant passage, with the moment when Dyagilev sent her out to take her curtain call. Pil′ts, she writes,

> mechanically assumed her pose of the victim ready for sacrifice, and stood amidst the thunder of applause and shouts of protest descending upon her from the auditorium. She did not move, standing just like an idol hewn from wood. Except that the tears flowed, making furrows in the greasepaint on her face. Fifty years later in Leningrad, in a room on Ligovsky Prospect which looked onto a rather gloomy courtyard, an old lady stricken with paralysis maintained a long and persistent silence, until she pronounced: 'Sergei Pavlovich pushed me onto the stage. I stood in the middle and just howled'.[32]

[29] Nijinska, *Early Memoirs*, 450.

[30] Teresa Billington-Grieg, *Suffragist Tactics Past and Present* (1912), in Marie Mulvey Roberts and Tamae Mizuta, eds, *The Militants: Suffragette Activism* (London: Routledge, 1994), 4.

[31] Robin H. Legge, 'Drury Lane Theatre', *Daily Telegraph* (26 July 1913).

[32] Vera Krasovskaya, *Nijinsky* (New York: Schirmer Books, 1979), 267.

Nizhinskaya believed that *Sacre* marked 'the beginnings of a new era for the ballet and for choreography'. What Krasovskaya identifies here is the experience of being in the absolute centre of this turbulent flux. Her writing bears witness to the overwhelming emotions Pil'ts experienced as she found herself as the figure at the heart of this dynamic shift when something new and unknown was beginning to appear—'the beginnings of a new era for the ballet and for choreography', as Nizhinksaya put it.[33] It is here that parallels with the suffragettes become relevant, as Emily Wilding Davison's act of sacrifice put her in a similar position at the centre of a traumatic moment of social rather than artistic transition.

WOMEN AND SACRIFICE

Emily Wilding Davison was a member of the Women's Social and Political Union (WSPU), formed in 1903 by Emmeline Pankhurst: disappointed with older suffragist organizations, WSPU members believed that militant actions were the only way to force politicians to give votes to women. Between 1905 and 1914, they campaigned against the Liberals, who as a party appeared to oppose giving votes to women, at two general elections and at intervening by-elections. In the early years, they heckled Liberal politicians at public meetings, but protests gradually became increasingly violent and destructive. Noting that the motto of the WSPU was 'Deeds not Words', Wendy Parkins argues that 'suffragettes did not simply *act* to become citizens or act *like* citizens, they acted citizenship'.[34] Many suffragettes were initially arrested for comparatively minor offences, but refused to pay fines or be bound over to keep the peace and were therefore sent to prison. Once there, they were rarely granted the status of political prisoner and given First Division privileges, as, for example, the Irish nationalist political leader, Charles Stewart Parnell, had been. In June 1909 Marion Dunlop, a Scottish artist, was the first Suffragette prisoner to go on hunger strike when her request for First Division privileges was denied. After refusing food for ninety-one hours, she was released, thus inspiring a number of other suffragettes to follow her example. In September that year, the Home Secretary Herbert Gladstone ordered that hunger-striking suffragettes should henceforth be force-fed.

Davison was imprisoned eight times for militant actions, and force-fed on many occasions, once even though she was not in fact on hunger strike. Her offences included stone-throwing, breaking windows, and setting fire to a post box. Because their voices were in effect silenced, Davison and others were extraordinarily inventive in finding other means, including non-verbal embodied ones, for formulating and signifying specifically female aspirations for change in a modern world. Davison, for example, hid in a cupboard in the House of Commons overnight to avoid the 1911 census. Ann Morley and Liz Stanley suggest that, together with her

[33] Nijinska, *Early Memoirs*, 471.

[34] Wendy Parkins, 'Protesting like a girl: Embodiment, dissent and feminist agency', *Feminist Theory*, 1 (2000), 63.

close friend Mary Leigh, Davison was one of the more independent and radical members of the WSPU. She 'had a habit of pioneering militant actions without recourse to leadership approval or even knowledge, and this was incompatible with employment by the WSPU'.[35] The escalating destructiveness—and self-destructiveness—of the methods adopted by the WSPU, and the brutal juridical processes including forced feeding that were used to suppress them, appear to have pushed Davison to further and further extremes, ending with her fatal intervention at the 1913 Derby. The radical extremes to which Pil'ts pushed her new, powerfully visceral dance movements produced a disturbing experience for many in her audience. Pil'ts's sacrificial solo and Davison's death made related revelations of what the body on its own can do.

The 21-year-old Rebecca West, at the start of her career as a journalist, wrote an angry article for *The Clarion,* a weekly socialist newspaper, inspired by her attendance at the funeral of Emily Davison. Noting that Davison's life was a tragedy 'which we ought not to have permitted', West, in an astonishing passage, points the finger of blame at the whole institution of government, which she compares with the nineteenth-century serial killer Jack the Ripper and accuses of taking pleasure in violence against women:

> Today Jack the Ripper works free-handed from the honourable places of government: he sits on the Front Bench at St Stephen's or in those vast public sepulchres of conscience in Whitehall, and works not in secret but through Home Office orders and scarlet-robed judges. Scotland Yard is at his service; the medical profession, up to the President of the Royal College of Surgeons, places its skills at his disposal, that his mutilations may be more ingenious. And for his victims he no longer seeks the shameful women of mean streets. To him, before the dull eyes of the unprotesting world, fall the finest women of the land.[36]

What is remarkable about this passage is West's recognition of the way the smooth and efficient functioning of the modern state can dehumanize bodies. West had become aware of what distinguishes human life from animal existence because Davison presented her with the terrible spectacle of the denial and removal of this human quality. West's article not only denounces the Government, but begins with a testament of her friendship with Davison. She describes her as someone who 'delighted by the world which her fine wits and her moral passion had revealed to her could not rest till you had seen it too'. Noting Davison's academic achievements—she gained honours in degrees at both Oxford and the University of London—West remembers her 'cheerfulness and her pyrotechnic intelligence blazing the brighter through a body worn thin by pain'.[37] West published an essay on

[35] Liz Morley and Ann Stanley, *The Life and Death of Emily Wilding Davison* (London: Women's Press, 2001), 114.

[36] Rebecca West, *The Young Rebecca: Writings of Rebecca West, 1911–17* (Basingstoke: Macmillan, 1982), 183.

[37] West, *The Young Rebecca*, 178, 179.

the Ballets Russes in 1919, and wrote about Nizhinsky towards the end of her life: it seems likely that she attended one of the London performances of *Sacre* a few weeks after she followed Davison's coffin through London.[38] If West saw the Chosen One's final solo, might she have felt that Pil′ts was carrying on a similar fight with equal determination?

The major point of commonality between Pil′ts's solo and Davison's final actions is the idea of sacrifice. During a suffragette riot in Holloway Prison in late 1912, Davison had thrown herself downstairs and nearly died. After her release, in an interview with the *Pall Mall Gazette*, she said, 'I did it deliberately and with all my power because I felt that by nothing but the sacrifice of human life would the nation be brought to realize the horrible torture our women face. If I had succeeded I am sure that forcible feeding could not in all conscience have been resorted to again.'[39] In an essay entitled 'The price of liberty', published posthumously in *The Suffragette*, Davison re-interpreted the New Testament parable of the pearl as an allegory of the suffragette struggle.[40] She compares women's liberty to winning a pearl of great price, in which 'the perfect Amazon is she who will sacrifice all even unto the last, to win the Pearl of Freedom for her sex... To lay down life for friends, that is glorious, selfless, inspiring! But to re-enact the tragedy of Calvary for generations yet unborn, that is the last consummate sacrifice of the Militant.'[41] Stanley and Morley argue that Davison was referring here to Emmeline Pankhurst, the founder and leader of the WSPU. It was, however, widely believed at the time that Davison's fatal intervention at the Derby was an act of sacrifice.

In *Sacre*, the Chosen One is expelled from her fictional community and dies through exhausting her body's vitality. This is her sacred gift. Since Hobbes, it has been assumed that communities have some kind of contract whereby members pay a due in return for protection. The Chosen One's gift should not, however, be conflated with a due paid in order to be part of a community. A gift is freely given, while a due is a compulsory deduction. The question of community is complicated in the case of the suffragettes. Their aim was to become fully enfranchised members of the national community: one of their complaints was that women were subject to taxation but could not vote for the parliamentary representatives who decided how their taxes were spent. The sacrifices that Davison and others made for the suffragette movement generated a sense of community within the movement itself, as exemplified by the large number of people who marched in procession behind Davison's coffin. Henri Hubert and Marcel Mauss have argued that there can be no sacrifice without a community.[42] Yet the effect of Davison's sacrifice on the national

[38] Rebecca West, 'The Russian Ballet', *The Outlook*, (7 June 1919), 568; and 'Nijinsky', *Sunday Telegraph*, (7 November 1971), quoted in Richard Buckle, *Nijinsky* (Harmondsworth: Penguin, 1975), 390.

[39] Emily Davison, 'Letter to the Editor', *Pall Mall Gazette* (19 September 1912), 4

[40] Carolyn Collette argues that the essay was also inspired by Chaucer's 'The Knight's Tale': see '"Faire Emelye": Medievalism and the Moral Courage of Emily Wilding Davison', *Chaucer Review*, 42 no. 3 (2008), 223–43.

[41] Emily Davison, 'The Price of Liberty', *The Suffragette* (5 June 1914), 129.

[42] Henri Hubert and Marcel Mauss, *Sacrifice: Its Nature and Function* (Chicago, IL: Chicago University Press, 1964).

community was to reveal its narrowness and limitations and thus articulate the absolute necessity of reimagining community in more open ways. The Chosen One's sacrifice in *Sacre* had a similar effect. What was so shocking about the latter was its modernist lack of sentiment. As Isabelle Launay proposes, what *Sacre* presents is neither a heroic sacrifice nor a redemptive Christian one: 'The sacrifice of this articulated body reaches the limits of its representation in order to allow a new body to appear.'[43] The avant-garde nature of the Chosen One's final sacrificial solo deconstructs ballet as a theatrical form in order to suggest new creative potentials for women as professional dancers performing in theatres.

I noted earlier that the Chosen One's solo was choreographed first, and used as a template or movement archive while making the rest of the ballet. As Launay points out, when this solo was finally performed, everything in it was already familiar in the movements of the community. The Chosen One's act of sacrifice was therefore one of selflessly embodying the gestures of others, giving her life to them and, by doing so, according to Hubert and Mauss, acquiring sacred value. The same happened when Pil′ts took her bow. She resumed her pose as the victim ready for sacrifice in order to become the focus for the conflicting hopes and fears that the ballet had stirred up in the audience. Similarly, Davison's gift became the focus for conflicting hopes and fears about women's enfranchisement. By donating herself as a sacred gift, Davison was reasserting her humanness—a quality that had been taken away from her by the State as it reduced her to mere biological existence through the dehumanizing practice of forced-feeding. Davison and Pil′ts's sacrifices transformed a due that had been a compulsory deduction into a freely given gift that was in excess of what the State had demanded. By doing so, their radical actions troubled and challenged their communities and created potential in them for something new.

This chapter has discussed how the freedoms expressed by the lawless bodies of Davison and Pil′ts were a source of unease in early twentieth-century Britain. Responses to modernist ballet, I have argued, were conditioned by attitudes towards modernity. What some feared, others eagerly embraced. Both Crawford Flitch and Leonard Inkster, for very different reasons, recognized that the qualities of modernist movement were the products of modern urban lifestyles. Inkster and Geoffrey Whitworth hoped that the new expressive power Nizhinsky was developing would have the potential to generate cultural renewal. Gross, Nizhinskaya, Pil′ts, and Rambert were also enthusiastic about the new possibilities that Nizhinsky's choreography offered to modern dancing bodies. As modern women, they had no investment in continuing to embody the status quo. What my comparison between Davison's intervention at the Derby and the final solo in *Sacre* reveals is the complex and disconcerting power of the idea of sacrifice. To embrace the new freedoms which modernity offered women was to risk having to pay the cost of losing community protection from male misogyny. Rebecca West characterized the latter as Jack the Ripper working with the acquiescent support of the male governing elite.

[43] 'Le sacrifice de ce corps articulaire atteint les limites de sa représentation pour laisser apparaître un nouveau corps' : see Isabelle Launay, 'Communauté et articulations: à propos du *Sacre du printemps* de V. Nijinsky', in Claire Rousier, ed., *Être ensemble: figures de la communauté en danse depuis le xxe siècle* (Paris: Centre national de la danse, 2003), 84.

Responses to the London performances of *Sacre* show that the British were prepared to accept that the revolutionary dancing bodies in Nizhinsky's modernist ballet were related to the modernism of post-impressionist and cubist painting. To British eyes, they were all equally foreign—something that may explain the relative lack of emphasis on the Russianness of the ballet. *Le Sacre du printemps*, like the suffragettes' militant campaign, confronted spectators with the unbearable necessity of accepting a dynamic shift when something new and unknown was starting to appear.

8

Russian Aesthetics in Britain

Kandinsky, Sadleir, and *Rhythm*

Caroline Maclean

In the fourth issue of the modernist magazine *Rhythm*, published in the spring of 1912, its editor, the aspiring art critic Michael Sadleir, declared that Vasily Kandinsky had 'voiced the inarticulate ideals of a multitude'.[1] The article in which this remark appeared, 'After Gauguin', claimed to describe Gauguin's legacy, but was in fact primarily a critique of Kandinsky's new book, *Über das Geistige in der Kunst*, published in Germany earlier that year. Sadleir's article was the first to introduce the British public to the Russian artist's aesthetics. Sadleir went on to translate *Über das Geistige in der Kunst*, which was published as *The Art of Spiritual Harmony* in 1914.[2]

Rhythm, published between 1911 and 1913, was one of the more aesthetically radical of the pre-war magazines that have shaped our understanding of the modernist period. I am using the term 'modernist magazine' in line with Peter Brooker and Andrew Thacker's recent critical and cultural history of modernist magazines, in which they argue for a heterogeneous field that includes avant-garde 'little magazines' (such as *Rhythm, BLAST*, and *The Egoist*) as well as the 'more neutral sounding' periodicals, journals, papers, and reviews (such as the *New Age*, *The Athenaeum*, and *The Criterion*).[3] Like other modernist magazines of the pre-war period *Rhythm* was keen to assert itself as avant-garde. In the first issue, the editor, John Middleton Murry, declared that 'Rhythm is a magazine with a purpose.' That purpose was to 'provide art, be it drawing, literature, or criticism, which shall be vigorous, determined, which shall have its roots below the surface, and be the rhythmical echo of the life with which it is in touch'.[4] And in a very early usage of the term, he declared that 'modernism' 'penetrates beneath the outward surface of the world' and 'disengages the rhythms that lie at the heart of things'.[5] However, *Rhythm*'s manifesto

[1] Michael T. H. Sadler, 'After Gauguin', *Rhythm*, 1, no. 4 (1912), 29. Michael T. H. Sadler changed his name to the older spelling of Sadleir in 1914 to differentiate himself from his father, Michael E. Sadler. Hereafter I will refer to Michael T. H. Sadler as Sadleir in the text to avoid confusion.

[2] Wassily Kandinky, *The Art of Spiritual Harmony*, trans. M. T. H. Sadler (London: Constable, 1914)

[3] Peter Brooker and Andrew Thacker, 'General Introduction', in *The Oxford Critical and Cultural History of Modernist Magazines* (Oxford: Oxford University Press, 2009), 13.

[4] [John Middleton Murry], 'Aims and Ideals', *Rhythm*, 1, no. 1 (1911), 36.

[5] John Middleton Murry, 'Art and Philosophy', *Rhythm*, 1, no. 1 (1911), 12.

appears modest alongside Wyndham Lewis's manifesto in *BLAST*, published two years later, which describes itself as 'an avenue for all those vivid and violent ideas that could reach the Public in no other way', or Dora Marsden's declaration in the *New Freewoman* in 1913 that 'in the clash of opinion we shall expect to find our values'.[6] *Rhythm*'s purpose was less combative; rather than spar with the European avant-garde, it sought to appropriate it to its own purposes.

Rhythm was first published in the summer of 1911, edited by Murry and Sadleir, with the Scottish painter John Duncan Fergusson as art editor. Murry's partner, Katherine Mansfield, became assistant editor on the fifth issue in July 1912. Breaking her connections with A. R. Orage's weekly, the *New Age*, Mansfield replaced Sadleir at the request of Charles Granville, of Stephen Swift and Co., who had published her first collection of short stories, *In a German Pension* (1911), and had now taken over the publication of *Rhythm*. Mansfield co-edited the February and March 1913 issues, before the journal folded due to severe financial difficulties after a total of fourteen issues.

Rhythm tends to be referred to as Bergsonian in philosophy and Scottish Fauvist in aesthetics, with a strong emphasis on French literature and art.[7] Its Fauvism was that of the Scottish colourists Fergusson and S. J. Peploe. Fergusson's close friend, Georges (Dorothy) Banks, and his partner of the time, Anne Estelle Rice, were also regular contributors. Fergusson's access to the Parisian art world resulted in the reproduction of works by artists associated with Fauvism including André Dunoyer de Segonzac, André Derain, Auguste Herbin, and Auguste Chabaud, as well as drawings by Picasso and Henri Gaudier-Brzeska. *Rhythm* published literary works by the Parisian-based writers Tristan Derème and Francis Carco in French. As Marysa Demoor has remarked, 'one is struck by the sheer number of French contributions to *Rhythm*'.[8] Less frequently discussed, though often noted, is the wider international focus of the magazine. In addition to the work coming out of Paris, *Rhythm* published Yone Noguchi's articles on Japanese aesthetics, and showed a particular interest in Russian art and literature: it printed prose by Leonid Andreev, drawings by Natal'ya Goncharova, reviews of productions by Sergey Dyagilev's Ballets Russes, and stories written in the style of Tolstoy and Dostoevsky. Two of the international-sounding authors, Boris Petrovsky and Lili Heron, were in fact Mansfield's pseudonyms, reminding us, as Faith Binckes notes, that 'cosmopolitanism, or internationalism, was also about image and performance'.[9]

Rhythm embraced its cosmopolitan status, listing both 'Agents for *Rhythm* Abroad' on the back cover and 'foreign correspondents' on the contents page.

[6] [Wyndham Lewis], 'Long Live the Vortex', *Blast*, 1 (1914), 7; Dora Marsden, 'Views and Comments', *New Freewoman*, 1, no. 2 (1913), 25.

[7] See Faith Binckes, *Modernism, Magazines, and the British Avant-Garde: Reading Rhythm, 1910–1914* (Oxford: Oxford University Press, 2010), Mark Antliff, *Inventing Bergson: Cultural Politics and the Parisian Avant-Garde* (Princeton, NJ: Princeton University Press, 1993), and Anna Gruetzner Robins, *Modern Art in Britain, 1910–1914* (London: Merrell Holberton, 1997).

[8] Marysa Demoor, 'John Middleton Murry's Editorial Apprenticeships: Getting Modernist "Rhythm" into the *Athenaeum*, 1919–1921', *English Literature in Transition, 1880–1920*, 52 (2009), 130.

[9] Binckes, *Modernism, Magazines, and the British Avant-Garde*, 81.

Agents in Paris, New York, Munich, and Berlin, and an American correspondent, were listed by the fifth issue. The critic and translator Floryan Sobieniowski was added as the Polish correspondent in the sixth issue, and by August 1912 agents in Warsaw, Krakow, and Helsinki were included. Mikhail Likiardopulo, the secretary to the directors of the Moscow Art Theatre, was added as the Russian correspondent, and Francis Carco, Tristan Derème, Georges Banks, and Anne Estelle Rice were all listed as French correspondents from August 1912.

The significance of Sadleir's article on Kandinsky can be understood only when it is read in conjunction with a cross section of articles in magazines from the same period. Kandinsky's book is not mentioned in other British magazines in early 1912 because it had only just been published in Germany. Sadleir was given advance notice because Kandinsky himself had mentioned it in a letter to him in October 1911.[10] By comparison, Huntly Carter's art column in the *New Age* on 7 March 1912, focused on the first futurist exhibition held at the Galerie Bernheim-Jeune in Paris. The 'Notes from Russia' column in the *The Athenaeum* on 9 March included information about the number of public libraries in Russia (six hundred and thirty-three) and the publication of the first volume of *The Fauna of Russia* detailing every species of fish in the 'Russian Empire'.[11] The March 1912 issue of the *English Review* published the first translation by Stephen Graham of an essay by Vyacheslav Ivanov on the 'Theatre of the Future' in which he wrote that the 'presence of rhythm is indispensable' in art.[12] *Rhythm*, we can see, was not unusual in its focus on Russian aesthetics, but Sadleir's personal connection with Kandinsky positioned the magazine at the heart of a new spiritually-inflected Russian aesthetics.

Brooker's and Thacker's history of modernist magazines, and the digitization of many of the publications themselves, has opened up scholarship into this 'dialogic matrix of modernism'. As Brooker and Thacker argue, magazines cannot be read in isolation, they function in (often competitive) dialogue with each other as a 'network of cultural formations'.[13] In light of this argument, this chapter will argue that the appearance of Kandinsky's aesthetics in *Rhythm* was not anomalous, but part of a wider network of aesthetic concerns in British periodicals during the pre-war period. Of particular interest is the way in which Russian culture and modernism were connected to a growing interest in spiritual aesthetics, an interest that grew from a mixture of sources, including the Victorian fashion for spiritualism, the turn-of-the-century theosophical movement, and a reaction—in some quarters—against empiricism.

[10] Kandinsky to Sadleir, 6 October 1911, in Wassily Kandinsky, *Concerning the Spiritual in Art*, trans. Michael T. H. Sadler (London: Tate, 2006), appendix B, letter 2, 115.

[11] Huntly Carter, 'Art and Drama in Paris', *New Age*, 10, no. 19 (1912), 443; 'Notes from Russia', *Athenaeum*, 4402 (1912), 279.

[12] Viacheslaf Ivanof, 'The Theatre of the Future', trans. Stephen Graham, *English Review*, 10 (1912), 634, 640.

[13] Brooker and Thacker, 'General Introduction', in *The Oxford Critical and Cultural History of Modernist Magazines*, 2.

RHYTHM'S RUSSIAN AESTHETICS

The December 1912 issue of *Rhythm* included two lithographs by Natal′ya Goncharova that were titled *La Vendange*, and are now known as *Women with Basket of Grapes* and *Men with Basket of Grapes*. Goncharova's rhythmic representation of the harvesting of grapes shows the arms of the harvesters in identical dance-like poses. The designs were based on the *Picking Grapes* polyptych (1911). As Anthony Parton suggests, the polyptych brought together Goncharova's neo-primitive research and practice within a Christian framework (Fig. 6).[14] The 'drawing' that appears a few pages later attributed to Mikhail Larionov depicts a typically Russian-looking scene. In fact, this was a lithograph based on Goncharova's *Autumn Study* (1911), created as a postcard for the Donkey's Tail exhibition in Moscow in 1912.[15] It shows a man on horseback and another man following through a pine forest, in which the rain is so heavy it bends the branches of the trees. The angle and thickness of the strokes of the pencil, like the brushwork in the painting, indicate rain and also fragment the composition into triangular sections (Fig. 7).

The December 1912 issue of *Rhythm* went to press after the opening of Roger Fry's *Second Post Impressionist Exhibition* on 5 October 1912, in which Goncharova and Larionov were to exhibit, although their works, along with those of some others, did not arrive in time for the opening, and were added to the exhibition in January 1913. It may have been coincidence that the editors of *Rhythm* wanted to include Fry's exhibitors, but it is likely that there was also a competitive element. Earlier in 1912 the opening of the exhibition of the 'Rhythmists' at the Stafford Gallery, which included Jessica Dismorr, Fergusson, Peploe, Rice, and Ethel Wright, had been postponed from June to October in order to coincide with Fry's exhibition. Anna Gruetzner Robins argues convincingly that this was likely to have been orchestrated by Sadleir and the director of the gallery, John Neville, for maximum impact.[16]

As well as reproducing Russian visual art, *Rhythm* printed poems and stories purporting to be by Russian writers. In the same issue in which Sadleir wrote about Kandinsky, Mansfield used her alias 'Boris Petrovsky' for the first time, claiming to be 'his' translator. Yet the poems by Petrovsky/Mansfield—'Very Early Spring' and 'The Awakening River'—draw on a range of national styles. They appear, first, to parody contemporary Georgian pastoral poetry, a volume of which was published the same year.[17] Mansfield's reference to the river running away with the birds to

[14] Anthony Parton, *Goncharova: The Art and Design of Natalia Goncharova* (Woodbridge, Suffolk: Antique Collector's Club, 2010), 173–8.

[15] See Yevgenia Petrova, ed., *Natalia Goncharova: The Russian Years* (St Petersburg: Palace Editions, 2002), cat. 244. I am grateful to Anthony Parton for pointing this out.

[16] Gruetzner Robins, *Modern Art in Britain*, 108.

[17] [Katherine Mansfield], 'Two Poems of Boris Petrovsky', trans. Katherine Mansfield, *Rhythm*, 1, no. 4 (1912), 30. See Edward Marsh, ed., *Georgian Poetry, 1911–1912* (London: Poetry Bookshop, 1912).

NATALIE GONTCHAROVA

THE OPAL DREAM CAVE

In an opal dream cave I found a fairy :
Her wings were frailer than flower petals—
Frailer far than snowflakes.
She was not frightened, but poised on my finger,
Then delicately walked into my hand.
I shut the two palms of my hands together
And held her prisoner.
I carried her out of the opal cave,
Then opened my hands.
First she became thistledown,
Then a mote in a sunbeam,
Then—nothing at all.
Empty now is my opal dream cave.

KATHERINE MANSFIELD

NATALIE GONTCHAROVA

SEA

The Sea called—I lay on the rocks and said :
"I am come."
She mocked and showed her teeth,
Stretching out her long green arms.
"Go away," she thundered.
"Then tell me what I am to do," I begged.
"If I leave you, you will not be silent,
But cry my name in the cities
And wistfully entreat me in the plains and forests ;
All else I forsake to come to you—what must I do ?"
"Never have I uttered your name," snarled the Sea.
"There is no more of me in your body
Than the little salt tears you are frightened of shedding.
What can you know of my love on your brown rock pillow . . . .
Come closer."

KATHERINE MANSFIELD

Fig. 6. Natal′ya Goncharova, *Women with Basket of Grapes* and *Men with Basket of Grapes*, after the motifs of the *Picking Grapes* polyptych (1911), Russkii muzei (Russian Museum), St Petersburg. Reproduced as *La Vendange* in *Rhythm*, 2, no. 11 (December 1912), 306-7. © ADAGP, Paris and DACS, London 2012.

the sea in 'Very Early Spring' gently mocks the tendency of pastoral poets to be seduced by nature. But they also bear a striking resemblance in theme and tone to Paul Selver's translation of the Polish poet, Kazimierz Przerwa-Tetmajer, whose lyrical 'Song of the Night Mists' was published in the *New Age* in January 1912. This was noted by the *New Age* contributor Beatrice Hastings (Emily Alice Haigh), who referred to the 'flapping and wappering' of the stanzas, and to the entire issue of *Rhythm* as 'dutifully imitative' of the latest issue of the *New Age*.[18] Selver's translation of Przerwa-Tetmajer's poem reads, 'Softly, softly, let us wake not streams that in the valley sleep, / Let us with the wind dance gently o'er the spaces wide and deep'. Three months later in 'Very Early Spring', Mansfield wrote, 'A wind dances over the fields. / Shrill and clear the sound of her waking laughter, / Yet the little blue lakes tremble'.[19] Given the contentious relationship between Mansfield and Hastings, and Mansfield's fondness for satire, it seems likely that these poems were intended to amuse readers of the *New Age* and *Rhythm*. Hastings asks, 'Aware that Miss Mansfield has, on occasions, a sense of humour, we wonder if it is all a joke; especially as the verse is solemnly asserted to be a translation from the Russian!'[20]

[18] Beatrice Hastings, 'Present-Day Criticism', *New Age*, 10, no. 22 (1912), 519.
[19] Kazimierz Przerwa-Tetmajer, 'Song of the Night Mists', trans. Paul Selver, *New Age*, 10, no. 13 (1912), 292; [Mansfield], 'Two Poems of Boris Petrovsky', 30.
[20] Hastings, 'Present-Day Criticism', 519.

Fig. 7. Natal′ya Goncharova, *Autumn,* after the motifs of *Autumn Study (Direct Perception)* (1911), Russkii muzei (Russian Museum), St Petersburg. Reproduced as Mikhail Larionov, *Drawing,* in *Rhythm,* 2, no. 11 (December 1912), 317. © ADAGP, Paris and DACS, London 2012.

Frank Harris published 'The Holy Man (After Tolstoi)', a version of Tolstoy's 'The Three Hermits', in the June 1912 issue of *Rhythm*. Tolstoy's story was based on a legend he had heard from a wandering storyteller in 1879, and had first been published in Britain in 1906 in *Twenty-Three Tales,* a collection of his stories translated by Louise and Aylmer Maude. Harris adapts the story for a British readership: he explains that 'Men are commonly called "souls" in Russia as they are called "hands" in England', and in case we might find the holy man who is the subject of the story too sincere for authenticity the Bishop protagonist tells us he was not trying to "show off" but that his "sincerity was manifest and his goodness too"'.[21] Whereas Tolstoy's Bishop asks that we pray for 'us sinners', Harris's Bishop is abandoned in mid-sentence at the end of the story to effect the transfer of the story from a nineteenth-century Russian context to a British modernist one: 'I only wish—.'[22] More important than the changes made by Harris to Tolstoy's tale, however, is the editorial decision to include a nineteenth-century spiritual Russian folk legend in

[21] Frank Harris, 'The Holy Man', *Rhythm,* 2, no. 5 (1912), 3, 7.

[22] Leo Tolstoy, 'The Three Hermits', in *Walk in the Light and Twenty-Three Tales,* trans. Louise and Aylmer Maude (Farmington, PA, and Robertsbridge, East Sussex: Plough Publishing House, 1998), 260; Harris, 'The Holy Man', 10.

the first place. Its publication was also likely to have been financially motivated. Binckes notes that, given Harris's financial contribution to the magazine, Murry owed Harris 'plenty of positive publicity'.[23] This argument is reinforced by the advertisement in the same issue for a talk at Claridge's by the 'greatest English master of the short story', none other than Frank Harris himself.[24]

Mansfield's 'Tales of a Courtyard' in the August 1912 issue have more in common with the moral ambiguity found in a Dostoevsky novel than the Tolstoyan spirituality of 'The Three Hermits'. The first story in the series involves a group of neighbours admiring a budding chestnut tree and jeering at the 'swollen distorted body' of a Russian girl walking out of the courtyard. The final story tells the story of Feodor, an aspiring poet who works as a doorman for a drapery establishment. He steals a book of poetry from an old man sitting on the stone bench in the courtyard. He is tortured by his theft but unable to return the book, only to discover the old man has died in the courtyard over night.[25] Moral degradation and spiritual inspiration are combined in Leonid Andreev's 'The Present', published in *Rhythm* two months later. A worker, Sazonka, visits his apprentice, Senista, in hospital and promises to return but instead spends his Easter holiday drinking. When he eventually returns to the hospital Senista is dead. Sazonka walks away from the city, lies down on a hill and falls 'upon his split lip, rigid, in a fit of silent despair.' But unlike 'Tales of a Courtyard', Andreev's story ends with the comfort of 'Eternal mother earth' who took 'her guilty son to her bosom and comforted his sad heart with the warmth of her love and hope. Far away in the city the Easter chimes were ringing gaily...'[26]

The Ballets Russes featured strongly in *Rhythm*, as they did in many publications of the period, for example the *New Age*, *The Egoist*, and the *Little Review*. Georges Banks illustrated and wrote *Rhythm*'s first review of the Ballets Russes for the July 1912 issue. *Petrushka*, wrote Banks, 'has the eternal something, the "incommunicable thrill of things," which belongs to all great art'. The reason for this, according to Banks, is the unity of sound and visual art, the music becomes '*visual* in form', and the feeling of 'world tragedy' is created by the 'designs in colour, line and music'.[27] In August 1912, Anne Estelle Rice described the visual impact of Leon Bakst's set for *Sheherazade* as though it were a post-impressionist painting: 'full of the visions of Asia, a tropical heat, not of stillness, but of new life born every instant, where realism and fantasy combine and multiply into a fluidity of moving reds, blues, oranges, greens, purples, triangles, squares, circles, serpentine and zig-zag shapes'. For Rice, Bakst's use of line and colour broke new ground, moving away from impressionism: 'Bakst takes all colours, every nuance of each colour from its extreme brilliancy downwards, and all directions of line and compositions of line, harmonizes everything; and by his simple but fully expressive effect, convinces the

[23] Binckes, *Modernism, Magazines, and the British Avant-Garde,* 102.
[24] [John Middleton Murry], 'Notes', *Rhythm,* 2, no. 5 (1912), 36.
[25] Katherine Mansfield, 'Tales of a Courtyard', *Rhythm*, 2, no. 7 (1912), 99–105.
[26] Léonide Andreieff, 'The Present', *Rhythm*, 2, no. 9 (1912), 213.
[27] Georges Banks, 'Pétrouchka—The Russian Ballet' *Rhythm*, 2, no. 6 (1912), 58, 60 (italics original).

spectator of the artist's belief in his power to create, as opposed to the apologetic grovelling of the aesthetic before nature.'[28] The Ballets Russes offered a powerful new aesthetic experience in which the boundaries between sound and image were no longer fixed.

Russian art and literature, therefore, served two very different functions in *Rhythm*. The inclusion of Russian visual art, including that of the Ballets Russes, established the magazine's position at the cutting edge of modernism, and contributed to the magazine's promotion of a distinctive interpretation of post-impressionism, made up of Anglo-American fauvists, Scottish colourists, and the Russian artists, Goncharova and Kandinsky. *Rhythm* claimed in the third issue, not without cause, that it had 'given the world better drawing than has been seen in one magazine before'.[29] The fourth issue advertised a case costing half a crown, designed 'in colours by J. D. Fergusson' for binding issues of *Rhythm*, indicating that it aspired to be an art work in itself rather than a disposable journal. By contrast, the Russian literary works, apart from the story by Andreeev, were simulated versions of Russian literature, mediated through Frank Harris and Katherine Mansfield. The creation of quasi-Russian literature in *Rhythm* points to both the editorial ambition for internationalism and a desire to experiment, sometimes playfully, across perceived national styles.

RUSSIAN ART IN BRITAIN

Before turning to Sadleir's interpretation of Kandinsky in *Rhythm*, the range of Russian art on show in early twentieth-century Britain should be established. In 1908 Frank Rutter held a small exhibition of Russian art called 'Modern Russian Arts and Crafts' in London as part of his first Allied Artists' Association (AAA) Salon. The establishment of the AAA was triggered by a conversation with the Russian sculptor Naum Aronson about the difficulty of exhibiting works in Britain, because the cost of shipping without guarantee of exhibition was prohibitive.[30] The aim of the Association was that artists might 'submit their work freely to the judgment of the public without the intervention of any middleman, be he dealer or artist'.[31] Although his account of the AAA does not refer directly to Dyagilev's 'Exhibition of Russian Art' (1906) in Paris, it is likely that Rutter was aware of it and it may have influenced his decision to include a special exhibition in the two South Galleries of the Royal Albert Hall of 'a clan of Russian artists wishing to advance national art in alliance with the traditions of the past'. Like Dyagilev, Rutter included works by Nikolay Rerikh (Roerich), ceramics by Mariya Tenisheva, and embroideries by the 'skilful hands of the little peasant women of Smolensk' from the School of Art at Talashkino. The other artists, none of whom had been previously exhibited in Britain, were Ivan

[28] Anne Estelle Rice, 'Les Ballets Russes', *Rhythm*, 2, no. 7 (1912), 108, 107.
[29] [John Middleton Murry], 'What We Have Tried To Do', *Rhythm*, 1, no. 3 (1911), 36.
[30] Frank Rutter, *Since I was Twenty-Five* (London: Constable, 1927), 180.
[31] 'Foreword', in *Allied Artists' Association Catalogue* (London: Royal Albert Hall, 1912), xiii.

Bilibin, Konstantin Raush fon Traubenberg, and the architects Vladimir Pokrovsky and Aleksey Shchusev. The Russian qualities of the artworks were heavily emphasized; for example, Rerikh was described in the catalogue as creating an 'evocation of the ancient world and of prehistoric pagan Russia'.[32]

In October 1910, a month before Fry's first post-impressionist exhibition, an exhibition of four hundred and thirty Russian artworks by ninety-three Russian artists was held at the Doré Gallery in Bond Street. In anticipation of the event, *The Times* described it as an exhibition of 'a novel and promising' character, which would include artists who had 'arrived' and those who had 'recently passed through the studios'.[33] In a review of the exhibition, the *Times* critic pointed out that the artists were keen to be known in the West where no Russian painter, save perhaps Vereshchagin, had a 'popular reputation'. Artworks singled out for comment included Vladimir Makovsky's paintings, Evgeny Lansere's bronze sculptures of Cossacks and horses, and a bust of Sof'ya Tolstoy by her son, Lev. However, the review concluded that if the artworks on display at the Doré Gallery were representative of contemporary Russian art, the genre had a 'long way to travel before she can meet Paris, London and Berlin on equal terms'.[34] Following Tolstoy's death in November 1910, an exhibition of portraits of Tolstoy was held at the Doré Gallery.

Roger Fry's decision to include a British and a Russian section alongside the critically accepted French works for his *Second Post-Impressionist Exhibition* of October 1912 was not unusual, given the number of exhibitions involving international art in London in the preceding years. Of a total of about two hundred and sixty artworks on view, thirty-five were by Russian artists and forty-eight by British artists. In his introduction to the catalogue, Fry wrote that it 'would of course have been possible to extend the geographical area immensely. Post-Impressionist schools are flourishing, one might almost say raging, in Switzerland, Austro-Hungary and most of all in Germany'. However, despite giving no rationale for his choice, he concluded with an air of having solved a mathematical problem: 'England, France and Russia were therefore chosen to give a general summary of the results up to date.'[35]

Fry's narrow selection of countries and artists did not go unnoticed. Rupert Brooke wrote in the *Cambridge Magazine* in November 1912, 'It is a pity that the committee could not have included works by, at any rate, Erbslöh, Jawlensky, and Kandinsky of Munich, Pechstein of Berlin, and Kokoschka of Vienna, who paint pictures at least as good and as interesting as most of those here.'[36] Kandinsky, in particular, is a surprising omission, given that he had exhibited at the Allied Artists' Association in London since 1909, and his theories were more accessible than those of most Russian artists because he wrote in German. However, the Russian artist Boris Anrep, who made the selection on behalf of Fry, may have been influenced by the trend for more nationalist

[32] *Allied Artists' Association Catalogue* (London: Royal Albert Hall, 1908), 147.

[33] 'Russian Art in London', *The Times* (26 October 1910), 6.

[34] 'Exhibition of Russian Art', *The Times* (1 November 1910), 11.

[35] Roger Fry, 'Introduction', in *Catalogue of the Second Post-Impressionist Exhibition*, in J. B. Bullen, ed., *Post-Impressionists in England* (London: Routledge, 1988), 348.

[36] Rupert Brooke, *Cambridge Magazine* (23 November 1912), 125–6 (30 November 1912), 158–9, in Bullen, ed., *Post-Impressionists in England*, 404.

strains in Russian art, which to a certain extent precluded those Russian artists living and working in Germany. We know that Anrep visited Larionov's studio in Moscow in the summer of 1912, the year after Larionov's break with the Jack of Diamonds group, with which Kandinsky had exhibited, and this meeting may have reinforced Anrep's position. Kandinsky and Aleksey Yavlensky were working in Germany and were more connected with the European avant-garde than the new Donkey's Tail neo-primitive movement, which drew on Russian folk art, children's art, and icons.

Michael Sadleir's first opportunity to view Kandinsky's work in Britain would have been at the second exhibition of the AAA in 1909, in the form of two paintings, *Murnau Landscape with Green House* (1908) and *Yellow Cliff* (1909), and twelve engravings. Kandinsky's work continued to be included in the AAA exhibitions (with the exception of 1912) until 1914 when the onset of war brought the larger AAA shows to an end, although smaller exhibitions were held at the Grafton Galleries until 1920. Sadleir bought six of Kandinsky's woodcuts from the 1911 AAA exhibition. They were part of the proofs for *Klänge*, a book of Kandinsky's poems and woodcuts that was published in Germany in 1913. Sadleir wrote in his memoir of his father that they 'were strange productions, semi-representational, and with an element of hieratic rigidity which presumably appealed at that time to some Schwärmerei of my own'.[37] Gruetzner Robins notes that Rutter must have written to Kandinsky about the sale, because Kandinsky wrote back in August 1911 sending '16 small texts' and an account of *Klänge*. He describes his 'compositions for the stage' which will consist of 'gesture (movement of "dance"), colour (movement of painting) and of sound (musical movement—this will be done by the famous composer Hartmann) on the principle of pure theatre'. Rutter replied to say that he had passed on the texts to Sadleir, who had bought the prints. [38]

On 2 October 1911, Sadleir wrote to Kandinsky to say how pleased he was to have the woodcuts and that he believed 'this artistic revolution' to be so important that he would like to 'reproduce one of them in my quarterly journal *Rhythm*'.[39] Kandinsky wrote back on 6 October:

> Thank you for sending me your periodical. I am very glad to give permission for the reproduction of my wood-cuts. I am very pleased that the so-called modern art movement is mirrored in your journal and meets with interest in England. Mr Brooke from Cambridge also told me about this last winter. I enclose for you the prospectus of the art periodical that I have founded, the first issue is due to appear in January. Also this month my book 'Über das Geistige in der Kunst' will be published. I will send you a copy. Please write back with your impression.[40]

[37] Michael Sadleir, *Michael Ernest Sadler, 1861–1943: A Memoir by his Son* (London: Constable, 1949), 237.

[38] Gruetzner Robins, *Modern Art in Britain*, 12. Kandinsky, Postcard to Rutter, 22 August 1911, in Kandinsky, *Concerning the Spiritual in Art*, appendix B, letter 1, 115.

[39] Quoted in Adrian Glew, '"Blue Spiritual Sounds": Kandinsky and the Sadlers, 1911–16', *Burlington Magazine*, 139, no. 1134 (1997), 602. Glew's article gives a thorough account of the relationship between the Sadlers and Kandinsky, including their visit to Kandinsky's house in Murnau in 1912.

[40] Kandinsky to Michael T. H. Sadler, 6 October 1911, in Kandinsky, *Concerning the Spiritual in Art*, appendix B, letter 2, 115. Glew points out that Rupert Brooke met Kandinsky while learning German in Munich in January–May 1911: see Glew, 'Blue Spiritual Sounds', 602, note 20.

Although he did not publish Kandinsky's woodcuts in *Rhythm*, Sadleir was made aware in October 1911 of two of Kandinsky's major theoretical works: *Über das Geistige in der Kunst* and the *Blaue Reiter* almanac, both of which were published in Germany in 1912. In December 1911 Kandinsky wrote to Sadleir that the 'great inner relationship of all arts is coming gradually ever more clearly to light'. And in the same letter he advised Sadleir to read the texts of *Klänge* without 'looking for an explicit narration' but to let them 'work on your feeling, on your soul' and then they will 'become clear'.[41]

KANDINSKY AND *RHYTHM*

In his article 'After Gauguin', published in the spring 1912 issue of *Rhythm*, Sadleir positioned Kandinsky and Derain as 'neo-primitive' successors to Paul Gauguin. Binckes argues that the article was primarily intended as a way to establish connections between *Rhythm* and 'related, high-caste, publishing ventures' including Kandinsky's *Der Blaue Reiter* and Apollinaire's *L'Enchanteur Pourrissant* (1909).[42] Although this was partly true, Sadleir's genuine enthusiasm for Kandinsky's theories of abstraction is clear. Sadleir summarized Kandinsky's aesthetics as 'virtually a statement of Pantheism', or a belief in 'a "something" behind externals, common to nature and humanity alike'. New art for Kandinsky, wrote Sadleir, will 'act as intermediary for others, to harmonize the *inneres klang* of external nature with that of humanity'.[43]

Sadleir's interpretation relies on a knowledge of Kandinsky's theories in *Über das Geistige in der Kunst*. One of the first theoretical discussions of abstract art, the book sets out to define what Kandinsky sees as the contemporary status of spiritualism in art. According to Kandinsky, the spirit of the age in the early twentieth century was connected to that of 'the Primitives' because artists from both periods were seeking to express 'internal truths' without concern for 'external form'. The souls of artists in the early twentieth century, argued Kandinsky, were emerging from the 'nightmare of materialism' towards 'subtler emotions'. Kandinsky argued that literature, music, and art were all approaching each other in terms of their 'spiritual development' because they were 'striving towards the abstract, the non-material'. Music, for Kandinsky, is the 'best teacher', because it reveals 'that modern desire for rhythm in painting, for mathematical, abstract construction, for repeated notes of colour, for setting colour in motion'. The second half of the book is devoted to the 'psychological working of colour' in which Kandinsky expounds his theory that different colours create different psychic effects, or 'spiritual vibration', and that different forms each have their individual 'spiritual value'.[44]

[41] Kandinsky to Michael T. H. Sadler, 7 December 1911, in Kandinsky, *Concerning the Spiritual in Art*, appendix B, letter 3, 116.

[42] Binckes, *Modernism, Magazines, and the British Avant-Garde*, 142.

[43] Sadler, 'After Gauguin', 24. Here, 'inneres klang' should read as 'innerer Klang' and translates as 'inner sound' or 'inner resonance'.

[44] Kandinsky, *Concerning the Spiritual in Art*, 6, 7, 40, 41, 49, 56.

Six months before writing his review of *Über das Geistige in der Kunst*, and around the time of his initial correspondence with Kandinsky, Sadleir revealed his interest in colour theories. In the autumn 1911 issue of *Rhythm* he reviewed the *Letters of Vincent Van Gogh*, and argued that Van Gogh never used colour to 'create illusion' but rather to 'suggest deeper meaning'. Sadleir was not in favour of the 'purposely divided' colour of the impressionists, which would 'fuse in the eye from the proper distance'. He attacked the impressionists' use of colour because the 'actual value' of 'each pure red or blue or yellow went to create another composite value, and there was no attempt beyond the creation of a suffused brilliance'.[45] By contrast, according to Sadleir, Fauvists kept the integrity of each colour by using definite slabs rather than creating an artificial surface.

However, Kandinsky's theory of synaesthesia or, in Sadleir's words, 'the possibility of hearing colour, seeing sound, touching rhythms, and so forth', was too systematic for Sadleir, who preferred the simpler idea that 'colour can convey a more immediate and subtle appeal to the inner soul than words'.[46] Sadleir argued that the 'deeper meaning' of colour should be apparent but not articulated. Synaesthesia had become an increasingly popular phenomenon at the beginning of the twentieth century, as epitomized by Aleksandr Skryabin's *Prometheus* (1910) for piano, orchestra, optional choir, and *clavier à lumières* (keyboard with lights). And later Duncan Grant's *Abstract Kinetic Collage Painting with Sound* or *The Scroll* (1914) involved an abstract pattern of painted rectangles on a scroll of paper to be viewed through an opening in a lit box to the sound of the Adagio from Bach's *First Brandenburg Concerto*. The availability of theories of synaesthesia is apparent in Yone Noguchi's throw-away comment in *Rhythm*: 'Oh how I wish to write my poetry to be smelled!'[47]

Before writing on Kandinsky in *Rhythm*, Sadleir reviewed *Über das Geistige in der Kunst* in *Art News* in March 1912. Again, Sadleir was critical of Kandinsky's system:

> I think Kandinsky inclines over-much to the scientific in some of his theories. Sane art need not mean scientific art, and the chief danger of this new idea is the growth of formulae, by which the impressions to be given by a picture will be manufactured from recipes. Such a line will excite, such a colour soothe.[48]

Having criticized Kandinsky for being too scientific in this review of 1912, in the introduction to his 1914 translation he attacked Kandinsky's lack of clarity: 'Philosophy, especially in the hands of a writer of German, presents inexhaustible opportunities for vague and grandiloquent language.'[49] Sadleir's criticisms of Kandinsky's prose were perhaps intended to achieve empathy with the general reader by acknowledging its difficulty and generating debate about Kandinsky's theories. But the criticism simultaneously fostered a sense of exclusivity amongst those who were able to appreciate Kandinsky's art. In his review in *Art News* in

45 Michael T. H. Sadler, 'The Letters of Vincent Van Gogh', *Rhythm*, 1, no. 2 (1911), 19; Michael T. H. Sadler, 'Fauvism and a Fauve', *Rhythm*, 1, no. 1 (1911), 16.

46 Sadler, 'After Gauguin', 26.

47 Yone Noguchi, 'From a Japanese Ink-Slab', *Rhythm*, 2, no. 14 (1913), 450.

48 Michael T. H. Sadler, 'Kandinsky's Book on Art', *Art News* (9 March 1912), 46.

49 Sadler, 'Introduction', in Kandinsky, *Concerning the Spiritual in Art*, xxviii .

1912, Sadleir adopts a belligerent tone and accuses those who object to new forms of art as being 'uneducated enemies' of the new movement. He challenges these 'enemies' to produce work themselves that creates the 'psychological effect given by the best work of the new school'. If they can, he writes that he will 'salute them as artists. If not, I would suggest that they mind their own business.'[50]

Kandinsky's theory of 'innerer Klang' and the 'inner need' of artists bolstered the Bergsonian aesthetics of *Rhythm*. Murry, we remember, stated that modernism 'penetrates beneath the outward surface of the world' and in the same article he indicated that *Rhythm*'s primary ambition was to spread the theories of Bergson to England.[51] Sadleir highlighted Kandinsky's idea that the artist 'in varying degree' is able to 'realize what lies underneath the life which inspires him'.[52] The aesthetic faculties of humanity, according to Bergson, prove that we are capable of accessing our intuition or inner life, demonstrated by the way in which an artist is able to understand life by 'placing himself back within the object' and by breaking down 'the barrier that space puts up between him and his model'. The idea of a common soul running through generations is also an important connection between Kandinsky's aesthetics and the Bergsonian philosophy so fundamental to *Rhythm*. Bergson's theory of evolution 'implies a real persistence of the past in the present, a duration which is, as it were, a hyphen, a connecting link'. Bergson builds on the notion of a connecting link to formulate his theory of transformism, which he defines broadly as 'a visible current' passing from generation to generation that 'has become divided amongst species and distributed amongst individuals without losing anything of its force'.[53] It was this concept of a 'visible current' that Murry used to represent art in his opening article for *Rhythm*, where he used an alchemical metaphor to define it as a 'golden thread that runs through a varied texture, showing firm, brilliant, and unbroken when the fabric has fallen away'.[54] Kandinsky argued for a 'vital impulse of life' and, like Murry's aesthetic golden thread, this impulse runs through the ages so that the relationship between art of different times 'is not a relationship in outward form but in inner meaning'. The artist, according to Kandinsky must 'watch only the trend of the inner need' as opposed to the 'conventions of form' and 'demands' of 'his particular age'.[55] Sadleir's version of Kandinsky's theories reinforced the idea of a spiritual life connecting art of all ages that had begun with the interpretation of Bergson's philosophy in the pages of *Rhythm*.

RHYTHM AND THE SPIRITUAL

Kandinsky's reference to 'that modern desire for rhythm in painting' draws attention to the widespread use of the term 'rhythm' that spanned art movements and

[50] Sadler, 'Kandinsky's Book on Art', 46.
[51] Murry, 'Art and Philosophy', 12.
[52] Sadler, 'After Gauguin', 25.
[53] Henri Bergson, *Creative Evolution*, trans. Arthur Mitchell (London: Macmillan, 1911), 186, 192, 24, 27.
[54] Murry, 'Art and Philosophy', 9.
[55] Kandinsky, *Concerning the Spiritual in Art*, 22, 69.

time periods.[56] Just weeks before the first issue of *Rhythm* was published, Roger Fry wrote in a discussion of post-impressionism that 'Rhythm is the fundamental and vital quality of painting, as of all the arts—representation is secondary to that, and must never encroach on the more ultimate and fundamental demands of rhythm.'[57] Although Fry would later move towards the idea of 'significant form' to define (with equal ambiguity) post-impressionism, at this stage rhythm was the fundamental principle of his aesthetics, a principle that defined the 'vital quality' of painting.

The idea and terminology of rhythm was such common currency amongst British art critics that D. S. MacColl, Keeper of the Tate Gallery, developed a theory of classic and romantic rhythms to categorize art of all ages. MacColl referred to the 'tyrannic imposition of rhythm' in Romantic drawing, 'a rhythm of the artist's excitement' rather than 'the rhythms of the objects' in classic art.[58] Laurence Binyon's *Flight of the Dragon* (1911), a formal analysis of Chinese and Japanese art, brought together rhythm and spirituality in its translation of the first principle of ancient Chinese art: 'Rhythmic Vitality, or Spiritual Rhythm expressed in the movement of life'.[59] Reviews of Fry's Post-Impressionist exhibitions routinely described the work of Matisse in terms of rhythm. Desmond MacCarthy, for example, referred to Matisse's search for 'an abstract harmony of line, for rhythm', and the *Times* reviewer observed that Matisse does not 'impose this rhythm' on his figures but 'has wrung it, as it were out of the figures themselves'. In fact, although the artists associated with *Rhythm* were keen to assert their independence from Fry's post-impressionism, to the wider public, post-impressionism and rhythm were considered synonymous. The art critic for *The Observer*, P. G. Konody, wrote in 1911 that 'Post-Impressionism has evidently come to stay. It now has its official organ in the shape of the new shilling quarterly "Rhythm".'[60] By 1912 Frank Rutter claimed that rhythm was 'the magic word of the moment'. Even if 'the numerous attempts made at defining it were not very convincing', he argued, 'one "knew what it meant"'.[61] The ambiguity of the term was clear when C. J. Holmes admitted in *Rhythm* itself that 'until it was suggested that I should write an article' on the subject 'it had never occurred to me to find out what the word "Rhythm" meant'.[62]

Ideas about spirituality, rhythm and art were evolving outside as well as inside the pages of *Rhythm*, then, and, as in *Rhythm*, Russian art was a particular focus for this complex of ideas. The art critic for the *New Age*, Huntly Carter, wrote in his book,

[56] Kandinsky, *Concerning the Spiritual in Art*, 41.

[57] Roger Fry, 'Post Impressionism', *Fortnightly Review*, 95 (May 1911), 856–67, in Bullen, ed., *Post-Impressionists in England*, 174.

[58] D. S. MacColl, 'A Year of Post-Impressionism', *Nineteenth Century* (1912), 285–302, in Bullen, ed., *Post-Impressionists in England*, 274.

[59] Laurence Binyon, *The Flight of the Dragon: An Essay on the Theory and Practice of Art in China and Japan, Based on Original Sources* (London: Murray, 1935), 13.

[60] Desmond MacCarthy, 'The Post-Impressionists', in *Manet and the Post-Impressionists* (1910); [Robert Ross?], 'A Post-Impressionist Exhibition: Matisse and Picasso', *The Times* (4 October 1912), 9; P. G. Konody, *Observer* (16 July 1911), 7, all in Bullen, ed., *Post-Impressionists in England*, 98, 363, 24.

[61] Frank Rutter, *Art in My Time* (London: Rich & Cowan, 1933), 132.

[62] C. J. Holmes, 'Stray Thoughts on Rhythm in Painting', *Rhythm*, 1, no. 3 (1911), 1.

The New Spirit in Drama and Art (1912), that 'the enormous importance of rhythm in life is already beginning to be felt'. Rhythm was one of Carter's four 'modern principles', alongside 'simplicity, unity, continuity' that distinguished the Moscow Art Theatre and the Ballets Russes from contemporary theatre in London and Paris. One of the reasons for this, according to Carter, was that the 'Russian decorators' have discovered, 'as the early Egyptians expressed it', that 'mysticism' is a 'definite thing, having strength and vitality, and enthroned in a blinding white light' rather than being 'necessarily vague and indefinite and buried in darkness'.[63]

Carter was an important figure for the *Rhythm* artists. His promotion of their work in his book is acknowledged by a sketch of Carter by Banks in the January 1913 issue of *Rhythm* called 'The New Spirit in Art and Drama'. Adrian Glew calls this sketch a 'Kandinsky-like skit' but the title must be a reference to Carter's book.[64] Carter had written of 'the strong direction of line and colour' in one of Banks's works that 'seems to proclaim the fact that the study is about to walk out of the frame'.[65] As though in response to Carter's remark, Banks's drawing of Carter appears to push against the edges of the sketch. In a review for *The Egoist* Carter compared Kandinsky's book with Clive Bell's *Art*, both published in the spring of 1914. Given Carter's admiration for spiritualism in art, and Russian art in particular, it is not surprising that he favoured Kandinsky—whom he called a 'spiritual harmonist' who (adding a touch of Bergson) believes that 'art passes through the world as a flux of spirit'—over Bell, who saw art as 'frame or form'.[66]

CONCLUSION

The importance of Sadleir's article 'After Gauguin' and his subsequent translation of *Über das Geistige in der Kunst* is evident in the contemporaneous reception of Kandinsky, and his current international status. The reviews of *The Art of Spiritual Harmony* were mixed. Solomon Eagle, the reviewer for the *New Statesman*, praised Kandinsky's sincerity and yet referred to his pictures as 'puzzling' because they reminded him of 'enlarged photographs of bacteria'. Eagle called Kandinsky's book the work of a 'single minded—though conceivably misdirected—artist', and argued that Kandinsky had difficulty 'convincing us that his forms really are abstract'. *The Saturday Review* complained that 'intelligent review of this book is not easy; it is vague and confusing, sincere, occult and idealistic; philosophical, psychological and dogmatic. In much it seems to us soundly critical, in much unsound in its philosophy.' The reviewer for *The Athenaeum* (probably Murry), praised Kandinsky's classification of colours, and yet inexplicably complained that 'he exaggerates the

[63] Huntly Carter, *The New Spirit in Drama and Art* (London: Frank Palmer, 1912), 4, 24, 25.

[64] Georges Banks, 'The New Spirit in Art and Drama', *Rhythm*, 2, no. 12 (1913), 339; Adrian Glew, 'Introduction', in Kandinsky, *Concerning the Spiritual in Art*, xxi.

[65] Carter, *The New Spirit in Drama and Art*, 221–2, 223.

[66] Huntly Carter, 'New Books on Art', *The Egoist*, 1, no. 12 (1914), 235, 236.

inertness of green', presumably referring to Kandinsky's theory that green is 'the "bourgeoisie"—self-satisfied, immovable, narrow'. For *The Athenaeum* the problem was 'one of planning', because Kandinsky 'has a mania for classifying in detail, but the main divisions are loosely related'. Frank Rutter was one of the only reviewers to praise Kandinsky's book unequivocally as 'the most lucid and best reasoned account of the aims of abstract painting that has yet been written'.[67]

The vorticist artist Edward Wadsworth reviewed Kandinsky's theories of aesthetics positively in the first issue of *Blast* in June 1914: 'This book is a most important contribution to the psychology of modern art.'[68] However, Wyndham Lewis was disparaging in the second issue. He was dismissive of Kandinsky's desire to be 'passive and medium-like', and argued that his art avoided 'almost all powerful and definite forms', and that he was 'at the best, wandering and slack'.[69] Henri Gaudier-Brzeska remarked in 1914 in *The Egoist*, 'I have been told that he is a very great painter', but that his own [i.e. Gaudier's] 'temperament does not allow of formless, vague assertions'.[70]

Kandinsky's reputation in London was enhanced by an endorsement from Fry, even though Fry and Anrep did not choose to include Kandinsky in the Russian section of the *Second Post-Impressionist Exhibition*. On 11 March 1913 Sadleir's father wrote to Kandinsky that, 'Mr Roger Fry has been staying with us and was deeply interested in your drawings. He asked if I would lend them for an exhibition which he and some friends are organizing next week in London, and of course I gladly consented.' Kandinsky was thus exhibited at the Grafton Group show at the Alpine Club Gallery in March 1913. When Fry went to the AAA exhibition later the same year, he wrote in his review for *The Nation* that 'by far the best pictures there seemed to me to be the three works by Kandinsky', because they had the most 'definite and coherent expressive power'. Fry described Kandinsky's paintings as 'pure visual music', and decided that he could not 'any longer doubt the possibility of emotional expression by such abstract visual signs'.[71]

Sadleir's interpretation of Kandinsky's spiritualist aesthetics in 1912 crystallized a set of aesthetic concerns that had been emerging and evolving in Britain since the late nineteenth century. Ideas about the spiritual vision of the artist and the vogue for Russian culture cut across literature, philosophy, and the visual arts, bringing

[67] Solomon Eagle, 'Current Literature, Books in General', *New Statesman*, 3, no. 56 (1914), 118; 'Art's Enigma', *Saturday Review* (15 August 1914), 203; Kandinsky, *Concerning the Spiritual in Art*, 76; [John Middleton Murry?], 'The Art of Spiritual Harmony', *The Athenaeum*, 4523 (1914), 24; Frank Rutter, 'Round the Galleries: Twentieth Century Art', *Sunday Times* (24 May 1914), quoted in Gruetzner Robins, *Modern Art in Britain*, 134.

[68] Edward Wadsworth, 'Inner Necessity', *Blast,* 1 (1914), 119.

[69] Wyndham Lewis, 'A Review of Contemporary Art', *Blast*, 2 (1915), 40.

[70] Henri Gaudier-Brzeska, 'Allied Artists' Association Ltd', *The Egoist,* 1, no. 12 (1914), 228.

[71] Michael E. Sadler to Kandinsky, 11 March 1913, Michael Ernest Sadler Collection, 8221/2/50, Tate Archive; Roger Fry, 'The Allied Artists', *The Nation* (2 August 1913), 676–7, in Bullen, ed., *Post-Impressionists in England*, (1988), 459.

together Bergsonian philosophy, ideas about rhythm in art, the Ballets Russes, synaesthesia, and colour theory. Sadleir's introduction of Kandinsky's aesthetics to the British public formed a significant contribution to *Rhythm*'s search for 'an art that strikes deeper, that touches a profounder reality, that passes outside the bounds of a narrow aestheticism, cramping and choking itself, drawing its inspiration from aversion, to a humaner and a broader field'.[72]

[72] [Murry], 'Aims and Ideals', 36.

9

Reading Russian

Russian Studies and the Literary Canon

Rebecca Beasley

The British canon of Russian literature was largely the creation of a small number of amateur translators and critics. They include, in the nineteenth century, John Bowring, William Ralston, Thomas Budd Shaw, Charles Turner, and Frederick Whishaw, and in the early twentieth century, Maurice Baring, Constance Garnett, Stephen Graham, Petr Kropotkin, Aylmer Maude, and Louise Maude.[1] Those who had not grown up in Russia or a Russian-speaking family (as Kropotkin, Louise Maude, and Whishaw had) learned Russian in a variety of ways: through visiting Russia, whether on business (Bowring), or to teach English (Aylmer Maude, Shaw, Turner), from private teachers in Britain (Baring, Graham), including British-based émigrés (Garnett), and through independent study (Ralston).[2] Engagement with Russian literature was both a motivation to and a means of learning the language: literary translation usually featured in tuition and self-tuition at an early stage. Stephen Graham, the author of travel books, histories and novels about Russia, recalled that, 'from a barrow I bought a tattered copy of *Crime and Punishment*... It resulted in my beginning to learn Russian, first from a grammar, then from Berlitz, and thirdly from a young Russian recommended to me by the Russian Consul.' This was Nikolay Lebedev, whose method of teaching included the recitation of passages of Turgenev, and the joint translation of Dostoevsky's *Unizhennye i oskorblennye* (*Humiliated and Insulted*).[3] Constance Garnett recorded that Feliks Volkhovsky, the émigré editor of *Free Russia*, 'suggested my learning Russian and gave me a grammar and a dictionary, and the first story I attempted to read—one of Stankevitch's'.[4]

[1] This list omits translators based in the United States who were nevertheless read in Britain, notably Nathan Haskell Dole, Isabel Hapgood, and Leo Wiener, and translators into French and German, who were also important conduits of Russian literature for British readers.

[2] Maurice Baring, *The Puppet Show of Memory* (London: Heinemann, 1922), 224, 260, Stephen Graham, *Part of the Wonderful Scene: An Autobiography* (London: Collins, 1964), 14, 16, Werner Lauter, *Die Bedeutung von W. R. S. Ralston als Vermittler russischer Literatur nach England* (Marburg: Philipps-Universität, 1962), 10.

[3] Graham, *Part of the Wonderful Scene*, 14–15.

[4] Richard Garnett, *Constance Garnett: A Heroic Life* (London: Sinclair-Stevenson, 1991), 75.

However, at the turn of the century the study of Russian was becoming professionalized, with increasing numbers of schools and universities offering courses in Russian. The biographical and scholarly focus on individual amateur translators has obscured the less obviously tangible impact of the institutions. Yet from 1904, when Russian was added to the Final Honour School of Medieval and Modern Languages at the University of Oxford, many translators and critics of Russian literature were no longer self or privately taught, they were the product of a small number of institutions.[5] By 1917 an aspiring Russophile could learn Russian at at least nine independent schools (the City of London School, Cheltenham College, Eton, the Holt School in Liverpool, the Leys School in Cambridge, Oundle, Repton, Princess Helena College, and Tonbridge School), attend courses at the universities and university colleges of Birmingham, Bristol, Cambridge, Durham, Liverpool, London, Manchester, Nottingham, and Sheffield, and the British Army training institution, the Staff College at Camberley, and take classes at technical colleges, commercial institutes, and Berlitz schools across the country.[6]

But what characterized the teaching in these institutions, and what was their impact on the dissemination of Russian literature? Following the lead of institutional histories, notably Gerald Graff's account of the development of English departments in the American academy, this chapter investigates debates about the teaching of Russian at the turn of the twentieth century.[7] Although certain individuals were undoubtedly responsible for the shape of the discipline in its early years, the attempt here is to analyse the variety of institutional forces that formed methodologies, curricula and canons. James Muckle's excellent study *The Russian Language in Britain* has excavated a wealth of information on the teaching of Russian, and it informs my enquiry throughout; however, the following discussion focuses specifically on the teaching of Russian literature, rather than Russian language or Russian studies more generally. The move of Russian into the universities took place at a point when the major works of Russian literature were still in the process of being translated into English for the first time, and this chapter examines the impact of the institutionalization of Russian studies on the creation of a British canon of Russian literature.

READING RUSSIAN

In 1906, Nevill Forbes graduated with a first class degree from Oxford's new Final Honour School of Medieval and Modern Languages, the first student to offer

[5] Charles Firth, *Modern Languages at Oxford, 1724–1929* (Oxford: Oxford University Press, 1929), 74–6.

[6] Modern Language Association Sub-Committee for Russian Studies, *The Teaching of Russian* (Cambridge: W. Heffer, 1917), 18–25; James Muckle, *The Russian Language in Britain: A Historical Study of Learners and Teachers* (Ilkeston: Bramcote Press, 2008), 32–3, 47–51, 59–65 [Addresses of teachers of Russian], *Russian Review*, 1, no. 3 (July 1912), 6.

[7] Gerald Graff, *Professing Literature: An Institutional History* (Chicago, IL: University of Chicago Press, 1989).

Russian. There had been, however, a series of annual or biennial lectures on Slavonic subjects in Oxford since 1870, when Forbes's teacher, William Morfill, delivered the first Ilchester lectures, funded by an endowment to promote the study of Slavonic languages, literature, and history. Morfill was appointed Reader in Russian and the Other Slavonic Languages in 1889, and Professor in 1900.[8] Although Cambridge's Medieval and Modern Languages Tripos preceded Oxford's Final Honours School by twenty years, its provision in Russian developed later: Ivan Nestor-Schnurmann provided Russian tuition from 1897 to 1899, and in 1900 Alexander Goudy, who had been teaching Russian at the University College of Liverpool, was appointed to the first University Lectureship. In 1907 Russian was added to the Medieval and Modern Languages Tripos, and Goudy was first listed as an examiner in 1910, but it was not until 1948 that Elizabeth Hill was appointed the first Professor of Slavonic Studies.[9] The first School of Russian Studies in Britain was founded in 1907 at the University of Liverpool by Bernard Pares, who had held appointments at the university in modern history from 1902 to 1908, when he became Professor of Russian History, Language, and Literature.[10] At the University of London, Russian had been taught at King's College since 1889, when Nicholas Orloff was appointed Lecturer in Russian in the School of Oriental and Colonial Languages, and in 1915 the university established a separate School of Slavonic Studies, to which Pares was appointed Professor of Russian in 1917.[11] Russian was also taught in the English department at the University of Manchester by W. J. Sedgefield, appointed as Lecturer in English Language in 1906, but also, the following year, University Lecturer in Russian, a post he held until 1919, when Mikhail Trofimov, Pares' former colleague at both Liverpool and the School of Slavonic Studies, took up the newly established post of Sir William Mather Professor of Russian. Before 1914, Russian could be studied at university level at only these five institutions.[12]

The professorial titles held by Morfill and Pares indicate some of the differences between the teaching of Russian in their universities. Morfill, Professor of Russian and the Other Slavonic Languages at Oxford, worked within a tradition of modern language teaching that was specifically philological. Francis Trithen and

[8] Firth, *Modern Languages at Oxford*, 59, Gerald Stone, 'The History of Slavonic Studies in Great Britain', in Josef Hamm and Günther Wytrzens, eds, *Beiträge zur Geschichte der Slawistik in nichtslawischen Ländern* (Vienna: Österreichischen Akademie der Wissenschaften, 1985), 376–89.

[9] Muckle, *The Russian Language in Britain*, 43, 45–6, J. R. Tanner, *The Historical Register of the University of Cambridge: Being a Supplement to the Calendar with a Record of University Offices, Honours and Distinctions to the Year 1910* (Cambridge: Cambridge University Press, 1917), 970; Elizabeth Hill, *Why Need we Study the Slavs? An Inaugural Lecture* (Cambridge: Cambridge University Press, 1951), 35, Anthony Cross, *Cambridge: Some Russian Connections: An Inaugural Lecture* (Cambridge: University Press, 1987), 28–9.

[10] Bernard Pares, *My Russian Memoirs* (London: Cape, 1931), 246–50, Bernard Pares, *A Wandering Student: The Story of a Purpose* (Syracuse, NY: Syracuse University Press, 1948), 98–9.

[11] I. W. Roberts and Roger Bartlett, *History of the School of Slavonic and East European Studies, 1915–2005*, 2nd edn (London: School of Slavonic and East European Studies, 2009), 2–4, 8, Pares, *A Wandering Student*, 275–6.

[12] Muckle, *The Russian Language in Britain*, 47, Henry Guppy, 'Notes and News', *Bulletin of The John Rylands Library, Manchester*, 29, no. 1 (July 1945), 13, W. K. Matthews, 'Professor M. V. Trofimov', *Slavonic and East European Review*, 27, no. 69 (1949), 575–6.

Max Müller, the first two Professors of Modern European Languages at Oxford (appointed in 1848 and 1854 respectively), were both trained in, and taught, comparative philology, and indeed the Professorship of Modern European Languages was abolished when in 1868 a Professorship of Comparative Philology was created for Müller, as more suited to his research interests.[13] Morfill, like many Slavonic scholars, had been trained as a classicist, and his Ilchester lectures show the influence of this language-focused training: the subject of his first series, in 1870, was 'Ethnology, early history, and popular traditions of the Slavonic nations', and that of his second series, in 1873, 'The best mode of beginning the study of the Slavonic languages'.[14] In his 1890 lecture delivered on his inauguration as Reader, 'An Essay on the Importance of the Study of Slavonic Languages', the only one of these lectures to have survived, Morfill gave three reasons for studying Slavonic languages: their significance for comparative philology ('the Slavonic languages occupy a middle position between the Western and Eastern branches of the great Aryan family'), the quality of their literature (of which he mentions their folk literature as of particular interest), and, more briefly, their practical use for diplomacy: 'In order to interpret properly the Eastern question, which never settled is still hovering over us, we must know the Slavonic mind, the Slavonic languages and literatures'.[15] His published works also testify to his linguistic and literary focus: he was the author of *Slavonic Literature* (1883), which prefaces its account by presenting August Schleicher's classification of Slavonic languages; three histories of Russia and one of Poland, three of which give particular prominence to literary history; grammars of Polish (1884), Serbian (1887), Russian (1889), Bulgarian (1897) and Czech (1899); two translations from Old Church Slavonic, and an edition of Elizabethan ballads.[16] Under Nevill Forbes, who succeeded Morfill in 1910, Russian in Oxford continued to be a primarily linguistic and literary subject. Forbes was best known for his translations for children and for his grammars and textbooks, including *Russian Grammar* (1914), *Elementary Russian Grammar* (1919), and four *Russian Books* (1915–18) of lessons, literary extracts, and exercises.[17] In his obituary, Pares described him as 'in the first place a comparative Slavonic philologist with a sound knowledge of the various

[13] Firth, *Modern Languages at Oxford*, 34.

[14] Stone, 'The History of Slavonic Studies in Great Britain', 379.

[15] W. R. Morfill, *An Essay on the Importance of the Study of Slavonic Languages* (London: Henry Frowde, 1890), 15, 17–29, 32.

[16] W.R. Morfill, *Slavonic Literature* (London: Society for Promoting Christian Knowledge, 1883), W. R. Morfill, *Russia* (London: Sampson Low, Marston, Searle, & Rivington, 1880), W. R. Morfill, *Russia* (London: T. Fisher Unwin, 1890), W. R. Morfill, *A History of Russia* (London: Methuen, 1902), W. R. Morfill, *Poland* (London: T. Fisher Unwin, 1893), W. R. Morfill, *A Simplified Grammar of the Polish Language* (London: Trübner, 1884), W. R. Morfill, *Simplified Grammar of the Serbian Language* (London: Trübner, 1887), W. R. Morfill, *A Grammar of the Russian Language* (Oxford: Clarendon Press, 1889), W. R. Morfill, *A Short Grammar of the Bulgarian Language, with Reading Lessons* (London: Trübner, 1897), W. R. Morfill, *A Grammar of the Bohemian or Čech Language* (Oxford: Clarendon Press, 1899), *The Book of the Secrets of Enoch*, trans. W. R. Morfill, ed. R. H. Charles (Oxford: Clarendon Press, 1896), 'The Apocalypse of Baruch', trans. W. R. Morfill, in Montague Rhodes James, ed., *Apocrypha Anecdota*, ii, *Texts and Studies: Contributions to Biblical and Patristic Literature*, 5.1 (Cambridge: Cambridge University Press, 1897), 96–102, W. R. Morfill, ed., *Ballads Relating Chiefly to the Reign of Queen Elizabeth* (London: Ballad Society, 1873).

[17] Nevill Forbes, *Word-for-Word Russian Story-Book* (Oxford: Blackwell, 1916), and the translations for his cousin Valery Carrick's *Picture Tales from the Russian* (Oxford: Blackwell, 1913), *More Russian Picture Tales* (Oxford: Blackwell, 1914), *Still More Russian Picture Tales* (Oxford: Blackwell, 1915), *Picture*

Slav languages', who 'wrote also several interesting literary studies in the *Russian* and *Slavonic Reviews*'. Drawing attention to the difference in their approaches, Pares noted somewhat disdainfully that Forbes' contribution to the co-edited *History of Russia from the Vangarians to the Bolsheviks* 'covered the middle period from John the Great to modern times, just that in which the Russian people found the least expression in the political history of the country'.[18]

Pares, Professor of Russian History, Language and Literature at the University of Liverpool, and Professor of Russian ('but really of Russian History', he later wrote) at the University of London, was, by contrast, a modern historian, although he had also studied Classics as an undergraduate. In his memoirs he emphasized that his first professorial title was carefully chosen, as 'it represented the principle of nation study, which is what I have always stood for; namely, that our teaching should not stop short at language and that, apart from provision for the teaching of philology, the language should also serve as a key to the study of literature, history, and economics'.[19] For Pares, the study of Russian was less a scholarly pursuit than an urgent political necessity: attending the first Duma in 1906, he became aware how few of the British Foreign Office employees could speak Russian well enough to understand the political situation, leaving them reliant on interpreters and other attendees who, he claimed, deliberately misinformed them.[20] Far more than Morfill, Forbes, Sedgefield, or even Hill, who set up the intensive Russian courses at Cambridge to train interpreters during the Second World War, Pares saw the study of Russian as providing preparation for political or commercial engagement with Russia, rather than linguistic or cultural knowledge for its own sake.[21] The distinction between his approach and that of the philological study in Oxford was explicit: 'Nine students out of ten really wish rather to know about the country than

Tales: Fourth Selection (Oxford: Blackwell, 1924), Nevill Forbes, *Russian Grammar* (Oxford: Clarendon Press, 1914), Nevill Forbes, *Elementary Russian Grammar* (Oxford Clarendon Press, 1919), Nevill Forbes, *First Russian Book: A Practical Manual of Russian Declensions* (Oxford: Clarendon Press, 1915), Nevill Forbes, *Second Russian Book: A Practical Manual of Russian Verbs* (Oxford: Clarendon Press, 1916), Nevill Forbes, *Third Russian Book: Extracts from Aksakov, Grigorovich, Herzen, Saltykov* (Oxford: Clarendon Press, 1917), Nevill Forbes, *Fourth Russian Book: Exercises on First and Second Russian Books* (Oxford: Clarendon Press, 1918), Raymond Beazley, Nevill Forbes, and G. A. Birkett, *Russia from the Varangians to the Bolsheviks* (Oxford: Clarendon Press, 1918). Forbes' other book publications were: Nevill Forbes and Captain Keyworth, *Easy Serbian for our Men Abroad, and How to Pronounce it* (London: Kegan Paul, 1915), Louis Cahen and Nevill Forbes, *English-Serbian Phrase-Book, with Easy Grammar* (Oxford: Blackwell, 1915), Nevill Forbes, *The Southern Slavs* (Oxford: Oxford University Press, 1915), Nevill Forbes, and others, *The Balkans: A History of Bulgaria, Serbia, Greece, Rumania, Turkey* (Oxford: Clarendon Press, 1915), Dragutin Subotić and Nevill Forbes, *Serbian Grammar* (Oxford: Clarendon Press, 1918), Dragutin Subotić and Nevill Forbes, *Engleska Gramatika* (Oxford: Clarendon Press, 1920). Forbes was also the general editor of the 'Oxford Russian Plain Texts' series, for which he also edited most of the texts published.

[18] Bernard Pares, 'Obituary: Nevill Forbes', *Slavonic and East European Review*, 7, no. 21 (March 1929), 702.

[19] Pares, *My Russian Memoirs*, 249–51; Pares, *A Wandering Student*, 276.

[20] Pares, *A Wandering Student*, 141. Bernard Pares, 'Mackay and the School of Russian Studies', in *A Miscellany Presented to John Macdonald Mackay, LL.D.* (Liverpool: *Liverpool University Press*/London: Constable, 1914), 48.

[21] Elizabeth Hill, *In the Mind's Eye: The Memoirs of Dame Elizabeth Hill*, ed. Jean Stafford Smith (Lewes: Book Guild, 1999), 230–9.

about the history of its language', he wrote, 'Business men would naturally prefer as their employees persons trained in this way: so would the diplomatic and consular services.'[22] Unsurprisingly, Pares is remembered less for his scholarship than his promotion of Russian studies in Britain, persuading local businessmen to fund lectureships and travelling fellowships, and founding and editing the first scholarly journals of Slavonic studies in Britain, the *Russian Review* (1912–14), and the *Slavonic* (from 1928 *The Slavonic and East European*) *Review* (1922–).[23] Though he produced three literary translations, he was relatively uninterested in, even antagonistic towards, the nineteenth-century prose his compatriots were discovering in the early twentieth century: reading the works of Turgenev, Tolstoy, Gogol', and Chekhov while he was learning Russian, he wrote in his memoirs, 'used to make me extremely angry—especially Tolstoy. Reading him at a snail's pace, one had forced in on one every ounce of his innate cynicism and, I would dare to add, his innate savagery'.[24] Bar his *History of Russia* (1931), described by his former colleague R. W. Seton-Watson in 1949 as 'probably still...the most practical textbook of Russian history coming from an English pen', his books consisted primarily of reflections on the contemporary history he viewed at first hand—as in *Russia and Reform* (1907), *The League of Nations, and Other Questions of Peace* (1919), *The Fall of the Russian Monarchy* (1939), *Russia* (1940), and *Russia and the Peace* (1944)—and explicitly autobiographical accounts of the political situation, such as *Day by Day with the Russian Army* (1915), and *Moscow Admits a Critic* (1936).[25] The School's secretary, Dorothy Galton, described him as 'not the sort of scholar who spent a great deal of time poring over books and papers; indeed I doubt very much if he ever did much work in the British Museum Library, for instance...He was more of a publicist, a disseminator of ideas and knowledge.'[26]

The teaching of Russian in Cambridge has been less fully recorded. Goudy published little—his one book-length contribution, produced with his colleague Edward Bullough, was an edition of Tolstoy's *Sevastopol'skie rasskazy* (*Sevastopol'*

[22] Pares, *My Russian Memoirs*, 250.

[23] Pares, *My Russian Memoirs*, 246–8, 251–3, 569, Pares, *A Wandering Student*, 98–102, 296–303.

[24] Pares, *My Russian Memoirs*, 38. Alexander Griboyedov, *The Mischief of Being Clever (Gore ot Uma)*, trans. Sir Bernard Pares (London: School of Slavonic Studies/ Eyre and Spottiswoode, [1925]), *Krylov's Fables*, trans. Bernard Pares (London: Jonathan Cape, 1926), N. Misheyev, *A Heroic Legend: How the Holy Mountains Let Out of Their Deep Caves the Mighty Heroes of Russia: A Modern Bylina*, trans. Gleb Struve and Bernard Pares (London: Centenary Press, 1935).

[25] R. W. Seton-Watson, 'Bernard Pares', *Slavonic and East European Review*, 28, no. 70 (November, 1949), 30. Bernard Pares, *A History of Russia* (London: Jonathan Cape, 1926), Bernard Pares, *Russia and Reform* (London: Constable, 1907), Sir Bernard Pares, *The League of Nations and Other Questions of Peace* (London: Hodder & Stoughton, 1919), Bernard Pares, *The Fall of the Russian Monarchy: A Study of the Evidence* (London: Jonathan Cape, 1939), Bernard Pares, *Russia* (Harmondsworth: Penguin, 1940), Bernard Pares, *Russia and the Peace* (Harmondsworth: Penguin, 1944), Bernard Pares, *Day by Day with the Russian Army, 1914-15* (London: Constable, 1915), Bernard Pares, *Moscow Admits a Critic* (London: Thomas Nelson, 1936). Pares also published two volumes of autobiography, *My Russian Memoirs* and *A Wandering Student*.

[26] D. Galton, 'Sir Bernard Pares and Slavonic Studies in London University, 1919-39', *Slavonic and East European Review*, 46, no. 107 (July 1968), 482.

Sketches).[27] The figure who had been expected to be appointed to Goudy's university post, Ellis Minns, had followed his undergraduate degree in Classics with studying Russian under Paul Boyer at the l'École des langues orientales in Paris, and research in Russian archaeology in St Petersburg. He was appointed College Lecturer in Russian at Pembroke in 1901, and Disney Professor of Archaeology in 1927.[28] Hill was one of the early graduates of Pares' School of Slavonic Studies, and wrote her doctoral dissertation there under D. S. Mirsky on the development of the nineteenth-century psychological novel. She was, a former student remembered, 'a poor teacher of literature, but, paradoxically, a powerful inspirer of love for the Russian writers, and also a brilliant, though terribly demanding, language instructor'.[29] Memories of her teaching collected for an eightieth birthday tribute recorded the centrality of literature in her teaching: 'nearly everything, Marshak's "Mister Tvister", Pushkin's "Evgeny Onegin", numerous songs and poems, stuck and a seed was sown', recalled Derek van Abbé, 'Do you still . . . get people to enjoy literature instead of just analysing it?', asked John Davidson.[30]

The differences between both individuals and institutions were in part generational. At the new University of Liverpool, which received its Royal charter only in 1903, Pares found himself 'in a hive of creation . . . Brilliant men from all quarters, Oxford, Cambridge, Scotland, Germany, were drawn hither by the attraction of writing a new word on a blank sheet.'[31] The aims and methods of university education were undergoing rapid change, as access to higher education expanded and new universities looked to different constituencies for both their students and their benefactors.[32] For many of these students, and the middle-class businessmen who funded their education, the vocational aspects of university courses became more relevant. The implications for the teaching of Russian, with its potential directly to facilitate new commercial and political opportunities, are strikingly apparent in Pares' account of the development of his department at Liverpool. Members of his staff, he wrote, 'had close relations with many business men and, were ready to answer any inquiries as to Russian trade; for these there was no fee, but we invited support for the school'. Alongside John Mackay, the Professor of History, the greatest assistance, both financial and advisory, was provided by the shipping magnates Alfred Jones and John Rankin. Although both initially refused assistance, Jones became more interested in supporting Pares' work following the visit of a delegation from the third Duma to Britain in 1909, which Pares organized and not only

[27] Leo Tolstoy, *Sevastopol*, ed. A. P. Goudy and E. Bullough (Cambridge: Cambridge University Press, 1916)

[28] Grahame Clark, *Prehistory at Cambridge and Beyond* (Cambridge: Cambridge University Press, 1989), 30–2, Hill, *Why Need we Study the Slavs?*, 35.

[29] A. D. P. Briggs, 'Obituary: Professor Dame Elizabeth Hill', *The Independent* (6 January 1997), 14.

[30] Quoted in Hill, *In the Mind's Eye*, 500, 497. See also Christopher N. L. Brooke, *A History of the University of Cambridge*, 4 vols (Cambridge: Cambridge University Press, 1988–1993), iv, 435–6.

[31] Pares, *My Russian Memoirs*, 53. See also Thomas Kelly, *For the Advancement of Learning: the University of Liverpool, 1881–1981* (Liverpool: Liverpool University Press, 1981).

[32] See 'Report on Commercial Education', *Modern Language Quarterly*, 3, no. 2 (December 1900), 151–3.

brought to Liverpool, but to the Liverpool Chamber of Commerce, where Jones, as President, 'made a short and typical speech: "We know you have got things that we want, and we believe we have got things that you want; let's see how we can be useful to each other."' Rankin's assistance, which included funding Pares' own post, was made possible after Pares was able to obtain Russian compensation for a ship belonging to his firm that had been sunk in 1905, during the Russo-Japanese war. The department's journal, the *Russian Review*, was edited by contacts Pares had made on his visits to Russia in 1905 and 1906: Harold Williams and Maurice Baring, the correspondents for the *Manchester Guardian* and the *Morning Post*, respectively, and Samuel Harper, son of the first President of the University of Chicago, who had studied Russian at the l'École des langues orientales in Paris from 1902 to 1904.[33]

Russian became established in the universities, then, at a point when ideas about what and who education was for were starting to transform the range of subjects available and how they were taught. Depending on the institution, Russian, as a new subject, could either be shaped to existing educational models, as at Oxford, or present a new model, as at Liverpool.

MODERNIZING MODERN LANGUAGES

The emergence of Russian as a subject in university also coincided with a change in language teaching in Britain, which sheds some light on the difference in approach between these institutions and these individuals. In the last two decades of the nineteenth century, the 'grammar-translation method' of teaching, based on the teaching of Greek and Latin, was largely replaced by the 'direct method' advocated by the reform movement, in which tuition was given in the foreign language rather than the mother tongue. Oral communication and accurate pronunciation became prioritized over reading and translating literary texts.[34] Reading over the contributions to the major British periodicals in modern language studies of the period, *Modern Language Quarterly* (1897–1904) and its successors *Modern Language Teaching* (1905–19) and *Modern Language Review* (1905–), one gains a sense of the scale of the change. *Modern Language Teaching*, the journal of the British Modern Language Association, was edited by Walter Rippmann (elsewhere Ripman), one of the early proponents of the reform movement in Britain, and from its inception the journal promoted the direct method and the use of phonetics in teaching. In 1905,

[33] Pares, *My Russian Memoirs*, 51, 254, 201, 246, 248, 90, 115; A. H. Milne, *Sir Alfred Lewis Jones, K.C.M.G.* (Liverpool: Henry Young, 1914), 70–1; Samuel N. Harper, *The Russia I Believe In: The Memoirs of Samuel N. Harper, 1902–1941*, ed. Paul V. Harper, with the assistance of Ronald Thompson (Chicago, IL: University of Chicago Press, 1945), 11–14, 29, 37–8. Russian at the University of Birmingham was funded on similarly commercial grounds: see R. E. F. Smith, *A Novelty: Russian at Birmingham University, 1917–67* (Birmingham: University of Birmingham, 1987), 2–9.

[34] For an overview of the changes in language teaching during the period, see Eric W. Hawkins, *Modern Languages in the Curriculum*, rev. edn (Cambridge: Cambridge University Press, 1987), 117–53.

MLT published a report on the ideal school curriculum in modern languages by a committee of the Assistant Masters' Association, to which Rippmann had been co-opted, which, as its introduction noted, 'goes very far in the direction of the reform movement'. It recommended 'as little as possible of the mother-tongue' in lessons, that grammar should be taught inductively, rather than through memorizing rules and exceptions, and that the teacher should have knowledge of the application of phonetics. It stated that the main aims of teaching a modern language (which it envisaged beginning when pupils were aged ten to twelve) as enabling pupils to acquire:

1. A good pronunciation.
2. Fluency in the use of a fair vocabulary of serviceable words.
3. Ease in the application of the elementary accidence and syntax of the foreign language.
4. A sympathetic attitude towards the foreign nation.

Translation and composition were only to be introduced at the intermediate stage. Even at the advanced stage, after pupils had studied the language for up to eight years, 'only the elements of historical grammar', were to be taught.[35]

The reform movement had significant implications for the place of literature in modern language tuition. In January 1901, W. Stuart Macgowan, a teacher at Cheltenham College, who was a central figure in the British reform movement, proposed a resolution to the Annual General Meeting of the Modern Language Association 'That the aim of modern language teaching should be literary rather than colloquial', and that rather than emphasizing the immediate utility of languages, teachers should devote themselves to 'the task of proving their literary value as instruments of humanistic culture'. But most of the audience argued that such a resolution would return them to an outmoded and ineffective curriculum. Rushton Parker remarked that if the early training was in the spoken language 'surely literature would take care of itself', and a Dr Abrahams agreed that 'they should give a practical knowledge of a language first, and let the literary knowledge follow'. Rippmann himself argued that 'it seemed to him utterly unfair to bring against the reformed mode the charge of neglecting the literary side of modern language teaching', but nevertheless that 'it was of immense value to attach importance to a spoken language in the early stage of teaching' and 'from such a groundwork there would be...a perfectly natural progress to the literary appreciation of the language'. An amended resolution was passed with precisely the opposite emphasis from Macgowan's original formulation: 'That the aim of modern language teaching should be colloquial as well as literary.'[36]

The reform movement's success in Western Europe was such that in France the direct method was imposed by ministerial decree in 1902. Only six years later,

[35] 'Suggestions for a Modern Language Curriculum', *Modern Language Teaching*, 1 (1905), 141, 142, 145.

[36] 'Report of the Annual General Meeting', *Modern Language Quarterly*, 3 (1900), 169, 173–4.

however, ministerial instructions re-introduced limited grammar teaching and translation into the mother tongue.[37] In Britain, too, Macgowan's critique of the reform movement's utilitarianism appeared to gain more adherents towards the end of the first decade of the twentieth century. In 1909 *Modern Language Teaching* initiated a discussion forum on 'The Teaching of Literature', because, the forum's editor F. B. Kirkman noted, 'though the Reform in England has already done much for the language, it has yet to win for the literature its rightful place'. Contributors responded to the questions, 'What are the best methods of giving our pupils a taste for reading the best foreign literature strong enough to endure beyond the end of the school period?', 'What conditions, if any, hinder our giving to the cultivation of literary taste the place it merits in modern foreign language instruction?', and 'What principles are to determine the suitability of the literary works to be read?' However, many of the respondents still took issue with the questions' assumption that schools should cultivate literary taste in their pupils at all: 'If by the cultivation of literary taste is meant teaching to read Racine, Pascal, and Goethe, I maintain that, with the usual exceptions, such taste does not and cannot exist at school', wrote W. Osborne Brigstocke of Berkhamsted School, 'It is ridiculous to attempt this with a class.' If literature was to be read, almost all contributors agreed with Hardress O'Grady of Goldsmiths' College that it should be only after doing 'a very great deal of spade-work' in learning vocabulary and pronunciation, which left little time for the discussion of literature. Several respondents noted that the difficulty in finding time for literary study was exacerbated by the necessity of teaching to exams, which required 'prepared books studied from the translation rather than from the literary point of view', as L. M. Grove of Redland High School remarked. As F. W. G. Foat of the City of London School and City of London College pointed out, 'suppose he does not know the English equivalent of the latter half of the fourth line, and the examiner should ask it? Ah! that is another story, and has little to do with literature, none at all with the cultivation of a lasting taste for good authors'. According to. L. Chouville of the Perse School, 'Assuming the study of a foreign literature to begin with pupils about sixteen years of age, they should be at least in the sixth year of the course, and should have reached such a standard as to enable them to read easily, write and speak with correctness, and follow a lesson given entirely in French or German, and that without fatigue'. Although C. R. Ash of St. Paul's Girls' School noted that 'for a form to find itself promoted to the reading of French literature after the drudgery of the middle-school means a quite extraordinary revival of interest in the whole subject', she also maintained that the study of literature was a means, rather than an end: 'it is as a stimulus to the study of the language, and interest in one's neighbours over the water, that an introduction to the foreign literature at school seems to me most valuable'. Most of her colleagues agreed: Harold W. Atkinson made the point even more explicitly: 'soberly considered, the chief aim of linguistic instruction at school is linguistic and not

[37] Hawkins, *Modern Languages in the Curriculum*, 130, Wilfried Decoo, *Systemization in Foreign Language Teaching: Monitoring Content Progression* (New York: Routledge, 2011), 59.

literary. The literary part should come incidentally in the course of the linguistic instruction.'[38]

These discussions focus almost exclusively on the teaching of French and, to a much lesser extent, German. The only discussion of Russian in *Modern Language Teaching* before 1914 is a 1911 article, 'Practical Training in Russian', by Mikhail Trofimov, then a member of Pares' department at the University of Liverpool, which provides an account of the language in the form of an introductory lecture. Although Trofimov does not discuss teaching methods, his focus on the history of the language, its grammar, and morphology aligns his approach to the grammar-translation method based on the study of Classics, rather than the new direct method. Following the outbreak of war, however, the teaching of Russian received much more attention. In *Modern Language Teaching*, the classicist Herbert A. Strong suggested that German would become less widely taught after the war, and that Russian might replace it: 'there is no language at once so simple, so rich, and so musical; nor is there any other European language which contains such a store of national songs and legends'.[39] In reply, W. H. D. Rouse, headmaster of the Perse School, advocated Italian as a replacement for German, rather than Russian, 'not only because the [Russian] language is more difficult than any of those mentioned, but because its literature is largely in the future. I am aware that Russian contains much that is worth studying now, but it cannot show any writers to rank with Dante, or even Boccaccio.'[40] Unsurprisingly, the Russian Lecturer at the University of Manchester, W. J. Sedgefield, argued the case for Russian and its literature, but thought the language's difficulty precluded it being studied in school apart from in the most advanced classes. Nevertheless, he wrote, 'the study of Russian must be taken up vigorously in this country' because 'there will be a great field for British capital and enterprise in the Russian Empire, which is incomparably endowed with natural resources hitherto hardly at all developed'.[41] The connection between education and commercial opportunity was made even more explicitly in the journal's report on the Conference of the United Kingdom Commercial Travellers' Association, which discussed how Britain could compete more effectively with Germany. The President, the industrialist and former Liberal M. P., William Mather, told the conference that 'of all the beneficial developments in foreign countries possible for us, the greatest was that of cultivating a close relationship with Russia in industrial, social and political efforts . . . Our Public Schools and Universities must apply themselves to this end by providing for Russian studies as they did for French and German.'[42]

It was at this point, when the legacy of the direct method's educational claims converged with the political and commercial opportunities presented by the Great

[38] 'Discussion Column: The Teaching of Foreign Literature', *Modern Language Teaching*, 5 (1909), 50–1, 86, 207, 85, 178, 146, 106, 204.

[39] Herbert A. Strong, 'German and Russian', *Modern Language Teaching*, 10 (1914), 183.

[40] W. H. D. Rouse, 'Italian v. German', *Modern Language Teaching*, 10 (1914), 222.

[41] W. J. Sedgefield, 'The Study of Russian', *Modern Language Teaching*, 10 (1914), 243–4.

[42] 'From Here and There', *Modern Language Teaching*, 11 (1915), 121.

War, that a report on 'The Position of Modern Languages in the Educational System of Great Britain' was commissioned from a committee chaired by Stanley Leathes, a former Cambridge historian who had become First Civil Service Commissioner in 1910. The report, commissioned in 1916 and published in 1918, was part of a broader examination of education in Britain, prompted by concerns that it was failing to teach the skills needed to keep British industry and commerce internationally competitive. While the Leathes Report affirmed what it called the 'idealistic aims of education'—the development of 'the higher faculties, the imagination, the sense of beauty, and the intellectual comprehension'—it was the immediate practical utility of modern languages that was emphasized. After the war, the report noted, 'lost ground must be recovered; new openings must be found; in countries where we felt secure we shall find our footing precarious... In a great part of our foreign trade a knowledge of languages, a knowledge of foreign countries and of foreign peoples, will be directly and abundantly remunerative.'[43]

The report encouraged the expansion of teaching of all languages, but while it found that 'school teaching in non-European languages is not necessary... the study of such language will as a rule be confined to adults', it recommended that Russian, alongside Italian and Spanish, should be established on an equal footing with German in schools and universities, and French, 'by far the most important language in the history of civilisation', should retain its priority. Amongst its recommendations for universities was that 'neither Latin nor Greek be compulsory for an Arts degree in any of our Universities', that within ten years from the end of the war, the staff in French, German, Spanish, Italian, and Russian should be increased from the current 31 to 55 professorships and 72 to 110 lectureships, in the areas of language and philology, literature, history and institutions, and economics, and that these areas should be considered within universities as 'an interdependent whole' with 'recent and present day conditions of each country studied' included as much as possible. This last recommendation is indicative of the report's support for what Pares called 'nation-study' and came to be called Area Studies: it advocated more collaboration between departments and remarked with regret that although departments of modern languages had been set up in a number of universities 'none of these has up to the present attempted to join all the studies connected with any one foreign country in a single enlightened and comprehensive School of Modern Humanities'.[44]

Throughout the report the discipline discussed was referred to as 'Modern Studies' rather than 'Modern Languages', which efficiently sums up the change it envisaged, especially in universities, in looking to History rather than Classics as a disciplinary model: 'All or nearly all of [the Honours Courses in Modern Studies] require of all their students some philology and some study of the ancient forms of the language. This we consider unnecessary. These branches should be optional. None of the courses give any adequate place to the history of the life, the thought,

[43] *Report of the Committee on the Position of Modern Languages in the Educational System of Great Britain* ['Leathes Report'] (London: His Majesty's Stationery Office, 1918), 15, 10.

[44] *Report of the Committee on the Position of Modern Languages*, 19, 64–5, 42, 4.

the institutions, of the foreign countries.' Although the authors of the report noted that 'it will not be expected of us that we should enter into a minute disquisition on the method of teaching Modern languages, or attempt to decide the many controversial points that are still debated under this head', they had 'no doubt that the introduction into teaching of what is called the Direct Method has removed a great obstacle from the path of teachers of modern languages', that is, the 'incessant intervention of English', used in the method of teaching Classics. The report also followed advocates of the direct method by proposing that 'teachers of Modern Languages should have a thorough training in phonetics' and 'oral examination should be used wherever possible'. But overall the approach supported by the report was a considerably modified version of the direct method appropriate to 'Modern Studies': the use of English was not prohibited—'it is probably impossible to carry language teaching far in schools without some reference to the mother tongue'—, and nor was reading literary texts in schools—'we feel bound to plead for more serious attention being given in the Upper Forms to the writings of French classical authors'. The report even suggested that after learning a first language 'one or more additional languages can be learnt with advantage for reading purposes only.... such passive knowledge is quite worth cultivating, though the student may never attain the stage of speaking and writing'. Languages, the report argued, 'are for use'.[45]

This brief history of the debates governing modern language teaching in the first two decades of the twentieth century indicates that by 1918, the date of the Leathes report, the role of literature in modern language study was being questioned on a number of fronts. In schools, literary study was seen as broadly desirable, but only for advanced students, because it was not conceived as contributing to language learning, and, according to proponents of the direct method, could impede it. The Leathes Report, while supportive of literary study as 'one of the most important sources of historical enlightenment', places its emphasis firmly on the contemporary political and commercial use of modern languages, rather than the broader cultural understanding of nations, to which literature might contribute.[46]

RUSSIAN LITERATURE IN THE CURRICULUM

Despite the political and popular interest in Britain's wartime ally, neither Russian literature nor Russian history was highly valued in the Leathes Report: 'though Russian literature of late years has attracted great interest and exercised some influence, we shall probably be right in conceding to it little educational value. Nor is Russian history a subject to be recommended for study in schools. At present it appears as amorphous, obscure, unaccented, and uninspiring.'[47] This was not the view of the Modern Language Association's Sub-Committee for Russian Studies

[45] *Report of the Committee on the Position of Modern Languages*, 48, 53–8.
[46] *Report of the Committee on the Position of Modern Languages*, 58.
[47] *Report of the Committee on the Position of Modern Languages*, 20.

whose 'Memorandum on the Teaching of Russian' was published in February 1917. Its secretary, Edward Bullough, taught French and German at Cambridge, and was a member of Leathes' committee. While the memorandum, like Leathes' report, demonstrated the profession's turn away from the philological teaching model, it argued that Russian literature was a particularly important source of historical, including contemporary historical, information:

> To speak of her literature may be superfluous. Its influence during the 19th Century, though small in this country, has been profound and lasting on the Continent. Some of its outstanding names—Púshkin, Lérmontov, Gógol, Dostoyévsky, Herzen, Turgénev, Tolstóy, Merezhkóvsky, Chékhov—are household words even here. To mention others, as yet unfamiliar to English ears, might savour of the foolish attempt to impress the reader with celebrities, to him unknown. They are, however, gradually coming into their own even among the general reading-public (as, for instance, Aksákov from among the older writers, or Kúprin among the moderns). But certainly two features in Russian literature of educational importance, deserve mention: the fact that Russian literature, by reason partly of its youth and partly of its circumstances, has hardly ever reached that degree of divorce from reality which Western literatures frequently display, and reflects, therefore, more directly currents of thought and problems of human life; the second feature is the delicate balance—one of its artistic triumphs—of realism, often frank and unflinching, and a spirituality which finds in it its emblem and embodiment.[48]

What, then, was actually studied by students of Russian? What proportion of the curriculum was devoted to literature, and which authors and works were dominant? The relative youth of Russia's literary history was a persistent point in discussion: was Bullough's positive interpretation of this reflected in a curriculum dominated by the nineteenth-century novel? Or did W. H. D. Rouse's negative interpretation (Russia 'cannot show any writers to rank with Dante, or even Boccaccio') provoke the creation of curricula asserting a longer literary tradition?[49]

In light of the evidence from *Modern Language Teaching*, which shows how little literature was taught in French classes in schools, it would seem unlikely that Russian literature was taught in the few schools that offered the language. However, School Certificate and Higher Certificate examination papers (usually for students of sixteen and eighteen respectively) tell another story. Those set by the Oxford and Cambridge Schools Examination Board between 1922 and 1925, for example, show that students taking the Higher Certificate were required to translate two passages from their prescribed texts, which were either Forbes' *Third Russian Book: Extracts from Aksakov, Grigorovich, Herzen, Saltykov* and Arshak Raffi's edition of two short stories by Turgenev, *Moo-Moo and The District Doctor*, or alternatively Goudy's and Bullough's edition of Tolstoy's Sevastopol sketches and Paul Selver's Chekhov collection, *The Chameleon and Four Other Tales*—all accented

[48] Modern Language Association Sub-Committee for Russian Studies, *The Teaching of Russian*, 11–12.
[49] Rouse, 'Italian v. German', 222.

Russian texts with Russian-English vocabularies.[50] For the School Certificate set by the Oxford and Cambridge Schools Examination Board, there appear to have been no prescribed texts, but students were required to produce unseen translations from literary authors: Turgenev, Pushkin, and Ostrovsky in 1923, Gogol′, Tyutchev, and Goncharov in 1924, and Dostoevsky, Pushkin (and the historian Moisey Ostrogorsky) in 1925.[51] From the academic year 1917–18, the Joint Matriculation Board prescribed a rotating series of Russian literary works for its School as well as its Higher Certificates, though no examination was actually set until a Higher Certificate in 1921, when the prescribed texts were J. H. Freese's edition of Ivan Krylov's fables, and Nevill Forbes' editions of short works by Mikhail Saltykov-Shchedrin and Dostoevsky.[52]

However, commenting on how demanding the examinations were, James Muckle remarks that 'other evidence suggests that these examinations were intended to matriculate Russian émigrés seeking entry to British universities, rather than home candidates, and it became necessary later to adjust standards'.[53] But there are other indications that literature was taught in schools. The preface to Eric Underwood's *A School Russian Grammar*, published in 1916, recommends using the grammar alongside 'an easy reading book such as *Dearmer and Tananévich's First Russian Reader*', which consisted of 'the easiest little stories from Tolstóy (who was a master of style even in his shortest and simplest writings)'; and the series of accented readers published in 'Kegan Paul's Russian Texts series' were advertised as 'for School Use'.[54] The examination for the Newcastle Russian Prize at Eton included translation from prescribed literary texts: in 1920, Gogol′'s *Starosvetskie pomeshchki* (*An Old-World Country-House*), edited by Forbes, and *Russian Lyrics*, edited by the Cambridge classicist, J. D. D. Duff.[55]

In the universities, the extent of, and approach to, the literary content on Russian courses was inevitably determined by the tutors' disciplinary background and their perspective on the changing profession. At Oxford, the course was notably

[50] Forbes, *Third Russian Book*, Ivan Turgenyev, *Moo-Moo and The District Doctor*, ed. A. Raffi (London: Kegan Paul, Trench, Trubner, [1917]), Tolstoy, *Sevastopol*, Anton Chekhov, *The Chameleon and Four Other Tales*, ed. P. Selver (London: Kegan Paul, Trench, Trubner, 1916).

[51] Box 1, Nevill Forbes Papers, Taylor Bodleian Slavonic and Modern Greek Library, University of Oxford.

[52] I. A. Kryloff, *Select Fables*, ed. J. H. Freese (London: Kegan Paul, Trench, Trubner, 1917), M. E. Saltykov, *Bogomoltsy, stranniki i proezzhie; Proshliya vremena* [*Pilgrims and Wayfarers; Bygone Times*] (Oxford: Tipografiya Klarendon, 1917), and F. M. Dostoevsky, *Elka i svad′ba; Chestnyi vor* [*A Christmas Tree and a Wedding; An Honest Thief*] (Oxford: Tipografiya Klarendon, 1917). The Saltykov-Shchedrin and Krylov volumes apparently replaced the two works that, with the Dostoevsky volume, were originally prescribed for that year, Karamzin's 'Bednaya Liza' and Pushkin's *Poltava*, perhaps due to difficulties in obtaining them, as there had been no recent editions of the Russian texts published in Britain. See *The Calendar of Joint Matriculation Board, 1921, Containing the Examination Papers and Lists of Successful Candidates for the Year 1920* (Manchester: Cornish, 1920), 54.

[53] Muckle, *The Russian Language in Britain*, 71. Muckle does not cite the evidence he refers to here.

[54] E. G. Underwood, *A School Russian Grammar* (London: Blackie and Son, 1916), [3]; Chekhov, *The Chameleon and Four Other Tales*, back matter.

[55] N. V. Gogol′, *Starosvetskie pomeshchki* [*An Old-World Country-House*] (Oxford: Tipografiya Klarendon, 1917), J. D. D. Duff, ed., *Russian Lyrics* (Cambridge: Cambridge University Press, 1917); Box 5, Nevill Forbes Papers.

literary and text-based. For the year 1905–1906, the year Forbes graduated, the Examination Statutes listed the subjects of examination (for all languages) as 'The Language as spoken and written at the present day', 'Works or portions of works written in the Language', 'The History of the Language', 'The History of its Literature' and 'A Special Subject of Language or Literature'. In Russian, the prescribed authors and texts were: the Gospel of St Mark in the Ostromir Codex; Karl Berneker's *Slavische Chrestomathie mit Glossaren* (1902); *Povest' vremennykh let* (the Primary Chronicle); *Puteshestvie igumena Daniila po Svyatoi zemle* (*The Travels of the Igumen Daniel in the Holy Land*); Nikolay Ustryalov's edition of *Skazaniya Knyazya Kurbskogo* (*Tales of Prince Kurbsky*, 1833); the *Domostroi*; Kotoshikhin; Kantemir; Gogol'; Pushkin (*Evgeny Onegin, Poltava, Tsygany, Boris Godunov*, lyrics); Lermontov; Turgenev (*Dvoryanskoe gnezdo* (*Home of the Gentry*); *Dym* (*Smoke*); *Senilia*).[56] The list remained identical until 1928, the year before Forbes died, as did the range of examined subjects, bar the addition in 1915–16 of 'The History, especially the Social History, of the corresponding country or countries of Europe during the prescribed period of Literature'.[57] This change in fact appears to have had little actual impact on the teaching or examinations: knowledge of social history was tested, both before and after 1916, in the two 'History of the Literature' papers, which required candidates to answer one question on history in addition to three on literature. But the fact that the study of history is highlighted in the list of subjects from 1915 reflects the wartime situation, and the intellectual and educational climate in which the Leathes Report was written.

In Cambridge, the emphasis of the Russian curriculum fell on later material than in Oxford, and Russian history received greater attention. In 1907, when Russian was added to the Tripos, the subjects for examination were 'Passages from Russian writers beginning with the nineteenth century for translation, with questions on language and metre', 'Alternative subjects for original composition in Russian bearing on Russian literature, history or institutions', 'Passages from English authors to be translated into Russian', 'Questions on Russian literature from the beginning of the eighteenth century with special reference to selected authors' (consistently Pushkin, Gogol', and Turgenev, with the addition from year to year of Griboedov, Krylov, Karamzin, Lomonosov, Fonvizin, Novikov, Aleksey Tolstoy, and Lev Tolstoy), 'Passages from selected works of Russian literature earlier than the eighteenth century for translation and explanation; with questions on the elements of historical Russian grammar, metre, and literary history' (consistently, the Chronicle of Nestor from 946 to 1015, *Slovo o polku Igoreve* (*The Tale of Igor's Campaign*), and either *Tales of Prince Kurbsky*, the *Domostroi*, or Kotoshikhin). The last area, the only one on literature before 1800, could be substituted by a paper on recent history: 'Questions on the outlines of the history of Russia (including social, political, and ecclesiastical institutions), especially in

[56] *The Examination Statutes, 1905–1906* (Oxford: Clarendon Press, 1905), 128, 130.
[57] *The Examination Statutes, 1915–1916* (Oxford: Clarendon Press, 1915), 142.

the nineteenth century'.[58] This alternative was offered only for students studying Russian, and it is not surprising that it calls to mind Bullough's words in the 1917 Modern Languages Association memorandum on Russian teaching, which represented Russian literature as 'reflect[ing]... more directly' contemporary history than did its 'Western' counterparts, since Bullough was one of the main agents in the reform of the languages curriculum in 1917.[59] After the Medieval and Modern Languages Tripos became the Modern and Medieval Languages Tripos that year, driven by the same combination of intellectual transition and wartime pressures that produced the Leathes Report, it was specified that the passages for translation would be from works written after 1800, and the subjects for original composition would be drawn from the nineteenth century. This firm positioning of the Russian literary canon in very recent history contrasts with the choice of periods for the other languages: for French, subjects were drawn from 1600–1700, for German from 1750–1850, for Italian from 1300–1400, and for Spanish from 1550–1650. The final year examinations in Russian, on 'Literature and History' and 'Historical and Comparative Philology', required some work in earlier periods, though the weight of the former still fell on the post 1700 period.[60] From its inception at Cambridge, Russian was the least philologically inflected course in the Medieval and Modern Languages Tripos, with the most contemporary literary and historical content.

The Russian departments run by Bernard Pares at the University of Liverpool and the School of Slavonic Studies were, as one would expect, less linguistic and literary in their outlook. At Liverpool, studying Russian as part of the first year course leading to the Intermediate Examination entailed 'translation from and into Russian; outlines of Russian historical grammar and literature; elementary philology or phonetics', alongside courses in history and economics. The second and third year course was examined in two parts, the first consisting of an oral examination, and one paper each in general Russian history, European history since 1682, Russian economics, Russian literature and Russian language, and the second consisting of a dissertation and oral examination, and a paper on a special period of Russian history, literature, or economics.[61] Although the historical study of language is not absent from the curriculum, and students can choose to specialize in

[58] *Ordinances of the University of Cambridge to 1 October 1907* (Cambridge: Cambridge University Press, 1907), 138–9, 'Subjects Proposed for the Medieval and Modern Languages Tripos, 1914', *Cambridge University Reporter*, 41, no. 43 (1911), 114–18, 'Subjects for the Medieval and Modern Languages Tripos, 1915', *Cambridge University Reporter*, 42, no. 39 (1912), 1070–3, 'Medieval and Modern Languages Tripos, 1917: Subjects', *Cambridge University Reporter*, 44, no. 40 (1914), 1103–6.

[59] Modern Language Association Sub-Committee for Russian Studies, *The Teaching of Russian*, 11; E. M. W. Tillyard, *The Muse Unchained: An Intimate Account of the Revolution in English Studies at Cambridge* (London: Bowes & Bowes, 1958), Brooke, *A History of the University of Cambridge*, iv, 434.

[60] *Ordinances of the University of Cambridge to 1 October 1920* (Cambridge: Cambridge University Press, 1920), 140–1.

[61] *The University of Liverpool Calendar, 1912* (Liverpool: Liverpool University Press, 1912), 229. 1912 is the first year the scheme of papers is listed, though the areas of study appear from 1911, and a brief syllabus first appeared in 1910, augmented in subsequent years.

literature, no other course in Russian gave so much space to history, let alone economics. As Pares later wrote,

> We were not a language school, though we hoped some day to have the language more creditably taught than it would be easy to do elsewhere. But the language was the most necessary of Hülfsmitteln for the study of all other subjects connected with Russia. Our plan, with any serious student, would be to pitch him straight into it. He would begin with almost daily language classes, with our very capable native teacher, who reported him as soon as possible to be ready for further work in his subject; he would then be given Russian books and told to read them. He would be little lectured, at first much tutored. Probably knowing almost nothing, not merely of Russia but of all that European atmosphere in which Russia has to be set, he might need at first many lectures on modern European history. But these lectures would hardly be lectures; at every point the teacher would stop to find out by questioning whether the pupil were losing his time, or whether he had to begin further back. The classes were, then, an examination of the student's reading, with which the teacher was kept in continual contact. Russian was learnt on the road.[62]

In contrast with the entries for other languages, no set books are listed for Russian in the *University of Liverpool Calendar*, and it is likely that the course had few enough students for not only the learning but the teaching to occur 'on the road'. Indeed, between 1907 and 1918, when Pares resigned his position to move to the University of London, an external examiner in Russian is listed in the Calendar only twice, Pavel Vinogradov appears in 1912 and W. J. Sedgefield in 1915, which suggests very few students indeed took university examinations in the subject.[63]

At the School of Slavonic Studies Pares put a similar curriculum in place for degrees in Russian (and in Polish, in Czech and Slovak, and in Serbo-Croat and Slovene). After passing the University Intermediate Examination at the end of their first year of study, students could choose to follow either a course in language and literature or in regional studies. The former course consisted of examinations in oral proficiency, translation, composition, literature, history of the language, and either comparative Slavonic philology or the history of Russian literary criticism. The course in regional studies also contained examinations in oral proficiency, translation, and composition, and in place of the language and literature examinations, papers in 'Russian history, with political geography', Russian laws and institutions, modern European history, and 'Russian literature (more particularly as one of the principal expressions of Russian social history)'.[64] The prospectus outlining the course does not list prescribed books, which could be obtained from the Academic Registrar, and the surviving examination papers, the language and literature papers taken by Elizabeth Hill and the regional studies papers taken by Joshua Cooper

[62] Pares, 'Mackay and the School of Russian Studies', 51–2.

[63] *The University of Liverpool Calendar, 1912,* 100; *The University of Liverpool Calendar, 1915–16* (Liverpool: Liverpool University Press, 1915), 123. However, Samuel Harper notes that Vinogradov visited Liverpool as an external examiner in 1911, see Harper, *The Russia I Believe In*, 71.

[64] *School of Slavonic Studies Prospectus, 1921–22* (London: University of London Press, 1921), 7–10, 11–12; *School of Slavonic Studies Prospectus, 1922–23* (London: University of London Press, 1922), 8–12.

in 1924, do not list them. The papers show, however, that extracts for translation by Hill were taken from Pushkin's correspondence with Petr Vyazemsky, from Dostoevsky's *Brat'ya Karamazovy* (*The Brothers Karamazov*), from Aleksey Tolstoy's poem, *Ioann Damaskin* (*John of Damascus*), and Chekhov's short story, 'Dom's mezoninom' ('The House with the Mezzanine'). Questions on other papers covered a wide range of subjects and authors, but particular works singled out were Gogol′'s *Peterburgskie povesti* (*Petersburg Stories*), Aleksandr Griboedov's play, *Gore ot uma* (*Woe from Wit*), and the essays *Chto takoe iskusstvo?* (*What is Art?*) by Tolstoy, and 'L. Tolstoy i Dostoevsky' ('L. Tolstoy and Dostoevsky') by Dmitry Merezhkovsky. The Regional Studies translation paper required Cooper to translate into Russian extracts from recent studies of Russia by the historian Pavel Vinogradov, and into English extracts from an essay by Gertsen (Herzen), and Gor′ky's *Detstvo* (*Childhood*). Its literature paper asked Cooper to, for example, 'Give an account of the „Слово о пълку Игоревѣ" [*Slovo o polku Igoreve* (*The Tale of Igor's Campaign*)] (*a*) from the poetical, and (*b*) from the political and historical point of view', and discuss 'The Russian upper classes as portrayed by Tolstoy (with special reference to „Война и Миръ" [*Voina i mir* (*War and Peace*)])' or 'Chekhov as the representative and the poet of the интеллигенція [intelligentsia]'.[65] The School of Slavonic Studies' lecture lists during the 1920s show that, after a somewhat generalist beginning, where Pares' and Seton-Watson's history lectures were supplemented by talks by the music critic Rosa Newmarch and Tolstoy's translator Aylmer Maude, Russian literature was taught by two substantial lecture series a year following the appointment of D. S. Mirsky in 1922, then 'the first and only full-time academic specialist in Russian literature in the country'.[66] However, according to the School's secretary, Dorothy Galton, though Pares gave the impression that the School was 'a hive of industry, with many students playing an important part in the life of the nation and empire; alas, the degree lists for the period (1922–39) tell a different story, and most of the staff were engaged in teaching of an elementary kind more appropriate to a secondary school'. Moreover, despite his commitment to the Regional Studies degree, 'the Regional Studies courses never had the same appeal for students as the more regular language and literature courses'.[67] The record of degrees bears out Galton's argument, which suggests that in fact despite the appearance of the curriculum and the lecture lists, students at the School of Slavonic received under D. S. Mirsky an education not substantially less literary, if notably more up-to-date, than those at Oxford and Cambridge, rather than the training in contemporary history offered by Pares.[68]

[65] Box 2, Nevill Forbes Papers.

[66] University of London, King's College and King's College for Women, 'Public Lectures and Arrangements in the Easter Term, 1922', Seton-Watson Collection (SEW 20/3/6), School of Slavonic and East European Studies Library, University College London; G. S. Smith, *D. S. Mirsky: A Russian-English Life, 1890–1939* (Oxford: Oxford University Press, 2000), 94.

[67] Galton, 'Sir Bernard Pares and Slavonic Studies in London University, 1919–39', 488.

[68] University of London, *The Historical Record, 1836–1926* (London: University of London Press, 1926).

BEYOND THE UNIVERSITY

It is, however, somewhat misleading to measure the teaching of Russian literature by degree courses and university examinations. Although the type of information available differs between institutions, the class lists for all the universities discussed show that the number of students taking degrees in Russian was extremely small: Muckle notes that only ten first degrees were awarded at the School of Slavonic Studies between 1920 and 1939, an average of less than one student a year was taking the Russian undergraduate course at Oxford, as late as 1933 there were only two registered degree students at Cambridge, and the department at Nottingham awarded no degree in almost two decades of teaching Russian, beginning in 1915.[69] Yet many more students were studying Russian for diplomas, certificates, and civil service exams, often as 'external students', and teachers of Russian, especially Pares, but also Mirsky and Forbes, gave a number of public lectures. Indeed, the School of Slavonic's lectures during this period were open to the public.[70]

But it was not necessary to attend classes or lectures to be taught Russian literature by the new generation of university teachers. Their influence was extended by a variety of publications that shaped the Russian literary canon in Britain. Their critical work was of course important: Mirsky's School of Slavonic lectures formed the basis of his enormously influential *History of Russian Literature*, the most significant work of literary criticism from this early period of university Russian studies.[71] Morfill was a prolific reviewer of new books in Slavonic studies for the *Academy* as well as for academic journals, Forbes published introductory articles on major Russian authors in Pares' *Russian Review*, and Mirsky wrote mainly on contemporary literature in journals from the *Times Literary Supplement* and *The Listener* to the *Nation and Athenaeum* to Pares' *Slavonic Review*. Pares' two journals themselves were the major conduits for new research in Russian and Slavonic studies, although in both cases, the literary content was subordinate to work on history and contemporary politics. A letter to Pares from his co-editor Seton-Watson written at some point during the Second World War discusses criticism from their colleague at the School of Slavonic and East European Studies, Gleb Struve, that the journal neglected literature and literary criticism.[72] But these first teachers were less important as critics than as facilitators of others' study of Russian literature. Part of the

[69] Muckle, 95–96, James Muckle, 'Russian in the University Curriculum: A Case-study of the Impact of the First World War on Language Study in Higher Education in Britain', *History of Education: Journal of the History of Education Society*, 37, no. 3 (2008), 372.

[70] Muckle, *The Russian Language in Britain*, 95–6; Smith, *D. S. Mirsky*, 95; Galton, 'Sir Bernard Pares and Slavonic Studies in London University, 1919–39', 482, 491.

[71] Prince D. S. Mirsky, *Contemporary Russian Literature, 1881–1925* (London: Routledge, 1926), Prince D. S. Mirsky, *A History of Russian Literature: From the Earliest Times to the Death of Dostoyevsky (1881)* (London: Routledge, 1927). The edition usually referred to as *A History of Russian Literature* (D. S. Mirsky, *A History of Russian Literature*, ed. and abr. Francis J. Whitfield (London: Routledge & Kegan Paul, 1949)), is an abridged version of these two volumes.

[72] Pares, 'Mackay and the School of Russian Studies', 54, Pares, *A Wandering Student*, 100–1; Seton-Watson Collection (SEW 18/2/3).

reason their significance has been obscured is that they were at least as likely to be editors as authors or translators, providing Russian literary texts for students of the language and literature.

Literary texts in Russian for English-speaking students had been available since the late nineteenth century: Henry Riola's *A Graduated Russian Reader* appeared in 1879, consisting of grammatical exercises followed by 'stories, extracts, etc., selected from the prose and poetry of the best Russian authors', including sections from Russian histories, as well as extracts from works by Ivan Dmitriev, Gogol', Krylov, Nikolay Karamzin, Lermontov, Pushkin, Tolstoy, Turgenev, and Mikhail Zagoskin, among others.[73] Ivan Nestor-Schnurmann brought out an edition of Lermontov's *Geroi nashego vremeni* (*A Hero of our Time*) in 1899 with an English translation on the page facing its accented Russian text, so that 'he who works carefully through this book, learning by heart, translating, and retranslating as he goes, cannot fail to pick up a great deal of Russian by the time he gets to the end of it'.[74] In 1902 Eduard Roller produced an English version of Gustav Werkhaupt's *Russisches Konversations-Lesebuch*, which consisted of very short extracts from poems and prose (Pushkin, Lermontov, and Tolstoy prominent again), with conversation practice based on the extracts' vocabulary and grammar.[75] The most substantial, and most respected, of these early Russian readers was the 1906 English edition of the 1905 *Manuel pour l'étude de la langue russe* by Paul Boyer and Nikolay Speransky, colleagues at l'École des langues orientales in Paris, adapted by their former pupil, Samuel Harper. It consisted of complete stories for children by Tolstoy, with the addition of his short story 'Tri smerti' ('Three Deaths'), described by Boyer in his introduction as 'perfect models of the language as actually spoken'.[76] In Forbes' 1914 *Russian Grammar*, it is the only reader in English recommended, alongside three German and four Russian volumes of accented texts.[77]

But during the war many more readers for English beginners were produced. Some were marketed at schools, such as the editions of stories by Chekhov, Garshin, Krylov, Lermontov, and Turgenev edited by Paul Selver, J. H. Freese, Roman Biske, and Arshak Raffi, respectively, and A. E. Semeonoff and H. J. W. Tillyard's *Russian Poetry Reader*, all of which were published in 'Kegan Paul's Russian Texts' series, advertised 'for School Use', and which included introductions, grammatical notes, and vocabularies.[78] Other series were directed at beginners more generally, such as

[73] Henry Riola, *A Graduated Russian Reader, with a Vocabulary of all the Russian Words Contained in It* (London: Trübner, 1879), iii.

[74] Ivan Nestor-Schnurmann, trans. and ed., *Russian Reader: Lermontoff's Modern Hero with English Translation and Biographical Sketch* (Cambridge: Cambridge University Press, 1899), vii–viii.

[75] G. Werkhaupt and Ed Roller, *Russian Reader: With Exercises of Conversation* (Heidelberg: Groos, 1902).

[76] Paul Boyer and N. Spéranski, *Manuel pour l'étude de la langue russe* (Paris: Colin, 1905), Paul Boyer and N. Speranski, *Russian Reader*, adpt. Samuel Northrup Harper (Chicago, IL: University of Chicago Press; London: Luzac, 1906), ii.

[77] Forbes, *Russian Grammar*, 5–6.

[78] Chekhov, *The Chameleon and Four Other Tales*, Vsyévolod Garshin, *The Signal, and Four Days on the Field of Battle*, ed. J. H. Freese (London: Kegan Paul, Trench, Trubner, [1918]), Kryloff, *Select Fables*, Michail Yurievitch Lermontoff, *Bela*, ed. R. Biske (London: Kegan Paul, Trench, Trubner, [1917]), Turgenyev, *Moo-Moo and The District Doctor*, A. E. Semeonoff and H. J. W. Tillyard, eds, *Russian Poetry Reader* (London: Kegan Paul, Trench, Trubner, 1917).

the accented texts in the 'Russkaya Biblioteka' series, edited by Roman Biske and published by Richard Jaschke, 'Bondar's Russian Readers', edited with a facing page translation, notes and vocabulary by the prolific David Bondar, and the 'Oxford Russian Plain Texts', edited by Nevill Forbes.[79] Several poetry readers were published with grammatical notes and vocabulary: as well as Semeonoff's and Tillyard's, beginners could turn to James Duff's *Russian Lyrics*, consisting primarily of poems and extracts by Pushkin, Aleksey Tolstoy, and Fedor Tyutchev, E. N. Steinhart's *Poems of Michael Lermontoff*, and Paul Selver's *Modern Russian Poetry*, whose collection of poetry by the Russian Symbolists was a rare departure from the dominance of Romantic poetry.[80]

However, the readers' editors differed in the extent to which they conceived of their volumes as an aid to language learning or as introductions to Russian literature. Steinhart remarks that 'whatever may be the purpose of the English student of Russian, whether a commercial or a purely literary one, he cannot penetrate as far as necessary into the language without studying its literature and, I am inclined to think, more especially its poetry'. Semeonoff and Tillyard agree that 'the perusal of verse has a recognized value in fixing grammatical forms and the stress-accents in the pupil's mind, especially if some of the poems are learnt by heart'. Selver,

[79] The 'Russkaya Biblioteka' series of 'abridged and accented' texts, with brief prefaces by Roman Biske, consisted of: A. S. Pushkin, *The Captain's Daughter: A Tale* (London: Jaschke, 1919), N. V. Gogol, *Dead Souls* (London: Jaschke, 1919), A. P. Chekhov, *Short Stories* 2 vols. (London: Jaschke, 1919), and I. V. Skvortsov, *Russian History*, 2 vols. (London: Jaschke, 1919). 'Bondar's Russian Readers' consisted of (in order of issue): A. S. Pushkin, *The Queen of Spades*, ed. D. Bondar (London: Effingham Wilson, 1915), A. P. Chekhoff, *Humorous Stories*, ed. D. Bondar (London: Effingham Wilson, 1916), L. N. Tolstoy, *Family Happiness*, ed. D. Bondar, 2 vols. (London: Effingham Wilson, 1916–17), N. V. Gogol, *The Inspector-General*, ed. D. Bondar (London: Effingham Wilson, 1917), A. E. Kouprin, *How I Became an Actor*, ed. P. Bondar (London: Effingham Wilson, 1919). Amongst Bondar's many other publications were (with Alfred Calvert), *Bondar's Simplified Russian Method (Conversational and Commercial)* (London: Effingham Wilson, 1911), and the *Russian Journal* (1916–17) and *Russian Pupil* (1918). The 'Oxford Russian Plain Texts' consisted of Dostoevsky, *Elka i svad'ba; Chestnii vor* [*A Christmas Tree and a Wedding, An Honest Thief*], V. M. Garshin, *Izbrannye razskazy: To, chego ne bylo, vstrecha, signal, chetyre dnya* [*What Never Happened, The Meeting, The Signal, Four Days*] (Oxford: Tipografiya Klarendon, [1920]), Gogol', *Starosvetskie pomeshchki* [*An Old-World Country-House*], I. A. Goncharov, *Slugi starogo veka* [*Men-Servants of Other Days*] (Oxford: Tipografiya Klarendon, [1918]), I. A. Krylov, *Izbrannye basni* [*Selected Fables*] (Oxford: Tipografiya Klarendon, [1918]), V. G. Korolenko, *Noch' yu, v noch' pod tsvetlyi prazdnik* [*In the Night, Easter Eve*] (Oxford: Tipografiya Klarendon, [1918]), M. Yu. Lermontov, *Izbrannye stikhotvoreniya* [*Selected Poems*] (Oxford: Tipografiya Klarendon, [1918]), A. S. Pushkin, *Boris Godunov: drama v stikhakh* (Oxford: Tipografiya Klarendon, 1920?], A. S. Pushkin, *Pikovaya dama* [*The Queen of Spades*] (Oxford: Tipografiya Klarendon, 1917), Saltykov, *Bogomoltsy, stranniki i proezzhie; Proshlie vremena* [*Pilgrims and Wayfarers; Bygone Times*], Lev Tolstoy, *Kavkazskii plennik: rasskaz* [*A Prisoner of the Caucasus*] (Oxford: Tipografiya Klarendon, 1917), I. S. Turgenev, *Pegas; Biryuk; Les i step'* [*Pegasus; Biryúk; Forest and Steppe*] (Oxford: Tipografiya Klarendon, 1917). All volumes were edited by Forbes, bar Tolstoy, *Kavkazskii plennik*, and Pushkin, *Pikovaya dama*, edited by E. G. Underwood, Turgenev, *Pegas; Biryuk; Les i step'*, edited by Underwood and Forbes, and Garshin, *Izbrannye rasskazy*, edited by Ivy Williams and Forbes. The volumes contained only accented texts, and the promise of the series list in the back pages, that 'Editions of the above will also be issued with introductions, notes, and vocabularies', was not realized.

[80] Duff, ed., *Russian Lyrics*, E. N. Steinhart, trans. and ed., *Poems of Michael Lermontoff* (London: Kegan Paul, Trench, Trubner, 1917), P. Selver, trans. and ed., *Modern Russian Poetry: Texts and Translations* (London: Kegan Paul, Trench, Trubner, 1917).

however, confines his introduction to comment on the literary and cultural value of his collection, hoping that it 'will convey a fairly adequate idea of the chief features in modern Russian poetry, a branch of Russian literature which has so far received very little serious attention in this country'.[81] Of the readers that anthologized extracts or short works by a variety of authors, Frank Freeth's *A First Russian Reader* provided no attributions, and made no distinction between short pieces presumably composed by the author and texts by, for example, Karamzin, Krylov, and Lermontov, which suggests that the texts operate entirely as examples of language use. Evelyn While's *Easy Russian Reader* attributes texts by, for example, Aleksandr Afanas'ev, Krylov, and Tolstoy, but not others, by Aleksey Pleshcheev and Vasily Zhukovsky. Mikhail Trofimov's *Elementary Russian Reader*, however, recommends study of the literary texts not only as 'one of the surest ways of strengthening and developing the stock of grammatical knowledge, and of mastering the means of expression peculiar to the language', but also as a means to bring the student 'into the field of national ideas and views of the Russian people'. Accordingly from the very beginning of his reader he uses attributed sentences and short paragraphs by Aleksandr Izmailov, Apollon Maikov, and Tolstoy to teach particular grammatical points, as well as providing more substantial texts by Aksakov, Chekhov, Krylov, and Turgenev as the lessons advance.[82]

It was professional teachers of Russian who were the principal disseminators of this material. As well as Boyer, Forbes, Harper, Goudy, Nestor-Schnurmann, and Trofimov, whose affiliations have been discussed, Riola appears to have taught at the Army Staff College, Bondar taught at the Manchester Municipal School of Commerce, and Raffi at the School of Slavonic Studies. Duff, Freese, and Tillyard were professional classicists (Duff and Freese at Cambridge, Tillyard at Edinburgh), but they also taught Russian. Making Russian-language literary texts available facilitated their own teaching, and made setting texts for national examinations possible, but as part of a network of scholarly activities that increasingly emanated from within the academy, it also put in place a particular canon, and certain ways of engaging with it.

CONCLUSION

The canon of Russian literature developed by the first generation of Russian teachers in schools and universities is distinct from that generated by their amateur predecessors in a number of ways. First, it contained more poetry. Although John Bowring's early nineteenth-century editions had introduced Russian poets to British readers at the very beginning of the translation of Russian literature into English, little

[81] Steinhart, *Poems of Michael Lermontoff*, vi; Semeonoff and Tillyard, *Russian Poetry Reader*, v; Selver, *Modern Russian Poetry*, 5.

[82] Frank Freeth, *A First Russian Reader* (London: Kegan Paul, Trench 1916), 56–61, 68–71, 72–9, Evelyn C. While, *Easy Russian Reader* (London: Kegan Paul, Trench, Trubner, 1919), 2, 8, Michael V. Trofimov, *Elementary Russian Reader* (London: Constable, 1917), 3.

poetry had been published since; even Pushkin, though frequently translated, was represented primarily by his prose. Professional Russian teachers drew attention to the poetry of Pushkin, Lermontov, Maikov, and Aleksey Tolstoy, in particular, and Selver's *Modern Russian Poetry* reader and Mirsky's lectures and criticism introduced the poets of the late nineteenth and early twentieth centuries. Poetry was, as Semeonoff and Tillyard pointed out, a useful tool in teaching pronunciation and consolidating grammar, the status of the genre supported a defence of Russian courses as sufficiently rigorous mental exercise, and lyrics, at least, were a convenient length for classroom teaching.[83] The latter reason also fostered the publication and teaching of short stories and fables: Krylov and, especially, Tolstoy had been translated in the late nineteenth century, and Chekhov's stories were becoming popular through, first, R. E. C. Long's and S. S. Kotelyansky's, and subsequently Constance Garnett's, translations at the same time that professional teachers were providing the Russian texts. To their short works, teaching materials added the writings of Aksakov, Saltykov-Shchedrin, and Garshin to the canon of easily available works. It is notable that the first generation of Russian teachers did not translate, nor produce editions, of longer works, even when they were taught on courses, as we know *Anna Karenina* was at Cambridge and *Brat'ya Karamazovy* (*The Brothers Karamazov*) was at the School of Slavonic Studies. Dostoevsky is in general surprisingly under-represented in the teaching canon, given that the period of the Great War was the height of 'the Dostoevsky cult', to use the phrase coined by Helen Muchnic, Mirsky's former graduate student.[84]

The canon of Russian literature was affected not only by the addition of certain texts produced in the course of the institutionalization of Russian teaching, but by the approach to literature in the new modern languages departments, generated in reaction against prior intellectual and educational models, chiefly Classics and philology, and attraction to more 'modern' subjects, chiefly history and English. (The picture, however, is far from consistent from institution to institution: in Cambridge, as Christopher Brooke has discussed, Classics represented the progressive literary model for modern languages, in reaction against the model of English, which was associated with Anglo-Saxon philology.)[85] The literary texts produced by professional teachers are evidence of the change in language teaching away from philological analysis to use of the foreign language, and literature is used in the new grammars to supply authentic examples of language use—'perfect models of the language as actually spoken', as Boyer wrote of Tolstoy's stories—in place of the contorted concoctions associated with grammars for the classical languages.[86]

[83] Semeonoff and Tillyard, *Russian Poetry Reader*, v.

[84] Helen Muchnic, *Dostoyevsky's English Reputation, 1881–1936*, Smith College Studies in Modern Languages, 20, no. 3/4 (Northampton, MA: Smith College, 1939), 63. The 'Dostoevsky cult' is Muchnic's phrase, but she derives it from D. S. Mirsky's description of 'the cult of Dostoevsky' in *The Intelligentsia of Great Britain*, trans. Alec Brown (London: Gollancz, 1935), 107.

[85] Brooke, *A History of the University of Cambridge*, iv, 434.

[86] Paul Boyer and N. Speranski, *Russian Reader*, ii.

In the case of Russian, this change in literature's use in language teaching has a particular force and interest. Since the first stage of extensive translation of Russian literary texts into English, during the Crimean war, Russian literature had been read as a window onto contemporary political history, reflecting 'more directly currents of thought and problems of human life' than other national literatures'.[87] In a sense, then, the role of Russian literature in grammars, to teach how the language was authentically used, and its role in courses inflected towards regional or nation studies, was a continuation or consolidation of its place in the popular or, at least, pre-professional culture. When Pares advocated teaching Russian literature as part of a regional studies programme, he may have been breaking with prevailing educational ideas of how one teaches foreign languages and literatures, but there was no break with the prevailing popular ideas of how one interprets a Russian novel. Of all the European literatures, Russian literature's use value was always the most evident. A circular logic is in play here: the British canon of Russian literature was established in the second half of the nineteenth century, when Russian writers, following the lead of their British and French contemporaries, were developing the realist novel; the Russian novel's realism was readily accepted by British readers seeking information about a political enemy, and eventually, ally.[88] In the first decades of the twentieth century, 'Russian literature', that is, the British canon of realist Russian nineteenth-century novels, was inevitably promoted as reflecting 'more directly currents of thought and problems of human life'. So even though the nineteenth-century realist novels were not moved into the canon by the institutionalization of Russian studies, that institutionalization—in which the connection between the wartime government and Russian studies via Pares played a significant part—consolidated their canonical position.

Yet in the immediate postwar period the ideas governing literary studies in Britain and the United States—and, briefly, in Russia—began to pull in the opposite direction, away from the study of literature as historical record and towards the study of literary form. To a certain extent, the literature that was valued in the subsequent four decades, particularly modernist literature, both contributed to and benefited from this shift. The fact that, from the 1930s, contemporary Russian literature was dominated by its ideological opposite, socialist realism, adds an external political factor to the native pressures with which this chapter has been primarily concerned. In recent years, critics such as Greg Barnhisel, Walter Kalaidjian, and Cary Nelson have shown how in the United States the autonomy of the literary artefact, as studied by formalist literary critics, came to stand for an assertion of American individualism against socialist realism and Marxist criticism during the Cold War.[89] Research on analogous allegiances in the British context is yet to be

[87] Modern Language Association Sub-Committee for Russian Studies, *The Teaching of Russian*, 11.

[88] Rebecca Beasley, 'Russia and the Invention of the Modernist Intelligentsia', in Peter Brooker and Andrew Thacker, eds, *Geographies of Modernism: Literatures, Cultures, Spaces* (London: Routledge, 2005), 19–30.

[89] Greg Barnhisel, '*Perspectives USA* and the Cultural Cold War: Modernism in Service of the State', *Modernism/Modernity*, 14 (2007), 729–54, Walter Kalaidjian, *The Edge of Modernism: American Poetry and the Traumatic Past* (Baltimore, MD: Johns Hopkins University Press, 2006), 128–56, Cary Nelson, *Repression and Recovery: Modern American Poetry and the Politics of Cultural Memory, 1910–1945* (Madison, WI: University of Wisconsin Press, 1989).

undertaken, though Ian Patterson's and James Smith's chapters in this volume begin that work. Certainly, there is much to say about the role of the School of Slavonic and East European Studies during the early years of the Soviet Union, and Pares' and Mirsky's increasingly opposed ideologies, as Mirsky became committed to communism. Mirsky's lecture series in spring 1931 was entitled 'Russian Literature in its Relation to Russian Social History (From 1860)', and ran from Dostoevsky to 'the Soviet Novel' via Tolstoy, 'The Radicals of the 'Sixties', 'Nekrasov and the *Narodniki*', Chekhov, Gor'ky, the Symbolists and Mayakovsky.[90] The same year, Pares published *My Russian Memoirs*, which contained the comments on Russian literature quoted at the beginning of this chapter. It is instructive that Pares' strongest invective is reserved for Tolstoy, and his highest praise for Chekhov, in whom, he writes, 'there is no shade of cynicism and hardly any of the unpleasant'.[91] The champion of regional studies and the integration of university disciplines, has, it turns out, a narrow and conventional conception of literary value. But Pares' literary taste, like the debates, curricula, examination papers, grammars, and teaching texts examined in this chapter, is both cause and effect in the development of the British canon of Russian literature. Literature is indeed 'one of the most important sources of historical enlightenment', to quote the Leathes Report once more—though, as even Pares knew, literature is not only that.[92]

[90] University of London, King's College and King's College for Women, 'Public Lectures and Arrangements in the Easter Term, 1931', Seton-Watson Collection (SEW 20/3/6), School of Slavonic and East European Studies.

[91] Pares, *My Russian Memoirs*, 38.

[92] *Report of the Committee on the Position of Modern Languages*, 58.

10

The Translation of Soviet Literature

John Rodker and PresLit

Ian Patterson

Soviet art and culture, including and perhaps especially literary culture, passed through a series of radical transformations in the two decades after the Bolshevik Revolution of 1917, but probably the most significant were the consolidation of literature as part of the state apparatus, and the reform of all aspects of its administration, the completion of which was marked by the First Congress of Soviet Writers in 1934. The high revolutionary ambitions of Proletkul′t, LEF, and the Russian Association of Proletarian Writers (Rossiiskaya assotsiatsiya proletarskikh pisatelei, RAPP) were officially abandoned by the Central Committee of the Communist Party of the Soviet Union on 23 April 1932, when they adopted a policy 'On the Reconstruction of Literary and Artistic Organizations', and put in place a vision of writing as craftwork devoted to the development of the new proletarian consciousness. RAPP was disbanded and replaced by the Union of Soviet Writers. As Maksim Gor′ky put it in his speech to the Union's first Congress, 'The proletarians' state must educate thousands of outstanding "craftsmen of culture", "engineers of souls".'[1] And as Andrey Zhdanov explained in his words of welcome at the start of the Congress, 'All the necessary conditions have been created to enable Soviet literature to produce works answering to the requirements of the masses': he exhorted those present to 'actively help to remould the mentality of people in the spirit of socialism'.[2] The policy shifts of the early 1930s were consolidated in the new Stalinist concept of socialist realism, which united instructive and instructional narrative with documentary methods and appropriate information in an attempt to create not only a new literature but also new writers and new readers, illustrative of the new society under construction in the Soviet Union. All the resources of state publishing, state libraries, and the new Union of Soviet Writers were devoted to the production of this literature and to its dissemination, at home and abroad. The organization known as VOKS (Vsesoyuznoe obshchestvo kul′turnoi svyazi s zagranitsei, or the All-Union

[1] Evgeny Dobrenko, *The Making of the State Writer: Social and Aesthetic Origins of Soviet Literary Culture*, trans. Jesse M. Savage (Stanford, CA: Stanford University Press, 2001), 358.

[2] A. Zhdanov, et al., *Problems of Soviet Literature: Reports and Speeches at the First Soviet Writers' Congress*, ed. H. G. Scott (London: Lawrence, [1935]), 23–4

Society of Cultural Relations with Foreign Countries), which had been set up in 1925 to develop support for the state among cultural figures in the West, came under increasing pressure to manufacture support for the regime, bringing prominent intellectual figures to the Soviet Union, and encouraging the publication of translations of Russian works abroad.[3] Although its origins are unclear, it seems likely that it was as part of this process of consolidation that a central literary agency to sponsor foreign publication was set up, and so the Press and Publisher Literary Service, Moscow, known by its ubiquitous Soviet shorthand as 'PresLit', came into being.

One of its immediate tasks was to establish competent and sympathetic representatives in Western capitals, and as their London representative, they found John Rodker. A marginal but crucial figure in British literary modernism, he was brought up in the East End of London in the early years of the previous century.[4] His parents were refugees from Russian anti-semitism, his father making his living as a corset-maker. As a teenager, Rodker had artistic ambitions, and made friends with a group of similarly aspirant young people in his neighbourhood, including the painters David Bomberg, Clara Birnberg, Mark Gertler, and Isaac Rosenberg (later to be better remembered as a poet), and fellow poets Joseph Leftwich and Sammy Winsten, a group these days generally referred to, somewhat exclusively, as 'the Whitechapel boys'. All were the children of Jewish immigrants, their parents having fled from Russia or Eastern Europe, and all had literary or artistic ambitions. They were also, most of them, involved in politics to a greater or lesser extent, particularly in the Young Socialist League, where they took what part they could in the political life of the area and also organized educational meetings on modern art and radical politics. They haunted Whitechapel Public Library, and the boys went for long walks across London during which they discussed every topic imaginable. It was Lazarus Aaronson, later a poet of some distinction, who 'converted' Rodker to socialism, but it was Joe Fineberg who was the most politically active of Rodker's friends, and who encouraged him to stand for offices such as Secretary of the local branch, or Vice-Chairman, of the London District Young Socialist League, responsibilities that Rodker took seriously, and which showed his flair for organization. Fineberg was older than Rodker by some seven or eight years and already a politically experienced member of the Social Democratic Federation. He was elected to the Executive of the British Socialist Party in 1914 as an opponent of the war, and worked for a while, after 1917, as secretary to Maksim Litvinov when he was appointed (unofficial) Soviet representative in Britain. After his return to Russia in 1918, Fineberg was involved in the foundation of the Communist International.[5]

[3] On VOKS, see Ludmila Stern, *Western Intellectuals and the Soviet Union, 1920–40: From Red Square to the Left Bank* (Abingdon: Routledge, 2007), 92–174.

[4] Information about Rodker's contacts in the Soviet Union, and his work with PresLit, and quotation from correspondence, including the correspondence with John Lehmann, derives from the John Rodker Papers at the Harry Ransom Humanities Research Centre (HRHRC) at the University of Texas, Austin. I am grateful to the staff there for their help, and for the award of a Dorot Fellowship in 1999, which made part of this research possible.

[5] See Walter Kendall, *The Revolutionary Movement in Britain, 1900–1921* (London: Weidenfeld and Nicolson, 1969), 32, 82, 328n.

Fineberg and his younger brother Abraham (Bram), who was closer in age to Rodker, were enthusiastic and committed supporters of the Russian Revolution; both brothers emigrated to the Soviet Union as soon as they could and spent much of their lives working as translators, Bram becoming Lenin's translator and the editor of his works. Bram and his wife continued to exchange letters with Rodker well into the 1920s, and he may well have kept in touch with them during his visits to the Soviet Union in the 1930s. At heart, Rodker was always more interested in art and bohemianism than in politics, but when conscription was introduced in 1916 he declined to take part in the war, and as a result was court-martialled and suffered periods of imprisonment. Winsten, too, was imprisoned for his pacifism. Rosenberg, also inclined to pacifism, joined up so that his desperately poor family could benefit from the soldier's wage, and was killed. There is no doubt that these experiences added to Rodker's dislike and distrust of the bourgeois state, and intensified his sense of himself as an outsider, but at the same time they intensified his desire to be successful, to be accepted by society, to escape from his origins. He was a deeply conflicted individual, full of contradictory impulses; even his name is mysterious, as he was registered on his birth certificate as Simon Solomon, and always retained Simon as his second name. (At some point early on in John's life, his father David must have changed the family name to Rodker, but it is not clear when.) Most people knew him as John, his East-End friends called him Jimmy; and to his family, he was Jack. He was adept, perhaps too adept, at compartmentalizing himself, which sometimes led others to accuse him of inauthenticity; certainly some people found him hard to pin down. Wyndham Lewis paints a cruel but accurate caricature of him as Julius Ratner in *The Apes of God*, where he is described as 'the eternal imitation-person in a word, whose ambition led him to burgle all the books of Western romance to steal their heroes' expensive outfits for his musty shop.'[6]

Despite his teenage involvement in socialism and his wartime pacifism, Rodker's own interests and ambitions after the armistice were almost exclusively literary. He had already published a volume of poems in 1914, and written more poems, a play, and a novel. He succeeded Ezra Pound as foreign editor of the *Little Review*, and by 1920 had established himself not only as a poet and critic, but with Mary Butts, to whom he was briefly married, had also set up the Ovid Press which published early books by T. S. Eliot, Wyndham Lewis, Ezra Pound, and Rodker himself, among others.[7] The Ovid Press ceased in 1920, but capitalizing on the expertise gained over two years operating his own hand press, he set up as a publisher of fine limited editions. The two imprints he ran until the early 1930s, John Rodker, and the Casanova Press, produced a substantial number of ambitiously produced fine and limited editions of original works, historical reprints, and translations, a few of a mildly salacious nature, many of them highly sought after by collectors. Among

[6] See Ian Patterson, 'John Rodker, Julius Ratner and Wyndham Lewis: The Split-Man Writes Back', in Andrzej Gasiorek, Alice Reeve-Tucker, and Nathan Waddell, eds, *Wyndham Lewis and the Cultures of Modernity* (Farnham: Ashgate, 2011), 95–107.

[7] See Gerald Cloud, *John Rodker's Ovid Press: A Bibliographical History* (New Castle, DE: Oak Knoll Press, 2010).

the earliest of them were the second and third impressions of James Joyce's *Ulysses*. But whatever he may have pretended to himself, he was never a successful businessman. Something about him courted bad luck; he was usually in debt, hoping that each increasingly expensive investment would pay enough dividends to bring him into the black and allow him to do more of what he wanted to do, which was to write, and to publish avant-garde writing, both Anglophone and in translation. But it never happened, and in the depressed business climate after 1929, life became increasingly difficult. It was also typical of his luck that three days after the Aquila Press published his major prose work, *Adolphe 1920*, it too went bust. By the end of the 1920s Rodker was contemplating the ruins of two promising careers, as a publisher and as a writer. His first novel had been published in French translation but not in Britain, the only manuscript of his second had been lost, his novella *Dartmoor* had also only been published in French, and his most important work was all but unobtainable. He had written no more than a handful of poems since the publication of his second book in 1920, and most of his stories, plays, articles, and sketches were failing to find publishers or readers. In addition, he had been forced to place the publishing companies into a form of administration, and almost all the money he earned went to the administrators who controlled his finances.

His interest in Russia began early, but it is difficult to gauge how much it meant to him at this stage of his life. His primary interests were cultural, especially avant-garde writing, art, dance, theatre, film, psycho-analysis, and publishing. He was, in all essentials, a modernist writer. He was also a translator, having early discovered a facility for languages. His first contacts with Russia, apart the circumstances of his family's exile, would have been through the other exiles and emigrés in Bethnal Green and Whitechapel—Rudolf Rocker's Socialist Club was next door to the house in Jubilee Street where he and his family lived, and much of his teenage political activity was focused there—and through the intellectual contacts he made in his late teens with 'progressive' figures like David Eder, his wife Edith, and her sister Barbara Low (who was later to become his psychoanalyst). Maksim Litvinov, living in exile in London, was soon to marry Barbara Low's niece Ivy. Rodker certainly knew Ivy, and probably saw her when he visited Moscow, where—like many other foreigners—she worked as a translator, although as Litvinov's wife, she enjoyed greater freedoms than most of her contemporaries.[8] But for all his youthful involvement with socialism, there is no evidence that Rodker was particularly enthusiastic about the 1917 Revolution, nor that he wanted to visit the new Soviet Union, although as time went on he did his best to be enthusiastic or at least optimistic about it. In 1931, he was already claiming a knowledge of Russian literature; reviewing a translation of Mikhail Saltykov-Shchedrin's *The Golovlyov Family* (*Gospoda Golovlevy*) in the *Spectator*, he wrote that it 'relentlessly depicts the Russia that so inevitably prepared the Revolution. The book is a classic in its own country, and it is obvious why.'[9] The sketches of Soviet life which he wrote in 1933 contain knowledgeable accounts of life in Moscow, Leningrad, and Kharkiv, an awareness

[8] John Carswell, *The Exile: A Life of Ivy Litvinoff* (London: Faber and Faber, 1983).
[9] J. Rodker, 'Fiction: Underdogs', *The Spectator*, 5391 (24 October 1931), 550.

of the housing shortage, and a decidedly non-idealistic, indeed managerial, view of work in the Soviet Union.[10] How much of this he owed to his friends there, how much to the same sort of guarded enthusiasm that emerges in his correspondence, how much to a genuine conviction that a new and better society was being built, it is hard to say. He may simply have seen the Soviet Union as a business opportunity. But there appears to have been more to it than that. From 1934, it is worth noting, his elder daughter Joan was living in the Soviet Union, travelling round collective farms in the Ukraine and elsewhere as part of a revolutionary theatre troupe.

Like many other people, Rodker was in financial difficulties in 1934; years of unsuccessful trading as a publisher had brought him little but debts, his *Memoirs of Other Fronts* had been rejected by over twenty publishers in Britain and the United States (and by one in Germany) before it was finally brought out (anonymously) in 1932, and even then the publishers were reluctant to advertise it.[11] Proposals for subsequent books met with polite expressions of interest and equally polite rejection; it was not a good time for modernist writers, especially writers whose only previous publishing record had been from specialist or private press imprints. Nor was it the most propitious time to take on the task of Soviet literary agent, as publishing was in the worst slump it had known for decades. But Rodker's own writing was not likely to bring in an income, his own publishing firms were in administration, and there was only so much money he could make from translating. Yet he was still capable of optimism. He was becoming increasingly sought after as a translator from the French (he translated seventeen books in all), but *Memoirs of Other Fronts* sold badly and he had to abandon its planned sequel, an autobiographical account of his years at the centre of literary modernism.[12]

Despite all the setbacks, he was writing a memoir of his childhood and reviewing fairly regularly for a range of papers. He was developing contacts with publishers around the world, travelling to Paris and New York and, more recently, to the Soviet Union. And despite a lack of financial independence, he was still running what was left of his publishing companies, and looking for new ventures. He had after all built up an impressive network of contacts. In the summer of 1933, he visited the Soviet Union, and when he returned he wrote the sketches he titled 'Russian Impressions'. There are several different manuscripts in the archive, showing that he reworked or reselected material from a larger store of notes or drafts, adjusting the length and content of the sketches for different potential readerships. Alongside the 'Impressions', there are 'Dostoievsky's Tomb', 'Two Cities' (an article structured round the contrast between Leningrad and Moscow), pieces on 'Harvest in the U.S.S.R.', and 'Work in the U.S.S.R.', and a satirical story called 'Five plates of soup'. He sent them round several magazines, including the *Weekend Review*, which published the piece on 'Dostoievsky's Tomb', but the others were rejected, either

[10] John Rodker, 'Russian Impressions (prose sketches)', John Rodker Papers, box 37, folder 2.

[11] [John Rodker], *Memoirs of Other Fronts* (London: Putnam, 1932).

[12] For a full account of Rodker's activities as a translator, see Ian Patterson, 'Writing on Other Fronts: Translation and John Rodker', in *Modernism and Translation*, special issue of *Translation and Literature*, 12, no. 1 (spring 2003), 88–113.

because they were too critical or because they were not critical enough, depending on the editorial standpoint. They are worth pausing over, though, as they provide a useful indication of his attitude to the Soviet Union at this point.

They are, as he says, 'impressions', and what impresses him first and most strongly when he arrives in Leningrad is 'the physical discomfort attached merely to keeping alive in the Soviet Union. The rutty roads, the yawning pavements full of holes, the crowded infrequent trams, the storms of dust, the queues for paraffin, bread and tobacco, sometimes a couple of yards in length, all tell their tale.' He notes the paucity of materials in the shops, the 'contemptible' quantity of vegetables for sale in the almost empty markets, 'even outside Moscow', the beggars and 'peasants in the street offering two lamp glasses and a stale bun, or boys selling cigarettes one by one.' In the second article, he dutifully repeats the official line, that the 1933 harvest was a bumper one, that all records had been broken, and the project of collectivization completely justified. He continues, 'It was a surprise therefore to find certain English newspapers on my return running stories to the effect that conditions little short of famine prevailed', and offers a series of official explanations given to him by 'a responsible member of the Party', all of which sound somewhat implausible, despite Rodker's ostensible mild approval of some of the other things he encountered, especially as he points out that the price of bread doubled the day he left. For all this, he concludes that he found Moscow 'as civilised and agreeable as I had found Leningrad dispiriting'. Uncharacteristically, the article on 'Harvest in the U.S.S.R.' reads more like straight propaganda; the widespread interest in Moscow in the wheat harvest and its likely yield is taken as evidence of the State's benevolent and rational attitude to farming rather than anxiety about the winter to come. He rejects all the rumours of famine he reads in the British press, with 'peasants reduced to eating grass and weeds and bark, when it is not each other' and announces that 'on all hands I saw the sincerest pleasure at the superb abundance of the harvest', and follows it up with a couple of pages of statistical and anecdotal evidence for the success of collectivization. In 'Dostoievsky's Tomb' he returns to his preferred ground of cultural complexity, and the conflict between 'bright open faces' and bureaucracy. He wanders through the monastery where Dostoievsky was buried, a place of 'macabre disrepair' with 'a stench of urine and excrement', but there is no sign of the tomb, and the 'sacristan' has never heard of him or it. 'It is true nobody in Russia reads him, they tell me. There is too much happening, too much work, they are too busy being extrovert to find time for him. Even they say there is no neurosis in Russia now. But later, when the culture comes, and the Pantheon has to be restocked, where will they dig him up?'[13]

It was at this point, in late 1933, that he was approached by the representatives of the Press and Publisher Literary Service in Moscow (PresLit), who wanted him to be their representative in London. After some negotiation, he signed a provisional agreement on 2 August 1934, in which he also agreed to edit the short-lived magazine *Soviet Culture* (it lasted five issues in 1934). A second contract was signed on 22

[13] John Rodker, 'Russian Impressions (prose sketches)', John Rodker Papers, box 37, folder 2.

May 1935 to take effect from 1 June, at which time he agreed to be the main agent for Russian books, and to use his best endeavours to get Soviet books published in English translation in London and New York. The terms of his contract were these:

He would have eight months in which to place a manuscript with a publisher;
He would receive 20% of all payments;
He would receive an extra 150 roubles in his Moscow bank account for every title placed;
He was to send accounts, press cuttings, and a monthly report to PresLit;
He was to be paid a minimum retainer of £10 per calendar month, whatever happens;
He was also to receive 30% on periodical placements, and 20% (later increased to 30%) on dramatic or musical material.

He continued to act as PresLit's agent, with increasing unhappiness, until five months after the outbreak of war, when he resigned his agency, writing that he now had 'no wish to continue with this work'.[14]

Why did PresLit choose Rodker for the job? He had no obvious qualifications for it, with little knowledge of Russian, a poor track record as a businessman, and no evident commitment to the communist cause. On the other hand, PresLit probably had enough Party contacts through Martin Lawrence (later Lawrence and Wishart) and needed somebody outside those circles to deal with non-communist publishing houses. Rodker was well enough disposed towards the Soviet Union, his daughter lived and worked there, he was charming and persuasive, well connected in the publishing world, knew people in Moscow, and was doubtless recommended by some of them. And he needed the money, so was not in a position to turn PresLit down. Indeed, it was not just the PresLit directors who saw him as a useful ally; there were others, and they would seem to confirm this account of him.

One of those who seem to have regarded him in this light was the American avant-gardist and anarchist Bob Brown, busy at the time setting up his Museum of Social Change at Commonwealth College in Mena, Arkansas, for which Rodker occasionally sent items. Brown was a friend of Rodker's former lover, Nancy Cunard, and an irregular correspondent of Rodker's for much of the 1930s. In 1935, visiting Russia and having just finished his book on communes and cooperation, *Can we Co-operate?*, Brown sent it to Rodker, who was already trying to find a British publisher for his *Wine Cook Book*, in the hope that he might be able to interest Gollancz in publishing it, writing optimistically, 'I still think that 7,000,000 co-operators can't be wrong, so here's hoping it sells.'[15] It did not, even when he published it himself five years later.[16] An earlier attempt to persuade Rodker to place the manuscript of *Nobody's Baby* had been unsuccessful the previous year, too. It may well be that in 1935 Rodker shared Brown's disenchantment with capitalist publishing. In fact,

[14] 'Contracts', John Rodker Papers, box 15, folder 1.
[15] Bob Brown, Letter to John Rodker, 1935, John Rodker Papers, box 1, folder 3.
[16] Bob Brown, *Can We Co-operate?* (Staten Island, NY: Roving Eye Press, 1940).

it would be surprising if he did not, after his recent experience. He may even have shared Brown's faith in the Soviet example: 'if neither the publisher nor the writer can make a living these days then it is high time that a more sensible system of writing and publishing be adopted—and the only successful system is that practiced in the Soviet Union under socialism, publication of books of the people, for the people and by the people'.[17] But to the enthusiastic Brown, with little experience of either Soviet socialism or trade publishing, Rodker as a sympathetic writer, with a long record in publishing and translating, as well as with good contacts in Russia, must have looked like a useful and reliable socialist agent. In reality Rodker was neither a member of the Communist Party, nor a sympathizer; and as time went on he became increasingly annoyed at the assumption that he must be, simply because he represented PresLit. Virginia Woolf, for example, described him as 'a communist', whereas he was in truth as apolitical as a former East-End Jewish anarchist-pacifist businessman ever could be.[18]

During the five or six years between 1934 and early 1940, Rodker played a central, complex and unacknowledged role in the Soviet Union's self-presentation in Britain. In a review of one of the first books he managed to place, for example, *Soviet Geography* by Nikolay Mikhailov, published by Methuen, Edgell Rickword calls it

> the most exciting book to have come out of Russia for some time, not forgetting *The Voyage of the Chelyuskin* or *The White Sea-Baltic Canal* [both also represented by Rodker]. Its title is the only dullish thing about it; its maps and statistics are alive, and it has been translated into real, crisp, natural English.... It reveals the beautiful organic unity of Soviet planning... It is a book which should inspire poems, for it glows itself with imaginative fervour. It materializes a real body for that spirit which was vocal for a brief moment in English poetry at the end of the sixteenth century, when the discovery of new lands where life was more luxuriant than under our pale sun fired the minds of poets.[19]

It is extraordinary that a literary magazine, even the *Left Review*, should have been so enthusiastic about such a book, but it does serve to remind us how important such books were as part of the Soviet Union's self-promotion, and as part of the vision of a future society that bound its sympathizers together. (One indication of the sheer unfamiliarity of the Soviet Union and its literature, even to those closest to it, can be seen in an interview that was given pride of place a year earlier, in the sixth issue of the *Left Review* in March 1935, between an unnamed questioner and 'Shokoloff', that is, Mikhail Sholokhov, the author of *And Quiet Flows the Don* (*Tikhii Don*).)[20] Books like this, of which there were many, should be seen as part of the project of socialist realism, given the extent to which the heroic achievements

[17] Bob Brown, 'The American Writer's Plight [letter]', *International Literature*, 11 (November 1935), 92.

[18] Virginia Woolf, *The Diary of Virginia Woolf*, v: *1936–41*, ed. Anne Olivier Bell and Andrew McNeillie (Harmondsworth: Penguin, 1985), 106.

[19] Edgell Rickword, 'Social Creativity', *Left Review*, 2, no. 6 (March 1936), 283.

[20] 'Shokoloff: An Interview', *Left Review*, 1, no. 6 (March 1935), 193–4.

they described were fictionalized. The White Sea-Baltic Canal project praised by Rickword, like other much praised achievements, was in reality an enormous and expensive failure: as Marshall Berman has remarked, 'the workers and the engineers were never allowed the time, money or equipment to build a canal that would be deep enough or safe enough to carry twentieth-century cargoes; consequently the canal has never played any significant role in Soviet commerce or industry. All the canal could support, apparently, were tourist steamers.'[21] But the book about it was a huge collaborative project, listing thirty-four co-writers on its title page, a work of revolutionary structure, 'a Socialist Realist plot in an avant-garde narrative structure—with documents built into the text... all of this arranged in montage fashion'.[22] Books like these were the only substantial source of information, however fallacious, about the new Soviet Union and about the literally and metaphorically vast new territory of socialism. They brought with them their own quality of truth, as news reports from the socialist future.

The emphasis on the grandeur, the heroism, the achievements, and the institutions of the Soviet Union was much more marked in the years after 1934 than previously, which is one of the reasons why PresLit needed Rodker. As recently as 1933, George Reavey had claimed in his foreword to *Soviet Literature: An Anthology* that the Five-Year Plan had given 'the phases and demarcations of Soviet Literature... added continuity and made its plot more dramatic', and insisted that the Soviet Union was best understood through its literary production.'[23] The last piece in the Reavey and Slonim anthology is the April 1932 resolution of the Central Committee of the Soviet Communist Party which abolished the Russian Association of Proletarian Writers and established the broader Union of Soviet Writers; between then and 1934, when the new official doctrine of socialist realism was promulgated, the Soviet leadership made a determined move to project their vision of the Soviet Union to readers abroad. The texts selected for translation and publication abroad were carefully chosen to create the strongest possible impression of a successful society. The construction of socialism involved the development of new and more socially-evolved humanity, celebrated in fiction, and sociological, historical, and documentary narratives. The representation of the Russian past was also subject to preferential treatment.

Without examining the PresLit archives themselves, it is not possible to ascertain the full range of titles Rodker was charged with placing in Britain, but it has proved possible to reconstruct a reasonably full list from Rodker's own papers.[24] It is worth following up all of his extant portfolio, though, as it reveals just how fragile and complex the decisions were about which texts were published. In addition to full-length

[21] Marshall Berman, *All that is Solid Melts into Air: The Experience of Modernity* (London: Verso, 1983), 76.

[22] Evgeny Dobrenko, *Political Economy of Socialist Realism*, trans. Jesse M. Savage (New Haven, CT: Yale University Press, 2007), 106–7.

[23] George Reavey and Marc Slonim, eds and trans. *Soviet Literature: An Anthology* (London: Wishart, 1933), 11.

[24] See appendices.

books, both fiction and non-fiction, Rodker was responsible for music, screenplays, short stories, essays, and general feature articles. So far as it has been possible to verify, in the entire period of his agency he successfully placed fewer than forty books with British publishers. But he tried to place considerably more than these; and was markedly more successful in placing short stories in specialized locations, particularly in the first two series of John Lehmann's *New Writing*. The salient question is why publishers wanted to take some books and not others. The list of rejected titles can tell us a great deal about the dominant attitudes to the Soviet Union in the mid-1930s, and the extent to which the market was made by readers broadly sympathetic to the least problematic or most encouraging versions of the Soviet experiment. Among the books which no British publishers were prepared to take were Aleksander Radishchev's *Journey from St. Petersburg to Moscow* (*Puteshestvie iz Peterburga v Moskvu*, 1790), *Kara-Bugaz* (*Kara-Bugaz*) by Konstantin Paustovsky, Viktor Shklovsky's *Marco Polo* (*Marko Polo*), Galina Grekova's *On Happiness* (*O schast′e*) and—perhaps less surprisingly—Andrey Vyshinsky on *Soviet Justice*. Unwin rejected *Jews in the Taiga* (*Evrei v taiga*) by Viktor Fink, Mikhail Kol′tsov's *A Spanish Diary* (*Ispanskii dnevnik*), and Boris Zhitkov's stories about animals. Typical of the complex and protracted negotiations which characterized Rodker's work on some of these titles was the attempt to find a publisher for *The Letters of Tsar Nicholas and Empress Marie: Being the Confidential Correspondence between Nicholas II, Last of the Tsars, and His Mother, Dowager Empress Maria Feodorovna*, edited by Edward J. Bing. An extensive and litigious correspondence about the translation—Bing was being difficult about money—between Erica Beale Ltd (who held some rights in the book), PresLit, and Rodker resulted in PresLit and Moura Budberg (who also had an interest in the book), finally placing the title with Nicholson and Watson, ceding all rights to Bing in exchange for a one-off payment, which meant abandoning PresLit's hopes of a lucrative sale of the serial rights. Bing, who worked for the Intercontinental Press in Zürich, subsequently succeeded in selling the copyright on to Longmans, Green and Co. in the United States, and with the help of his friend Eugene Lyons, to Hearst Newspapers.[25] On the other hand, Rodker did try to get the rights to several other interesting titles, including Evgeny Zamyatin's *We* (*My*), which had been published in French translation (as *Nous autres*) in 1929; but PresLit did not want the book published, and Dutton may, in any event, have held all English-language rights since they had already published a translation in New York in 1924.[26]

As a general rule, rejections outnumbered acceptances by a substantial ratio. The sale of the film rights for Anatoly Vinogradov's *Black Consul* (*Chernyi konsul*), a novel about Toussaint l'Ouverture, was in the air during April 1935, but it proved impossible to obtain a firm commitment from film companies. In the middle of negotiations, Rodker went to Russia for six weeks; he came back on 31 May 1935

[25] See general correspondence folders, Byng [*sic*], Edward J., John Rodker Papers, box 13, folder 13–14, box 14, folder 1, and Erica Beale Ltd, John Rodker Papers, box 14, folder 6.

[26] See correspondence with Allen & Unwin, John Rodker Papers, box 14, folder 9.

to discover that the texts and synopses of fourteen works which he had sent to RKO pictures had all been returned. They expressed possible interest in only one of them, the 1926 play *Lyubov' Yarovaya*, by Konstantin Trenev. Eighteen months later Rodker was hopeful of setting up an arrangement to distribute Soviet films in association with Arcos, a Russian-run trade organization based in Bush House. Nothing seems to have come of this idea, either. Outlining the situation on New Year's Day 1937, in a letter to one of PresLit's assistant directors, A. Yevnovitch, he grumbles, 'There is not enough [work] to keep me fully occupied, and as I have often complained the returns have not been sufficient to provide me with a reasonable livelihood. On the contrary I have been out of pocket by it'.[27]

The work was not all one-way. Rodker also acted as an emissary for English-language books to the Soviet Union. As part of the second contract with PresLit, he undertook to send news of English books and to suggest articles suitable for reprinting in the journal *Za rubezhom*, which had already commissioned him to read British magazines and send them interesting material. Almost as soon as he agreed, Rodker talked about giving it up, and seems to have sent very little. It has been possible to trace only a couple of pieces by John Langdon-Davies and 'Frank Pitcairn' (a pseudonym for Claud Cockburn), which he sent in late in 1936.[28]

Reading through the incomplete file of correspondence between Rodker and the Soviet authorities, one very rapidly gets the impression that being their agent in the mid-1930s was more problematic than the mere 'niggling annoyance' that he described it as being. It involved almost endless processes of negotiation with publishers and agents, mostly by letter, with hardly any human contact, as well as legal wrangling over the precise sums of money due to the Moscow publishers, and sometimes over procedural matters. When Rodker sold the stage rights to Aleskandr Afinogenov's *Distant Point* (*Dalekoe*) to Norman Marshall's Gate Theatre Studio in 1937, a slightly acrimonious correspondence ensued with both the Assistant Director of PresLit, D. Umansky, and with M. Grimev at the Soviet Embassy in London, because he had not shown them the staging contract before agreeing to it.[29] At the same time he was liable to get requests to expedite the American edition of a book he had only just placed with an English publisher. This sort of bureaucratic control made Rodker's job more difficult than it otherwise might have been, and the length of time it sometimes took to get official agreement to publishers' contracts could result in the loss of a sale. All this, Rodker felt, was out of proportion to the sums involved: PresLit's total commission in the two and a half years to the end of 1937 amounted to a total of £211. 19*s*., almost a tenth of which came from the contested production of *Distant Point*.

On behalf of PresLit, Rodker also occasionally represented writers living in exile in Moscow; he tried to interest John Lehmann in Adam Scharrer's story 'Hans Zäuner wird Soldat', published in the German edition of the 'Organ of the International

[27] See 'Films, Soviet', John Rodker Papers, box 14, folder 7.

[28] See '*Za Rubezhom*, S. Gurevitch, ed., 1935–6', John Rodker papers, box 15, folder 9.

[29] See general correspondence folder Afinogenov, A., *Distant Point*, 1935–61, John Rodker Papers, box 13, folder 11.

Union of Revolutionary Writers', *International Literature*, in July 1938. (Lehmann himself wrote several reports on the British literary left for *International Literature*, and was better informed about German and Austrian left-wing writers than Rodker.) It therefore seems likely that other pieces by German anti-fascist exiles may have come through Rodker as well, although of course Lehmann had his own contacts. But as he explained to Rodker when *New Writing* was still in the planning stage, 'I want to see the S.[oviet] U.[nion] [as] well represented [in *New Writing*] as possible, but I think you'll see that as translation always means paying more, heavy fees simply mean less taken—until Lane gives me more money to chuck about.'[30] At the end of the year Rodker noted that *New Writing*'s publisher, the Bodley Head, was in receivership, so John Lane had no money at all to spend on translations. After the first two issues, Lehmann moved the magazine to Lawrence & Wishart, then after three more numbers, he moved again, to the Hogarth Press. In his autobiography, he recalls wryly how little help he had from Moscow, and how 'practically all the Soviet material...came from enthusiasts in England'.[31]

Despite its peripatetic existence, *New Writing* was a fruitful source of commissions, as well as of translation work for Rodker himself. In the first five issues (the first series) there is a total of eighteen stories or other pieces which come through Rodker's agency, starting with the anonymously translated story 'Sour Grapes—and Sweet' ('Vinograd') by Nikolay Ognev (reprinted in the first issue of *New Writing*'s successor, *Penguin New Writing*), 'The Tea-Khan at "The Pond of the Emir"' ('Chaikhana u Lyabi-Khouza') by Nikolay Tikhonov, translated by Alec Brown, and Boris Pasternak's poem '1905' (*Devyatsot' pyatyi god*), also translated by Brown. The second number carried Vasily Grossman's 'In the Town of Berdichev' ('V gorode Berdichev'), for which no translator was credited, and another story by Tikhonov, 'Nights in a Persian Garden', translated by Brown. In the third, there were three stories: 'The Lord of Lashkheti' by Sergo Kldiashvili and 'The Road to Affluence' by Panteleimon Chikvaidze (both Georgian tales translated from Russian versions by Stephen Garry (Henry Charles Stevens)), and Yury Olesha's 'Love' ('Lyubov''), translated by Anthony Wolfe (Robert Payne). Stephen Garry translated Tikhonov's 'Morale' ('Podvig') in the fourth number of *New Writing* and 'The Cup' by M. Javakhishvili (again, a Georgian original, but translated from the Russian), but no translator is credited for Sholokhov's 'The Father' ('Semeinyi chelovek'). Number five of the first series contains another translation of Yury Olesha by Anthony Wolfe, 'Liompa' ('Liompa'), and Mikhail Zoshchenko's 'The Housing Crisis' ('Krizis'), translated by the indefatigable Stephen Garry, who also contributes a translation of 'Shock Tempo' by Fedor Gladkov. In the new series, which ran from autumn 1938 to Christmas 1939, the first number featured just one contribution from a Russian writer, Tikhonov's 'Story with a Footnote' ('Rasskaz s primechaniem'), translated by Garry, and the second number carried an anonymous translation of an Evenk folk tale, 'Vladimir in the Taiga'. The third has

[30] See correspondence with Lehmann, John Rodker Papers, box 1, folder 3, and box 7, folder 9.
[31] John Lehmann, *The Whispering Gallery* (London: Longmans, Green, 1955), 286.

Nikolay Virta's anonymously translated 'On a Journey', and 'An Airwoman over Mayday' by Marina Raskova, in another Stephen Garry translation.[32]

The quality of the translations was a constant source of friction. 'This business of translation is a very *vexed* one, hellish even', Rodker wrote to Lehmann in July 1936:

> For between ourselves, [Ralph] Fox has translated a collection of Zoshchenko's stories for Wishart that this firm is not at all comfortable about. The fault may be in the author or the translator, but anyhow the publisher is bothered about it. So we get yourself wondering whether Payne has got Envy straight, Lane bothered about Brown and Wishart bothered about Fox. And the Moscow translations are on the whole pretty unsatisfactory. So where in a manner of speaking are we...?[33]

PresLit sent in nineteen pages of corrections to Payne's draft translation of Olesha's *Envy* (*Zavist'*), published by Hogarth Press in 1936, and consequent negotiations between Rodker and Leonard Woolf took 'several months'.[34] Later, in his autobiography, Lehmann would write that 'with the first number of *New Writing*, my long, truceless war with translators had begun' (though he made an exception for Rodker himself).[35] In fact the translators working for Rodker out of Russian, Polish, and German were on the whole a quite exceptional group of writers: not only James Cleugh, and Sholokhov's translator Stephen Garry, who also translated from Polish, but major figures like Alec Brown, who translated a huge number of books, articles, and stories, some from Serbo-Croat and Polish as well as Russian, and who published seven very interesting novels, a work of sociology, and two books of poetry during the 1930s. Other translators included Charles Ashleigh, author of the semi-autobiographical *Rambling Kid*, one of the best novels about the Industrial Workers of the World, and a very accomplished translator, and Rodker's old acquaintance, Ivy Low. Brown and Ashleigh were both members of the Communist Party, and Ivy Low was living in Moscow. Yet one can sympathize with Lehmann's sense that it could be difficult to exercise proper critical independence; he expressed annoyance early on that PresLit wanted to approve the English translations of Russian works when, as he put it, 'I don't in any case think they know what good English is'. In the early days of *New Writing*, the proprietor wanted to intervene too, as Rodker learned from Lehmann in July 1936. 'Lane has kicked up a fuss about Alec Brown's translation of this last Tikhonov story... It makes going on with Brown rather difficult... It's a great pity, as his Pasternak translation was so good, I thought.' It is Lehmann himself, though, who rejects a story by Zoshchenko that Rodker offers ('I've seen better by him'); he also rejects a piece by Eugen Leviné on the grounds that it is too old to be in *New Writing*. He also, rather tantalizingly and not entirely convincingly, writes at the end of one letter, 'I wish I could help you about the

[32] For bibliographical details, see Ella Whitehead, ed., *John Lehmann's 'New Writing': An Author-Index, 1936–1950* (Lampeter: Edwin Mellen, 1990).

[33] John Rodker Papers, box 1, folder 3, and box 7, folder 9.

[34] J. H Willis, *Leonard and Virginia Woolf as Publishers: The Hogarth Press, 1917–41* (Charlottesville, VA: University Press of Virginia, 1992), 283.

[35] Lehmann, *The Whispering Gallery*, 240.

Russian Operetta' (possibly a reference to Dmitry Shostakovich's *Lady Macbeth of Mtsensk*, which Rodker eventually persuaded the BBC to broadcast).[36]

For a number of reasons, it was not always easy for Rodker to keep control of the publication of writers represented by PresLit. In some cases, publishing arrangements had been made in earlier years, in others it was rumour, non-delivery, or a change of policy in Britain or in the Soviet Union. Take the case of one of the most accomplished Russian writers, Isaak Babel′. On 25 October 1935, Babel′ confirmed an agreement which appointed Rodker and Baroness Moura Budberg as his joint British representatives. Budberg, born into the Russian aristocracy, left Russia in 1920 and thereafter led a peripatetic life, as Gor′ky's lover and later as a lover of H. G. Wells, living by her wits and her contacts; Rodker and she had worked together several times on projects, and knew one another quite well.[37] Rodker then negotiated with Putnam to publish a volume of Babel′'s stories. The agreement, though, was conditional upon Putnam also getting Babel′'s 'big novel', which was to be finished in 1936; since the late twenties, Babel′ had been said to be working on a novel, *Kolya Topuz,* about a conman who overcomes his criminal tendencies thanks to his work for socialist construction. Whether any of it was actually written, though, or whether it was just a cover story, a suitable subject to be writing about during the Five-Year Plan, is unclear.[38] The novel failed to materialize, so the contract with Putnam came to nothing. Lehmann rejected an offer of Babel′'s stories, and of work by Boris Pil′nyak, saying 'Babel is, of course, excellent, but Contemporary Prose and Poetry [*sic*] seems to have made a corner in him'. Rodker appears to have been unaware that pirated translations of Babel′'s work had been appearing in Roger Roughton's little magazine, *Contemporary Poetry and Prose,* since he had recently sent the volume of Babel′'s stories to Ralph Fox asking him to consider translating it. Lehmann then seems to have had a change of heart: in late 1936 he went to Moscow and while he was there had a meeting with D. A. Umansky, who promised that Rodker could let Lehmann have three stories by Babel′, and stories by Virta, David Kldiashvili, Paustovsky, and others, described as 'undecipherable from Umansky's scribble'. This seems to have provided some temporary reassurance, but six months later he tells Rodker, 'As usual, I'm in despair about Russian stuff, and distressed that your visit to Moscow did not have more positive results. But perhaps you found a lot of new novels?'[39]

Nikolay Virta provoked further anxiety. No decision could be made about a story of his called 'Solitude' ('Odinochestvo') because Edgell Rickword, responsible at Lawrence and Wishart for approving *New Writing*'s content, was away for several weeks. Then it seemed that Moscow might be withdrawing it. A week later he wrote to thank Rodker for sending a Babel′ story and some volumes by Leonid Leonov,

[36] John Rodker Papers, box 1, folder 3, box 7, folder 9.

[37] See Nina Berberova, *Moura: The Dangerous Life of the Baroness Budberg*, trans. Marian Schwartz and Richard D. Sylvester (New York: New York Review Books, 2005).

[38] See Patricia Blake, 'Researching Babel's Biography', in Gregory Freidin, ed., *The Enigma of Isaac Babel: Biography, History, Context* (Stanford, CA: Stanford University Press, 2009), 4.

[39] John Rodker Papers, box 1, folder 3, box 7, folder 9.

and adds 'Good news about Virta' whose story had obviously been approved. Nothing by him appeared in *New Writing*, though, until the end of 1939. The uncertainty over Virta's story is symptomatic of a larger and more unusual problem, associated with Soviet politics, which Rodker's English clients had to deal with: as the political fortunes of the writers rose or fell, so did the agency's willingness to see their work in print. This, too, may have affected publishers' choices. There is one further complication in unravelling this story: John Lehmann had plans, which were agreed in July 1937, to set up a Lawrence and Wishart 'New Writing Library' to publish, among other things, translations of Russian books. It did not materialize, but was another factor is deciding what to print in the magazine for the next year or so. Meanwhile Lehmann was also looking for titles to publish through the Hogarth Press, where in 1938 he became managing director, but they had to be fairly short. Kol′tsov's *Spanish Diary* (already rejected by Unwin) was too long for them. In the event, Hogarth published none of the titles that Rodker suggested.

One area where Rodker had some early success was with plays and with books about film: Vsevolod Pudovkin's *Film Technique* (containing *Kinorezhisser i kinomaterial* and *Kinotsenarii: teoriya tsenariya*) was already in print before Rodker started the agency, but his *Film Acting* (*Akter v fil′ me*), which Rodker handled, had equal success for Newnes. Newnes were also the publisher of Vladimir Nil′sen's *The Cinema as a Graphic Art* (*Izobrazitel′ noe postroenie fil′ ma: teoriya i praktika operatorskogo masterstva*), in Stephen Garry's translation. Plays, being more specialized, were more difficult to place. Some plays didn't attract enthusiasm: Alec Brown's translation of Alexey Tolstoy's play for children, *The Little Golden Key, or The Adventures of Buratino* (*Zolotoi klyuchik, ili priklyucheniya Buratino*, a Russian adaptation of the Pinocchio story) was 'reluctantly' rejected by A. & M. Heath; nothing came of his attempts to sell 'Bulgakov's Molière' (also known as *The Cabal of the Hypocrites* (*Kabala svyatosh*)), but he had more success with Bulgakov's adaptation of Gogol′'s *Dead Souls* (*Mertvye dushi*) which imagined Gogol′ as a visitor to the modern Soviet Union. The play was first produced at the Moscow Arts Theatre in 1932, and was successfully produced several times in Britain and the United States, as was Afinogenov's *Distant Point*, which Rodker's own Pushkin Press published in 1941.[40] But success also brought its own set of complications. The BBC's production, on 18 March 1936, of Shostakovich's opera, *Lady Macbeth of Mtsensk* (*Ledi Makbet Mtsenskogo uezda*) is a case in point. It was a important event, with several preview articles (including one by the poet J. F. Hendry in *Left Review*), but in its wake Rodker had to deal with interminable legal wrangles about broadcast royalties, publication rights, and recording rights.[41] At the end of that year he writes to Umansky, asking for a list of musicians represented by PresLit, 'so that I can send it to the BBC and thus avoid the sort of complication we have had recently in connection with Shostakovich's Piano Concerto'.

[40] John Rodker Papers, box 15, folder 2; 'Bulgakov, M.A., *Dead Souls*, translated by Alec Brown', John Rodker Papers, box 15, folder 10; Afinogenov, A., *Distant Point*, 1935–61 (re Pushkin Press 1941 edition), John Rodker Papers, box 13, folder 11; folder 13.13, 14.15.

[41] James Findlay Hendry, 'Lady Macbeth of Mzensk', *Left Review*, 2, no. 6 (March 1936), 272–3.

The trouble was that PresLit wanted Rodker to represent the whole breadth of cultural production, whether he knew the field or not. And although he had a huge network of contacts, national and international, they had their own operating constraints. The contacts included Harold Matson (at the literary agency, Ann Watkins Inc, New York), whom he had met through Bob Brown, and who worked intermittently with him on PresLit representation throughout the thirties, and other agents in most European countries. In December 1936, for example, he was trying to place the work of five Soviet composers in Paris; while elsewhere Alexander Marton, an agent in Budapest, was unable to find a publisher for Sholokhov's *The Soil Upturned* (*Podnyataya tselina*); David Grünbaum in Copenhagen couldn't place *Antonina* by Yury German; Ahlen and Sonero in Stockholm couldn't place Boris Zaitsev's *Anna*.[42]

By the end of 1939 dealings between Rodker and Moscow were becoming increasingly awkward, and Rodker's view of the agency was increasingly jaundiced. The frustration he was already experiencing at the difficulty of placing books is likely to have been increased by the outbreak of war, and then further compounded by the Molotov-Ribbentrop non-aggression Pact. Then, in a letter dated 31 December, the President of Mezhdunarodnaya Kniga (the newly formed official organization that dealt with foreign publication and the import and export of books, into which PresLit had been absorbed) wrote Rodker a letter, accusing him of violating his agreement with them and of withholding moneys. This was the final straw, and Rodker, weary and angry, terminated his association with PresLit for good on 25 January 1940.[43]

But that didn't mark the end of Rodker's Russian connections. On the wave of enthusiasm for the Soviet Union as an ally in the war against fascism, his knowledge and experience of Soviet literature made him an obvious choice to edit a book of Soviet short stories for Jonathan Cape, published in 1943 as the *Soviet Anthology*. He did not contribute any editorial comment to the book, but the selection of stories is informed and interesting. The idea of the anthology was to bring together a varied group of stories, covering 'the whole period of the Soviet regime from the chaos of revolution, through the constructive fever of the Five Year plans, to the "Life is good, brothers!" of the epoch immediately preceding the war', and to communicate the humanity of the Soviet citizen and 'something of that vast hinterland which produced the heroic fighters of to-day'.[44] The contributors included Babel′, Zoshchenko, Paustovsky, Grossman, Gor′ky, Pil′nyak, Virta, and Mark Volosov. One of the stories, 'In the town of Berdichev' by Grossman, was reprinted from *New Writing*, and most were translated by the writers Rodker used regularly in the 1930s, with ten by Alec Brown and four by Stephen Garry. Of the rest,

[42] 'Agents, 1934–38', John Rodker Papers, box 1, folder 3.

[43] 'Correspondence & royalty statements, 1934–43', John Rodker Papers, box 15, folder 2; 'Contracts', John Rodker Papers, box 14, folder 17.

[44] John Rodker, ed., *Soviet Anthology* (London: Cape, 1943), dust jacket. See '*Soviet Anthology*, 1942–7', John Rodker Papers, box 12, folder 3.

Moura Budberg translated two and Alfred Fremantle one; other translators were anonymous.

Rodker's newest publishing venture, after he had finally emerged from the trammels of financial administration in the late 1930s and started up again on his own account, was named the Pushkin Press, and its first two titles were Pushkin's *Eugene Onegin* (*Evgeny Onegin*) and Afinogenov's *Distant Point*. This did not, however, mean that he still had a fondness for Russia, nor did it guarantee impeccable editorial taste: he wrote to Moura Budberg in 1939, rejecting a new author whom she thought might be of interest to him: Vladimir Nabokov. 'As for *The Real Life of Sebastian Knight*', he explained, 'I am afraid I really have not been able to read very much of it. I think the author has possibilities but the content seems lacking. There just isn't enough backbone to it.'[45] The Pushkin Press ceased publication in 1948.

[45] 'Budberg, Moura, 1935–61', John Rodker Papers, box 1, folder 12.

APPENDICES

The two appendices given here are derived from documents in the John Rodker Papers in the Harry Ransom Humanities Research Center at the University of Texas at Austin. Appendix 1 is a list of the memoranda of agreement signed between British publishers and John Rodker, acting on behalf of PresLit, based on a document entitled 'Memoranda of agreement with J. R. as agent', with further information added from papers contained in box 14, folder 17 and box 15, folder 1, 'Contracts'. Appendix 2 is the transcription of a table compiled by John Rodker of books successfully placed with British publishers, also contained in box 15, folder 1. Neither list is a complete record. As appendix 2 is a direct transcription of an original document, names and titles have not been adapted to the system of transliteration used in this volume; however, as appendix 1 is a composite document, Russian names have been transliterated systematically.

APPENDIX 1: MEMORANDA OF AGREEMENT SIGNED WITH BRITISH PUBLISHERS

Boosey and Hawkes	
19.5.36	Lev Shvarts, 'Soir dans le steppe de Turkmanie', publ. as *Evening in the Turkestan Steppe*, 1937
19.5.36	Sergey Vasilenko, 'Seven Russian Dances' (not publ.)
15.6.36	Dmitry Shostakovitch, 'Lady Macbeth of Mtsensk', (not publ., perhaps owing to copyright reasons)
Boriswood	
29.6.36	Yury Tynyanov, *Death and Diplomacy in Turkey*, trans. and abbr. Alec Brown, 1938
Chatto and Windus	
12.12.34	*Voyage of the Chelyuskin, by Members of the Expedition*, trans. Alec Brown, 1935 (also contracted to Macmillan, New York)
11.6.36	Grekova, 'On Happiness' (not publ., agreement revoked)
Edward Arnold	
4.4.39	M. Yu. Bal'shin, 'Powder metallurgy' (not publ.)
George Allen and Unwin	
9.9.35	Aleksey Novikov-Priboy, *Tsushima*, trans. Eden and Cedar Paul, 1936
10.2.36	Boris Zaitsev, *Anna*, trans. Natalie Duddington, 1937
4.6.35	Aleksandr Voronsky, *Waters of Life and Death*, trans. L. Zarine, 1936
20.7.36	Vitaly Bianki, *Mourzouk, The Story Of A Lynx*, trans. Ivy Low [Litvinov], 1937
13.1.37	Vitaly Bianki, *Forest News*, trans. Ivy Low [Litvinov], introd. Rose Fyleman, 1938
George Newnes	
23.10.34	V. I. Pudovkin, *Film Acting. A Course of Lectures Delivered at the State Institute of Cinematography, Moscow*, trans. Ivor Montagu, 1935
8.10.35	Vladimir Nil'sen, *The Cinema as a Graphic Art. On A Theory of Representation in the Cinema*, trans. Stephen Garry [Henry Charles Stevens], with editorial advice from Ivor Montagu, 1937

(*Continued*)

(*Continued*)

Hutchinson	
19.9.33	Vikenty Veresaev, *Sisters* (not publ.)
Kegan Paul, Trench, Trübner	
2.9.36	Yu. P. Frolov, 'On Professor Pavlov', publ. as *Pavlov and his School: the Theory of Conditioned Reflexes*, trans. C. P. Dutt, 1937
9.11.36	Yu. P. Frolov, 'Encounters with Animals', publ. as *Fish who Answer the Telephone, and Other Studies in Experimental Biology*, trans. Stephen Graham, introd. Eleanor Graham (1937)
Lane: Bodley Head	
22.6.34	'Baltic—White Sea Canal', publ. as *The White Sea Canal. Being an Account of the Construction of the New Canal Between the White Sea and the Baltic Sea*, ed. Maksim Gor'ky, L. Averbach and S. G. Firin. English edn prepared from the Russian and ed., introd. Amabel Williams-Ellis, 1935
Lovat Dickson	
21.6.34	Leonid Sobolev, 'Capital Repairs', publ. as *Storm Warning*, trans. and abbr. Alfred Fremantle, 1935
17.5.35	Leonid Leonov, *Skutavrevsky*, trans. Alec Brown, 1936
18.3.36	Vsevolod Ivanov, *I Live a Queer Life: An Extraordinary Autobiography*, 1936
Methuen	
4.12.34	N. Mikhailov, 'New Economic Geography of the USSR', publ. as *Soviet Geography*, 1935
Putnam	
14.1.37	Petr Shiraev, *Taglioni's Grandson*, trans. Alfred Fremantle, 1937
30.3.38	Fedor Panferov, 'Bruski [vol. 4]', publ. as *And Then the Harvest*, trans. Stephen Garry, 1939
Routledge	
5.2.37	Yury German, 'Our Acquaintances' (not publ.)
15.5.37	Petr Pavlenko, 'On the East', publ. as *Red Planes Fly East*, trans. Stephen Garry, 1938
24.7.37	Petr Skosyrev, 'Your Humble Servant' (not publ.)
18.11.37	Sofiya Mogilevskaya, 'A Camp on the Ice', publ. as *The Camp on the Icefield*, trans. Stephen Garry, 1938
1.3.38	Arkady Perventsev, 'Kochubei', publ. as *Cossack Commander*, trans. Stephen Garry, 1939
1.2.39	Vera Chaplina, 'Animals I Have Reared', publ. as *My Animal Friends*, trans. Stephen Garry, 1939
4.4.39	Yury German, *Aleksey Zhmakin*
Secker & Warburg	
16.6.36	Nikolay Ostrovsky, *How Steel Was Tempered* (not publ.)
23.9.36	Evgeny Tarle, *Bonaparte*, trans. John Cournos, 1937
25.9.37	Vladimir Arsen'ev, *Travelling Through Ussourisk* (not publ.)
Stanley Nott	
9.12.35	Anton Makarenko, *The Road to Life*, trans. Stephen Garry (1936) (taken over within a year by Lindsay Drummond, after the bankruptcy of Stanley Nott)

(*Continued*)

(*Continued*)

Victor Gollancz		
	6.6.34	Anatoly Vinogradov, *Black Consul*, trans. Emile Burns (1935 [1934])
	28.11.35	A. Y. Vyshinsky, *Soviet Justice* (not publ.)
	1.9.36	G. N. Serebrennikov, 'Woman's Labour in the USSR', publ. as *The Position of Women in the USSR*, 1937
	12.3.37	*Bolshevo* (not publ., no information: perhaps a projected book on the Bolshevo Labour Colony for Criminals)
	13.7.37	L. Brontman, 'Conquest of the North Pole', publ. as *On Top of the World: the Soviet Expedition to the North Pole, 1937*, ed. O. J. Schmidt, 1938
	24.7.37	M. I. Bogolepov, 'The Financial System of the USSR' (not publ., possibly the work published as *The Soviet Financial System: What it is and How it Works*, Lindsay Drummond, 1945)
	8.8.39	Vladimir Kokkinaki, 'The Route East', ed. L. Brontman (transl. not publ.)
Wishart		
	5.7.34	Karl Radek, *Portraits and Pamphlets*, trans., introd. A. J. Cummings, notes by Alec Brown, 1935 [unknown date], and Mikhail Zoshchenko, 'Restored Youth', trans. Ralph Fox (not publ., translation deemed unsatisfactory)
Lawrence & Wishart		
	30.3.36	Mikhail Romm, *The Ascent of Mount Stalin*, trans. Alec Brown, 1936

This list omits A.N. Afinogenov's *Distant Point*, performed at Norman Marshall's Gate Theatre Studio in November and December 1937, and later published by Rodker's own Pushkin Press, and several other titles mentioned in PresLit correspondence.

APPENDIX 2: 'BOOKS PLACED BY JOHN RODKER AS AGENT FOR PRESS AND PUBLISHER LITERARY SERVICE, MOSCOW'. UNDATED LIST

Author:	**Book:**	**Publisher:**
Arsenyev	Dersu, the Trapper	Secker & Warburg
Anon	Belomor	The Bodley Head Ltd.
Bianchi	Mourzouk	Allen & Unwin
do.	Forest News	do.
Brontman	On the Top of the World	Gollancz
Chaplina	My animal friends	Routledge
Anon	The Voyage of the Chelyuskin	Chatto & Windus
Frolov	Pavlov	Routledge
do.	Fish who answer the telephone	do.
Hermann	Our Acquaintances	do.
do.	Alexei Zhmakin	do.
Ivanov	I live a queer Life	Lovat Dickson

(*Continued*)

(*Continued*)

Author:	Book:	Publisher:
Leonov	Skutarevsky	do.
Makarenko	Pedagogical Poem	Nott
Mikhailov	Economic Geography of USSR	Methuen
Mogilevskaya	A Camp on the Ice	Routledge
–	The Letters of Tsar Nicolas & Empress Marie	Nicholson & Watson
Nilsen	The Cinema as a Graphic Art	Newnes
Novikov-Priboy	Tsushima	Allen & Unwin
Ostrovsky	The Making of a Hero	Secker & Warburg
Panferov	And then the Harvest	Putnam
Pavlenko	War in the East	Routledge
Perventsev	Cossack Commander	do.
Pudovkin	Film Acting	Newnes
Radek	Pamphlets and Portraits	Wishart
Romm	Ascent of Peak Stalin	Lawrence & Wishart
Serebrennikov	Womens Labour in USSR	Gollancz
Shirayev	Taglioni's Grandson	Putnam
Sobolev	Storm Warning	Dickson
–	Soviet Union Comes of Age	Hodge
Tarle	Napoleon	Secker & Warburg
Tynyanov	Death and Diplomacy in Persia	Boriswood
Vinogradov	The Black Consul	Gollancz

11

Russia and the British Intellectuals

The Significance of *The Stalin-Wells Talk*

Matthew Taunton

In the interwar years, Soviet Russia posed a number of problems for British intellectuals, especially those who were in principle sympathetic to socialism. Visiting the country to judge for oneself the extent to which communism was a success or otherwise became a popular pursuit among left-leaning intellectuals and workers' delegations. In his book *Political Pilgrims*, Paul Hollander examines the phenomenon of 'political tourism' to the Soviet Union, China and Cuba, asking why intellectuals 'tended to be so harsh on their own societies, and surprisingly indulgent of as well as uninformed about others'.[1] The diverse reports that came back from the Soviet Union tended to demonstrate that even going there to see it with one's own eyes could not guarantee an objective view—even the bare facts of the case were hotly debated. No doubt this was to some extent due to the fact that the Bolsheviks often staged theatrical spectacles of communist prosperity for visitors, or simply concealed some of the harsh realities of communism from them. Visitors from Western Europe, on the other hand, proved exceptionally pliable, to the extent that—as Patrick Wright has written of the British Workers' Delegation that visited in 1927—'it might be thought that they never really reached Russia at all, and only toured their own ardent preconceptions'.[2] One of the subjects of this chapter, John Maynard Keynes—hostile in principle to Marxism but certainly no friend of the tsars—wrote that: 'almost everything one can say about the country is true and false at the same time—which is the reason why friendly and hostile critics can each in good faith produce totally different pictures of the same thing'.[3]

In 1934, H. G. Wells travelled to Moscow to interview Stalin, and on his return a verbatim transcript of the interview was published in the *New Statesman and Nation*. Keynes and George Bernard Shaw responded in the same journal, and the

[*] I should like to thank Professor Morag Shiach for reading and commenting insightfully on a draft of this chapter, and the Leverhulme Trust for funding the research project of which it forms a part.

[1] Paul Hollander, *Political Pilgrims: Travels of Western Intellectuals to the Soviet Union, China, and Cuba, 1928–1978* (New York: Harper Colophon, 1981), 3.

[2] Patrick Wright, *Iron Curtain: From Stage to Cold War* (Oxford: Oxford University Press, 2007), 261.

[3] John Maynard Keynes, *A Short View of Russia* (London: Hogarth Press, 1925), 19.

resulting exchange of views was subsequently published as a pamphlet under the title *The Stalin-Wells Talk*. Wells, Shaw, and Keynes had all visited Russia before and written about their experiences, although arriving at different conclusions. This chapter sets the discussions surrounding the talk into the context of a longer debate that had, in effect, started in 1917. The triangular relationship between Wells, Shaw, and Keynes reveals much about the contested status of Soviet Russia in interwar Britain, especially for those seeking to bring about social and economic changes at home. As I have argued elsewhere, the Soviet Union had become in this period 'a kind of fantasy space' where British writers and intellectuals could stage their debates, and onto which they could project their desires.[4]

As with all three of the intellectuals under discussion here, Wells's opinion of Soviet Russia had developed in important ways since 1917. Wells visited first in 1914, and returned in 1920 when the country was still ravaged by civil war. In his account of his travels, *Russia in the Shadows*, Wells described terrible poverty, but asserted that 'this desolate Russia is not a system that has been attacked and destroyed by something vigorous and malignant. It is an unsound system that has worked itself out and fallen down'. Given these bleak conditions he regarded the newly founded workers' state as an 'emergency Government' that was 'the only possible government in Russia at the present time'. He acknowledged that the Red Terror was 'cruel and frightful', but also that 'it did on the whole kill for a reason and to an end'.[5] Wells was far from holding up Bolshevism as an ideal, but on the other hand he saw it as the only hope for the reconstruction of Russia. It is indicative of the state of political debate at this time that *Russia in the Shadows* was criticized from both sides: Trotsky accused Wells of bourgeois 'condescension', while friends at home thought he had blindly signed up to the Bolshevik programme.[6] In an increasingly polarized debate the truth was somewhere in between, and Wells's case highlights some of the difficulties with trying to occupy such a position in this period.

By 1934, when he went to meet Stalin, Wells's opinion of Soviet communism had changed. He had recently returned from the United States where he had met Roosevelt, and the interview with Stalin was conceived as a kind of foil to this meeting, with both men being treated as potential sources of ideas and inspiration for Wells's socialist project. Writing in *The New America: The New World* (1935), Wells compared his two trips to Russia: 'When I was in Russia last year I was enormously impressed by the changed morale since my former visit in 1920. Then there was danger, hardship, heroism, hope and a sense of limitless effort and adventure; now under the honest but uncreative fidelity of Stalin, cynicism and a widespread self-satisfied fatuity prevail.'[7] In the account of this meeting in his *Experiment in Autobiography* (1934), Wells states that he started out with 'a certain amount of

[4] Matthew Taunton, 'Cottage Economy or Collective Farm? English Socialism and Agriculture Between Merrie England and the Five-Year Plan', *Critical Quarterly*, 54, no. 3 (2011), 18.

[5] H. G. Wells, *Russia in the Shadows* (London: Hodder and Stoughton, 1920), 27, 11–12, 64.

[6] John Batchelor, *H. G. Wells* (Cambridge: Cambridge University Press, 1985), 124.

[7] H. G. Wells, *The New America: The New World* (London: Cresset Press, 1935), 18.

suspicion and prejudice' about Stalin, expecting a 'very reserved and self-centred fanatic' and, moreover, 'inclined to take the part of Trotsky against him'. And yet, as he went on, 'I had to recognize that under [Stalin] Russia was not being merely tyrannized over and held down; it was being governed and it was getting on.'[8]

The interview with Stalin lasted a little under three hours, with a translator present, and the *New Statesman and Nation* published a verbatim transcript of the whole interview.[9] This magazine was one of the key organs of the British left. The *New Statesman* had been established as a Fabian weekly by Bernard Shaw and Sidney and Beatrice Webb in 1913. At the time of the Stalin-Wells talk (and since its merger with Keynes's liberal *Nation and Athenaeum* in 1931), its chair was John Maynard Keynes and its editor Kingsley Martin.[10] The *New Statesman* was criticized for being too indulgent in its coverage of the Soviet Union, but its pages contained genuine debate. This was exemplified when Keynes reviewed *Low's Russian Sketchbook* (1932) for the magazine, a book of illustrations by David Low with text by Kingsley Martin, documenting their visit to Soviet Russia. Keynes was polite, but argued that Martin was 'a little too full perhaps of good will' in forming judgements about the 'Russian experiment', and that any doubts he had experienced had been 'swallowed down if possible'. Martin was deeply offended but printed the review, while Keynes accused him in a private letter of double standards: 'I should like to see for once the kind of leader which you would write if the Government in England were to do the kind of things in matters of justice and liberty... in the same kind and scale as events in Russia.'[11] Martin discredited himself a few years later by refusing to print Orwell's anti-Soviet dispatches from the Spanish Civil War.[12] So while the *New Statesman and Nation* undoubtedly showed a pro-Soviet bias in many of its editorial choices, it was also—as the Stalin-Wells talk shows—willing at times to accommodate genuine debate about the political morality of Stalinism.

The Stalin-Wells talk exposes conflicts both at the magazine and within the British left as a whole. Wells was criticized for the reverence with which he addressed Stalin; George Orwell, for example, observed that Wells had found Stalin 'human, simple, and likeable'. Orwell went on: 'Is it not also recorded that Al Capone was the best of husbands and fathers?'[13] But Wells also contradicts Stalin and tries to put across his own view. Indeed, Shaw—a jingoistic Stalinist at this stage of his career—found Wells rather *too* irreverent, claiming that he had implied that Stalin was 'a second-rate person' and concluding that 'frankly, he had better apologize to Stalin and take it out

[8] H. G. Wells, *Experiment in Autobiography: Discoveries and Conclusions of a Very Ordinary Brain* (London: Faber & Faber, 1984), ii, 800.

[9] Richard Nickson, 'The Lure of Stalinism: Bernard Shaw and Company', *Midwest Quarterly*, 25, no. 4 (1984), 423.

[10] Adrian Smith, *The New Statesman: Portrait of a Political Weekly, 1913–1931* (London: Frank Cass, 1996), 43, 245.

[11] John Maynard Keynes, *The Collected Writings of John Maynard Keynes*, xxviii: *Social, Political and Literary Writings*, ed. Donald Moggridge (London: Macmillan, for the Royal Economic Society, 1982), 15, 18.

[12] Smith, *The New Statesman*, 246.

[13] George Orwell, review of Eugene Lyons, *Assignment In Utopia*, in Peter Davison, ed., *Orwell and Politics*, (London: Penguin, 2001), 34.

on me to his heart's content'.[14] With Keynes also engaged in the debate, the editor Kingsley Martin was delighted to find Britain's three most prominent intellectuals involved in a battle of wit and eloquence in the pages of his magazine, and asked them all permission to reprint the correspondence in pamphlet form. Wells immediately agreed, saying that 'Shaw has behaved like a cad and ought to be exposed', while Shaw—claiming to be acting in the interests of his 'old friend H. G.'—was initially reluctant, giving the go-ahead only because Wells and Keynes were willing 'to exhibit themselves at their worst'.[15] Shaw wrote to Keynes that 'I am not at all easy about Kingsley Martin's proposal to reprint the stuff in *The New Statesman*. I should put my foot down on it at once but for H. G. who has an infatuated belief that he has put Stalin in his place and given me an exemplary drubbing, whereas it is equally clear to me that he has made a blazing idiot of himself.'[16] Martin's amusing account of this episode in his autobiography, *Editor*, demonstrates just how juvenile the argument became. He concludes perceptively that 'in these comic rows Shaw usually scored because to him it was all a fine game of wits, while Wells was always deeply and personally involved'.[17]

The dispute revealed not only differences in opinion, but also fundamental uncertainties about whether genuine debate was possible. Shaw complains that 'Wells is a very good talker; but he is the worst listener in the world.' Keynes responds by comparing Stalin to a 'gramophone': in the interview, Wells was trying 'to coax the needle off the record and hear it—vain hope—speak in human tones'. And Wells, frustrated by Shaw's unswerving adherence to Stalinist dogma, characterizes him as 'practically stone deaf'.[18] These communication problems were symptomatic of the uncertainties that plagued the wider conversation about the Soviet Union in Britain, which had become the focal point on which the left-wing thinkers of the day were converging, but one on which few could agree. This was borne out by the constant stream of books about the Soviet Union in this period, containing wildly divergent accounts. There were books by sympathizers, such as Sidney and Beatrice Webb, whose *Soviet Communism: A New Civilisation?* (1935) tellingly dropped the question mark from its title in subsequent editions. There were also books by left-wing visitors who were horrified by what they saw, such as Malcolm Muggeridge's *Winter in Moscow* (1934), a novel that drew on the author's experience of working as a foreign correspondent in the Soviet Union at the time of the terror-famine of 1932-4. Muggeridge and Gareth Jones published the first reports of the famine in the *Manchester Guardian* (which were—to Muggeridge's consternation—toned down by the communist-sympathizing editor). These reports, which we now know to be all too true, were widely and publicly disputed by the Webbs, Shaw, and

[14] George Bernard Shaw, and others, *Stalin-Wells Talk: The Verbatim Record and A Discussion by G. Bernard Shaw, H. G. Wells, J. M. Keynes, Ernst Toller and others* (London: New Statesman and Nation, 1934), 40.

[15] Kingsley Martin, *Editor: A Second Volume of Autobiography* (London: Hutchinson, 1968), 85–6.

[16] George Bernard Shaw to John Maynard Keynes, 30 November 1934, in Keynes, *Social, Political and Literary Writings*, 37.

[17] Martin, *Editor*, 87.

[18] Shaw, and others, *Stalin-Wells Talk*, 22, 30, 37.

other leading figures of the British left, often in the pages of the *New Statesman and Nation*. An exasperated Muggeridge responded to his erstwhile mentor Beatrice Webb's denial of the famine and continued enthusiasm for Soviet communism, addressing her in a letter as 'Aunt Bo': 'I'd hate to think of you upholding something that I know you'd hate if you knew its real character.'[19] Squabbles like this one, which are internal to the left, are this chapter's primary concern, but the new fixation on the Soviet Union was not confined to the left. Indeed, it is worth noting briefly that the Conservative press too was filled with ardent and rarely well-informed denunciations of Soviet socialism that frequently connected it (not entirely without justification) to the programme of the Labour party. Indeed, as Ross McKibbin has recently argued, the electoral success of the Conservative Party in the inter-war period was partly attributable to their 'mobilization of a new anti-socialist majority'.[20] Across the political spectrum, the Soviet Union had become a crucial reference point against which individual positions could be defined.

One should not seek to excuse the execrable behaviour of apologists like the Webbs and Bernard Shaw ('after Stalin the most hated man in Russia', as Gareth Jones wrote).[21] Neither must one blind oneself to the strategic role played by Conservative anti-socialism, based as it was on a partly imaginary description of the Soviet Union that was powered by ideology and political expediency. But it must be conceded that the 'real character' of the Soviet regime, which Muggeridge urged Webb to see, was for practical and perhaps for psychological reasons difficult to access, even for those who made the journey to the promised (or abominated) land. Keynes wrote that 'a belt of fog separates us from what goes on in the other world where the Union of Soviet Socialist Republics rules and experiments and evolves a kind of order'.[22] The Stalin-Wells talk highlights the polarizing nature of a new geopolitical order, which increasingly impelled commentators to choose between two 'implacably opposed political systems'.[23] The choice was becoming a starker one: either endorse Stalin's regime and tolerate its methods, or reconcile oneself to the capitalist West and renounce socialism entirely. This is a choice that Wells refused to make, which explains why he was often attacked from both sides.

For Wells, the failure of communication was internal to the Soviet Union as well as being a feature of its relationship with Western Europe: 'This is the outstanding difference... between the constructive effort in Washington and Moscow. The one is a receptive and co-ordinating brain-centre; the other is a concerted and personal direction.'[24] In particular, Wells's interest in communication problems was linked to his concerns about the restrictions on freedom of expression that existed in the Soviet Union. Wells concludes the interview by suggesting that the Soviet Writers'

[19] Quoted in Richard Ingrams, *Muggeridge: The Biography* (London: Harper Collins, 1995), 65.

[20] Ross McKibbin, *Parties and People: England 1914–1951* (Oxford: Oxford University Press, 2010), 181.

[21] Gareth Jones, 'Famine in Russia. Englishman's Story. What He Saw on a Walking Tour', *Manchester Guardian* (30 March 1933), 12.

[22] Keynes, *A Short View of Russia*, 11.

[23] Wright, *Iron Curtain*, 164.

[24] Wells, *Experiment in Autobiography*, ii, 792.

Union might want to affiliate with the PEN Club, an institution which stood for free speech and of which he himself was President. Asked directly about free speech in the Soviet Union, Stalin responds: 'We Bolsheviks call it "self-criticism". It is widely used in Russia.'[25] 'Self-criticism' (*samokrikita*) had little to do with free speech: it was 'a ritual whereby delinquent comrades were made to confess their errors and to subscribe to the "correct" line before a Party meeting'.[26] The freedom of expression that prevailed under the democratic system in the United States, Wells believed, played a crucial role in enabling Roosevelt to act as 'a receptive and co-ordinating brain centre'. Stalin had isolated himself from critical voices at home, but the Stalin-Wells talk highlights an intriguing feature of his rule: that he would willingly engage in dialogue with a foreign intellectual for consumption abroad.[27]

This touches on one of the substantive points of disagreement between Wells, Shaw, and Keynes: the question of internationalism. Wells's belief that the New Deal and the Five-Year Plan were augurs of global economic rationalization was a key element of his internationalism in this period. He had been deeply impressed with New Deal America on his visit earlier in 1934, finding in Roosevelt's Brains Trust 'a view of the world... which seemed to contain all I had ever learnt and thought, but better arranged and closer to reality'.[28] His first question to Stalin posits a genuinely international project in which both Stalin and Roosevelt can participate: 'It seems to me that what is taking place in the United States is a profound reorganisation, the creation of planned, that is, socialist economy. You and Roosevelt begin from two different starting points. But is there not a relation in ideas, a kinship of ideas and needs, between Washington and Moscow?'[29]

Wells was a committed cosmopolitan throughout his career, and increasingly argued that the formation of a world state was an essential goal of socialism.[30] He proposes to Stalin that 'instead of stressing the antagonism between the two worlds, we should, in the present circumstances, strive to establish a common tongue for all the constructive forces'.[31] Stalin responds by insisting that Roosevelt's reforms were palliative measures designed to defend the capitalist system from the revolutionary socialism that was its only cure. Stalin's insistence on the reality of the 'antagonism between the two worlds' reflects that fact that the Soviet Union had adopted his patriotic slogan of 'socialism

[25] Shaw, and others, *Stalin-Wells Talk*, 18.

[26] Martin Malia, *The Soviet Tragedy: A History of Socialism in Russia* (New York: Free Press, 1994), 267.

[27] In fact, as Sheila Fitzpatrick has shown, miscommunication between Stalin and his mid-level bureaucrats was a deliberate feature of his leadership style: his statements of policy were usually obscure and often secret. This allowed Stalin to play the 'good tsar' while blaming state oppressions on lower-level officials who had misinterpreted his cryptic ukases. Sheila Fitzpatrick, *Everyday Stalinism: Ordinary Life in Extraordinary Times: Soviet Russia in the 1930s* (Oxford: Oxford University Press, 1999), 28.

[28] Wells, *Experiment in Autobiography*, ii, 785. Roosevelt was also a great admirer of Wells, and wrote to him in praise of the *Experiment in Autobiography*, claiming that 'your direction and mine are not so far apart', quoted in Norman and Jeanne MacKenzie, *The Life of H. G. Wells: The Time Traveller*, rev. edn (London: Hogarth Press, 1987), 384.

[29] Shaw, and others, *Stalin-Wells Talk*, 4.

[30] John S. Partington, *Building Cosmopolis: The Political Thought of H. G. Wells* (Aldershot: Ashgate, 2003), 1.

[31] Shaw, and others, *Stalin-Wells Talk*, 5–6.

in one country' in 1924.[32] According to this mantra, the Soviet Union should 'create the preconditions of socialism by its own unaided efforts' rather than waiting for the revolutions in the capitalist West which Trotsky and Zinov'ev thought were vital for its long-term survival. This was in part an expedient response to the failure of revolution elsewhere in Europe and also a way of countering Trotsky, whose persistent internationalism could thus be labeled unpatriotic: he 'cared less about Russia than about Europe', Stalin's followers claimed.[33] But the belief in the West that 'Russian shirts and balalaikas... are integral parts of socialism' existed even before Stalin moved the Bolshevik ideal of global revolution down the agenda.[34] As Patrick Wright argues, 'years before Stalin committed Soviet Russia to the idea of "Socialism in one country", the spirit of "international" revolution was already fervently identified with the ground on one side of this new division between states'. Hence the habit that new arrivals had of kissing the hallowed soil of the socialist heartland, the first instance of which was the arrival of the USS *Buford*—also known as the 'Red Ark'—which brought Alexander Berkman, Emma Goldman, and other exiled radicals from the United States to Russia in January 1920.[35] Wells deplored the fact that under Stalin the Soviet Union had become 'militantly patriotic', and lacking in internationalist spirit.[36]

Shaw's response is in keeping with the wholehearted endorsement of Stalinism that characterized this period of his career. He had always been a statist, arguing in 1889 that under socialism the state would take on the 'whole work of organizing the national industry, thereby making it the most vital organ in the social body'.[37] Yet, perhaps because of a lingering commitment to Fabian gradualism, he was initially dismissive of the Bolsheviks, and wrote in 1924 that

> the members of the Third International do not know even the beginning of their business as socialists; and the proposition that the world should take its orders from a handful of Russian novices, who seem to have gained their knowledge of modern Socialism by sitting over the drawing room stove and reading the pamphlets of the liberal revolutionists of 1848-70, makes even Lord Curzon and Mr. Winston Churchill seem extreme modernists in comparison.[38]

Shaw even went on to say that Trotsky 'has allowed himself to speak of Mr. H. G. Wells with a contempt which shows that he has not read Mr. Wells' *Outline of History*, and has therefore no suspicion of what an enormous advance on *Das Kapital* that work represents'.[39] Wells quotes this passage back at Shaw in his final, exasperated contribution to the debate—Shaw had long since seen through Bolshevik jingoism, so why was he now allowing it to spout immoderately from

[32] Richard Sakwa, *The Rise and Fall of the Soviet Union, 1917–1991* (London: Routledge, 1999), 160–2.

[33] Sheila Fitzpatrick, *The Russian Revolution*, 3rd edn (Oxford: Oxford University Press, 2008), 115.

[34] Arthur Koestler, 'Soviet Myth and Reality, in *The Yogi and the Commissar* (New York: Macmillan, 1946), 188.

[35] Wright, *Iron Curtain*, 156.

[36] Wells, *The New America*, 19.

[37] George Bernard Shaw, *Essays in Fabian Socialism* (London: Constable, 1961), 67.

[38] Shaw, and others, *Stalin-Wells Talk*, 45.

[39] Shaw, and others, *Stalin-Wells Talk*, 45.

his pen? Why go back to Marx, when he had already accepted the more advanced Wellsian view of history? Shaw's conversion to Soviet communism occurred for a range of reasons too complex to be investigated in detail here. Shaw and the Webbs had begun to feel that 'Fabian gradualism had been getting to seem all too gradual'.[40] Frustration with the failure of Ramsay MacDonald's Labour government to establish socialism in Britain combined with a lingering investment in the concept of the *Übermensch* and a predilection for demagogic rule.[41] He argued in his 1931 introduction to a reprint of his *Fabian Essays in Socialism* that 'Labor Governments, like other governments, end in disappointment and reaction with their millennial promises unfulfilled; whilst the revolutionary Left and the Fascist Right are supplied with daily evidence as to the futility of parliamentary action at home, and the swift effectiveness of hard knocks abroad.'[42]

This impatience with the slowness of democratic means of implementing socialism was shared by many advocates of socialism in one country. Those in a hurry to effect change were more apt to abandon the undeniably idealistic goal of achieving it multilaterally in collaboration with workers' parties and liberals from abroad, preferring to establish socialism at home by whatever means possible in the hope that other countries would follow. The Soviet Union positioned itself as a blueprint for change, and socialists the world over duly obliged by identifying it as the homeland of socialism. Shaw's 1931 trip to Stalin's Soviet Union—described in an appalling unfinished book entitled *The Rationalization of Russia*—was representative of a certain way of thinking about communism in the 1930s, precisely because the ideal society was no longer a utopian fantasy existing only in a mass of dense and often contradictory pamphlets. Socialism and the Soviet Union had become identical. If something was true of the Soviet Union it became true of socialism, and vice versa.

Shaw takes the side of Stalin and endorses the doctrine of socialism in one country whilst deriding the impracticality of Wells's internationalism. Stalin, Shaw writes, 'is a practical Nationalist statesman recognising that Russia is a big enough handful for mortal rulers to tackle without taking on the rest of the world as well (Wells will have nothing short of a World State)'.[43] Shaw is unapologetic about the nationalist direction that Soviet communism had taken, exhorting those on the left simply to identify their interests with the socialist heartland; anything else would be tantamount to siding with the forces of conservatism. The fact that this profoundly polarized understanding of global politics exists at this early stage tends to support Patrick Wright's hypothesis of the 'long Cold War'.[44] In this theory, the destructive mental habit of dividing Europe into two opposed blocs separated by an 'iron curtain' preceded (and indeed helped to precipitate) the First World War, rather than, as the conventional historical narrative has it, being inaugurated by Winston Churchill's use of the term in a speech in Fulton, Missouri in 1946. The controversy

[40] Nickson, 'The Lure of Stalinism', 422.

[41] Gareth Griffith, *Socialism and Superior Brains: The Political Thought of Bernard Shaw* (London: Routledge, 2003), 132–3.

[42] Shaw, *Essays in Fabian Socialism*, 308.

[43] Shaw, and others, *Stalin-Wells Talk*, 26.

[44] Wright, *Iron Curtain*, 18.

surrounding the Stalin-Wells talk is a site at which this proto-Cold-War polarization of political discussion rubs up against a lingering internationalism, redolent of an earlier period. Perhaps this goes some way towards explaining the problems of communication that afflicted these three writers when they turned their minds towards Soviet Russia. The geopolitical map was in the process of being redrawn, and the three men differed in their perceptions of its contours.

Wells's continuing commitment to internationalism was in some ways admirable, but there are hints that he had failed to tailor his ideas to the realities of the new international situation. During his visit to America he explained to Roosevelt:

> If it were not . . . for questions of mere political mechanism, stale traditions, the mental childishness of our British Foreign Office and what not, it would be perfectly possible even now for the English speaking masses and the Russian mass, with France as our temperamental associate, to be made to say effectively that Peace shall prevail throughout the earth. And it would prevail.[45]

Wells's belief in humankind's ability to see through 'stale traditions' and accept that common sense is best served by the formation of a socialist world state starts to look a little naïve in the context of the 1930s. Orwell thought so, arguing that the problem of nationalism was a more intractable one: Wells was 'incapable of understanding that nationalism, religious bigotry and feudal loyalty are far more powerful forces than what he himself would describe as sanity'.[46] For Orwell, Wells's internationalism was laudable enough in itself, but the nationalism he despised was not likely to be dispelled by simply trying to convince various world leaders that a world state is a good idea.

John Maynard Keynes had been making the case for international cooperation at least since his account of the disaster of the Versailles treaty, *The Economic Consequences of the Peace* (1919). Keynes had forecast in that book that the failure of the peace conference to arrive at a settlement that could secure the economic stability of Europe would leave its impoverished and desperate citizens vulnerable to 'counsels of despair and madness', implicitly Bolshevism.[47] He criticized the allied blockade that was dividing Europe and amplifying the suffering of the Russian people, and wrote in favour of international cooperation.[48] Keynes's contribution to this debate does not address Shaw's advocacy of socialism in one country, a policy that continued in the polarizing spirit of Versailles, in its division of Europe into two opposed blocs. Instead, Keynes focuses on the economic arguments into which Wells, Stalin and Shaw enter, and to which I now turn.

The second major point of disagreement between the participants in the debate turns on their conflicting economic theories, and in particular on their theories of class. Wells held that the Marxist insistence on 'class-war' was a particularly outmoded element of Stalinist doctrine. He dismissed Marx as 'a Bore of the extremest

[45] Wells, *Experiment in Autobiography*, ii, 796.
[46] George Orwell, 'Wells, Hitler and the World State', in *Essays* (London: Penguin, 2000), 193.
[47] John Maynard Keynes, *The Economic Consequences of the Peace* (London: Macmillan, 1919), 235.
[48] Keynes, *The Economic Consequences of the Peace*, 276.

sort' in 1920, deriding the 'crude Marxist philosophy which divides all men into bourgeoisie and proletariat, which sees all social life as a stupidly simple "class war"'.[49] He explained to various Bolsheviks that, rather than the increasing division of society into two antagonistic classes that Marx had predicted, 'in England there were two hundred different classes at least'.[50] Moreover, Wells's assertion that the New Deal and the Five-Year Plan tended towards the same goal implied that on the level of economics the two systems were similar. In this analysis, Stalin's 'Marxist imagery was little more than verbal camouflage on a system that was essentially state-capitalist'.[51] Two of the world's most powerful nations were evolving systems of state-socialism, but Stalin's doctrinaire insistence on the rhetoric of class war was obscuring the basic homology between the two systems and creating a hostile rivalry.

Wells challenged Stalin on the issue of class-war, arguing that Soviet valorization of the proletariat could alienate the 'technical intelligentsia', which he saw as playing a crucial role in the planning of the socialist future. He said, 'I think that class-war propaganda may detach from Socialism just those educated people whom Socialism needs.'[52] Technical and scientific progress were central to the vision of the socialist future set out in Wells's utopian writings. In his vision, 'bourgeois' scientists and engineers were not—as Stalinist dogma would have it—the enemies of socialism. On the contrary, they were at the very vanguard of socialist progress. The importance Wells placed on the 'technical intelligentsia' had been a point of disagreement with Fabian orthodoxy for many years. Beatrice Webb recorded her frustrations with Wellsian socialism in her diary as early as February 1902, complaining that a 'world run by the physical-science-man is [Wells's] ideal'.[53]

Here, there is evidence of continuity between the Fabianism of the Edwardian period and the bureaucratic Stalinism of the thirties. Stalin dissents from Wells's view of the 'technical intelligentsia' in Webb's terms, arguing that this class has no independent contribution to make and can be of use only as the instrument of the proletariat which, under communism, holds enough political power to dominate it.[54] In his response Shaw jokily refers to Wells's beloved technical intelligentsia as 'Clissolds', alluding to Wells's partially autobiographical novel, *The World of William Clissold*: 'Stalin gallantly admits that these Clissolds could organise, but adds that the problem is how to organise *them*, which is precisely the problem that the Soviet has successfully solved, though not on the basis of private property, and not in all cases without a gentle but persistent pressure of a pistol muzzle on the

[49] Wells, *Russia in the Shadows*, 67, 46.

[50] Wells, *Russia in the Shadows*, 77. This issue was debated in the *New Statesman and Nation* in 1934, for example in an unsigned article, 'The Revolutionary Middle Class', *New Statesman and Nation*, NS 7, no. 167 (5 May 1934), 664–5. G. D. H. Cole, a frequent contributor to the *New Statesman* who was considered for the editorship in 1930, had written that year on precisely this subject in *What Marx Really Meant* (London: Gollancz, 1934).

[51] MacKenzie, *The Life of H. G. Wells*, 380.

[52] Shaw, and others, *Stalin-Wells Talk*, 11, 15.

[53] Beatrice Webb, *The Diary of Beatrice Webb*, ii: *1895–1905*, ed. Norman and Jeanne MacKenzie (London: Virago, 1983), 240.

[54] Shaw, and others, *Stalin-Wells Talk*, 10–11.

Clissold occiput.'[55] This attitude of Stalinism to the technical intelligentsia—its determination to direct science in the interest of 'the people'—led to the disaster of Lysenkoism and 'proletarian science'. It was destined, as Louis Althusser argued, to alienate the Western scientific community from Marxism.[56] Arthur Koestler, an ex-communist with a strong scientific background (and, admittedly, a growing interest in the pseudo-science of parapsychology) was particularly scathing of the way the Communist Party of the 1930s dismissed any scientific thinking that was not congruent with the party line as 'bourgeois objectivism'.[57] Shaw's justification of the Bolsheviks' use of violent coercion against the Clissolds demonstrates that he was not ignorant of the methods by which Stalinist policies were implemented, but he was prepared to tolerate them. Indeed elsewhere he seemed to revel in them: 'what we are confronted with now is a growing perception that if we desire a certain type of civilization and culture we must exterminate the sort of people who do not fit into it'. Only Soviet Russia had fully grasped this, and realized that it was the 'kulak' and the bourgeois that needed to be exterminated.[58]

Shaw was also blind to the chronic scarcity of food and other essentials in the Soviet Union. He remarked that during his 1931 visit to Russia he 'saw no underfed people there; and the children were remarkably plump'. At most, he was willing to grant that a certain amount of belt-tightening in the name of the 'sacrifice of the present to the future' was necessary.[59] He retained a belief in the prosperity of the Soviet Union, and argued in his final missive in the *New Statesman* controversy that it justified the despotism of the regime. 'Mussolini, Kemal, Pilsudski, Hitler, and the rest can all depend on me to judge them by their ability to deliver the goods, and not by Swinburne's comfortable Victorian notions of freedom. Stalin has delivered the goods in to an extent that seemed impossible ten years ago; and I take my hat off to him.'[60]

Stalin had apparently made a scientific discovery in the field of economics that Wells was simply unwilling or unable to grasp. As Shaw put it, 'Stalin, with invincible patience, again gives Wells a lucid elementary lesson in post-Marxian political science.' 'Science' is a crucial category in the part of this controversy that concerns economics. Responding to Keynes, Shaw writes: 'I admit that he really made me laugh by calling Stalin a gramophone. Stalin will not mind; we are all gramophones when it comes to the multiplication table.'[61] For Shaw, Marxist science has provided the answer to the economic question, and once one is in possession of that knowledge—which is effectively grasped as an *a priori* truth—one no longer needs

[55] Shaw, and others, *Stalin-Wells Talk*, 22.

[56] See Louis Althusser, 'Introduction: Unfinished History', in Dominique Lecourt, *Proletarian Science? The Case of Lysenko* (London: NLB, 1977), 7–16.

[57] Arthur Koestler, *The Invisible Writing* (London: Vintage, 2005), 317.

[58] George Bernard Shaw, *Plays Political: The Apple Cart, On the Rocks, Geneva* (London: Penguin, 1986), 146, 164–5.

[59] Shaw, *Plays Political*, 168.

[60] Shaw, and others, *Stalin-Wells Talk*, 47.

[61] Shaw, and others, *Stalin-Wells Talk*, 21, 41.

to listen to alternatives. Dialogue is useless: one might as well debate the validity of the three times table.

Keynes also believed that he was confronting an irrational ideology with reasoned scientific logic, but this time it was Shaw and Stalin who had discarded empirical science in favour of dogmatic mysticism. In *A Short View of Russia*, his dissatisfaction with the manner in which capitalism was being conducted elsewhere led him to 'sympathise with those who seek for something good in Soviet Russia'. Surely, if nothing else, Bolshevism would compare favourably to tsarism: 'out of the cruelty and stupidity of Old Russia nothing could ever emerge, but... beneath the cruelty and stupidity of New Russia some speck of the ideal may lay hid'.[62] Writing in 1919 in *The Economic Consequences of the Peace*, Keynes had suggested that the Russian Revolution should be explained as a consequence of the vast increase in population.[63] Keynes's interest in the effects of population growth is no doubt part of his debt to Malthus, whose work has an intrinsic importance in contributing to Keynes's theoretical differences from Stalinist economics but also, extrinsically, symbolizes a tradition of economic thought that Marx deliberately set himself against.[64] If *The Economic Consequences of the Peace* saw unchecked increases in population as a threat to political order, then it also stressed the idea that economic prosperity and political stability are closely related. Failure to secure the economic future of Europe would have disastrous consequences, and the book is haunted by the spectre of desperate, malnourished people across Europe, stricken by unemployment and susceptible to dangerous revolutionary ideologies. The stability of political systems, for Keynes, depended on the success of their economic model.

Unlike Shaw, though, Keynes was not inclined to sacrifice liberty at the altar of prosperity: 'Comfort and habits let us be ready to forgo, but I am not ready for a creed which does not care how much it destroys the liberty and security of daily life, which uses deliberately the weapons of persecution, destruction and international strife.' Moreover, for Keynes, there was nothing less likely to bring about economic prosperity than Bolshevik Marxism: 'How can I accept a doctrine which sets up as its bible, above and beyond criticism, an obsolete economic textbook which I know to be not only scientifically false but without interest or application to the modern world?' At the same time, like Wells, Keynes objected to the Bolsheviks' valorization of the industrial proletariat: 'How can I adopt a creed which, preferring the mud to the fish, exalts the boorish proletariat above the bourgeois and the intelligentsia who, with whatever faults, are the quality in life and surely carry the seeds of all human advancement?'[65] Whatever Keynes may have admired in the buoyant idealism of Bolshevism, he shared with Wells a fundamentally Edwardian faith in the

[62] Keynes, *A Short View of Russia*, 13, 28.

[63] Keynes, *The Economic Consequences of the Peace*, 12–13.

[64] Robert Skidelsky, *John Maynard Keynes, 1883–1946: Economist, Philosopher, Statesman* (Basingstoke: Pan Macmillan, 2004), 462–5. Wells was also impressed by Malthus's *Essay on the Principle of Population*, and argued that the utopian society must 'control the increase of its population' along Malthusian lines (H. G. Wells, *A Modern Utopia* (London: Penguin, 2005), 105).

[65] Keynes, *A Short View of Russia*, 13–14.

culture and values of the progressive middle class. The Clissolds were the driving force of progress: to persecute them as the Bolsheviks did was folly.

By 1934 any hope that 'the speck of the ideal' might reside in Bolshevism had disappeared from Keynes's writing. Shaw's initial response to the interview implied that the Marxism-Leninism to which he and Stalin subscribed hinged on a fundamentally different, more scientific view of economics than the 'standard system' taught in schools and universities. Keynes counters:

> Shaw has forgotten that he and Stalin are just as completely under the intellectual dominance of that standard system as are Asquith and Inge. The system bred two families—those who thought it true and inevitable, and those who thought it true and intolerable. There was no third school of thought in the nineteenth century. Nevertheless, there is a third possibility—that it is not true. A most upsetting idea to the dogmatists—no one would be more annoyed than Stalin by that thought—but hugely exhilarating to the scientists.[66]

The 'standard system' to which Keynes refers is the classical economics of Ricardo, a system with which, he thought, Marxism had never decisively broken. Nineteenth-century economic thought had taken a wrong turn when the abstractions of Ricardo had won out over the sound good sense of Malthus. As Keynes wrote in his essay on Malthus: 'If only Malthus, instead of Ricardo, had been the parent stem from which nineteenth-century economics proceeded, what a much wiser and richer place the world would be today!' In a private letter to Shaw dated 1 January 1935, Keynes promised that his *General Theory of Employment, Interest and Money*—to be published just over a year later, in February 1936—'will largely revolutionise... the way the world thinks about economics'. Crucially, he went on, 'the Ricardian foundations of Marxism will be knocked away'.[67]

There is not space here to describe exactly how Keynes went about this or to assess the success or failure of the enterprise (needless to say, in the specialist economic literature on the subject this is not a matter of consensus). Nevertheless, the fact that '*The General Theory* arose from Keynes's deep anti-Marxism as well as from his opposition to laissez-faire economics' has frequently been overlooked.[68] This is particularly important in understanding the triangular relationship between the views of the Soviet Union held by Keynes, Shaw, and Wells. Keynes argued that Marxism and laissez-faire capitalism shared a common basis in the economics of Ricardo, and that they were therefore 'based on intellectual error'.[69] In opposition to these fundamentally similar systems, Keynes constructed his *General Theory*. Wells, as I have already explained, thought that a globally planned economy was the future end towards which all contemporary developments tended: Roosevelt's New Deal was analogous to Stalin's Five-Year Plan. For Wells, it was only communism's dogmatic insistence on outmoded ideas about class war and its jingoistic

66 Shaw, and others, *Stalin-Wells Talk*, 26, 33.

67 Skidelsky, *John Maynard Keynes*, 463, 518.

68 Donald Markwell, *John Maynard Keynes and International Relations: Economic Paths to War and Peace* (Oxford: Oxford University Press, 2006), 176.

69 Shaw, and others, *Stalin-Wells Talk*, 33.

nationalism that were making the two systems seem opposed. Of the three, it was only Shaw who believed in this opposition, with Wells and Keynes instead pointing out continuities between the two seemingly incongruous worlds.

Keynes's disdain for theoretical Marxism was accompanied by the belief that the real economic basis of the Soviet Union bore scant relation to the model upon which it purported to be based. Writing in 1925, he observed that six-sevenths of the Soviet population lived in rural, agricultural conditions, and one-seventh in urban and industrial. Bolshevism, Keynes argued, had secured its stability by pandering to the industrial proletariat and exploiting the peasantry. This exploitation was implemented thorough the state's monopoly over import and export trade and the pricing policy that it pursued, buying grain from the peasant at well below the world price, and selling him textiles and other industrial products at well above the world price. As well as 'pampering' the proletariat, the difference was used to fund the state's high running costs and compensate for 'the general inefficiency of manufacture and distribution'.[70]

Believing it to be intrinsically flawed in theory and brutal in its application, Keynes 'could never take [Marxism] seriously as a science. But he did take it seriously', as Robert Skidelsky puts it, 'as a sickness of the soul.'[71] It was Keynes's firmly held conviction that the appeal of Bolshevism was to be explained primarily in religious terms. Keynes argued that for the young atheist intellectuals of the 1930s—raised in a world that was freer from moral strictures than that inhabited by Keynes and his peers, and less intoxicated by the spirit of transgression—Marxism had moved into the space vacated by Christianity.[72] It is this analysis that underpins Keynes's response to Shaw, which more than simply dissenting from the tenets of Bolshevism, gives an account of its psychological appeal:

> On the surface Communism enormously overestimates the significance of the economic problem. The economic problem is not too difficult to solve. If you will leave that to me, I will look after it. But when I have solved it, I shall not receive, or deserve, much thanks. For I shall have done no more than disclose that the real problem lying behind is quite different and further from solution than before. Underneath, Communism draws its strength from deeper, more serious sources. Offered to us as a means of improving the economic situation, it is an insult to our intelligence. But offered as a means of making the economic situation *worse*, that is its subtle, its almost irresistible, attraction.
>
> Communism is not a reaction against the failure of the nineteenth century to organise optimal economic output. It is a reaction against its success. It is a protest against the emptiness of economic welfare, an appeal to the ascetic in us to all other values. It is the curate in Wells, far from extinguished by the scientist, which draws him to take a peep at Moscow. It is Shaw, the noblest old curate in the world and the least scientific, who rallies to the good cause of putting the economist in his place somewhere underground.[73]

[70] Keynes, *A Short View of Russia*, 20–1.
[71] Skidelsky, *John Maynard Keynes*, 515.
[72] Keynes, *A Short View of Russia*, 6–7.
[73] Shaw, and others, *Stalin-Wells Talk*, 35–6.

For Keynes, Shaw's unswerving insistence on the economic triumphs of Bolshevism merely shows how profoundly his perceptions of the Soviet Union have been distorted by an underlying psychological complex. The true appeal of Soviet communism lay not in its economic success, but in its economic failure.

Wells, unlike Keynes, had come to believe at least in the efficiency of Stalinist economics, claiming that 'everything I had heard in favour of the First Five-Year Plan I had put through a severely sceptical sieve, and yet there remained a growing effect of successful enterprise'.[74] In private, Keynes told Virginia Woolf that Wells was 'a little squit' and despite his efforts to defend him from some of Shaw's vitriol, he was in reality far from taking his side.[75] These three thinkers were never likely to agree on the morality of Stalinism. But the startling reality is that they could not agree on the basic facts of the case, even where it came to economic 'science', or judging the degree of prosperity in Russia. It may have been true that, as Keynes wrote, 'Wells is fully conscious... and justly so, that his own mind dwells with the future and Shaw's and Stalin's with the past'. Yet Wells had no real programme to propose. Keynes goes on:

> Shaw writes that Wells 'has not come to be instructed by Stalin, but to instruct him'. Nothing could be more untrue. On the contrary. It is Wells's trouble that he has never yet found a satisfactory instruction to give. He has nothing to offer Stalin. That is what Stalin might have pointed out, if gramophones could hear.[76]

This passage sums up perfectly the problems raised by the Stalin-Wells talk. The British left were disappointed by the progress made by social democracy, as represented by the Labour government of Ramsay MacDonald. The choice was becoming a starker one between two increasingly polarized political systems, identified as two geographically distinct spheres. But it would be overly schematic to divide the left intelligentsia of the period into two opposed blocs: the Soviet-sympathizers (which would contain writers as diverse as Shaw, the Webbs, and the young W. H. Auden, Stephen Spender, and C. Day Lewis) versus the anti-communists (including Orwell, Muggeridge, Rebecca West, Havelock Ellis, and Keynes). The triangular relationship revealed by the debate surrounding the Stalin-Wells talk works against any such reductive account of the cultural politics of the 'long' Cold War, at least in the British context. Instead, it testifies to the diversity and complexity of the ways in which British intellectuals negotiated their relationship to the Soviet Union. Shaw fitted in most easily with the emergent polarizing worldview, enthusiastically backing Stalin. Wells, meanwhile, seemed by 1934 to have accepted the idea that the Soviet Union was 'being governed and... getting on'.[77] Yet he also tried to retain his socialist internationalism and his belief in freedom of expression, in the face of divisive Soviet nationalism and the empty 'self-criticism' that stood in for real debate there. Keynes was working on his *General Theory*, which would oppose

[74] Wells, *Experiment in Autobiography*, ii, 800.
[75] Skidelsky, *John Maynard Keynes*, 516.
[76] Shaw, and others, *Stalin-Wells Talk*, 34, 33.
[77] Wells, *Experiment in Autobiography*, ii, 800.

the revolutionary collectivism of the Soviet Union with a vision of a mixed economy, in which 'the necessary measures of socialisation can be introduced gradually and without a break in the general traditions of society'.[78]

The *General Theory* was to be the definitive economic textbook of the post-war period, establishing the basis of Western social democracy until the OPEC crisis of 1973. As this chapter has shown, some if its ideas were formed in an intense debate with some of the century's most prominent imaginative writers. The inter-war debate about the Soviet Union, as exemplified by the Stalin-Wells talk, suggests that in this period there was a closer, more interactive relationship between literary writers and the levers of power—between the intelligentsia and the state—than has sometimes been assumed.

[78] John Maynard Keynes, *The General Theory of Employment, Interest and Money* (Basingstoke: Palgrave, 2007), 378.

12

The Tempo of Revolution

British Film Culture and Soviet Cinema in the 1920s

Laura Marcus

In the 1920s the new Soviet cinema had an influence in Britain which somewhat displaced the earlier enthusiasm, amongst those turning to film as a new artistic medium, for German Expressionist cinema. Films such as Robert Wiene's *The Cabinet of Dr Caligari* (*Das Cabinet des Dr. Caligari*, 1919) had, for many viewers, represented the birth and development of 'film as an art' in the early 1920s. Soviet cinema began to make its mark towards the end of the decade. This chapter explores the impact of Soviet cinema and film theory on British film culture, and the routes through which knowledge of Soviet film and theory (in particular that of Sergey Eizenshtein and Vsevolod Pudovkin) entered Britain. It looks at developments in writing about cinema, the establishment of film fora, including film societies, and the anti-censorship movements of the period, and suggests that negotiations with and around censorship contributed in important ways to the shaping of film aesthetics and film theory in its early years. One of the express functions of the film journals which were set up in the late 1920s and early 1930s (which included *Close Up*, *Film Art*, and *Experimental Cinema*) was to provide some visual access to films for which it was difficult to gain exhibition or which had been banned by the censors. This was particularly significant for the reception of Soviet cinema in Britain, during a period in which censorship laws did much to prevent the screening and viewing of Soviet film.

The entry of images from the films of Eizenshtein or Pudovkin into twentieth-century art and literature, and into the cultural imaginary more broadly, was often mediated through the film still or strip. For the artist Francis Bacon, images from Eizenshtein's 1925 film *Battleship Potemkin* (*Bronenosets Potemkin*), acted as a permanent touchstone—not least those of the sides of rotten, maggot-infested meat which, in the film, lead the sailors to mutiny. As Martin Harrison records, Bacon's 'working documents' included a torn leaf from Roger Manvell's *Film* (1944, revised edition 1946), with stills from *Potemkin*'s 'Odessa Steps' sequence.[1] In 1949, the critic Robert Melville noted the relationship between Bacon's *Head VI* and this

[1] Martin Harrison, *Francis Bacon: Photography, Film and the Practice of Painting* (London: Thames and Hudson, 2005), 96.

sequence, a connection confirmed when Bacon painted his *Study for the Nurse in the Film 'Battleship Potemkin'* (1957). Bacon returned obsessively to the image of the screaming schoolteacher, the figure he interpreted as a nurse, focusing in earlier paintings on the open mouth (which would also recapitulate the image of the gaping mouth of the woman who appears earlier in the sequence, and which David Mellor describes as the 'primordial cinematic scream for Bacon'), and later on the shattered pince-nez. Discussing his series of paintings of screaming Popes, Bacon told David Sylvester: 'I wanted to paint the scream more than the horror'.[2]

The pince-nez of *Battleship Potemkin* would also play a prominent role in Samuel Beckett's silent *Film* (1965). *Film*, which revolves around scenarios of looking (or staring) and looking away, reveals the influence of Dziga Vertov's *Man with a Movie Camera* (*Chelovek s kinoapparatom*, 1929), in particular its image of the 'kino-eye', and was, indeed, filmed by Vertov's brother, Boris Kaufman. The echoes of *Potemkin* emerge in Beckett's replication of Eizenshtein's transfer of the eyeglass between figures on the screen, and in its staging of a sequence in which a woman, wearing a pince-nez, opens her mouth in an expression of horror which mirrors or mimics that of Eizenshtein's wounded schoolteacher. In a later sequence in *Film*, an elderly woman collapses on the stairs of a house, while, at the film's close, the face of Buster Keaton (the central figure in the film) is shown wearing a single eyepatch which becomes a visual reference to the damaged eye and shattered eyeglass of the figure in *Potemkin*.

Bacon's most direct reworkings of Eizenshtein's imagery, like those of Samuel Beckett, were produced two or three decades after the period on which this chapter focuses—the late 1920s, when Eizenshtein's films were first shown in Britain, in restricted conditions and after many battles with the censors. Eizenshtein's images of revolution, war, and violence were overlaid for Bacon by the imagery of the Second World War, including Nazi imagery, becoming a palimpsest of the violence of the twentieth century. It seems likely, however, that Bacon would first have encountered *Battleship Potemkin* at the Film Society screening in London on Sunday 10 November 1929, where it was shown in a programme which included *Drifters* by the British documentarist, John Grierson. The screaming mouths of the 'Odessa steps' sequence and the tempo of the 'storm', which brings to a close Pudovkin's epic film about Genghis Khan, *Storm over Asia* (as *Potomok Chingiskhana* (*The Heir to Genghis Khan*) was retitled in Britain), became the most emphatic images or markers of Soviet politics and of the power of the cinema to reorder reality and move the spectator. For this reason, they were among the elements of Soviet film most disturbing to the censors.

The censorship of Soviet films, in Britain, continental Europe, and America, played a determining role in the ways in which film culture developed in the 1920s and 1930s. The theatre and film critic Huntly Carter, who travelled widely through Eastern Europe in the 1920s, gathering material on the new Russian theatre and

[2] Quoted in Matthew Gale and Chris Stephens, eds, *Francis Bacon* (London: Tate Publishing, 2008), 21, 59, 94–5.

cinema, wrote in *The New Spirit in the Cinema* (1930): 'The Art of the Cinema tendency is to-day a very involved one owing to its close association with the crusade against censorship'. 'The Bolshevist pictures', in Carter's words, 'had the effect of inciting the aesthetes into rebellion against the censorship. The English censor's attitude towards revolutionary pictures lashed them into fury. Then came the "Talkie" to add fuel to the flame.'[3] The cinematic institutions which developed significantly as a response to, or way of skirting, censorship, included the film journal *Close Up*, which ran from 1927 to 1933, and which published the first English translations of articles by Eizenshtein, as well as numerous stills from the new Soviet cinema. Its editors were the young Scottish artist Kenneth Macpherson and the writer Bryher (Winifred Ellerman), who was also the author of one of the earliest studies of this cinema, entitled *Film Problems of Soviet Russia* (1929).

Close Up was edited in Switzerland, where it was possible to see French, German, American, and British films in the same week, as the poet H. D. (Hilda Doolittle), one of the journal's central contributors in its first years, noted. The editors' frequent visits to Berlin provided them with much of their copy, and the city (of speed and spectacle) itself became for them an image of the Kino. While censorship certainly operated in Germany at this time, with *Potemkin* being drastically re-edited at junctures throughout the late 1920s, it was still possible to see a range of Soviet films that had not been cleared for exhibition in Britain. In the words of Huntly Carter: 'Several revolutionary pictures have been established in Berlin which have not been permitted to be shown in this country. Owing to the fairly large number of Bolshevist pictures exhibited in Berlin, that city has of late become the Mecca of the aesthete in search of adventures among revolutionary films, and of evidence by which he may slay the British censor.'[4]

The late 1920s and early 1930s were the 'Berlin years' of W. H. Auden, Stephen Spender, and Christopher Isherwood, for whom the experience of the city was not only highly sexualized ('To Christopher, Berlin meant Boys', Isherwood wrote) but also cinematic: the question of censorship and repression, and the freedom from their constraints represented by Weimar Berlin, prevailed in both arenas.[5] Spender later described the significance of the Russian films he and Isherwood saw at this time, including *Earth* (*Zemlya*), *The General Line* (*Staroe i novoe,* literally *The Old and the New*), *Mother (Mat')*, *Potemkin*, *October: Ten Days that Shook the World* (*Oktyabr': Desyat' dnei, kotorye potryasli mir*), and *The Way into Life* (*Putevka v zhizn'*):

> These films, which form a curiously isolated episode in the aesthetic history of this century, excited us because they had the modernism, the poetic sensibility, the satire, the visual beauty, all those qualities we found most exciting in other forms of modern art, but they also conveyed a message of hope like an answer to *The Waste Land.* They extolled a heroic attitude which had not yet become officialized; in this they foreshadowed the defiant individualism of the Spanish Republicans. We used to go

[3] Huntly Carter, *The New Spirit in the Cinema* (London: Harold Shaylor, 1930), 277, 284.
[4] Carter, *The New Spirit in the Cinema*, 277.
[5] Christopher Isherwood, *Christopher and his Kind* (London: Methuen, 1977), 10.

> long journeys to little cinemas in the outer suburbs of Berlin, and there among the grimy tenements we saw the images of the New Life of the workers building with machine tools and tractors their socially just world under the shadows of baroque statues reflected in ruffled waters of Leningrad, or against waving, shadow-pencilled plains of corn.[6]

Soviet films, Spender suggested, played a central role in their 'restless and awakening mood', projecting images of a different kind of landscape and a different organization of society in, and onto, the decaying facades of Berlin.

In 1929 Eizenshtein and Pudovkin visited Britain and lectured in London, in the months during which *Battleship Potemkin* was screened at the Film Society. The Film Society was another significant institution which emerged as an attempt to bypass local and governmental controls of film exhibition: it was set up by a group of young cineastes in 1925, foremost among them Ivor Montagu. Montagu, the 'youngest son', the title he gave his autobiography, of an aristocratic family (his father was the banker Louis Montagu, Lord Swaythling), became a member of the Communist Party in 1929. He travelled to the Soviet Union for the first time in 1925, soon after leaving Cambridge and visiting Berlin to find about its film culture, though he was unsuccessful in his attempts to arrange, with the Soviet film industry, exhibition through the Film Society: 'I tried hard to explain censorship restrictions on public shows in Britain, the commercial control of cinemas and all the familiar rest, but the idea of a special society that might be outside the operation of the market, and laws that might exempt it from control or censorship, was quite untranslatable into terms credible to Soviet understanding.'[7]

Montagu returned from this and subsequent trips to the Soviet Union with numerous film stills, which, in the mid-late 1920s, he used to illustrate articles on the cinema to which access was still being denied in Britain. He also became the translator of a number of works by Soviet directors and theorists, most notably Pudovkin in the early 1930s. In 1929, he published a pamphlet on 'The Political Censorship of Films', a topic on which his frequent dealings with the London County Council and the British Board of Film Censors had made him highly expert. The British Board of Film Censors Report for the year ending 31 December 1928 gives an indication of the topics to which 'exceptions' might be taken (I have selected from a much longer list):

> Exceptions taken:
>
> Political:
>
> 1. References to H.R.H. the Prince of Wales
> 2. Libellous reflections on Royal Dynasties
> 3. British Possessions represented as lawless sinks of iniquity

[6] Stephen Spender, *World within World: The Autobiography of Stephen Spender* (London: Hamish Hamilton, 1951), 132–3.

[7] Ivor Montagu, *The Youngest Son: Autobiographical Characters* (London: Lawrence and Wishart, 1970), 301.

4. Themes likely to wound the just susceptibilities of Friendly Nations
5. White men in state of degradation amidst Far Eastern and Native surroundings
6. Equivocal situations between white girls and men of other races

Social:

3. Girls and women in state of intoxication
23. Son falling in love with his father's mistress
24. Employee selling his wife to employer to cover defalcations

Questions of Sex:

9. Indecorous bathroom scenes.[8]

1929 was also the year in which Montagu became actively involved in the London Workers' Film Society and joined the Executive Council of the newly founded Federation of Workers' Film Societies (along with John Grierson, Henry Dobb, Oswell Blakeston, Ben Davies, and Ralph Bond), although he retained a seat on the Film Society council. The Film Society's original patrons were prominent figures on the social scene and in the arts and politics; it had a strong Bloomsbury presence and was set up, in large part, to show the new European avant-garde and experimental cinema at a time in which the question of whether film was an art was becoming central. It was the arrival of the new Soviet cinema in the mid-1920s that turned the focus towards politics as well as aesthetics. The Film Society's screenings of Soviet films were instrumental in shaping an emergent film criticism: as one writer for *Close Up* noted, 'when Pudovkin's Mother was shown by the Film Society it set London agog for a week. The weekly ration of film news in every paper was largely taken up with Russian films and their producers'.[9]

The London Workers' Film Society, and the numerous film societies that grew up in this period in Britain (in Birmingham, Manchester, Salford, Glasgow, Edinburgh), following their establishment in a number of West European countries, were overtly political from the outset. They were founded, as the Dutch film historian Bert Hogenkamp notes (and as James Smith discusses in the next chapter of this volume), 'as a direct response to the censorship's interference with the exhibition of Soviet films. The film society as a legal and organisational form offered the possibility to get round censorship measures; bourgeois film societies had proved that this could be done in the name of Art.' The Soviet films, Hogenkamp further argues,

> acted as the workers' film society movement's indispensable 'capital'. They shaped the image of the societies towards the membership, the press, and last but not least the authorities. The Soviet films were appreciated for a complex of political and artistic reasons which it is not easy to disentangle.[10]

[8] Ivor Montagu Collection, British Film Institute, Item 63.
[9] Hay Chowl, 'Propaganda', *Close Up*, 4, no. 1 (January 1929), 27.
[10] Bert Hogenkamp, *Deadly Parallels: Film and the Left in Britain 1929–39* (London: Lawrence and Wishart, 1986), 31, 65.

Hogenkamp, and other film historians, have drawn a sharp divide between the 'bourgeois film societies'—the London-based Film Society foremost among them—and the Workers' Film Societies. It is certainly the case that the Film Society, with its higher subscription rates, was from its inception in 1925 allowed by the London County Council. to show uncensored films to its members, and that it gained permission to screen films—*Potemkin* and *Mother* amongst them—which was frequently denied to the Workers' Film Societies and to groups such as the Masses Stage and Film Guild. Yet Huntly Carter, as a contemporary observer of the scene, if a somewhat eccentric one, noted the 'strangely variegated legion' that had arisen among three organizations in the late 1920s 'for the purpose of making war on censorship... [and] of exhibiting moving pictures with a cinematographic, social or revolutionary interest'.[11] The three groups Carter referred to were the Film Society and, by association, *Close Up* (which he placed on the political Right), the Masses Stage and Film Guild (Centre), and The Federation of Workers' Film Societies' (Left). Carter's schema here is in fact reproduced from his earlier study, *The New Theatre and Cinema of Soviet Russia* (1924), in which he divided the new theatre of the Soviet Union into the same divisions, defining 'the Right Group' as including 'all theatres which are tolerated rather than sanctioned by the Government and Left extremists'.[12]

From the perspectives of the censors and government bodies wary of the ways in which Soviet cinema might impact on British politics, *Close Up*, the Film Society, and the Workers' Film Societies were certainly connected. A memorandum, issued by the Conservative Party Headquarters, 'on revolutionary film propaganda, carried out in England by direction of the Soviet government, 1927–May 1930', linked the activities of *Close Up* and the Film Society (along with Ralph Bond's Atlas Films Ltd and the London Workers' Film Society) to those of 'the Communist Party of Great Britain supported by the Komintern'.[13] A reference to 'this accelerated "tempo" of propaganda', instanced by addresses to the Film Society by Pudovkin and Eizenshtein, suggests that the activity around Soviet cinema (including anti-censorship campaigns) was itself perceived as if it were a Soviet film: a *Potemkin*, perhaps, celebrated for its 'rhythm' and 'tempo', whose banning by the Home Secretary Sir William Joynson-Hicks had outraged writers and intellectuals on the Left. *Battleship Potemkin* had first arrived in Britain during September 1926, a few months after the General Strike in May 1926: the censor chosen to view the film was General J. C. Hanna, who was, as James Richardson has written, 'notoriously unsympathetic to revolutionary tendencies', and the film was rejected after BBC consultation with Joynson-Hicks, 'who was hostile to the cinema in general'.[14]

It was Montagu's persistence that finally led to the acquisition of a print of the film, procured from the Soviet film delegation, in Berlin, and its screening at the

[11] Carter, *The New Spirit in the Cinema*, 285.

[12] Huntly Carter, *The New Theatre and Cinema of Soviet Russia* (London: Chapman and Dodd, 1924), 256.

[13] Conservative Party Memorandum, Film Society Collection, British Film Institute, Item 16.

[14] James C. Robertson, *Hidden Cinema: British Film Censorship in Action, 1913–1972* (London: Routledge, 1993), 29–30.

Film Society in November 1929—its last significant exhibition before the Second World War. The programme notes which accompanied the screening on this occasion, written by Montagu, gave an account of the film's vicissitudes at the hands of the censors:

> The negative has so often been cut and matched to meet the requirements of various countries that it is now more difficult to draw a perfect positive and the present print is not entirely satisfactory. It is shown by courtesy of the U.S.S.R. Trade Delegation on Berlin and Messrs. Brunel and Montagu Ltd, and, unlike any other copy previously shown outside Russia, is complete; following, in arrangement and colour, the original nearly exactly.

The notes called attention to the divergence between 'the story shown in the film' and 'the historical incident'. While 'the cause and course of the mutiny are exact', Montagu wrote, the film re-ordered events: in the historical incident, the exposure of the slain soldier on the Mole at Odessa 'led to riots in the town culminating at night in the arson of a part of the dockyard. The massacre on the flight of steps, which appears in the film as entirely wanton, was subsequent to the burning of the dockyard.' One can only speculate about Montagu's emphases here, but it would seem that he was striving for an effect of political neutrality: the massacre on the Odessa steps was in fact a fictional dimension of Eizenshtein's film.

Montagu's programme notes continued with an account of the film's techniques: 'In viewing this film it must be recalled that "Potemkin" was the first Russian film in which those remarkable methods of expression—the use of non-acting materials and the incitement to hysteria by means of rhythmic cutting—were attempted... It is important to note that the work of Eisenstein and Alexandrov, unlike that of Pudovkin, contains rarely any content effective in itself: its effect depends nearly entirely on the technical visual rhythm.' It is for this reason, Montagu concluded, that the films 'are most effective only when this visual rhythm is emphasized by aural rhythm', and to Edmund Meisel's music, composed specially for the film and to be conducted at the Film Society's performance, 'is attributed much of the success of "Potemkin" outside U.S.S.R. Indeed it is recorded that at Stuttgart, though the film itself was permitted, the music was forbidden as *staatsgefährlich*!'[15]

Montagu's emphasis on *Potemkin*'s affect is significant, as is his use of the term 'hysteria', which arises time and again in discussions of the cinema of this period, sometimes as 'screen hysteria'. Bryher made the term the target of her attack on censorship laws, and the furore over Soviet cinema, in her introduction to *Film Problems of Soviet Russia*: 'the stock phrase of Fleet Street is "the enjoyment of Russia films is a species of hysteria"'. For the critics, she writes, 'Russian films are not art, they are hysteria partially induced by mass-feeling and hysterical music'. It was impossible, she argues, to have a neutral discussion of Russian film art: 'Either, it appears, you must be prepared to bayonet your aunt because she wont [*sic*] read Karl Marx, or else you must leave the room because *Potemkin* is mentioned.'[16]

[15] *The Film Society Programmes, 1925–1939* (New York: Arno Press, 1972), 130, 131.

[16] Bryher, *Film Problems of Soviet Russia* (Territet: POOL, 1929), 12, 11.

The term 'hysteria' had been present in some of the earliest discussion of cinema, and in a variety of contexts: the American writer on film and theatre Victor Freeburg, for example, wrote in the early 1920s of the ways in which film's speed, quick close-ups, 'large violent movements on the screen', and stark contrasts between black and white tones 'hurt the eyes', producing 'pictorial hysterics'.[17] In a different context, Huntly Carter, in his *The New Spirit in the Cinema*, quoted an article from the *Daily Express*:

> We are still overshadowed by the hysteria and the urge to live recklessly for the moment that were bred in the days of the Great War. Physical life becomes infinitely precious in the face of death; and though we are ten years away from that period of ecstasy and animalism we have not emerged from the mental morass which it engendered. Sex in all its attributes was summoned to the surface by the war; and we still move and think—aided by books, films, and plays—in a welter of sex.[18]

While the Soviet director Abram Room's film *Bed and Sofa* (*Tret'ya meshchanskaya*), which centres upon the relationship that develops between a woman and the male friend of her husband who comes to stay in their small flat, came up against the British censors on the grounds of its sexual candour ('Subject: Overcrowding: wife alternates with husband's friend: Exception: Offensive to English moral code'), it was, by and large, Hollywood cinema, not Soviet film, which was represented as a sex-machine. Soviet cinema represented a different, and perhaps more dangerous form of arousal. It too, however, was rendered in strongly physiological and somatic terms (as it was in Eizenshtein's film theories), so that the dangers of sexual and political 'arousal', the 'rhythms' of arousal, were more intertwined than they might at first appear.

Attack and defence at this time moved back and forth between the question of Soviet cinema and politics, and Soviet cinema and film technique, though for Eizenshtein the two were not, of course, separable. While support for Soviet film art came to be at the heart of *Close Up*'s project, its editors tended to steer a middle line politically, arguing for Russian films as 'art' and as 'truth'. H. D. wrote, in an article on 'Russian Films', that 'the greatness of the Moscow art productions that it was my unique privilege to see last month in Berlin, puts the question of the Russian film ... on a plane transcending politics. These films do not say to the British or the American workman, go and do likewise. They say look, we are your brothers, and this is how we suffered.'[19]

Bryher's *Film Problems of Soviet Russia* was one of the earliest English-language studies of Soviet film: Huntly Carter's *The New Theatre and Cinema of Soviet Russia* (1924) had devoted only one chapter to the cinema. Bryher's study was a striking achievement, in its coverage of a very large number of Russian films, many of which she viewed in Berlin in under a year. The book devoted individual chapters

[17] Victor O. Freeburg, *Pictorial Beauty on the Screen* (New York: Macmillan, 1923), 36.

[18] F. G. H. Salusbury, *Daily Express* (11 September 1929), quoted in Carter, *The New Spirit in the Cinema*, 174–5.

[19] H. D., 'Russian Films', *Close Up*, 3, no. 3 (September 1928), 25.

to the directors Lev Kuleshov, Eizenshtein, Pudovkin, and Room (from whom, Bryher writes, she gathered 'biographical data' wherever possible), while other chapters explore 'the sociological film', the Ukrainian film organization 'the Wufku' (short for Vseukrains'ke fotokinoupravlinnya, the All-Ukrainian Photography and Cinema Administration), and 'educational films'. The dominant purpose of *Film Problems of Soviet Russia* was to introduce British readers to a film culture to which they were denied access and, in tandem with *Close Up*'s censorship petition, alongside other similar initiatives, to promote a reform of the censorship laws as they related to cinema.

In her introduction Bryher wrote: 'The present attitude to Russian films in England is dangerous on account of the inconceivable stupidity of the authorities. They are investing a work of art with the terror and power which the forest negro credits to a fetish.' She returned repeatedly to the position that no revolution had fomented in Germany and Austria, despite the relative ease of access to the Soviet cinema. She argued, moreover, that the average complacent and insular British audience would, in all likelihood, remain untouched by a *Potemkin* if it were to be freely screened. At points in the text she insisted that Russia was not England, and would never follow the same path; at others she wrote (as in her discussion of Pudovkin's *Mother*) that one should 'forget about Russia and remember that *Mother* fundamentally is the story of many English homes, with disease or stagnation, or the Colonies as a substitute for the ending'. 'One of the great film problems of Russia', she argued, was that the universal situations its films depicted (she instanced the father and son relationship in Yury Stabavoy's *Two Days,* a film banned in Germany at the time of her writing) were censored purely because they were set 'in the environment of the Revolution'. As she noted towards the close of the book, only twenty or so of the hundred to hundred and fifty films made in the Soviet Union were available abroad, chiefly in Germany: 'It is to be hoped that united protest by English desirous of intellectual liberty will remove the barrier to our cinematographic development and that we shall be able to study the new Russian films as they appear.'[20]

For the most part Bryher's critical approach was descriptive, thematic and sociological (though Huntly Carter accused her of shifting the focus from sociology to aesthetics), focusing on the history of the film industry in the Soviet Union, the specificities of Soviet film technique, in particular 'cutting', and, most particularly, the questions of education (which she differentiated from politics) and of women's social situation. Nonetheless, her detailed, linear accounts of Soviet films (which 'walk' readers through films that they are presumed not to have seen) also sought to convey their power and drama: Eizenshtein's *October: Ten Days that Shook the World* is 'all rhythm, all movement...of all the films I know, I feel it to be the greatest...There is not a shot in the picture that has not been created by mind alone.' In her account of Pudovkin's *The End of St Petersburg* (*Konets Sankt-Peterburga*), she returned to, and redefined, the terms of 'hysteria', in relation to

[20] Bryher, *Film Problems of Soviet Russia,* 11, 56, 116.

the film's representations of 'war hysteria', drawing upon the imagery of the close of *Storm over Asia*:

> The cumulative effect upon the spectator of the scenes of hysteria upon the outbreak of war, followed by the trenches and Lebedeff sequence cross cutting with each other, cannot be described. Pudovkin is vehement, personal, the Euripides of the screen, where Eisenstein is the Aeschylus. Where injustice has burnt him, he cannot let his anger go. He is at his best with storm, following an emotion, loosing his visual sense in a hurricane till everything but the bones of the incident are swept away in the wind.[21]

Storm over Asia was particularly charged for British spectators, and British censors, because of its attacks on colonialism and its perceived anti-British sentiment. ('Subject: Mongol overthrow of foreign adventurers. Exception: Conduct of troops in British uniform'). Leonard and Virginia Woolf saw the film in Berlin in 1929, in the company of Vanessa Bell, Duncan Grant, Edward Sackville-West, Vita Sackville-West, and Harold Nicolson. In a letter to Roger Fry, Vanessa Bell described the experience, and its stormy, or 'thundery', aftermath:

> The film seemed to me extraordinary—there were the most lovely pictures of odd Chinese types, very well done. I enjoyed it immensely & was under the impression that everyone else did too until we got out on into the street when it appeared that feeling was running very high on the question whether it was anti-British propaganda! No doubt it was—at least the feeblest part of it consisted of the flight of soldiers in British uniforms flying from Asiatics. Vita again enraged Leonard by asking him 6 times whether he thought they were meant for Englishmen—she and Harold both thought they weren't but managed to quarrel with each other all the same. The discussion went on & on, all standing in the melting snow, & the general rage & uneasiness was increased by Eddy who was also of the party... Never have I spent quite such a thundery evening.[22]

The image of the storm as a way of representing the overwhelming impact of the new Soviet cinema emerged repeatedly in the film criticism of the time, with *Close Up* contributors giving their articles titles such as 'Storm over Berlin' and 'Storm over London'. In his *Close Up* review, '*Storm over Asia*—and Berlin!', Kenneth Macpherson wrote of the film (with reference to the censors), 'however they quieten it and calm it down it will remain Storm, with lightning and thunder and rain and wind and fury'.[23] Robert Herring's article, 'Storm over London', by contrast, shifted the terms of the debate to Pudovkin's visit to London, and in particular his lecture material on sound imagery and contrapuntal sound (in which sound would be non-coincident with visual imagery): 'Pudovkin would combine the fury of an angry man with the roar of a lion. Think what that means.'[24] Herring's discussion

[21] Bryher, *Film Problems of Soviet Russia*, 37–8, 60.

[22] Quoted in Quentin Bell, *Virginia Woolf: A Biography*, 2 vols (London: Hogarth Press, 1972), ii, 142. In a footnote, Bell writes of his mother's letter: 'I do not think that Harold Nicolson doubted that the film was an attack upon British Imperialism in Asia. Vita may have had her doubts. Harold's position was made painful by the fact that he was his country's representative and that at the end of the film there was a small demonstration in the audience which could have been considered anti-British'.

[23] Kenneth Macpherson, 'Storm over Asia—and Berlin!', *Close Up*, 4, no. 1 (January 1929), 39.

[24] Robert Herring, 'Storm over London', *Close Up*, 4, no. 3 (March 1929), 38.

thus translated the terms of radical politics into film technique, while at the same time it repeated from Pudovkin's lecture, subsequently published in *The Cinema* on 6 February 1929, an image ('I can join the fury of a man to the roar of a lion') that would inevitably have conjured up one of the most striking montage sequences in Eizenshtein's *Potemkin*: that of the 'sleeping' stone lions on the Odessa Steps awakened and become rampant.

Huntly Carter was critical of the Film Society for 'pos[ing] as a harmless school of technique', as a way of evading the censors.[25] The Marxist film critic Harry Alan Potamkin, writing in the American film journal *Experimental Cinema,* took Bryher's *Film Problems of Soviet Russia* to task for representing the Russian film as 'entirely harmless . . . But the Russian idea is dangerous, decidedly dangerous to the prevailing acceptations. The dangerous idea creates the dangerous, or heroic structure—ultimately'.[26] It is, in this light, surprising that *Experimental Cinema*, whose politics and whose editor, Seymour Stern, were avowedly Marxist, should have, in their numerous discussions of Soviet film, included so many articles whose approach seemed so purely formalist. The film theorist and historian Lewis Jacobs wrote in the first issue of *Experimental Cinema*, in February 1930:

> It was not until the projection of the Soviet film 'Potemkin' that the cinema became aware of its individuality . . . Eisenstein achieved his results not by any emphasis of actor or acting, plot or setting, but by an *arithmetical relationship* of the projection of images in *time, movement* and *image content*: each projection of *image* in *movement and time* paralleled and reverted and carried the component projections in a rhythmic, and psychological relation to one another, and at the same time unreeled Eisenstein's 'theme' in cadences strictly cineplastic . . . . Omitting the few abstract films for the moment, 'Potemkin' was the beginning of aesthetic form in the cinema insofar as it was the first instance of a film which expressed the essential idea (theme) in terms of cinema and came into existence only and entirely through the particular of its medium—the film.

This emphasis on medium-specificity, evidenced in many of the articles in *Experimental Cinema*, might seem like a typically modernist gesture (and one, incidentally, at odds with Eizenshtein's insistence in his lectures and essays on the continuities between film and the other arts—literature, painting, theatre, music.) It can also be understood, however, in more strategic terms. Jacobs' discussion included a '*Censorship note*', in which he wrote: 'An alteration of any unit in such an ensemble would destroy the existing relations and ruin that particular psychological and cineplastic unity. It is this combination of all forms that constitutes value, aesthetically important in proportion as the synthesis is complete.'[27] While arguments for Soviet cinema on formal and aesthetic grounds might have been a way of distracting from the political content, it may also have been the case that arguments made on these terms—the claim that each

[25] Carter, *The New Spirit in the Cinema*, 290.

[26] Harry Alan Potamkin, review of Bryher, *Film Problems of Soviet Russia*, in *Experimental Cinema: A Monthly Projecting Important International Film Manifestations*, 1, no. 1 (February 1930), 3.

[27] Lewis Jacobs, 'The New Cinema: A Preface to Film Form', *Experimental Cinema*, 1 (February 1930), 14.

element of the film is essential to its aesthetic 'unity', that in Soviet montage meaning derives not from individual shots but from the relationships between images—were attempts to defend against the censors' scissors. As Herbert Jehring wrote of the cuts and excisions made to *Battleship Potemkin* in Germany in 1926:

> The whole structure, the phenomenal dynamism of the action, the intercutting of portraits and mass meetings, the contrast of the menacingly calm march of the Cossacks with the alarmed population, the rhythm, the inflammable power—all have been lost. The best proof of the merit of the film and of the mediocrity of its re-editing is that with the destruction of its human rationale it also lost its artistic quality. Eizenshtein's work was killed for Germany. Precisely because the effect of the film is calculated and arranged with such subtlety, it was possible to make cuts only with great prudence (as was done in the first German re-editing).[28]

In sum, we might note the strongly, if covertly, political dimensions of the formalist approach, and the profound impact on film aesthetics of both Soviet film and of the censorship which sought to suppress it.

The lectures given in London by Eizenshtein and Pudovkin in 1929 played a significant role in the intellectual and political understanding of Soviet cinema and film theory. In February 1929, Pudovkin came to London's New Gallery Cinema at the invitation of Ivor Montagu for the first British screening of *The End of St Petersburg*.[29] During this visit Pudovkin also delivered an address to the Film Society on 'Types as Opposed to Actors', which became central to the tenets of the British documentary film movement. The talk was an explication of 'montage principles', and included a description of the Kuleshov-Pudovkin experiments with cutting between static, inexpressive close-ups of an actor's face and various shots—a bowl of soup, a dead woman in a coffin, a little girl playing with a toy bear. Audiences, it was said, found in the actor's blank expression the intense emotions of hunger, grief, and joy respectively. Pudovkin linked this to his preferred use of non-actors in films: he discussed the acting 'honours' of the Mongols in his *Storm over Asia*.[30] He ended the talk with a discussion of the use of sound in film (the material to which Robert Herring referred in his 'Storm over London') and the potential for non-synchronous and contrapuntal sound; the most influential account of this had come in the joint statement written by Eizenshtein, Pudovkin, and Aleksandrov, published for the first time in the October 1928 issue of *Close Up*, and taken up in the national and regional press. The questions of sound working contrapuntally to sight, and of 'sound used not realistically but as a kind of expressive commentary on visual action', proved to be powerful concepts.[31] They would find expression in the literature of the 1930s (in, for example, the work of Virginia Woolf and Graham Greene) and in a number of British documentary films, in which the conventional 'Voice of God' commentary was supplemented, and at times undermined, by more radical and experimental uses of sound.

[28] Herbert Jehring, *Berliner Börsen-Courier,* July 28, 1926, quoted in Herbert Marshall, ed., *The Battleship Potemkin* (New York: Avon Books, 1978), 144.

[29] See Amy Sargeant, *Storm over Asia* (London: I. B. Tauris, 2007), 68.

[30] V. I. Pudovkin, *Film Technique*, trans. Ivor Montagu (London: George Newnes, 1933), 143.

[31] Charles Davy, *Yorkshire Post* (29 October 1929).

The concept of 'types' and 'typage' which Pudovkin explored would also become central to the British documentarists' theory and practice. For the documentary film-maker and theorist Paul Rotha, 'if there are human beings they are secondary to the main theme. Their private passions and petulances are of little interest. For the most part they perform their natural behaviour as in normal life... They are types selected from the many, portraying the mind and character of this or that social group.' The tenets of 'typage' would, however, be contested, both in the Soviet Union and elsewhere, and Rotha himself came to feel that audience identification required a focus on the individual story: 'If the masses are interested in seeing individuals and following their emotions on the screen, then documentary must embrace individuals... We must go into the streets and homes and factories to meet them.'[32]

The articles containing the substance of Eizenshtein's 1929 London lectures were 'The Principles of Film Form', 'The Filmic Fourth Dimension', and 'Methods of Montage', which were later published in the collection *Film Form*, but made their first appearance in the pages of *Close Up*, with 'The Principles of Film Form' also appearing in *Experimental Cinema*. The lectures themselves were later recalled by the literary critic Jack Isaacs and the documentary film-maker Basil Wright, in a BBC radio broadcast. As Isaacs stated, 'here was someone laying down, (and we must remember laying down for the first time), the laws and principles of the youngest of the arts, an art no older than most of us in the audience'. Wright and Isaacs noted Eizenshtein's insistence on film as a 'synthetic' art, and his argument that 'film montage was the *cinematic* aspect of a particular form of expression used by artists in other media—particularly poetry, painting, drama and the novel'. They also recalled his emphasis on the hieroglyph or ideogram—and the 'overtone'—'a term for that unanalysable element—that rare and wonderful aesthetic impact which comes to us only too seldom from the screen'.

In the broadcast, Wright further discussed the significance of Eizenshtein's 'instinctive' approach to film-making, 'the making of a film *to an idea*'. In making his own documentary film *Song of Ceylon*, Wright was, he stated

> working, through Eisenstein's conception of montage, to shoot everything to a central idea. By this I mean that all the filmic material—the many, many strips of celluloid depicting different scenes—was related to a central conception—no, less definite than that—a deep *feeling* about this particular island. I couldn't then, any more than I can now, express this feeling in words. It belongs strictly to the flow and movement of film visuals, and could only be expressed in that manner.

He also recalled Eizenshtein's insistence on the relationship between different levels of montage, the development of a line from the most basic to the most complex of styles and effects.[33]

The Film Society programme for Sunday 10 November 1929 included not only *Battleship Potemkin* but, screened before it, John Grierson's *Drifters*, a film on the

[32] Paul Rotha, *Documentary Film* (London: Faber, 1936), 142, 182.

[33] *Eisenstein's Lectures in London: A Reconstruction by Basil Wright and J. Isaacs* (BBC Third Programme, 17 December 1949, 10.05–10.45 p.m.), transcript in the Film Society Collection, British Film Institute.

home fishing industry which Grierson had been commissioned to make in late 1927. Grierson's indebtedness to Eizenshtein and other Soviet film-makers, and the milieu of the screening, helped situate *Drifters*, one of the first 'documentary' films, in the context of European avant-garde film culture. It is said of the Film Society screening, however, that Eizenshtein perceived Grierson's act of homage to be rather more a theft of his thunder.

The conjunction of the two films is significant. While researching in the United States, Grierson had worked on the English subtitling of *Battleship Potemkin* for American distribution, and on a critical commentary on the film. He returned to Britain in 1927, taking up employment under Stephen Tallents at the recently established Empire Marketing Board (EMB), whose role was to promote trade and economic relations between Britain and the countries of the Empire, with an initial commission to explore international developments in film-making and to set up screenings of documentary and narrative films, including Soviet cinema. In outlining his plans for the EMB to its Film Committee, he presented Soviet cinema as a model to follow, in its departure 'from the tyranny of individualism'. Describing the Broadway run of *Potemkin*, which lasted for a couple of months, he wrote that

> the film inspired more enthusiasm among its admirers than any film has ever done before. The spectator however individualistic in his outlook will dispense temporarily with an emphasis on personal fortunes the moment a picture touches the sources of his pride. A few appreciated 'Potemkin' critically for its cinematic values, but the general audiences which cheered their way through the film did so for the revolutionary cause it espoused and the pride of class to which it appealed.

Grierson made no reference to the censorship battles that had been fought in Britain and Germany the previous year. His concern, and apparently that of the Empire Marketing Board, seemed to be exclusively that of rendering popular those films which would represent to the public 'the progress of industry, the story of invention, the pioneering and developing of new lands and the exploration of lost ones, the widening horizons of commerce, the complexities of manufacture, and the range of communications: indeed in all the steam and smoke, dazzle and speed, of the world at hand, and all the strangeness and sweep, of affairs more distant'.[34] (Even Grierson's memos read like voice-over commentaries.)

'One cannot do less when recording a world revolution', Grierson wrote of *Potemkin*, 'than develop a tempo to take it, and that is what Eisenstein did more than anyone before him—from the smashing of the plate that starts and symbolizes the rebellion, through the cumulative flow of the procession in the streets of the city, to the violence and the clash of boots and faces on the stairs of Odessa'.[35] 'Quiet movement succeeding stormy movement, or stormy movement mounting to movement still stormier', he wrote of *Potemkin* in a review announcing its screening at the Film Society along with his own *Drifters*.[36] Combining Flaherty's representations of

[34] John Grierson, 'Notes for English Producers', John Grierson Archive, University of Stirling, G2A: 2:15, 12.

[35] John Grierson, 'Eisenstein and Documentary', in Marshall, ed., *The Battleship Potemkin*, 156.

[36] John Grierson, 'Films and Talkies', *The Clarion*, NS 1, no. 11 (November 1929), 11.

the natural world with the dynamic editing and symphonic structure of *Potemkin*, '*Drifters*', Grierson wrote, 'is about the sea and about fishermen, and there is not a Piccadilly actor in the piece':

> The life of Natural cinema is in this massing of detail, in this massing of all the rhythmic energies that contribute to the blazing fact of the matter. Men and the energies of men, things and the functions of things, horizons and the poetics of horizons: these are the essential materials. And one must never grow so drunk with the energies and the functions as to forget the poetics.

His discussion of the film, from which this quotation is drawn, was first published in the Left journal *The Clarion* and reprinted in *Close Up*, under the title 'Making a Film of the Actual: A Problem in Film Construction'. Grierson wrote that he had learned what he knew of cinema 'partly from the Russians, partly from the American westerns, and partly from Flaherty... The net effect of this cinematic upbringing was to make me want a storm: a real storm, an intimate storm, and if possible a rather noble storm.' The storm at sea and the physical 'agonies' of the fishermen return at the close of the film, intercut with shots of the marketplace and the 'boxing and barrelling' of the fish and, by extension, of the men's labour: 'the frenzy of a market in which said agonies are sold at ten shillings a thousand, and iced, salted and barrelled for an unwitting world'.[37]

The author of the lead article in the inaugural issue of *Workers' Cinema* (the 'Official Organ of the Federation of Workers' Film Societies'), which appeared in November 1931, wrote:

> In the Soviet Union, the film has been perfected as a social weapon—this time on behalf of the workers there and throughout the world. We have learned to borrow that weapon from out of their hands and to use it in our own struggles. Films which tell us of the world as it really is from the workers' viewpoint, films which encourage him in his struggle to possess it... *We must make more of our own films—about our own struggles and our own problems.*[38]

Reports from the regional Workers' Film Societies noted both the successful screening of Soviet cinema and continued struggles over the exhibition of banned films. The censorship battles over Soviet films in Britain continued to be a shaping influence on British film culture into the 1930s and beyond. *Potemkin* remained banned from public cinemas until 1954, when it was finally passed for exhibition by the British Board of Film Censors with an 'X' certificate.

Soviet cinema and theory also fed directly into British film and literature, creating, in Grierson's term, 'a documentary idea'. At times Grierson expressed doubts about 'the fake climax of Revolution' in the films of Pudovkin and Eizenshtein, but he nonetheless argued that the position of Soviet cinema remained unassailed.[39] As he wrote in an article on the occasion of the re-issue of Pudovkin's *Film Technique* in 1933:

[37] John Grierson, *Grierson on Documentary*, ed. Forsyth Hardy (London: Faber, 1979), 20, 19.

[38] 'The Film is a Weapon', *Workers' Cinema*, 1, no. 1 (November 1931), 2.

[39] John Grierson, 'Films and Talkies: Cinema of State', *The Clarion*, NS 2, no. 8 (August 1930), 235.

> Perhaps the one thing which the Russians have most plainly taught us in the past is that cinema has a life of its own: that objects and events should not be dumbly *reproduced* on the screen, but should be *recreated* by the screen. It is the same essential distinction which divides representational painting from the genuine work of art. On this understanding of cinema, the emphasis falls naturally on the special capacities which the cinema has for shaping movements and moods and vitalities; and the cutting bench, not the studio, becomes the holy of holies of film composition. It is the place where the different aspects of the object, or the movement, or the mass, or the mood, are brought together; where they are given cinematic identity.[40]

Grierson's assertions indicate the complex ways in which concepts of film realism and filmic construction, the given and the made, would develop, as a 'recreation of the world in its own image'.[41] The impact of Soviet film on British documentary film culture was a powerful one, shaping not only its ideas about realism but its discussions and uses of film 'symbolism', film 'rhythm' and 'tempo', the use of sound in relation to the visual image, the relationship between private and public, the question of individuals and individualism, and critiques of the 'story-film' and the film star. More broadly, the extraordinary flourishing of Soviet film and film theory in the 1920s, in the years before the increasing repression of the Stalinist era, and at a time when there was all to play for in the new medium of the cinema, created new syntheses between art and politics, avant-gardism and realism, which would have deep and lasting significance for the cultures of modernity.

[40] John Grierson, 'A First Principle of Criticism', *New Britain*, 2, no. 27 (22 November 1933), 14.

[41] André Bazin, 'The Myth of Total Cinema', in *What is Cinema?*, ed. and trans. Hugh Gray, i (Berkeley and Los Angeles, CA: University of California Press, 1971), 21.

13

Soviet Films and British Intelligence in the 1930s

The Case of Kino Films and MI5

James Smith

In her chapter in this volume, Laura Marcus details the impact Soviet film had on British film culture during the 1920s and 1930s, and suggests that the 'censorship of Soviet films... played a determining role in the ways in which film culture developed' in Britain. In this chapter, I wish to take a closer look at how one of these key censorship battles was fought, and expose the hitherto little-known role that Britain's covert intelligence and policing agencies played in attempts to suppress the dissemination of Soviet works in Britain.[1] Recent releases from the archives of the Security Service, MI5, Britain's domestic intelligence agency, have revealed the extent to which MI5 and the Metropolitan Police Special Branch were involved in surveillance of the film industry and the ostensibly independent censorship process, particularly when this concerned films deemed politically subversive or presenting propaganda material favourable to the Soviet regime. Though what is available in these archival releases is far from a complete picture, it is evident that such attention ranged from police surveillance of small amateur shows through to long-term files being maintained on key film industry figures such as Ivor Montagu, as well as records being accumulated on individual films, societies, and companies which were regarded as part of the Comintern's networks.

This chapter presents a case study of the files MI5 maintained on Kino Films, a left-wing film distribution organization that operated in Britain, under several name variations, between 1933 and 1939.[2] Founded with the expressed aim of bringing Soviet films to British audiences, but later expanding to distribute and produce a wider range of leftist feature and documentary films, Kino represented a significant cultural institution of the 1930s. Due to its success in circumventing the reach of the film censors, Kino was able to establish a nationwide film-hire network

[1] While British film censorship was supposedly conducted without governmental involvement, scholars have shown cases of Home Office intervention in the censoring of politically controversial films. For an account that examines the Home Office role in censoring *Battleship Potemkin*, see Temple Willcox, '*Soviet Films, Censorship and the British Government: A Matter of the Public Interest*', *Historical Journal of Film, Radio and Television* 10, no. 3 (1990), 275–92.

[2] The file kept on Kino Films is preserved in The National Archives in the Records of the Security Service: Organisation (OF series) Files, KV 5/42–5 (hereafter KV 5 followed by folder number).

to bring previously inaccessible Soviet films to working-class and leftist audiences in local halls and meeting places, aptly promoted with the slogan 'Show the Best Films in the World YOURSELVES'.[3]

Such commitments also meant that Kino received substantial attention from state-security organs.[4] The released MI5 file, consisting of four separate folders, contains a wide variety of material: surveillance-derived items such as intercepted letters, transcripts of tapped telephone calls, and Special Branch reports on film showings; a significant range of ephemera such as Kino's film-hire catalogues and publicity material; and also wider correspondence showing how MI5 coordinated with other organizations such as the Home Office, provincial police forces, and the British Board of Film Censors, in order to assess and respond to Kino's activity.[5] It thus presents probably the single most comprehensive source as yet available that shows security intelligence concerns with the film industry in Britain.

This chapter will therefore proceed with two aims. First, while the operations of Kino have previously attracted scholarly attention, the wide range of material accumulated by MI5, whether overtly or covertly, presents an important new source for understanding the organization and operations of Kino itself.[6] Thus this chapter will begin by outlining the context of Kino's formation, its structure and methods of operation, and its particular role in contesting film censorship in the 1930s and facilitating widespread access to important Soviet films. Second, this chapter will examine the specific surveillance activity of MI5 and the assessments that were made, in order to understand how British security agencies reacted to the attempts to disseminate Soviet films. Through this, this chapter will develop an understanding of the dynamic of covert security intelligence involvement in the monitoring and censorship of Soviet film in Britain, and contribute to the growing scholarly debate about the role western intelligence agencies played in contesting the international influence of Soviet culture.

THE ESTABLISHMENT OF KINO AND THE CONTEXTS OF FILM CENSORSHIP

In May of 1933 the Moscow Congress of the International Union of Revolutionary Theatres urged its delegates to establish film sections in their national organizations, in order to exploit the propaganda potential of film.[7] Within a few months

[3] Kino promotional flyer, c. early 1935, KV 5/42.

[4] MI5 had its origins in 1909, and from 1931 was elevated to being the main agency that monitored subversive threats occurring within Britain. Special Branch, a section of the Metropolitan Police, specialized in policing political and espionage threats.

[5] The files were released in June 2006 and consist of KV 5/42–45.

[6] For discussion of the Kino organization see, for example, Bert Hogenkamp, *Deadly Parallels: Film and the Left in Britain, 1929–1939* (London: Lawrence and Wishart, 1986).

[7] As Trevor Ryan has shown, this was not the first time that such organizations had been launched in this way: see Ryan, '"The New Road to Progress": The Use and Production of Films by the Labour Movement, 1929–39', in James Curran and Vincent Porter, eds, *British Cinema History* (London: Weidenfeld and Nicolson, 1983), 113–15.

arrangements had been made for such an organization to be launched in Britain with the formation of Kino, which was established as the film section of the Workers' Theatre Movement. Kino was initially structured as a cooperative society keeping offices at 33 Ormond Yard WC1, and was organized by Charles Mann (an influential member of the Workers' Theatre Movement) and Ivan Seruya (a Regent Street Polytechnic student involved with the Friends of the Soviet Union and the Young Communist League), and backed by Ivor Montagu. The formation was publicly announced in an article in the *Daily Worker* on 7 November 1933, with Kino's films described unequivocally as a 'weapon in the struggle', and the organization promoting itself as offering 'direct propaganda', as well as attempting to establish 'a united front of revolutionary film art together with all interested art, cultural, educational, trade union and professional organisations'. The article also set out Kino's specific mode of action, that 'starting with *Potemkin*, it is hoped soon to have ready a whole library of Soviet films available for 16 mm. apparatus', and the 'development of production groups' was also announced as a way for Kino to create its own political films in Britain.[8]

The fact that Kino was launching with *Battleship Potemkin* (*Bronenosets Potemkin*), and doing so via the mode of 16 mm film, signalled that it intended a direct challenge to the convoluted system by which British film censorship operated. While at the turn of the century the British cinema industry was largely unregulated, the introduction of the Cinematography Act of 1909 brought the public display of cinema under specific government control. The Act was initially intended only to regulate the safety of cinema venues, particularly given that the standard 35 mm film stock was highly inflammable. However, the loose wording of this act, specifying that 'inflammable films...shall not be given...elsewhere than in premises licensed for the purpose', gave local authorities the power to grant or withhold venue licenses, while leaving it open to each individual authority to determine what the actual licensing criteria should be. As a consequence, the conditions imposed quickly moved beyond issues of fire safely and into monitoring the actual content of films that the venue displayed, with each authority free to apply different standards in assessing a given film.[9]

Faced with this commercially damaging uncertainty, and fears that the Home Office could impose an even more cumbersome official state censor, the British film industry established the British Board of Film Censors (BBFC) in 1912, an ostensibly non-government body charged with viewing each film before its release and recommending its classification. Most local authorities, happy to be unburdened of the time-consuming censorship responsibility, chose to defer their decisions to the BBFC, and thus an unlegislated but largely unified film censorship regime operated in Britain. Films were liable to be censored or banned on a variety of grounds; particularly controversial was the BBFC's proclivity to censor cinema on political

[8] KV 5/42, serial 1a.

[9] See James C. Robertson, *The Hidden Cinema: British Film Censorship in Action, 1913–1975* (London: Routledge, 1989).

topics for reasons including being 'Bolshevik propaganda' or an 'incitement to class hatred'.[10] The extent of this censorship on the dissemination of important Soviet works of cinema in Britain was severe, to the extent that Aldgate and Robertson have asserted that 'between the two world wars no Soviet feature of any genre was shown in a British licensed public cinema outside London'.[11]

As Laura Marcus's chapter in this volume details, such censorship did not go uncontested, and indeed it was one of the major contributors to the growth of an avant-garde film culture in the country. Campaigns by influential journals such as *Close Up* made available still images from prohibited films and agitated to overturn the BBFC's bans. Organizations such as the London Film Society, established in 1925 by Ivor Montagu, functioned as private film clubs that managed to secure exemptions from their local authorities to show films otherwise prevented from release. However, while these organizations did indeed allow some circulation of this restricted Soviet cinema amongst the British public, only a small number of people had access to these showings.

Other organizations, however, lobbied not so much for reform or exemptions as for ways to escape entirely the censorship regime enabled by the 1909 Act, and it is here the specific genesis of Kino's activity becomes clear, and the significance of its 16 mm film stock becomes apparent. As 16 mm 'substandard' film was non-inflammable, any films shown on this medium appeared to be beyond the scope of the 1909 Act and its licensing criteria, leaving open the possibility of transferring banned 35 mm Soviet films to the 16 mm format, and thus escaping any formal control. The British Government had been aware of this potential loophole for several years, with questions asked of the Home Secretary in the House of Commons in 1931 and 1934 on film licensing legislation and the status of 16 mm films, but the legal position as to the exact status of the medium remained vague, and thus in the early years of its existence Kino operated in an uncertain political and censorship climate.[12] Cannily, though, Kino used the continued censorship of 35 mm film to its great advantage, with publicity pamphlets specifically emphasizing that all Kino's films were in the unrestricted 16 mm format. Nonetheless many police forces were unaware of the legal position of 16 mm films and continued to threaten prosecutions against showings of films in unlicensed premises. A range of reports submitted to MI5 detailed police attempts to shut viewings down, the most significant such attempt being the prosecution launched by the Durham police against showings of *Potemkin* in 1934, with the case of an unlicensed 16 mm showing at Boldon Colliery eventually going against the police in the Jarrow-on-Tyne court.[13]

With courts upholding the 'non-flam' status of 16 mm film, and pressure being put on the Home Office to resist any legislative change, it was gradually conceded

[10] John Trevelyan, *What the Censor Saw* (London: Michael Joseph, 1973), 39.

[11] Anthony Aldgate and James C. Robertson, *Censorship in Theatre and Cinema* (Edinburgh: Edinburgh University Press, 2005), 49.

[12] See, for example, 'Cinematograph Films', Hansard, HC (series 5) vol. 256, cols. 1280–1 (21 September 1931); 'Cinematograph Industry', Hansard, HC (series 5) vol. 293, cols. 339–40 (1 November 1934).

[13] Cross-reference report 'Exhibitions of 16 mm Films', 30 January 1935, KV 5/42, serial 60a.

by governmental agencies that 16 mm versions of otherwise banned films were indeed exempt, and the documents in the Kino file record the transition in police attitudes as this recognition was made. By April 1935, detectives attending a Kino showing of Vsevolod Pudovkin's *Mother* (*Mat'*, 1926) were reporting back to MI5 the 16 mm films used meant 'no licence being required or notice given to the Police' (although they still contacted the Customs and Excise Authorities to ascertain whether showings would be liable for entertainment tax, indicating another mode of potential intervention).[14] In July of the same year MI5 would inform other enquiring police forces that they 'cannot prevent' the display of 16 mm Kino films, marking a significant point in the history of film censorship in Britain;[15] although, as will be seen, the legality of Kino's operations certainly did not mark the end of MI5's interest in the Kino organization.

THE OPERATIONS OF KINO

Thus free from the censor's control, Kino underwent a period of rapid growth. Within a few years the organization had built up a large collection of 16 mm film far beyond its meagre launch with *Potemkin*. In April 1935 the Kino catalogue could boast a wide range of major feature films, listing Pudovkin's *Storm over Asia* (*Potomok Chingiskhana*, literally *The Heir of Genghis Khan*,1928) and *Mother* (1926), Grigory Kozintsev's and Leonid Trauberg's *New Babylon* (*Novyi Vavilon*, 1929), and Grigory Aleksandrov's and Sergey Eizenshtein's *The General Line* (*Staroe i novoe*, literally *The Old and the New*, 1929), as well as a range of shorter Soviet documentaries with titles such as *A Trip to Russia*, *Isotov the Bolshevik*, *Soviets Conquer the Stratosphere*, *Oil Symphony*, and the cartoon *Little Screw*. Kino would also offer the hire of its own short productions such as three *Workers' Newsreels* and *Hunger March 1934*. Within this list costs varied from £1 12*s*. 6*d*. to hire the eight reel and 110 minute *Storm over Asia*, to just 5*s*. for the single reel, 20 minute *Hunger March 1934*.[16]

By the start of 1937 Kino had acquired its first sound films, and by the peak of Kino's operations in late 1937 and early 1938, the catalogue had further swelled to contain Soviet features such as Pudovkin's *Deserter* (*Dezertir*, 1933) and *The End of St Petersburg* (*Konets Sankt-Peterburga*, 1927), Abram Room's *Ghost that Never Returns* (*Privedenie, kotoroe ne vozvrashchaetsya*, 1929), Aleksandrov's and Eizenshtein's *October: Ten Days that Shook the World* (*Oktyabr': Desyat' dnei, kotorye potryasli mir*, 1928), Viktor Turin's *Turksib* (*Turksib*, 1929), Yakov Protazanov's and Porfiry Podobed's *Marionettes* (*Marionetki*, 1934), Nikolay Ekk's *Road to Life* (*Putevka v zhizn'*, 1931), and the A. Shafron and Mark Troyanovsky documentary *Heroes of the Arctic* (*Geroi Arktiki*, 1934), as well as a range of other short propaganda films and documentaries. The catalogue also listed international films from countries other

[14] Report from Commercial Street Station, 15 April 1935, KV 5/42, serial 69a.

[15] Letter from MI5 to Chief Constable Sheffield, 12 July 1935, KV 5/43, serial 78a.

[16] The titles and prices are contained in a police extract taken from Kino film price list number 2, dated April 1935: KV 5/42, serial 68b.

than Soviet Russia, such as Georg Pabst's *Comradeship* (*Kameradschaft*, 1931) and Slatan Dudow's *Soap Bubbles* (*Seifenblasen*, 1934), and there were numerous propaganda pieces covering events such as the Spanish Civil War. Besides these international offerings, Kino also continued to distribute a number of locally-made films, such as a two-minute propaganda film for the *Daily Worker* that was distributed free to any interested organization, or *News Review 1937*, a 30-minute silent film that covered leftist trade union activity in London, British Union of Fascists demonstrations, and international events such as strikes in Trinidad.

The expansion in its film list was matched by a nationwide growth in the Kino network. Within a few years of its foundation Kino had agents in numerous regional cities, and many ordinary commercial firms would carry out shows for Kino, too.[17] Besides the large number of screenings organized by Kino itself, Kino's films were promoted for hire through Party channels, with Kino's films often booked by Communist Party branches and other Party-affiliated organizations such as the Friends of the Soviet Union and the National Unemployed Workers' Movement. However Kino would also supply a wide range of broad left-wing groups, such as Labour Party branches meetings, the Left Book Club, and trade union groups.[18] This fulfilled the aim (suggested in Kino promotional material) for such viewings not just to function as entertainment for those already allied to the Communist Party, but to act specifically as a mechanism for attracting new, unaffiliated workers to the entertainment and thus engage them with strong propaganda.[19]

Kino's activities were not just limited to providing film reels to such groups, but also extended to making available mobile film apparatus and operators, making it both legally and financially possible for small unlicensed organizations almost anywhere in the country to show films that were still banned from the standard cinema venues. In many cases Kino provided operators and 16 mm projector apparatus for those hiring its films, and Kino also organized regional tours, such as the 1935 'Summer tour of the North of England' (a tour promoted by the Central Committee of the CPGB), when Kino film operators travelled to venues with *Storm Over Asia*, offering discounted viewing and requiring branches only to arrange a darkened hall in advance for a film showing.[20] Kino was well practised in maximizing the propaganda potentialities of its network, offering to print discounted publicity handbills and posters for individual showings when bookings were made. Additionally, the London office issued regional agents a monthly bulletin advertising new films, providing advice on marketing and propaganda, and requesting feedback as to how the operation could be modified. Individuals who were organizing Kino showings were given material explaining how to maximize the propaganda effectiveness of the event, down to details such as specifying that they should 'have the hall decorated gaily with banners, posters, bunting and where possible, flowers. It pays in every way to make a meeting bright and gay and to get your audience in

[17] A copy of the Kino agent list is in KV 5/44, serial 164c.

[18] See Hogenkamp, *Deadly Parallels*, 141, for a breakdown of Kino's audiences.

[19] KV 5/43, serial 120a.

[20] Copy of interdicted Kino letter, 25 May 1935, KV 5/43, serial 71a.

as receptive a mood as possible'.[21] Consequently, the Kino network rapidly turned into a well-organized means for local organizations to view Soviet films and organize fundraising events. Trevor Ryan estimates that up to 100,000 people viewed a Kino film during the year from March 1935 until February 1936 (including both the showings put on by Kino itself and the showings organized by other groups in which Kino's films were used), and possibly up to 200,000 during 1938.[22]

While primarily a film distributor, at several stages in its life Kino was also involved in production activities. The first attempt to set up a production group would result in the formation of the Workers' Film and Photo League, which would split off from Kino in 1934, but would still supply Kino with its key early local documentary material such as the *Workers' Newsreel*.[23] In April 1936 Kino formed another production committee with the aim to 'discuss and determine themes and treatments for films of social significance' and to 'form units throughout the country for their production, on sub-standard stock, and to act as a co-ordinating body to all such units and give assistance in every possible way'.[24] Later Kino would also employ professional camera operators, as well as set up a club for amateur enthusiasts, in order to facilitate further production of films capturing British working-class activity.[25] In addition, the main Kino company had off-shoots such as 'International Films–Kino Exhibitors', established to make 'certain short films' which the main Kino branch did not want to produce, and the Progressive Film Institute, which was established as a separate limited liability company in 1935 to deal specifically with 35 mm film (and indeed became a major left-wing organ in Britain involved in the independent 35 mm film trade). The fact that it shared the same address as Kino indicates the close links between the two.[26]

THE DECLINE OF KINO

If Kino was successful in beating the British censors and setting up a wide network for the distribution of its films, sustaining these operations appears to have been a far more difficult affair, with the documents in the MI5 files suggesting a volatile organization which struggled to maintain any financial viability. Within a few months of its establishment, Kino was near financial collapse, due to non-payment of outstanding accounts, and this was not helped by a management dispute in which a member of the organization seized the film stock and was expelled from the group.[27] This led

[21] 'It's Simple to Run a Successful Film Show!', KV 5/45, serial 200a.

[22] Ryan, 'The New Road to Progress', 124–5.

[23] See Victoria Wegg-Prosser, 'The Archive of the Film and Photo League', *Sight and Sound*, 46, no. 4 (1977), 245–7.

[24] These plans are set out on a Kino document in KV 5/43, serial 112a.

[25] Special Branch report, 25 March 1938, KV 5/44, serial 175a.

[26] Cross reference report, 9 April 1935, KV 5/42, serial 68a; Special Branch report, 22 November 1937, KV 5/44, serial 161a.

[27] One of the more interesting documents recording Kino's financial difficulties is an intercepted letter from Kino on 25 March 1934 to Nancy Cunard, begging her to settle her outstanding account, KV 5/42, serial 22b.

to a series of rapid organizational and name changes, with Kino's stationery quickly shifting to 'Kino Amateur Film Federation' and then 'Kino Film Hire Service' over the next year, before finally being registered as the formal limited liability company 'Kino Films (1935) Ltd'. But significant problems still plagued the group. While the central Kino office and the Communist Party of Great Britain (CPGB) leadership hoped that film showings would be financially beneficial for Party branches, material in the MI5 file records a different story. One letter to an official of the CPGB complained of the 'lousy' collections a group had made when showing Kino films at a Congress, and that the showing 'nearly broke us financially' due to the loss of over thirteen pounds incurred.[28] This cannot have been the only incident of branch-level dissatisfaction with Kino, as in 1937 Kino registered a loss of over £263 in its yearly accounts, clearly showing an unsustainable operation and necessitating another management reshuffle.[29] By late 1937, Special Branch reported that the South African Max Sempton was taking a 'leading part in the direction of the affairs', while the company chairman Basil Burton (who was also involved in another company, Unity Films) now controlled the film purchases.[30] By this time Kino had also accumulated an eminent General Council, listing J. D. Bernal, Aneurin Bevan, the Bishop of Birmingham, Alberto Cavalcanti, Stafford Cripps, Maurice Dobb, Havelock Ellis, Victor Gollancz, Viscount Hastings, Lancelot Hogben, Julian Huxley, H. Levy, Ivor Montagu, D. N. Pritt, Joseph Reeves, Paul Rotha, Bertrand Russell, Lord Strabolgi, and H. G. Wells.[31] From the material evident in the MI5 files, apart from Montagu, members of this council had little to do with the day-to-day running of Kino's affairs, but they nonetheless represented an influential public mark of support for Kino.

But again, despite this restructure, it appears that little could be done to steady Kino's position, as by mid 1938 Special Branch were receiving information that the company 'is experiencing a period of depression; its sales have slumped during the last few months and two of the technical staff... have been discharged'.[32] By early 1939 even close political allies had begun to avoid dealings with Kino, with an intercepted letter between the Friends of the Soviet Union and Russia To-Day Society discussing the establishment of film organizations with the Left Book Club so as to be 'independent from Kino Film and give... the possibility to work on cheaper rates, if Kino film is not able, to give sufficient cheap prices for smaller shows'.[33] The company of Kino Films (1935) Ltd finally collapsed in September 1939, going into voluntary liquidation after an extraordinary general meeting. The final balance sheet for the company, submitted in November 1938, showed that Kino had made a loss of £188 for the year. It was suggested by Special Branch that the stock of the liquidated Kino company was to be taken over by another mutation of the group,

[28] Interdicted letter to George Allison, 28 October 1936, KV 5/43, serial 123a.

[29] Special Branch report, 25 May 1938, KV 5/44, serial 179a.

[30] Special Branch report, 23 November 1937, KV 5/44, serial 162a.

[31] Special Branch report, 17 August 1937, KV 5/44, serial 144x. From cross-references on this document, it is evident that MI5 already possessed records on most of those on the General Council.

[32] Special Branch report, 24 May 1938, KV 5/44, serial 178a.

[33] Cross reference report, 8 May 1939, KV 5/45, serial 203a.

this one incorporated as Kino Film Services Limited.[34] MI5's tap on the phone-line at the King Street Headquarters of the Communist Party of Great Britain recorded a cryptic discussion about a 'skeleton service' and 'keeping the name [Kino] and whoever was there should sign letters as from [Kino]' as 'the service would have an address 8 Red Lion Square... So the world wouldn't know that it would be in the same office.'[35] A later telecheck clarified that this was referring to a takeover of the Kino organization by the Russia To-Day Society, and a Special Branch report suggests that another company, Mobile Publicity Limited, was used as the vehicle for continuing the organization's activity.[36] But this final manoeuvre appears to have effectively spelt the end of Kino as a distinct organization. The final substantive report on the aftermath of the Kino company was filed in 1941, marking an end of direct security intelligence concern, and the end of an organization that had fundamentally altered the paradigms of the reception of Soviet film in Britain.

METHODS OF MI5 SURVEILLANCE

The previous section has discussed the overt activity and significance of the Kino organization, and I will now focus more specifically on the nature of the MI5 surveillance itself, to understand the precise concerns that policing and intelligence agencies displayed about Soviet and left-wing film, and more generally the processes of surveillance deployed by state agencies at this time to tabulate these Soviet-linked cultural forms deemed to present a potential risk.

Information on Kino was gathered by a range of means. There is an abundance of documents originating from the covert methods: intercepted mail, tapped telephones, reports from secret informers, and undercover police monitoring operations all functioned as valuable sources. But by no means was all the information gathered by MI5 obtained by secret activity. MI5 and Special Branch kept keenly abreast of many developments in the film industry simply by consulting the published industry journals and news. Some copies of *Kino News* were obtained and kept, articles about Kino in the communist newspaper *Daily Worker* were clipped out and put in the file, and catalogues and pamphlets were collected and read for their updates on Kino's film library. It is important to note that much of the generated informational traffic on Kino did not necessarily come from the conduct of specific operations against Kino, but rather from the standing surveillance maintained against CPGB premises and personnel. This meant that any time a member of the Kino organization wrote to the Communist Party headquarters at King Street, the letter was liable to be opened and copied into a file—an established

[34] Special Branch Report, 28 October 1939, KV 5/45, serial 205b. These facts tend to counter Hogenkamp's view that Kino 'adapted itself remarkably well to the special needs' of the late 1930s. See *Deadly Parallels,* 196.

[35] Transcript of telecheck on King Street, 14 November 1939, KV 5/45, serial 205c.

[36] Transcript of telecheck on King Street, 1 December 1939, KV 5/45, serial 207a; cross reference report, 21 February 1941, KV 5/45, serial 211a.

process of activity that suggests how tightly and comprehensively MI5 was able to monitor not just left-wing film associations, but any aspect of the broader cultural flow that crossed into what was regarded as 'extremist' or Soviet-linked networks of the time.

The volume of material precludes a single chapter discussing every document of significance, so here I am more interested in discussing several main trajectories of interest that stand out for examination. Amongst the volume of material, in broad terms, security concerns fell into two overlapping but separate spheres. First, MI5 were concerned that Kino was a communist organization with strong links to the CPGB and potentially with Comintern networks originating from Moscow, and thus they instigated investigations of this network of risk to see where the money, communication, or company paper trail led. Second, there were concerns that the films themselves were propaganda and potentially subversive, and thus MI5, in conjunction with the policing services and the BBFC, coordinated steps to monitor the consumer-level distributions and showings of films, and attempted to negotiate a satisfactory policing and censorship response to the developments in Kino's operations.

The picture MI5 developed of Kino's place within left-wing networks and associations was comprehensive. Even before the *Daily Worker* had publicly announced the launch of Kino, MI5 had already gathered considerable information on the organization, and was disseminating this intelligence through policing and censorship channels. The first record contained in the Kino file dates from September 1933, reporting on a letter written by Ivan Seruya and sent from the headquarters of the Workers' Theatre Movement, which was duly intercepted en route, copied, and provided to MI5 for analysis. This letter provided basic details about the formation of the Kino organization, and explained that the films would be 'suitable for showing either in a hall, which need not be licensed, or actually in the open, at the street corners'. The contents of the letter were extracted by MI5 and inserted in Seruya's personal file, and later added as one of the initial documents in the Kino organizational file.[37]

What appears to have sparked definite MI5 action was a second intercepted letter, sent by Charles Mann to the Cinema Bureau of the International Union of Revolutionary Theatres in Moscow—a postal address that guaranteed the letter would be opened by British security agencies before it had left the country. Shortly after receiving the intercept, MI5 used the letter to compile a detailed report for the BBFC, with the Home Office also receiving a copy. The report informed the BBFC about the background to Kino and its links to the Moscow-based International Union of Revolutionary Theatres and the Friends of the Soviet Union, information which clearly situated Kino as a possible Comintern-front organization and thus the subject of security interest and potentially close attention by the BBFC. The tone of the report was unequivocal in expressing MI5's distrust. For example, noting that Kino was producing a ten-minute cartoon 'in a humorous style', the report implied such humour masked Kino's true intentions, and was indeed a ploy

[37] Cross reference report, 22 September 1933, KV 5/42, serial 0a.

to allow propaganda to slip through: 'These early cartoons are apparently to be used to make exhibitions of the 16 mm film *Soviet Russia—Past and Present*, produced by E. Wurzel, more attractive to audiences.' It was not just the presentation of otherwise banned Soviet material, or potential links with the Comintern, however, that appears to have interested MI5, considerable space was also given to Kino's innovative new methods of establishing mobile film viewing:

> Wurzel has produced a small projector enclosed in a box of the type carried by travelling salesmen...They have got hold of a motor car and, using the accumulator on the car as the source of power, have given a number of open-air shows to workers in the East End of London actually in the streets, with Mann as the lecturer and Wurzel as the operator. In a report to Moscow they comment on the opportunities of getting films to the masses which this method provides.[38]

The MI5 reports were evidently considered very seriously by the BBFC, since Brooke Wilkinson, secretary of the BBFC, asked the reporting officer, Captain H. Miller, to lunch, as he 'would very much like to have an opportunity of talking over the subject matter of your communication with you'.[39]

The interception of mail gave MI5 perhaps the most ubiquitous sources of intelligence on Kino over the life of the file, providing them with information not only on the business directions, the thinking of the company management, and the current film lists being posted out to subscribers, but also the names and addresses of many of those in the network of communication with Kino—names and addresses that were each duly annotated, carded, and entered in the MI5 registry as individuals with suspected extremist associations. Other valuable information was also gained by informers who were in a position to monitor the management discussions of the organization and report them back to either MI5 or Special Branch handlers.[40] In the later stages of Kino's existence, phone taps deployed by MI5 on the CPGB headquarters picked up several calls originating from Kino's Gray's Inn Road premises. While much of this information was only of marginal value, it was through such phone taps that MI5 gained information about the break-up of the Kino company after its liquidation, in that case providing key information that effectively confirmed for MI5 the end of Kino's organizational life.

But despite the range of information gathered on Kino, its exact links to the Communist Party or Comintern were never clear to MI5. There was strong evidence that rendered Kino open to suspicion, such as correspondence from the Central Committee of the Party urging all branches and districts to increase their use of Kino films.[41] There were also some links to the Soviet trading company Arcos, the company

[38] MI5 report to Brooke Wilkinson (BBFC), 14 October 1933, KV 5/42, serial 0b.

[39] Extract from letter from Brooke Wilkinson to H. Miller, 22 November 1933, KV 5/42, serial 3b.

[40] For example, such a report was received in November 1933 from a source (designated 'Casual') who appears to have been present at one of the first meetings of Kino's management: see KV 5/42, serial 3a.

[41] An interesting example of this is an interdicted 1 September 1937 letter found at KV 5/44, serial 148a, where the Propaganda Department of the CPGB Central Committee, in a letter to all the CPGB branches and districts, remarked on the fact that non-Party hire of Kino films had increased at a far greater rate than that of the Party, and urged renewed efforts to arrange Kino film showings.

that was the major site of inter-war Soviet espionage in Britain. Customs officers reported to Special Branch details of certain Kino films that were shipped from Moscow to the London Arcos premises, while other reports suggested that there might be some form of financial link between the Kino office and Arcos.[42] But for MI5 this was not conclusive in establishing that there was any controlling interest, and later in the file officers would note that they had 'no evidence that any subsidy was made' to Kino by Moscow, and that 'of the seven members of the first Council of Management of Kino Films 1935 Ltd, only one, Ivan Seruya, is a member of the Communist Party'.[43] The assessment settled on was that although it was not 'quite justified' to consider Kino one of 'those organisations affiliated to or financed by the Comintern', it nonetheless deserved 'a certain amount of attention' from other intelligence services.[44]

SURVEILLANCE OF FILM SHOWINGS

Even if Kino was not a Comintern-controlled organization, security forces were still worried about the subversive risk Kino posed, with the file indicating the extensive concerns held (particularly by Special Branch) about the use and impact of film at its point of audience consumption. Officers from Special Branch routinely attended showings of Kino films and filed reports of their impressions (as did, to a lesser extent, detectives from the provincial police), providing MI5 with a de facto film reviewing and audience research system. Many times, such reports recorded even the most banal events, resulting in comical documents, but ones that have also unwittingly recorded for posterity not just details of films shown by Kino on certain occasions, but the wider activities, costs of seats, level of attendance, disposition, and response of the crowds at such events. An interesting early example of such as report was compiled in July 1934, after Special Branch officers monitored a Kino-sponsored 'Film Festival and Fun Fair' at King Alfred School Gardens, London, NW11. It appeared to be a rather dispiriting affair. The officer recorded that 'only 25–30 persons attended' during the first five hours of the festival, spending their time mostly 'in groups talking or in wandering around the grounds' until at a 'later stage in the afternoon, many of them engaged in sports and games...with little or no enthusiasm'. The officer did not record whether he joined the groups in the games or observed from the sidelines, but he evidently persevered in his watch, eventually being rewarded for his stoic surveillance effort when the main event took place:

> Between 8pm and 8.30 pm about twenty more persons arrived on the grounds, and preparations were made for an open air film show. A film apparatus was mounted on

[42] For the details of the Customs report, see Metropolitan Police Telegram, 15 January 1937, KV 5/44, serial 130a. The evidence of financial links to Arcos was derived from information received by Special Branch that the Progressive Film Institute (which shared offices with Kino) submitted monthly balance sheets to Arcos: see Special Branch report, 7 December 1937. KV 5/44 serial 164a.

[43] Note on Kino, 1 January 1936, KV 5/43, serial 108a.

[44] This was the view MI5 passed to Indian Political Intelligence, 2 January 1936, KV 5/43, serial 109a.

> a table, and the pictures were projected on a darkened screen which was hung on the wall of one of the buildings. Ivan Seruya and one or two assistants were in charge of the apparatus, and the show consisted of shewing [*sic*] scenes from various parts of the world, including Russian life, all of which had some bearing on the conditions of either peasants or industrial manner of living.

While the report was entitled 'Extremists', giving a clear indication of what Special Branch suspected they would find, there was little evidence of extreme activity during the day, with the officer writing that 'the people who patronized the festival did not appear to devote their attention to any act of a revolutionary nature; there was little indication of Communist support, and no speeches came under notice'. Having thus maintained surveillance over this small gathering for over eight hours, the officer was able to conclude that 'there was no disorder throughout the proceedings, and the crowd left the grounds at 10.30 pm'.[45]

While the diligence of this Special Branch officer was certainly overzealous, the report remains in many ways an important and indicative document. For example, the focus of the detective's concerns gives us an insight into what police viewed as the specific danger posed by such films. The officer reported very briefly on the basic topic of the film, but seems uncurious about what would strike us now as central facts, such as the specific title of the film being shown. Nonetheless, this was not due to the officer being inattentive, as in other sections of the report the watcher specifically identified prominent known communists attending and organizing the day's events; these names in the report were duly marked by an MI5 hand and annotated with identifying file numbers, indicating that MI5 too regarded their presence as significant. Thus it appears, for this Special Branch officer at least, the actual content or qualities of the film itself were of less concern than its appearance in an event they feared could spill over into unrest, the identity of the organizers and disposition of the crowd the key facts to be reported rather than the ideological or aesthetic content of the film.

While the particular officer attending the fun fair seemed to find little to object to in the conduct of the day's events, other officers were more concerned about the ability of Kino's films to provoke public unrest. One such example of this can be seen in a 1937 case when an officer, after filing a detailed report on the content of the films *Call to Arms* and *Torn Shoes*, specifically registered that such films risked making unemployed people 'very bitter indeed'. He evidently feared that these films could not just provoke unrest but serve as a training tool for leftists seeking the most effective disruptive techniques, and stated that the film's depiction of 'children as a kind of shield in front of strikers... might be adopted at some time by extremists [who] view this film'. Interestingly, though, this officer moved beyond simple description of content into some attempts to assess the aesthetic quality of the film. Noting that 'the full significance of the film is lost because of the foreign dialogue', it was reported that the aesthetic quality of the film still rendered it a dangerous artefact: 'the clever editing, the use of children, the superimposed

[45] Special Branch report, 21 July 1934, KV 5/42, serial 33a.

English titles, and the vibrant musical accompaniment, still make it possible for a considerable amount of the Communist propaganda contained in the film to get across to audiences'.[46]

Other examples of the development of Special Branch officers as more nuanced film critics can be found in a report on a showing of *Madrid Today* and *China Fights for Freedom.* It was described in this report that *Madrid Today* was a 'significant piece of propaganda' with the tempo of the film 'very skilfully... increased as women are shown assisting men in the trenches near Madrid', and the picture 'heightened by a dramatic, tense commentary spoken by a cultured, restrained American voice'. While the latter film achieved Special Branch praise for its 'excellent scenes of Mongolia—camels, camel caravans, followed by a map of China and "4,500,000 square miles, 450,000,000 population" superimposed and illustrated by the crowded conditions of Shanghai and the International Settlement', the detective equally commented that the 'last sequence of the film... [was] emphasized by the most skilful editing, [and] shows the war scenes of the present conflict in China'.[47] It is notable, then, that even within the scope of the Kino file itself, a growing sophistication can be discerned in Special Branch's understanding of film as a specific aesthetic medium, as it shifts away from judging a film solely judged on its immediate effect in crudely provoking a given crowd into disorderly action, towards a far more detailed understanding of how the components of a film combined to create a work that might subtly persuade or shape political opinion.

THE IMPACT OF SURVEILLANCE AND CENSORSHIP ON LEFTIST FILM CULTURE

While MI5 was able to develop this comprehensive intelligence profile of Kino and its associations, and clearly judged it to be involved in activities that formed a security concern, an obvious but nonetheless crucial question to ask is, what impact or effect the agency actually had in altering any aspect of Kino's operations. The paradox of the file is that while MI5 had the ability to gather and assess wide-ranging information on Kino's activity, it was relatively impotent in its powers to directly intervene, functioning only in an advisory capacity without the executive powers to arrest or prosecute. Nonetheless, there were several modes of influence that MI5 can be seen to have asserted over Kino and the wider cinema industry at the time. For one, the role of MI5 did not end in simply gathering and processing such information (whether by overt or covert means), but in disseminating it back out to executive agencies, thereby coordinating an informed security and censorship response to the appearance of Soviet and left-wing film. MI5 sat at the centre of a hub with spokes disseminating information to a wide range of bureaucratic agencies—to the BBFC and Home Office it reported, for example, on the recent

[46] Special Branch report, 3 March 1937, KV 5/44, serial 137a.
[47] Special Branch report, 14 December 1937, KV 5/44, serial 167a.

intelligence gathered from postal intercepts, to the Chief Constables of provincial cities it gave information about the possible showing of *Potemkin* in their jurisdictions, and to the British external intelligence agencies such as SIS (more commonly known as MI6) and Indian Political Intelligence, it provided tips about the international operations of the Comintern that intelligence gathered on Kino revealed.

Secondly, while by 1935 it was largely recognized that 16 mm film was not unlawful, surveillance activity on individuals involved in Kino's showings by no means decreased. An interest in organizing or attending such films could potentially lead to security records being kept on an individual, and such records could later be used to deny such a person access to areas of government or military work. One example to be found in the file occurred in June 1937, when the Chief Constable of Berkshire contacted MI5 over a local request to screen *The End of St Petersburg*, *The Defence of Madrid*, and *The International Brigade* at the Guildhall in Abingdon. After receiving information from MI5 that such showings were not illegal, the police decided that they would not oppose the application to screen the films but nevertheless made 'arrangements to note the names of local people attending the performances'.[48] In another case, the Chief Constable of Plymouth was asked to inform MI5 if 'any members of His Majesty's Forces are noticed to have been present' at any showing of Kino's 'propaganda films' in the city.[49] Another example found in the file showed Charles Fraser receiving attention from MI5 when his name was submitted on a BBC vetting list, after MI5 noted him as being 'Film Secretary of the New Art Cinema Movement'.[50] In other cases those involved in the running of Kino were subject to Special Branch reports detailing their itineraries when leaving the country to travel abroad.[51] We do not as yet have wide access to the personal files of many of the left-wing film-society figures, but a major question yet to be answered is how these records of involvement in such film organizations affected the fortunes of talented individuals seeking to undertake wartime work for agencies such as the BBC or Ministry of Information.

But perhaps the most fascinating aspect of the influence MI5 was able to wield lies in its communications outside the government-security networks into the industry domain, specifically in its remarkably close interactions with the ostensibly independent BBFC.[52] From the early stages of Kino's emergence it is clear that the BBFC was granted privileged access to intelligence communications, as officers from MI5 passed to Brooke Wilkinson information from 'a specially secret source' to be treated 'in its present form as highly confidential' that provided detail about

[48] Ba/1 report on visit to Chief Constable, Berkshire, 2 June 1937, KV 5/44, serial 142a.

[49] Letter from MI5 to Chief Constable, Plymouth, 17 August 1934, KV 5/42, serial 35b.

[50] Extract from BBC vetting list, January 1937, KV 5/44, serial 158a.

[51] Extract from BBC vetting list, January 1937, KV 5/44, serial 158a; see, for example, a 22 July 1938 Special Branch report that recorded several people passing through the Port of Dover, of interest because they had already 'come under the notice of Special Branch in connection with Kino Films Limited', KV 5/44, serial 182a.

[52] As other scholars have noted, many of the BBFC's officials came from military or intelligence backgrounds: see Nicholas Pronay and Jeremy Croft, 'British Film Censorship and Propaganda Policy during the Second World War', in Curran and Porter, eds, *British Cinema History*, 145–6.

the background of Kino.[53] MI5 often provided the BBFC with the same updates on Kino's activities and financial status as it provided the Home Office, and would pass on to the BBFC details of Customs officers' reports about Soviet films imported from Moscow to London.[54] When further companies were established that had links with Kino, the BBFC was kept closely informed by MI5, and the BBFC were advised on the details of the pending collapse of the Kino organization and the likely rise of a new organization to take its place.[55] In other instances MI5 would alert the BBFC to material in more readily available publications, by passing them articles from the *Daily Worker* discussing news films produced by Kino, or lending them copies of periodical such as *The Camera Forward* and *Kino News*.[56]

However, the BBFC was not a passive receiver of intelligence: at times it functioned as a de facto intelligence agency, responding to requests by MI5 for information and undertaking activities to obtain new intelligence material. When in March 1934 MI5 had received information about an A. D. Frischmann, who had agreed to work with Kino to reduce Soviet films to 16 mm format, MI5 wrote to the BBFC stating that 'we should welcome very much anything that you might be able to tell us about him'. Wilkinson promptly responded to MI5 to inform them that 'I am making one or two private enquiries and should I receive any information I will immediately communicate with you again.'[57] Another case saw the BBFC forwarding to MI5 copies of film publications for perusal, as well as providing MI5 with 'a copy of all the correspondence' the BBFC had received from the film studio owner Mrs Earle, who had contacted the BBFC to express her fears about the activity of Kino, so long as it was treated 'as very specially confidential'.[58] In other instances, the BBFC was the instrument through which MI5 tried to shut down film industry activity that was judged politically undesirable. For example, when MI5 provided the BBFC with information from a 'casual source' detailing how the photographic dealers Wallace Heaton Ltd were 'pushing Kino films through the Home Film Library',[59] Brooke Wilkinson confirmed to MI5 that the company had indeed 'included in their library... some of the Soviet Films to which my Board has in the past taken exception', but was evidently confident that he could wield his influence for a result desired by MI5: 'I will make some diplomatic enquiries about

[53] Letter from MI5 to Brooke Wilkinson (BBFC), 14 December 1933, KV 5/42, serial 7a.

[54] See, for example, letters from MI5 to Newsam (Home Office) and Brooke Wilkinson, 6 April and 23 July 1934, KV 5/42, serials 25a and 34a. The details of the Customs report were passed on in a 19 January letter from MI5 to Brooke Wilkinson, KV 5/44, serial 131a.

[55] See, for example, the letter from MI5 to Brooke Wilkinson, 26 November 1937, which informed the BBFC of the founding of the Progressive Film Institute and the fact that it shared offices with Kino: KV 5/44, serial 163a; letter from MI5 to Brooke Wilkinson, 15 November 1939, KV 5/45, serial 206a.

[56] Letters from MI5 officers to Brooke Wilkinson, 4 September 1934, 3 October 1935, 18 December 1935, KV 5/42, serial 37a, KV 5/43, serial 91a, and KV, 5/43 serial 105a, respectively.

[57] Letter from MI5 to Brooke Wilkinson, 21 March 1934, KV 5/42, serial 22a; letter from Brooke Wilkinson to MI5, 24 March 1934, KV 5/42, serial 23a.

[58] Letter from Brooke Wilkinson to MI5 (forwarding copy of *Home Movies*), 4 April 1934, KV 5/42, serial 24d; report on meeting with Brooke Wilkinson, 2 July 1936, KV 5/43, serial 117a.

[59] Letter from MI5 to Brooke Wilkinson, 11 January 1937, KV 5/43, serial 129a.

this matter, as I did some years ago in connection with Messrs. Houghton Ltd., with, I hope, equally satisfactory results.'[60]

The extent of the close relationship between the two agencies can be seen in the arrangement of joint viewings between MI5 and BBFC officers in order to assess films. One instance occurred in September 1934 when the BBFC became aware of Kino's *Workers' News Reel*, at that time being advertised in *The Daily Worker* but not submitted to the BBFC for review. As it was uncertain whether the film's news content rendered it liable to BBFC classification, Brooke Wilkinson asked MI5 about the possibility of the intelligence agency 'securing a copy so that it may be seen privately at our Offices'.[61] After Special Branch detectives hired the film, a viewing was attended by officers of MI5 and members of the BBFC at the offices of the censors, and evidently those watching from both agencies were little impressed with what they saw. An MI5 officer derided it as 'a deplorable exhibition from a pictorial, constructive and revolutionary point of view', but concluded after discussions with Brooke Wilkinson that unless Kino obtained 'the services of a really first-rate producer, it is much better that they should be left alone', with the canny decision that 'publicity is a thing they very much want, but they are not likely to obtain it unless it is given to them by the authorities'.[62]

The assessment of this officer—that government repression and free publicity were essentially different sides of the same coin—provides us with a neat final point to consider. On the one hand, as this chapter has shown, the MI5 files reveal a widespread and sustained pattern of covert government attempts to monitor and suppress pro-Soviet films and related film societies—all at a time when the Home Secretary was emphatically informing Parliament that the government should play no role in the censorship of cinema. But on the other hand, British censorship had created the very space for organizations such as Kino to thrive, one in which MI5 and the BBFC, whatever their manoeuvres, found themselves relatively impotent to act. Ironically, then, the surveillance that MI5 maintained on Kino not only failed to curtail its operations in the 1930s, it preserved an archive of information that might otherwise have been lost, which now shows us just how large the spectre of Soviet film had seemed to those working within the darker corridors of the British state.

[60] Letter from Brooke Wilkinson to MI5, 18 January 1937, KV 5/44, serial 133a.

[61] Letter from Brooke Wilkinson to MI5, 6 September 1934, KV 5/42, serial 38a.

[62] Report on film viewing, 30 October 1934, KV 5/42, serial 47a.

Afterword

A Time and a Place for Everything: On Russia, Britain, and Being Modern

Ken Hirschkop

In 1925–26, Stuart Young tells us in his chapter, the Russian director Fedor Komissarzhevsky staged an avant-garde production of Nikolay Gogol′'s *The Government Inspector* (*Revizor*) in Barnes, an attractive but sleepy suburban village in southwest London. Although the Barnes Theatre was small and remote from the bright lights of the West End, the production was in fact hugely successful, attracting excellent reviews and starring, amongst others, Claude Rains and a very young Charles Laughton.[1] For all its success, however, it doesn't register on the modernist map like another 1926 production of *The Government Inspector*: the one directed by Vsevolod Meierkhol′d at the Moscow Arts Theatre, which Young himself calls 'seminal'. That production was attended by Walter Benjamin who was in Moscow to meet intellectuals, discuss Goethe, and chase, rather hopelessly, the elusive Asja Lacis.[2] If the present volume were about the old 'international modernism', it's Benjamin and Meierkhol′d we'd be talking about, the intersection between a great modernist critic and a great modernist director, between Berlin and Moscow, the moment when experiments in politics and art seem to walk hand-in-hand. We wouldn't be talking about Barnes.

Or, to put it another way, this volume would be called 'From Leningrad to London', not 'Russia in Britain'. The internationalism of modernist art has always been one of the features that was supposed to distinguish it from its nineteenth-century precursors, but this internationalism depended on the metropolitan location of modernist art, its flourishing in London, Paris, New York, Berlin, and that place in Russia that morphed from St Petersburg to Leningrad (via Petrograd) and back again. At some point the modern metropolis had become, in Raymond Williams' words, 'much more than the very large city', now 'the place where new social and economic and cultural relations, beyond both city and nation in their older senses, were beginning to be formed'.[3] These new relations were to a great

1 'Barnes Theatre: The Government Inspector', *The Times* (29 April 1926), 14.

2 Benjamin saw the production on December 19 1926 and described it in his diary: see 'Moscow Diary', trans. Richard Sieburth, *October*, 35 (1985), 32-4.

3 Raymond Williams, 'Metropolitan Perceptions and the Emergence of Modernism', in Tony Pinkney, ed., *The Politics of Modernism* (London: Verso, 1989), 44.

extent the simple consequence of the kind of 'creative clustering' effect that urban theorists today claim for places like Silicon Valley. The metropolises were where the money and power was, and in cultural terms they were where the art galleries, publishing houses, and concert halls were, however orthodox in taste these may have been. Perhaps more importantly, the great cities were places where—again Williams—'small groups in any form of divergence or dissent could find some kind of a foothold, in ways that would not have been possible if the artists and thinkers composing them had been scattered in more traditional, closed societies'.[4] The result was immigration, both from the provinces and from other nations, to cities where a network of avant-garde writers or painters could support themselves, to a place like—to cite the exemplary case—Paris.

But there was more to it than simple proximity. The great city had also, so the argument goes, invented, or at least hosted, a qualitatively new, distinctively 'modern' kind of experience, based on constant overstimulation, the overwhelming presence of strangers, and the excitements made possible by urban geography. This modernity expressed itself in *flânerie*, in what Simmel called the 'blasé attitude', and in a posture of ironic detachment and distance.[5] The metropolis made the settled routines, the habits of behaviour and discourse that helped define an everyday national space, strange and conventionalized, comprehensible only by reference to universal features of human psychology or sociology. Modern life was found in the metropolises, not in particular nations: like the proletariat, it had no country.

Russia in Britain is about a *national* modern life. True, most of the events recorded and discussed in this volume take place in London. Most, not all: it's probably significant that it's the film screenings discussed by Laura Marcus and James Smith that traverse Britain as a whole, while the dance, theatre, painting, and publishing discussed elsewhere remain locked into the capital. But even if it's the same old place, the perspective is different: in the contributions to this collection London appears not as the modernist metropolis, but as the capital of Great Britain, absorbed, entranced, and frightened by the representatives and representations of Russia that make their way towards it. If modernism is international, here it is international in the most literal sense, as something that takes place in a space between nations and not in a space above all nations. Sergey Eizenshtein's films, the writings of Isaak Babel′ and Mikhail Zoshchenko, the painting of Vasily Kandinsky, the dancing of Vatslav Nizhinsky, and the avant-garde theatre of Komissarzhevsky are all very *Russian*, and their strangeness and avant-gardism is associated with the remoteness and strangeness of that country rather than with a generally estranging 'modernity'.

Russia in Britain therefore sounds like it is of a piece with the kind of internationalism more characteristic of the so-called new modernist studies, the trend which urges us to think of modernism as a much larger range of cultural forms emerging in a much larger range of countries. The new modernist studies doesn't like the universalist pretensions of the old modernist internationalism—its practitioners

[4] Williams, 'Metropolitan Perceptions', 45.

[5] Georg Simmel, 'The Metropolis and Mental Life', in Kurt H. Wolff, ed. and trans. *The Sociology of Georg Simmel* (Glencoe, IL: Free Press, 1950), 413.

prefer to talk of a 'transnational turn' or of a distinctively modernist cosmopolitanism.[6] To be cosmopolitan is not to rise above one's national or ethnic identity, not to live as a representative of the universal, but to move between or among national or otherwise local identities. 'Another way to put the contrast,' says Bruce Robbins, 'is to say that instead of an ideal of detachment, actually existing cosmopolitanism is a reality of (re)attachment, multiple attachments, or attachment at a distance', a kind of qualified belonging to a nation, or a belonging qualified by its dispersion among several nations.[7]

Rebecca Walkowitz has argued that this new 'critical' conception of cosmopolitanism should take its cue from the stylistic achievements of classical high modernists like Conrad, Woolf, and Joyce. Their cosmopolitanism is manifest in tactics or 'cultural strategies of posture' that emphasize 'adverse or quotidian experiences of transnational contact'.[8] Focusing on the trivial, or altering the manner in which we direct our attention, has the effect of 'testing and redefining what can count as international politics: they may emphasize incidents that seem to be trivial in order to reject wartime values of order and proportion, or they emphasize what seem to be only personal experiences in order to expand what we know of global processes'.[9] On this account cosmopolitanism entails a change in the terms of national affiliation and a conscious rejection of nationalist politics in favour of a more nuanced kind of commitment. To be cosmopolitan is not to be universalist but to practice a distanced, modernist kind of association with the nation state and its politics.

This doesn't seem quite right, either. As a case in point we might look at the cosmopolitanism of Oscar Wilde, whose 'late-Victorian tradition of aesthetic decadence' is a crucial ingredient in Walkowitz's recipe for a critical cosmopolitanism.[10] As Michael Newton and Laurence Senelick show us in this volume, when Wilde embarked on his first attempt at 'political prophecy' he drew on the celebrated case of Vera Zasulich, a young Russian populist (later Menshevik) acquitted for the shooting of a leading Russian general, an act which she, along with her comrades at the time, justified as revenge against manifest injustice. Newton describes the resulting work, Wilde's *Vera; or the Nihilists*, as 'a play set in Russia, about Ireland, written first for the British public, and then eventually played in the United States where its target audience included the Irish diaspora. It is a work that migrates between international and local contexts, responses, and meanings'—in other words, just the sort of thing that today's theorists of a critical or modern cosmopolitanism had in mind. But what the drama reaches for in its Russian setting, what it appropriates as a lever with which to shift British sentiment, is not a larger and more expansive definition

[6] Douglas Mao and Rebecca L. Walkowitz, 'The New Modernist Studies', *PMLA*, 123, no. 3 (2008), 738.

[7] Bruce Robbins, 'Introduction, Part I: Actually Existing Cosmopolitanism', in Bruce Robbins and Pheang Cheah, eds, *Cosmopolitics: Thinking and Feeling Beyond the Nation* (Minneapolis, MN: University of Minnesota Press, 1998), 3.

[8] Rebecca L. Walkowitz, *Cosmopolitan Style: Modernism Beyond the Nation* (New York: Columbia University Press, 2006), 15, 17.

[9] Walkowitz, *Cosmopolitan Style*, 10.

[10] Walkowitz, *Cosmopolitan Style*, 12.

of politics, one found in the interstices of quotidian existence, but a more dramatic version of politics. *Vera; or the Nihilists* is a kind of faux-Shakespearean tragedy, in both its awkward, elaborate diction, and its plotting, in which erotic passion and political passion collide, with predictably fatal results. What Russia contributes to the exercise is not merely, as Wilde put in a letter twice quoted in this collection, a 'fiery and fervent background' for his characters, but a political scene driven by fierce, uncompromising, moral passions, passions that will drive a heroic, individualist, and 'irrational' kind of political action. The kind of politics, you might say, that one was unlikely to encounter in the world's oldest parliamentary democracy.

Or you could say that what Russia, or at least its image, contributed was politics as such. Pierre Rosanvallon has described the 'disappointment' that attended the invention of representative democracies in the nineteenth century, which promised to express a national will that nonetheless seemed forever lost in petty political wrangling. As a result, Rosanvallon comments, 'politics often seems simultaneously like an irritating residue, to be eliminated if possible, and like a tragically lacking dimension of life, a cruelly absent grandeur'.[11] What Russian nihilism offered to the British audience—which, according to Laurence Senelick's contribution, spent much of the 1880s watching dramas with nihilist plots and characters—was the spectacle of such a grand politics. Unfortunately, the result seems not have been tragic grandeur, but corny and unpersuasive melodrama. That's probably because in the end, however generally 'tragic' the diction is (and in Wilde's case it came complete with the requisite archaisms: 'mayest', 'methinks', 'spake', and so on), the passions ended up looking a bit like personal obsessions, as if everything had to be folded back into the everyday life from which it was supposed to be an exit. Newton persuasively argues that Wilde's *Vera; or the Nihilists* was in fact making a case for Irish politics, where political assassination was also part of politics, but which was viewed as savage by the civilized and parliamentary English. But one can also see Wilde having a go at the late Victorian version of quotidian experience from two directions: by means of the self-conscious and cynical wit paraded by the immoral Prince Paul and by means of the spectacle of a moral and dramatic politics unavailable to the British.

In an astute essay, Amanda Anderson has described the 'distinctly casual normativity of the cosmopolitan'. Advocates of the cosmopolitan point of view, she notes, want to press their general, universalizing claims 'through a process of incremental, casual description rather than philosophical justification'. Such descriptions, typically made from the 'perspective of the participant as he or she negotiates a dense array of affiliations and commitments' find their natural métier 'in genres more classically literary or eclectic: the essay, the autobiography, travel writing, and works of literature generally'.[12] A very shrewd observation, which leads, however, to a

[11] Pierre Rosanvallon, 'Inaugural Lecture, Collège de France', in Samuel Moyn, ed., *Democracy Past and Future* (New York: Columbia University Press, 2006), 55.

[12] Amanda Anderson, 'Cosmopolitanism, Universalism, and the Divided Legacies of Modernity', in Robbins and Cheah, *Cosmopolitics*, 275.

significant qualification. Are all literary genres equally suited to the cosmopolitan task? Wilde's attempt at tragedy indicates this may not be the case.

Franco Moretti has argued that literary genres, far from operating within some agreed division of literary labour, often struggle with one another for dominance. In twentieth-century Europe this struggle pitted tragedy against the novel, the former focusing on the crisis point as a moment of truth, the latter on the elaboration of an interesting everyday life, animated by conversation and compromise. Britain and France, with great novelistic traditions, were hostile to the tragic (hence the furious response to Ibsen); Germany became tragedy's great champion. To have a great novelistic tradition, however, is not the consequence of artistic genius: it depends on strong, durable state structures, beneath which everyday life can go about its business with some measure of security and predictability. Germany, latecomer to statehood and buffeted by challenges to the state from both Left and Right, is the place where the exceptional moment and the exceptional hero hold court.

How does Russia fit into Moretti's typology? Russia only comes up in a brief discussion of Anton Chekhov, who, Moretti argues, had to battle with the 'weight of the Russian narrative tradition' when trying to develop some kind of tragic form.[13] In his chapter on Russian performances in Britain, Laurence Senelick has shown how central a figure Chekhov was in this respect, confirming that this most novelistic of playwrights had a natural affinity with an audience schooled on novels. But the Russian Empire was not the British Empire or the French Republic, and its political instability and radical politics would have seemed to place it closer to the 'tragic' camp. And so it did: for what Russian autocracy fostered was not a secure sphere of civil society, where a meaningful everyday life could be cultured, but a national culture divided between elaborations of a pointless everyday life, rich in event and empty of substance (embodied in the 'superfluous man' and *Oblomovshchina*), and the invention, *within* the novel form, of the 'novel-tragedy', as Vyacheslav Ivanov put it: the prose genre that looked like a novel, but was in actuality a tragedy—in a word, Dostoevsky.[14]

The appearance of Russian nihilism as a theme, and melodrama as a form, within the British theatre scene might therefore signify a significantly different kind of cosmopolitanism: literary in genre, but dramatic, rather than incremental, in its implicit claims. Looking at the range of Russian material described in this volume, it's hard not to conclude that this dramatic cosmopolitanism was the rule rather than the exception. The radically 'violent' and graceless choreography for *The Rite of Spring* that Ramsay Burt describes for us, the orchestral music that, as Philip Ross Bullock notes, embodied a suspiciously popular 'vehement emotional spontaneity' and 'orgiastic frenzy', and the violent, striking images of Pudovkin and Eizenshtein that Laura Marcus finds transposed into British and Irish art and writing were understood by British audiences as emblems of a more dramatic and spontaneous

[13] Franco Moretti, 'The Moment of Truth', in *Signs Taken for Wonders*, rev. edn (London: Verso, 1988), 255.

[14] See Ilya Kliger, 'Dostoevsky and the Novel-Tragedy: Genre and Modernity in Ivanov, Pumpiansky and Bakhtin', *PMLA*, 126, no. 1 (2011), 73–87.

culture than that on offer at home. Attempts to borrow, integrate, and adapt Russian and Soviet-Russian material might have entailed something different than negotiating a 'dense array of affiliations and commitments' in Anderson's terms, because the Russian material's 'commitment' and 'affiliation' might have been different *in kind* from that of the British context that played host to it. National belonging in Britain could find expression in what Walkowitz calls 'local authenticities': habits of dress, deportment, speech, behaviour, and interior decoration that suffused the civil society of middle-class England (we will leave aside, for the moment, the fact that Britain hosted different classes of such authenticities).[15] In the Russian Empire, where nationality was officially defined for most of the nineteenth century by the notorious triad of 'Orthodoxy, Autocracy, and Nationality', the commitments that ensured national belonging were necessarily quite different.

What filled the gap of middle-class affiliation in Russia was to a great extent the first leg of the triad: orthodox religion, with all the rhetoric of the Russian *dusha* (soul) that was attached to it. When spirit or soul became the force behind the artwork, the usual and habitual rhythms of everyday life had to give way to something more unpredictable and amorphous. Thus, as Caroline Maclean demonstrates, spirituality in Kandinsky found expression not in distinct representational forms but in the abstract principle of 'rhythm'. When put on stage or printed in books, spirit took the shape of Russian characters that had neither airs nor graces and were marked by an astonishing directness. In her account of the 'Russian point of view', Woolf could only imagine such individuals as the consequence of a metaphorical railway accident that suspended the niceties of ordinary existence: 'Men reft of their coats and manners, stunned by a railway accident, say hard things, harsh things, unpleasant things, difficult things, even if they say them with the abandonment and simplicity which catastrophe has bred in them.'[16]

The two terms that recur throughout this volume in British descriptions of Russian cultural forms are 'violence' and 'formlessness'. This violence and formlessness, at least in the early decades of the century, was not the violence and formlessness of an artistic avant-garde: it was not, if the phrase makes any sense, a 'meaningless' formlessness. Rather it appeared as violence born of passions—moral, erotic, political, and religious—unrestrained by any kind of civility. Vera and her nihilist kin were violent on the basis of their devotion to the people, their hatred of the autocracy, and a wide-eyed *eros* that had neither shading nor development. The Chosen One in *The Rite of Spring* was the victim of pagan religious passion that was at one with the rhythms of the earth. And given how dependent the narrative forms of nineteenth-century fiction, theatre, and ballet were on the idea of passions gradually sculpted and pressed into social form—the structuring idea of the *Bildungsroman*—it is hardly surprising that unrestrained passions had as their correlate apparently formless artworks. As Rebecca Beasley shows in her contribution,

[15] Walkowitz, *Cosmopolitan Style*, 49.

[16] Virginia Woolf, 'The Russian Point of View', in *The Common Reader*, 2nd edn (London: Hogarth Press, 1925), 222.

Russian writing was celebrated for this formlessness, which could be taken as an index of its immediacy, its lack of 'divorce from reality'.

That these passions and their ensuing violence were to be found in the art of an imperial rival was, of course, convenient. There's more than a whiff of Orientalism in the British description of barbarous, wild, and abandoned Russians. The North/South axis that lies behind much current thinking about cosmopolitanism can obscure the fact that Britain had Others that were different in kind and status from its Asian, Middle Eastern, and African colonies. Russia in particular seemed to combine Asian barbarousness and despotism with an unnerving imperial power; it was at once alien and, being a rival empire, similar. The Great Game played between Britain and the Russian Empire for much of the later nineteenth century, after all, ended in an Entente guaranteeing that the two empires, Western and Eastern, would run smoothly at the expense of their colonial possessions. But Russia's Orientalism was not merely a sign of its relative backwardness: it also made it a resource for modernism. 'The concept of the Orient', in Peter Wollen's words, 'was the rallying cry for those who wanted to create an alternative aesthetic', and Nizhinsky, Dyagilev, and the Ballets Russes led the charge.[17] When performances by the Ballets Russes were described as barbaric, 'what the critics really meant was that the ballet eroticized the body and flooded the stage with colour and movement'.[18] Ramsay Burt's essay in this volume takes the argument one step further. The female body eroticized in the productions of the Ballets Russes (Mariya Pil′ts as the Chosen One in *Le Sacre*, Ida Rubinshtein in the performance of *Schéhérazade* discussed by Wollen) also had a modern political resonance, echoing the violent and 'graceless' self-sacrifice of the suffragette Emily Howard Davison. Although Orientalism presented its objects as if their sensuality and directness were a mark of backwardness, these same qualities could be recoded as something modern and avant-garde, as a sign of an emancipated body and sensibility.

The female body was not the only occasion on which aesthetic objections seemed to morph into political ones. In his chapter on Russian drama, Stuart Young notes how deeply works depicting Russian poverty such as Maksim Gor′ky's *The Lower Depths* (*Na dne*) and Lev Tolstoy's *The Power of Darkness* (*Vlast′ t′my*) offended—but also fascinated—bourgeois taste. Works celebrated for their naturalism, which harmonized with British conventions, were at the same time condemned for that which they represented naturalistically: 'swinish drunkenness and satyr-like lust and fiendish crime', 'coarse oaths and torrents of vile abuse', in short, 'the degradation of the lower classes in Russia'. These objectionable scenes arrived, of course, at the very moment when middle-class Londoners were having difficulties with their own 'lower depths'. The final edition of Charles Booth's *Life and Labour of the People in London* was published in 1902–3, C. F. G. Masterman's *Of the Abyss* in 1902, both providing vivid accounts of London's poor, accounts that were to play a role in the hesitant steps towards a welfare

[17] Peter Wollen, 'Out of the Past: Fashion/Orientalism/the Body', in *Raiding the Icebox: Reflections on Twentieth-century Culture* (London: Verso, 1993), 26.

[18] Wollen, 'Out of the Past', 26.

state taken in the first two decades of the twentieth century.[19] The formlessness, the lack of narrative pace that British audiences deplored in Russian drama about peasants and proles, was echoed in the formlessness of London's 'abyss', a world that for many Edwardians would have been as alien as the steppes.

In that sense, it's tempting to say that Russia was *already* in Britain, its appearance in imported plays, films, and ballet obliquely reminding its audience that Britain was a more confused space than they were willing to admit. When *The Lower Depths* appeared in book form the translation made sure to indicate, via systematic 'misspelling', that the characters could not and did not speak in the received middle-class manner. But the accent that was conveyed orthographically was not Russian, but Cockney, dropped aitches and all.[20] If Britain was a modern and civilized nation, how could it have places that would be considered backward if they had been found abroad? Or was it possible that the 'abyss' of the East End and South London was part and parcel of modernity? What Russian art and literature subtly suggested was that there might be a different way of being modern and that this modernity split the nation instead of internationalizing it.

Split the nation: not so much culturally as politically. The cosmopolitanism discussed in these pages was not obliquely political, but, for the most part, explicitly political, and it is symptomatic that some of the institutions discussed here (the Free Library in Whitechapel and Kinofilm, for instance) were the objects of state surveillance. Of course, after 1917 the issue wasn't 'Russia in Britain', but 'Soviet Russia in Britain', or even 'the Soviet Union in Britain'. Here was a nation that announced that it was a political entity even in its name. But was the Soviet Union a *nation*? Some claim it was just the Russian Empire dressed up in socialist garb (although, to be fair, the United Kingdom wasn't simply a nation, either, but four nations yoked together by a single state). But to belong to the Soviet Union, or Soviet Russia, was not so much a matter of cultural affiliation as political commitment. Ian Patterson's chapter on John Rodker makes the point neatly: Rodker's sketches of Russian life, his 'Russian Impressions', are more precisely Soviet impressions, evaluations of the success or failure of the communist enterprise, and his promotion of Russian writing was inevitably the promotion of Soviet arguments. To have an interest in Soviet culture was to ally oneself with a nation that was not simply a political enemy of the British nation as a whole, but a political enemy that threatened to divide Britain politically, to set one class within it against another.

What happens when the nation to which the cosmopolitan reaches out is defined not in ethno-cultural terms, but in political ones? What if the thing one belongs to is not simply Russia or France, but the Soviet Union or the Third Republic? The

[19] Charles Booth, *Life and Labour of the People in London*, 17 vols (London: Macmillan, 1902–3); [C. F. G. Masterman], *From the Abyss: Of its Inhabitants By One of Them* (London: R. B. Johnson, 1902). An excellent account of middle-class confusion over the lower depths is Gareth Stedman Jones, *Outcast London: A Study in the Relationship Between Classes in Victorian Society* (Oxford: Oxford University Press, 1971).

[20] Maxim Gorki, *The Lower Depths*, trans. Laurence Irving (London: T. Fisher Unwin, 1912). A characteristic rendering: "Ow yer ever 'ave managed, you poor soul, to live with such a beast?' (14).

'affiliations and commitments' recent theories of cosmopolitanism ask us to negotiate are modeled on national or ethnic cultures, not on states and political systems. For it's not at all clear how one can suspend or relativize one's commitment to, say, a republican government. While it's fair to say one can think and feel like a republican, or that being a republican is in part a matter of thinking and feeling, to be a citizen of a republican government (or the subject of a constitutional monarchy, or vassal to a feudal lord) is not a matter of thinking and feeling, in the sense that you can't feel it less or in a distanced or ironic manner. Those kinds of attachments don't have the kind of play built into them that cultural identities do. And where literary forms are intimately bound up with problems of the state, where they cannot devote themselves to the comings and goings of life in a stable civil society, they may be less amenable to any kind of 'transnational' blending.

Russia was certainly Britain's Other in cultural terms, but to Wells, to Rodker, to the workers' film societies and Tolstoyan communes, even to Wilde perhaps, it was also the political laboratory of Europe, from which emerged strange and wondrous compounds: Tolstoyanism, Nihilism, Bolshevism... Such creations could not be wholly embodied in forms of art and fiction, and much of what captured the imagination of British subjects was communicated to them through news reports (of Zasulich's action and trial), through non-fiction journalism and debate (such as Wells' interview with Stalin in *The New Statesman*), and though public lectures and commentary. What could be captured culturally was the kind of social space and the kind of social and political time within which these creations lived, a space and time different from that of the host British culture, 'modern', 'modernist', or 'melodramatic' in a distinctive manner.

The spatial peculiarities are well conveyed by Mikhail Bakhtin's description of the social world of Dostoevsky's novels. In justifying Dostoevsky's description of himself as a 'realist in the higher sense'—a realist, that is, who doesn't expend effort on social descriptions, but goes straight for the soul (*dusha*, the obscure object of so much Russian desire)—Bakhtin claims that in Dostoevsky's novels 'the relations of this *I* with an *other* and with *others* take place directly on the terrain of ultimate questions, bypassing all intermediate and immediate forms'.[21] The terrain of ultimate questions: it's hard to imagine describing any of the available British *milieux* in quite those terms, which is why Woolf herself could only imagine such a place as the scene of an accident or catastrophe. T. S. Eliot had come to more or less the same conclusion and thought the ultimate questions could only be approached by subsuming the available *milieux* in a mythic poem that would endow them with a more profound layer of meaning. I imagine Bakhtin, and Dostoevsky as well, also thought this terrain depended on a religious or sacred conception of space, but in truth nothing could have been more modern. For the terrain of Dostoevsky's prose and the people in it are urban, creatures of St Petersburg. Petersburg was both paradigmatically and uniquely modern, in that it threw modernized subjects—subjects

[21] M. M. Bakhtin, *Problemy tvorchestva Dostoevskogo* (Leningrad: Priboi, 1929), 240–1.

with talents, aspirations, democratic manners—into a world without 'intermediate and immediate forms', that is without the institutions and the pathways through them that make for careers open to talent. The result was a series of melodramatic collisions (the prince and the nihilist, the student and the prostitute), a hypertrophic ethics of conviction, and the high pathos of actions that ignore consequences.

The received line on such peculiarities is that they are the result, the precipitate of Russian backwardness, its failure to develop a proper sphere of civil society, a mature bourgeoisie and middle class, and the kind of constitutional arrangements that 1848 delivered for Europe. It was a line propounded by Russians as much as anyone else. But it was possible to construe this backwardness not as a permanent condition or merely as a deficit that at some point would have to be made up, but as an opportunity to defy the logic of incremental progress and overleap the nations of Western Europe, achieving in one great dramatic bound what they planned to accomplish by a series of measured steps. Vera Zasulich herself carried on a famous correspondence with Marx in which she managed to extract from him the acknowledgement that the 'archaic' Russian rural commune might be made the direct basis of a new socialist society, without first going through a stage of capitalist dissolution.[22] There were predictions of a Third Rome, a Third Renaissance, in which Russia would take up the civilization betrayed by the European West and lead it to a great conclusion. Russia was the land in which time was out of joint, but this could be turned to advantage. Indeed, the belief that it could be turned to advantage was one of the defining features of the kind of modernism pioneered in Russia.

One could take this one step further and say that the belief that social and cultural development did not progress by a gradual incline but by leaps and vaults, by shortcuts and zig-zags, was what made Russia in some sense *more* modern than Britain. 'Progress' had been the colour Britain nailed proudly to its mast, and its critique in the early twentieth century left that standard looking frayed and a little sad. That critique did not have an unambiguous direction; it did not mean merely breaking with a tired and spent Victorianism in order to embrace a radically different future. It could mean Spengler and Eliot, as well as Benjamin or Mayakovsky, fascism as well as socialism and social democracy. In the Russian culture that travelled to Britain between 1880 and 1940, it was embodied in the juxtaposition of the most ancient and the most modern, in ballets where modern angularity depicted ancient rites, in films where rapid cutting and montage stood in for continuity editing, in novels that were—as Woolf said of Dostoevsky's—'seething whirlpools, gyrating sandstorms, waterspouts which hiss and boil and suck us in'.[23] It envisaged—Bakhtin again, this time writing on the novel—'not changes within the limits of a given life (progress, decline), but the possibility of a life different in principle, with different scales and dimensions': sudden transformations, reversals of fortune, the irruption of the future in the present.[24]

[22] Letter from Marx to Vera Zasulich, 8 March 1881, in Karl Marx and Friedrich Engels, *Collected Works*, xlvi (New York: International Publishers, 1992), 71–2.

[23] Woolf, 'The Russian Point of View', 226.

[24] M. M. Bakhtin, 'O Flobere' ['On Flaubert'], in *Sobranie sochinenii*, v (Moscow: Russkie slovari, 1996), 132.

It's not at all clear whether some kind of compromise or negotiation could fuse this kind of time and space with the local variant, although British Whiggishness was already being challenged from within. Perhaps the difficulty of the task can be gauged by the temporary and provisional nature of so many of the projects recounted in this collection. The Tolstoyan collectives faded away, Rodker lost his job, Wells' dreams came to naught, Russian drama remained—outside Chekhov, Turgenev and Bulgakov's *Days of the Turbins* (*Dni Turbinykh*)—an alien body, and Kinofilms went bust. For sure, those who wanted to learn from Russia made progress, the most visible instance being Grierson's adaptation of Russian film technique. But a healthy and productive hybrid?: maybe not. For Russian culture may not have been the kind of material its host culture could adapt or amalgamate. Perhaps it was, in fact though not in intention, the critique of Britain's modernity, to be accepted or rejected. From the evidence of this volume, the critique did not fall on deaf ears, but those who listened most attentively were not in a position to make it stick.

Bibliography

ARCHIVES

Archives nationales, Paris (AN)
  Police Géneral Collection, Sous série F7
British Broadcasting Corporation (BBC)
  The Proms Archive, <http://www.bbc.co.uk/proms/archive>
British Film Institute, London (BFI)
  Film Society Collection
  Ivor Montagu Collection
The British Library, London
  Analytical Programmes and Words of the Queen's Hall Promenade Concerts, h.5470
Gosudarstvennyi arkhiv rossiiskoi federatsii (State Archive of the Russian Federation), Moscow (GARF)
  A. L. Teplov Collection, f. 1721, op. 1.
Gosudarstvennyi muzei L. N. Tolstogo (State Tolstoy Museum), Moscow (GMT)
  Letters from Ernest Howard Crosby to Tolstoy, TS 211/25-27
  Letters from John Morrison Davidson to Tolstoy, TS 231/19
  Letters from John Kenworthy to Tolstoy, TS 223/78-80
  Letters from Percy Redfern to Tolstoy, TS 235/54
Michigan State University Library
  Ernest Howard Crosby Papers
The National Archives, London (TNA)
  Records of the Security Service, KV
Stanford University, Hoover Institution Archives (HIA)
  Okhrana Records, 1883–1917, 26001
Stepney Libraries and Museums Committee, London
  Registers of Donations, 1891–1922, STE/731
Tate Archive, London
  Michael Ernest Sadler Collection
University College London, School of Slavonic and East European Studies Library
  Seton-Watson Collection
University of Leeds, Brotherton Library
  Tuckton House Papers
University of Nottingham
  Harold F. Bing Collection
University of Oxford, Taylor Bodleian Slavonic and Modern Greek Library Nevill Forbes Papers

University of Stirling
John Grierson Archive
University of Texas at Austin, Harry Ransom Humanities Research Center
John Rodker Papers
Victoria and Albert Museum, London (V&A)
Department of Theatre and Performance Collections

PUBLISHED SOURCES

Acocella, Joan, introduction in Joan Acocella, ed., and Kyril Fitzlyon, trans. *The Diary of Vaslav Nijinsky: Unexpurgated Edition* (New York: Farrar, Strauss and Giroux, 1999), vii–xlvi.

Adams, Byron, '"Thor's Hammer": Sibelius and British Music Critics', in Daniel M. Grimley, ed., *Jean Sibelius and His World* (Princeton, NJ: Princeton University Press, 2011), 125–57.

Addams, Jane, 'A Book that Changed My Life', *Christian Century* (13 October 1927), 1196–8.

_____ *Twenty Years at Hull House* (New York: Macmillan, 1911).

[Addresses of teachers of Russian], *Russian Review*, 1, no. 3 (July 1912), 6.

Adlam, Carol, and Juliet Simpson, eds, *Critical Exchange: Art Criticism of the Eighteenth and Nineteenth Centuries in Russia and Western Europe* (Oxford: Peter Lang, 2009).

Agate, James, *The Amazing Theatre* (London: G. G. Harrap, 1939).

_____ *At Half-Past Eight: Essays of the Theatre, 1921–1922* (London: Jonathan Cape, 1923).

_____ *The Contemporary Theatre, 1925* (London: Chapman and Hall, 1926).

_____ *The Contemporary Theatre, 1926* (London: Chapman and Hall, 1927).

_____ 'An Early Masterpiece', review of *The Storm*, Everyman, 1929, *Sunday Times* (8 December 1929), 6.

_____ review of *A Month in the Country*, Westminster, 1936, *Sunday Times* (4 October 1936), 6.

_____ review of *The Seven Who Were Hanged*, Yiddish Art Theatre, New Scala, 1924, *Sunday Times* (18 May 1924), 6.

_____ *A Short View of the English Stage, 1900–1926* (London: Herbert Jenkins, 1926).

Albertson, Ralph, 'The Christian Commonwealth in Georgia', *Georgia Historical Quarterly*, 29 (September 1945), 125–42.

Aldgate, Anthony, and James C. Robertson, *Censorship in Theatre and Cinema* (Edinburgh: Edinburgh University Press, 2005).

Alekseev, M. P., *Russko-angliiskie literaturnye svyazi (XVIII vek-pervaya polovina XIX veka)*, Literaturnoe nasledstvo 91 (Moscow: Nauka, 1982).

Allied Artists' Association Catalogue (London: Royal Albert Hall, 1908).

Allied Artists' Association Catalogue (London: Royal Albert Hall, 1912).

Althusser, Louis, 'Introduction: Unfinished History', in Dominique Lecourt, *Proletarian Science? The Case of Lysenko* (London: NLB, 1977), 7–16.

'American Affairs', *Birmingham Daily Post* (29 September 1883), 5.

'The American-Irish Press', *The Times* (21 June 1882), 5.

Ames, Ernest, 'The Brotherhood Church', *The Tolstoyan*, 1, no. 6 (April 1903), 217–25.

Anderman, Gunilla, *Europe on Stage: Translation and Theatre* (London: Oberon, 2005).

Anderson, Amanda, 'Cosmopolitanism, Universalism, and the Divided Legacies of Modernity', in Bruce Robbins and Pheang Cheah, eds, *Cosmopolitics: Thinking and*

Feeling Beyond the Nation (Minneapolis, MN: University of Minnesota Press, 1998), 265–89.
Andreieff, Léonide, 'The Present', *Rhythm*, 2, no. 9 (1912), 207–13.
Andreyev, Catherine, and Ivan Savický, *Russia Abroad: Prague and the Russian Diaspora, 1918–1938* (New Haven, CT: Yale University Press, 2004).
Antliff, Mark, *Inventing Bergson: Cultural Politics and the Parisian Avant-Garde* (Princeton, NJ: Princeton University Press, 1993).
'The Apocalypse of Baruch', trans. W. R. Morfill, in Montague Rhodes James, ed., *Apocrypha Anecdota,* ii, *Texts and Studies: Contributions to Biblical and Patristic Literature,* 5.1 (Cambridge: Cambridge University Press, 1897), 96–102.
Archer, William, *About the Theatre: Essays and Studies* (London: Unwin, 1886).
Armfelt, Count E., 'Russia in East London', in *Living London: Its Work and its Play, its Humour and its Pathos, its Sights and its Scenes,* i (London: Cassell, 1901), 24–8.
Armytage, W. H. G., 'J. C. Kenworthy and the Tolstoyan Communities in England', in W. Gareth Jones, ed., *Tolstoi and Britain* (Oxford: Berg, 1995), 153–83.
'Art's Enigma', *Saturday Review* (15 August 1914), 202–3.
'Austria', *The Times* (9 May 1882), 5.
'Ball for the Russian Library', *The Times* (7 February 1921), 8.
Bakhtin, M. M., 'O Flobere', in *Sobranie sochinenii*, v (Moscow: Russkie slovari, 1996), 130–7.
_____ *Problemy tvorchestva Dostoevskogo* (Leningrad: Priboi, 1929).
Banks, Georges, 'The New Spirit in Art and Drama', *Rhythm*, 2, no. 12 (1913), 339.
_____ 'Pétrouchka—The Russian Ballet' *Rhythm*, 2, no. 6 (1912), 57–63.
Baring, Maurice, *The Grey Stocking and Other Plays* (London: Constable, 1911).
_____ *The Puppet Show of Memory* (London: Heinemann, 1922).
'Barnes Theatre: The Government Inspector', *The Times* (29 April 1926), 14.
Barnhisel, Greg, '*Perspectives USA* and the Cultural Cold War: Modernism in Service of the State', *Modernism/Modernity*, 14 (2007), 729–54.
Barratt, Andrew, 'Leonid Andreyev's *He Who Gets Slapped*: Who Gets Slapped?', in Robert Russell and Barratt, eds, *Russian Theatre in the Age of Modernism* (Houndmills: Macmillan, 1990), 87–105.
Barta, Peter I., with Ulrich Goebel, eds, *The European Foundations of Russian Modernism* (Lampeter: Mellen, 1991).
Bartoshevich, Alexei, 'The "Inevitability" of Chekhov: Anglo-Russian Theatrical Contacts in the 1910s', in Patrick Miles, ed., *Chekhov on the British Stage* (Cambridge: Cambridge University Press, 1993), 20–8.
_____ 'Theodore Komisarjevsky, Chekhov, and Shakespeare', in Laurence Senelick, ed., *Wandering Stars: Russian Emigré Theatre, 1905–1940* (Iowa City, IA: University of Iowa Press, 1992), 102–15.
Bashford, Christina, 'Not just "G": Towards a History of the Programme Note', in Michael Musgrave, ed., *George Grove, Music and Victorian Culture* (Basingstoke: Palgrave, 2003), 115–42.
Bassett, Kate, review of *Plasticine*, Royal Court Upstairs, 2002, *Independent on Sunday* (23 March 2002), in *Theatre Record*, 22, no. 6 (2002), 343.
Bassnett, Susan, *Comparative Literature: A Critical Introduction* (Oxford: Blackwell, 1993).
Batchelor, John, *H. G. Wells* (Cambridge: Cambridge University Press, 1985).
B[aughan], E. A., 'What is "Classical"', *Musical Standard*, 9, no. 221 (26 March 1898), 194–5.
'Bawdsey', *The Ipswich Journal* (22 July 1882), 9.
Bazin, André, 'The Myth of Total Cinema', in *What is Cinema?*, ed. and trans. Hugh Gray, i (Berkeley and Los Angeles, CA: University of California Press, 1971), 17–22.

Beasley, Rebecca, 'Modernism's Translations', in Mark Wollaeger and Matt Eatough, eds, *The Oxford Handbook of Global Modernisms* (New York: Oxford University Press, forthcoming 2012), 551–70.

_____'On Not Knowing Russian: The Translations of Virginia Woolf and S. S. Kotelianskii', *Modern Language Review*, 108, no. 1 (2013), 1–29.

_____'Russia and the Invention of the Modernist Intelligentsia', in Peter Brooker and Andrew Thacker, eds, *Geographies of Modernism: Literatures, Cultures, Spaces* (London: Routledge, 2005), 19–30.

_____ 'Vortorussophilia', in Mark Antliff and Scott Klein, eds, *Vorticism: New Perspectives* (Oxford: Oxford University Press, 2013).

Beasley, Rebecca, and Philip Ross Bullock, eds, *Translating Russia, 1890–1935*, special issue of *Translation and Literature*, 20, no. 3 (2011).

Beazley, Raymond, Nevill Forbes, and G. A. Birkett, *Russia from the Varangians to the Bolsheviks* (Oxford: Clarendon Press, 1918).

Beckson, Karl, *Oscar Wilde: The Critical Heritage* (London: Routledge & Kegan Paul, 1970).

_____ *The Oscar Wilde Encyclopedia* (New York: AMS Press, 1998).

Beecham, Thomas, *A Mingled Chime* (New York: Putnam's, 1943).

Beerbohm, Max, 'The Stage Society', *Saturday Review* (3 December 1904), in *Last Theatres, 1904–1910* (New York: Taplinger, 1970), 113–15.

_____ 'Two Plays', *Saturday Review* (18 June 1898), in *More Theatres, 1898–1903* (New York: Taplinger, 1969), 36–9.

_____review of *The Lower Depths*, Stage Society, 1903, *Saturday Review* (5 December 1903), 699–700, reprinted in *Around Theatres* (London: Rupert Hart-Davis, 1953), 302–5.

_____review of *The Power of Darkness*, Stage Society, 1904, *Saturday Review* (31 December 1904), 823–4.

Bell, Quentin, *Virginia Woolf: A Biography*, 2 vols (London: Hogarth Press, 1972).

Benjamin, Walter, 'Moscow Diary', trans. Richard Sieburth, *October*, 35 (1985), 9–135.

Berberova, Nina, *Moura: The Dangerous Life of the Baroness Budberg*, trans. Marian Schwartz and Richard D. Sylvester (New York: New York Review Books, 2005).

Bergman, Jay, *Vera Zasulich: A Biography* (Stanford, CA: Stanford University Press, 1983).

Bergson, Henri, *Creative Evolution*, trans. Arthur Mitchell (London: Macmillan, 1911).

'Berlin Experts' Cure for Anarchy', *Daily Express* (7 January 1911), 1.

Berman, Marshall, *All that is Solid Melts into Air: The Experience of Modernity* (London: Verso, 1983).

Berry, Lloyd E., and Robert O. Crummey, eds, *Rude & Barbarous Kingdom: Russia in the Accounts of Sixteenth-Century English Voyagers* (Madison, WI: University of Wisconsin Press, 1968).

Bibbee, Jeffrey, 'The Church of England and Russian Orthodoxy: Politics and the Ecumenical Dialogue, 1888–1917', PhD thesis, University of London, 2008.

Billington-Grieg, Teresa, *Suffragist Tactics Past and Present* (1912), in Marie Mulvey Roberts and Tamae Mizuta, eds, *The Militants: Suffragette Activism* (London: Routledge 1994), 1–14.

Binckes, Faith, *Modernism, Magazines, and the British Avant-Garde: Reading Rhythm, 1910–1914* (Oxford: Oxford University Press, 2010).

Bing, Harold F., 'Tolstoyans in England', *One and All* (May 1972), 6.

Binyon, Laurence, *The Flight of the Dragon: An Essay on the Theory and Practice of Art in China and Japan, Based on Original Sources* (London: Murray, 1935).

'The Blackburn Brotherhood', *New Order*, NS5, no. 19 (August 1899), 115–16.

Blake, Patricia, 'Researching Babel's Biography', in Gregory Freidin, ed., *The Enigma of Isaac Babel: Biography, History, Context* (Stanford, CA: Stanford University Press, 2009), 3–15.

Blakesley, Rosalind P., *The Arts and Crafts Movement* (London: Phaidon, 2006).

_____ and Susan E. Reid, 'A Long Engagement: Russian Art and the "West"', in Rosalind P. Blakesley and Susan E. Reid, eds, *Russian Art and the West: A Century of Dialogue in Painting, Architecture, and the Decorative Arts* (Dekalb, IL: Northern Illinois University Press, 2007), 3–20.

'Blood Relations and Brothers', *Punch* (13 December 1879), 275.

Bondar, D., and Alfred Calvert, *Bondar's Simplified Russian Method (Conversational and Commercial)* (London: Effingham Wilson, 1911).

The Book of the Secrets of Enoch, trans. W. R. Morfill, ed. R. H. Charles (Oxford: Clarendon Press, 1896).

'Books for Russian Emigrants', *The Times* (4 November 1912), 4.

Booth, Charles, *Life and Labour of the People in London*, 17 vols (London: Macmillan, 1902–3).

Booth, Michael R., *English Melodrama* (London: Jenkins, 1965).

Bowers, Faubion, *Scriabin: A Biography*, 2nd edn, 2 vols (New York: Dover, 1996).

Boyer, Paul, and N. Spéranski, *Manuel pour l'étude de la langue russe* (Paris: Colin, 1905).

_____ *Russian Reader*, adpt Samuel Northrup Harper (Chicago, IL: University of Chicago Press; London: Luzac, 1906).

Bozóki, András, and Miklós Sükösd, *Anarchism in Hungary: Theory, History, Legacies* (Boulder, CO: Social Science Monographs, 2006).

Bratton, J. S., 'Theatre of war: The Crimea on the London stage, 1854–5', in David Bradby, Louis James, and Bernard Sharratt, eds, *Performance and Politics in Popular Drama: Aspects of Popular Entertainment in Theatre, Film and Television, 1800–1976* (Cambridge: Cambridge University Press, 1980), 119–37.

Brereton, Austin, 'Dramatic Notes, 1881', in *Dramatic Notes: A Chronicle of the London Stage, 1879–1882* (London: Bogue, 1883), 17.

Brewster, Dorothy, *East-West Passage: A Study in Literary Relationships* (London: George Allen and Unwin, 1954).

Briggs, A. D. P., 'Obituary: Professor Dame Elizabeth Hill', *The Independent* (6 January 1997), 14.

Brock, Peter, trans. and ed., *Life in an Austro-Hungarian Military Prison: The Slovak Tolstoyan Dr. Albert Škarvan's Story* (Syracuse, NY: Syracuse University Press, 2002).

_____ 'The Škarvan Case: The Trial and Imprisonment of a Slovak Tolstoyan', in *Against the Draft* (Toronto, ON: University of Toronto Press, 2006), 172–87.

_____ 'Tolstoyism and the Hungarian Peasant', *Slavonic and East European Review*, 58, no. 3 (July 1980), 345–69.

_____ 'Tolstoyism, Cultural Nationalism, and Conscientious Objection: A Slovak Case Study', in *Freedom from War: Non-Sectarian Pacifism, 1814–1914* (Toronto, ON: University of Toronto Press, 1991), 230–46.

Brody, Ervin C., *The Demetrius Legend and its Literary Treatment in the Age of the Baroque* (Madison, NJ: Fairleigh Dickinson University Press, 1972).

Brooker, Peter, and Andrew Thacker, eds, *The Oxford Critical and Cultural History of Modernist Magazines* (Oxford: Oxford University Press, 2009).

Brooke, Christopher N. L., *A History of the University of Cambridge*, 4 vols (Cambridge: Cambridge University Press, 1988–93).

Brooks, Peter, *The Melodramatic Imagination: Balzac, Henry James, Melodrama and the Mode of Excess* (New Haven, CT: Yale University Press, 1995).

Brown, Bob, *Can We Co-operate?* (Staten Island, NY: Roving Eye Press, 1940).

_____ 'The American Writer's Plight', *International Literature*, 7 (November 1935), 92.

Brown, Catherine, *The Art of Comparison: How Novels and Critics Compare* (London: Legenda, 2011).

_____ 'The Russian Soul Englished', *Journal of Modern Literature,* 36, no. 1 (Fall 2012), 132–49.

Brown, Ivor, review of *The White Guard,* Phoenix, 1938, *The Spectator* (14 October 1938), 603.

Brown, Nathalie Babel, *Hugo and Dostoevsky* (Ann Arbor, MI: Ardis, 1978).

Bryher, *Film Problems of Soviet Russia* (Territet: POOL, 1929).

Buckle, Richard, *Nijinsky* (Harmondsworth: Penguin, 1975).

Buckler, Julie A., 'Melodramatizing Russia: Nineteenth-century Views from the West', in Louise McReynolds and Joan Neuberger, eds, *Imitations of Life: Two Centuries of Melodrama in Russia* (Durham, NC: Duke University Press, 2002), 55–78.

Bullen, J. B., ed., *Post-Impressionists in England* (London: Routledge, 1988).

Bullock, Philip Ross, ed. and trans. *The Correspondence of Jean Sibelius and Rosa Newmarch, 1906–1939* (Woodbridge: Boydell, 2011).

_____ '"Lessons in Sensibility": Rosa Newmarch, Music Appreciation and the Aesthetic Cultivation of the Self', in Stefano Evangelista and Catherine Maxwell, eds, *The Arts in Victorian Literature,* special issue of *Yearbook of English Studies,* 40, nos 1–2 (2010), 295–318.

_____ *Rosa Newmarch and Russian Music in Late Nineteenth and Early Twentieth-Century England* (Farnham: Ashgate, 2009).

Burchard, Amory, *Klubs der russischen Dichter in Berlin, 1920–1941: Institutionen des literarischen Lebens in Exil* (Munich: Sagner, 2001).

Burnett, Leon, and Emily Lygo, eds, *The Art of Accommodation: Literary Translation in Russian Culture* (Oxford: Peter Lang, 2013).

Burtsev,V. L., *Za sto let 1800–1896. Sbornik po istorii politicheskikh i obshchestvennykh dvizhenii v Rossii* (London: Russian Free Press Fund, 1897).

Byukling [Byckling], Liisa, *Mikhail Chekhov v zapadnom teatre i kino* (St Petersburg: Akademicheskii proekt, 2000).

Cahen, Louis, and Nevill Forbes, *English-Serbian Phrase-Book, with Easy Grammar* (Oxford: Blackwell, 1915).

Cain, Jimmie E., Jr., *Bram Stoker and Russophobia: Evidence of the British Fear of Russia in 'Dracula' and 'The Lady of the Shroud'* (Jefferson, NC: McFarland, 2006).

Calderon, George, *The Little Stone House* (London: Sidgwick and Jackson, 1913).

The Calendar of Joint Matriculation Board, 1921, Containing the Examination Papers and Lists of Successful Candidates for the Year 1920 (Manchester: Cornish, 1920).

Cambrensis, 'Scriabin's Music and the Three Choirs Festival', *Musical Times,* 63, no. 948 (1 February 1922), 124.

Capell, Richard, 'Cannibal music: Amazing production of Russian Ballet', *Daily Mail* (12 July 1913), 5.

Carswell, John, *The Exile: A Life of Ivy Litvinoff* (London: Faber and Faber, 1983).

Carrick, Valery, *More Russian Picture Tales* (Oxford: Blackwell, 1914).

_____ *Picture Tales: Fourth Selection* (Oxford: Blackwell, 1924).

_____ *Picture Tales from the Russian* (Oxford: Blackwell, 1913).

_____ *Still More Russian Picture Tales* (Oxford: Blackwell, 1915).

Carter, Huntly, 'Art and Drama in Paris', *New Age,* 10, no. 19 (1912), 443.

_____ 'New Books on Art', *The Egoist,* 1, no. 12 (1914), 235–6.

_____ *The New Spirit in Drama and Art* (London: Frank Palmer, 1912).

_____ *The New Spirit in the Cinema* (London: Harold Shaylor, 1930).

_____ *The New Theatre and Cinema of Soviet Russia* (London: Chapman and Dodd, 1924).

'The Case of Hammond', *New Order*, 3, no. 3 (March 1897), 17–20.

Chekhov, Anton, *The Chameleon and Four Other Tales*, ed. by P. Selver (London: Kegan Paul, Trench, Trubner, 1916).

_____ *Humorous Stories*, ed. D. Bondar (London: Effingham Wilson, 1916).

_____ *Short Stories*, 2 vols (London: Jaschke, 1919).

_____ *Letters of Anton Chekhov*, ed. Simon Karlinsky, trans. M. H. Heim in collaboration with Simon Karlinsky (London: Bodley Head, 1973).

_____ *Polnoe sobranie sochinenii i pisem*, xiii (Moscow: Nauka, 1986).

Chertkov, Vladimir, 'Words to Vegetarians', *New Order*, 4, no. 11 (December 1898), 117–19.

Chowl, Hay, 'Propaganda', *Close Up*, 4, no. 1 (January 1929), 27–32.

Churchill, William, review of Maurice Baring, *The Russian People* (1911), *Bulletin of the American Geographical Society*, 44, no. 3 (1912), 218.

'Cinematograph Films', Hansard, HC (series 5) vol. 256, cols 1280–1 (21 September 1931).

'Cinematograph Industry', Hansard, HC (series 5) vol. 293, cols 339–40 (1 November 1934).

Clapp, John Bouvé, and Edwin Francis Edgett, *Plays of the Present* (New York: Dunlap Society, 1902).

Clark, Grahame, *Prehistory at Cambridge and Beyond* (Cambridge: Cambridge University Press, 1989).

Clark, Katerina, *Moscow, the Fourth Rome: Stalinism, Cosmopolitanism, and the Evolution of Soviet Culture, 1931–1941* (Cambridge, MA: Harvard University Press, 2011).

Cloud, Gerald, *John Rodker's Ovid Press: A Bibliographical History* (New Castle, DE: Oak Knoll Press, 2010).

Cole, G. D. H., *What Marx Really Meant* (London: Victor Gollancz, 1934).

Collette, Carolyn P., '"Faire Emelye": Medievalism and the Moral Courage of Emily Wilding Davison', *Chaucer Review*, 42, no. 3 (2008), 223–43.

Cooper, Sandi, *Patriotic Pacifism: Waging War on War in Europe, 1815–1914* (Oxford: Oxford University Press, 1991).

Cornwell, Neil, *James Joyce and the Russians* (Basingstoke: Palgrave, 1992).

Crawford Flitch, J. E., *Modern Dancing and Dancers* (London, Grant Richards, 1912).

Cross, Anthony, *Anglo-Russica: Aspects of Cultural Relations between Great Britain and Russia in the Eighteenth and Early Nineteenth Centuries* (Oxford: Berg, 1993).

_____ *Cambridge: Some Russian Connections: An Inaugural Lecture* (Cambridge: University Press, 1987).

_____, ed., *'A People Passing Rude': British Responses to Russian Culture* (Cambridge: Open Book Publishers, 2012).

_____ *The Russian Theme in English Literature from the Sixteenth Century to 1980: An Introductory Survey and a Bibliography* (Oxford: Meeuws, 1985).

Dale, Catherine, *Music Analysis in Britain in the Nineteenth and Early Twentieth Centuries* (Aldershot: Ashgate, 2003).

Dalgarno, Emily, *Virginia Woolf and the Migrations of Language* (Cambridge: Cambridge University Press, 2012).

Damrosch, David, *What is World Literature?* (Princeton, NJ: Princeton University Press, 2003).

Danson, Lawrence, 'Wilde as Critic and Theorist', in Peter Raby, ed., *The Cambridge Companion to Oscar Wilde* (Cambridge: Cambridge University Press, 1997), 80–95.

Davie, Donald, ed., *Russian Literature and Modern English Fiction: A Collection of Critical Essays* (Chicago, IL: University of Chicago Press, 1965).

Davison, Emily, 'Letter to the Editor', *Pall Mall Gazette* (19 September 1912), 4.

_____ 'The Price of Liberty', *The Suffragette* (5 June 1914), 129.

Decoo, Wilfried, *Systemization in Foreign Language Teaching: Monitoring Content Progression* (New York: Routledge, 2011).

Demoor, Marysa, 'John Middleton Murry's Editorial Apprenticeships: Getting Modernist "Rhythm" into the *Athenaeum*, 1919–1921', *English Literature in Transition, 1880–1920*, 52 (2009), 123–43.

'Discussion Column: The Teaching of Foreign Literature', *Modern Language Teaching*, 5 (1909), 50–1, 84–7, 105–9, 144–8, 177–9, 202–7.

Disher, Maurice Willson, *Blood and Thunder: Mid-Victorian Melodrama and its Origins* (London: Muller, 1949).

_____ *Melodrama: Plots That Thrilled* (London: Rockliff, 1934).

Dobrenko, Evgeny, *The Making of the State Writer: Social and Aesthetic Origins of Soviet Literary Culture*, trans. Jesse M. Savage (Stanford, CA: Stanford University Press, 2001).

_____ *Political Economy of Socialist Realism*, trans. Jesse M. Savage (New Haven, CT: Yale University Press, 2007).

Doctor, Jennifer, *The BBC and Ultra-Modern Music, 1922–1936: Shaping a Nation's Tastes* (Cambridge: Cambridge University Press, 1999).

_____ and David Wright, eds, *The Proms: A New History* (London: Thames & Hudson, 2007).

Dodgson, Charles Lutwidge, *The Russian Journal and Other Selections from the Works of Lewis Carroll*, ed. John Francis McDermott (New York: Dutton, 1935).

Donohue, Joseph, 'Wilde and the Idea of a Theatre', in C. George Sandulescu, ed., *Rediscovering Oscar Wilde*, (Gerrards Cross: Colin Smythe, 1996), 118–26.

Dostoevsky, F. M., *Elka i Svad' ba; Chestnyi vor* (Oxford: Tipografiya Klarendon, 1917).

Doyle, Laura, and Laura Winkiel, eds, *Geomodernisms: Race, Modernism, Modernity* (Bloomington and Indianapolis, IN: Indiana University Press, 2005).

'The Drama in America', *The Era* (8 September 1883), 3.

'Dramatic Notes', *Funny Folks* (10 March 1883), 78.

Drummond, Pippa, *The Provincial Music Festival in England, 1784–1914* (Farnham: Ashgate, 2012).

Duff, J. D. D., ed., *Russian Lyrics* (Cambridge: Cambridge University Press, 1917).

Dukes, Ashley, *Modern Dramatists* (London: Frank Palmer, 1911).

'Dynamite Done Up', *Funny Folks* (17 September 1881), 291.

E., St. J., review of *He Who Gets Slapped*, Everyman, 1927, *The Observer* (13 November 1927), 15.

_____ review of *Paul I*, Court, 1927, *The Observer* (9 October 1927), 15.

Eagle, Solomon, 'Current Literature, Books in General', *New Statesman*, 3, no. 56 (1914), 118.

Edgerton, William B., 'The Artist Turned Prophet: Leo Tolstoj after 1880', in W. E. Harkins, ed., *American Contributions to the Sixth International Congress of Slavists*, ii: *Literary Contributions* (The Hague: Mouton, 1968), 61–85.

_____ 'The Social Influence of Lev Tolstoj in Bulgaria', in Jane Gary Harris, ed., *American Contributions to the Tenth International Congress of Slavists: Literature* (Columbus, OH: Slavica, 1988), 123–38.

_____, ed., *Memoirs of Peasant Tolstoyans in Soviet Russia* (Bloomington, IN: Indiana University Press, 1993).

Elkin, Robert, *Queen's Hall, 1893–1941* (London: Rider, 1944).

Ellmann, Richard, *Oscar Wilde* (London: Hamish Hamilton, 1987).

Etkind, Alexander, *Internal Colonization: Russia's Imperial Experience* (Cambridge: Polity, 2011).

The Examination Statutes, 1905–1906 (Oxford: Clarendon Press, 1905).
The Examination Statutes, 1915–1916 (Oxford: Clarendon Press, 1915).
'Exhibition of Russian Art', *The Times* (1 November 1910), 11.
'Exodus of the Æsthetes', *Funny Folks* (7 January 1882), 4.
Fairclough, Pauline, 'The Old Shostakovich: Reception in the British Press', *Music and Letters*, 88, no. 2 (2007), 266–98.
Fanger, Donald, *Dostoevsky and Romantic Realism* (Cambridge, MA: Harvard University Press, 1965).
Fawkes, Richard, *Dion Boucicault: A Biography* (London: Quartet Books, 1979).
Fillion, Michelle, *Difficult Rhythm: Music and the Word in E. M. Forster* (Urbana, Chicago, and Springfield, IL: University of Illinois Press, 2010).
'The Film is a Weapon', *Workers' Cinema*, 1, no. 1 (November 1931), 2.
The Film Society Programmes, 1925–1939 (New York: Arno Press, 1972).
Fink, Hilary L., *Bergson and Russian Modernism, 1900–1930* (Evanston, IL: Northwestern University Press, 1999).
Firth, Charles, *Modern Languages at Oxford, 1724–1929* (Oxford: Oxford University Press, 1929).
Fitzgerald, Percy, 'Nadjezda', *The Theatre* (1 February 1886), 104–5.
Fitzpatrick, Sheila, *Everyday Stalinism: Ordinary Life in Extraordinary Times: Soviet Russia in the 1930s* (Oxford: Oxford University Press, 1999).
_____ *The Russian Revolution*, 3rd edition (Oxford: Oxford University Press, 2008).
Fleming, Peter, review of *The White Guard*, Phoenix 1938, *The Spectator* (14 October 1938), 603.
Fletcher, John, *The Loyal Subject: A Tragi-Comedy*, in *The Works of Mr. Francis Beaumont and Mr John Fletcher*, 7 vols (London: Jacob Tonson, 1711), ii, 923–1016.
'Floats and Flies', *Fun* (30 November 1881), 228.
'Floats and Flies', *Fun* (14 December 1881), 248.
Foot, Michael, *H. G.: The History of Mr. Wells* (London: Black Swan, 1996).
'For the Cause of Education in East London', *Free Russia*, 13, no. 6 (1 June 1902), 68.
Forbes, Nevill, *Elementary Russian Grammar* (Oxford Clarendon Press, 1919).
_____ *First Russian Book: A Practical Manual of Russian Declensions* (Oxford: Clarendon Press, 1915).
_____ *Fourth Russian Book: Exercises on First and Second Russian Books* (Oxford: Clarendon Press, 1918).
_____ *Russian Grammar* (Oxford: Clarendon Press, 1914).
_____ *Second Russian Book: A Practical Manual of Russian Verbs* (Oxford: Clarendon Press, 1916).
_____ *The Southern Slavs* (Oxford: Oxford University Press, 1915).
_____ *Third Russian Book: Extracts from Aksakov, Grigorovich, Herzen, Saltykov* (Oxford: Clarendon Press, 1917).
_____ *Word-for-Word Russian Story-Book* (Oxford: Blackwell, 1916).
Forbes, Nevill, and others, *The Balkans: A History of Bulgaria, Serbia, Greece, Rumania, Turkey* (Oxford: Clarendon Press, 1915).
Forbes, Nevill, and Captain Keyworth, *Easy Serbian for our Men Abroad, and How to Pronounce it* (London: Kegan Paul, 1915).
Foster, D. B., 'Notes from Leeds', *New Order*, 4, no. 5 (June 1898), 55.
_____ *Socialism and the Christ: My Two Great Discoveries in a Long and Painful Search for the Truth* (Leeds: D. B. Foster, 1921).
Foster, R. F., *Modern Ireland, 1600–1972* (London: Penguin, 1988).

Franklin, Peter, 'Sibelius in Britain', in Daniel M. Grimley, ed., *The Cambridge Companion to Sibelius* (Cambridge: Cambridge University Press, 2004), 182–95.

Freeburg, Victor O., *Pictorial Beauty on the Screen* (New York: Macmillan, 1923).

Freeth, Frank, *A First Russian Reader* (London: Kegan Paul, Trench 1916).

'French authors and English adapters', *The Theatre* (1 December 1878), 329–32.

Friedberg, Maurice, *Literary Translation in Russia: A Cultural History* (University Park, PA: Pennsylvania State University Press, 1997).

Friedman, Susan Stanford, 'Periodizing Modernism: Postcolonial Modernities and the Space/Time Borders of Modernist Studies', *Modernism/Modernity*, 13, no. 3 (2006), 425–43.

Frolova-Walker, Marina, 'Against Germanic Reasoning: the Russian Search for an Alternative Means of Symphonic Development', in Harry White and Michael Murphy, eds, *Musical Constructions of Nationalism: Essays on the History and Ideology of European Musical Culture, 1800–1945* (Cork: Cork University Press, 2001), 104–22.

'From Here and There', *Modern Language Teaching*, 11 (1915), 119–22.

'The fusion of music and dancing: "Le sacre du printemps"', *The Times*, (26 July 1913), 8.

Fry, Roger, 'Stage Setting', *New Statesman* (27 June 1914), 2.

Gale, Matthew, and Chris Stephens, eds, *Francis Bacon* (London: Tate Publishing, 2008).

Galton, D., 'Sir Bernard Pares and Slavonic Studies in London University, 1919–39', *Slavonic and East European Review*, 46, no. 107 (July 1968), 481–91.

Garafola, Lynn, *Diaghilev's Ballets Russes* (New York: Oxford University Press, 1989).

Garnett, Richard, *Constance Garnett: A Heroic Life* (London: Sinclair-Stevenson, 1991).

Garshin, V. M., *Izbrannye razskazy: To, chego ne bylo, vstrecha, signal, chetyre dnya* (Oxford: Tipografiya Klarendon, [1920]).

_____*The Signal, and Four Days on the Field of Battle*, ed. J. H. Freese (London: Kegan Paul, Trench, Trubner, [1918]).

Gassert, Imogen, 'Charles Daniel: Maverick Pacifist Publisher in the First World War', *Publishing History*, 48 (2000), 5–40.

Gaudier-Brzeska, Henri, 'Allied Artists' Association Ltd', *The Egoist*,1, no. 12 (1914), 227–8.

Gettmann, Royal A., *Turgenev in England and America* (Urbana, IL: University of Illinois Press, 1941).

Gibian, George, and H. W. Tjalsma, *Russian Modernism: Culture and the Avant-Garde, 1900–1930* (Ithaca, NY: Cornell University Press, 1976).

Gibson, Aleksey, *Russian Poetry and Criticism in Paris from 1920 to 1940* (The Hague: Leuxenhoff, 1990).

Gleason, John Howes, *The Genesis of Russophobia in Great Britain: A Study of the Interaction of Policy and Opinion* (Cambridge, MA: Harvard University Press, 1950).

Glew, Adrian, '"Blue Spiritual Sounds": Kandinsky and the Sadlers, 1911–16', *Burlington Magazine*, 139, no. 1134 (1997), 600–15.

Gogol', N. V., *Dead Souls* (London: Jaschke, 1919).

_____ *The Inspector-General*, ed. D. Bondar (London: Effingham Wilson, 1917).

_____ *Starosvetskie pomeshchki* (Oxford: Tipografiya Klarendon, 1917).

Goncharov, I. A., *Slugi starogo veka* (Oxford: Tipografiya Klarendon, [1918]).

Goring, Jack, 'Wickford Notes', *New Order*, 4, no. 7 (August 1898), 76.

Gorki, Maxim, *The Lower Depths*, trans. Laurence Irving (London: T. Fisher Unwin, 1912).

Gosse, Edmund, 'Mr. Baring's Plays: They Show a Decided Improvement on His Previous Work (From the *Morning Post*)', *New York Times Review of Books* (21 April 1912), 247.

Graff, Gerald, *Professing Literature: An Institutional History* (Chicago, IL: University of Chicago Press, 1989).

Graham, Stephen, *Part of the Wonderful Scene: An Autobiography* (London: Collins, 1964).

Gray, Cecil, *Sibelius* (London: Oxford University Press, 1931).

_____*A Survey of Contemporary Music* (London: Oxford University Press, 1924).

_____'The Task of Criticism', *The Sackbut*, 1 (1920), 9–13.

Gregory, James, *Victorians and Vegetarians: The Vegetarian Movement in Nineteenth-Century Britain* (London: I. B. Tauris, 2007).

Grein, J. T., review of *The Brass Paperweight*, Apollo, 1928, *The Sketch* (31 October 1928), 246.

_____review of *The Storm*, Everyman, 1929, *The Sketch* (18 December 1929), 604.

Griboyedov, Alexander, *The Mischief of Being Clever*, trans. Sir Bernard Pares (London: School of Slavonic Studies/Eyre and Spottiswoode, [1925]).

Grierson, John, 'A First Principle of Criticism', *New Britain*, 2, no. 27 (22 November 1933), 14.

_____'Films and Talkies: Cinema of State', *The Clarion*, NS 2, no. 8 (August 1930), 235.

_____'Films and Talkies', *The Clarion*, NS 1, no. 11 (November 1929), 11.

_____*Grierson on Documentary*, ed. Forsyth Hardy (London: Faber, 1979).

Griffith, Gareth, *Socialism and Superior Brains: The Political Thought of Bernard Shaw* (London: Routledge, 2003).

Grigoriev, S. L., *The Diaghilev Ballet, 1909–1929* (Harmondsworth: Penguin, 1960).

Gross, John, review of *Black Milk*, Royal Court Upstairs, 2003, *Sunday Telegraph* (9 February 2003, in *Theatre Record*, 23, no. 3 (2003), 127.

Groys, Boris, *The Total Art of Stalinism: Avant-Garde, Aesthetic Dictatorship, and Beyond*, trans. Charles Rougle (Princeton, NJ: Princeton University Press, 1992).

Gruetzner Robins, Anna, *Modern Art in Britain, 1910–1914* (London: Merrell Holberton, 1997).

Guppy, Henry, 'Notes and News', *Bulletin of The John Rylands Library, Manchester*, 29, no. 1 (July, 1945), 1–47.

H. D., 'Russian Films', *Close Up*, 3, no. 3 (September 1928), 18–29.

H., H., review of *The Storm*, Everyman, 1929, *The Observer* (8 December 1929), 15.

Habets, Alfred, *Borodin and Liszt*, trans. Rosa Newmarch (London: Digby, Long, 1895) [Fr. orig. *Alexandre Borodine d'après la biographie et la correspondance publiées par M. Wladimir Stassoff* (Paris: Fischbacher, 1883)].

Hall, Bolton, *What Tolstoy Taught* (London: Chatto and Windus, 1913).

Harper, Samuel N., *The Russia I Believe In: The Memoirs of Samuel N. Harper, 1902–1941*, ed. Paul V. Harper, with the assistance of Ronald Thompson (Chicago, IL: University of Chicago Press, 1945).

Harris, Frank, 'The Holy Man', *Rhythm*, 2, no. 5 (1912), 2–10.

Harrison, Martin, *Francis Bacon: Photography, Film and the Practice of Painting* (London: Thames and Hudson, 2005).

Hastings, Beatrice, 'Present-Day Criticism', *New Age*, 10, no. 22 (1912), 519.

Hatton, Joseph, *By Order of the Czar: A Drama in Five Acts* (London: Hutchinson, 1904).

Hawkins, Eric W., *Modern Languages in the Curriculum*, rev. edn (Cambridge: Cambridge University Press, 1987).

Hemmings, F. W. J., *The Russian Novel in France, 1884–1914* (Oxford: Oxford University Press, 1950).

Henderson, Robert, 'Aleksei Teplov and the Free Russian Library in Whitechapel', *Solanus*, NS, 22 (2011), 5–26.

_____'Russkaya besplatnaya biblioteka v Ist-Ende', in O. Morgunova, ed., *Russkoe prisutstvie v Britanii* (Moscow: Sovremennaya ekonomika i pravo, 2010), 59–68.

Hendrix, Henriette, *Een Week in de Kolonie te Blaricum* (Amsterdam: Cohen Zonen, 1901).
Hendry, James Findlay, 'Lady Macbeth of Mzensk', *Left Review*, 2, no. 6 (March 1936), 272–3.
Hermans, Theo, ed., *The Manipulation of Literature: Studies in Literary Translation* (London: Croom Helm, 1985).
Herring, Robert, 'Storm over London', *Close Up*, 4, no. 3 (March 1929), 34–44.
Higgins, A. G., *A History of the Brotherhood Church* (Stapleton: Brotherhood Church, 1982).
Hill, Elizabeth, *In the Mind's Eye: The Memoirs of Dame Elizabeth Hill*, ed. Jean Stafford Smith (Lewes: Book Guild, 1999).
_____ *Why Need we Study the Slavs? An Inaugural Lecture* (Cambridge: Cambridge University Press, 1951).
Hingley, Ronald, *Nihilists: Russian Radicals and Revolutionaries in the Reign of Alexander II, 1855–81* (London: Weidenfeld and Nicolson, 1967).
Hobhouse, Stephen, *Forty Years and an Epilogue* (London: James Clarke, 1951).
Hodgson, W. Earl, *A Night With A Nihilist* (Cupar: Fifeshire Journal, 1886).
Hogenkamp, Bert, *Deadly Parallels: Film and the Left in Britain, 1929–39* (London: Lawrence and Wishart, 1986).
Holah, Florence, 'Money—An Instrument of Compulsion', *New Order*, 4, no. 12 (January 1899), 5.
_____ "The Root of All Evil', *New Order*, NS 5, no. 18 (July 1899), 101.
Hollander, Paul, *Political Pilgrims: Travels of Western Intellectuals to the Soviet Union, China, and Cuba, 1928–1978* (New York: Harper Colophon, 1981).
Holman, M. J. de K.,'The Purleigh Colony: Tolstoyan Togetherness in the late 1890s', in W. Gareth Jones, ed., *Tolstoi and Britain* (Oxford: Berg, 1995), 135–51.
_____ 'Translating Tolstoy for the Free Age Press: Vladimir Chertkov and his English Manager Arthur Fifield', *Slavonic and East European Review*, 66, no. 2 (April 1988), 184–97.
Holmes, C. J., 'Stray Thoughts on Rhythm in Painting', *Rhythm*, 1, no. 3 (1911), 1–3.
Holroyd, Michael, *Lytton Strachey: A Critical Biography*, 2 vols (New York: Holt, Rinehart and Winston, 1968).
Howard, Cecil, 'Siberia', *The Theatre* (2 January 1888), 45–6.
_____ 'Vera', *The Theatre* (1 August 1890), 35–6.
Hubert, Henri, and Marcel Mauss, *Sacrifice: Its Nature and Function* (Chicago, IL: Chicago University Press, 1964).
Hughes, Meirion, and Robert Stradling, *The English Musical Renaissance, 1840–1940: Constructing a National Music*, 2nd edn (Manchester: Manchester University Press, 2001).
Hughes, Michael, *Diplomacy before the Russian Revolution: Britain, Russia and the Old Diplomacy, 1894–1917* (Basingstoke: Macmillan, 2000).
_____ 'The English Slavophile: W. J. Birkbeck and Russia', *Slavonic and East European Review*, 82, no. 3 (2004), 680–706.
_____ 'Searching for the Soul of Russia: British Perceptions of Russia during the First World War', *Twentieth Century British History*, 20, no. 2 (2009), 198–226.
Hutchings, Stephen C., *Russian Modernism: The Transfiguration of the Everyday* (Cambridge: Cambridge University Press, 1997).
Hyde, H. Montgomery, ed., *The Annotated Oscar Wilde* (New York: Clarkson N. Potter, 1982).
_____ *Oscar Wilde: A Biography* (New York: Farrar, Straus, and Giroux, 1975).
_____ *The Trials of Oscar Wilde* (New York: Dover, 1973).
Ingrams, Richard, *Muggeridge: The Biography* (London: Harper Collins, 1995).

Inkster, Leonard, 'The Russian ballet, I', *New Statesman* (5 July 1913), 406–8.
_____ 'The Russian ballet, II', *New Statesman* (19 July 1913), 469–70.
_____ 'The Russian ballet: A postscript', *New Statesman* (26 July 1913), 501.
'Ireland', *Bristol Mercury and Daily Post* (16 September 1881), 2.
'Ireland', *Trewman's Exeter Flying Post or Plymouth and Cornish Advertiser* (21 September 1881), 8.
'Ireland: The State Prosecutions', *The Times* (14 January 1881), 10.
Isherwood, Christopher, *Christopher and his Kind* (London: Methuen, 1977).
Ivanof, Viacheslaf, 'The Theatre of the Future', trans. Stephen Graham, *English Review*, 10 (1912), 634–50.
Jacobs, Lewis, 'The New Cinema: A Preface to Film Form', *Experimental Cinema*, 1 (February 1930), 13–14.
Jameson, Fredric, *A Singular Modernity* (London: Verso, 2002).
Jans, Rudolf, *Tolstoj in Nederland* (Bussum: P. Brand, 1952).
Järvinen, Hanna, 'The Myth and Genius in Movement: Historical Deconstruction of the Nijinsky Legend', PhD thesis, University of Turku, 2003.
_____ 'The Russian Barnum: Russian Opinions on Diaghilev's Ballets Russes, 1909–1914', *Dance Research*, 26, no. 1 (2008), 18–41.
Jennings, Richard, review of *Red Rust*, Little Theatre, 1929, *The Spectator* (16 March 1929), 417.
Jones, Gareth, 'Famine in Russia. Englishman's Story. What He Saw on a Walking Tour', *Manchester Guardian* (30 March 1933), 12.
Jones, W. Gareth, 'George Eliot's "Adam Bede" and Tolstoy's Conception of "Anna Karenina"', *Modern Language Review*, 61, no. 3 (1966), 473–81.
_____ ed., *Tolstoi and Britain* (Oxford: Berg, 1995).
Jones, Susan, 'Diaghilev and British Writing', *Dance Research*, 27, no. 1 (2009), 65–93.
_____ 'Virginia Woolf and the Dance', *Dance Chronicle*, 28, no. 2, (2005), 169–200.
Jordan, Stephanie, *Stravinsky Dances* (London: Dance Books, 2007).
Julien, Adolphe, 'Musique', *Journal des débats* (8 June 1913), 1–2.
Kalaidjian, Walter, *The Edge of Modernism: American Poetry and the Traumatic Past* (Baltimore, MD: Johns Hopkins University Press, 2006).
Kandinsky, Wassily, *The Art of Spiritual Harmony*, trans. M. T. H. Sadler, (London: Constable, 1914).
_____ *Concerning the Spiritual in Art*, trans. Michael T. H. Sadler (London: Tate, 2006).
Kanevsky, B. P., 'Russkaya kniga v Britanskom muzee v XIX veke', in *Gosudarstvennaya biblioteka SSSR im. V. I. Lenina: Trudy* (Moscow: Kniga, 1969), xi, 106–5.
'Karma', 'Exiles', *The Theatre* (New York) (1890), 59.
Katarsky, I. M., *Dikkens v Rossii* (Moscow: Nauka, 1966).
Katz, Daniel, *American Modernism's Expatriate Scene: The Labour of Translation* (Edinburgh: Edinburgh University Press, 2007).
Kaye, Peter, *Dostoevsky and English Modernism, 1900–1930* (Cambridge: Cambridge University Press, 1999).
Kaznina, O. A., *Russkie v Anglii: Russkaya emigratsiya v kontekste russko-angliiskikh literaturnykh svyazei v pervoi polovine XX veka* (Moscow: Nasledie, 1997).
Kelly, Catriona, ed., *Utopias: Russian Modernist Texts, 1905–1940* (London: Penguin, 1999).
Kelly, Thomas, *For the Advancement of Learning: the University of Liverpool, 1881–1981* (Liverpool: Liverpool University Press, 1981).
Kendall, Walter, *The Revolutionary Movement in Britain, 1900–1921* (London: Weidenfeld and Nicolson, 1969).

Kenworthy, John, 'A Change of Name', *New Order*, 3, no. 10 (October 1897), 73–4.
_____ 'The Basic Christian Principle', *New Order*, 3, no. 11 (November 1897), 80–1.
_____ 'Man and the Animals', *New Order*, NS 5, no. 15 (April 1899), 56–8.
_____ *A Pilgrimage to Tolstoy* (London: Brotherhood Publishing Co., 1896).
_____ *My Psychic Experiences* (London: Office of 'Light', 1901).
_____ *Tolstoy: His Life and Works* (London: Walter Scott, 1902).
Keynes, John Maynard, *The Collected Writings of John Maynard Keynes*, xxviii: *Social, Political and Literary Writings*, ed. Donald Moggridge (London: Macmillan, for the Royal Economic Society, 1982).
_____ *The Economic Consequences of the Peace* (London: Macmillan & Co., 1919).
_____ *The General Theory of Employment, Interest and Money* (Basingstoke: Palgrave, 2007).
_____ *A Short View of Russia* (London: Hogarth Press, 1925).
Kliger, Ilya, 'Dostoevsky and the Novel-Tragedy: Genre and Modernity in Ivanov, Pumpiansky and Bakhtin', *PMLA*, 126, no. 1 (2011), 73–87.
Koestler, Arthur, *The Invisible Writing* (London: Vintage, 2005).
_____ 'Soviet Myth and Reality', in *The Yogi and the Commissar* (New York: Macmillan, 1946), 131–92.
Kolehmainen, John I., 'When Finland's Tolstoy met his Russian Master', *American Slavic and East European Review*, 16, no. 4 (December 1957), 534–41.
Komisarjevsky, Theodore, *Myself and the Theatre* (London: William Heinemann, 1929).
Korolenko, V. G., *Noch'yu, v noch' pod tsvetlyi prazdnik (In the Night, Easter Eve)* (Oxford: Tipografiya Klarendon, [1918]).
Kouprin, A. E., *How I Became an Actor*, ed. by P. Bondar (London: Effingham Wilson, 1919).
Krasovskaya, Vera, *Nijinsky* (New York: Schirmer Books, 1979).
Krylov, I. A., *Izbrannye basni* (Oxford: Tipografiya Klarendon, [1918]).
_____ *Krylov's Fables*, trans. Bernard Pares (London: Jonathan Cape, 1926).
_____ *Select Fables*, ed. J. H. Freese (London: Kegan Paul, Trench, Trubner, 1917).
Lambert, Constant, *Music Ho! A Study of Music in Decline* (London: Faber & Faber, 1934).
Langley, Leanne, 'Building an Orchestra, Creating an Audience: Robert Newman and the Queen's Hall Promenade Concerts, 1895–1926', in Jenny Doctor and David Wright, eds, *The Proms: A New History* (London: Thames & Hudson, 2007), 32–73.
_____ 'Joining Up the Dots: Cross-Channel Models in the Shaping of London Orchestral Culture, 1895–1914', in Bennett Zon, ed., *Music and Performance Culture in Nineteenth-Century Britain: Essays in Honour of Nicholas Temperley* (Farnham: Ashgate, 2012), 37–58.
Launay, Isabelle, 'Communauté et articulations: à propos du *Sacre du printemps* de Nijinsky', in Claire Rousier, ed., *Être ensemble: figures de la communauté en danse depuis le XXe siècle* (Paris: Centre national de la danse, 2003), 65–88.
Lauter, Werner, *Die Bedeutung von W. R. S. Ralston als Vermittler russischer Literatur nach England* (Marburg: Philipps-Universität, 1962).
Lawrence, D. H., *The Letters of D. H. Lawrence*, iii, *1916–21*, ed. James T. Boulton and Andrew Robertson (Cambridge: Cambridge University Press, 1984).
Leatherbarrow, W. J., ed., *Dostoevskii and Britain* (Oxford: Berg, 1995).
'Leeds Notes', *New Order*, 4, no. 10 (November 1898), 116.
Lefevere, André, *Translation, Rewriting and the Manipulation of Literary Fame* (London: Routledge, 1992).
Legge, Robin H., 'Drury Lane Theatre', *Daily Telegraph* (26 July 1913).
Lehmann, John, *The Whispering Gallery* (London: Longmans, Green, 1955).
'Letter of an Englishman', *Daily Mail* (19 July 1913).

Lermontoff, Michail Yurievitch, *Bela*, ed. by R. Biske (London: Kegan Paul, Trench, Trubner, [1917]).

_____ *Izbrannye stikhotvoreniya* (Oxford: Tipografiya Klarendon, [1918]).

Levidou, Ekaterini, 'The Encounter of Neoclassicism with Eurasianism in Interwar Paris: Stravinsky, Suvchinsky and Lourié', DPhil thesis, University of Oxford, 2008.

[Lewis, Wyndham], 'Long Live the Vortex', *Blast*, 1 (1914), 7–8.

Lewis, Wyndham, 'A Review of Contemporary Art', *Blast*, 2 (1915), 38–47.

Livak, Leonid, *How it was Done in Paris: Russian Émigré Literature and French Modernism* (Madison, WI: University of Wisconsin Press, 2003).

_____ *Russian Émigrés in the Intellectual and Literary Life of Inter-War France: A Bibliographical Essay* (Montreal, QC: McGill-Queen's University Press, 2010).

'London Gossip', *Hampshire Telegraph and Sussex Chronicle* (7 December 1881), 3.

'The Lower Depths', *The Times* (22 November 1911), 11.

Lubbock, Percy, *George Calderon: A Sketch from Memory* (London: Grant Richards, 1921).

_____ 'George Calderon', *Dictionary of National Biography, 1912–1921* (Oxford: Oxford University Press, 1927), 105.

M., 'Mrs. Rosa Newmarch', *Musical Times*, 52, no. 818 (1 April 1911), 225–9.

Macdonald, Nesta, *Diaghilev Observed by Critics in England and the United States, 1911–1929* (New York: Dance Horizons, 1975).

[MacCarthy, Desmond], 'The Post-Impressionists', in *Manet and the Post-Impressionists* (London: Ballantyne & Company, 1910), 7–13.

MacKenzie, Norman and Jeanne, *The Life of H. G. Wells: The Time Traveller*, rev. edn (London: Hogarth Press, 1987).

Macpherson, Kenneth, 'Storm over Asia—and Berlin!', *Close Up*, 4, no. 1 (January 1929), 37–46.

Macqueen-Pope, W., *Haymarket: Theatre of Perfection* (London: Allen, 1948).

Malia, Martin, *The Soviet Tragedy: A History of Socialism in Russia* (New York: Free Press, 1994).

Mansfield, Katherine, *In a German Pension* (London: Penguin Books, 1964).

[Mansfield, Katherine], 'Two Poems of Boris Petrovsky', trans. Katherine Mansfield, *Rhythm*, 1, no. 4 (1912), 30.

_____ 'Tales of a Courtyard', *Rhythm*, 2, no. 7 (1912), 99–105.

Mao, Douglas, and Rebecca L. Walkowitz, 'The New Modernist Studies', *PMLA*, 123, no. 3 (2008), 737–48.

Marcus, Laura, *The Tenth Muse: Writing about Cinema in the Modernist Period* (Oxford: Oxford University Press, 2007).

Marks, Steven, *How Russia Shaped the Modern World: From Art to Anti-Semitism, Ballet to Bolshevism* (Princeton, NJ: Princeton University Press, 2003).

Markwell, Donald, *John Maynard Keynes and International Relations: Economic Paths to War and Peace* (Oxford: Oxford University Press, 2006).

Marsden, Dora, 'Views and Comments', *New Freewoman*, 1, no. 2 (1913), 23–5.

Marsh, Cynthia, *File on Gorky* (London: Methuen, 1993).

_____ *Maxim Gorky: Russian Dramatist* (Bern: Peter Lang, 2006).

Marsh, Edward, ed., *Georgian Poetry, 1911–1912* (London: Poetry Bookshop, 1912).

Marshall, Herbert, ed., *The Battleship Potemkin* (New York: Avon Books, 1978).

Marshall, Norman, *The Other Theatre* (London: John Lehman, 1947).

Martin, Kingsley, *Editor: A Second Volume of Autobiography* (London: Hutchinson, 1968).

Marx, Karl, and Friedrich Engels, *Collected Works*, xlvi (New York: International Publishers, 1992).

Mason, Stuart, *Bibliography of Oscar Wilde* (London: T. Werner Laurie, [1914]).

[Masterman. C.F.G.], *From the Abyss: Of its Inhabitants By One of Them* (London: R. B. Johnson, 1902).

Matthews, W. K., 'Professor M. V. Trofimov', *Slavonic and East European Review*, 27, no. 69 (1949), 575–6.

Maude, Louise, 'The Root of All Evil', *New Order*, NS 5, no. 17 (June 1899), 79.

Maugham, Somerset, *Ashenden or the British Agent* (London: Heinemann, 1928).

May, Rachel, *The Translator in the Text: On Reading Russian Literature in English* (Evanston, IL: Northwestern University Press, 1994).

Mazer, Cary M., 'New Theatres for a New Drama', in Kerry Powell, ed., *The Cambridge Companion to Victorian and Edwardian Theatre* (Cambridge: Cambridge University Press, 2004), 207–21.

McKibbin, Ross, *Parties and People: England 1914–1951* (Oxford: Oxford University Press, 2010).

McReynolds, Louise, and Joan Neuberger, eds, *Imitations of Life: Two Centuries of Melodrama in Russia* (Durham, NC: Duke University Press, 2002).

'Meetings and Lectures', *Free Russia*, 13, no. 3 (1 March 1902), 36.

Mensiaux, Marie de [Clement Scott?], 'The Red Lamp', *The Theatre* (1 June 1887), 335–9.

Merkle, Denise, 'Secret Literary Societies in Late Victorian England', in Maria Tymoczko, ed., *Translation, Resistance, Activism* (Amherst and Boston, MA: University of Massachusetts Press, 2010), 108–28.

'Michael Strogoff', *The Theatre* (1 April 1881), 240–3.

Mierop, Lodewijk van, 'Geen Tolstoyaan maar Christen', *Vrede*, 2, no. 15 (15 May 1899), 108–10.

Miles, Patrick, *Chekhov on the British Stage, 1909–1987: An Essay in Cultural Exchange* (Cambridge: Sam & Sam, 1987).

_____ ed., *Chekhov on the British Stage* (Cambridge: Cambridge University Press, 1993).

Milne, A. H., *Sir Alfred Lewis Jones, K.C.M.G.* (Liverpool: Henry Young, 1914).

Mirsky, D. S., *Contemporary Russian Literature, 1881–1925* (London: Routledge, 1926).

_____ *A History of Russian Literature*, ed. and abr. Francis J. Whitfield (London: Routledge & Kegan Paul, 1949).

_____ *A History of Russian Literature: From the Earliest Times to the Death of Dostoyevsky (1881)* (London: Routledge, 1927).

_____ *The Intelligentsia of Great Britain*, trans. Alec Brown (London: Gollancz, 1935).

_____ *Modern Russian Literature* (London: Oxford University Press, 1925).

Misheyev, N., *A Heroic Legend: How the Holy Mountains Let Out of Their Deep Caves the Mighty Heroes of Russia: A Modern Bylina*, trans. Gleb Struve and Bernard Pares (London: Centenary Press, 1935).

'A Mixed bag: Sporting Stories from Here and There', *The Tatler*, no. 546 (13 December 1911), 106.

Modern Language Association Sub-Committee for Russian Studies, *The Teaching of Russian* (Cambridge: W. Heffer, 1917).

Modjeska, Helena, *Memoirs andImpressions* (New York: Macmillan, 1910).

Montagu, Ivor, *The Youngest Son: Autobiographical Characters* (London: Lawrence and Wishart, 1970).

Morard, Annick, *De l'émigré au déraciné: la 'jeune génération' des écrivains russes entre identité et esthétique (Paris, 1920–1940)* (Lausanne: L'Age d'Homme, 2010).

Moretti, Franco, 'The Moment of Truth', in *Signs Taken for Wonders*, rev. edn (London: Verso, 1988), 249–62.

Morfill, W. R., ed., *Ballads Relating Chiefly to the Reign of Queen Elizabeth* (London: Ballad Society, 1873).

_____ *An Essay on the Importance of the Study of Slavonic Languages* (London: Henry Frowde, 1890).
_____ *A Grammar of the Bohemian or Čech Language* (Oxford: Clarendon Press, 1899).
_____ *A Grammar of the Russian Language* (Oxford: Clarendon Press, 1889).
_____ *A History of Russia* (London: Methuen, 1902).
_____ *Poland* (London: T. Fisher Unwin, 1893).
_____ *Russia* (London: Sampson Low, Marston, Searle, & Rivington, 1880).
_____ *Russia* (London: T. Fisher Unwin, 1890).
_____ *A Short Grammar of the Bulgarian Language, with Reading Lessons* (London: Trübner, 1897).
_____ *A Simplified Grammar of the Polish Language* (London: Trübner, 1884).
_____ *Simplified Grammar of the Serbian Language* (London: Trübner, 1887).
_____ *Slavonic Literature* (London: Society for Promoting Christian Knowledge, 1883).
Morley, Liz, and Ann Stanley, *The Life and Death of Emily Wilding Davison* (London: Women's Press, 2001).
'The Mormon Embargo', *The Examiner* (16 August 1879), 1050.
Morrison, Simon, *The People's Artist: Prokofiev's Soviet Years* (New York: Oxford University Press, 2009).
'Mr. Oscar Wilde's Play, *North-Eastern Daily Gazette* (22 August 1883), 3.
Muchnic, Helen, *Dostoyevsky's English Reputation, 1881–1936*, Smith College Studies in Modern Languages, 20, no. 3/4 (Northampton, MA: Smith College, 1939).
Muckle, James, 'Russian in the University Curriculum: A Case-study of the Impact of the First World War on Language Study in Higher Education in Britain', *History of Education: Journal of the History of Education Society*, 37, no. 3 (2008), 359–81.
_____ *The Russian Language in Britain: A Historical Study of Learners and Teachers* (Ilkeston: Bramcote Press, 2008).
Muir, Stephen, '"About as Wild and Barbaric as Well Could be Imagined...": The Critical Reception of Rimsky-Korsakov in Nineteenth-Century England', *Music and Letters*, 93, no. 4 (2012), 513–42.
[Murry, John Middleton], 'Aims and Ideals', *Rhythm*, 1, no. 1 (1911), 36.
_____ 'Notes', *Rhythm*, 2, no. 5 (1912), 36.
_____ 'What We Have Tried To Do', *Rhythm*, 1, no. 3 (1911), 36.
Murry, John Middleton, 'Art and Philosophy', *Rhythm*, 1, no. 1 (1911), 9–12.
_____ 'The Art of Spiritual Harmony', *The Athenaeum*, 4523 (1914), 23–4.
'Music and the Drama', *The Illustrated Police News* (22 September 1883), 2.
Nelson, Amy, *Music for the Revolution: Musicians and Power in Early Soviet Russia* (University Park, PA: Pennsylvania University Press, 2004).
'A new spectacular play: the success of "Michel Strogoff" in Paris', *New York Times* (9 December 1880), 1.
Neilson, Keith, *Britain and the Last Tsar: British Policy and Russia, 1894–1917* (Oxford: Clarendon Press, 1995).
Nelson, Cary, *Repression and Recovery: Modern American Poetry and the Politics of Cultural Memory, 1910–1945* (Madison, WI: University of Wisconsin Press, 1989).
Nestor-Schnurmann, Ivan, trans. and ed., *Russian Reader: Lermontoff's Modern Hero with English Translation and Biographical Sketch* (Cambridge: Cambridge University Press, 1899).
Newmarch, Rosa, 'Moussorgsky's Operas', *Musical Times*, 54, no. 845 (1 July 1913), 433–9.
_____ 'The Promenade Concerts', in *BBC Handbook, 1928* (London: British Broadcasting Corporation, 1928), 101–4.

_____ 'A Requiem for the Allied Heroes', *Musical Times*, 58, no. 897 (1 November 1917), 496–7.

_____ 'Russian Opera in Paris: Moussorgsky's "Boris Godunov" ', *Monthly Musical Record*, 38, no. 451 (July 1908), 147–9.

'News of the Day', *Birmingham Daily Post and Journal* (8 May 1882), 5.

Newsky, Pierre, *Les Danicheff: Comédie en quatre actes* (Paris: Calmann Lévy, 1879).

_____ 'Various dramatic topics', *Musical World* (6 January 1877), 27.

Nickson, Richard, 'The Lure of Stalinism: Bernard Shaw and Company', *Midwest Quarterly*, 25, no. 4 (1984), 416–33.

'Nihilism in Russia', *Pall Mall Gazette* (10 December 1866), 1.

Nijinska, Bronislava, *Early Memoirs* (London: Faber and Faber, 1981).

Nijinsky, Romola, *Nijinsky* (London: Sphere Books, 1970).

Nijinsky, Vaslav, 'M. Nijinsky's critics: "The word 'grace' makes me feel seasick" ', *Daily Mail* (14 July 1913), 7.

Noguchi, Yone, 'From a Japanese Ink-Slab', *Rhythm*, 2, no. 14 (1913), 449–52.

Nokkala, A., *Tolstoilaisuus Suomessa* (Helsinki: Kustannusosakeyhtiö Tammi, 1958).

'The No Money Movement', *New Order*, NS 7, no. 35 (May 1901), 51.

Norris, Gerald, *Stanford, The Cambridge Jubilee and Tchaikovsky* (Newton Abbot, London, and North Pomfret: David & Charles, 1980).

'Notes from Russia', *Athenaeum*, 4402 (1912), 279–80.

'The old ballet and the new: M. Nijinski's revolution', *The Times* (5 July 1913), 11.

Ol'khovik, P., *Een Volgeling van Jezus: Peter Olchowik. Een jonge Russische boer* (The Hague: Vrede, 1899).

_____ 'Letters of P. V. Olkhovik', *New Order* (June 1899), 84–5 (July 1899), 102–3 (August 1899), 109–11.

_____ *Lettres de Pierre Olchowik, paysan du gouvernement de Kharkoff, qui a refusé de faire son service militaire en 1895* (Geneva: M. Fischer, 1898).

_____ *Pis'ma P. V. Ol'khovika, krest'yanina Khar'kovskoi gubernii, otkazavshegosya ot voinskoi povinnosti v 1895 godu* (London: V. Tchertkoff, 1897).

'Omicron', review of *The Brass Paperweight*, Apollo, 1928, *Nation and Athenaeum* (27 October 1928), 141.

_____ review of *The Government Inspector*, Barnes, 1926, *Nation and Athenaeum* (22 May 1926), 176.

_____ review of *He Who Gets Slapped*, Everyman, 1927, *Nation and Athenaeum* (19 November 1927), 277.

_____ review of *Paul I*, Court, 1927, *Nation and Athenaeum* (15 October 1927), 84.

Ordinances of the University of Cambridge to 1 October 1920 (Cambridge: Cambridge University Press, 1920).

Orwell, George, review of Eugene Lyons, *Assignment In Utopia*, in Peter Davison, ed., *Orwell and Politics* (London: Penguin, 2001), 31–4.

_____ 'Wells, Hitler and the World State', in *Essays* (London: Penguin, 2000), 188–93.

Oswald, Peter, *Vaslav Nijinsky: A Leap into Madness* (New York: Citadel Press, 1991).

'Oscar Interviewed', *Punch* (14 January 1882), 14.

'Oscar's "Vera" ', *Moonshine* (1 September 1883), 112.

'Our Chicago Trip', *The Social Gospel* (December 1898), 21–2.

'Our Omnibus-Box', *The Theatre* (1 March 1883), 190–1.

Paddock, Troy R. E., *Creating the Russian Peril: Education, the Public Sphere, and National Identity in Imperial Germany, 1890–1940* (Columbia, SC: Camden House, 2010).

Palmer, John, 'Gorki's Masterpiece', review of *The Lower Depths*, Kingsway, 1911, *Saturday Review* (9 December 1911), 730–1.

Paperno Irina, and Joan Delaney Grossman, eds, *Creating Life: The Aesthetic Utopia of Russian Modernism* (Stanford, CA: Stanford University Press, 1994).

Pares, Bernard, *Day by Day with the Russian Army, 1914–15* (London: Constable, 1915).

_____ *The Fall of the Russian Monarchy: A Study of the Evidence* (London: Jonathan Cape, 1939).

_____ *A History of Russia* (London: Jonathan Cape, 1926).

_____ *The League of Nations and Other Questions of Peace* (London: Hodder & Stoughton, 1919).

_____ 'Mackay and the School of Russian Studies', in *A Miscellany Presented to John Macdonald Mackay, LL.D.* (Liverpool: Liverpool University Press/London: Constable, 1914), 48–55.

_____ *Moscow Admits a Critic* (London: Thomas Nelson and Sons, 1936).

_____ *My Russian Memoirs* (London: Cape, 1931).

_____ 'Obituary: Nevill Forbes', *Slavonic and East European Review*, 7, no. 21 (March 1929), 702.

_____ *Russia* (Harmondsworth: Penguin, 1940).

_____ *Russia and the Peace* (Harmondsworth: Penguin, 1944).

_____ *Russia and Reform* (London: Constable, 1907).

_____ *A Wandering Student: The Story of a Purpose* (Syracuse, NY: Syracuse University Press, 1948).

Parkins, Wendy, 'Protesting like a girl: Embodiment, dissent and feminist agency', *Feminist Theory*, 1 (2000), 59–78.

Parry, C. Hubert H., *Style in Musical Art* (London: Macmillan, 1911).

_____ *Summary of the History and Development of Mediæval and Modern European Music*, rev. edn (London: Novello, 1905).

Partington, John S., *Building Cosmopolis: The Political Thought of H. G. Wells* (Aldershot: Ashgate, 2003).

Parton, Anthony, *Goncharova: The Art and Design of Natalia Goncharova* (Woodbridge, Suffolk: Antique Collector's Club, 2010).

Patterson, Ian, 'John Rodker, Julius Ratner and Wyndham Lewis: The Split-Man Writes Back', in Andrzej Gasiorek, Alice Reeve-Tucker, and Nathan Waddell, eds, *Wyndham Lewis and the Cultures of Modernity* (Farnham: Ashgate, 2011), 95–107.

_____ 'Writing on Other Fronts: Translation and John Rodker', in *Modernism and Translation*, special issue of *Translation and Literature*, 12, no. 1 (spring 2003), 88–113.

Pavis, Patrice, *Theatre at the Crossroads of Culture*, trans. Loren Kruger (London: Routledge, 1992).

Pearson, Hesketh, *The Life of Oscar Wilde*, rev. edn (London: Methuen, 1954).

Pemberton, T. Edgar, *The Life and Writings of T. W. Robertson* (London: Bentley, 1893).

Peter, John, review of *Plasticine*, Royal Court Upstairs, 2002, *Sunday Times* (31 March 2002), in *Theatre Record*, 22, no. 6 (2002), 346.

'Peter the Painter', *Daily Express* (6 January 1911), 1.

'Peter the Painter', *Daily Express* (31 March 1911), 2.

'"Peter the Painter" in Paris', *Daily Express* (7 January 1911), 1.

Petrova, Yevgenia, ed., *Natalia Goncharova: The Russian Years* (St Petersburg: Palace Editions, 2002).

Phelps, Gilbert, *The Russian Novel in English Fiction* (London: Hutchinson's University Library, 1956).

'The Philistine Lover to his Æsthetic Fair', *Funny Folks* (10 December 1881), 386.

Pieper, Antje, *Music and the Making of Middle-Class Culture: A Comparative History of Nineteenth-Century Leipzig and Birmingham* (Basingstoke: Palgrave, 2008).

'Pilferings from Funny Folks', *Bristol Mercury and Daily Post* (4 June 1881), 6.
Pine, Richard, *The Thief of Reason: Oscar Wilde and Modern Ireland* (Dublin: Gill and Macmillan, 1995).
'Playhouses Without Plays', *Sporting Times* (15 September 1883), 3.
Pollock, John, review of *Fear*, Stage Society, 1932, *Saturday Review* (3 December 1932), 588.
Polonsky, Rachel, *English Literature and the Russian Aesthetic Renaissance* (Cambridge: Cambridge University Press, 1998).
Popovsky, Mark, *Russkie muzhiki rasskazyvayut: posledovateli L. N. Tolstogo v Sovetskom Soyuze, 1918–1977: dokumental' nyi rasskaz o krest' yanakh-tolstovtsakh v SSSR po materialam vyvezennogo na Zapad krest' yanskogo arkhiva* (London: Overseas Publications Interchange, 1983).
Potamkin, Harry Alan, review of Bryher, *Film Problems of Soviet Russia*, in *Experimental Cinema: A Monthly Projecting Important International Film Manifestations*, 1, no. 1 (February 1930), 3.
Pougin, Arthur, *A Short History of Russian Music*, trans. Lawrence Haward (London: Chatto & Windus, 1915) [Fr. orig., *Essai historique sur la musique en Russie* (Paris: Fischbacher, 1904)].
Powell, Kerry, *Oscar Wilde and the Theatre of the 1890s* (Cambridge: Cambridge University Press, 1990).
Pozefsky, Peter C., *The Nihilist Imagination: Dmitrii Pisarev and the Cultural Origins of Russian Radicalism, 1860–1868*, Middlebury Studies in Russian Language and Literature, 27 (New York: Peter Lang, 2003).
'Private Correspondence', *Birmingham Daily Post* (5 December 1881), 5.
Pronay, Nicholas, and Jeremy Croft, 'British Film Censorship and Propaganda Policy during the Second World War', in James Curran and Vincent Porter, eds, *British Cinema History* (London: Weidenfeld and Nicolson, 1983), 144–63.
Przerwa-Tetmajer, Kazimierz, 'Song of the Night Mists', trans. Paul Selver, *New Age*, 10, no. 13 (1912), 292.
'Public Amusements', *Reynolds's Newspaper* (9 September 1883), 5.
'Public Feeling in America and on the Continent', *Daily News* (9 May 1882), 6.
Pudovkin, Vsevolod, *Film Technique: Five Essays and Two Addresses*, trans. and ed. Ivor Montagu (London: Newnes, 1933).
_____ *On Film Technique: Three Essays and an Address*, trans. and ed. Ivor Montagu (London: Gollancz, 1929).
_____ *Selected Essays*, ed. Richard Taylor (London: Seagull Books, 2006).
Pushkin, A. S., *Boris Godunov, Drama v stikhakh* (Oxford: Tipografiya Klarendon, 1920?].
_____ *The Captain's Daughter: A Tale* (London: Jaschke, 1919).
_____ *Pikovaya Dama* (Oxford: Tipografiya Klarendon, 1917).
_____ *The Queen of Spades*, ed. D. Bondar (London: Effingham Wilson, 1915).
Pyman, Avril, *A History of Russian Symbolism* (Cambridge: Cambridge University Press, 1994).
Raby, Peter, ed., *The Cambridge Companion to Oscar Wilde* (Cambridge: Cambridge University Press, 1997).
Rainey, Lawrence, *Institutions of Modernism: Literary Elites and Public Culture* (New Haven, CT, Yale University Press, 1998).
Ram, Harsha, *The Imperial Sublime: A Russian Poetics of Empire* (Madison, WI: University of Wisconsin Press, 2003).
Rambert, Marie, *Quicksilver* (Basingstoke: Macmillan, 1972).
Reavey, George, and Marc Slonim, eds and trans. *Soviet Literature: An Anthology* (London: Wishart, 1933).

'The Reception of the News in Ireland', *The Belfast News-Letter*, 2nd edn (8 May 1882), 6.
'Reception of the News on the Continent', *Daily News* (8 May 1882), 5.
Redfern, Percy, *Journey to Understanding* (London: Allen and Unwin, 1946).
_____ *Tolstoy: A Study* (London: A. C. Fifield, 1907).
Renfrew, Alastair, and Galin Tihanov, eds, *Critical Theory in Russia and the West* (London: Routledge, 2010).
'Report of the Annual General Meeting', *Modern Language Quarterly*, 3 (1900), 157–88.
Report of the Committee on the Position of Modern Languages in the Educational System of Great Britain (London: His Majesty's Stationery Office, 1918).
'Report on Commercial Education', *Modern Language Quarterly*, 3, no. 2 (December 1900), 151–3.
'"Resting" and Revelling in the Simple Life: Princess Bariatinsky Prepares for a Strenuous Autumn', *The Tatler*, no. 633 (13 August 1913), 204.
Review of *Anna Karenina*, Ambassadors, 1913, *Illustrated London News* (6 December 1913), 976.
Review of *Bargains in Brides*, Charta Theatre, 1933, *The Times* (10 April 1933), 10.
Review of *The Bezsemenovs*, Mermaid Society, 1906, *The Times* (24 April 1906), 12.
Review of *Crime and Punishment*, Century Theatre, 1927, *The Times* (8 February 1927), 12.
Review of *Fear*, Stage Society, 1932, *The Times* (28 November 1932), 12.
Review of *He Who Gets Slapped*, Everyman, 1927, *Sunday Times* (13 November 1927), 6.
Review of *He Who Gets Slapped*, Everyman, 1927, *The Times* (9 November 1927), 12.
Review of *The Idiot*, Barnes, 1926, *The Times* (24 August 1926), 8.
Review of *The Lower Depths*, Kingsway, 1911, *Illustrated London News* (9 December 1911), 976.
Review of *The Lower Depths*, Kingsway, 1911, *The Times* (4 December 1911), 6.
Review of *The Marriage*, Prague Group, Garrick, 1928, *The Times* (21 April 1928), 10.
Review of *The Marriage*, Westminster, 1938, *Illustrated London News* (25 June 1938), 1180.
Review of *Nachtasyl*, Great Queen Street Theatre, 1906, *The Times* (17 February 1906), 6.
Review of *Poverty is No Crime*, Prague Group, 1928, *The Times* (14 April 1928), 14.
Review of *The Power of Darkness*, Stage Society, 1904, *The Times* (21 December 1904), 13.
Review of R. E. C. Long's translation of Chekhov's short stories, *Outlook* (14 November 1903), 433, in Victor Emeljanow, ed., *Chekhov: The Critical Heritage* (London: Routledge and Kegan Paul, 1981), 69–70.
Review of *Rasputin*, Stage Society, 1929, *The Times* (23 April 1929), 14.
Review of *Red Rust*, Little Theatre, 1929, *The Times* (1 March 1929), 14.
Review of *Resurrection*, Royalty, 1906, *Illustrated London News* (24 February 1906), 258.
Review of *The Sabine Women*, Everyman, 1928, *The Times* (4 April 1928), 12.
Review of *The Storm*, Everyman, 1929, *The Times* (4 December 1929), 12.
'The Revolutionary Middle Class', *New Statesman and Nation*, NS 7, no. 167 (5 May 1934,), 664–5.
Rice, Anne Estelle, 'Les Ballets Russes', *Rhythm*, 2, no. 7 (1912), 106–10.
Richardson, Dorothy, *Pilgrimage*, 4 vols (New York: Knopf, 1967).
Riley, Matthew, ed., *British Music and Modernism, 1895–1960* (Farnham: Ashgate, 2010).
Riola, Henry, *A Graduated Russian Reader, with a Vocabulary of all the Russian Words Contained in It* (London: Trübner, 1879).
_____ *How to Learn Russian: A Manual for Students of Russian, Based Upon the Ollendorffian System of Teaching Languages, and Adapted for Self-Instruction* (London: Kegan Paul, Trench, Trübner, 1878).

Rickword, Edgell, 'Social Creativity', *Left Review*, 2, no. 6 (March 1936), 283.
Robbins, Bruce, 'Introduction, Part I: Actually Existing Cosmopolitanism', in Bruce Robbins and Pheang Cheah, eds, *Cosmopolitics: Thinking and Feeling Beyond the Nation* (Minneapolis, MN: University of Minnesota Press, 1998), 1–19.
Roberts, I. W., and Roger Bartlett, *History of the School of Slavonic and East European Studies, 1915–2005*, 2nd edn (London: School of Slavonic and East European Studies, 2009).
Robertson, James C., *The Hidden Cinema: British Film Censorship in Action, 1913–1972* (London: Routledge, 1989).
Robertson, T. W., *Ours*, in *The New York Drama*, 4, no. 43 (Washington, DC: Wheat & Cornett, 1878).
_____ *Plays by Tom Robertson*, ed. William Tydeman and Martin Banham (Cambridge: Cambridge University Press, 1982).
Rodker, J., 'Fiction: Underdogs', *The Spectator*, 5391 (24 October 1931), 549–50.
_____ *Memoirs of Other Fronts* (London: Putnam, 1932).
_____,ed., *Soviet Anthology* (London: Cape, 1943).
Rodmell, Paul, ed., *Music and Institutions in Nineteenth-Century Britain* (Farnham: Ashgate, 2012).
Ronen, Omry, *The Fallacy of the Silver Age in Twentieth-Century Russian Literature* (Amsterdam: Harwood Academic Press, 1997).
Rosanvallon, Pierre, 'Inaugural Lecture, Collège de France', in Samuel Moyn, ed., *Democracy Past and Future* (New York: Columbia University Press, 2006), 31–58.
Rosenthal, Bernice Glatzer, *New Myth, New World: From Nietzsche to Stalinism* (University Park, PA: Pennsylvania State University Press, 2002).
_____ ed., *Nietzsche and Soviet Culture: Ally and Adversary* (Cambridge: Cambridge University Press, 1994).
Rotha, Paul, *Documentary Film* (London: Faber, 1936).
Rouse, W. H. D., 'Italian v. German', *Modern Language Teaching*, 10 (1914), 222.
Rowell, George, 'The Truth About *Vera*', *Nineteenth Century Theatre*, 21, no. 2 (1993), 94–100.
Rubenstein, Roberta, *Virginia Woolf and the Russian Point of View* (Houndmills: Palgrave, 2009).
Rubins, Maria, ed., *Twentieth-Century Russian Émigré Writers*, Dictionary of Literary Biography 317 (Detroit, MI: Thomson Gale, 2005).
Runciman, John F., 'The Most Modern Musicians', *Saturday Review of Politics, Literature, Science and Art*, 117, no. 3055 (16 May 1914), 629–31.
'Russian Art in London', *The Times* (26 October 1910), 6.
'Russian Ballet."Le Sacre de Printemps"', *Daily Telegraph* (12 July 1913).
'Russian Nihilists and Irish Land Leagues', *Hull Packet and East Riding Times* (10 December 1880), 4.
'Russian Opera and Ballet at Drury Lane', *Musical Times*, 54, no. 846 (1 August 1913), 535–6.
'Russian Refugees in England', *The Observer* (5 November 1905), 7.
'Russian Rivalry', *Musical Times*, 38, no. 650 (1 April 1897), 234.
Rutter, Frank, *Art in My Time* (London: Rich & Cowan, 1933).
_____ *Since I was Twenty-Five* (London: Constable, 1927).
Ryan, Trevor, '"The New Road to Progress": The Use and Production of Films by the Labour Movement, 1929–39', in James Curran and Vincent Porter, eds, *British Cinema History* (London: Weidenfeld and Nicolson, 1983), 113–28.
S., E. F., ('Monocle'), review of *The Lower Depths*, Kingsway, 1911, *The Sketch* (13 December 1911), 298.
Sabaneyeff, Leonid, *Modern Russian Composers* (London: Lawrence, [1927]).
Sadler [Sadleir], Michael T.H., 'After Gauguin', *Rhythm*, 1, no. 4 (1912), 23–9.

_____ 'Fauvism and a Fauve', *Rhythm*, 1, no. 1 (1911), 14–18.

_____ 'Kandinsky's Book on Art', *Art News* (9 March 1912), 45–6.

_____ 'The Letters of Vincent Van Gogh', *Rhythm*, 1, no. 2 (1911), 16–19.

_____ *Michael Ernest Sadler, 1861–1943: A Memoir by his Son* (London: Constable, 1949).

Safiullina, Nailya, 'Window to the West: From the Collection of Readers' Letters to the Journal *Internatsional' naya literatura*', *Slavonica*, 15, no. 2 (2009), 128–61.

Safiullina, Nailya, and Rachel Platonov, 'Literary Translation and Soviet Cultural Politics in the 1930s: The Role of the Journal *Internacional' naia literatura*', *Russian Literature*, 72, no. 2 (2012), 239–69.

Sakwa, Richard, *The Rise and Fall of the Soviet Union, 1917–1991* (London: Routledge, 1999).

Salomoni, Antonella, *Il pensiero religioso e politico di Tolstoj in Italia, 1886–1910* (Firenze: L. S. Olschki, 1996).

Saltykov, M. E., *Bogomoltsy, stranniki i proezzhie; Proshliya vremena* (Oxford: Tipografiya Klarendon, 1917).

Sandulescu, C. George, ed., *Rediscovering Oscar Wilde* (Gerrards Cross: Colin Smythe, 1994).

Sargeant, Amy, *Storm over Asia* (London: I. B. Tauris, 2007).

Savinkova, S. A., 'Na volosok ot kazni. (Vospominan'ya materi)', *Byloe*, 1 (January 1907), 247–71.

_____ 'A Russian Mother: A Personal Narrative (1897–1905)', trans. Constance Garnett, *Albany Review*, 1, no. 1 (April–May 1907), 86–101, 214–40.

Saxon, A. H., *Enter Foot and Horse: A History of Hippodrama in England and France* (New Haven, CT: Yale University Press, 1968).

_____ *The Life and Art of Andrew Ducrow & the Romantic Age of the English Circus* (Hamden, CT: Archon Books, 1978).

Scheijen, Sjeng, *Diaghilev: A Life*, trans. Jane Hedley-Prôle and S. J. Leinbach (London: Profile Books, 2009).

Schlögel, Karl, ed., *Russische Emigration in Deutschland, 1918–1941: Leben im europäischen Bürgerkrieg* (Berlin: Akademie Verlag, 1995).

Scholl, Tim, *From Petipa to Balanchine: Classical Revival and the Modernization of Ballet* (London: Routledge, 1994).

School of Slavonic Studies Prospectus, 1921–22 (London: University of London Press, 1921).

School of Slavonic Studies Prospectus, 1922–23 (London: University of London Press, 1922).

Schroeder, Horst, *Additions and Corrections to Richard Ellmann's Oscar Wilde*, 2nd edn (Braunschweig: privately printed, 2002).

Scott, Clement, *The Drama of Yesterday & To-day*, 2 vols (London: Macmillan, 1899).

Sealey Rahman, Kate, 'Ostrovskii on the British Stage: 1894–1928', *Toronto Slavic Quarterly*, 9 (Summer 2004), <http://www.utoronto.ca/tsq/09/rahman09.shtml>.

Sedgefield, W. J., 'The Study of Russian', *Modern Language Teaching*, 10 (1914), 243–4.

Sedlak, Francis, 'My Military Experiences', *New Order*, NS 6, no. 27 (May 1900), 81–3.

Segel, Harold B., *Twentieth-Century Russian Drama: From Gorky to the Present* (New York: Columbia University Press, 1979).

Selver, P., trans. and ed., *Modern Russian Poetry: Texts and Translations* (London: Kegan Paul, Trench, Trubner, 1917).

Semeonoff, A. E., and H. J. W. Tillyard, eds, *Russian Poetry Reader* (London: Kegan Paul, Trench, Trubner, 1917).

Senelick, Laurence, *The Chekhov Theatre: A Century of the Plays in Performance* (Cambridge: Cambridge University Press, 1997).

Seton-Watson, R. W., 'Bernard Pares', *Slavonic and East European Review*, 28, no. 70 (November, 1949), 28–31.

Shaw, Bernard, *The Drama Observed*, iv: *1911–1950*, ed. Bernard F. Dukore (University Park, PA: Pennsylvania State University Press, 1993).

_____ *Essays in Fabian Socialism* (London: Constable and Company, 1961).

_____ *Plays Political: The Apple Cart, On the Rocks, Geneva* (London: Penguin, 1986).

_____ and others, *Stalin-Wells Talk: The Verbatim Record and A Discussion by G. Bernard Shaw, H. G. Wells, J. M. Keynes, Ernst Toller and others* (London: New Statesman and Nation, 1934).

Shaw, Nellie, *Whiteway: A Colony on the Cotswolds* (London: C. W. Daniel, 1935).

Shkarvan, A. [Škarvan, Albert], *Moi otkaz ot voennoi sluzhby: zapiski voennogo vracha* (Purleigh: V. Tchertkoff, 1898).

_____ 'The Peace Movement in Holland', *New Order*, 3, no. 13 (January 1898), 97–8.

'Shokoloff: An Interview', *Left Review*, 1, no. 6 (March 1935), 193–4.

'Should I use Money? Correspondence between X who uses it, and E who does not', *New Order*, NS 5, no. 16 (May 1899), 70.

Siljak, Ana, *Angel of Vengeance: The 'Girl Assassin,' the Governor of St. Petersburg, and Russia's Revolutionary World* (New York: St. Martin's, 2008).

Simmel, Georg, 'The Metropolis and Mental Life', in Kurt H. Wolff, ed. and trans. *The Sociology of Georg Simmel* (Glencoe, IL: Free Press, 1950), 409–24.

Skidelsky, Robert, *John Maynard Keynes 1883–1946: Economist, Philosopher, Statesman* (Basingstoke: Pan Macmillan, 2004).

Skvortsov, I. V., *Russian History*, 2 vols (London: Jaschke, 1919).

Smith, Adrian, *The New Statesman: Portrait of a Political Weekly, 1913–1931* (London: Frank Cass, 1996).

Smith, G. S., *D. S. Mirsky: A Russian-English Life, 1890–1939* (Oxford: Oxford University Press, 2000).

Smith, Philip E., and Michael S. Helfand, eds, *Oscar Wilde's Notebooks: A Portrait of Mind in the Making* (New York and Oxford: Oxford University Press, 1989).

Smith, R. E. F., *A Novelty: Russian at Birmingham University, 1917–67* (Birmingham: University of Birmingham, 1987).

Smylie, Patrick, ' "Socialism of a mild type" ': The Political Thought and Action of Reverend J. Bruce Wallace and Radical Politics in Belfast, 1884–91', MA Thesis, Queen's University Belfast, 2008.

'Spanish Opinion on the Explosion', *Freeman's Journal and Daily Commercial Advertiser* (Dublin) (20 March 1883), 7.

Spargo, John, 'My Visit to the "Tolstoyan Colony" Whiteway', *Social Democrat* (15 September 1901), 275.

Spender, Stephen, *World within World: The Autobiography of Stephen Spender* (London: Hamish Hamilton, 1951).

'Spies in London: Watching Russian Refugees', *London Daily News* (27 January 1905), 6.

Spivak, Gayatri, *Death of a Discipline* (New York: Columbia University Press, 2003).

'The Stage', *Bell's Life in London and Sporting Chronicle* (26 November 1881), 11.

'The Standard Theatre', *The Times* (27 December 1881), 4.

'The State of Ireland', *Hampshire Telegraph and Sussex Chronicle* (26 October 1881), 3.

'The State of Ireland', *Liverpool Mercury* (16 September 1881), 6.

Stead, W. T., *The Truth about Russia* (London: Cassell, 1888).

Stedman Jones, Gareth, *Outcast London: A Study in the Relationship Between Classes in Victorian Society* (Oxford: Oxford University Press, 1971).

Steeves, Paul D., 'Tolstoyans in Russia and the USSR', in Joseph L. Wieczynski, ed., *The Modern Encyclopaedia of Russian and Soviet History*, xxxix (Gulf Breeze, FL: Academic International, 1985), 114–21.

Steinhart, E. N., trans. and ed., *Poems of Michael Lermontoff* (London: Kegan Paul, Trench, Trubner, 1917).

Stepniak, Sergei, *The New Convert: A Drama in Four Acts*, trans. Thomas B. Eyges (Boston: Stratford, 1917).

_____ *Underground Russia: Revolutionary Profiles and Sketches from Life* (London: Smith, Elder, 1883).

Stern, Ludmila, *Western Intellectuals and the Soviet Union, 1920–40: From Red Square to the Left Bank* (Abingdon: Routledge, 2007).

Stone, Gerald, 'The History of Slavonic Studies in Great Britain', in Josef Hamm and Günther Wytrzens, eds, *Beiträge zur Geschichte der Slawistik in Nichtslawischen Ländern* (Vienna: Österreichischen Akademie der Wissenschaften, 1985), 360–98.

Strong, Herbert A., 'German and Russian', *Modern Language Teaching*, 10 (1914), 183.

Subotić, Dragutin, and Nevill Forbes, *Engleska Gramatika* (Oxford: Clarendon Press, 1920).

_____ *Serbian Grammar* (Oxford: Clarendon Press, 1918).

'Suggestions for a Modern Language Curriculum', *Modern Language Teaching*, 1 (1905), 241–5.

'Swinburne and Water', *Punch* (23 July 1881), 26.

Tanner, J. R., *The Historical Register of the University of Cambridge: Being a Supplement to the Calendar with a Record of University Offices, Honours and Distinctions to the Year 1910* (Cambridge: Cambridge University Press, 1917).

Taruskin, Richard, *Stravinsky and the Russian Traditions: A Biography of the Works through 'Mavra'*, 2 vols (Oxford: Oxford University Press, 1996).

Taunton, Matthew, 'Cottage Economy or Collective Farm? English Socialism and Agriculture Between Merrie England and the Five-Year Plan', *Critical Quarterly*, 54, no. 3 (2011), 1–23.

Thacker, Joy, *Whiteway Colony: The Social History of a Tolstoyan Community* (Stroud: J. Thacker, 1993).

Thames, Jean-Marie, *Le Mélodrame* (Paris: Presses universitaires de France, 1984).

'The Theatres', *Daily News* (23 July 1883), 2.

'The Theatres', *Daily News* (21 November 1881), 2.

'Theatres', *The Graphic* (26 November 1881), 534.

'Theatres', *The Graphic* (28 July 1883), 94.

'Theatres', *The Graphic* (25 August 1883), 187.

'The Theatres', *The Times* (22 July 1936), 10.

'The Theatres: Avenue', *The Times* (15 June 1898), 13.

'The Theatres: Gogol's Marriage', *The Times* (6 June 1938), 8.

'Theatrical Gossip', *The Era* (26 November 1881), 5.

'Things New: At the Theatres', review of *The Brothers Karamazov*, Stage Society, 1913, *The Sketch* (26 February 1913), 236.

Thomas, Gareth James, 'The Impact of Russian Music in England, 1893–1929', PhD thesis, University of Birmingham, 2005.

Tillyard, E. M. W., *The Muse Unchained: An Intimate Account of the Revolution in English Studies at Cambridge* (London: Bowes & Bowes, 1958).

Tihanov, Galin, 'The Birth of Modern Literary Theory in East-Central Europe', in *History of the Literary Cultures of East-Central Europe*, i, ed. M. Cornis-Pope and J. Neubauer (Amsterdam: John Benjamins, 2004), 416–24.

_____ 'Why Did Modern Literary Theory Originate in Central and Eastern Europe? (And Why Is It Now Dead?)', *Common Knowledge*, 10, no. 1 (2004), 61–81.

'Tolstoy staged', *The Independent* (1903), 344–46.

Tolstoy, Leo,'The Beginning of the End', in *On Civil Disobedience and Non-Violence* (New York: Bergman, 1967), 9–28.

_____ *The Christian Teaching* (London: Brotherhood Publishing Company, 1898).

_____ *The Death of Ivan Ilyitch and Other Stories*, trans. Constance Garnett (London: Heinemann, 1902).

_____ *Family Happiness*, ed. D. Bondar, 2 vols (London: Effingham Wilson, 1916–17).

_____ *The Inevitable Change* (Saxmundham and Thorpeness: Peace Pamphlets by Ruth Fry, 1937).

_____ *Kavkazskii plennik: rasskaz* (Oxford: Tipografiya Klarendon, 1917).

_____ *The Kingdom of God and Peace Essays* (London: Oxford University Press, 1935).

_____ *Polnoe sobranie sochinenii* (Moscow: Khudozhestvennaya literatura, 1935–64).

_____ *Sevastopol*, ed. A. P. Goudy and E. Bullough (Cambridge: Cambridge University Press, 1916).

_____ 'The Three Hermits', in *Walk in the Light and Twenty-Three Tales*, trans. Louise and Aylmer Maude (Farmington, PA, and Robertsbridge, East Sussex: Plough Publishing House, 1998), 253–60.

_____ *Tolstoy's Letters*, ii: *1880–1910*, ed. R. F. Christian (London: Athlone, 1978).

_____ *War and Peace*, trans. Constance Garnett, 3 vols (London: Heinemann, 1904).

_____ *What is Art?* (London: Brotherhood Publishing Company, 1898).

Tolz, Vera, *Russia's Own Orient: The Politics of Identity and Oriental Studies in the Late Imperial and Early Soviet Periods* (Oxford: Oxford University Press, 2011).

Tomaszewski, Fiona, *A Great Russia: Russia and the Triple Entente* (Westport, CT: Praeger, 2002).

Torgovnick, Marianna, *Gone Primitive: Savage Intellects, Modern Lives* (Chicago, IL: University of Chicago Press, 1990).

Tree, Maud, 'Herbert and I', in Max Beerbohm, ed., *Herbert Beerbohm Tree: Some Memories of Him and His Art* (New York: Dutton, n.d.), 1–170.

Trevelyan, John, *What the Censor Saw* (London: Michael Joseph, 1973).

'A Trip up the Volga to the Fair of Nijni-Novgorod', *Daily News* (19 September 1874).

Trofimov, Michael V., *Elementary Russian Reader* (London: Constable, 1917).

Turgenef, Ivan, *Fathers and Sons*, trans. Eugene Schuyler (New York: Leypoldt & Holt, 1867).

_____ *Moo-Moo and The District Doctor*, ed. A. Raffi (London: Kegan Paul, Trench, Trubner, [1917]).

_____ *Pegas; Biryuk; Les i step'* (Oxford: Tipografiya Klarendon, 1917).

_____ *Pères et enfants*, ed. Prosper Mérimée (Paris: Charpentier, 1863).

Turton, Glyn, *Turgenev and the Context of English Literature, 1850–1900* (London: Routledge, 1992).

Tynan, Kenneth, *Tynan on Theatre* (Harmondsworth: Penguin, 1964).

Underwood, E. G., *A School Russian Grammar* (London: Blackie and Son, 1916).

The University of Liverpool Calendar, 1912 (Liverpool: Liverpool University Press, 1912).

The University of Liverpool Calendar, 1915–16 (Liverpool: Liverpool University Press, 1915).

University of London, *The Historical Record, 1836–1926* (London: University of London Press, 1926).

Van der Veer, J. K., 'Brieven uit Engeland', *Vrede*, 2, no. 5 (15 December 1898), 38–40, 2, no. 7 (15 January 1899), 52–3, 2, no. 9 (15 February 1899), 67–9, 2, no. 10 (1 March 1899), 76–8, 2, no. 13 (15 April 1899), 100–2, 2, no. 14,(1 May 1899), 102–4, 2, no. 18 (1 July 1899), 133–5, 2, no. 21 (15 August 1899), 156–8, 3, no. 1 (15 October 1899), 7–8.

Velikanova, N., and R. Whittaker, eds, *Tolstoy i SShA* (Moscow: IMLI RAN, 2004).

Venturi, Franco, *Roots of Revolution: A History of the Populist and Socialist Movements in Nineteenth Century Russia*, trans. Francis Haskell (London: Weidenfeld and Nicolson, 1960).

Venuti, Lawrence, *The Translator's Invisibility: A History of Translation* (London: Routledge, 1995).

Verdonk, Dirk Jan, *Het Dierloze Gerecht: Vegetarische Geschiedenis van Nederland* (Amsterdam: Boom, 2009).

Verne, Jules, and Adolphe d'Ennery, *Michel Strogoff*, ed. Louis Bilodeau (Exeter: University of Exeter Press, 1995).

Vishnevetsky, I. G., *'Evraziiskoe uklonenie' v muzyke 1920–1930-kh godov: istoriya voprosa, stat' i i materialy A. Lur' e, P. Suvchinskogo, I. Stravinskogo, V. Dukel' skogo, S. Prokof' eva, I. Markevicha* (Moscow: Novoe literaturnoe obozrenie, 2005).

Vogüé, E. M. de, *Le Roman russe* (Paris: Plon, 1886).

______ *The Russian Novel*, trans. H. A. Sawyer (London: Chapman and Hall, 1913).

_____ *The Russian Novelists*, trans. Jane Loring Edmands (Boston, MA: Lothrop, 1887).

W., F. E., 'Meetings and Partings II', *Focus* (February 1926), 97–107.

Wachtel, Andrew, *Plays of Expectations: Intertextual Relations in Russian Twentieth-Century Drama* (Seattle, WA: University of Washington Press, 2006).

_____ 'Translation, Imperialism, and National Self-Definition in Russia', in Dilip Parameshwar Gaonkar, ed., *Alternative Modernities* (Durham, NC: Duke University Press, 2001), 58–85.

Waddington, Patrick, *From 'The Russian Fugitive' to 'The Ballad of Bulgarie': Episodes in English Literary Attitudes to Russia from Wordsworth to Swinburne* (Oxford: Berg, 1994).

_____,ed., *Ivan Turgenev and Britain* (Oxford: Berg, 1995).

_____ *Turgenev and George Sand: An Improbable Entente* (Basingstoke: Macmillan, 1981).

_____*Turgenev in England* (London: Macmillan, 1980).

Wadsworth, Edward, 'Inner Necessity', *Blast*, 1 (1914), 119–25.

Walker, Samuel, 'George Howard Gibson, Christian Socialist Among the Populists', *Nebraska History*, 55, no. 4 (Winter 1974), 553–65.

Walkowitz, Rebecca L., *Cosmopolitan Style: Modernism Beyond the Nation* (New York: Columbia University Press, 2006).

Wallace, John Bruce, 'Tolstoyism and its English Parody', *Brotherhood* (October 1897), 63.

_____ *Towards Fraternal Organisation: An Explanation of the Brotherhood Trust* (London: Brotherhood Trust, [1894]).

Waller, W. F., 'Fédora', *The Theatre* (1 February 1883), 85–93.

_____ 'Fédora', *The Theatre* (1 June 1883), 362–9.

Wearing, J. P., *The London Stage: A Calendar of Plays and Players* (Metuchen, NJ: Scarecrow Press, 1981–90).

Webb, Beatrice, *The Diary of Beatrice Webb*, ii: *1895–1905*, ed. Norman and Jeanne MacKenzie (London: Virago, 1983).

Wegg-Prosser, Victoria, 'The Archive of the Film and Photo League', *Sight and Sound*, 46, no. 4 (1977), 245–7.

Wells, H. G., *Experiment in Autobiography: Discoveries and Conclusions of a Very Ordinary Brain*, ii (London: Faber & Faber, 1984).

_____ *A Modern Utopia* (London: Penguin, 2005).

_____ *The New America: The New World* (London: Cresset Press, 1935).

_____ *Russia in the Shadows* (London: Hodder and Stoughton, 1920).

Werkhaupt, G., and E. Roller, *Russian Reader with Exercises of Conversation* (Heidelberg: Groos, 1902).

_____ *Russian Reader: With Exercises of Conversation* (London: Nutt, 1902).

West, Rebecca, 'The Barbarians', *New Republic* (9 January 1915), 19–21.

_____ 'The Russian Ballet', *The Outlook* (7 June 1919), 568.

_____ 'Nijinsky', *Sunday Telegraph* (7 November 1971).

_____ *The Young Rebecca: Writings of Rebecca West, 1911–17* (Basingstoke: Macmillan, 1982).

While, Evelyn C., *Easy Russian Reader* (London: Kegan Paul, Trench, Trubner, 1919).

White, Jack, *Misfit* (London: Jonathan Cape, 1930).

Whitehead, Ella, ed., *John Lehmann's 'New Writing': An Author-Index, 1936–1950* (Lampeter: Edwin Mellen, 1990).

Whitworth, Geoffrey, *The Art of Nijinsky* (New York: Benjamin Blom, 1972).

Wilde, Oscar, *The Complete Letters of Oscar Wilde*, ed. Merlin Holland and Rupert Hart-Davis (London: Fourth Estate, 2000).

_____ *Complete Short Fiction*, ed. Ian Small (London: Penguin, 2003).

_____ *The Complete Works of Oscar Wilde*, i: *Poems and Poems in Prose*, ed. Bobby Fong and Karl Beckson (Oxford: Oxford University Press, 2000).

_____ *The Letters of Oscar Wilde*, ed. Rupert Hart-Davis (New York: Harcourt, Brace & World, 1962).

_____ *More Letters of Oscar Wilde*, ed. Rupert Hart-Davis (New York: Vanguard Press, 1985).

_____ *Oscar Wilde's 'Vera; or, The Nihilist'*, ed. Frances Miriam Reed (Lampeter: Edwin Mellen, 1989).

_____ *Selected Journalism*, ed. Anna Clayworth (Oxford: Oxford University Press, 2004).

_____ *Selected Letters of Oscar Wilde*, ed. Rupert Hart-Davis (Oxford: Oxford University Press, 1979).

Willcox, Temple, 'Soviet Films, Censorship and the British Government: A Matter of the Public Interest', *Historical Journal of Film, Radio and Television*, 10, no. 3 (1990), 275–92.

Williams, Harold, 'Notes from Holland and Germany', *New Order*, NS 7, no. 40 (June–July 1901), 73–4.

Williams, Raymond, 'Metropolitan Perceptions and the Emergence of Modernism', in Tony Pinkney, ed., *The Politics of Modernism* (London: Verso, 1989), 37–48.

_____ 'When Was Modernism?', *New Left Review*, 175 (1989), 48–52.

Williams, Robert C., 'The Russian Soul: A Study in European Thought and Non-European Nationalism', *Journal of the History of Ideas*, 31, no. 4 (1970), 573–88.

Williamson, Audrey, *Theatre of Two Decades* (London: Rockliff, 1951).

Willis, J. H., *Leonard and Virginia Woolf as Publishers: The Hogarth Press, 1917–41* (Charlottesville, VA: University Press of Virginia, 1992).

Wilson, Keith, *The Policy of the Entente: Essays on the Determinants of British Foreign Policy 1904–1914* (Cambridge: Cambridge University Press, 1985).

Witt, Susanna, 'Between the Lines: Totalitarianism and Translation in the USSR', in Brian James Baer, ed., *Contexts, Subtexts and Pretexts: Literary Translation in Eastern Europe and Russia* (Amsterdam: Benjamins, 2011), 149–70.

Wolff, Janet, *Feminine Sentences: Essays on Women and Culture* (London: Polity Press, 1990).

Wollaeger, Mark, and Matt Eatough, eds, *The Oxford Handbook of Global Modernisms* (Oxford: Oxford University Press, 2011).

Wollen, Peter, 'Out of the Past: Fashion/Orientalism/the Body', in *Raiding the Icebox: Reflections on Twentieth-century Culture* (London: Verso, 1993), 1–34.

Wood, Henry J., *My Life of Music* (London: Gollancz, 1938).

Woods, Joanna, *Katerina: The Russian World of Katherine Mansfield* (Auckland: Penguin, 2001).

Woolf, Virginia, 'Modern Fiction', in *The Common Reader* (London: Hogarth Press, 1925), 184–95.

_____ 'The Russian Point of View', in *The Common Reader*, 2nd edn (London: Hogarth Press, 1925), 219–31.

_____ *The Diary of Virginia Woolf*, v: *1936–41*, ed. Anne Olivier Bell and Andrew McNeillie (Harmondsworth: Penguin, 1985).

Wright, Patrick, *Iron Curtain: From Stage to Cold War* (Oxford: Oxford University Press, 2007).

Y.-B., F., review of *Paul I*, *The Spectator* (15 October 1927), 603.

Yao, Steven G., *Translation and the Languages of Modernism: Gender, Politics, Language* (Basingstoke: Palgrave, 2002).

Young, Stuart, 'A Month in the Country in the British Theatre', *New Zealand Slavonic Journal* (1994), 207–27.

Zhakkar, Zh.-F. [Jean-Philippe Jaccard], A. Morar [Annick Morard] and Zh. Tassis [Gervaise Tassis], eds, *Russkie pisateli v Parizhe: vzglyad na frantsuzskuyu literaturu, 1920–1940* (Moscow: Russkii Put′, 2007).

Zhdanov, A., and others, *Problems of Soviet Literature: Reports and Speeches at the First Soviet Writers' Congress*, ed. H. G. Scott (Martin Lawrence, [1935]).

Zograf, N., *Aleksandr Pavlovich Lensky* (Moscow: Iskusstvo, 1955).

Zvavich, I., 'Russkaya kniga v Anglii (Pis′mo iz Londona)', *Pechat′ i revolyutsiya*, 6 (1923), 98–114.

Zverev, Aleksey, *Zhizn′ russkogo literaturnogo Parizha, 1920–1940* (Moscow: Molodaya gvardiya, 2003).

Index